SCHOOLS FOR SPECIAL NEEDS

Tomorrow's Achievers...

...or society's misfits?

Today's gifted children should be among the outstanding entrepreneurs, business leaders, scientists and artistic performers of the 21st century.

Sadly, many are at risk of falling by the wayside or, through lack of fulfilling outlet, turning their talents to crime. Gifted children often go unrecognised at school, where they may become bored, isolated and disruptive. Some are dyslexic; others are loners and may be bullied or ostracised by classmates. Others deliberately underachieve so as not to be different.

In the two years since its launch, Tomorrow s Achievers — a programme of specialist day and residential master classes — has changed the lives of many gifted children. As news of its success has spread, the scheme has expanded into some of the UK s most deprived areas, opening up a new world of learning to inspire and challenge the most able minds.

Tomorrow s Achievers, endorsed by the Government, exists only through the support we receive from sponsors. By investing in today s children, you can make a vital contribution by giving them the tools to become tomorrow s success stories.

"NAGC gives Gabbitas its wholehearted support in this vitally needed initiative." Peter Carey, Director, National Association for Gifted Children.

All donations will be very gratefully received and should be sent to:
Gabbitas, Truman & Thring Educational Trust
Carrington House, 126-130 Regent Street, London W1B 5EE
Tel: 020 7734 0161 Fax: 020 7437 1764 Email: admin@gabbitas.co.uk

SCHOOLS FOR SPECIAL NEEDS

8TH EDITION

A COMPLETE GUIDE

GABBITAS
Educational Consultants

KOGAN
PAGE

Photographs on front cover supplied with kind permission of (left to right) St Vincent's School for Blind and Partially Sighted Children, Liverpool; Headlands School, Penarth, South Glamorgan; and Exhall Grange School, Coventry.

First published in 1995
This edition published in 2002

Kogan Page Ltd
120 Pentonville Road
London N1 9JN

E-mail: kpinfo@kogan-page.co.uk

© Gabbitas and Kogan Page 2002

British Library Cataloguing in Publication Data
A CIP record for this book is available from the British Library
ISBN 0 7494 3812 6

Typeset by Bibliocraft Ltd, Dundee
Printed and bound in Great Britain by Bell & Bain Ltd, Glasgow

Contents

PART TWO:
DIRECTORY OF SPECIAL SCHOOLS AND COLLEGES

PART THREE:
PROFILES OF SPECIAL SCHOOLS AND COLLEGES

PART FOUR:
INDEPENDENT MAINSTREAM SCHOOLS
WITH SPECIALIST PROVISION

PART FIVE:
REFERENCE SECTION

PART ONE: SPECIAL NEEDS – GUIDANCE FOR PARENTS

1.1
Introduction

Gabbitas Educational Consultants

Special educational needs remain the focus of much debate. Developments in recent years reflect the increasing attention now paid to the important tasks of assessing and defining the educational needs of each child and ensuring that suitable provision is made.

Parents, however, often face difficulties and frustrations during the complex and sometimes lengthy process of assessment, agreement on the nature of provision required, and identification of a suitable school.

Schools for Special Needs – A Complete Guide is designed specifically for parents, offering a step-by-step guide to all aspects of finding the right school for a child with special educational needs, including essential information on parents' rights and the duties of the Local Education Authority. We are delighted that it has met with so much interest and appreciation from parents and professionals alike.

This eighth edition has been fully revised and updated in line with the latest developments.

The bibliography in Part Five offers suggestions for further reading and has been compiled with the kind assistance of our editorial contributors.

Part One

Part One of the guide provides parents with extensive guidance written by experts on the many aspects of assessment, statementing and provision as well as on choice of schools, special arrangements for examinations, education planning at 16+, social security benefits for children and carers and advice for parents overseas.

Part Two

Information about individual special schools is given in Part Two, which contains a comprehensive directory of independent and non-maintained special schools, plus details of colleges and other establishments providing training and support services for students aged 16+. Each entry includes the name, address and telephone number of the school or college; the name of the Head or Director; the sex, number and age range of pupils or students; whether residential accommodation is available; and details of all the types of special needs for which the school or college provides. There is a separate section for state schools, which includes details of those that responded to our request for information. For ease of reference, the primary or principal need catered for is shown in bold (wherever this information was made available). Entries also indicate which schools offer 52-week care.

Part Three

The listings in Part Three are contributed by schools and offer more detailed information about individual special needs establishments.

Part Four

Part Four contains a directory, profiles and indexes of independent mainstream schools. The vast majority of these schools do not take children with statements, but offer provisions for a limited range of special needs. The most frequently available provision is for specific learning difficulties or dyslexia, although some can also offer help in other areas (see Part 4.1). Each school listed has been asked to classify the level of provision offered for individual special needs in order to help parents identify appropriate options.

Part Five

In Part Five parents will find a quick reference guide to independent and non-maintained special schools and colleges catering for specific types of need, together with suggestions for further reading, an extensive list of useful addresses and associations and details of schools registered under CReSTeD (Council for the Registration of Schools Teaching Dyslexic Pupils).

We are indebted to all those who have helped us in the preparation of this guide, as advisors and authors, and to the Heads and Principals who contributed so much information about their schools, colleges and support services, without which publication would not have been possible.

We should particularly like to acknowledge with thanks the support given to us by the following:

AFASIC

British Epilepsy Association

Dr Steven Chinn
Principal, Mark College, Somerset

Dr Deborah Christie, C Clin Psychologist AFBPsS
Consultant Clinical Psychologist, Department of Child and Adolescent Psychological Services, Middlesex Hospital

Mr Steve Cliffen, Principal, Coxlease School, Hampshire
Executive Committee member NAES (National Association of EBD Schools)

CreSTeD (Council for the Registration of Schools Teaching Dyslexic Pupils)

Cystic Fibrosis Trust

Disability Alliance

Down's Syndrome Association

Mr Ken Dutton, Principal Educational Psychologist, Scottish Borders Council

The Dyslexia Institute

The Dyspraxia Foundation

John Friel, Barrister-at-Law, Gray's Inn
Member of the Governing Council of Dyslexia Institute
Former Chair of the Advisory Centre for Education Council
Chair of the Special Needs Group of the Educational Law Society
Trustee, Dyslexia Institute Bursary Fund

Lyn Fry, MA, DipEdPsych, AFBPsS, Cpsychol, Chartered Educational Psychologist

Joint Council for General Qualifications

Dr Richard Lansdown, Chartered Psychologist

Muscular Dystrophy Campaign

The National Autistic Society

Nigel Pugh
The British Dyslexia Association

Arno Rabinowitz, BA, AFBPsS, Cpsychol
Chartered Educational Psychologist
Specialist Psychological Services

Liz Ranger
National Deaf Children's Society

Royal Association for Disability and Rehabilitation

Royal National Institute for the Blind (RNIB)

SCOPE (formerly the Spastics Society)

SKILL (National Bureau for Students with Disabilities)

David Urani, Chartered Educational Psychologist

Gill Winfield, Information Manager
Association for Spina Bifida and Hydrocepalus (ASBAH)

Gabbitas Educational Consultants

Having celebrated its 125th year in 1998, Gabbitas is uniquely placed to offer parents a wealth of professional expertise, an understanding of their concerns and a personal knowledge of independent schools throughout the UK. Each year Gabbitas helps thousands of parents and students in the UK and abroad who seek guidance at all stages of education:

- choice of independent preparatory and senior boarding and day schools;
- choice of independent sixth form or further education colleges;
- educational assessment services;
- sixth form options – A and AS Levels, the International Baccalaureate, vocational courses;
- university and degree choices and UCAS applications;
- careers assessment and guidance.

Familiar with the requirements of students from overseas, Gabbitas also advises on specialist areas such as transferring into the British education system, guardianship for children from overseas attending boarding schools in the UK and testing for overseas students in English, Maths and Science.

   In this guide we aim to provide a comprehensive and practical source of advice based on our knowledge and experience – a unique reference source to help you through all stages of your search for the right school for your child.

Gabbitas Educational Consultants

May 2002

1.2
Sources of Help: A Guide for Parents

Arno Rabinowitz, Chartered Educational Psychologist,
Specialist Psychological Services

There are many sources of help for parents who are worried about any aspect of their child's development. The range can often seem bewildering. With so many professions that exist to help children it is important for parents to know what each does and how to access this help if they are to gain access to the right support for their children and themselves. The list that follows is not exhaustive but includes the main groups with whom parents might come into contact during the course of an assessment of their child's needs.

Educational psychologists

Educational psychologists (EPs) are trained to understand how young children learn, think and behave. All EPs are trained teachers who have taught for a minimum of two years and, in many cases, very much more. Their training begins with an Honours degree in Psychology and then, after teaching experience, further postgraduate training lasting a year.

Most EPs work for Local Education Authorities, but some – an increasingly large number – work privately. They use a variety of tests and techniques to find out the general level of a child's ability to learn, and whether the child has any areas of specific learning difficulty. Referral to sources of help, including Child and Family Consultation Services, can be arranged through EPs and some are actually based at these centres. EPs have special knowledge of schools and similar provision and play a key part in the formulation of psychological advice that contributes to a Statement of Special Educational Needs. EPs who work for Local Education Authorities cannot normally help children who attend non-maintained schools. In such cases an independent EP will have to be approached. Independent EPs can also help in presenting cases to, and supporting parents at, Special Educational Needs Tribunals.

Clinical psychologists

Clinical psychologists work more from the perspective of health and community care. They are not trained teachers but their training, like that of EPs, is long and rigorous. Clinical psychologists usually work in the health service, in health centres, GP surgeries, hospitals and outpatient clinics.

Both clinical and educational psychologists are members of a profession, which is strictly regulated and chartered. Only people recognised by the British Psychological Society can call themselves chartered psychologists – a legally recognised title authorised by the Privy Council. They have agreed to follow a strict code of conduct and are answerable to a disciplinary system in which non-psychologists are in the majority when complaints are considered.

Child psychotherapists

Child psychotherapists work in Child and Family Consultation Centres (or Child Guidance Centres as they were more generally called) and also in health centres, hospital wards and centres for adolescents. Their work is mainly with children, teenagers and their parents, and their training gives them a particular understanding of the inner worlds of children and of how early childhood experience influences everyday life. Most child psychotherapists work with children individually, though some may work with groups of children and families. A number of child psychotherapists work independently but the majority are employed within the health service.

Child and Family Consultation Services

Child and Family Consultation Services (CFCS) are centres where parents can discuss worries about their children and where a range of professional workers can co-operate to help the child and family resolve problems. In most CFCS you will find an EP or clinical psychologist, a psychotherapist, a child psychiatrist, a specially trained social worker, a community psychiatric nurse and other specialised therapists. They work as a team to address problems but usually only one worker will work with a child or his or her family. CFCS are free and open to all. The service is confidential except where a child is at risk. Referral can be arranged through a GP, social worker, EP or teacher and many CFCS accept self-referral from families.

Child psychiatrists

Child psychiatrists are doctors who are specially trained to work with children who show signs of emotional distress or difficulty. They work within teams in clinics and hospital departments and will usually offer treatment or therapy in clinical settings or schools. Working with them may be a similarly trained range of specialised medical personnel: nurses, social workers and sometimes occupational and speech and language therapists.

Occupational therapists

Occupational therapists are trained in understanding how the body functions and how it works as a system. They can assess the way a child interacts with the physical world around him and can arrange therapy where this is needed. Usually they work within health centre or hospital settings but an increasing number work independently.

Speech and language therapists

As their name implies, speech and language therapists are concerned not only with articulation but also with the development and extension of language abilities and skills. They are, as are all the workers mentioned here, members of a carefully regulated profession with high professional standards of conduct. They work on programmes for individual children that can be implemented in school, as well as provide individual therapy in appropriate cases.

All the workers mentioned above are there to help and support parents. Sometimes, though, the most valuable help comes through contact with parents and others who have had similar experiences. Finding these groups is not always easy. Each Local Authority, at your town, county or shire hall, has a list of voluntary groups. As well as the groups and organisations listed at the end of this book, there are many umbrella groups which exist to inform parents about help available.

Contact-a-Family (020 7608 8700) has links with about 9000 independent self-help and mutual support groups and contacts throughout the country. Young Minds (020 7336 8445) and the Advisory Centre for Education (020 7354 8321) can help parents find similar groups in the field of mental health and education. For help with children in any form of education in London, Parents in Partnership (020 7735 7735) has many contacts and there are many similar organisations that offer support for parents of children with special needs. Network 81 (01279 647415) is a national network of support groups of parents of children with special educational needs while In Touch (0161 905 2440) offers information and contact for children who have rare handicapping conditions. Specialist Psychological Services (020 8874 1569) can help in finding the most appropriate professional for your child. The most important thing for parents is to find information and, for once, the truism is accurate: if you seek, you will find!

1.3
A Guide to the Classification
of Special Needs

Attention Deficit/Hyperactivity Disorder
(Lyn Fry, MA, DipEdPsych, AFBPsS, C.Psychol)

Do you recognise this child?

- Jo can't dress himself in the morning because he gets distracted by anything that is around him.
- Alex can't stay at a meal table without constantly getting up.
- Sarah has always had teachers writing in her reports that she must learn to concentrate.
- David's teachers complain because he daydreams.
- Homework is a nightmare with Sam. He can't settle to it and then he keeps popping up unless supervised by an adult.
- Jacob is just like his Dad. Both of them talk constantly and are always on the go.
- Victoria drives other kids mad because she is always touching their things.
- Other children don't like Ben because he spoils their games. He does silly things and forgets about rules.

From time to time all children have difficulty in sitting still, listening to what the teacher says, or being distracted by their friends. For those children with Attention Deficit Disorder (ADD), the difficulties are more pervasive. Because of this, they have considerable difficulty in keeping their behaviour under control. ADD is not easy to diagnose and can often be confused with other conditions. Children whose behaviour is not well managed, those with a language disorder, or those who are deaf, for example, often have difficulty in staying focused in class.

The American Psychiatric Association has a Diagnostic and Statistic Manual (DSM-IV) that attempts to break all conditions down into their key requirements, in order to differentiate them from other conditions. For attention-deficit/hyperactivity disorder they divide it into two parts: 'Inattention' and 'Hyperactivity-Impulsivity'. For Inattention, they require that 'at least six of the following symptoms of inattention have persisted for at least 6 months to a degree that is maladaptive and inconsistent with developmental level:

a)   often fails to give close attention to details or makes careless mistakes in schoolwork, homework, or other activities;
b)   often has difficulty sustaining attention in tasks of play activities;
c)   often does not seem to listen to what is being said to him/her;
d)   often does not follow through on instructions and fails to finish schoolwork, chores, or duties in the workplace (not due to oppositional behaviour or failure to understand instructions);
e)   often has difficulties in organising tasks and activities;
f)   often avoids or strongly dislikes tasks (such as schoolwork or homework) that require sustained mental effort;
g)   often loses things necessary for tasks or activities (eg school assignments, pencils, books, tools or toys);
h)   is often easily distracted by extraneous stimuli;
i)   is often forgetful in daily activities.

For Hyperactivity-Impulsivity they require that 'at least four of the following symptoms of hyperactivity-impulsivity have persisted for at least 6 months to a degree that is maladaptive and inconsistent with developmental level:

a)   often fidgets with hands or feet or squirms in seat;
b)   leaves seat in classroom or in other situations in which remaining seated is expected;
c)   often runs about or climbs excessively in situations where it is inappropriate (in adolescents or adults, may be limited to subjective feelings of restlessness;
d)   often has difficulty playing or engaging in leisure activities quietly.

Impulsivity:

e)   often blurts out answers to questions before the questions have been completed;
f)   often has difficulty waiting in lines or awaiting turn in games or group situations.

In addition, symptoms should have been present before the child turns 7 and must be present in two or more situations. The latter is particularly important, since children frequently show their symptoms in one situation (such as home) but not in another (such as school). DSM-IV goes on to stress that the disturbance must cause 'clinically significant distress or impairment in social, academic or occupational functioning'.

It is important for parents to appreciate that children with ADD are not always hyperactive. In fact, some children cause considerable concern to their teachers by daydreaming or showing poor concentration in class without ever being overactive or impulsive. In addition, children do tend to become less hyperactive as they get older (usually after about 7 or 8 years of age) although difficulties with concentration will remain into adulthood.

The troublesome thing about ADD is that it does not occur all the time. Many children have no difficulties watching television or videos or playing computer games. These are highly visually stimulating with images changing many times every minute.

Causes

The cause for this condition is not fully understood. It clearly has a neuro-biological basis. Research has also shown that there is a genetic link. Thus, many children with ADD also have parents who have similar difficulties.

Making The Diagnosis

A number of steps need to be taken before a firm diagnosis can be made. Parents should start with a medical opinion about the child's physical health, in order to exclude any obvious causes like vision, hearing or thyroid dysfunction. Other medical conditions should also be considered.

There are a variety of ways of going about assessing for ADD. These include:

- In-depth interview with the parents, looking at the child's development, education and behavioural history.
- Evidence from the child's school or social groups.
- Use of a checklist such as the Conners' Checklist. The Conners' Checklist is a set of questions that differentiates between diagnoses of ADD (distinguishing between with hyperactivity and with distractibility/impulsivity) and other conditions such as oppositional defiant disorder, cognitive and learning problems, social difficulties.
- Observation in a clinical setting, together with testing that looks at a child's hyperactivity, distractibility and impulsivity in a standardised way.

Assessment of pre-schoolers is particularly difficult, since most of them are very active at one time or another. They also develop at different rates, so that while they may be very immature at one point they will then go through a developmental spurt and calm down. Nevertheless, there are some pre-schoolers who are very much more active, unable to entertain themselves, demanding and more easily bored than others.

In about 30 per cent of cases ADD exists alongside another problem, such as a specific learning difficulty or dyslexia.

Treatment For Attention Deficit Disorder

It is very important that the appropriate steps are taken in finding suitable help for a child, since inappropriate treatment and continuation of the disorder can lead to poor self-esteem, academic under-achievement and social isolation.

There has been considerable research interest in ADD since it was first identified a hundred years ago. Some approaches have been scientifically proven to be effective while others have been shown to have little or no effect. Those that are effective include:

- Parent training in behaviour management techniques
- Appropriate measures taken in the classroom
- Counselling and therapy for the individual or the family
- Medication if necessary. Between 70 to 80 per cent of children with ADD do respond well to medication.

All other treatments have either been shown to have little impact or have been researched inadequately.

Factors that have been shown to have an occasional or small impact, such as the levels of sugar, food additives and colouring in the diet, are being studied.

What can be done at school?

It is important that the teacher sees this as a situation that needs to be attended to, and not something that is simply going to improve by telling the child to concentrate.

Through the Educational Research and Improvement Clearing House, the US Department of Education has summarised the research and has come up with a variety of recommendations for teachers. They suggest that:

1. *The 'proper learning environment' must be established.* This means that children with ADD should be seated away from distractions in the classroom. They should be near the teacher's desk but as much apart from the class as possible. They should be surrounded by good role models. They have difficulty in handling change well, so need to be carefully supervised at transition times in class and in the less structured lessons.

2. *Instructions must be given carefully* to children with ADD. The teacher should be making eye contact with the child, keeping directions clear and concise and repeating the instructions if necessary. Sometimes it is important to get feedback from the child, to ensure that they have heard the whole instruction. A daily assignment notebook may help. The teacher should check that homework is written down correctly. This notebook may also be used for communication with parents.

3. *Giving assignments.* Only one task at a time should be given. The teacher should be monitoring frustration, since this may lead to a breakdown in good behaviour patterns. The child may need extra time for some tasks. Many children cope better if the assignment is broken down into manageable parts, often called 'chunks'. For example, a teacher wants a class to do 20 sums. For the ADD child, however, she might ask them to do 5 and then show them to her. This sets a reasonable target and gives the child an acceptable way to have a short break.

4. *Modifying behaviour and enhancing esteem.* The teacher needs to remain calm and have pre-established consequences for behaviour. It is important for the teacher to remember that this is not the child's fault and if things are not going well then other behavioural strategies will need to be considered. It is often best for a teacher to reward outcomes (such as completion of a task) rather than on task behaviour, since praise at this point may serve to distract the child. ADD children often respond better when inattention is drawn to their notice. Response/cost programmes will often work well. Children do need to be rewarded more frequently than they are punished. The child needs to be encouraged frequently and aspects of success need to be drawn to the attention of the whole class. It is also important for a teacher to be wary of using the child's name too often as a means of helping them to refocus. Constantly hearing one child's name can make the rest of the class increasingly aware of his unacceptable behaviour. Children with ADD need frequent feedback about when they are on task.

5. It is important to have an *individual education plan* with a specific plan for modifying unacceptable behaviour. This should be reviewed at approximately two-weekly intervals so that changes can be made if necessary. It is also important to keep trying for this period of time before judging a programme to be a failure.

Some children respond to social skills training. This will often help them to be less impulsive and socially inappropriate in a group.

Children with ADD do not cope well with team sports such as football, since they have difficulty in sustaining concentration for that length of time. They often do better at individual sports, such as tennis, gymnastics, skiing, swimming, karate.

Parenting The Child With Attention Deficit Disorder

Children with ADD present a special challenge for parents. Reasoning and explaining are poor techniques, since these children have difficulty in listening carefully.

Above all, these children respond well to clear rules and routines. They do not cope well with sudden changes of plan. Using charts and other reward systems will work well, as long as the parents start by tackling small targets. It is also important that parents should start with the most important issues first, such as temper tantrums or rudeness. These two issues will undermine any behaviour management systems. Thomas Phelan devised a system called "1,2,3, Magic!" for use with ADD children with behaviour management difficulties, which has been shown to be very successful over the years.

Homework is often a problem. This needs to be done in a distraction free environment. It should always be done with the television off (as should most other activities for ADD children). There should be a set time during which absolutely nothing else happens. Parents also need to look after each other. It is a stressful business having a child who is hyperactive, distractible and impulsive.

Where Can I Get More Information?

One of the best places for parents to find extra help is through the Internet. They should start with the C.H.A.D.D. Website, which can be found on www.chadd.org. This has a variety of fact sheets, research bulletins and information, including contacts for parents.

- "Is your Child Hyperactive, Inattentive, Impulsive, Distractible: Helping the ADD/ Hyperactive Child" by Stephen Garber, Marianne Garber and Robyn Spizman, 1990, Villard Books, Random House.
- "Power Parenting for Children with ADD" by Grad L Flick, Prentice Hall International, 1996
- "1,2,3, Magic!" by Thomas Phelan, Child Management Incorporated, 1996.
- "Understanding A.D.H.D." Christopher Green, Kit Chee, Roger Roberts, Random House, 1998.

References

American Psychiatric Association (1994). *Diagnostic and Statistical Manual of Mental Disorders*. Fourth Edition. Washington, DC: American Psychiatric Association.

Autism

(Information supplied by the National Autistic Society)

Autism is a complex developmental disability that affects social and communication skills. People with autism can often have accompanying learning disabilities but everyone with the condition shares a difficulty in making sense of the world. In most children with autism, some types of skills will be better than others so that their development will not only be slower than usual but will also be uneven and different from that of other children with learning disabilities.

An autistic spectrum disorder is a life-long disability and is not, at present, curable, but there are ways of helping, especially if a child is diagnosed and receives appropriate intervention early in life. Specialised education and structured support can really make a difference to a child's life, helping to maximise skills and achieve full potential in adulthood.

Autism affects the way a child communicates and relates to people around him or her. Although it describes a condition with wide ranging degrees of severity (hence the description, 'autistic spectrum disorder'), all those affected have a triad of impairments. These affect

- social interaction (difficulty with social relationships, eg appearing aloof and indifferent to other people around them or making odd, one-sided, naïve social approaches);
- social communication (difficulty with verbal and non-verbal communication, eg not really understanding the meaning of gestures, facial expressions or tone of voice);
- imagination (difficulty in the development of play and imagination, eg having a limited range of imaginative activities, possibly copied and pursued rigidly and repetitively).

In addition to this triad, repetitive behaviour patterns and a resistance to change in routine are notable features.

Particular points are worth noting. Firstly, the severity of impairment differs from person to person, and different aspects of the behaviour pattern are more obvious at some ages than at others. In addition, three-quarters of children with autism also have mild or severe learning disabilities. A child's personality, education and social environment can also markedly affect their behaviour. Finally, children with autism may also have other associated disabilities including epilepsy, cerebral palsy and sensory impairments.

Autism also includes the condition known as Asperger Syndrome. This term is used to describe people at the higher functioning end of the autistic spectrum. Most are of average or above average intelligence and generally have fewer problems with language, often speaking fluently, though their words can sometimes sound formal or stilted. Unfortunately, because their disability is often less obvious, a person with Asperger Syndrome may be more vulnerable. They can, sadly, be an easy target for teasing or bullying at school. The exact cause of autism has not yet been fully established. It is, however, evident from research that autism can be caused by a variety of conditions which affect brain development and which occur before, during or after birth. They include, for example, maternal rubella, tuberous sclerosis, lack of oxygen at birth and complications of childhood illness such as whooping cough and measles. In many instances, genetic traits appear to be important, though the sites of the relevant genes have yet to be identified.

As yet there is no cure for autism, but specialised education and structured support can help maximise a child's skills and minimise any behaviour problems. The right kind of education and care programme is essential. They make a real difference to the child's life enabling each individual, whatever their level of disability, to achieve as great a degree of independence as possible.

It is crucial that autism is recognised early in a child's life to enable effective intervention and management of the condition. Early diagnosis and intervention are also essential to ensure that families and carers have access to appropriate services and professional support.

Certainly the signs are there to be recognised. In most cases, the triad of impairments emerges in the first two to three years of life. Indeed, there are often indications of developmental problems within the first year. However, because autism is a complex condition it is easy to miss important clues.

Autism is a pattern of abnormal development which unfolds over time, so diagnosis depends upon obtaining a detailed history of the child's development and a careful assessment of skills and abilities.

In infancy one of the most important indications that autism could be present is the absence, or very delayed development, of drawing the attention of parents and others to objects or events. In normal childhood development, by 12–18 months, children are usually pointing at things and trying to engage the interest of the person they are with to invite them to look too. They can also gain attention by bringing toys and making eye contact when doing so. If this behaviour does not occur or begins very late and is limited to the child's own interests, an autistic disorder should be suspected.

If you suspect that autism is present it is essential that you refer the child for a specialist diagnosis and assessment as early as possible – either to your local GP, the Child Development Centre or Child and Family Guidance Centre, or, if you are a teacher, to your Local Education Authority's educational psychologist.

The National Autistic Society runs 21 education and adult centres for people with autism, supports local authorities in the development of specialist services, provides publications, conferences and training programmes, offers specialist diagnosis and assessment services and supports local groups and families around the country. For more information, please contact the National Autistic Society, 393 City Road, London EC1V 1NG, tel: 020 7833 2299, fax: 020 7833 9666, Website: www.nas.org.uk Email: nas@nas.org.uk

Cerebral Palsy
(Information supplied by SCOPE, formerly The Spastics Society)

Cerebral palsy is not a disease or an illness. It is the description of a physical impairment that affects movement. The movement problems vary from barely noticeable to extremely severe. No two people with cerebral palsy are the same – it is as individual as people themselves.

Cerebral palsy is most commonly the result of failure of the part of the brain to develop, either before birth or in early childhood. This is sometimes because of bleeding or blocked blood vessels, complications in labour, or extreme prematurity. Infections during pregnancy, eg rubella, or infancy and early childhood, eg meningitis or encephalitis, can also lead to cerebral palsy. Occasionally it is due to an inherited disorder. In such cases genetic counselling may be helpful. It is sometimes possible to identify the cause of cerebral palsy, but not always.

The main effect of cerebral palsy is difficulty in movement. Many people with cerebral palsy are hardly affected, others have problems walking, feeding, talking or using their hands. Some people, for example, are unable to sit up without support and need constant enabling.

Sometimes other parts of the brain are also affected, resulting in sight, hearing perception and learning difficulties, and some people are also affected by epilepsy.

People with cerebral palsy often have difficulty controlling their movement and facial expressions. This does not necessarily mean that their mental abilities are in any way impaired. Some are of higher than average intelligence, other people with cerebral palsy have moderate or severe learning difficulties, although most people with cerebral palsy are of average intelligence.

Cerebral palsy includes a variety of conditions. The three main types correspond to injuries on different parts of the brain and many people will have a mixture of the following types and effects:

- People with spastic cerebral palsy find that some of the muscles become very stiff and weak, especially under effort. This can affect their control of movement.
- People with athetoid cerebral palsy have some loss of control of their posture, and tend to make unwanted movements.
- People with ataxic cerebral palsy usually have problems with balance. They may also have shaky hand movements and irregular speech.

The needs of children with cerebral palsy are very wide and often very complex. Some are able to integrate into mainstream schools with minimal support whilst others require the help of a welfare assistant, special furniture and adaptations to the environment. The mainstream experience can vary greatly according to the individual challenges faced by each child, the available expertise, resources and environment and the commitment of all involved. However, the needs of some children cannot easily be met with integrated mainstream provision.

In many cases, it is the complexity of needs as a result of cerebral palsy, for example communication, visuo-motor and visual perceptual problems, physical ability and medical conditions such as epilepsy and dietary needs that lead parents to seek out specialist education.

It is now widely agreed that early intervention is very important. The early diagnosis of a disability, coupled with appropriate specialist intervention, can do much to lessen its effects upon the development of children, and thus reduce the potential of the disability to result in functional handicap. This is no less true in the case of cerebral palsy than of any other disability.

The effectiveness of such a strategy in the early years is enhanced greatly by the active participation of the parents and family of a disabled child. Their involvement is central to the success of such programmes. During recent years, there has been a recognition of the role of parents as the prime educators of young children with whom other professional groups must work in genuine partnership.

Access to the National Curriculum is enhanced when children with cerebral palsy have opportunities to develop stable sitting, head control, hand/eye co-ordination, gross/fine motor skills, effective communication, independence in standing, walking and self-help skills.

Many children need additional time to achieve writing and manipulation activities and, in order to keep pace with their peers, require up to date micro technology and/or communication aids to support their learning.

Methods of teaching vary and professionals from many disciplines can be involved, eg teachers, occupational therapists, physiotherapists, conductors, nursery nurses, speech and language therapists, psychologists, as well as a variety of medical professionals. There are traditional educational methods within mainstream and special schools. Some mainstream schools have special units attached. Multi-disciplinary teams of staff are involved in teaching and providing for the needs of individual children. Children attending a mainstream school will usually require time out to attend therapy sessions. This may be within the school or can involve attendance at a child development centre.

Children attending a special school will usually receive their therapy support in the school. Some therapists see the children in their classroom as well for individual sessions. Another option is Conductive Education, developed by Professor Andra Peto in Hungary. Conductive Education is a holistic learning system which incorporates teaching and learning, and may help some children with cerebral palsy to become as independent as possible, encompassing all their learning needs.

For further information on cerebral palsy and SCOPE, contact the Cerebral Palsy Helpline, SCOPE, PO Box 833, Milton Keynes, MK12 5NY. Telephone 0808 800 3333 (freephone).

Cystic Fibrosis
(Information supplied by the Cystic Fibrosis Trust)

Cystic Fibrosis (CF) is the UK's most common inherited, life-threatening disease, affecting about 1 in 2,500 children. CF affects the glands which secrete body fluids, causing damage to major organs including the lungs, pancreas and liver and the digestive and reproductive systems. Before the discovery of antibiotics children with CF did not live very long. However, modern treatment means that today most live into adulthood with the condition kept under control. CF affects children in different ways and can vary in severity from one month to the next, so it is important to examine the special needs of each child on an individual basis.

One person in 25 is a carrier of the faulty gene which can cause CF in their children. Carriers are, however, completely healthy because they also have a normal gene which overrides the defective gene. If both parents are carriers of CF, any child they have has a 25 per cent chance of having CF (by inheriting faulty genes from both parents), a 50 per cent chance of being completely healthy but being a carrier (by inheriting a faulty gene from one parent and a healthy gene from the other) and a 25 per cent chance of being completely unaffected (by inheriting normal genes from both parents). Screening is now possible to enable prospective parents to find out if either is a carrier.

Medical complications

Children born with CF produce an abnormally thick mucus in the lungs which can block smaller airways and cause infections, leading to long-term damage. The most noticeable effect is a persistent cough which is non-infectious but may cause distress in front of classmates, particularly if severe, which may lead to coughing up mucus. Digestive problems, in widely varying degrees, may be caused as a result of damage to the pancreas, which produces insulin to regulate sugar levels in the blood and enzymes which aid digestion.

Other less common health problems associated with CF include sinusitis, hayfever, arthritis, diabetes, heart strain and cirrhosis of the liver. Sexual maturity may be delayed and boys with CF may become sterile.

Treatment for cystic fibrosis

Treatment for CF aims to keep the lungs functioning as normally as possible. Physiotherapy and breathing exercises to clear the lungs of any harmful mucus are a vital part of each child's daily routine. Many will require it two or three times a day, from 15 minutes to an hour at a time, depending on the child's needs. Parents are taught to do physiotherapy as soon as CF is diagnosed, but older children can do part of the treatment themselves and often become completely independent.

Physiotherapy may be combined with nebuliser treatment, in which liquid medication is converted to a fine mist which is inhaled and works directly in the lungs. Antibiotics are also taken regularly to prevent or treat infections. Digestive problems can be alleviated by replacing missing enzymes with a substance called pancreatin, taken with meals to aid good absorption of food.

Special Educational Needs

A child with CF may have special educational needs if the condition prevents or hinders him or her from making use of educational facilities of a kind provided for children of the same age in schools covered by the Local Education Authority. Most children with CF can be provided for within a mainstream school without the need for a statement. Schools should, of course, involve parents and seek their views at all stages.

All schools have the service of a Medical Officer or equivalent, but not always on site. Teachers, therefore, must be willing to allow parents or other helpers to come into school when a child requires treatment. The school's medical room or another suitable room will need to be made available.

Teachers may also need to arrange supervision at mealtimes to ensure that children eat well and take any necessary medication and food supplement capsules.

CF does not affect a child's intellectual or academic abilities but may mean long periods away from school because of chest infections or hospital stays. However, schools may be able to set work to be done at home or in the hospital if the child is well enough.

Physical exercise is usually very good for children with CF because it helps to loosen mucus in the lungs, but teachers should be aware that children may feel unusually tired after a cold or chest infection. Teachers should remember that children with CF may need to use the toilet urgently and more frequently than other pupils. Therefore, consideration should be made for them to leave the classroom for privacy to cough and visit the toilet.

Children with CF may be teased at school because of their persistent cough and the fact that they may be small for their age. Some may find it embarrassing to take medication in front of their classmates. Friends must be supportive and encouraged to understand the importance of physiotherapy sessions which may sometimes interfere with the social timetable. The adolescent years can be particularly traumatic. Some teenagers may display rebellious behaviour by neglecting physiotherapy and diet and refusing to recognise the potential seriousness of the condition. Sympathetic counselling can be valuable to help teenagers cope with the stresses associated with delayed sexual maturity, to advise girls of the risks associated with pregnancy and offer support to boys who face possible sterility.

The pressures of coping with CF place great strain on family life and relationships. Brothers and sisters may feel resentment at the attention given to their sibling with CF and may feel guilty as a result. This can give rise to bad behaviour, withdrawal or other problems at school. All members of the family will be affected by the psychological pressures arising from the severe nature of CF, uncertainty about the future, genetic aspects and tiring routines. Families may also have to face the prospect of death. Medical advice, support and bereavement counselling are available to help families to cope with these pressures.

Teachers can help by meeting parents before a child comes into class and by understanding the problems which may arise within the family. They may be able to offer practical help by administering medication or supervising children taking it. There are no national guidelines for teachers on giving medication to children at school and teachers are not obliged to do so. If parents consent, however, there is no reason why teachers should not help in this way, provided they are insured by their employer. Teachers can also explain to classmates the reasons for coughing, physiotherapy and so on and encourage a positive attitude.

Special arrangements can be made for candidates with CF taking GCSE examinations. Additional time and supervised breaks may be allowed, or permission given for candidates to take examinations in hospital or at home (see section on GCSE & GCE examinations – Special Arrangements for Candidates with Special Assessment Needs).

For further information parents should contact the Cystic Fibrosis Trust, 11 London Road, Bromley, Kent BR1 1BY, tel: 020 8464 7211, fax: 020 8313 0472, E-mail: enquiries@cftrust.org.uk Website: www.cftrust.org.uk

Down's Syndrome
(Information provided by the Down's Syndrome Association)

Down's syndrome is the most common form of learning disability (previously known as mental handicap). It is caused by an accident before or around the time of conception, which gives rise to an extra number 21 chromosome in each of the person's cells. Instead of the usual 46 chromosomes, a person with Down's Syndrome has 47 chromosomes. This results in a disruption of the growth of the developing embryo, and a degree of developmental delay in the child.

The presence of the extra chromosome also gives rise to a number of physical characteristics, which are often shared by people who have the condition. These include:

- short stature;
- eyes that slant upward and outward – the eyelids often have an extra fold of skin (epicanthic fold) which appears to exaggerate the slant. (This does not mean there is anything wrong with the eyes – they just look different.);
- small ears;
- short fingers;
- poor general muscle tone, although this tends to improve as the child grows.

The presence or absence of these characteristics bears no relation to the child's intellectual ability. It cannot be stressed enough that each child will have his or her own personality and traits of character, just like any other child.

Certain medical problems are more common among people with Down's Syndrome than in the rest of the population. These include:

Hearing loss

Children with Down's Syndrome are particularly prone to colds and often find them more difficult to 'shake off'. The Eustachian tubes which connect the ear to the nose can be particularly narrow in children with Down's Syndrome and become easily blocked with mucus. This, in turn, can lead to middle ear infections (otitis media) and cause temporary deafness. Usually, when the cold gets better, the Eustachian tube clears and the mucus which caused the infection drains away.

Sometimes, however, a single infection, or repeated upper respiratory infections such as colds, or infected or enlarged adenoids, can cause more long-term obstruction of the middle ear space which never drains away. The fluid in the ear gradually changes from a watery substance to become more like jelly (or glue) and hearing is affected, a condition known as 'glue ear'. This can happen in all children, but is more frequent in children with Down's Syndrome.

Vision Problems

Many children wear glasses, but a small proportion of children with Down's Syndrome also have a degree of visual impairment. However, this is far less common than hearing problems. As with other pupils who wear glasses, teachers must make sure that the child actually does wear them when necessary. Visually-impaired children have a partial or total lack of vision in both eyes. Most LEAs employ advisory teachers for visually-impaired students, and these specialists will be able to give guidance to teachers in mainstream schools. It is estimated that 75–80 per cent of classroom activities are based on vision, so a child who is visually disadvantaged will need considerable support.

Lack of muscle tone

Many babies with Down's Syndrome have poor muscle tone and tend to be 'floppy' (hypotonic). In most cases, this characteristic reduced muscle tone improves as the child grows. However, in some children, it can contribute to a delay in acquiring fine and/or gross motor skills. This means that skills such as running, skipping, throwing and catching may cause a child with Down's Syndrome more difficulty than the other children in the class, but there is nothing to prevent that child from acquiring these skills eventually. As with all children, the opportunity to practise these skills is necessary and it is important not to restrict such opportunities because the child is perceived to have certain limitations.

Poor muscle tone can also affect fine motor skills such as writing. Again, most children will eventually be able to write quite well, but may take longer to acquire such skills.

Heart defects

It is estimated that about 40 per cent of children born with Down's Syndrome also have a heart defect. Such defects can range from relatively minor problems to severe malformations of the heart, which can require surgery and/or medication. Most children of school age who have an operable defect should already have undergone surgery. Successful treatment will allow the child to lead as active a life as he/she wants.

Speech and language problems

Nearly all children with Down's Syndrome have significant delay in language acquisition and understanding. This is caused by a combination of factors, some of which are purely physical and some due to the overall developmental delay that usually accompanies the condition.

The main physical obstacle is the ratio between the size of the tongue to the size of the mouth. Many children with Down's Syndrome have a small mouth cavity which means that their tongues seem too big for their mouths. This, along with poor muscle tone in the tongue and mouth, can cause children varying degrees of difficulty in actually producing the sounds required for talking clearly.

Other speech and language problems of children with Down's Syndrome stem from delayed understanding of language or difficulty in processing words. It is common for children with Down's Syndrome to have problems with auditory short-term memory, which has limited capacity for storing and processing information they hear. This difficulty can sometimes make the child seem disobedient or stubborn when, in fact, he or she has been given too much information at once and is unable to process it. This can be helped in a number of ways, principally by breaking down information into smaller units which the child can deal with more easily, giving him/her time to process the information and respond. Speech and language therapists will be able to suggest strategies for improving any language problems.

Since the 1981 Education Act, the trend has been towards the integration of children with Down's Syndrome into ordinary schools rather than special schools. However, a significant number of children with Down's Syndrome are successfully placed in special schools and some will spend time in both.

The variance in the abilities of children with Down's Syndrome means that they are as individual as members of the general population and should be assessed as such when a choice of school is made.

Dyscalculia
(Information supplied by Dr Steve Chinn, Mark College, Somerset)

Dyscalculia is a specific learning difficulty which hinders the learning of mathematics. It may occur as a single learning difficulty for a child or it may co-occur with other specific learning difficulties, the most likely of which are dyslexia and dyspraxia.

Research on dyscalculia is minimal, though Prof. Brian Butterworth now has a team in London researching this fascinating topic. The research that does exist suggests that dyscalculia as a single, non co-occurring problem affects around 3 per cent of the population, which would represent a large number of pupils. As a co-occurring problem with dyslexia, Joffe suggested 60 per cent, but Miles and Chinn both suggest that the figure is much closer to 100 per cent. Who can guess the percentage of the population who say that they 'can't do maths'?

For this article I shall interpret dyscalculia as a resistant learning difficulty with maths, primarily with numeracy.

There has been some recent research which suggests that maths difficulties may have a genetic factor. There is also work in Europe looking at the areas of the brain which are active when performing mathematical tasks. It is difficult to separate the inherent problems of a child from the influences and experiences of his or her environment. It is likely that problems are cumulative. For example it has been shown that maths anxiety impacts negatively on working memory. Maths makes significant demands on short term and working memory so anxiety exacerbates any difficulties that pre-exist.

It is worth considering the interactions between the pupil and the subject for any learning difficulty. Maths is a developmental subject. Early experiences focus on numeracy and many of the concepts for algebra, calculus and other topics are dependent on early learning experiences. Attitude and anxiety also interact with learning and maths can create anxiety beyond any other subject. Indeed society has dealt with this by allowing us to confess that we 'can't do maths' without losing any social status. The same is not true of reading.

Since numeracy dominates the child's early experiences of maths, it seems likely that the root causes of dyscalculia start with numbers. Most learners can look at a random display of three, four, five or six objects and identify the number of objects correctly. Some cannot and Butterworth is proposing that this is one significant factor in predicting dyscalculia. His diagnostic test will be published by NFER-Nelson in 2002.

I would consider that memory and spatial skills are the key issues contributing to difficulties in maths. Dyslexics tend to have a weak short-term memory, for example a 15 year old boy who can only reliably recall three items and processes information in maximum chunks of three. It would be more typical for that number to be around seven. It is obvious that this deficit will have a significant impact on mental arithmetic tasks. For example to be able to add 137 and 484 mentally requires several steps, each making demands on memory. It is also likely that the answer will be computed from units to tens to hundreds, which will require the child to reverse the digits for the final answer.

Difficulties with long-term memory are less predictable. Some years ago Elaine Miles corrected me when I said dyslexics have poor long-term memories. She pointed out that the long-term memory is not for everything and this seems to be the case for most if not all learning difficulties. Certain maths facts seem to be difficult to hold in and retrieve from long term memory. The most common of these are basic facts, but for an able mathematician with dyslexia problems it is naming formulae.

There are three areas of impact for pupils who cannot (quickly) access basic facts. One is a sense of failure and loss of self-confidence. The second is the number of inaccuracies that will result in low scores for any work. The third is slow speed of working.

The attitude to learning basic facts is based on two premises. 'I had to do it and it didn't hurt me.' 'If you can't learn these facts you can't do maths'.

The first premise makes the dangerous assumption that everything works for everyone. The second premise overlooks the benefits of pupils learning alternate strategies based on building on the more easily remembered facts (such as doubles, tens and fives). A full description of these strategies is available in the 'What to do when you can't . . .' books.

Spatial skills may prevent a child from mastering the key concept of place value. This deficit may also hinder his attempts to line up digits in vertical sums or understand angle work or co-ordinates. Pupils may cope with co-ordinates when both values are positive, but may experience a disproportionate difficulty when one or both co-ordinates become negative.

One of the (inexplicable to me) demands of maths is speed of working. A child with difficulties works more slowly. If pressured to work more quickly then anxiety increases as does the error rate. One of the easier differentiations a teacher can make is to adjust the number of examples his slower pupils are required to do whilst keeping the range of learning experience the same.

Sometimes a pupil can start maths quite successfully and then, inexplicably, fail. For example a child may be happy when little written work is demanded and then fail when he is required to document his methods. Or a child may be surviving early demands for learning facts but not be able to appreciate or absorb the patterns and generalisations, which can be used to organise information into more manageable and memorable forms. Maths is a developmental subject and any area of failure or insecurity can have severe implications for future progress.

The vocabulary of maths can create problems. For example there are several words we can use to imply $+ - \times$ and $\div$. But then the language of maths can be used so that these words mean the opposite operation. Pupils with learning difficulties like the world to be consistent and maths is more inconsistent than we may appreciate. For example, until we meet fractions $+$ means add, but with $\frac{1}{4} + \frac{1}{4}$ the $+$ only operates on the top numbers. I firmly believe the equation 'Fractions = Anxiety'.

Children who are failing in maths will first of all need an understanding of their individual problems. They will need encouragement and the experience of success. Clear explanations (not just slow and repeated louder) of fundamental ideas using structured multisensory, multicognitive methods are essential.

Dyslexia
(Information supplied by the Dyslexia Institute)

Dyslexia is a specific learning difficulty, which hinders the learning of literacy skills. The problem of managing verbal codes in memory is neurologically based and tends to run in families. Other symbolic systems, such as mathematics and musical notation, can also be affected.

Dyslexia can occur at any level of intellectual ability. It can accompany, but is not a result of, lack of motivation, emotional disturbance or meagre opportunities.

About one child in every twenty-five is affected to some degree and will need specialist tuition at some point in their school career.

It has long been established that there is a genetic disposition to dyslexia and this has been confirmed by recent research. Environment, both before and after birth, also plays a part. Most importantly, it is known that environmental enrichment, including focused teaching, can bring about change in an individual's ability to learn and to succeed.

It is the tiny neurological differences present in specific areas of the brains of dyslexic people that create difficulties with processing information. Research has established that there are differences in lower levels where sensory information is coming into the brain and in higher levels where languages and codes are being organised, sequenced and retrieved.

Pre-school dyslexic children will often have difficulties with spoken language. They may be late in learning to talk and in learning common sequences, and may confuse sounds.

Typically, at five years dyslexic children will have problems with letter knowledge, in linking sounds with symbols and in blending letters. They are also likely to have difficulty in learning by heart such things as the months of the year, and songs and rhymes, and they frequently find it difficult to organise themselves. As a result difficulties arise in reading, spelling and learning to do sequential activities like learning tables. They may become increasingly reluctant to go to school during the first few years, or may develop emotional or behavioural problems.

Unidentified early problems persist and become more complex as they undermine the learning process. Children with dyslexia are puzzling to their parents and to their teachers. Often they appear (because they are) much more able than their work suggests. Occasionally it is only the more complex writing and comprehension tasks required at secondary school which expose the problems.

Dyslexia affects some people more severely than others. This depends on the amount of neurological difference and whether they have received the support that they need. The greater the difference, the greater the help required. The later the condition is identified, the greater its impact is likely to be. Success breeds success; conversely, failure breeds failure. Degrees of difficulty should be identified as early as possible so that effective remediation can be put in place.

The effects of dyslexia can be alleviated by skilled specialist teaching and committed learning. All children benefit from well-structured, phonically-based early learning at school; all benefit from practice to make the learning permanent. Dyslexic children must have this type of teaching and, because of their difficulties, a multi-sensory approach which integrates seeing, hearing and doing is critical to them.

If by the age of six a child is failing to gain early reading, writing and spelling skills (or earlier if dyslexia exists in the family), a psychologist's assessment should be considered. An assessment by an experienced specialist teacher can also be very valuable in the early years. The aim is to identify strengths and weaknesses and make recommendations for appropriate helping strategies.

The majority of dyslexic children can, and should, be educated in ordinary schools alongside their peers. They will benefit from specialist teaching to enable them to reach their full potential. Only a tiny minority with severe and complex problems, which are frequently exacerbated by other conditions such as attention deficit hyperactivity disorder or dyspraxia, need to be educated in specialist schools. The key is the quality of teaching by the specialist teacher.

Dyslexic children must be identified and given focused specialist teaching as early as possible. Wherever possible they should be placed in schools which can nurture their latent talents as they frequently have strong creative and lateral thinking abilities. If their education is well-managed and they are prepared to work hard they can, and do, succeed in a wide range of careers.

Dyspraxia
(Information supplied by the Dyspraxia Foundation)

The Dyspraxia Foundation defines dyspraxia as 'an impairment or immaturity of the organisation of movement and, in many individuals, there may be associated problems with language, perception and thought'.

The term normally used is Developmental Dyspraxia or Developmental Co-ordination Disorder.

The condition is thought to affect up to 10 per cent of the population in varying degrees. It is probable that there is at least one dyspraxic child in every classroom requiring access to a specific treatment programmes.

Symptoms are evident from an early age. Youngsters are generally irritable from birth and many exhibit significant feeding problems. They are slow to achieve expected developmental milestones, often not sitting independently by the age of 8 months. Many fail to go through the crawling stage as babies, preferring to 'bottom shuffle' and then walk. Children with dyspraxia usually avoid tasks which require good manual dexterity and depend upon well developed perceptual skills. Inset puzzles, Lego and jigsaws are difficult.

Between the ages of 3 and 5, children with dyspraxia may demonstrate the following types of behaviour:

- Very high levels of motor activity, including feet swinging and tapping when seated, hand clapping or twisting and an inability to stay in one place for more than 5 minutes.
- High levels of excitability, with a loud/shrill voice. Children may be easily distressed and prone to temper tantrums.
- Awkward movement. Children may constantly bump into objects and fall over. Associated mirror movements, hands flap when running.

- Difficulty pedalling a tricycle or similar toy.
- Poor figure and ground awareness. Children may lack any sense of danger, illustrated, for example, by jumping from an inappropriate height.
- Continued messy eating. Children may spill liquid from drinking cups and prefer to eat with their fingers.
- Avoidance of constructional toys, such as jigsaws or building blocks.
- Poor fine motor skills, demonstrated by difficulty in holding a pencil or using scissors. Drawings may appear immature.
- Lack of imaginative play. Children may show little interest in 'dressing up' or playing appropriately in a home or Wendy House.
- Limited creative play.
- Isolation within the peer group. Rejected by peers, children may prefer adult company.
- Laterality still not established. Problems crossing the mid-line.
- Persistent language difficulties. Children are often referred to a speech therapist.
- Sensitivity to sensory stimulation, including high levels of noise, being touched or wearing new clothes.
- Limited response to verbal instruction. Children may exhibit a slower response time and problems with comprehension.
- Limited concentration. Tasks are often left unfinished.

If the condition is not identified, problems can persist throughout school life causing increasing frustration and a lowering of self-esteem.

Between the ages of 5 and 7, behaviour may include the following traits:

- Problems adapting to a more structured school routine
- Difficulties with PE (Physical Education)
- Slow at dressing and inability to tie shoe laces
- Barely legible handwriting
- Immature drawing and copying skills
- Limited concentration and poor listening skills
- Literal use of language
- Inability to remember more than 2–3 instructions
- Slow completion of class work
- Continued high levels of motor activity
- Motor stereotypes – hand flapping or clapping when excited
- Tendency to become easily distressed and emotional
- Problems co-ordinating a knife and fork
- Inability to form relationships with other youngsters, isolation in class
- Sleeping difficulties, including wakefulness at night and nightmares
- Reporting of physical symptoms, such as migraine, headaches or feeling sick

Poor handwriting is one of the most common symptoms of dyspraxia and, as the child progresses through the education system, requirement for written work increases. By the age of about 8 or 9 the children may have become disaffected and poor school attendance is much in evidence in secondary education.

With access to appropriate treatment, the majority of dyspraxic youngsters could have their needs accommodated within the mainstream setting.

Parents concerned about their children should refer to their GP or health visitor if the child is aged under five or the special needs co-ordinator if in full-time schooling. A referral may then be made to an outside professional, for example, a paediatrician, educational psychologist, physiotherapist, occupational therapist or speech therapist for assessment.

When an appointment has been made, write down all your concerns. In an unfamiliar setting your child may not behave in the expected manner or give sufficient attention to the tasks set. Assessment usually involves giving a detailed account of your child's developmental history, examination of gross and fine motor skills and a test of intellectual ability.

Treatment is available from specialists in health and education when the condition has been identified. Movement programmes may be offered by therapists and additional support can be made available in school.

If you require further information about dyspraxia or how to help your child, contact the Dyspraxia Foundation, 8 West Alley, Hitchin, Herts, SG5 1EG, tel: 01462 454 986.

Epilepsy
(Information supplied by the British Epilepsy Association)

Epilepsy is a tendency for the brain to experience recurrent seizures in which total or partial consciousness may be lost. The brain is a complex sensitive organ carefully protected inside the bony skull. It regulates and controls everything we do. To accomplish its many functions the brain's nerve cells (neurones) must work in smooth harmony. An epileptic seizure is caused by a brief disruption of brain function involving abnormal electrical activity in the nerve cells.

Epilepsy can begin at any age, but the incidence is high in childhood. Some children have epilepsy as a result of damage to the brain through, for example, injury, birth trauma or stroke (symptomatic epilepsy). Others have no known or identifiable cause but have epilepsy as a result of being born with a low epileptic seizure threshold (idiopathic epilepsy). Everyone has a seizure threshold; having a low seizure threshold means that a person has a lower resistance to seizures than people in general.

Children who have 'uncomplicated epilepsy', that is those without any additional physical disability or mental handicap, have exactly the same range of intelligence and abilities as unaffected children. For this reason the majority of children with epilepsy are educated in mainstream schools, usually without any extra educational provision. A number of children with epilepsy do experience behavioural problems and/or learning difficulties. However, the possible causes for this vary. The following factors may have a bearing:

- The severity of the epilepsy. If seizures occur frequently, a child's everyday life may well be affected.
- As epilepsy is a symptom rather than a condition in itself, it may well be that any damage to the brain may cause learning difficulties as well as epilepsy.

- The type of seizure. For example, when someone is experiencing a complex partial seizure they may appear to others as if their behaviour is strange or abnormal.
- Subclinical seizure activity, that is ongoing epileptic activity which is taking place in the brain without any obvious outward signs. This may also affect a child's learning or behaviour.
- The duration of seizures. Prolonged seizure activity (non-convulsive status epilepticus) may be accompanied by confusion, inappropriate behaviour, etc.
- Anti-epileptic medication. This may also be a possible cause for behaviour problems/learning difficulties and therefore needs careful monitoring by the child's specialist.
- Psychological and social factors, such as family and peer attitudes as well as self-image.

There is also some evidence to suggest that some children with uncomplicated epilepsy do experience specific learning problems with particular subjects, often reading or arithmetic. For all these children, it is important that individual educational assessments are made, together with advice from the relevant education professionals to ensure that all children achieve their full potential.

Finally, there are some children with epilepsy who will need to attend schools particularly for children with this condition. There are very few schools in this category, but the following are specialist centres for children with epilepsy and associated problems: The National Centre for Young People with Epilepsy (NCYPE), St Piers Lane, Lingfield, Surrey RH7 6PW tel: 01342 832243; St Elizabeth's School, South End, Much Hadham, Herts SG10 6EW tel: 01279 844270; and the David Lewis School, Mill Lane, Warford, Nr Alderley Edge, Cheshire SK9 7UD tel: 01565 872613.

Further information about epilepsy and education can be obtained from the British Epilepsy Association Helpline (0808) 800 5050. The Helpline has a 24-hour answering machine, on which a message can be left to obtain the information you require. Alternatively, you can speak directly to an Advice and Information Officer. This service is available from 9.00am to 4.30pm Monday to Thursday and 9.00am to 4.00pm on Friday.

Gifted children
(Arno Rabinowitz, Chartered Educational Psychologist, Specialist Psychological Services)

In every group of children there are some who show more creativity, have more interest in learning and who are quicker to learn. Researchers estimate that these children make up about 2 per cent of the school population and these are the ones that are often called gifted. The word gifted, though, is not so often used now: schools prefer to use more accurate terms like able and talented or exceptionally able. Whatever term is used, the education of these children poses many special problems. The first problem is identifying the child with unusual or special abilities. From the very beginning the child will have been specially responsive to new ideas and insatiably curious, often severely testing the limits of parents' patience. A powerful sense of observation, an early ability to use logic and to read, an easy growth of lateral thinking and usually a good ability to express ideas and feelings are other early indictors of exceptional ability. Sometimes too, allied with these, is early development of good co-ordination, ingenuity in managing mechanical problems and a degree of determination and persistence that can be exhausting for the adults involved. If you link this with a special interest and ability ahead of usual developmental levels in activities such as music, you have a good profile of an average child with special abilities. The main thing to remember, though, is that there is no average specially able child. Each one is very different and has very different needs.

Once the child gets to school he or she may be quite quickly recognised as specially able by alert teachers. They will notice that the child is good at reasoning and dealing with abstract ideas and can do both of these remarkably quickly The child's vocabulary and ability to use it will be better than most. Reading will have usually developed easily and quickly, but this does not always happen. There are many dyslexic gifted children. For most, though, problem-solving appears to be a pleasure, as is the ability to put solutions into effect. Linked with this is often a very low boredom threshold and consequent displacement behaviour. The more able are not always the best behaved in class.

As a result, problems do sometimes arise. Teachers, particularly those who lack appropriate resources and training, may misinterpret signs of exceptional ability if a child is naughty or disruptive or has learning difficulties such as dyslexia or dyspraxia or conditions such as Asperger Syndrome (see p15) which gives rise to additional frustrations for the child. If parents believe that their child's exceptional abilities have not been recognised at school, tact, diplomacy and persistence will be required in tackling this issue.

Tests by educational psychologists, arranged through the school or through one of the relevant organisations, can give a very good idea of the child's academic potential. They can show, too, if a child is underachieving. However, a combination of the observations of parents and teachers, together with formal tests, is usually the best way of achieving a clear idea of a child's ability. What is particularly important in all testing is that any results are related to the National Curriculum and the levels to be expected. If this does not happen then it is very difficult for schools to make proper use of any estimations of potential ability.

Identification is the first problem. The second is understanding the need for these special children to have as normal a childhood as possible. Without this it is difficult for the child, as an adult, to make complete use of his or her special abilities.

Although more able children learn more quickly, their rate of emotional development is not always equally swift. For intellectual activities the child may need to be in a group doing higher level work but will still require the friendship, companionship and stimulation of a group of people of the same age and social interests.

People often think that the best way to help more able children is to accelerate them through classes so that they spend time learning with older and higher-achieving children. This is not always the right course. An enhanced curriculum, for which the National Curriculum makes good provision, is usually better for the child's development. The more able also need more opportunities for activities and the development of interests so as to prevent the onset of boredom. The most helpful way to provide this is often through evening and weekend clubs at school and activities organised by the major voluntary societies.

When the child reaches secondary school the extension of the curriculum is easier to organise. This can be arranged through the provision of differentiated work in conjunction with a school extension programme for the most able. Some schools allow the student to work with more advanced groups while retaining a link with their class or tutor group. Some can arrange for students to work at a local college for part of the curriculum. What is needed is a degree of imagination and resourcefulness in curriculum design while at the same time remembering the important principle that the normal process of personal and emotional development needs to be given as much care as does the narrowly academic process.

Sometimes difficulties arise when more able children show behaviour problems or appear to be unrecognised or underachieving. If this should happen, the first approach for parents should be to the child's tutor or to the school's special educational needs co-ordinator. Discussion should result in some agreement about the child's ability and needs. If not, parents should ask the school to bring in an educational psychologist (EP) to observe or test the child . It is sensible to ask for a copy of the school or LEA policy as soon as possible. Sometimes, if there is no agreement or if the school has no access to a psychologist, parents arrange for an independent assessment. This can be organised through the National Association for Gifted Children (01908 673677). The British Psychological Society (0116 254 9568) publishes a list of chartered psychologists and this is usually available in public libraries.

It is important that able children are helped to achieve everything they can. It is equally important that, in doing this, they do not become isolated from their friends and from groups in school; otherwise they will lose as much as they may have gained from early achievement. Balance, as in all things, is very important. Finding out your child's capabilities, working with the school to ensure that the child is stretched but not isolated, and allowing the child as much of a normal childhood as possible is the ideal prescription, the one to be aimed at. Intelligence and wisdom are two very different qualities. Finding the right prescription for a child will mean that these qualities both grow together and result in happiness and appropriate achievement.

[The Gabbitas, Truman and Thring Educational Trust manages a programme of masterclasses and residential courses for exceptionally able children. For details of 'Tomorrow's Achievers' and a list of courses contact Patricia Morse (see p.viii)

Deafness/Hearing Impairment
(Information provided by the National Deaf Children's Society [NDCS])

Types of deafness

Conductive deafness is the most common type. It means that sounds cannot pass efficiently through the outer and middle ear to the cochlea and auditory nerve. This is often caused by fluid in the middle ear (glue ear).

Sensori-neural deafness, or nerve deafness as it is sometimes called, usually means that the cochlea is not processing the sound effectively. Often the cause of sensori-neural deafness is not known, but hereditary factors are often present. Deafness may be passed down in families even if there is no apparent history of deafness. Infectious diseases such as rubella, mumps, measles or meningitis can also cause deafness. Another cause could be a shortage of oxygen in the bloodstream at birth or some other birth trauma. Premature babies are more at risk of being deaf.

Few children are totally deaf. Most children will have some hearing at some frequencies if the sound is made loud enough.

Communication methods

Children naturally try to learn a language that enables them to be understood. The communication method used by a deaf child will depend on a number of factors, such as the level of their hearing loss and which method they feel most comfortable with. The most common types of communication used by deaf children are summarised below:

Auditory-oral approaches to communication emphasise encouraging listening skills. These approaches maintain that, with the use of technology such as hearing aids, radio aids and cochlear implants to amplify residual hearing, children can develop their listening skills and therefore develop a spoken language. They do not use sign language or fingerspelling to support the understanding of spoken language.

Lip-reading is the ability to read lip patterns. Many deaf children will naturally try to lip-read when they are communicating. However it would be difficult for most deaf children to understand fully a conversation through lip-reading alone. The best possible conditions would need to be in place e.g. a quiet space and good lighting. This would allow them to concentrate and follow what is being lip-read. Lip-reading would usually be used in line with other communication approaches.

British Sign Language (BSL) is used by over 70,000 people within the British Deaf Community. It is a visual language using hand-shapes, facial expressions, gestures and body language to communicate. BSL is an independent, complete language with a unique vocabulary. The grammatical structure of BSL is different from that of written and spoken English. Just like other languages, BSL has evolved over time and developed regional and national dialects. **Fingerspelling** is a technique in which each letter of the alphabet is given its own sign (using fingers and palms). It is used for signing names, places or words that do not have a sign.

Deafness in education

Deafness itself is not defined as a special educational need. However, there are needs arising from deafness, whether it is temporary or permanent, which may require special educational provision. For example, a deaf child's language and communication development can often be affected by their deafness. They may need extra provision in the form of support from a specialist teacher of the deaf, regular speech and language therapy and specialist equipment such as a radio aid system.

There are various issues to consider when a deaf child attends a school such as: appropriate teaching methods, technical support, language and communication support as well as social and emotional development.

Educational support for deaf children

The National Deaf Children's Society (NDCS) has produced *Quality Standards in Education*, which sets out a number of recommendations for education services and schools working with deaf children and their families. These standards are particularly useful when considering what support deaf children will need at school. Such support is likely to include:

Teachers of the deaf

Teachers of the deaf support deaf children in a variety of ways:

- Home visits to newly diagnosed and pre-school children to help parents develop involvement in their child's early education and social development.
- The development of language, whether signed or spoken or both (as in Total Communication approaches).
- Checking of audiological equipment (although parents, support staff and deaf young people could be taught to check hearing and radio aids).
- Advising and training school staff to identify and meet the needs of individual deaf children.

Speech and language therapy

Speech and language therapists will have specialist knowledge about speech and language development (which goes beyond teaching the child to articulate sound) and may work with oral or signing children to develop some competence in lip-reading or British Sign Language (BSL). Some may use Signed Supported English, which is where a sign is used to follow the significant words in an English sentence.

Specialist equipment

There is a range of technical support now available for deaf children. Such technology can be used to make the teaching and learning process easier. At school a deaf child may use a radio aid system with their hearing aids or cochlear implants. A radio aid will help them to pick out the teacher's voice and cut out background noise.

An acoustically treated environment

The layout and type of classroom can make it easier or harder for a deaf child to learn. An acoustically treated environment is particularly important. Background noise makes it difficult for pupils who use hearing aids or cochlear implants, because their microphones amplify all noise.

It is very important that there is a whole school approach to the education of deaf children. This means that all members of staff need to be aware of the needs of deaf children and how to meet these needs. It is also essential that there is a commitment within the school to make sure that a deaf child has an equal opportunity to participate in every aspect of school life.

Deaf Friendly Schools is a booklet produced by the NDCS for teachers and governors. It provides information and guidance about working with deaf children. If you would like a copy then please contact the Freephone Helpline.

For further information, please contact:

The National Deaf Children's Society
Freephone helpline: 0808 800 8880 (voice and text). Open 10 am–5 pm, Monday – Friday
Fax: 020 7251 5020
Email: helpline@ndcs.org.uk
Web Site: www.ndcs.org.uk

Leukaemia
(Dr Deborah Christie, C. Clin. Psychologist AFBPsS, Consultant Clinical Psychologist, Middlesex Hospital Adolescent Unit)

Leukaemia is a cancer of the blood where the white blood cells stop working properly. The malfunctioning (malignant) cells can also invade internal organs and can get into the central nervous system. Early symptoms include anaemia, problems with infection and abnormal bruising. Current treatment for leukaemia has resulted in up to 80 per cent of children achieving cure. The treatment involves intensive chemotherapy, which will last up to two years. The child may also undergo radiotherapy. The small number of children who relapse will undergo additional chemotherapy and/or radiotherapy. They may also be given a bone marrow transplant.

Associated learning difficulties

Associated learning difficulties on treatment may include tiredness, nausea, poor appetite and hair loss, which are the most common acute side effects of the drugs. Some children can lose a lot of weight. Steroids may cause dramatic weight increases and irritable behaviour. Regular hospital appointments in addition to these side effects can make getting back to school difficult for the recently diagnosed child. Children on treatment must also be careful to avoid direct contact with certain viral illnesses, a factor which will also disrupt regular school attendance.

Children can have different emotional reactions to their diagnosis. Some children become angry, argumentative and demanding. Other children become withdrawn, anxious and depressed. Both reactions are quite normal and usually lessen as time goes on. All these problems can make it hard to concentrate, learn and participate in 'normal' school life.

Accurate and honest information about the disease is important for everyone in the school. While the child is in hospital, the school might send a tape, video or newsletter about what is happening. The school can also help by sending class work to the child at home. Liaison with the hospital school can reassure children that they will not fall behind in topic work during admissions or time at home. A school assembly about cancer can help classmates (and parents) understand what is happening to their friend and answer some fantasies and worries they may have (for example, classmates may be worried about catching the cancer). Advance warning about the possible changes may help them to be less frightened by changes in appearance. This can also reduce the incidence of teasing or bullying. Working closely with parents can also help reassure teachers about how much to expect of the child.

Research has shown that the combination of chemotherapy and radiotherapy caused learning difficulties in up to 40 per cent of children treated for leukaemia. For children who receive a second course of treatment the chance of developing learning difficulties is much higher. Many children experience a similar pattern of difficulties.

The most common problem is a drop in overall intellectual ability (IQ). The two most important factors in predicting long term effects of treatment are (a) age at treatment and (b) gender. Children treated at a younger age are more likely to develop problems than older children. In particular they may have difficulty with abstract verbal reasoning. Girls show greater vulnerability to treatment effects than boys, whatever their age at treatment. They develop impairments in a wider range of intellectual functions, with a selective reduction in verbal skills compared with non verbal abilities.

For those children who appear to maintain their overall IQ levels, short term memory, attention and concentration can often be selectively impaired. Many children have problems remembering several instructions or have difficulty processing and remembering visual information. This may make it difficult for them to copy quickly and accurately from the blackboard. Children with attention or concentration problems may be unable to concentrate for more than a few minutes or have problems completing or finishing tasks. This will make it difficult for them to keep up with lessons or complete assignments. Their behaviour can be seen as deliberately naughty or disruptive which results in them being constantly criticised. This can cause them to be unhappy and demotivated.

Curriculum

In many children the consequence of this pattern of cognitive impairment occurs in tandem with levels of reading, spelling and maths that are well below that which might be expected given their IQ. Some children will have problems in all areas of the curriculum while others will have specific problems with reading and spelling, making them appear to be like children who are dyslexic.

Many children find it difficult to learn how letters and sounds go together while other children with a poor visual memory struggle to remember how a word 'looks'. Maths may cause particular problems as short term memory and poor sequencing can contribute to difficulties with written maths and automatic memory-based number skills like learning tables. Older children may struggle to copy information from the blackboard quickly and accurately. Understanding and remembering class work or homework may also be difficult. Although, as mentioned above, having leukaemia may mean missing quite a lot of school, this is not the major contribution to these problems. The children who show the greatest difficulties in school have usually been diagnosed and treated before they began attending school.

The best way to address these problems is to try and determine levels of ability at time of diagnosis. Regular monitoring of progress is required and at the first signs of difficulty the school should set up additional support. A detailed neuropsychological assessment can help identify patterns of strengths and weaknesses that may be related to treatment (Christie et al, 1995).

Emotional concerns

Emotional concerns should also be taken into account. As children get older and the illness becomes ever more part of the past they may still have worries about how it has affected them. They may also worry about the cancer coming back. If their friends do not know about the cancer children may worry about them finding out. Being worried or anxious can make it difficult to concentrate in class. Some children may appear to have a 'short fuse' and lose their temper more easily than other children. For all children, being unable to 'keep up' feeds into a vicious cycle of failure and poor self esteem. This can produce emotional adjustment difficulties that make the learning difficulties more entrenched and severe.

The majority of children can remain in mainstream schooling with varying degrees of support. Some children however may develop moderate to severe learning difficulties that make it harder for them to function in a mainstream school without intensive teaching support and will require a special needs environment. It is possible to identify and assess those children who are at greatest risk for developing problems as they progress through the education system. Appropriate long term remedial support can help children readjust their learning strategies and develop compensatory strategies to help them deal with difficulties that are the consequence of treatment.

References

Christie, D, Leiper, AD, Chessells, J M and Vargha-Khadem, F. 'Intellectual Performance after presymptomatic treatment for lymphoblastic leukaemia: effects of age, time since treatment and sex'. *Archives of Disease in Childhood* 1995 (73) 136–140.

Loss of, or damage to, limbs
(Information supplied by the Royal Association for Disability and Rehabilitation)

Children may be born without a limb or part of one (limb deficiency), or they may lose all or part of a limb as a result of an accident, or through medical necessity (amputation).

Artificial limbs (prostheses) are usually provided for young children, both to encourage development of strength in the muscles and patterns of movement and, perhaps most importantly, to encourage independence. Learning to use artificial limbs is self-evidently not a natural process and takes time and practice, according to the motivation and skills of each child. Some may need encouragement, whilst others may need help to prevent them being too ambitious. For children born with digits missing or who have a partial hand, prostheses are not available or appropriate.

Staff will need to be aware of a child's needs before they start school. Parents will be able to advise on the medical aspects of the limb loss and in most instances a child will be able to explain their own needs, eg how he or she operates the arm, what he or she can and cannot do and how much help might be needed. It is important for a pupil to be given the opportunity to say when he or she prefers to wear or remove the artificial limb, for example for PE, or during hot weather when the residual limb may become uncomfortably hot in the prosthesis.

A child who is fitted with a prosthesis will be in regular contact with a prosthesist, who will be able to advise on any problems in using the prosthesis, or in new tasks to be learned. As children grow, prostheses need to be replaced regularly. If the child has had an amputation, they may need surgery from time to time to check the growth of the residual limb.

There are no learning difficulties specifically associated with limb deficiency or amputation. However, teachers may have to seek extra time for students sitting examinations if it is considered that the student's writing speed is affected by the limb loss. Written forms of language can be produced on typewriters, personal computers or a voice-activated computer system, and access to word-processing can be tailored to the requirements of the pupil. Other solutions include accessing the word processor via single or multiple switches, which may be in the form of rollerballs or joysticks.

The artificial arms usually supplied to children are made of metal or plastic and have a grasp mechanism. They are normally covered in foam and toning plastic to improve the appearance. With practice pupils develop the skills needed to use the arm and grasp mechanism. Most children do not learn to write with their artificial arm. Some prefer to use their own ways of managing instead of, or as well as, using an artificial arm. A pupil's preference is important but it is also advisable to check with the parents, prosthesist and/ or occupational therapist to ensure a consistent approach.

Children with no upper limbs who do not use artificial arms have to learn methods of managing their own personal needs. Initially they may require assistance, but with time many of them develop the skills needed to be fully independent. Children who have lost one or both legs, above or below the knee, will be able to use artificial limbs, but are still likely to have some mobility difficulties. Some may use sticks or crutches and some may use a wheelchair. Mobility needs should be taken into account when considering emergency procedures.

Children who have limb deficiency should be encouraged to take part in PE as far as possible. Physical fitness is as important for these pupils as for all others. Children will often develop strategies for participating within their limits but may need encouragement. If advice is needed a physiotherapist will be able to help. If the child chooses to participate without the artificial limb, it is important it is stored safely and securely. If the limb is hidden as a prank this can be very distressing for the child.

Children who lose a limb following an accident or through medical necessity often find it difficult to adjust to their impairment and changed body image. They, their parents and possible siblings may need counselling to help them work through the emotional stress of the loss of a limb. Emotional stress is an almost universal experience amongst amputees, their families and carers.

Any child who is physically 'different' is at risk of being teased. It may be helpful to ensure that the child concerned has a simple explanation and is ready to satisfy the curiosity of their peers. A matter-of-fact attitude on the part of the adults will help to reduce any embarrassment felt by a pupil and their peer group.

Good communication between parents, professionals and the pupil must be encouraged to ensure proper resources are in place. The expertise of parents and pupil should be utilised, and inter-agency collaboration will help smooth the way for the pupil's academic and social development. The transition from school to adult life can often be a stressful time and the process of transitional planning is therefore essential.

Further information is available from:

The National Co-ordinator
REACH – Association for Children with Hand or Arm Deficiency
12 Wilson Way
Earls Barton
Northamptonshire
NN6 0NZ
Tel: 01604 811041

Limbless Association
Roehampton Rehabilitation Centre
Roehampton Lane
London
SW15 5PR
Tel: 020 8788 1777

Muscular dystrophy
(Information supplied by the Muscular Dystrophy Campaign)

Muscular dystrophy (MD) is a name given to many different conditions which have in common the breakdown of muscle fibres leading to weak and wasted muscles. More than 20,000 children and adults in the UK have MD or a related neuromuscular condition.

Each of these neuro muscular conditions has a different cause; they are mostly genetic, but some are autoimmune (where a person's immune system attacks healthy cells within the body itself). Symptoms of some disorders show very early on, even at birth, but in others symptoms may only start to show later in childhood or adulthood. Severity is variable: several conditions are very disabling or life-threatening; the rest can cause moderate or mild disability. Most of the conditions cause progressive weakening of the muscles but some remain stable. Different conditions affect different muscles and various other body systems. The inheritance risks vary. There can also be a wide variation in the degree of severity not only between one type of dystrophy and another but also between individuals with the same type.

In some conditions, particularly Duchenne muscular dystrophy (DMD) and myotonic dystrophy, some individuals may have a degree of intellectual impairment. This may be reflected particularly in poor reading ability, word comprehension and memory skills. This intellectual impairment is not directly related to muscle weakness, however, and is not progressive.

Children's educational needs depend, of course, on the individual concerned and the nature of their condition and disability. Some children may need to attend special schools but many will be able to continue with mainstream schooling right through to college or university. Help needed within school will also vary widely depending on the physical limitations of the individual. Many children with a significant disability will need a great deal of support.

Some conditions also have other complications which need to be carefully monitored, such as heart and breathing problems and allergy to anaesthesia. Muscle weakness can also cause additional mobility problems such as contractures (tightening of joints) and scoliosis (curvature of the spine).

Anyone can be affected by these conditions. They are usually inherited from the parent(s) but can appear out of the blue, in a family with no history of the condition. Males and/or females can be affected depending on the genetic cause of the condition. For example, DMD is usually inherited from the mother by the son. Apart from very rare exceptions females are the only carriers of DMD and are not affected themselves. In myotonic dystrophy either the mother or the father is affected and can pass the gene on. In spinal muscular atrophy neither parent is affected but both must carry the faulty gene for it to be passed on to their children. The conditions are not infectious.

It is not possible to 'catch' muscular dystrophy or any of the related conditions. However, if someone is found to be affected, their relatives might also have the condition because the disrupted gene may run in the family.

Although there are as yet no treatments or cures available for the majority, physiotherapy is helpful and symptoms can be alleviated through careful management. However, it is possible to treat the symptoms of myotonia congenita effectively. Immunological treatment is possible for polymyositis, dermatomyositis, myasthenia gravis and other immunological neuromuscular conditions. These treatments may involve the use of immunosuppressive drugs such as steroids, plasma exchange and intravenous immunoglobin.

Researchers are trying to find treatments and cures for the rest. Where the cause is genetic, identification of the genetic fault is the first vital step towards understanding the condition and then finding a treatment. Muscular Dystrophy Campaign researchers are at the forefront of international research; they already know the genetic faults responsible for several conditions and are investigating several possible treatments.

A fact sheet entitled 'Children with muscular dystrophy in mainstream schools' is available from the Muscular Dystrophy Campaign, 7–11 Prescott Place, London, SW4 6BS Tel: 020 7720 8055.

Speech and language difficulties
(Information supplied by Afasic)

The ability to use language and communicate effectively is the basis of all learning and social interaction. Without these skills, education will not achieve its goals. It follows that the development of language and communication skills is central to all education.

The vast majority of children with special educational needs have one or other kind of communication difficulty. There is also a group of children who do not develop language skills normally, irrespective of any obvious intellectual or physical disability. These children are often said to have a specific or primary speech or language impairment, which may be in isolation or alongside another disability.

It is estimated that 1 in 500 school-age children will have severe long-term impairments, while at least 6 per cent will experience some degree of difficulty at some time which could interfere with his or her educational progress.

Characteristics

Some children are unable to understand or express themselves clearly, while others have near normal understanding but experience difficulty in speaking intelligibly. Some may not be able to form words and sentences correctly, have limited vocabulary, may produce strings of unintelligible sounds or repeat spoken language correctly without knowing the meaning of what they say. Some will have difficulty with the beginnings and endings of words. Others may display 'autistic tendencies'.

Identification of difficulties

Any of the following can be an indication of a language impairment:

- late onset of speech;
- a discrepancy between verbal and non-verbal skills or between receptive and expressive language;
- lack of concentration;
- history of 'glue-ear';
- difficulty with fine and/or gross motor skills;
- short-term memory;
- word-finding difficulties;
- poor interaction with peers.

As language skills develop very rapidly in the early years, much is gained if difficulties are identified as early as possible. 2–3 years of age is not too early. Where help is provided at this age, a child is often able to join a mainstream school at 5 years of age. If the difficulties are not tackled in the early years, and the child struggles through primary schooling, difficulties can be seriously compounded by the time secondary age is reached. In a mainstream school the child is unlikely to be able to master the necessary conceptual understanding and complex social interactions expected in such a setting and may well become confused, disorientated, suffer emotional stress and succumb to bullying. Special schooling is then likely to be the only way to begin to provide effective help.

Assessment of difficulties

If there is cause for concern and a speech and language therapist has not already been seen, referral should be arranged following discussion with parent(s). It is obviously important to identify a child's particular strengths and weaknesses at the first possible opportunity. Speech and language therapists have the skills to undertake such an assessment and to advise how any weakness may be overcome. Where a child's difficulties are particularly severe it is likely that a full assessment has taken place, or is underway, and that a statement has been drawn up.

Ways to help

Those with severe difficulties are best helped in a special school or language unit or class, with teachers and speech and language therapists working very closely in partnership. In the latter, intensive language work can take place with integration into the host school as and when appropriate. There are about 400 such units throughout the country, but few, as yet, are available for secondary-aged pupils.

Even where difficulties are not said to be severe, input from a speech and language therapist is recommended, as different approaches and programmes can be discussed, the most appropriate selected and queries clarified. Advice from an occupational and/or physiotherapist should be sought for those with co-ordination difficulties.

Because these children do not acquire language spontaneously as others do, they need to be taught appropriate skills in a structured setting.

- A planned approach should be used to teach speaking and listening skills and reading and writing for all pupils.
- Activities should encourage the development of turn-taking, rhythms and rhyme and the building up of self-esteem and confidence.
- Where a child has difficulty in learning the order of a task, it helps to structure the sequence of skills and to simplify each step.
- The use of computers and a combination of sight, sound, touch or movement can be valuable.
- Small group work (4–8 pupils) is essential to achieve national curriculum targets successfully.
- Social skills and the use of social or functional language must be developed.

It can be especially helpful to relate work to a child's own interests or family.

For further information please send a stamped, addressed envelope to Afasic, 69–85 Old Street, London EC1V 9HX.

Spina Bifida and/or Hydrocephalus

(Information supplied by the Association for Spina Bifida and Hydrocephalus)

What is Spina Bifida?

Spina bifida is a congenital disability that affects babies very early in pregnancy. It is a fault in the development of the spine, when one or more vertebrae fail to close properly. Spina bifida usually affects the lower limbs, where there will be a lack of sensation of pain and temperature and perhaps problems with circulation. Many people with spina bifida will have continence problems, which need to be managed effectively if self-image is not to be damaged.

What is Hydrocephalus?

Hydrocephalus happens when the fluid in the brain cannot drain away into the blood-stream because the normal pathways are blocked. The excess pressure must be relieved quickly to minimise brain damage.

New drainage pathways are opened, either by inserting a fine tube (called a shunt) inside a space in the brain or by making a small hole in the floor of one of these spaces, this operation is called a ventriculostomy.

Many people with spina bifida also have hydrocephalus, but it can occur by itself, especially after meningitis, a head injury, stroke, or in babies born prematurely.

Hydrocephalus may affect motor skills, vision, speech and language, and behaviour.

Neither spina bifida nor hydrocephalus is associated with any particular level of general intelligence.

Educational issues for children with spina bifida and/or hydrocephalus

Time off in hospital

Children with spina bifida and/or hydrocephalus may require repeated admission to hospital or hospital visits as out-patients. During prolonged stays in hospital, arrangements will probably need to be made for formal education to be continued.

Physical access

Consideration may need to be given to access issues, especially wheelchair access, or access to the curriculum through specialist equipment or classroom assistance before a child starts at a particular school. Accessible toilet facilities may also be necessary. For pupils who manage their own continence, or need assistance with this, the privacy of toilet facilities must also be considered.

Learning

Hydrocephalus, whether it has or has not been shunted, may affect (1) a child's co-ordination and visual-spatial perception, (2) short-term memory and ability to solve problems, and concept of time and (3) social and emotional development.

(1) Co-ordination and perception

Some children appear to be clumsy and have balance problems. Many tire very easily. Hand-eye co-ordination may be poor, and there is often a weak handgrip.

Visuo-spatial perception may be affected, resulting in a distorted view of the world. There may, for instance, be difficulty in distinguishing between a step and a line drawn on the ground. Many children have squints, some may have tunnel vision, or nystagmus. Work in mathematics and geography may be affected.

For some children, some abilities can improve through time, although appropriate experiences should be provided at an early age. However, careful observation is needed to identify ways in which residual visual problems (squints, tunnel vision) may be affecting a child's performance, eg in copying from the blackboard and organising their belongings.

Help and understanding may be needed in the following situations:

- walking long distances and walking down stairs
- colouring-in and hand-writing; using scissors and other tools; fastening buttons; tying laces
- moving in crowded spaces without bumping into furniture or other people
- 'finding' objects that are mixed up with other objects, interpreting diagrams and maps
- noticing things on their desk and table, which are immediately in front, or to one side
- 'tuning in' to one voice, against a background of chatter and hypersensitivity to noises like clapping, laughter or lawn mowers.

(2) Memory, problem-solving and concept of time

Long-term memory for details of events is usually very good. However, many children have short-term memory problems, especially in retaining spoken words long enough to understand what they mean. The 'verbal' ability of many children can lead others to presume that they understand the instructions and conversations when this may not be so. Most children will have short concentration spans. Many will have problems in self-correcting, expressing observations and giving explanations, and these children will find it difficult to 'make connections' between different items of information. Most children will need extra time and help to learn new ideas, and to develop the thinking strategies they need to deal with unfamiliar information.

Again for some children, some abilities can improve if appropriate experiences are provided. However, unless they are also helped to recognise their own competencies and what is expected of them, many still experience a great deal of anxiety in relatively unfamiliar situations, which may include formal tests.

Help and understanding may be needed in the following situations:

- concentrating on tasks, and self-monitoring
- switching from one activity to another
- finding their way in an unfamiliar environment
- understanding and remembering verbal instructions
- giving clear accounts – there can be a tendency to focus on isolated, unconnected details
- self-organisation – where to start, what to do next
- problem-solving – reluctance to engage in 'difficult' work without help
- thinking ahead – tendency to act or speak before they think.

(3) Social and Emotional Behaviour

Hydrocephalus is sometimes linked with developmental delay in physical development in infancy and also in language development.

Although children with hydrocephalus are very 'sociable', some may have problems in adjusting their own behaviour to different social contexts. Some can tend to treat everyone as a 'friend'. Some may be very shy, or overly domineering with their peers. Lack of self-esteem is common and some people become withdrawn and depressed, while others show challenging behaviours.

Children with hydrocephalus can be helped to learn social skills and have more confidence in themselves, and the chances of this teaching being effective are greater if begun before the beginning of Key Stage 2.

Help may be needed to develop skills in the following areas:

- self-inhibition, eg learning to wait their turn to speak
- addressing different people in appropriate ways
- peer relationships
- anticipating unfamiliar situations
- participating in family and classroom chores

Support in mainstream schools

Behavioural problems may be evident in school but not at home, and vice versa. It is important not to attribute blame in either context. Open and trusting relationships between parents and teachers are essential, as is a problem-solving approach to any perceived difficulties.

Good school-home partnerships will ensure that information relating to possible medical problems and physical difficulties is shared and understood, and that the 'strategies' to be used to solve behavioural problems are consistent. No strategy will succeed unless the child is also involved.

If learning support assistant time is available in class, target it on developing the skills the children will need to work and socialise independently. This may be a matter of gradual withdrawal of support, eg as children develop the ability to listen to whole-class instructions and carry them out, the assistant may begin to use prompts instead of repeating the whole instructions on a one-to-one basis.

Making a point of observing and noting the outcomes of the approaches that are used, and to modify them as necessary after discussions. If the children can begin to think positively about the skills and knowledge they are developing, this will provide the confidence for more difficult tasks.

ASBAH produces a pack of ten topic sheets, a book titled Hydrocephalus and You. These are available from: Information, ASBAH House, 42 Park Road, Peterborough, PE1 2UQ, Tel: 01733 555988, Email: gillw@asbah.org

Gilles de la Tourette Syndrome
(Dr Deborah Christie, C. Clin. Psychologist, AFBPsS, Consultant Clinical Psychologist, Middlesex Hospital Adolescent Unit)

Gilles de la Tourette Syndrome (TS) was first identified over 100 years ago. It is an inherited condition. There are often other members of the family who will have either TS themselves or some of the symptoms. It is associated with dysfunction in areas of the brain responsible for movement and the control of inhibition and impulsivity. These difficulties are thought to be connected with an excess of a brain chemical (neurotransmitter) called Dopamine. Medication which alters the amount of Dopamine in the brain can often help reduce many of the symptoms.

TS is found in three times as many boys as girls. Peak onset is around seven years of age and for many children a period of inattentiveness and impulsiveness precedes the onset of the tics. This may often be diagnosed as attention deficit disorder (ADD) – with or without hyperactivity, although over time it becomes clear that the attentional problems are not the primary difficulty. Very often the medication prescribed for ADD can exacerbate or initiate the onset of tics.

Tics

The main symptom in TS is the involuntary movements (motor) or noises (vocal) known as tics. These can be simple (eye blinks, head nod, sniffs, grunts) or complex (twirling, jumping, shouting or repeating things). One feature of the tics is their tendency to change over time. They may become more or less frequent or intense or may alter completely.

Attentional problems

Children with Tourette's syndrome can have problems with attention or concentration. It is estimated that 50 per cent of children with TS may be inattentive and overactive, which are the core manifestations of AD/HD (see p.10). This does not necessarily mean the child has AD/HD. He or she may be unable to concentrate for more than a few minutes or have problems finishing tasks. This will make it difficult for the child to keep up with lessons or complete assignments. Teachers may see behaviour as deliberately naughty or disruptive, which may result in the child being constantly criticised.

Obsessive Compulsive Behaviour

Beside the tics, 50–70 per cent of children with TS suffer from obsessive compulsive behaviour. An obsession is an overwhelming thought or image that produces significant distress and anxiety. To reduce this anxiety the individual feels a compulsion to complete a stereotyped behaviour or action. Children with TS may be unable to stop themselves touching something (or someone). They may need to do things in a particular way. These could be short routines, like flicking light switches, counting up to a certain number all the time or turning taps on and off. They may need to get dressed in a certain way. If anyone interrupts the routine, they may have to start all over again. Teachers may see this as stubborn or awkward behaviour. It can also cause conflicts with classmates.

Making friends

Many children with TS have problems making and keeping friends. They may not know how to 'stick to the rules', how to start a conversation, take turns or listen. Children with TS may have a 'short fuse' and lose their temper more easily than other children of the same age. Sometimes other children make fun of the habits and behaviours. Whatever the reason, having TS can make it hard to make friends.

Emotional problems

Although the motor and vocal tics (or habits) may not cause specific learning difficulties, they may result in emotional problems. The psychological sequelae of TS include aggressive behaviour, social difficulties, poor peer relationships, low self esteem, anxiety and depression. These can be both a part of the disorder and a response to how adults and other children respond to it. Teasing and bullying before or after being diagnosed can make the child feel bad about themselves. They may be withdrawn and unhappy at school or at home. Some children become defensive and angry in response to comments about habits or behaviour over which they have no control.

Intelligence

Although most children with TS are of normal intelligence, there is a tendency for verbal skills to be better developed than non verbal ones. They may also have specific problems with organising work, memory and copying. This means they may have difficulty copying information quickly and accurately from the blackboard. Maths may cause particular problems. There may also be difficulty in understanding and remembering class work or homework. A clinical or educational psychologist can complete a comprehensive assessment to see if your child has some of the difficulties that are often described in children with TS.

Living with tics

Although the tics described are involuntary, many children are also able to suppress them. The effect of this, however, is rather like putting a cork into the mouth of a kettle. There is a gradual increase in pressure (usually paralleling a wearing off of medication) and for many children there is an explosion of symptoms when they get home. The physical and psychological effort of suppressing the tics during the school day can cause children to be totally exhausted when they get home. They may also get a release of high levels of aggressive thoughts/behaviours that they have also been holding on to during the day. This can make it very difficult for homework to be completed efficiently or easily.

It is essential that parents and teachers work closely together to support and manage challenges created by Tourette's Syndrome. Once a diagnosis has been made it can be helpful to have regular meetings with the family, the school and the clinic staff to ensure everybody is working together and is aware of the resources that might be helpful. Parents may find some sessions of counselling helpful as a way of problem solving and identifying successful strategies for living with Tourette's Syndrome.

The relationship between stress, anxiety and the symptoms can be used to help children. Relaxation sessions in drama can help reduce tension (and stress). An accepting environment which acknowledges and responds sympathetically to the symptoms can initially produce an increase in tics as the child feels less need to suppress the movements/behaviours. Ultimately, however, the child becomes so comfortable that the frequency of the tics does reduce without the accompanying build-up of pressure. Another way of helping is building energy breaks into the day to help the child expel some of the built-up anxiety.

Parents may find it helpful to contact the Tourette's Syndrome (UK) Association, PO Box 26149, Dunfermline KY12 9WT. Email: enquiries@tsa.org.uk

Visual impairment
(Information supplied by the Royal National Institute for the Blind)

There are more than 24,000 blind and partially sighted children and young people under the age of 16 in the UK today.

While visual impairment is a 'low incidence' disability with only about two children in every thousand being blind or partially sighted, these children have very individual and important information and support needs.

Although a few children have no sight at all, most have some vision. For example, some can tell the difference between light and dark, some have central vision and can only see things in front of them, while others can see out of the sides of their eye but not the middle.

Some people see everything as a vague blur, others as a patchwork of blanks and defined areas. Some see better in bright light, some when it is darker, and others find it impossible to adjust between light and dark.

Children with a sight impairment but no other significant additional needs

It is increasingly common for blind as well as partially sighted children to be included in mainstream schools. For some children, inclusion will be appropriate throughout their education. Others may need special schooling for part or all of their school lives. Some children move in and out of mainstream education as their needs change.

Many children do need some level of special school education. Depending on the individual, this may be in a school for blind and partially sighted pupils or in another type of special school.

Each child should be assessed as soon as possible so that the level of educational support needed can be planned in conjunction with the local education authority (LEA) visual impairment specialist. The RNIB can provide names of local LEA visual impairment specialists and also offers a wide variety of assessment services.

Whether the child is in a mainstream or special school, he or she will need some specialised materials, equipment, or adaptations to the standard of work of sighted children in order to follow the National Curriculum fully.

Children with some residual vision may be able to use enlarged materials, whether enlarged on a photocopier or specially printed in a larger print size. Some examination boards provide pre-enlarged exam papers, and all Key Stage examination papers are available in both enlarged and modified enlarged formats.

If visual impairment prevents a child from reading enlarged print, he or she may learn to read and write braille and may also make extensive use of audio tapes. There are organisations, including the RNIB, which can supply text books to blind and partially sighted children spanning a wide range of subjects at all levels.

Computers and other technology are also valuable supplements to a child with impaired vision. There are many different ways for blind and partially sighted children to use technology. Examples include:

- a closed-circuit television (CCTV). This enables a student to place a regular piece of print underneath a small moving camera, while the CCTV shows the enlarged print on a monitor. The student can then move the camera across a page and read a whole page of standard print.
- computer packages which can convert words on a computer screen into synthesised speech, and read computer files back to a blind or partially sighted student.
- devices which can be attached to a computer and allow the user to have a braille display of what is on the computer screen.
- packages which can convert computer text into a braille print-out. One device allows a child to braille onto a Perkins brailler, then produce a print copy for a sighted teacher.
- portable braille note-takers, which allow individuals to braille information into a small machine and retrieve it later by hooking it to a computer.

The RNIB offers advice to LEA staff, in-service training, and help in setting up new inclusion schemes. For individual schools and pupils, the RNIB has facilities for trying out special equipment and can help with particular aspects of the curriculum.

Blind and partially sighted children with additional needs

More than one child in every three with a visual impairment also has additional disabilities. Due to the range of causes of visual impairment, a child may also have a hearing impairment, learning difficulty, physical difficulty or a combination of impairments.

A full multi-disciplinary assessment of all of the child's educational needs will determine whether a special or mainstream school is most appropriate. There is a small number of specialist schools for blind and partially sighted children with additional needs, including four RNIB schools which cover the 3–9 age range. The RNIB also offers assessment services for children who have a complex range of impairments.

Technology is also used extensively with multiply-disabled children, particularly in the form of multi-sensory rooms using lights and sounds to stimulate the sensory-impaired child or touch screens and switch technology to help develop communication skills and provide access to the National Curriculum.

A large number of books and factsheets have been published by the RNIB and others about the education of blind and partially sighted children, many of which are available from the RNIB. For details of any aspect of the education of a blind or partially sighted child, including the services mentioned above, please contact the RNIB Helpline Tel: 0845 766 9999.

1.4

Emotional and Behavioural Difficulties: Some reflections, ideas and perspectives

Steve Cliffen
Principal of Coxlease School, Hampshire
Executive Committee member NAES
(National Association of EBD Schools)

Definitions

Emotional and Behavioural Difficulties can appear in a whole range of human expressions and feelings. Consequently there has always been a variety of definitions. The spectrum of EBD is indeed wide and ranges from deviant to disturbed, from straightforward naughtiness through to quite complex psychiatric disorders and from nuisance value to challenging in the extreme.

The revised SEN Code of Practice (DfES 2001) Section 7:60, provides a protracted definition including the terms withdrawn, isolated, disruptive, disturbing, hyperactive, lacking concentration and presenting challenging behaviour. It also creates new terminology by naming Behavioural, Emotional and Social Development as being one of the new four areas of Special Educational Needs.

For the terminology EBD to be used in its generally accepted form, quite severe recurring emotional or behavioural problems must occur in home, social or school situations. Perhaps the best definition that is applicable to most children with EBD would be that due to an emotional difficulty or disturbance they refuse or cannot make full use of the educational opportunities offered to them and are consequently difficult or challenging to manage. In addition to this the majority of these children have parallel difficulties within their families and communities. They are frequently 'at the end of the line' in one or more areas of their lives.

Looked After Children, namely those involved with or under the care of Social Services are a major group in any specialist provision for EBD pupils. The lack of a stable home environment is also becoming an increasingly common feature, particularly in cases of more complex difficulties. In the author's own school, 90 per cent of pupils fall into the category of Looked After Children. The difficulty of identifying suitable foster placements for challenging children also makes for a small group that have no identified care base whatsoever.

It is important to point out, however, that not all children with EBD have these difficulties because of their family background or social environment. EBD is also associated with some genetic or biological conditions – such as Attachment Disorders, Gilles de la Tourette Syndrome, Fragile X, Attention Deficit (Hyperactivity) Disorder or Asperger's Syndrome – the symptoms and effects of which may cause the child frustration and distress leading to the development of EBD. Similarly, EBD may also be associated with exceptionally high levels of ability. In cases of genetic or biological conditions, the management of a child's associated EBD difficulties will normally form part of a wider programme of special education that addresses all of his or her particular needs. This will be provided either in a mainstream school – if suitable provision can be made – or in a special school with appropriate expertise.

Groups and causes

A review of the research over the last 20 years clearly indicates that EBD tends to be prevalent amongst certain groups:

- teenage boys
- Afro-Caribbean children
- those living in deprived inner city areas
- looked after children
- children who experience literacy and numeracy difficulties

The causes of EBD can be specific or various.

Family

They may revolve around the family:

- divorce or separation
- bereavement
- conflict, violence or mental health problems all of which could lead to lack of care and supervision.

Parents, carers or family members may have emotionally, physically or sexually abused a child.

Environment

Children may experience or be exposed to:

- inadequate, overcrowded housing
- vandalism and arson
- drug use and dealing
- theft
- violence and assaults (often related to alcohol use)
- anti-social behaviour.

Personal difficulties

The child may have experienced personal difficulties (often associated with genetic or biologocal conditions) such as:

- sensory
- physical
- mental health
- developmental
- learning.

How can parents help?

Schools working with parents to help reduce the negative effects of EBD can be of great value. Apart from the specific individual work and direct parental intervention carried out by some special schools, a number of key parenting skills can be pointed out and reinforced:

- try to understand the nature of individual difficulties;
- plan and create situations where a child can experience success;
- use positive reinforcement in the first instance but make any appropriate sanctions fair and consistent;
- be interested in educational activities and support the school;
- try to ensure adequate provision of activities and friends;
- be firm, clear and consistent towards the breaking of 'house rules';
- avoid aggression and threats of violence – only consider the use of physical interventions when a child is being dangerous to themselves or others;
- display emotional warmth, join in and value all achievements and improvements;
- do not show favouritism in dealing with siblings;
- wherever possible try to be a positive role model;
- do not be over concerned if you get things wrong – do not hesitate to seek advice or further help;

At the far end of the scale parents seen as being uninvolved can be forced to take greater responsibility for their child's behaviour through parenting orders that were introduced by the Crimes and Disorder Act (Home Office 1998). Such orders often require parents to attend behaviour management sessions and ensure a child's attendance at school.

Inclusion or Segregation – Mainstream or Special?

When the Green Paper *Excellence for All Children: Meeting Special Educational Needs* (DfEE 1997) recommended that all children, irrespective of the nature of their behaviour, should be considered as viable candidates for inclusion, a debate that had been going on for many years reached a seriously high level. There is little doubt that this statement is philosophically sound but there are a number of practical difficulties.

School performance 'league tables' and the increased level of parental choice have created 'sink' schools in many areas. As Armstrong and Galloway (1994) state, 'the very presence of large numbers of children with special needs, particularly those whose needs arise from learning and/or behaviour difficulties, may be seen as harmful to a school's performance.'

Both practitioners and parents know that bad behaviour 'rubs off' and it is easy to identify why Kathy Bull, a well respected HMI EBD specialist, states that 'EBD is the only contagious category of Special Educational Needs'.

With a range of local initiatives, often funded through LEA Behaviour Support Plans and successful bids for Standard Fund resources direct from the DfES, the inclusion movement has gathered pace over the last three to four years. There are many examples of excellence throughout the country where programmes are based on careful planning of the required support procedures combined with the contingency strategies to be used when things start to break down or do not go according to plan. The increasing use of dual placements where a child with Special Educational Needs attends both a special school and a mainstream school can also be very effective.

Of course, many would view the direct opposite to inclusion as full time attendance at a segregated special school. Although perhaps philosophically unsound, there is little doubt this part of a balanced continum of EBD provision can often be extremely effective. Regardless of some high quality inclusion programmes, there will always be the recognised need that many children will be advantaged by making a fresh start by attending either a smaller special day school or, for wider social factors, appropriate residential provision.

A well managed EBD Special School will have favourable staff:pupil ratios that can help develop the positive and stable relationships that are often difficult to establish in a large mainstream school. Specialist, skilled and committed staff teams will have the flexibility to provide individually tailored programmes to assist in meeting children's emotional and cognitive needs.

The decision making surrounding whether a child should attend a special school must be an extremely careful process. Some children will have experienced enormous problems and failing situations in one or more mainstream schools. Some will have refused to attend local schools as a result of extremely low self-esteem, others will have been involved in confrontations and even offending in their local neighbourhood, giving rise to intolerable levels of stress in school.

As clearly identified in *Inclusive Schooling – Children with Special Educational Needs* (DfES, November 2001), many such children will benefit from a well supported maintained Special School or a proficient Approved Independent or Non-Maintained Special School. There is little doubt that special schools will have a continuing and vital role to play within an inclusive education system. However, the decision to place a child in such a school should only be made after all the benefits of an ever-increasing range of provisions have been investigated.

Good practice in schools

Curriculum

As Circular 9/94 (DFEE 1994) accurately reports, EBD pupils in special schools will span the same range of ability as children in mainstream schools. Therefore the planning and presentation of an imaginative and sensitive curriculum is essential for pupils with EBD. In all schools this can be achieved through appropriate differentiation that often involves cross curricular initiatives, good use of ICT, tasks that can be broken down into small steps or 'chunks', built-in success strategies and a hands-on approach.

Although resistance to learning can frequently occur, nearly all pupils want to learn and make progress. Behind the confrontation and conflict that EBD pupils are capable of bringing into formal learning situations, there usually lies a desire to be viewed as 'normal'. In essence this means the same access to the National Curriculum as their peers without Special Educational Needs. The comment of Wilson and Evans (1980) is still significant, 'children who are not taught are entitled to feel that they are too dull, too bad or too mad for their teachers to take them seriously.'

Although many EBD pupils who are underachievers would view GCSEs as beyond their grasp, it is not unusual for pupils to exceed their expectations. For those who struggle with traditional academic subjects the flexibility available at Key Stage 4 – in the plethora of practical and vocational choices, combined with the range of relevant nationally accredited courses available – is highly attractive.

Counselling and Therapy

The special relationship that can be formed between child and trained counsellor or therapist in formal sessions can be of immense value in addressing complex cases. This can be of particular value in helping young people who may have been sexually abused, those recovering from a particularly traumatic event or those at the psychiatric end of the EBD spectrum. Work by therapists and counsellors can carry the potential for real change and the benefits of integrated therapy plans that are carried out as part of a 24 hour curriculum in residential settings can be of particular benefit.

Effective therapeutic interventions create situations in which emotions and strong feelings are aroused but contained. This can enable a child to see similar opportunities in different situations. As Youell (2000) points out the work of the therapist is 'often mistakenly characterised as being to do with going back and excavating the past and then restructuring it. In practice, successful work, particularly with acting out children, needs to be thought of as helping the child or adolescent to make use of current opportunities with a view to a better future.'

Many staff in EBD schools, whether support assistants, residential care staff or teachers, are often particularly skilled at talking and listening as part of informal counselling. This general reflection, exploration of feelings and interest in children's lives is essential in building positive and trusting relationships.

Effective Strategies

The last 15 years has seen a high number of EBD special schools experiencing difficulties due to poor OfSTED inspection reports. Such schools often felt unsupported by LEAs and encountered problems in keeping pace with the implications of a wide range of Government initiatives and legislation. This led to a number of schools being placed in 'special measures' and others being closed down altogether. Fortunately, as outlined by OfSTED (1999), the overall situation has improved and it is recognised that broader knowledge, skills and understanding are essential features in a more balanced provision for pupils with EBD. As Fogell and Long (1999) so aptly state, 'the school which makes effective provision for children with emotional and behavioural difficulties is just like any other school only more so.'

The SEN Code of Practice (DfES 2001) accurately identifies that pupils with EBD may require help or counselling including some, or all, of the following:

- flexible teaching arrangements;
- help with the development of social competence and emotional maturity;
- help in adjusting to school routines;
- help in acquiring the skills of positive interaction with peers and adults;
- specialised behavioural and cognitive approaches;
- re-challenging or re-focusing to diminish repetitive or self-injurious behaviour;
- provision of class or school systems which control or censure negative or difficult behaviours and encourage positive behaviour;
- provision of a safe and supportive environment.

Of a more specific nature are the results of research carried out by Harris (1995) on practitioners who worked with children who displayed quite challenging behaviour. Strategies identified as being most likely to be effective include the following:

- forming positive relationships with one particular adult;
- examining and amending the system of rewards and sanctions;
- matching learning tasks to known strengths of the pupil;
- focusing on teaching language and communication;
- working on language and communication necessary for meeting individual needs in everyday settings;
- helping the child to anticipate sequences of events in activities;
- allowing the child to opt out of specific activities;
- conveying adult expectations clearly and providing constant feedback;
- ensuring staff are aware of new working methods or behavioural plans;
- providing a written protocol to all staff describing how to respond to each challenging behaviour.

Alongside effective management and high quality teaching, the ethos of any school can greatly influence behaviour. Disruption and anti-social behaviour can be exacerbated by inappropriate, punitive, coercive and exclusive policies. Rigid streaming in a comprehensive school has always had the potential effect of creating a lower stream anti-social culture. On the other hand, a number of approaches and measures can promote positive behaviour and attitudes amongst school populations including:

- rewarding achievement, progress and positive behaviour;
- provision of opportunities for pupils to exercise responsibility, e g school councils;
- effective and efficient pastoral and referral systems to prevent and reduce problems through early identification and intervention;
- good leadership and management that involves staff in determining policies and procedures;

- high quality care of the school environment, e.g. on-going redecoration programmes, instant removal of graffiti and speedy repairs;
- positive staff role models who are organised, plan well and are punctual.

If more mainstream schools were able to emulate the positive features of a well managed, proficient and effective provision for EBD pupils, then they would perhaps be faced with fewer problems from their own challenging population.

The future agenda

A whole range of on-going challenges will always exist for the providers and policy makers involved in meeting the needs of EBD pupils. Much has recently been achieved through a range of Government initiatives and developments combined with some excellent practice in schools. However, it has never been more necessary to move forward and establish an appropriate, high quality, worthwhile and coherent range of provision that offers all pupils with EBD the opportunity to make real progress. For this to stand any chance of success a number of factors are essential:

- an ongoing emphasis that ensures high standards in EBD provision through a transparent supportive system incorporating Ofsted and the National Care Standards Commission;
- the establishment of peer consultancy and mentoring systems for EBD managers in order to reduce isolation and share good practice;
- the co-ordination and organisation of training, support groups and conferences on a regional and national basis, for specific issues relating to EBD;
- more work on definitions to provide clarity between disaffection and statemented EBD;
- increased levels of consultation between policy makers and key practitioners such as EBD school Headteachers;
- the provision of sound and realistic guidance concerning the use of physical interventions in EBD settings;
- continued work on the early recognition and identification of emotional difficulties;
- greater attention towards Emotional Literacy/Emotional Intelligence, so that children can develop a greater ability to recognise, understand, handle and express emotions;
- further investigation into the possibilities of staff working in mainstream schools spending periods of time in specialist EBD provisions;
- greater emphasis during initial teacher training on providing strategies to prevent and respond assertively to difficult classroom behaviour;
- increased levels of real and practical collaboration and co-operation between Education, Health and Social Services.

There will always be a variety of provision for EBD pupils. If the envisaged improvements in dealing with difficult classroom behaviour combined with relevant approaches and philosophies can be incorporated more consistently into mainstream school provision, we are likely to see higher levels of inclusion. However, there will always be some pupils who will fail to thrive unless they attend a small special school where time and expertise can be devoted to their needs. These schools must be forward thinking in their planning, appropriate in their ethos and determined in providing education, welfare and care of the highest standards.

References

Armstrong D and Galloway D (1994) 'Special educational needs and problem behaviour in the classroom' in Riddell S and Brown S (eds) *Special Educational Needs Policy in the 1990s* London, Routledge.

Cole T, Visser J and Upton G (1998) *Effective Schooling for Pupils with Emotional and Behavioural Difficulties* London, David Fulton.

DfE (1994) *The Education of Children with Emotional and Behavioural Difficulties* Circular 9/94. London, DfE

DfEE (1997) *Excellence for All Children. Meeting Special Educational Needs* London, DfEE

DfES (2001) *Inclusive Schooling – Children with Special Educational Needs* (ref: DfES 0774/2001) London, DfES.

DfES (2001) *Special Educational Needs Code of Practice (ref: DfES/581/2001)*. London, DfES.

Fogell J and Long R (1999) *Supporting Pupils with Emotional Difficulties – Creating a Caring Environment for All* London, David Fulton.

Harris J (1995) Responding to children with severe learning disabilities, who present challenging behaviour *British Journal of Special Educational Needs* Volume 22, No. 3 NASEN.

Home Office (1998) *Crime and Disorder Act 1998* London, HMSO

OfSTED (1999) *Principles into Practice: Effective Education for Pupils with Emotional and Behavioural Difficulties* London, OfSTED.

Wilson M and Evans M (1980) *Education of Disturbed Pupils, Schools Council Working Paper 65* London, Methuen.

Youell B (2000) 'Psychoanalytical Psychotherapy with Children with EBD' *The Journal of the Association of Workers for Children with Emotional and Behavioural Difficulties* Volume 5, No1 Spring 2000.

1.5

The New Special Educational Needs Code of Practice

John Friel, Barrister-at-law, Gray's Inn

The Special Educational Needs (SEN) Code of Practice was introduced as part of a substantial reform by the 1993 Education Act. For parents of children with special educational needs, the 1993 Act gave both parents and children new specific rights including rights of appeal. Alongside those rights of appeal was the Code of Practice, which provided guidance to all schools. The initial Code, to be used by parents and all concerned, was issued in 1994. It was replaced by a revised Code of Practice in November 2001.

The 1996 Education Act clarified previous Education Acts, but has now been subject to later variations. These include the Learning Skills Act 2000 and the Special Educational Needs and Disability Discrimination Act 2001. For the purposes of this book, it is not relevant to look at the new second Code of Practice in relation to Disability Discrimination.

The purpose of the Code of Practice is to give practical guidance on the discharge of functions in relation to children with special educational needs (under the Education Act 1996), to LEAs, governing bodies of all maintained schools, teachers, parents and all interested parties. The Code sets out guidance on policies and procedures aimed at enabling pupils with special educational needs to reach their full potential.

The Code makes it clear that the vast majority of children will be assisted in a mainstream setting. Additionally some children at some time will require further help from SEN services and other agencies.

A small minority of children who have special educational needs of a severe or complex nature will need Statements. The basic intention behind the Code is to set out guidelines in order to ascertain:

- whether children have special educational needs;
- whether they require special educational provision;
- if so at what level;
- and if a Statement is eventually or immediately necessary, provide guidance on this issue.

Principles of the new Code of Practice

The new Code is intended to help schools and LEAs obtain the best value from the considerable resources and expertise they invest in helping children with special educational needs. It now considers the new rights and duties introduced by the 2001 Act and Regulations, as well as the Learning Skills Act 2000.

Fundamental principles

The general principles are that:

- A child with special educational needs should have their needs met.
- The special educational needs of children will normally be met in mainstream schools or settings.
- The view of the child should be sought and taken into account.
- Parents have a vital role to play in supporting a child's education.
- Children with special educational needs should be offered full access to a broad, balanced and relevant education, including an appropriate curriculum at foundation stage and the National Curriculum.

The Code sets out a number of critical success factors, which are as follows:

- All resources in a school setting should be managed and deployed to ensure that all children's needs are met.
- LEA schools and settings should work together to ensure that any child's special educational needs are identified early.
- LEA schools and settings should exploit best practice when devising their interventions.
- The wishes of the child concerned should be taken into account in the light of their age and understanding.
- Parents and professionals should work in partnership.
- The views of individual parents should be taken into account.
- Interventions for each child should be reviewed regularly and assessed for their impact and effectiveness.
- There should be close co-operation between all relevant agencies together with a multi-disciplinary approach.
- LEAs should meet the prescribed time limits set out in the regulations.
- Where children require Statements these should be clear and detailed, the LEA should meet the prescribed time limits and should monitor the arrangements and review the Statement annually.

The Code of Practice defines the role of the LEA and its statutory duties far more extensively than before. Equally it defines the role of the school governing body and its statutory duties. It considers SEN policies in early education settings at schools and includes a useful table (paragraph 1.39) of roles and responsibilities.

The new Code is far more detailed and complex than the earlier Code. The 1994 Code provided a clear five stage assessment of children with special educational needs. Stages 1 and 3 were the school-based interventions (stage 3 bringing in outside intervention). Stages 4 and 5 were statutory assessment and a Statement. The current Code introduces the idea of school action and school action plus, which are much vaguer concepts than a five stage Code of Practice.

The Code is divided into a number of sections. The first defines principles and policies and thereafter outlines the system of identification and intervention. It begins with identification, assessment and provision in early education settings, then in the primary phase and finally in the secondary sector. Statutory assessments are dealt with in Chapter 7 of the Code. Statements of Special Educational Needs are dealt with in Chapter 8 and annual reviews in Chapter 9. Chapter 10 describes working in partnership with other agencies, including where a child transfers from the school sector into further education.

Overall, the Code is seeking to make schools more accountable for children with special educational needs and the funds invested in them. The previous Code could be described as far more precise about intervention on behalf of the child and more concerned with ensuring that some definition of his or her learning difficulties is set out. The current Code has abandoned the useful detailed guidance on certain learning difficulties contained in Chapter 3 of its predecessor.

Significant criticisms were made of the new Code of Practice in its draft form, and it was withdrawn in draft on a number of occasions. Some of these criticisms were valid. Firstly it is too complicated for parents and for teachers. Secondly, it uses unnecessarily complicated language. Overall, the document is far more concerned with administration and accountability than the first Code.

The new Code places greater obligations on all schools to make sure that the Special Educational Needs Co-ordinator (SENCO) in primary and secondary schools is given a substantial management role and has sufficient time to carry out the required duties. In seeking greater levels of accountability and clearer evidence of intervention, the Code is likely to create problems in cases where schools do not comply with its requirements. Local Education Authorities may well claim in cases where parents seek Statements of Special Educational Needs, that there is insufficient information. However, the legal position is that a Statement depends not on the availability of information, but on whether a Statement is necessary for the child (Section 323, the assessment provisions, and section 324, the Statement provisions of the 1996 Act make this quite clear).

School Action and School Action Plus

The new Code incorporates a two-stage procedure: school action and school action plus. Although the criteria for primary and for secondary level differ slightly, the overall principles are the same.

School action depends on the identification by the SENCO or a member of staff that the child requires an intervention additional to, or different from, that normally provided by the school. The criteria outlined at secondary level are that the child:

- Makes little or no progress even when teaching approaches are targeted particularly at a pupil's identified area of weakness.
- Shows signs of difficulty in developing literacy or mathematics skills that result in poor attainment in some curriculum areas.
- Has persistent emotional and/or behavioural difficulties which are not ameliorated.
- Has sensory or physical problems and continues to make little or no progress despite specialist equipment.

- Has communication and/or interaction difficulties and continues to make little or no progress despite the provision of a differentiated curriculum.

The Code provides for consultation and co-operation with parents. It also requires an individual education plan, examples of which are found in the SEN Toolkit and associated document published by the Department for Education and Skills (DfES). The Individual Education Plan should include information about:

- The short-term targets set for or by the pupil.
- Teaching strategies to be used.
- Provision to be put in place.
- When the plan is to be reviewed.
- Success and/or exit criteria.
- Outcomes.

The next stage is school action plus. This stage follows a review of intervention under school action, which would normally bring in, when needed, external support services provided by the LEA and/or outside agencies. The triggers for this are defined in the Code of Practice at secondary level (Chapter 6.64) as being that the child:

- Continues to make little or no progress in specific areas over a long period.
- Continues working at National Curriculum level substantially below that expected of pupils of a similar age.
- Continues to have difficulty in developing literacy and mathematics skills.
- Has emotional or behavioural difficulties which substantially and regularly interfere with their own learning and/or that of the class group despite intervention.
- Has sensory or physical needs that require additional specialist equipment or regular advice or visits providing direct intervention of pupil or staff.
- Has ongoing communication or social interaction difficulties that impede the development of social relationships and cause substantial barriers to learning.

The Code of Practice allows that for a very small number of pupils the help given by schools through action plus may not be sufficient to enable the pupil to make adequate progress. Schools can now themselves seek a statutory assessment. The terms upon which they can seek such an assessment are defined in pages 72 and 73 of the Code of Practice (Chapter 6.72).

It should be noted that the expectation of the Code of Practice is for a very complex and sophisticated intervention at action plus. Practical experience suggests that this may not be available in all cases. For example, where children or staff require specific help or disability equipment, they may in reality only be provided with aids as a result of a Statement or a statutory assessment under Section 323. The current Code of Practice expects an enormous amount of schools. It remains to be seen whether schools can deliver such a sophisticated service.

Statutory Assessment and Statement

Chapter 7 of the Code deals with the statutory assessment of special educational needs, the evidence to be provided by the school or the early education setting and referral by another agency. Considerations for parents who wish to request an assessment are important in this section (pages 78–79 of the Code Chapter 7.21 to 7.29). Many of the parents consulting this Guide will be considering making such a request.

Chapter 7.23 sets out the principles on which parents should request an assessment. Firstly, parents should believe that their child's needs are not being met through school-based intervention or that the needs are so substantial that a mainstream school could not meet them effectively without the use of outside resources. The Code points out that parents should clearly set out the reasons for their request. They should also provide information about the provision that the child has already received. However, the Code is silent on issues arising from certain cases which frequently come to the attention of LEAs, and the Special Educational Needs Tribunal. These are cases where children have not received any or adequate intervention because their problems have been under-estimated or missed altogether.

The previous Code included detailed criteria for dealing with individual categories of disability, i.e. emotional and behavioural difficulties and specific learning difficulties including dyslexia. The new Code does not address matters in similar detail. However the previous Code omitted some obvious categories.

The new Code provides an improvement on the previous version in that it includes a section on children who need an immediate referral for a statutory assessment. Obviously this refers to children with the most severe difficulties, and this new, more substantial section of the Code is a welcome addition.

Evidence in deciding whether to make a statutory assessment

Pages 81–89 of this Code cover the evidence that an LEA should consider before making a decision to conduct a statutory assessment. This includes, with guidance, some consideration of certain learning difficulties, but not in the same detail or complexity as the previous Code.

The evidence to be considered by the LEA includes:

- Evidence that the school has responded appropriately to requirements of the National Curriculum especially in relation to inclusion.
- Evidence provided by the child's school, parents and other professionals involved with the child as to the nature, extent and cause of the child's learning difficulties.
- Evidence of action already taken by the child's school to meet and overcome those difficulties.
- Evidence of the rate and style of the child's progress.
- Evidence that where some progress has been made, it has been the result only of additional efforts and instruction at a sustained level not usually commensurate with provision through school action plus.

The Code clearly requires specific evidence of attainment and requires LEAs to seek clear, recorded evidence of the child's academic attainment. Overall, the LEA should consider the case for a statutory assessment, where the balance of evidence presented to, and assessed by it suggests that the child's learning difficulties:

- Have not responded to relevant and purposeful measures taken by the school or by an external specialist.
- May call for special educational provision that could not reasonably be provided within the resources normally available to mainstream maintained schools and settings in the area.

The new document improves on the previous Code by seeking the child's views. It also points out that each child is unique and that the questions asked by the LEA should reflect the particular circumstances of that child.

The Code then covers some areas of strengths and difficulties such as: communication and interaction; vocation and learning behaviour; emotional and social development; sensory and/or physical needs; and medical conditions. However it covers these issues in a much broader sense than the previous Code and the guidance it gives is far more general. For example autism, dyslexia, dyspraxia and hearing impairment are covered in Chapter 7.55 to 7.57. The previous Code covered specific learning difficulties including dyslexia, very effectively and accurately in greater depth.

Criteria for considering intervention

In dealing with children with, for example dyslexia, dyspraxia, language delay, other learning difficulties and language and communication problems, the types of intervention are set out as follows:

- Flexible teaching and arrangements.
- Help in acquiring, comprehending and using language.
- Help in articulation.
- Help in acquiring literacy skills.
- Help in using augmentative and alternative means of communication.
- Help to use different means of communication confidently and competently for a range of purposes including formal situations.
- Help in organising and co-ordinating oral and written language.
- Support to compensate for the impact of communication difficulty on learning in English as an additional language.
- Help in expressing, comprehending and using the child's own language, where English is not his or her first language.

The Code goes on to state that if some or all of these programmes can be provided for a child by the school in collaboration with the LEA or external services, then the LEA may conclude that intervention should be provided at school action plus and monitored to see if that action is effective. It would then be appropriate for the LEA to conclude that a statutory assessment was not necessary. If, on the other hand, the school support and services had already provided these interventions through school action plus and the child had not made acceptable progress, then a statutory assessment should be considered.

There is one difficulty with the Code worth noting here. It makes no reference to the necessity of a Statement in cases where there has been no intervention and where there is evidence that sufficient support is not available. In most such cases a Statement should be necessary, but the Code does not address this point.

If one turns to the provision for Statements in Chapter 8 of the Code, particularly the criteria for deciding to draw up a Statement, and contrasts this with the provisions relating to a statutory assessment, it is clear that where children will require greater intervention than is normally available, a Statement should be made. There is therefore a clear internal conflict in the Code between cases in which there is lack of evidence of adequate intervention by the school together with insufficient evidence that there will be future adequate intervention, and cases where the LEA is bound to draw up a Statement.

Generally speaking, the new Code seems to over-emphasise the requirement of a school to provide detailed documentation in compliance with the Code, and to give insufficient emphasis to the child's interest. The law, however, lies clearly in the other direction. The statutory considerations in Sections 323 and 324 are based on the whole child R v. Secretary of State for Education ex parte E (1992) FLR p377.

The test as outlined by the Court of Appeal in that leading case is far more simple. As Balcombe LJ in ex parte E pointed out, the real test is whether the school, with or without assistance on assessment from the LEA, can provide from its own resources (which includes the resources normally provided to the school through LEA services) adequate intervention to deal with the child's needs. If so, no Statement is necessary. If, however, outside intervention over and above that which is normal is required, then a Statement is necessary.

The current Code has made the test extremely complex, and to some degree ignores the guidance of the Courts on these issues.

In outlining considerations for a Statement, the Code accurately sets out the law. A Statement makes a diagnosis of the child's learning difficulties and the prescription to meet their needs. If the LEA can provide what is needed together with the school within the normal resources, no Statement is necessary. If it cannot, then a Statement is necessary. Normally of course, Statements are required, as the Code makes clear, for children with severe and complex learning difficulties, but a Statement can be required for a child solely with a severe learning difficulty or a complex learning difficulty.

Chapter 10 of the Code discusses partnership with other agencies and covers future progress. It is to be noted that the new Connexions service brought in under the Learning Skills Act is an important development. The intention of this Chapter is to make sure that for children with Statements there is smooth co-operation between other agencies, particularly for the more disabled child who will require continuous support, and for those who will require support well into further and higher education. To this extent, again the Code is a great improvement.

1.6
Children with Special Educational Needs: The Legal Implications

John Friel, Barrister-at-law, Gray's Inn

The Special Educational Needs and Disability Act 2001 has made some amendments to rights and duties in relation to children in this field. In particular, it brings into play the Disability Rights Commission and the provisions of the Disability Discrimination Act 1995 in education when education has previously been exempt.

There is a Code of Practice on disability discrimination in education, but in relation to the issues arising for parents reading this Guide disability discrimination issues will normally not be particularly relevant. The new Act effectively:

- Strengthens the specific duty to educate in a mainstream school, if the child can be so educated, and if the parents so wish.
- Creates a needed mediation system, to which parents may have recourse when they are in dispute with an LEA over a Statement. However, the mediation system should not delay or deny an appeal.
- Brings in rights to raise disability discrimination issues in exclusion appeals. Parents who are paying fees for an independent school education may note that these schools are now subject, like state schools, to claims that they have discriminated against disabled children. While damages cannot be claimed, extensive changes may be required by the school to meet a disability discrimination claim.
- Brings the full weight of the Disability Discrimination Act into further and higher education, an area in which, it is likely to have a long-term substantial effect.

How do you enforce your rights?

Despite alterations to the law, and two new Codes of Practice, the principles as to how parents can obtain adequate assistance for their children remain unchanged. In some cases, the new Code of Practice may be of assistance, for example, if a school is discriminating against particular disabilities by making no provision for them. Therefore the Code of Practice on Disability Discrimination should not be ignored and should be obtained. However, the chief concern for parents reading this Guide is clearly the enforcement of their child's rights.

For parents of children with more severe disabilities there will probably be no debate about whether or not a Statement is required. The issue in this case will be how the child's difficulties are to be addressed, and where should he/she be educated? For parents of children who have obviously severe and complex learning difficulties (but not profound and multiple handicaps), and who will go on, if assisted properly, to take a role in normal life, the situation will not be the same as for a severely disabled child. The school may, of course, identify the child's problem, but it may not. Thus the parent may be seeking a statutory assessment under s.323, or alternatively, having reached the point where everybody agrees a Statement is necessary, be seeking to argue that they require much more for their child than the LEA is prepared to offer.

The principles upon which parents should prepare a case are exactly the same whether the issue concerns the necessity of a Statement or its content. However, the considerations and the level of preparation will be different if there is no Statement.

Preparation of your case

Before a parent or an education authority can know whether there is a legal obligation to make provision (under the Education Act 1996, s.324) for a Statement of Special Educational Needs or even for a statutory assessment, the child's needs must first be assessed.

Identification of children with special educational needs

The Code of Practice and the 1996 Act require an LEA to exercise its powers with a view to securing or identifying that those children who have special educational needs and for whom it is necessary for the authority to determine the special educational provision required are so identified. If the authority forms the opinion that the child's special educational needs requires, or probably requires, a Statement then they will conduct an assessment. The school itself can now request an assessment.

However, a major problem arises where the LEA has failed to identify children with special educational needs. Many requests for Statements still come from parents. Thus where a parent requests statutory assessment, unless that parent has evidence that it is required, the LEA will inevitably refuse. The terms of the new Code of Practice make it clear that the LEA will be entitled to refuse unless the request is supported by substantial evidence.

The 2001 Act allows schools to request a statutory assessment as well as permitting LEAs to conduct an assessment under s.323. Therefore it is likely to be more rather than less difficult for parents to obtain a statutory assessment and/or a Statement in circumstances where neither the LEA nor the school has requested an assessment. Regrettably, this can only be done if the case is prepared properly by the parent.

Preparing a request for an assessment

If possible, a parent who can afford independent advice should consider such advice essential. Where there is no support or little support by a school for a statutory assessment and evidence that the school has simply not fulfilled its role adequately, or where the LEA requires clearly identified intervention by the school and there is none, parents will not be able to obtain a Statement or even a statutory assessment unless they are prepared to obtain adequate independent reports.

Regrettably, for parents who have limited means, this is difficult. For those who are on Income Support, the legal help scheme (available from some specialist solicitors) provides a means whereby independent reports can be obtained. However, parents seeking such advice should ideally use specialist education solicitors because the Legal Services Commission has changed matters and procedure in legal aid cases. Legal aid is now only available from approved solicitors. For parents with very limited means, (i.e. those on Income Support), this remains one route.

For parents who have limited income, the National Health Service can be used. A number of hospitals – for example the Munro Centre, 66 Snowsfields, London, SE1 3SS and Liverpool Alder Hey – have clinical/educational psychologists who can provide a detailed and appropriate report. There are also some charities that provide assessments or funds for them. An example is the Dyslexia Institute Bursary Fund, which will provide funds for an assessment. However, this and other charities do not generally provide such assessments for the purposes of seeking a statutory assessment but in order to establish a level of need. IPSEA (The Independent Panel of Special Needs Advisors) remains a valuable service.

On the assumption that adequate funds are available, reports must be obtained. It should be remembered that experts need to earn a living but are not, in comparison with other services today, generally expensive. Independent experts should be used.

Parents should also bear in mind that they are asking the LEA to provide, in the form of a Statement, a potential substantial and valuable benefit. The cost of education at the state schools listed in this Guide or the independent schools with specialist help is considerable. All these schools provide a sophisticated, expensive and complex service to assist children with varying learning difficulties. Nobody would approach a claim where, for example, they had been run over in the street and suffered substantial damages, on the basis of amateur and inadequate preparation. Parents must take great care to prepare their child's case adequately.

Many children with special educational needs have conditions that require medical treatment or the supervision of doctors. In all such cases medical reports should be obtained. For those with physical difficulties and associated brain damage, that may include reports from a paediatrician, physiotherapist, occupational therapists and speech therapists. However it should be borne in mind that increasingly NHS speech therapy reports do not advise on the child's level of need, but rather what is on offer from the Local Health Service. Because provision from Local Health Services varies nationally, the advice also varies in quality. In some cases it is excellent, in others the Authority may only say what will be made available, not what is needed.

The legal duty of the Local Education Authority is to provide for the special educational needs of the child. Thus what is on offer from the Health Service is not necessarily what a Local Education Authority is obliged to provide. In cases of Statements of Special Educational Needs, the law requires the LEA to pay for a provision irrespective of resources. If provision is not locally available the LEA must pay for the provision to be made from elsewhere, see East Sussex County Council ex parte T (1998) Education Law Reports p198. The House of Lords differentiated the duties in education from duties in social services.

The Courts have strengthened parents' rights in this field. A Statement must have a diagnosis of and a prescription of the child's special educational needs R v. Secretary of State for Education ex parte E (1992) Family Law Reports p377. Further Statements must be specific so that provision in a Statement is ascertainable, identifiable and quantified. Although the Code of Practice and the Regulations make this point quite clearly, the major failing by LEAs is to so identify the provision. In L v. Clarke & Somerset (1998) Education Law Reports p128 and Bromley v. The SENT (1999) Education Law Reports p260 CA, both the High Court and the Court of Appeal confirmed that Statements must be detailed, quantified and specific.

This is an important consideration in dealing with a child's learning difficulties. Parents will need to seek evidence – both at the assessment stage and the statementing stage – that the intervention is detailed, sufficiently quantified, and sufficiently specific to ameliorate the child's learning difficulties. Evidence that such intervention is not available provides grounds for a case for a statutory assessment and means that it should succeed, irrespective of the vagueness of the Code of Practice on this issue. It should also establish a case for the parent on an appeal against a Statement.

Thus the expert must address the following questions:

- What are the child's needs in the area of expertise required? For example an educational psychologist will need to comment on requirements for specialist reports, for example from speech therapists, occupational therapists etc.
- What is the provision required to meet the needs?
- What provision is available at the local school?
- What provision is required for the child, if this is an assessment case, is this likely to be available in the local school or LEA?
- What provision does the expert advise?

As far as occupational therapists, physiotherapists, speech therapists, paediatricians and other specialists are concerned, the same questions arise within their area of expertise. In cases of autistic children or children with emotional and behavioural problems or mental health problems, reports from consultant child psychiatrists or child and adolescent psychiatrists can be essential. Regrettably, there are few good experts available nationally. However in cases where such a skill is involved, attention should be given to such reports.

Involvement of the child and the role of social services and educational welfare services

The Code of Practice now requires the views of the child to be sought. While this is a good and appropriate development, it can lead to difficulties. Parents may be understandably over anxious. At the same time there is a risk that schools and LEAs may put pressure on children to make statements in support of the institution.

Where children are capable of expressing their views – and some children may not be able to do so – use of the guidance given in the Children Act for the interviewing of young people by the LEA is essential. This guidance is to ensure that children are not over influenced by the interviewer, or pressurised into saying things with which they do not agree. Recent experience has shown that attempts have been made both by parents and local authorities to influence children in expressing their views. Children with special educational needs are generally vulnerable and may well be unduly subject to pressure.

Regrettably, social services intervention is often notable by its absence. Children with considerable learning difficulties who are likely to be disabled for life or for a substantial period often have no social services care plan or intervention in place for them. Section 17 of the Children Act provides a general power to assess children who are in need. Assessment provisions of the Act normally require that children should be assessed at the same time as a Statement of Special Educational Needs is put in to place or a statutory assessment takes place.

In London Borough of Bromley v. The SENT (1999) Education Law Reports p260 the Court of Appeal emphasises that there is no border between social services needs, medical needs and educational needs which are clear and defined. Children who require waking day curriculum or a 24-hour curriculum may be as much in need of a whole multi-professional approach (educational, medical and practical) as they are in need of education. Less able children will develop independence skills and communication skills but may never be fully independent or fully able to communicate, and thus the working day curriculum is educational.

If available, reports should be sought from social services. In more complex cases involving children with severe and complex difficulties, an independent social worker's report may be required if the social services reports are inadequate or if there has been no social services intervention.

What is a Statement?

A Statement is a document that clearly defines a child's educational needs and the intervention to meet those needs. It must be specific, quantified and effective. Case law in this area has been considered above.

The process of assessment

The process of assessment is governed by Regulation. The LEA should normally seek:

- educational advice;
- advice from an educational psychologist;
- advice from social services;
- medical advice;
- advice from any specialist services providing assistance to the child.

The Act creates a definite timetable that is often dishonoured. The Code of Practice timetable is set out at the end of this chapter and is laid out clearly in the current Regulations and in the Code of Practice. The Education (Special Educational Needs) England Consolidation Regulations 2001 SI 3455 clearly states the time limits. Once a local authority has completed an assessment it is under obligation to serve a draft Statement. The parent then has the right to require meetings and representations. It is at this time, once a Statement has been finalised, that mediation should be considered. The time limits for an appeal to the Tribunal are extremely strict. Appeals should be made within 2 months of the date of service of the final Statement, and it is only in exceptional circumstances that a Tribunal can extend the time.

The structure of the Act requires the parent to prepare the case in advance. If the parent is seeking to catch up, difficulties will ensue.

Experts

A major difficulty of seeking expert advice is that even though there are a large number of psychologists available for private consultation, few are prepared to assist in special educational needs appeal cases. Some who offer their services in these instances do not have the forensic skills to do so. Parents seeking to put forward a case in support of an application for a place at one of the schools in this Guide are well advised to seek expert legal guidance. If that is not available to them, advice from charities that have good working knowledge of complex difficulties should be sought. For example the British Dyslexia Association provides an advisory and representation service, as does the National Autistic Society. Parents should appreciate that these are complex, difficult and sophisticated cases which normally require expert preparation and support.

Experience suggests that the documents from the Special Educational Needs Tribunal indicating that parents can easily prepare a case and can represent themselves, are unrealistic. Children who require Statements will normally have complex difficulties. Although it is possible for parents to prepare cases properly, experience has shown that the task is often substantially underestimated. Many appeals to the High Court have arisen where parents were unrepresented, and for that reason the Tribunal has not been able to address key issues in their case and consequently has made quite substantial mistakes. The Tribunal system is obviously designed to hear very complex cases and decide them quickly. It does so without great cost in comparison to normal cases of this complexity and importance. However because the documentation of the Tribunal attempts to help parents – and ensure that cases are decided quickly and efficiently in the child's interest – it disguises the basic complexity of many cases. Some cases will be simple but a parent reading this publication would require expensive specialist provision. Cases of this nature are not easy, and few parents have been able to come away from a Tribunal feeling that they have handled cases on their own adequately. A number have complained after the hearing that the Tribunal publications on this issue are misleading and that they did not understand the difficulty and complexity of cases. For the reader of this Guide cases should be presented either with legal assistance, or at least with assistance from one of the major charities who provide representation of an experienced and competent nature.

A surprising number of appeals to the High Court are settled resulting in a rehearing. If argued, they have usually resulted in a remission to the Special Educational Needs Tribunal. The overall experience indicates that parents are better at preparing cases like this with professional legal advice and with adequate reports then they are attempting to prepare without such guidance. The Tribunal carries out good work, in difficult circumstances, to the best of its ability.

The Code of Practice Timetable

The LEA must decide whether or not to make a statutory assessment within six weeks of the date that the request was lodged. The LEA then has ten weeks to undertake the statutory assessment process. The decision about whether or not to make a Statement must be finalised within two weeks of completing the statutory assessment, allowing eight weeks to gather information, seek professional advice and make a decision. The LEA then has a further two weeks to notify the parents of its decision and to make a proposed Statement if appropriate. Otherwise a note in lieu, explaining why the Statement was refused, must be provided. A final Statement must be agreed within eight weeks of the issue of the proposed Statement.

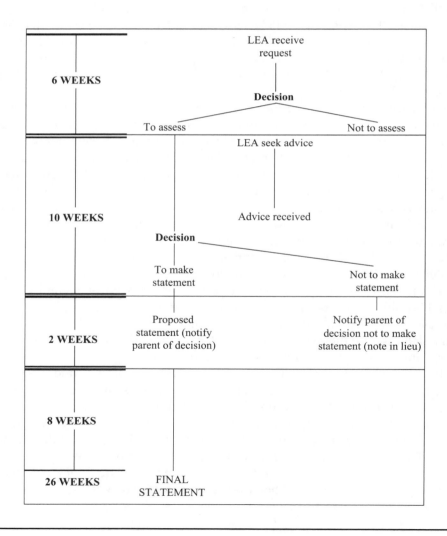

1.7
Special Educational Needs in Scotland

Ken Dutton,
Principal Educational Psychologist[1] – Scottish Borders Council

The Education Committee of the Scottish Parliament recently completed a comprehensive review of provision for special needs in Scottish schools, and collated its recommendations in a consultative report, 'Assessing our children's educational needs: The Way Forward?' Significant changes are proposed, particularly in the way needs are defined, identified, assessed, reported and recorded, and new legislation is currently being drafted. The recommendations, presently under consultation with local authorities, are described in some detail at the end of this article.

The description that follows outlines the present existing legal framework and arrangements for children with special educational needs. It is, however, fair to say that policies and support frameworks in Scotland are in a significant state of flux at the time of writing (March 2002).

The current existing legislative system

The special needs system in Scotland broadly follows similar principles and processes to the parallel requirements in England. However, this is defined by separate law in Scotland (the Education (Scotland) Act 1980, as amended by the 1981 Act) and the detail of the process is different in many significant ways. In general, the processes tend to be less bureaucratic than their English law counterparts.

Assessing and documenting special educational needs

The principal vehicle, currently, for the definition of needs in Scotland is the Record of Need process which is the equivalent of the Statementing practice, south of the border. Most authorities in Scotland have a staged system for supporting all pupils, similar to the 'Code of Practice' (COP) in England and Wales. There are recommended stages listed in the equivalent Scottish 'Manual of Good Practice', but this is guidance for authorities rather than the legally enforced prescriptive practice laid out in the Code of Practice.

Most school-age children with learning difficulties requiring the protection of a Record of Need would be identified in schools via the various staged systems of

---

1 Ken Dutton is Principal Psychologist at Scottish Borders Council; the article, however, is written in a private capacity and the views expressed are not necessarily those of the Council or Education Department.

identification, assessment and support. The local authority must open a Record of Need for any child who has severe, specific or complex needs which are required to be kept under review by the local authority.

Education Departments are required to identify and record children with severe and complex needs from the age of two. Such children, not yet within the formal school system, are usually brought to the attention of the authorities by multi-agency links with paediatric services, GPs & health visitors, visiting paediatric therapists and, often, parents themselves.

Any parent can request a multi-disciplinary assessment to see if a Record of Needs is necessary for their child. An authority must carry out such an assessment unless it feels it is an unreasonable request, and clearly must have evidence to support such a decision. If a parent does not accept an authority's decision either to carry out, or not to carry out, an assessment, they may appeal to the Scottish Executive Education Department (SEED) to have that decision scrutinised.

If the assessment is carried forward then an authority must obtain reports from the school the child attends, the school's educational psychologist and school clinical medical officer/paediatrician. The local authority must also seek the parents' views as to what they consider to be the best for their child. Since the enactment of the Children (Scotland) Act 1995, the child's own views must also be obtained, directly if they are over 12 years of age and able to express their views, or via their parents if younger or not considered able to express their own views.

When all the reports have been obtained, the authority collates them and makes a decision whether to open, or not to open, a Record. If it decides to proceed, a draft version of the Record of Need is then sent (or, in some authorities, taken by the educational psychologist) to the parents for their approval. If approved this is then issued as a final version Record of Need. If there are aspects that require editing or altering, this is negotiated between parents and authority.

The final Record of Needs is copied to parents, school and local authority; copy information can be provided to medical officers on request (normally a standardised system for such requests exists). Further copies to other personnel can be provided only with parental permission or after a parental request.

Appeals system

Parents retain rights of appeal about the various sections of the final Record of Need, if complete agreement proves difficult. The local authority appeals committee, sheriff, or Scottish Executive Education Department (depending on the specific area of disagreement) can variously hear these appeals. There is, at present, no equivalent to the tribunal system as in England & Wales though the notion of such a body has been debated as part of the (Scottish) parliamentary review of the special needs systems. Meanwhile an independent body 'Enquire', part of the Children in Scotland organisation, has been commissioned by the Scottish Executive to act in a conciliation role in the case of major disputes (which are rare, relative to the activity of the English tribunal system).

Reviewing needs

It is considered good practice to review Records of Need regularly and this is usually done via the child or young person's school, annually. Parents or other professionals involved can request a review at any time, but an authority does not have to carry out such a review unless it has been at least 12 months since the previous review.

Education authorities will formally review a child's Record of Needs, as a minimum, at key transition points e g transfer between nursery and primary stages, midway through the primary stages and at the primary/secondary transfer point.

The authority must, by law, carry out a Future Needs Review as a child approaches school leaving age (in the year prior to their 16th birthday, the point at which a child becomes legally referred to as a 'young person'). This meeting would typically involve teachers, educational psychologist, careers officer, medical officer and social worker (if they are likely to have a statutory responsibility to provide services for the young person as he/she moves into the adult world). Any other professionals who may have been providing services to the young person would also be invited to either attend or provide reports. Usually representatives from the local further education college, which may offer courses appropriate to the young person's needs, will also attend. The aim of the Future Needs Review is to offer the young person (and their parents) advice on what is available for them in the period beyond school, as they move into adulthood, and to plan that transition to ensure it is both smooth and effective for the young person.

As the young person leaves formal school education the Record of Need is discontinued, but kept in file archives for up to five years. This is so that the young person, further education establishment or other statutory bodies may obtain required information or later references from this (but only with the young person's knowledge and permission).

Supporting individual needs

Provision of support for children with special needs varies, both in terms of the type of need a child has and the different local authorities' responses to education provision. Different authorities' responses are varied as a result of geography/demography as well as historical, political and philosophical standpoints.

Sparsely populated areas, such as the Highlands and the border areas (Scottish Borders and Dumfries & Galloway Councils), typically tend to make provision in locally based schools and specialist provision attached to mainstream schools. Dedicated specialist centres are often non-viable both in terms of pupil numbers and the costs of establishing and running them. Some densely populated inner-city areas, such as Glasgow City, have large dedicated specialist schools as well as a spectrum of locally based and individual support arrangements.

A number of specialist independent centres exist throughout Scotland providing very specialist (frequently residential) support for children with complex, severe low-incidence needs, occasionally involving care and welfare as well as educational decisions. Some of the schools are listed elsewhere in this guide, but would include the Royal Blind School, Donaldsons School for the Deaf, Craighalbert Centre (offering Peto-type provision for children with motor impairment), etc.

Current developments

Recently enacted legislation (Standards in Scotland's Schools etc Act 2000), requires education authorities to ensure that education is directed to the development of the personality, talents and mental and physical abilities of the child to his or her fullest potential. Reflecting the move to inclusive policies in authorities, this has enshrined a requirement for 'presumption of mainstream' schooling as the starting point for meeting a child's needs. Only in exceptional or complex cases, or following parents' requests, would children be considered for specialist schools or resourced provision placements (which may or may not be provided locally by an education authority).

Other legislation, the UK-wide Special Educational Needs Disability Rights in Education 2001 Act – soon to be contextualised within Scotland via the Education (Disability Strategies & Pupils' Records) Bill – has also underlined the need for authorities to anticipate barriers to learning for a range of children with complex needs. Education Departments will be required to audit and plan strategically and proactively to make schools disability-friendly and the curriculum accessible, rather than the historic reactive ways of working. The changes will encompass teacher development and training, school policy-making as well as physical alterations to ensure accessibility to school buildings.

Future developments

The Scottish Executive document, 'Assessing our children's educational needs: The Way Forward?' is a response to a comprehensive two-year review of SEN provision across Scotland. (The complete document is available via the Internet at the Scottish Executive website at www.scotland.gov.uk – under 'publications'.)

The proposed changes try to find a middle ground between the opposing views of the main protagonists in the ongoing debate: those who wish to see the cumbersome bureaucratic systems dismantled completely with the adoption of an 'entitlement for all' philosophy, and those who feel the rights of children with special needs require an increased regulatory and legislative framework to protect them.

Key proposed changes are:

- The widening of the criteria for support needs – to include those children for whom English is an additional language, gifted children, travellers and those children with problems outside school contexts.
- The shifting of emphasis from local authority to schools as the key co-ordinators for the assessment and monitoring process for children with support needs. Only in exceptional and complex cases would centralised services become involved in assisting schools providing for support needs.
- A requirement for authorities and schools to have a staged intervention process building on and expanding information and planning routinely applied to existing systems for children's Personal Learning Plans (PLPs), individualised educational plans (IEPs), etc.
- The replacement of the Record of Needs with a Co-ordinated Support Plan (CSP), which would only apply when a mainstream school was unable to provide for a child from within its own resources.

- The CSP would be a flexible and responsive document, complementary to school plans, not a separate and cumbersome bureaucratic process, duplicating work in many instances. It would focus on the supports needed for the achievement of outcomes, rather than personalised to a child's strengths, deficiencies and weaknesses. It may involve other aspects of a child's development beyond purely educational requirements.
- A requirement for the active participation of children and young people in the processes of identifying and providing for their needs, through the appointment of a key 'named individual' adult within each school community to act as a support for each child.
- A proposed key-worker system for young people making the transition from secondary school, following them into employment, training, further education and higher education.
- CSPs should form an integral modular part of other support plans which may apply in some children's lives (e.g. care plans).
- Early identification and intervention should be built into pre-school systems.
- An earlier involvement of multi-agency workers (e.g. social workers and other non-education staff) to explore interventions and alternative pathways to solutions.
- Psychological and medical assessments would no longer be compulsory aspects of the assessment process, only being undertaken if required, or when requested by parents.
- A proposal for parent partnership services in local authorities to support and guide parents in all aspects of their child's support needs, including provision of interpreters/translators where required.
- A mandatory requirement for authorities to have a mediation service to try to resolve informally disputes prior to formalised appeals proceedings, leading into independent expert tribunal system for resolution of appeals, independent of the Scottish Executive (the present ultimate arbiter of disputes).

1.8
How Parents Can Help

Nigel Pugh, The British Dyslexia Association

Nigel Pugh is an experienced lay advocate helping parents through the complex and often frustrating legal and administrative processes of special education. Here he offers some practical advice to parents seeking suitable education provision for their child and emphasises the importance of an organised and positive approach.

All references to the Code are the 2001 SEN Code of Practice unless otherwise stated. Figures in brackets are the paragraph number within the Code.

The term 'he' means 'he or she'.

Being a parent is the most difficult job in the world! When your child has, or you believe that he has, Special Educational Needs then parenting becomes that much more difficult. You want an education that meets all of your child's needs. Some parents take the view that they will pay for their child's education. This is not an option to be undertaken lightly. Remember that you will have to pay out, over a number of years, a considerable sum of money. Generally speaking it is cheaper to place a child at the most expensive private school than in a specialist school. Most parents come to the conclusion that the only other alternative way forward is to gain the agreement of the Local Education Authority (LEA) to pay for the specialist provision. All LEA's are under considerable pressure to restrain costs. At the same time they are required to identify and meet children's needs with appropriate provision. All LEA's therefore have clear mechanisms to manage the SEN process based on law and regulation. This article aims to give you a basic framework to manage the process for your child. Good luck!

We shall start at the beginning of the process; don't worry if you come to it part way through. Your job will be to work within the SEN process by managing and directing it to produce the outcome desired by you. The professionals with whom you will come into contact will have considerable knowledge of the SEN process. It is essential to ensure that, as far as possible, you have equal knowledge.

To do so you must get a copy of the Special Educational Needs Code of Practice, DfES reference DfES/581/2001 and SEN Toolkit DfES/558/2001, both available free from the DfES publications branch on 0845 602 2260 or from the DfES web site. As knowledge equals power you need to find out as much as possible about the Law, the Code, the procedures involved and your child's learning difficulties and/or disabilities. Good books to start with are "Taking Action" by John Wright and David Ruebain or "Children with Special Educational Needs – Caught in the Act" by John Friel.

General points

LEAs have a responsibility to meet the needs of all children within their area. They have to be seen to manage the process equally for all parents and their processes are largely paper – based so you need to get organised to manage this information. The following may help:

- Keep a large ring binder file with all reports and correspondence in date order. Don't sub divide it. If you want to identify all the Individual Education Plans (IEPs) use coloured tags. Don't be tempted to stuff all correspondence in a drawer! Send letters to confirm in writing what has been said at meetings and on the phone and keep copies both on paper and on a PC.
- Keep a diary. We advise getting an A4 Date-a-Day diary.

  - Keep the top third of each page as a diary – who you spoke to, what you agreed, when they were going to action that point.
  - Try and keep notes of all telephone calls. So, if an LEA officer agreed to do something by the 15th, make an entry on that day calling forward the previous entry – the day of the call. If you are really keen, call the person 48 hours beforehand and remind them of their agreed action. If there is going to be a delay, for whatever reason, agree the new date and bring that forward in the diary.
  - In the bottom part of the diary run a behaviour log. Do not try and write *War and Peace* each day. What you need is a short daily comment about how your child has fared that day. What's gone well, what's gone badly, what caused it? Make notes of the things your child says about his or her problems.

Prepare for meetings using the ideas in this article. It is a good idea to send a letter beforehand saying what you would like to discuss at the meeting. If you can, agree an agenda. Give the school copies of any evidence in advance. There is no point asking people for their comment on new information in a meeting when they have not had time to consider it. The focus of the meeting should be your child. It is very easy to get distracted by a discussion about who said what and when or delays in the procedure, and find that you have not said anything about what really worries you about your child's difficulties.

If at all possible take someone with you to make sure the meeting sticks to the point and take notes. At times you may feel angry or upset if there are disagreements, but try to stay calm. Send a letter afterwards noting what was said.

You have a right to express your concerns and your views should be heard. Get in contact with the LEA Parent Partnership Officer who will give you neutral impartial advice as to how the SEN process works within your LEA (Chapter 2 of the Code). They should be able to help by offering an Independent Parental Supporter to work with you throughout the time that your child has SEN.

You now have a right to enter into dispute resolution with an independent conciliator (Chapter 2). They will try and help you reach agreement with the LEA or school as to how to proceed. Use of this service will not at any time prejudice your right of access to the Special Educational Needs Tribunal. It is free to use.

You know your child. You cannot solve all of his or her problems on your own but you can do your best to make sure that all those difficulties are fully understood and that he or she receives the right sort of help. So how do you achieve this?

First concerns

Chapters 4, 5 & 6 of the SEN Code of Practice discuss the identification, assessment and provision in the early years, primary and secondary sectors. The chapters are almost exactly duplicated. So for ease of reference we have focused on the primary phase, Chapter 5.

Whatever the triggers are for the concerns you may have about your child's progress you should always seek to talk to the child's tutor or class teacher. Schools should be 'open and responsive to parents' concerns (5.14). Many teachers misunderstand parents at this stage and believe that parents are saying that they are bad teachers. You must be very careful in what you say and how you say it. You need to be clear about your child's exact difficulties and what you want the school to do to address these difficulties. Even at this early stage it is important to be as clear as possible about what difficulties you think he or she has and why you are worried. Research the disability with the relevant national charity and get their advice on how to present the information effectively.

If you are not sure you have all the information about the child you can ask for a copy of the school files on your child, with certain exceptions. The request should be in writing and the school has to provide the information within 15 working days, see School and Pupil Information Regulations 2000 (Section five). There may be a charge for this information.

All schools should provide special help within the normal curriculum framework and monitor and review the effectiveness of this additional help. This is done through the Individual Education Plan (IEP). You need to see the IEP. This stage is now known as School Action. It replaces the old Stages 1 & 2. When the action that the school has carried out at this stage has not been effective then the school draws on the external specialists within the LEA e.g. educational psychologists, advisory teachers etc. This stage is called School Action Plus and is the replacement for the old Stage 3. Parents should contribute to the information gathered (2.2). The school must inform you that your child has special educational needs (Section 317A Education Act 1996).

Independent reports, for example from an educational psychologist or speech and language therapist, stating that your child has severe SEN, should be taken seriously by the school and by the LEA. If not, you should write to the school asking why they disagree with professional advice about both your child's difficulties and the help he or she needs. Insist on a reply in writing. LEAs must have due regard to the private advice; they cannot ignore it.

It is usually, but not always, easier to find agreement on a child's difficulties than the sort of help he or she should have. School governors have a statutory duty to 'use their best endeavours to secure that if any registered pupil has special educational needs the special educational provision which his learning difficulty calls for is made' (Section 317, 1996 Education Act).

The big question in most cases is: who pays? School or LEA? The key point here is how severe are the needs? If meeting those needs is going to cost more than a mainstream school might reasonably be expected to manage then a statutory assessment is called for.

The statutory assessment

One of the major changes under the SEN and Disability Act 2001 is the right of parents to appeal. If a school makes a request for statutory assessment and the LEA refuses this assessment, the parents now have a right of appeal to the Special Educational Needs Tribunal (SENT) against the decision. Regulations state that the LEA has to make its decision within six weeks of the request.

If the parents make the request then the LEA only has to comply with the request to start a statutory assessment 'if it is necessary'. Your view of what is necessary and theirs may well be some distance apart. It is not enough to write a polite letter asking for an assessment. You must gather evidence and demonstrate that it is *really needed*, that everything else has been tried and that your child needs help that his school cannot provide. Once you write the letter asking for an assessment you are on a strict timeline. Make sure you have the information first rather than trying to find it out later.

If the school makes the request the LEA will have a form to be completed by the Head. Try and work with the school to complete this form. Get as much information as possible to support your case. Make sure that the rate of progress through the IEP's is included. Make sure that all of the additional help that the school is providing is included; if possible state the cash value of this help.

It is important to describe in detail all the difficulties you know your child experiences. If he or she has difficulties with reading, for example, describe these very precisely. What happens when he can't read a word? Does he guess wildly? Does he attempt to work it out? How successfully? In continuous reading, does he make errors; e.g. miss words or syllables (beginning, middle, and end)? Can he read for information? A bus timetable? A computer game manual? The *TV Times*? Does he seem to be concentrating so hard on decoding, or reading so slowly, that he can't remember what he has read? Can he remember/understand a sentence/page/chapter? What strategies does he use to avoid reading? What help does he need? If certain activities at home are helpful, say so, e.g. 'If I read the textbook to him he can do the homework'. Examples of a child's work are useful evidence.

You may find it helpful to use headings to describe each of his difficulties. An example of possible headings is given below in the section about analysing a statement. Don't rely on your independent evidence to speak for you. Use it instead to back up what you say. Think carefully about the help your child needs and say why. Say also why his local school cannot provide it. Remember that you are describing a 'difficulty in learning' or a disability that 'prevents or hinders' your child from making use of educational facilities, not simply his scores on certain tests (Section 312, 1996 Education Act).

Once the LEA has agreed to start the assessment it will seek more advice from parents, educational advice from the child's school, medical advice and psychologist advice. The LEA psychologist must consult with other psychologists involved with the child, including your independent psychologist.

The quality of advice varies enormously, but The Education (Special Educational Needs) (England) (Consolidation) Regulations 2001, printed at the back of the Code of Practice, are quite specific:

The regulations (Section 7(2)) state that advice, including parents' advice, shall relate to:

a)   the educational, medical, psychological or other features of the case (according to the nature of the advice sought) which appear to be relevant to the child's educational needs (including his future needs).

b)   how these features could affect the child's educational needs and

c)   the provision which is appropriate for the child in the light of those features of the child's case.

When you receive all the differing advice you should check that it has properly detailed what your child's difficulties are and that it specifies the help he needs. If it does not you should challenge the view in writing immediately.

If, after making the assessment, the LEA decides that an ordinary school can meet your child's needs it may decide not to make a statement. In this case they will issue a 'note in lieu' saying what his needs are and the help he requires. If you do not accept that this amount of help is adequate you have a right to appeal to the SEN Tribunal (see Part 1.5 and 1.6 for further information).

Analysing the statement

Once the LEA has decided 'it is necessary' for it to make a statement it will first send you a proposed statement, with all the advice gathered during the assessment. You have a right to make representations and to have a meeting to discuss the statement (Schedule 27, 1996 Education Act).

The Code is very specific about what is required within a statement (8.29 and 8.32/8.33 forward). A judge has described Part two of the statement, which covers the special educational needs or difficulties, as a 'diagnosis' and Part three, which specifies provision, as a 'prescription'. Part two must therefore describe 'all the child's needs'. All means all – each and every one of the needs, not just the one that the school can easily manage. Where behaviour is an issue then it should explain how the behaviour is going to be managed. Part three must make provision 'for each and every one' of the needs described in Part two. Provision, how the needs shall be met, should normally be quantified (e.g. in terms of hours of provision, staffing arrangements etc.) (8.37).

A good statement is one that enables anyone reading it, e.g. a supply teacher who does not know your child, to understand what his special educational needs are and makes it clear what sort of help he will receive. There should be no doubt about what is going to happen, who is going to do it and how often.

It is essential to analyse the proposed statement carefully. There are two ways of doing this, a paper method or using a PC spreadsheet; the methodology is the same.

First make a copy of the statement and all reports. You need one working copy. Put the original away in a safe place. Number the pages on the working copy. Then take three different coloured highlighter pens. Go through all the reports, including the one you wrote yourself and your independent evidence. With one colour, highlight any descriptions of your child's experiences. With another, highlight any proposed provision. With the third, colour anything with which you disagree. Assign a number along side each highlighted point. It does not matter that the numbers on the page are in sequence. You have now created a reference system so that you can refer to each point quickly in the future e.g. 15 /2, page 15, highlighted item 2.

Use a separate sheet of paper for each of your child's special educational needs and give each a heading. For example, for a dyslexic or dyspraxic child they may be: reading, writing, spelling, maths, memory, organisation, motor skills, language skills, social skills, self-esteem, confidence, behaviour and abilities. Other learning difficulties or disabilities will have similar characteristics that your child may or may not share.

Fold the paper in half, so that you have one half for descriptions of difficulties (SEN) and one half for the suggested provision for that particular difficulty or aspect of his disability.

Go through all the reports again. Copy each highlighted phrase of a description of difficulty on to the relevant page and similarly any advice about provision (noting the reference number). You may also wish to note who said what. Don't worry if the same need or provision appears in two different columns.

You now have a list of what everyone says about each of your child's educational needs and the help they say he or she requires. Check this list against the statement. This preparation will be invaluable when you meet with the LEA. You can also, using the vocabulary from the reports, draft a proposed statement of your own to be used as the basis of discussion.

You will be asked to state a preference for a maintained school. You have the right to make representations for an independent school. The LEA, in that case, only has to support your request if it cannot meet your child's needs in a maintained school (mainstream). You need to prove that a mainstream maintained school cannot meet those needs.

The LEA has eight weeks in which to finalise the statement. You have a right to meet with an LEA officer to discuss the draft statement. If, after trying to negotiate, you find you still disagree with the statement you have a right to appeal to the SEN Tribunal (see Part 1.5 and 1.6) about the description of needs and/or provision and the name of the school.

Reviews

A statement has to be reviewed at least annually. That means every 12 months, not 15 or 18 months. The Code of Practice describes what should happen at the review. Most of this is endorsed by regulations, printed at the back of the Code. You will be asked to give your views. If you do not feel that the statement is adequate or wish to move to an independent school you will need to think about your report in much the same way as described for the statutory assessment. The review report, written after the meeting, should recommend amendments to the statement but the LEA does not have to follow this advice.

If the statement is amended, but you are still not satisfied, you have a right to appeal to the SEN Tribunal about the contents of the statement, including the name of the school (see Part 1.5 and 1.6 for further information).

And finally!

Keep encouraging your child and show him or her plenty of love. Home is where your child should be safe and happy, however hard things may be at school. Try and keep any frustrations or anxieties to yourself and allow yourself to escape from the pressure sometimes. Join a support group!

1.9
An introduction to assessment
Dr Richard Lansdown MA, PGCE, DipPsych, PhD, FBPsS
Chartered Educational and Clinical (Child) Psychologist

The psychological assessment of a child thought to have special educational needs is an exercise in problem solving.

First one has to pose a 'why' question, examples of which are:

Why is s/he not reading as well as we expect?
Why is s/he unable to get on well with other children?
Why is s/he having such difficulty with written work?

The problem then is to answer these questions in a way that will give indications for the child's educational future.

The first step

The very first step is to gather some general information, which involves taking a brief medical, social and educational history. Information on milestones like walking and talking, hearing and vision, serious illnesses or accidents is essential. Whether there is a history of learning difficulties of any kind in the family may be relevant and details on how many schools have been attended are also sought.

Next comes current information: what do the present teachers say about the child's attainment and behaviour? Is there any specific concern, e.g. maths or reading, or is the worry more general? What are the child's interests? What is the child's behaviour like at home? Are there any problems with sleeping or eating or with making and keeping friends?

The first hypothesis

Once this information has been gathered, a preliminary hypothesis can be made. For example, consider these four nine year olds:

Peter Doe was born after a difficult delivery and he has always been slow in his milestones. His hearing and vision are normal but he has not been able to keep up with his peers in school work and has been kept down a year in primary school. He prefers to play with younger children. He used to sleep well but now says that it is hard to get to sleep, especially in term time.

Mary Doe was a normal toddler, very bubbly and outgoing as a young child, who has always had a wide circle of friends. She was a little late in talking but is very agile and swims like a fish. She has recently been reluctant to go to school, complaining of headaches or tummy aches and her reports have been encouraging but consistent in pointing to a difficulty with reading and spelling.

Jenny Doe has severe cerebral palsy and has no speech. She can swipe at an object with a closed fist but cannot hold or manipulate a pencil. Her parents report that she seems able to understand a great deal but they admit that they may be biased.

John Doe is described as having been a good baby, but not at all cuddly, with normal motor milestones, no illnesses but some language delay. He is solitary at school and has only one friend in the neighbourhood who shares his interest in trains. By choice, he reads nothing but train books, including out of date timetables, and will spend hours at a station. He hates change of any kind.

Each of these yields a different hypothesis. The next step is to test them, using tests and/or observations.

Testing the hypotheses

An intelligence test is the usual starting point for children with learning difficulties of any kind. Two are commonly used in the UK: the Wechsler Scales and the British Ability Scales. Both follow the same pattern of asking that children undertake a range of tasks which include verbal and non-verbal reasoning, memory, general knowledge, vocabulary and so on. The results are then aggregated to yield an IQ, with 100 as an average score. About 80 per cent of children score between 80 and 120. As a very rough rule of thumb, a score below 70 is an indication of learning difficulties, but it is of the utmost importance to note that this is only an indication, not a ticket to a special school.

There has been much criticism of intelligence tests and it is true that they have to be used with caution, especially with children from cultures different from that on which the test was standardised. Caution has to be exercised also when quoting an overall IQ since these can mask significant differences between verbal and non-verbal skills. What is more, an IQ is not as precise a measure as height or weight: there is an expected variation of plus or minus about 6 points, so a given IQ of 100 could be seen to represent a 'true' score of between 94 and 106.

It should be remembered that the tests have been devised for and standardised on able bodied children, so if one is assessing a child with disabilities, one is comparing that child with children without disabilities.

Much can be learned from the scores on such a test, but also from the way the child approaches the task. Does he rush at everything, showing no sense of planning or reflection on what he is doing? Does she persist, even when the tasks are getting hard? How does he react to failure?

But an IQ is only a beginning. One needs next to look at other relevant areas, depending on the question asked.

Peter: global or specific problems?

Peter's history suggests global difficulties, but to check on this one would supplement the intelligence test with others which look at reading and maths, writing and drawing. If they all point in the same direction, one begins to firm up on a diagnosis of learning difficulty, but it may be helpful also to consider his behaviour. Here there are two approaches. One is to rely on observations from the teachers, the parents and the psychologist carrying out the assessment. The other is to use a standardised rating scale which usually consists of a series of statements about children, with boxes to tick if they are appropriate for that child. This allows one to compare the child in question with others on whom the test was standardised, giving some indication of how serious any behaviour problems may be. Apart from anything else, it is useful to have data on behaviour when considering which school will be appropriate.

Mary: dyslexia?

Mary is reported to have problems with reading and spelling, so one must test those skills. Here we run into the difficulty of defining what we mean by reading. Some tests simply look at the child's ability to read single words out of context; this is useful as a screen but if there are difficulties it should be supplemented with a test of reading comprehension: how well does the child understand what is read? How much can he/she use context to guess at difficult words or phrases? Spelling mistakes can also give a clue to the next area of investigation: a child who writes 'mite' for might and 'dun' for done may have a weakness in visual memory.

If Mary's reading and/or spelling are poor when compared with her IQ, and if there are no reasons in her educational, medical or social history to explain the discrepancy, then the hypothesis of specific reading difficulty or dyslexia is likely to be upheld. It is common at this stage to assess the child's phonological awareness, which means in essence finding out how well she copes with language related sounds. There are batteries of tests to examine this, most of which include asking the child to detect words which rhyme, picking out words according to their ending sound or saying as many words as possible that begin with a certain letter in a short time. The rationale is that children diagnosed as dyslexic have often been found to have a weakness in such skills.

If it is thought that she has a memory weakness, then there are tests which examine children's memory, differentiating between visual and auditory channels.

A rating of Mary's behaviour may also be helpful, but equally important may be to look at how she sees herself. Here one uses a self concept scale, which gives some idea of whether she perceives herself as socially or academically a success, or possibly whether she feels supported at home.

A note on dyscalculia. Much is made of dyslexia, less of the maths equivalent which is known as dyscalculia. Relatively little work has been done in this area, there is some suggestion that it is related to spatial skills. The approach is similar to that used for dyslexia, with more detailed assessments of mathematical knowledge being carried out.

Jenny: a test for the tester

Jenny is quite a different matter. There are no tests standardised on children with cerebral palsy and so one normally uses instruments devised for the able bodied and interprets them in the light of the child's disability. At first it may seem impossible even to begin testing a child with no language and no hand control but much can be learned if the child can point, and swiping with a fist is often enough. For example, the British Picture Vocabulary Test consists of a series of pages with four pictures on each. The tester says a word and the child has to indicate the appropriate picture on that page. In this way one can assess vocabulary even in a child who has no speech at all. There are similar tests for spatial skills, and even one new scale which claims to assess general intelligence.

The interpretation of such tests is very much a matter of experience, for one has to take into account the fact that children with physical disabilities have not necessarily had the same breadth of life experience that their able-bodied peers have and may therefore not have a comparable range of vocabulary.

John: autism?

From his history, John is possibly autistic. Here one starts, not with any formal testing, but with a careful and detailed consideration of what he has done in the past and what he does now. Observations from teachers and parents are all important. One approach is to take the criteria for autism given in one of the classification[1] systems, and to look to see to what extent the child's behaviour matches them.

Once it has been established that a child can be so classified, tests can be useful, and indeed are essential, to allow recommendations for the type of school that will be the best. Standard intelligence and attainment tests can often be used, although it may be necessary to rely on non-verbal scales for some children.

Behaviour ratings are also helpful, especially those which focus on activity levels, for autistic children are often overactive.

These four examples have been chosen to show that not only are different tests used according to the question put, different weights are assigned to tests or assessment approaches as well. The art of assessment is not simply in coming up with answers, it lies crucially in asking the right questions.

Questions and answers

1. *A note on the IQ (intelligence quotient) and a reading age.*

Psychologists usually report the results of intelligence tests using an IQ or standard score. This computation allows an age correction to be applied to children's responses: a six year old answering 20 out of 30 items correctly is clearly brighter than a nine year old who has the same raw score. Reading test results are sometimes expressed as standard scores as well (and the purists say they should be) but they are often given as a reading age which indicates the level reached by an average child of those years.

2. *What effect is there when a child feels unwell, or if he or she does not like the psychologist?*

It is unwise to test a child who is unwell, and most unwise to rely on scores on one who is emotionally upset. The personality of the psychologist can make a difference but if he or she has been properly trained this should be relatively small.

---

1   There are two classification systems in use in the UK. DSM IV is American, ICD X is European. They both give detailed lists of criteria for the whole range of psychiatric disorders.

3. Are scores stable over time?

The older the child, the more stable the IQ will be. But a test is a snapshot, taken at one time, giving a picture of a child on that occasion and although large changes are relatively unusual in older children, they can occur and a retest after two years is advisable.

NB There can also be a practice effect on tests, that is if a child is given the same test within a few weeks the scores on the second occasion tend to be higher by up to 8 points on the full scale IQ.

4. Is IQ that important in explaining school success or failure?

Yes and no. There is no doubt that in general children with high IQs do better in school than those at the lower end. Hardly surprising, but factors within children such as motivation, organisation and persistence play a major part, as do good teaching and support from home.

5. Do all intelligence tests give similar IQ scores?

Again, yes and no. They are likely to give more or less similar scores but the variation can be considerable. The IQ is basically a figure derived from a comparison of the child being tested with the sample on whom the test was standardised. So test A, standardised on group A, will not necessarily give the same results as test B, standardised on group B.

Of relevance here is the fact that tests get out of date and should be restandardised every twenty years or so.

6. What does an IQ of 100 really mean?

For the WISC-III^{UK} it indicates that a child has scored in the average when compared with a sample of children chosen in 1991 to be representative of the whole of the UK, geographically, ethnically and socially.

7. Why are IQ scores generally preferred to mental ages?

Mental ages are sometimes helpful but they can be misleading. Say three children have a mental age of a nine year old. There is all the difference in the world between a four year old, a nine year old and a fifteen year old with that mental age.

8. Does IQ predict success in areas other than the academic?

Not really; many other factors come into play, like the ability to get on with other people and creative ability.

9. Should we, then, talk of many different types of intelligence?

Some authorities say we should: we should distinguish, for example, between practical and academic abilities: one person may be outstanding at running a greengrocery business, always giving the right change and managing to balance the books, but may have been hopeless at the more sophisticated maths at school.

Musical or artistic skills also seem frequently to be distinct, ie a child can be very talented in either of these areas but not necessarily do well in mainstream school subjects.

1.10
Choosing a School for your Child's Special Educational Needs

David Urani, Chartered Educational Psychologist

The new Special Educational Needs Code of Practice, which came into effect on January 1st 2002, defines special educational needs in the following way: 'Children have special educational needs if they have a learning difficulty which calls for special educational provision to be made for them.'

The general principal underpinning special needs education today is one of 'inclusion'. The belief is that the majority of children with special educational needs can and will be catered for within a mainstream Local Education Authority (LEA) or independent school. However situations do arise whereby a child's special educational needs cannot be met within a mainstream context, and a range of more specialist provision needs to be considered.

Types of Specialist Provision

Special Needs Units

Units are based on mainstream school sites. They enable children to access specialist support from the unit, as well as having the possibility of regular integration into a mainstream class. In some cases children can be enrolled in the unit, but in fact spend most of their time in mainstream.

LEA Special Schools

Some children may require the intensive and specialist support provided by special schools. LEA special schools (including grant maintained special schools) offer smaller classes, teachers with specialist training, high levels of one to one and small group support including on site input from therapists and other professionals where necessary. Special schools usually have the resources to cater for children with more severe learning, emotional/behavioural or medical needs.

Special schools fall into two broad categories. Some specialise in dealing with a specific need, for example dyslexia or autism. Other schools cater for a variety of children who may have different specific diagnoses but come under a more general description, such as moderate learning difficulties (MLD) or severe learning difficulties (SLD).

In the main, LEA special schools are day schools where the child attends on a daily basis. In some cases where the special need is relatively rare, very complex or the appropriate school is not available near the child's home, residential provision can be offered.

Depending on the child's progress, some children in special schools can be given the opportunity to integrate into local mainstream schools with support. In a few cases, it is possible for the child to return to full-time mainstream education with support.

Independent Special Schools

There are a comparatively smaller number of independent special schools in the UK that can offer specialist provision for children with more complex educational needs.

Being independent, fees are charged for children to attend. Whilst some schools will accept private fee paying students, in the main the costs are too prohibitive for most parents. Many independent special schools have a policy of only considering children who have a Statement of Special Educational Needs, where the child's LEA is in a position to fund the placement. In some instances, funding may be arranged through other agencies such as Social Services or the Department of Health, depending upon the specific needs and circumstances of the child.

Independent special schools have usually been designated or approved by the Secretary of State for Education and are recognised by LEAs as providing for a particular aspect of special needs education. In cases where the school does not have official approval to take a certain category of special need child, LEAs will not be in a position to support the placement. In exceptional circumstances, it is possible to gain permission from the Secretary of State for a child to attend a non-designated school.

Another category of independent special schools, Non-Maintained Special Schools, are also approved by the Secretary of State but are wholly funded by charitable organisations (e.g. Barnardo's, National Autistic Society).

Alternative Provisions

In very exceptional circumstances, such as chronic illness, some children's learning needs cannot be met in a school setting. With prior approval from the LEA, tuition can be offered at home or in hospital. Tuition however is often only provided on a part-time basis, and is seen as a short-term arrangement.

Some parents choose to implement an intensive home based programme, supervised by a non-LEA organisation. An example of this is the Lovaas/Applied Behavioural Analysis interventions used for young autistic children. These programmes are either self-funded by parents or can be funded by the LEA through a child's Statement.

Selecting a School

Parents are frequently put in a position of having to access the suitability of a school in meeting their child's special needs. The decision as to which school to choose can be a daunting task. The following are some aspects to consider prior to contacting schools directly:

- What is the LEA recommending as suitable to your child's needs? Is there a choice? Do you accept that the school/s being offered are appropriate?
- What are the opinions of professionals such as teachers, educational psychologists, therapists or medical consultants regarding the type of school needed for your child?
- Many support groups (e g ADHD) or professional organisations (e g Royal Institute for the Blind) exist to help parents and are able to offer advice in their area of expertise.
- Consulting organisations such as Gabbitas or IPSEA for a list of possible schools can be a good place to start a search.
- Most schools publish prospectuses for parents. Has the school had a recent OFSTED inspection and is the report available for you to see? (OFSTED publishes its reports on the Internet).

Once you have narrowed down the schools you think may be suited to your child's needs, the next step is to visit the schools and see what they have to offer. It is advisable not to take your child on an initial visit, as it may establish within the child unrealistic expectations of attending the school.

The following are a few things to consider:

- Don't limit your list to only one school. The more schools you see, the greater your chances are of finding the best school for your child.
- The most vital question to ask before taking things further is ascertaining if in fact the school actually has a place to offer. Many schools are often full, or may have long waiting lists.
- How far is the school from home? Will transport be an issue? Will boarding need to be considered?
- Does the school only cater for your child's specific area of need (e.g. visual impairment) or is it more generalist (e g MLD)?
- What is the physical learning environment like? Is the school modified for children with physical impairments? Is the playground safe and easy to supervise?
- Is the school well resourced in terms of learning materials and teaching aides? What level of access is there to computers and IT?
- What are the class sizes, the pupil to staff ratio, the training and expertise of the teaching and support staff? Is there access to other professionals such as psychologists and therapists if needed?
- Are there opportunities for mainstream integration? If so, are there children in the school who are on an integration programme?
- Were you able to see children in a lesson? If so did the children appear to be stimulated and interested? How did the teacher deal with unforeseen circumstances such as a child misbehaving?
- With boarding, what are the residential facilities like? Are there extra curricular activities on offer?
- What access is there to the National Curriculum? With older children, is there a work experience/life skills component to the curriculum? What links does the school have with post-secondary colleges?

It is more likely that you will have further questions to ask after seeing a school for the first time. A second visit is always a good idea, especially if you're unsure. If you feel certain of your choice, take your child along. Ultimately he/she is the one who will be attending and it may well be that you haven't considered some aspect from his/her perspective. For support, it is also helpful to take a friend or a trusted professional who knows your child and can provide an objective opinion.

Making an Application to a School

If as parents you are paying the fees, the application process is relatively uncomplicated and made directly to the school.

With a Statemented child the situation is very different. You will need to ascertain if the LEA is prepared to fund a place in the school you have chosen. Even when you have found a school, and the school is prepared to offer a place, an LEA is under no obligation to support the placement if it believes that similar provision can be found from within the LEA's own resources.

Disagreements between parents and LEAs regarding school placement can in some instances lead to an appeal by parents to an independent Special Educational Needs Tribunal. This can be a very drawn out and expensive option. Advice from professionals such as solicitors or educational psychologists experienced in tribunals is strongly recommended before embarking on an appeal process.

1.11
Social Security Benefits

Disability Alliance

Many families with a child with special needs are not aware of how the social security system could help them. This article is a brief introduction to the benefits that you may be able to claim if your child has a physical disability, a learning disability, developmental delays or behavioural problems.

Getting advice

The benefits system need not be daunting or confusing. You can get information and advice from a number of sources. In the first instance you can contact your local Department for Work and Pensions (DWP) office, or call the Benefit Enquiry Line on 0800 882200. This is a national telephone helpline about benefits for people with disabilities.

You can get independent advice from a Citizens' Advice Bureau or local advice centre. There is also a number of books that give information or advice about benefits. The Disability Alliance provides information and advice about the social security benefits that disabled people can claim and publishes the *Disability Rights Handbook* and a range of other publications every year as well as providing a free telephone helpline (see useful addresses at the end of this book).

The information in this chapter uses the benefit rates current from April 2002. In addition, several of the rules affecting disability benefits for children and young people changed in April 2001. This is a short summary of those changes.

- In July 2001, the Department for Work and Pensions (DWP) replaced the Department of Social Security.
- From April 2002 the rules regarding the work that you can do while retaining an Incapacity Benefit changed.
- April 2002 introduced a £10 a week disregard from child maintenance payments for new claims of income support and income-based Jobseeker's Allowance; the 'child maintenance premium'.

Benefits for your child

Child Benefit
You are entitled to receive child benefit for your dependent children, regardless of your other income or savings. You do not have to be the child's parent, but you do have to be responsible for him or her. You can receive child benefit for a child aged under 16, or aged under 19 and who is studying for more than 12 hours per week. You may not be entitled to child benefit if your child is in local authority care for more than 8 weeks, or if you receive a fostering allowance for that child.

Amounts
Only or eldest child	£15.75
Lone parent rate	£17.55 (*only paid to claimants who were already receiving the higher rate in April 1998*)
Each other child	£10.55

To claim child benefit, ask for a claim pack from your local office.

Children's tax credit
Since April 2001 a new children's tax credit has been introduced. You can claim if you pay tax and you have at least one dependent child under 16 living with you.

The credit is available to married or unmarried couples and single parents, and it is worth up to £520 off the tax you have to pay. If the person who receives the credit does not pay enough tax to use all the credit, they will be able to transfer the unused credit to their partner after the end of the tax year. If you or your partner pay higher tax rate, the partner with the larger income must claim the credit. When the person claiming the tax is a higher tax rate payer (on an individual income of around £32,785) the amount of the credit will be reduced. The credit of £520 is reduced at the rate of £1 for every £15 of income taxed at the higher rate. This means that you are unlikely to receive any credit if your income is around £41,000.

To claim the children's tax credit you will need to fill in a claim form available from your tax office.

Disability Living Allowance
The most important benefit for those looking after a child with disabilities is Disability Living Allowance. It is assessed purely on your child's needs – your financial circumstances are irrelevant. The benefit is assessed and paid in two parts. The care component helps with the extra costs of providing personal care, and the mobility component helps with the extra costs of going out.

The care component can be paid if your child needs supervision or extra attention in connection with their bodily functions during the day or night. It can be claimed at any age, but your child must have needed extra care for three months before any benefit is paid. All children obviously need different amounts of care at different stages in their development, and it can be difficult to explain to the DWP the amount of care that your child needs. You have to show that your child needs care or attention *substantially in excess* of that needed by other children of the same age and sex. The care component is paid at three different rates, depending on the amount of extra care needed.

The mobility component is paid at two different rates and is designed to help with the costs of going out and getting around. The higher rate can be paid from the age of three and is for children who have physical problems walking. The lower rate can only be claimed from the age of five, and is for those children who may be physically able to walk, but need extra guidance or supervision out of doors (again substantially in excess of what other children need). If you get the higher rate of mobility component you will also be entitled to exemption from road tax for one car, and you may be able to hire or buy a car under the motability scheme. You can also apply to your local authority for a blue badge for concessionary parking. Even if you don't get the higher rate mobility component you may be able to get a blue badge if your child has very substantial difficulty walking or is registered blind.

Amounts

Care Component		Mobility Component	
Higher	£56.25	Higher	£39.30
Middle	£37.65	Lower	£14.90
Lowest	£14.90		

The Benefits Agency will normally award Disability Living Allowance to your child for fixed periods. You will need to re-apply when the award expires. It is common for benefit to be renewed at *milestone* ages – five, eleven and sixteen.

Whether you are working or unemployed you should be aware of Disability Living Allowance. It is not means-tested or taxable, and it is paid on top of any other benefits you may receive. In fact your other benefits may actually be increased when you receive Disability Living Allowance.

If you think your child may be entitled, you should lodge a claim. Phone the Benefit Enquiry Line on 0800 882200 and ask them to send you the claim forms. If you are awarded benefit it can be paid from the date of this phone call. The claim forms can seem quite complicated, so seek advice if you are not sure how to fill them in.

Benefits your child can claim at age 16

On reaching age 16 a disabled child can claim benefit in his or her own right. If s/he receives benefit s/he will cease to be your dependent and you can no longer claim Child Benefit for him or her. The benefit will be paid in his or her name, but if the young person is unable to handle his or her own claim you may apply to be their appointee and act for them.

If your child is coming up to 16 there is a very useful booklet, written by the Family Fund, entitled 'What Next'. It is full of practical advice on education and training opportunities as well as information on benefits and services. The booklet is available free to young disabled people and their carers from The Family Fund, PO Box 50, York YO1 2ZX.

Incapacity Benefit

A disabled young person can claim Incapacity Benefit under a special route for people who become incapable of work before the age of 20. It is very important to claim before his or her 20th birthday, because after that age s/he will only be able to receive incapacity benefit if s/he has been employed and paid a sufficient number of national insurance contributions. There is some protection for young people in education to allow them to make a claim under these rules up to the age of 25, as long as their course of education or training began at least three months before their 20th birthday, and they claim incapacity benefit within two years of the course ending.

A young person will only be entitled to Incapacity Benefit after s/he has been incapable of work for 28 weeks. It is possible for these weeks to be before the young person's 16th birthday, so s/he can claim as soon as the age of 16 is reached. S/he will need a medical certificate from the doctor, and if Incapacity Benefit is to start straight away, the certificate will need to be backdated for at least 28 weeks. It is also possible for a new claim for Incapacity Benefit to be backdated for up to three months, as long as the claimant would have qualified for it at that time.

Incapacity Benefit is paid at three different rates depending how long your child has been claiming it. For the first 28 weeks of a claim the short-term lower rate is paid, from 29 weeks up to the 51st week of the claim the short-term higher rate is paid, and once your child has been on Incapacity Benefit for one year, the long-term rate is paid. A person receiving the higher rate care component of Disability Living Allowance will receive the long term of Incapacity Benefit after 28 weeks. An age addition is also payable with the long term rate.

Amount – Incapacity benefit
Short term lower rate   £53.50
Short-term higher rate   £63.25
Long-term rate   £85.85
(£70.95 + £14.90 age addition if under 35)

Full time education

Incapacity Benefit and Severe Disablement Allowance cannot be paid to a student under 19 who is at school or college and is attending classes for more than 21 hours every week. When calculating the 21 hours you should ignore any time spent in study that would not be suitable for a person of the same age and sex who does not suffer from a physical or mental disability. So, if a disabled young person receives a lot of support to follow a course, or if the course is taught in such a way that would make it unsuitable for a non-disabled person, then he/she may still be able to get benefit in spite of the 21 hour rule.

Income support

A disabled young person over the age of 16 may also be able to claim Income Support. With Income Support, it doesn't matter if s/he is attending school or a training centre. If your child is still at school, s/he will have to show that s/he would be unlikely to get a job in the next year. If s/he has left school, s/he will need to be accepted by the DWP as incapable of work. In both cases, the young person should give in a medical certificate from his or her GP.

Income Support includes a personal allowance and extra amounts called premiums. A young person will be entitled to a disability premium if s/he has been incapable of work for 52 weeks, is registered blind, or gets a Severe Disablement Allowance or any rate of Disability Living Allowance. The enhanced disability premium is payable to a person receiving the highest rate care component of Disability Living Allowance. Income Support cannot be paid to a young person who has more than £8000 savings. Any saving between £3000 and £7999 will reduce the amount of benefit paid.

Amounts

Income Support personal allowance (under 25)	£42.70
Disability premium	£23.00
Sub-total (if not entitled to enhanced disability premium)	£65.70
Enhanced disability premium	£11.25
Total (if enhanced disability premium payable)	£76.95

If a disabled young person receives Income Support, s/he will also be able to apply for help from the Social Fund for certain one-off expenses.

Benefits for carers

Invalid Care Allowance

You can claim this if your child receives Disability Living Allowance care component at the middle or higher rate. You must be looking after him or her for at least 35 hours every week. You can claim even if your partner is in full-time work.

You cannot receive Invalid Care Allowance (ICA) if you are in full time education (21 hours of study per week) or earning above £75 net per week. It does not matter for how many hours you work, as long as you are still caring for at least 35 hours per week. To calculate your net earnings deduct tax, National Insurance contributions and half of your contributions towards an occupational or personal pension. You are also allowed to deduct care costs up to a maximum of half your net earnings. This includes care for the disabled person for whom you claim ICA, or for any child under 16 for whom you claim Child Benefit, as long as the care is not provided by a close relative of yours or of the person cared for.

Invalid Care Allowance is paid at £42.45 per week, and while you are receiving the allowance your National Insurance Contribution record will be protected. Your Invalid Care Allowance will be taken into account if you or your spouse or partner are also claiming Income Support or Job Seeker's Allowance, but your overall benefit will include a carer's premium worth £24.40 per week.

To claim, get a claim form from your local office or from the Invalid Care Allowance unit on 0235 856123.

Other benefits

National Insurance contributory benefits

If you are incapable of work, unemployed, widowed or retired, you may be entitled to some benefits because of the National Insurance you have paid.

Incapacity Benefit, contribution-based Job Seeker's Allowance, Bereavement Benefit (for widows and widowers), Maternity Allowance and Retirement Pension can be paid if you have paid enough National Insurance contributions (in the case of Bereavement Benefit your late husband or wife's contributions are relevant).

If you qualify for them these benefits are paid to you as an individual (although you can in some circumstances claim increases for dependents). It does not matter if you have savings or a spouse who is in full time work.

However, if these benefits are your family's only or main source of income you will usually need to claim a top-up from a means-tested benefit, such as Income or Housing Benefit, as well.

Income Support and income-based Job Seeker's Allowance

Income Support and income-based Job Seeker's Allowance are the benefits for people who do not have enough money to live on and who are not in full time work. You will not be entitled to these benefits if you have capital above £8,000 (£12,000 if aged over 60), and if you have savings of more than £3,000 (£6,000 if over 60) your benefit will be reduced.

You claim benefit for yourself and your family. If you have a partner you will have to claim as a couple. In most cases it will not matter which of you makes the claim, but if one of you receives Invalid Care Allowance or is incapable of work because of illness, it is usually better if that person is the claimant. This is because they may be entitled to extra amounts and may not be required to register as available for work.

Income Support can be paid to lone parents, carers, people who are incapable of work, or people over 60. Some people from abroad, who are entitled to no other benefits, may be entitled to a reduced rate of Income Support. If you do not fit in to any of the categories listed above you cannot claim Income Support and you will have to claim income-based Job Seeker's Allowance instead.

Income-based Job Seeker's Allowance is paid to people under pension age who are required to be available for and actively seeking work. You can be sanctioned, and have your benefit reduced or taken away altogether, if you refuse the offer of a job or leave a job without *just cause*.

If you own your home, Income Support and income-based Job Seeker's Allowance are particularly important as they are the only benefits which provide any help with your mortgage costs.

If you receive Income Support or income-based Job Seeker's Allowance you will be entitled to free school meals, milk tokens for children under 5, free prescriptions, NHS dental treatment and vouchers for glasses, wigs and fabric supports. You can also claim a refund of your fares to hospital. You can also apply for grants and loans from the Social Fund for one-off expenses.

Benefits in Work

If you are working for 16 hours or your partner is working for 24 hours or more per week, you are considered to be working full-time and you cannot claim Income Support or Job Seeker's Allowance. Depending on your family's circumstances you may be able to claim an in-work benefit to top up your earnings.

You can claim Working Families Tax Credit if you are working for over 16 hours a week and you have at least one dependent child. The amount that you receive depends on your family circumstances and the level of your earnings. It is awarded at a fixed rate for a period of 26 weeks, and the amount will not generally be increased or reduced if your circumstances change. Benefit can end before 26 weeks in some circumstances – for example, if your only child leaves school.

If you or your partner have a disability you may be better off claiming Disabled Person's Tax Credit instead, which is assessed in a similar way.

You can claim either tax credit from a JobCentre, DWP office or Inland Revenue Enquiry Centre. There is also a Tax Credit helpline on 0845 605 5858, which can advise you on how much you may be entitled to.

If you are thinking about coming off benefit and claiming a Tax Credit instead, you can ask the Benefits Agency or a local advice centre to do a 'better off' calculation, comparing your current rate of benefit with what you could be entitled to once you start work. You will need to know roughly how much you will be earning, and how much your weekly rent and council tax bills are.

When you make your decision remember to take into account your extra expenses and costs of going out to work, as well as other factors such as the loss of free school meals and milk tokens, and the loss of access to grants and loans from the Social Fund. If you own your own home remember that Income Support and income-based Job Seeker's Allowance are the only benefits that provide any help with mortgage interest.

Housing Benefit and Council Tax Benefit

These benefits are administered by your local council. You can claim them whether you are working or on benefits. Housing Benefit helps with your rent if you are a tenant. Council Tax Benefit helps with your Council Tax bill. It does not matter whether you are an owner-occupier or a tenant.

If you are on Income Support or income-based Job Seeker's Allowance you will be entitled to the maximum allowable Housing and Council Tax Benefit. Otherwise the amount of help you get will depend on the level of your family's income. The amount you get will be reduced if you have any non-dependent adults living with you.

Contact your local authority for their claim forms.

Health Benefits

- If you receive Income Support or income-based Job Seeker's Allowance you will automatically qualify for help with prescription charges, hospital travel costs, dental treatment and glasses.
- If you receive Working Families Tax Credit or Disability Person's Tax Credit you may be able to get free NHS prescriptions and optical and dental treatment, but it is not an automatic entitlement. The decision on whether or not you will be exempt from NHS charges is based on how your tax credit has been worked out – your tax credit award letter should tell you whether or not you are exempt.
- If you are not on these benefits you can still claim this help on low income grounds. Claim on form HC1.

Getting further advice

This article can only give a very brief introduction to the benefits to which you may be entitled. If you want to find out more speak to a local advice centre or Citizens' Advice Bureau.

If you believe that the Benefits Agency has made a mistake about your benefit you should contact them and tell them why you think their decision is wrong. You may be able to appeal to an independent tribunal but there are very strict limits – get independent advice.

1.12
GCE (General Certificate of Education), VCE (Vocational Certificate of Education) GCSE (General Certificate of Secondary Education) and GNVQ (General National Vocational Qualification) assessment: special arrangements for candidates with particular requirements

(Information supplied by the Joint Council for General Qualifications)

Awarding bodies for GCE, VCE, GCSE and GNVQ recognise that there are some candidates who have coped with the learning demands of a course but for whom the standard arrangements for the assessment of their attainment may present a barrier. This applies both in the case of candidates with known and long-standing learning problems and candidates who are affected at or near the time of assessment. This section offers a summary of the special arrangements procedures operated in common by the awarding bodies. It is based on the Joint Council for General Qualifications (JCGQ) booklet *GCE, VCE, GCSE and GNVQ: Regulations and Guidance relating to Candidates with Particular requirements – 1 September 2000 to August 2001*. Copies of this are available direct from any of the awarding bodies, or can be downloaded from their websites. Contact details are available at the end of this section. An updated edition is issued at the start of each academic year.

Awarding body principles relating to special arrangements

In providing special arrangements for assessment, awarding bodies seek to:

- give special consideration to the performance in assessment where specific circumstances have arisen at or near to the time of assessment that were not provided for by prior special arrangements;
- ensure that neither a special arrangement nor special consideration gives an unfair advantage over other candidates;
- ensure that special arrangements do not reduce the validity or reliability of the examination or assessment;
- ensure that the provision for special arrangements and special consideration does not mislead the users of the qualification about the candidate's attainment;

- ensure that the provision for special arrangements and special consideration does not compromise the integrity or credibility of the qualification;
- determine special arrangements and special consideration in relation to the defined needs of individual candidates;
- consider the candidate's usual methods of learning and producing work when making decisions on special arrangements.
- approve valid special/alternative arrangements for access to examinations and assessment.

Principles for centres relating to special arrangements

The centre should:

- choose the qualification – or the option(s) within a qualification – which is most appropriate for the candidate with a known long-term or permanent disability or learning difficulty;
- diagnose the requirements of each candidate individually, making use of specialist advice from external sources as appropriate;
- ensure that all applications for special arrangements and special consideration are supported by the Head of the centre;
- ensure that the arrangements requested will assist the candidate to demonstrate his/her attainment without affecting or circumventing assessment requirements;
- consider the candidate's normal way of learning and producing work as a basis for special arrangements provided that this would not give the candidate an unfair advantage or compromise the integrity of the examination or assessment;
- ensure that the candidate has experience of and practice in the use of the arrangements requested;
- consult the relevant awarding body at the earliest opportunity if there is any doubt surrounding the acceptability of proposed arrangements for a particular candidate.

Centres should note that a candidate with a Statement of Special Educational Needs does not qualify automatically for special arrangements.

Types of special arrangements

These are summarised below. However, it should be noted that the kinds of special arrangements which are appropriate for one subject, may not be appropriate for other subjects. Separate arrangements exist for examinations in GCSE English and English Literature and awarding bodies will be able to supply details. The JCGQ *Regulations and Guidance* booklet has more detailed information on how these arrangements might apply to particular needs.

Time allowance

Additional time may be allowed in timed components in most subjects, including English, Irish and Welsh. Additional time will not normally be permitted on the basis of disability alone.

The amount of additional time granted must reflect the extent to which the completion of the examination is affected by the candidate's condition. For example, a candidate with a learning difficulty requiring additional time for writing should not be given additional time for examinations of a predominantly practical nature.

An additional allowance of up to 25 per cent of the total examination time should meet most needs. An allowance of more than 25 per cent may be permitted in exceptional cases with the prior approval of the awarding body.

Means of access to questions

Modification to the way the examination questions are presented may be required to enable them to be understood by candidates with particular requirements.

Modifications to the visual presentation of papers can be arranged for visually impaired candidates whose impairment is not corrected by spectacles or other forms of vision aid. Four types of modification are available:

- enlarged or large print papers
- modified print (simplification of eg layout or items of visual complexity)
- Braille version of papers
- tactile enhancement

Low vision aids and other technological devices, such as closed circuit television, OCR (Optical Character Recognition) scanners may also be permitted.

Modifications to the language used in papers may be required by severely hearing-impaired candidates who are pre-lingually deaf or hearing impaired from such an early age that vocabulary and understanding syntax are limited. Some material cannot be modified in this way, however:

- technical terms in any subject
- text and stimulus material in English and Welsh examinations
- text in the foreign language in modern foreign language papers
- literary extracts
- source material where understanding of the original material is specifically being assessed.

Reading of questions may be permitted if access to the paper is not possible through other means, except where understanding of the written word is an assessment objective.

In exceptional circumstances, the signing of questions or the oral presentation of questions using the oral/aural approach may be permitted if either approach is the usual method of communication in the classroom and access to the examination cannot be achieved by other means.

When hearing impaired candidates are taking aural tests, special amplification or reading the tests to enable lip reading is allowed on application to the awarding body with the necessary evidence.

In mental arithmetic tests, the use of flashcards or other visual presentation is allowed for hearing-impaired candidates.

Some visual difficulties are normally corrected by the use of tinted spectacles or coloured overlays and permission for the use of these aids does not have to be sought from the awarding body.

Candidates whose first language is not English, Irish or Welsh may be permitted to use bilingual translation dictionaries (ie without explanation of terms) in examinations other than in English, Irish or Welsh and in examinations in the candidate's first language. Under exceptional circumstances use of a prompter is permitted.

Means of presenting responses

The general principle applied to the presentation of responses is that candidates should use the method of answering which is quickest and most fluent for them.

For visually impaired candidates, responses may be given in Braille, although the centre must provide a transcript.

Candidates who are unable to write may use a typewriter or word processor, although they may not normally have access to any spell check, grammar check, thesaurus or other such facilities. If responses cannot be communicated through such means either, then an amanuensis may be used. Dictation of responses onto tape is not generally considered to be in the best interests of the candidate and would therefore be permitted only in the most exceptional of circumstances. In the case of a candidate's handwriting being difficult to read, the school or college may provide a transcript of the paper along with the candidate's original work.

In oral examinations, candidates who have difficulties with speech may be permitted to use augmentative speech equipment. However, it is possible that by doing so they may not be able to meet all the relevant assessment criteria.

In practical examinations or tests, use of a practical assistant or helper is allowed to ensure the candidate's safety and to support the candidate by assisting with those elements of the tasks which are not the focus of the assessment. The practical assistant must not perform tasks for which the candidate is given credit.

Alternative accommodation arrangements

It may be possible for candidates to take examinations outside the normal centre, for example at home or in hospital, provided that the relevant security and supervision requirements can be met.

Coursework

The relevant awarding body should be consulted as soon as possible if a candidate is unlikely to be able to fulfil all coursework requirements. An extension may be granted to the permitted time for completion of the coursework, but this must be formally agreed with the awarding body in advance.

Exemption

Candidates unable to fulfil a particular assessment objective may be given a special award to compensate for the missing element. However, an appropriate indication of the exemption will be recorded on the certificate.

Spelling, punctuation and grammar in GCSE

In examinations where spelling, punctuation and grammar form part of the assessment, all candidates will be assessed under the same nationally agreed criteria.

It is not considered to be in the interests of candidates to be exempted from this assessment, but if a candidate is eligible for exemption, and compensation is given in the form of an adjustment to marks, there will be an indication on the certificate that the candidate was exempt from fulfilling one of the assessment criteria in the subject.

If, in exceptional circumstances (for example, for a child with a severe physical disability or a candidate with a broken arm) permission is given for the use of an amanuensis, the candidate will not be normally be expected to dictate spelling and punctuation. If reliable alternative evidence is available, such as examples of the candidate's written work under controlled conditions, special consideration procedures will be applied to enable an assessment to be made.

Quality of language in GCE

Where this forms part of the assessment, all candidates are assessed under the same nationally agreed criteria, and no exemptions allowed.

Applying for special arrangements

Permission to allow some special arrangements is delegated to centres; in other instances form JCGQ/SA/01 must be submitted to the relevant awarding body. A copy of the form is provided in the Regulations and Guidance booklet, along with full details of evidence requirements and deadlines for applications.

Special Consideration

Special consideration is given following an examination or assessment to ensure that a candidate who has a temporary illness, injury or indisposition at the time it is conducted is given some compensation for those difficulties and the circumstances.

Further information

Parents should note that only Heads of Centre or their authorised representatives must deal directly with Awarding Bodies about matters to do with internal candidates. The school should see that early notice to the Awarding body about special arrangements is in the interest of the candidate. For more detailed guidance on special arrangements and special consideration, please contact the school or college in the first instance, since all applications must come from there.

Awarding body contact details:

Edexcel
Stewart House
32 Russell Square
London
WC1B 5DN
Tel. 0870 240 9800
Website: www.edexcel.org.uk

**Northern Ireland Council for the
Curriculum Examinations and
Assessment**
29 Clarendon Road
Belfast
BT1 3BG
Tel. 01232 261 200
Website: www.cea.org.uk

OCR
Syndicate Buildings
1 Hills Road
Cambridge
CB1 2EU
Tel. 01223 553998
Website: www.ocr.org.uk

**The Assessment and Qualifications
Alliance**
Stag Hill House
Guildford
Surrey
GU2 5XJ
Tel. 01483 506506
Website: www.aqa.org.uk

**The Assessment and Qualifications
Alliance**
Devas Street
Manchester
M15 6EX
Tel. 0161 953 1180
Website: www.aqa.org.uk

Welsh Joint Education Committee
245 Western Avenue
Cardiff
CF5 2YX
Tel. 02920 265000 (main switchboard)
or
Tel. 02920 265150 -155 (GCSE administration)
Website: www.wjec.co.uk

1.13
Children with Special Educational Needs: Guidance for Families Overseas*

Leaving the UK

Parents leaving the UK, for example on a temporary posting, face key decisions about their children's education, including whether or not their child should accompany them or, alternatively, remain at a boarding school in the UK. In cases where a child has special educational needs, wider issues must also be considered. If you expect to live overseas for a period, the following points may be helpful in planning your child's education.

Whether your child will accompany you or remain in the UK for his or her education depends on many factors, including:

- your individual circumstances;
- expected length of stay outside the UK;
- continuity – are you likely to move again before returning to the UK?
- your child's age;
- the nature and severity of your child's special needs;
- availability and accessibility of suitable education provision and, where appropriate, medical provision and therapy in the UK and in the host country;
- your child's ability to cope with change.

It is also wise to ensure that you have a thorough understanding of the culture and attitudes towards special needs or disabilities in the country in which you will be living. You may also wish to check the general levels of physical access available to people with mobility difficulties; some travel guides provide good information on this point.

If your child has a Statement of Special Educational Needs, check with your local authority the position with reference to the maintenance of that Statement. This may vary from one local authority to another and according to your/your child's individual circumstances. If your child has been attending a day school, for example, will the LEA maintain a residential place for him or her while you are away from the UK? What happens upon your return? Depending upon circumstances, funding may be shared between education, health and welfare departments, and arrangements may be complex.

If you plan to take your child with you, life in your host country may offer a number of pros and cons. The benefits might include, for example:

---

* This article was originally compiled with the kind assistance of Jennifer Steeples, Founder of the Special Needs support group at the Diplomatic Service Families Association, now of the London Dyslexia Association Resource Centre.

- better salary and employment conditions;
- better climate;
- availability of domestic help;
- good provision for your child's particular needs;
- local tax concessions;
- higher welfare benefits;
- better housing;
- travel opportunities that will broaden your child's horizons and experiences.
- better medical provision

Against this, however, there may be drawbacks, including:

- isolation;
- absence of support groups;
- lack of family support;
- language barriers;
- loss of welfare benefits;
- limited special needs provision;
- lack of facilities for the disabled;
- climate;
- housing (perhaps in a flat with no garden);
- setbacks in development;
- lack of networking opportunities to share help and ideas.
- poorer medical provision

Above all, avoid making hasty decisions. Give yourself time to make an informed choice and to consider the pros and cons for the whole family.

Points to remember

1) It may prove very helpful for your child to have a full educational and medical assessment in the UK and to have an Individual Education Plan (IEP) drawn up before you leave the UK. The IEP can then be adjusted at any new school in whichever country you settle.

2) Find out as much as you can with reference to the country in which you expect to live, for example:

- What provision is available in the host country for your child's needs?
- Is there an appropriate centre/support group where you can obtain information and advice?
- Is your child/are you entitled to any state benefits or tax concessions?

Some countries may offer highly advanced provision, others almost none. Your support group in the UK, if one exists, may be able to advise you or put you in touch with 'sister groups' in the host country or with other members of the association who have lived abroad. If experienced in working in the host country, your employer/your partner's employer may be able to guide you. It may also be worth consulting international organisations such as the

European Dyslexia Association or the British Embassy or British Council office in your host city/country, as well as the internet, for any other useful information.

3) If you know the area in which you will be living, try to make contact with sources of help, such as:

- a local doctor or hospital;
- local town hall/authority or equivalent;
- any English-speaking organisation, for example an expatriates' or women's club;
- any organisation for the disabled. Even if it does not focus specifically on your child's particular needs it may still be able to offer support and direct you to other appropriate organisations.

4) You may wish to consider educating your child at home. If so, make sure you have all the support you need before committing yourself. The internet is a good source of help, but check whether you will have access to it in your new destination. At the time of writing there are several useful website addresses with details of the National Curriculum and support groups. For general information try the websites for the Department for Education and Skills at www.dfes.gov.uk or for the Qualifications and Curriculum Authority at www.qca.org.uk.

5) Even if your child has little speech, talk over the move and possible changes in routine. Take care also to talk to siblings about their concerns.

6) Keep a clear diary of the help you seek, names and contact numbers.

7) Try to obtain some basic training in the treatment of the type of special needs presented by your child and research why your child has the condition or learning difficulty.

8) Keep your employer and/or your partner's employer fully briefed about your child's special needs. Most companies now have a Family Friendly Policy. Might either employer offer any help to meet additional costs associated with your child's education?

9) Take with you any reference books about the condition or learning difficulty that affects your child.

10) Join any organisation in your home country that can keep you up to date with developments and improvements in provision for the special needs your child has.

11) State clearly what you want and need for your child. Do not assume that friends and colleagues understand the kind of help and support you and your child require. Remember too that you will not be alone: at least 20 per cent of children will at some time in their lives present special needs in some form.

12) Finally, be realistic about the level of involvement you have had with your child's needs and the extent of support given by the school and other sources. How will your child cope under different circumstances?

Returning to the UK

If you are returning to the UK after being resident abroad, it is wise to contact in advance the local education authority (LEA) for the area in which you intend to live and ask for an assessment of your child's needs. At the same time, contact your support group in the UK to ensure that you are fully up to date with Department for Education and Skills (DfES) regulations on special needs provision.

Educating your child in the UK

If you live overseas, either as a British expatriate or as a citizen of another country, but wish to have your child educated in the UK, there are a number of points to consider.

The UK offers a variety of boarding education options. The independent (fee-paying) sector offers a wide choice of boarding education with varying levels of provision for special needs. Few mainstream independent schools accept children with Statements of Special Educational Needs. Many, however, will accept children with mild or moderate specific learning difficulties provided that applicants can fulfil the normal academic entry criteria for the school. The level of provision and the number of pupils with learning difficulties admitted varies widely from school to school, and parents should take care to establish the nature and extent of special tuition available. Some schools have dedicated units to cater for children requiring special tuition and usually operate on a withdrawal basis, which means that children are withdrawn from certain lessons during the school day to have special tuition for their particular needs. Other schools offer more limited assistance, for example through extra lessons from a visiting teacher. Annual fees at independent boarding schools in 2001–2002 generally range from £8,500–£12,000 at preparatory level and from £13,000–£16,750 at senior level.

Where a child's needs are more complex or severe, and where a child has a Statement of Special Educational Needs, a special school may be more appropriate. Residential special schools usually provide for a particular type of special need. Because of the highly specialist teaching and facilities offered by independent special schools, fees are often substantial. Where the local education authority agrees that a child should attend a particular school, it will normally pay the fees (sometimes in conjunction with social services or health services), provided that the school is one that has been approved by the Secretary of State for Education and Employment. In some cases, the fees are paid by parents. Parents with no right of abode in the UK should expect to meet the full cost of fees.

State-maintained boarding schools are few in number and are open only to UK and EU nationals and others with a right of residence in the UK. Fees are charged only for the cost of boarding at these schools, while tuition is free. Annual fees are therefore generally no more than £6,000 and in some cases considerably less. As indicated above, parents should take care to find out exactly how much help will be offered to a child with special needs.

In most cases, parents based overseas should expect to meet the cost of the fees for a boarding place. A boarding allowance is made for British parents employed by the Foreign & Commonwealth Office or by HM Forces. British parents living overseas *may* be eligible for local authority support for a child being educated in the UK, but are strongly advised to take independent advice in accordance with their individual circumstances.

Non-British children of statutory school age, who are nationals of a member state of the European Union (EU) or of Iceland, Norway or Liechtenstein and who are being educated in the UK (whether accompanied by their parents or not), have the same rights to education in the UK as British citizens. Under reciprocal arrangements within the EU, those who hold the equivalent of a Statement of Special Educational Needs made in another EU country may be eligible for support from the local education authority covering the area of the UK in which they will be living, and parents should seek advice according to their particular circumstances. In practice, children who come to the UK unaccompanied may be more likely to attend a boarding school in the independent sector, for which parents will normally be required to meet the fees.

Unaccompanied children of statutory school age who do not have a right of abode in the UK are not normally allowed entry to take up a place at a state-maintained school. Entry to the UK for purposes of receiving an education is only permitted if the student can demonstrate that he or she has been accepted for a course of study at an independent educational institution.

It may be helpful to obtain a clear assessment of a child's needs in the home country for use in finding suitable UK schools. Some schools will reassess the child before offering a place.

Points to remember about boarding education in the UK for parents resident overseas

The choice of a suitable boarding school requires careful research. As well as providing suitable provision for your child's special needs, the school must meet your child's wider needs and offer an environment in which he or she will feel happy and at home. Find out as much as possible about schools in which you are interested and visit them before making a choice. Consider in particular:

- **Your child's academic background**
  If your child has been educated in the British system, it should not be difficult to join a school in the UK. Entry from a different national system is possible but may be less straightforward.
- **Your child's level of English**
  Is additional support required?
- **Length of stay**
  If the stay in the UK is expected to be relatively short, an international school may be more appropriate.
- **Location**
  You may prefer a location that enables your child to be near friends or relatives, but most parts of the UK are well served by air, road and rail links, so it is not necessary to limit your search to schools close to major airports.

Further advice on the choice of a suitable mainstream school is given in Part 4.1.

Also bear in mind the following points:

- If your child is attending a boarding school in the UK while you are overseas, he or she must have a guardian in the UK, preferably living near the school, who will take responsibility for your child at weekends and other times when your child is out of school. While some residential special schools offer 52-week placements, most schools have three school holidays plus half term holidays and exeats (weekends out of school). You may have friends or relatives in the UK able to care for your child during these periods, but this arrangement is not always suitable and may limit your choice of schools. If you have no contacts in the UK, talk to a reputable guardianship service provider who can find a family able to offer your child a safe and welcoming home-from-home and may also take care of other travel and administrative arrangements.

- Your child may require an escort during travel, which will incur additional costs. Some airlines issue a card to travellers who require special care and will provide the facilities requested free of charge each time a booking is made. Children with parents in the Forces may be entitled to have escorts provided by the British Red Cross or the Soldier, Sailor and Airforce Families Association (SSAFA).
- While you should receive regular progress reports from your child's school and guardian, communication with your child on a day-to-day basis may be difficult if his or her special needs give him or her limited or no speech.

Children accompanying their parents to the UK

Children accompanying parents who have the right of abode in, or leave to enter, the UK will normally be treated as dependants. Upon taking up residence in the UK, overseas parents living in the UK have the same right as anyone else with a right of abode in the UK to apply for a place at a maintained school. They also, therefore, have the same entitlement to have their child's educational needs met by their local education authority.

Whatever your requirements, you are strongly advised to seek specialist guidance in accordance with your own individual circumstances and the specific needs of your child. Further information may be available from your child's school, from any parents' support group to which you currently belong or from one of the associations listed at the back of this book.

1.14
Education and Training for Young People with Disabilities or Learning Difficulties After Age 16

SKILL (National Bureau for Students with Disabilities)

If you are nearly 16 years old, you will probably be thinking about education and training options ahead. You will need to consider what you are best at and what you would most like to do. You may also need to consider any extra support that you may need because of your disability or learning difficulty. This article explains the options available to you and the support you should expect because of your disability or learning difficulty.

What choices are available at 16?

School

You may be able to stay at the same school if it accepts students beyond age 16. You could take an academic course such as A levels, or you might wish to take a work-based course (General National Vocational Qualifications or GNVQs). You might want to consider changing to a different sixth form for a better course or better support. Your school should be able to advise you about what is best. If you are leaving your school, your local careers service or Connexions personal adviser can help you to find a new place to learn or train (see below).

Link courses

Many schools offer what are called 'link courses'. These courses are based at school, but students attend a local further education college for part of their studies.

Further education colleges

You may find that your local further education college offers a wider range of courses than is available at your school. These might include:

- academic courses (GCSEs, A and AS levels)
- work-based courses (National Vocational Qualifications or NVQs, including RSA, Edexcel or City and Guilds Institute qualifications)
- general courses to prepare you for adult life. These courses may not always lead to a qualification.

It is important to find a course that appeals to you and to ensure that the college can offer you any extra support required because of your disability or learning difficulty.

Specialist colleges

You may find that your support needs cannot be met in a local school or college. If this is the case, there are specialist colleges which have extensive experience of teaching students with one type of disability or a range of different disabilities. These courses are located around the country and recruit nationally, so you may have to travel to get there. Such colleges are often residential. A specialist college can help you to learn to live away from home. Some colleges offer a range of education options, including those listed above under Further education colleges.

Information on specialist residential colleges is given in the COPE Directory (Compendium of post-16 education and training in residential establishments for young people with special needs). Your local careers/Connexions service should have a copy and they should be able to help you find the best option. You can also contact the Association of National Specialist Colleges (NATSPEC) for details of their colleges.

Higher education

If you decide to do A levels or GNVQs, you may want to go on to higher education to study for a degree or a Higher National Diploma (HND). To find out more about how to apply for higher education, seek advice from your school or college. You may also find it helpful to consult the article which begins on p 120 (1.15).

Work-based learning opportunities

Work-based learning for young people is organised by the Learning and Skills Council (LSC), which has replaced the Further Education Funding Council. Young people are able to take up work-based learning at 16 or 17 years when they have left school.

- **Modern Apprenticeships** give training to school leavers at a higher level within an industry; there are two levels, Foundation, which provides training up to NVQ level 2 and Advanced, which provides training to at least NVQ level 3.
- **Other training** includes NVQ below level 2 and above level 3
- **Employment preparation** which does not necessarily lead to a particular qualification, e.g. life skills training

For further information you would need to contact your local LSC or careers/Connexions service. The Employment Service runs training programmes for adults. You would need to contact your local jobcentre for further information.

Paid time off for study or training

If you are 16 or 17, in employment and not yet qualified to level 2, you will be able to get 'reasonable' paid time off from work to study. The types of qualification you could study for include GCSEs, NVQs, intermediate GNVQs and BTECs. The study or training could be done at a local college, by distance learning or in the workplace. Contact your local careers/Connexions service for further information.

How do I find out what's available? Can anyone help me?

Careers education at school

Once you reach year 9 at school, you should be given help to prepare for your future. There may be a teacher who is responsible for careers education. The school should give you access to careers information, such as books and leaflets about further education, training and careers. You should be able to get information in the same format as your other school work. For example, if you read Braille, you should be given access to this information in Braille.

Guidance on careers and future learning

From year 9 you may need independent information and advice on your future work or learning. This is available from the new Connexions service, in areas where this is already running, or from your local careers service. Connexions services are replacing careers services around the country and should be in place nationwide by September 2003. Both of these services will be able to advise you about different jobs and the type of training courses required for the job of your choice. They should be able to tell you about local courses in schools and colleges. Connexions or careers services can also let you know where to find your local careers library. You should be given the opportunity to write a Career Action Plan, which includes your goals in education and employment and the steps you should take to get there. You will have to register with the Connexions or careers service, if you wish to claim:

- Jobseeker's Allowance
- Bridging Allowance
- Extended Child Benefit.

Transition plan

If you have a statement of special educational needs, it should be reviewed every year. When you are 14, you should be involved in writing a transition plan. This should help you to think about what to do when you reach 16. It is important that a careers adviser helps you to go through the options. You can telephone in advance to say that you would like help from a careers adviser, who then has a duty to attend. He or she should help you to find another school, college, or training course if you are unable to stay at your school after 16. If you have a disability or learning difficulty, you are also entitled to additional advice and an assessment of your needs. Your careers service can help if you are having problems obtaining what you need from your school or LEA. Parents or guardians should also be involved in ensuring that there is a good transition plan. In Scotland a Future Needs Assessment should be done. The Department for Education and Skills in England produces a booklet entitled *Special Educational Needs: Parents' Guide*. In Scotland, a useful publication is *Your Future Needs Assessment*, published by the Children in Scotland Special Needs Forum.

The Learning and Skills Act 2000 (covering England and Wales) has increased the powers of the state to meet the needs of disabled students. Section 140 of the Act states that in the last year of compulsory education, an assessment must be carried out on students under the age of 19 who have a Statement, and who are likely to go on to further education. This will set out the student's learning needs and the provision required to meet those needs.

How do I contact my local careers or Connexions service?

Local careers and Connexions services should be listed in the telephone directory. The service may have a different name, such as 'Lifetime Careers', but check under 'careers services' or 'Connexions' first. Your school or college should also know which careers officer is responsible for young people in the area. You may also use the following website: www.connexions-card.gov.uk to carry out a search for your local service. Each area must have a specialist careers adviser who has experience of advising people with disabilities. You can request an interview with the specialist adviser if you have questions about how your disability will affect your career choices.

Social worker

Local social services or social work departments are required to provide certain services to young people and adults with disabilities. If you have a statement of special educational needs, your LEA must liaise with the local social services department about your needs. This should happen when you have your transition plan written and again when you are due to leave school. This will enable them to decide whether or not you need any help from the social services or the social work department. You, or your parent or guardian may make direct contact with the social services or the social work department if you are worried that the department is not getting involved.

Health authority

If you need medical help, you may have to seek assistance from the local health authority and social services as well as funding from your LEA or the Learning and Skills Council (LSC). Funding for education, personal care and medical care comes from different sources, which means that arrangements can be complicated. It is very important that the careers service helps you; they can speak to the different agencies involved and ensure that everything is paid for before you begin your course.

How do I find out about courses?

National Database of Vocational Qualifications

There is a detailed database of vocational qualifications. You should be able to use this database at your local careers service.

UK Course Provider

This is a CDROM database with information of full-time courses in universities and colleges in the United Kingdom. It also gives information about access and extra support for students with disabilities in colleges and universities. You should be able to use UK Course Provider at your local careers services and there may be a copy in your school or college.

Learndirect freephone (0800 100 900)

This is a free telephone helpline set up by the Government. The helpline can give general advice about courses anywhere in the United Kingdom. It is a useful means of finding out about courses available locally, but will not provide detailed advice on disability-related support.

Will I be able to get the support or help I need because of my disability or learning difficulty?

What happens to my statement when I reach age 16?

If you have a statement of special educational needs, this will set out the types of educational support you need at school. The school has a legal duty to provide the support specified in your statement. When you reach 16, the statement will only continue to be a legal document if you stay on in a school. If you go to college, you are still entitled to disability support, but your statement will cease to give you a legal right to this support.

School

If you stay on in the same school or move to a different school, the support you have had up until now should still be available to you. As long as you remain at a school, your awarding authority (LEA, education department or education and library board) must ensure that you receive the support you need.

Local further education colleges

Local further education colleges receive money from their funding bodies to pay for additional support needed by students with disabilities or learning difficulties, for example, additional teaching for dyslexia students, an interpreter for deaf students or materials in alternative formats. Most further education colleges also offer study pro-grammes specifically for people with learning difficulties, which include specialist help. These may be Basic Skills courses, which aim to develop numeracy and literacy skills or Independent Living Skills courses, which prepare students generally for adult life. There is a Disability or Learning Support Co-ordinator at all local further education colleges, whose job it is to co-ordinate disability support within the college. You should contact this person to discuss individual support arrangements.

Specialist further education colleges

Specialist further education colleges provide education exclusively for people with disabilities. Some specialist colleges cater for students with any type of disability, whilst others provide mainly for those with specific disabilities. You may have access to helpful equipment or support teaching that you cannot access in a local college.

Work-based learning

If you opt for work-based learning, you should be given enough support to enable you to take part in and complete successfully the training outlined in your Individual Training Plan. The Employment Service has stated that extra support should be given to allow people with disabilities to take part in mainstream training. Where this is not possible, there should be residential training available with disability-related support. You may also be able to claim back any extra money you have to spend on travelling to your training placement. For further information, contact your local LSC or the Disability Employment Adviser at your local Employment Service.

The Disability Discrimination Act (DDA) 1995

At present, publicly funded education is excluded from the provisions of the DDA 1995. However, from September 2002, the amended part IV of the DDA will come into force, providing legal rights for disabled people in education. Part IV will cover education provided by local further education and sixth form colleges. School sixth form education will also be covered by part IV of the Act, but in the pre-16 section. Work-based learning held at a private training provider will be covered by part III of the Act. For more information on the Act, you should contact Skill's Information Service or the Disability Rights Commission.

How is education and training after the age of 16 paid for?

Education up to 19

Sources of funding for education up to the age of 19 vary according to the type of education chosen.

School

If you stay at a school until you are 19, the local awarding authority (LEA, education department or education and library board) pays for your education. Any statement or record of special educational needs will still legally apply. Everyone is entitled to full-time education funded by the LEA up to the age of 18.

Local further education colleges

In **England**, further education colleges receive most of their funding from the Learning and Skills Council (LSC), previously known as the Further Education Funding Council. The

LSC inspects colleges to make sure they 'have regard to' the needs of students with learning difficulties and/or disabilities before they allocate funding. The funding body for further education in **Wales** works in a similar way and is now known as the National Council for Education and Training.

In **Scotland**, further education colleges receive funding from the Scottish Further Education Funding Council (SFEFC).The SFEFC must also have regard to the needs of students with learning difficulties and/or disabilities.

If you are studying full time in a further education college and are aged 16–19 years in England and Wales or between 16–18 years in Scotland, you will not have to pay any tuition fees. A college should not accept you unless it can offer the support that you need because of your disability or learning difficulty and must provide any equipment or extra support services you need. An assessment may be needed to find out exactly what is required.

Education over 19

Funding for education should not stop when you reach 18 or 19. If you start a full-time course before you are 19, you should be funded until the end of your course. If you start a course once you are over 19, you may be exempt from paying tuition fees. Colleges operate a fee waiver scheme, whereby students on certain means-tested benefits do not have to pay tuition fees. Sometimes individual colleges will also waive or reduce the fees for students who do not receive any of these benefits but who nevertheless find it difficult to meet their course fees.

Independent specialist colleges

If your disability-related needs can be met at a local further education college, then it is unlikely that you will receive government funding for a place at a specialist college. However, the Learning and Skills Council has a **duty** to fund a specialist place for a student under the age of 19 whose needs cannot be met in local colleges. It also has the **power** to fund a specialist place for a student between the ages of 19 and 25 whose needs cannot be met elsewhere. You would need to provide certain forms of evidence that your needs cannot be met in a local further education college. It is advisable to discuss this with your specialist careers adviser/personal adviser, who can approach the funding bodies on your behalf.

Social Services may also pay or contribute towards a specialist place where the provision includes a strong care component.

In Scotland you may be able to obtain funding for a placement in an independent college through a bursary from the education department of your local council.

Transport help and costs

Unfortunately there is no legislation in place as yet to ensure the provision of transport to further education colleges for students aged 16 and over. Whilst several bodies have the 'power' to provide transport, no-one has the 'duty' to do this. Local education authorities are obliged to treat further education college students 'no less favourably' than people of the same age studying at their schools. Social services also have the power to pay for transport, but may take their resources into account when deciding whether to make this provision. The government is aware of the gap in the provision of transport to college for students with disabilities. It has been conducting a transport study which places particular emphasis on improving the support available to this group of people.

Further education colleges have Access Funds for students who face financial hardship. If your transport costs are very high, you can apply to the Access Fund for extra money. In Scotland you would need to contact your college to see if you can get help with travel costs through a bursary.

Benefits

When you are 16, you may be able to claim certain benefits in your own right, even if you are still studying. These include

- Incapacity Benefit
- Income Support
- Disability Living Allowance

If you are confused by the calculations or what you can claim, you should contact a local welfare rights unit or a Citizens Advice Bureau for independent help with claiming benefits. You may also find it helpful to consult the article which begins on page 000.

Education Maintenance Allowances (EMAs)

The EMA is a weekly allowance that aims to encourage more young people to stay on in further education. It is being piloted in 56 areas of the country and is available to students aged 16 to 19. The amount you receive depends on your household income: in most areas the maximum amount is £30 per week. In order to qualify for an EMA, you and a parent or guardian, must sign a Learning Agreement with the school or college, and stick to the steps it sets out. To find out which areas are running EMAs you can contact your local education authority, careers service or visit the Connexions Card website at www.connexionscard.gov.uk. For details of whether or not you are eligible for the EMA, contact your local education authority.

Useful publications

For a list of useful publications see the Bibliography in Part 5.

If you have any questions regarding the choices available for disabled people in post-16 education, training and employment, contact Skill's Information Service on 0800 328 5050 (voice) or 0800 068 2422 (text) (open Monday to Friday 1.30–4.30pm) or write to:

Skill
Chapter House
18–20 Crucifix Lane
London SE1 3JW

Alternatively, visit Skill's website at www.skill.org.uk, or email info@skill.org.uk

1.15
Applying to Higher Education:
Guidance for Disabled People

SKILL (National Bureau for Students with Disabilities)

For many people the prospect of going to university is becoming more and more attractive. Every student seeking entry to higher education should ask questions about courses and facilities in colleges. Disabled students should ask the same questions, but will probably have other concerns too. These might include, for example, provision of learning materials in Braille, wheelchair access to lecture halls or the extent to which an institution will understand the difficulties encountered by a dyslexic student. These concerns are very important, but the usual concerns of all students are just as important to disabled students as they are to non-disabled students. These include what to study and where.

What is higher education?

Higher education is any course that leads to a certain level of qualification. It includes the following:

Undergraduate studies leading to:

- a first degree (BSc, BA, BEd, LLB, BEng, BMus)
- a diploma of higher education (DipSW, DipHE)
- a Higher National Diploma (HND)

Postgraduate studies leading to:

- a master's degree (MA, MSc, MEd, MPhil)
- a doctorate (PhD)
- a Postgraduate Certificate of Education (PGCE)
- other postgraduate diplomas

These courses are offered in universities and colleges around the country. Some further education colleges also offer higher education courses.

Higher education – is it for me?

You could go into higher education for a number of reasons. This might be in preparation for a chosen career, for the experience or as a way of empowering yourself as a disabled person. Higher education can give you the chance to learn new subjects and obtain qualifications. It can also offer opportunities to take up other activities, develop new skills, gain new experiences and meet new people.

Will I get the funding I need?

Money is a big issue for all students. If you have specific needs because of your disability you will also need to consider sources of funding for these. Universities and colleges do not always provide or pay for all the support or equipment you may need. You will need to check whether or not you can claim Disabled Students' Allowances to help pay for support costs.

How do I choose the right course?

You should start your search for a university or college like any other student – by choosing a course of study. There are several questions to consider, including:

- Is the course essential for your proposed work or career plans? Would it be helpful?
- Could you still pursue your ambitions with a degree or HND in any subject?
- Which subject interests you? Is the content of a course you have in mind appropriate for this interest?
- Would you prefer to study full-time or part-time?
- Which teaching methods are used?
- Which assessment methods are used?
- What level of course do you require?
- Can you fulfil the entry requirements? Is there a related course with different requirements?
- Are you seeking a course which includes work experience or study abroad?

Where should I study?

You may be tempted to apply only to institutions which have good provision for disabled students. But take care – choosing the right institution and course for you as an individual is very important. A good way to start is to prepare a list of places which offer the courses that interest you. Then think through the following issues:

Academic considerations:	Facilities and reputation of the college? Academic support, eg personal tutor? Library facilities?
Location:	Should the institution be near your home, or not? Campus or city site?
Student community:	How many students are there? What age?
Recreation and leisure:	Town facilities, sports, hobbies, students' union?

Access:	To lecture theatres and teaching rooms? To a parking space? To the bar and canteen? To sports facilities? In other ways, eg induction loops, good signage.
Experience:	Other disabled students? Staff attitude to you as a disabled person?
Accommodation:	Is it accessible? Will you be integrated with other students? Can equipment be installed or adaptations made? Will a room be provided for your personal assistant?
Support facilities:	Talk to the disabled student's adviser about the support available. Is there a suitable centre available locally for medical treatment? Any particular facilities for disabled students? eg Braille embosser, dyslexia support tutor, sign language interpreter unit, campus minibus, note-takers. If these are not available, can they be arranged in time for the start of your course?

How do I find out more about a college or university?

The prospectus

All prospectuses provide information about the general facilities in colleges or universities as well as course details. Most also give some details of facilities for disabled students. They may also give a contact name for the disability co-ordinator.

Disability statements

By law, publicly funded higher education providers in England, Wales, Scotland and Northern Ireland (and also further education providers in England, Wales and Northern Ireland) have to produce a statement of their facilities for disabled students. This should include specific support services as well as general accessibility of college premises. When requesting a prospectus, ask for a copy of the statement, plus any other information produced by the institution about its services for disabled students.

Student union or association

The student union or association may produce its own information about the college or university and may have its own disability support structures and policy.

Making contact

If your questions are not answered by the prospectus or other written information, telephone or write to the institution. For information on disability related provision contact the disability co-ordinator who is responsible for services for disabled students. The internet is another useful source. Most universities have websites that contain general information and details of courses and facilities.

Making a visit

The best way to find out what a university or college is like is to visit. Many places welcome early informal 'information visits'. Try to visit during term time or semester, when you are more likely to meet other students with disabilities and will be able to form a more accurate picture.

How do I apply?

The application form

Applications for most courses are made through the Universities and Colleges Admissions Service clearing house (UCAS). Application forms are available from careers services or directly from UCAS.

Your disability or impairment

Most application forms ask for details of any disability and associated individual needs. Many people worry that disclosing a disability or impairment at this stage may leave them vulnerable to discrimination. However, the following points should be kept in mind:

- Being fair to yourself: you do not want to spend the first week of term setting up support while everyone else is going to parties and making new friends.
- Being fair to the college: changes may need to be made or staff may need training before you arrive.
- Explaining something: you may need to mention your disability or impairment in order to explain something. For example your disability may have affected your school career or you may have done exams later than most other people.
- Providing the information yourself: headteachers or tutors writing your confidential reference may mention your disability if they think it is significant.
- Discrimination: although this does still exist, more and more colleges realise that disability and inability are not the same thing. As a failsafe, UCAS and other clearing houses allow you an extra choice of college if you receive a rejection because of your disability. This will change for people applying after September 2002, when university education will be covered by the amended part IV of the Disability Discrimination Act 1995. From this time, universities and colleges will not be allowed to treat a disabled applicant 'less favourably' than a non-disabled applicant for reasons related to his or her disability, without 'justification'.

The decision about what to write is yours and you must feel comfortable with it. Beware of using terms which admissions tutors may not understand. The institution is interested in two things: how your disability or impairment may affect your studies and what they need to know to give you the right support.

If you cannot fill in the form yourself, ask someone to type or write your answers for you. Your referee can explain in his or her confidential report the method used and the reasons for it.

Selection interviews

If you are invited to attend an interview, let the institution know if you need any particular arrangements. You may be asked about your disability, for example about adapting course material to suit your needs. Be prepared to speak clearly and confidently about potential problems and solutions. It is best if these points have already been discussed during your information visit.

Offers

Admissions tutors decide whether to offer you a place and the offer will usually be a conditional offer. This means that your exam results must meet the grade requirements of the course.

Rejections

Institutions rarely give reasons for a rejection. If you think you have been rejected because of your disability, contact the institution to find out. If they confirm that they have rejected you because they do not have the facilities for your needs, UCAS will give you another choice.

What support is available?

Do not be afraid to use support. It does not make you different from other students; it is intended to help you study at the same level. You can always change your support arrangements eg if your needs change or if the support turns out to be the wrong type.

How do I find out more?

There are many directories of higher education courses. A list of suggested titles is given in the Bibliography in Part Five. These can be found in careers, and local libraries.

For further information about higher education for disabled people, contact Skill's information service on 0800 328 5050 (voice) or 0800 068 2422 (text) Monday to Thursday 1.30–4.30pm; or write to Skill at:

Skill
Chapter House
19–20 Crucifix Lane
London SE1 3JW

Alternatively visit their website at www.skill.org.uk or email: info@skill.org.uk

Expert, personal guidance on issues of interest to any student planning to enter higher education, including choice of courses and universities, gap year options, UCAS applications and interview techniques, is also available from:

Gabbitas Educational Consultants
Carrington House, 126–130 Regent Street, London W1B 5EE
Tel: 0207 734 0161 Fax: 0207 437 1764
Email: admin@gabbitas.co.uk Website: www.gabbitas.co.uk

PART TWO: DIRECTORY OF SPECIAL SCHOOLS AND COLLEGES

A note on the directories and key to abbreviations

Part Two of *Schools for Special Needs – A Complete Guide* contains three directories covering establishments in England, Scotland, Northern Ireland and Wales.

1. Independent and non-maintained special schools

2. Colleges and other provision at 16+

Every attempt has been made to compile a comprehensive list of independent and non-maintained schools, and support services for students aged 16+. Each entry includes, where known, the name, address and telephone number of the school, the name of the Head, Principal or Director, the age range of students and the numbers accepted, with the number of boys and girls (B/G) or male and female students (M/F) given where available. Where applicable the number of boarding pupils or residential students is also given. Within the schools directory these are sometimes divided into full boarders (F) and weekly boarders (W).

The types of need for which the school or college makes provision are shown in abbreviated form. A key to the abbreviations is given below. The principal types of special needs catered for, where known, are shown in bold.

Schools may be Independent, DfES Approved Independent or Non-maintained or, in Scotland, Voluntary or Grant-aided. The status of each school is given where known. Entries also indicate whether a school offers 52-week care.

3. State Maintained Schools by Education Authority
Maintained schools are listed by Local Education Authority. An index of Local Education Authorities and their corresponding page numbers appears on p177. This is not a comprehensive list, but includes information on all schools that replied to requests from Gabbitas for information.

Each school's entry includes, where known, the name, address and telephone number of the school, the name of the Head, Principal or Director, the age range and number of students accepted. Where applicable the number of residential students is also given. The number of pupils is given for both boys and girls (B/G), where known.

The types of need for which the school or college makes provision are shown in abbreviated form. A key to the abbreviations is given below. The principal types of special needs catered for, where known, are shown in bold.

Key to abbreviations used in the directories

ADD	Attention Deficit Disorder	MLD	Moderate Learning Difficulties
ADHD	Attention Deficit/Hyperactivity Disorder	PH	Physical Impairment
		PMLD	Profound and Multiple Learning Difficulties
ASP	Asperger Syndrome		
AUT	Autism	SLD	Severe Learning Dificulities
CP	Cerebal Palsy	SP&LD	Speech & Language Dificulties
DEL	Delicate	SPLD	Specific Learning Dificulties
DOW	Down's Syndrome	TOU	Tourette's Syndrome
DYC	Dyscalculia	VIS	Visual Impairment
DYP	Dyspraxia	W	Wheelchair access
DYS	Dyslexia	†	Registered with CReSTeD (see Part 5.2)
EBD	Emotional/Behavioural Difficulties		
EPI	Epilepsy	*	School Profile in Part Three or Part Four
HI	Hearing Impairment		

2.1
Directory of Independent and Non-maintained Special Schools

ENGLAND

BERKSHIRE

ANNIE LAWSON SCHOOL*
Nine Mile Ride, Ravenswood Village,
Crowthorne, Berkshire RG45 6BQ
Tel: (01344) 755508
Head: Mr M Hughes
Type: Co-educational Boarding and
Day 11–19
No of pupils: 23 *No of Boarders:* F20
Special Needs: PMLD SLD W
Approved Independent
52-week care

**HIGH CLOSE SCHOOL
(BARNARDO'S)***
Wiltshire Road, Wokingham,
Berkshire RG40 1TT
Tel: (0118) 978 5767
Head: Mrs R Mahony
Type: Co-educational Boarding and
Day 6–16
No of pupils: 64 *No of Boarders:* W44
Special Needs: **EBD** MLD W
Non-Maintained

**THE MARY HARE GRAMMAR
SCHOOL FOR THE DEAF**
Arlington Manor, Newbury,
Berkshire RG14 9BQ
Tel: (01635) 244200
Head: Dr I G Tucker
Type: Co-educational Boarding and
Day 11–19
No of pupils: 210 *No of Boarders:* F208
Special Needs: **HI**
Non-Maintained

PRIORS COURT SCHOOL*
Hermitage, Thatcham, Berkshire
RG18 9NU
Tel: (01635) 248209
Head: Mr R G Hubbard
Type: Co-educational Boarding and
Day 5–16
No of pupils: B31 G6
No of Boarders: F13 W19
Special Needs: **AUT** SLD
Independent

BRISTOL

BELGRAVE SCHOOL
10 Upper Belgrave Road, Clifton,
Bristol BS8 2XH
Tel: (0117) 973 9405
Head: Mrs P Jones
Type: Co-educational Day 7–12
No of pupils: 24
Special Needs: ADD DYC DYP DYS
MLD SPLD
Independent

ST CHRISTOPHER'S SCHOOL*
Carisbrooke Lodge, Westbury Park,
Bristol BS6 7JE
Tel: (0117) 973 3301
Head: Ms O Matz
Type: Co-educational Boarding 6–19
No of pupils: B33 G15
No of Boarders: F48
Special Needs: AUT CP EPI PMLD
SLD SP&LD W
Independent
52-week care

THE SHEILING SCHOOL*
Thornbury Park, Thornbury, Bristol
BS35 1HP
Tel: (01454) 412194
Type: Co-educational Boarding and
Day 6–19
No of pupils: B25 G15
No of Boarders: F30 W2
Special Needs: ADHD AUT DEL DOW
EBD MLD SLD
Independent

BUCKINGHAMSHIRE

THE CHARMANDEAN DYSLEXIA CENTRE*
Tile House Mansion, Lillingstone
Dayrell, Buckingham,
Buckinghamshire MK18 5AN
Tel: (01280) 860182
Head: Mrs J P Hawkins
Type: Co-educational Day 8–16
No of pupils: B74 G25
Special Needs: DYC DYP DYS
Independent

MACINTYRE SCHOOL WINGRAVE*
The Old Manor House, Wingrave,
Aylesbury, Buckinghamshire
HP22 4PD
Tel: (01296) 681274
Acting Head: Mr S Smith
Type: Co-educational Boarding 10–19
No of pupils: 34 *No of Boarders:* F34
Special Needs: **AUT EPI** PMLD **SLD**
SPLD SP&LD
Approved Independent
52-week care

PENN SCHOOL*
Church Road, Penn, High Wycombe,
Buckinghamshire HP10 8LZ
Tel: (01494) 812139
Head: Mrs M Richardson
Type: Co-educational Boarding and
Day 11–18
No of pupils: 26
Special Needs: AUT CP DEL DYC DYS
DYP EPI HI MLD PH SLD SPLD
SP&LD TOU VIS W
Non-Maintained

CAMBRIDGESHIRE

CHARTWELL HOUSE SCHOOL
Goodens Lane, Newton, Wisbech,
Cambridgeshire PE13 5HQ
Tel: (01945) 870793
Head: Mr C E Wright
Type: Boys Boarding 10–16
No of pupils: 7 *No of Boarders:* F7
Special Needs: ADD DYS EBD
Independent
52-week care

CHESHIRE

CHAIGELEY SCHOOL
Lymm Road, Thelwall, Warrington,
Cheshire WA4 2TE
Tel: (01925) 752357
Head: Mr D Crawshaw
Type: Boys Boarding and Day 8–16
No of pupils: 72 *No of Boarders:* W24
Special Needs: ADD ADHD **EBD**
Non-Maintained

THE DAVID LEWIS SCHOOL
Mill Lane, Warford, Cheshire
SK9 7UD
Tel: (01565) 640066
Head: Mr C D Dean
Type: Co-educational Boarding and
Day 7–19
No of pupils: B42 G22
No of Boarders: F55
Special Needs: **EPI** MLD PH **SLD**
SP&LD W
Non-Maintained
52-week care

DELAMERE FOREST SCHOOL
Blakemere Lane, Norley, Frodsham,
Warrington, Cheshire WA6 6NP
Tel: (01928) 788263
Head: Mr H Burman
Type: Co-educational Boarding and
Day 6–17 (Jewish boarders only)
No of pupils: B21 G2
No of Boarders: W13
Special Needs: ADD ADHD **ASP** DEL
DOW DYP DYS EBD EPI **MLD**
SP&LD SPLD TOU
Non-Maintained

LAMBS HOUSE SCHOOL
Buxton Road, Buglawton,
Congleton, Cheshire CW12 2DT
Tel: (01260) 272089
Head: Mrs M S Lee
Type: Co-educational Boarding and
Day 5–16
No of pupils: 39
No of Boarders: F12 W8
Special Needs: **AUT**
Independent

ROYAL SCHOOL FOR THE DEAF (MANCHESTER)*
Stanley Road, Cheadle Hulme,
Cheadle, Cheshire SK8 6RQ
Tel: (0161) 610 0100
Head: Mrs H Ward
Type: Co-educational Boarding and
Day 5–20
No of pupils: B40 G26
No of Boarders: F11 W23
Special Needs: AUT CP EPI HI MLD
PH PMLD SLD SPLD SP&LD TOU
VIS W
Non-Maintained
52-week care

THE ST JOHN VIANNEY SCHOOL
(Lower School), Didsbury Road,
Heaton Mersey, Stockport, Cheshire
SK4 2AA
Tel: (0161) 432 0510
Head: Mr M M O'Donoghue
Type: Co-educational Day 5–11
No of pupils: 69
Special Needs: **ADD** ADHD ASP AUT
CP **DOW** DYP **MLD** SP&LD W
Non-Maintained

CUMBRIA

EDEN GROVE SCHOOL*
Bolton, Appleby, Cumbria CA16 6AJ
Tel: (01768) 361346
Head: Mr I McCready
Type: Boys Boarding and Day 8–19
No of pupils: 78
Special Needs: ADD **ADHD ASP** AUT
EBD EPI HI MLD SP&LD TOU W
Approved Independent
51-week care

LOWGATE HOUSE SCHOOL
Levens, Kendal, Cumbria LA8 8NJ
Tel: (01539) 560124
Head: Mrs J Richardson
Type: Boys Boarding and Day 7–13
No of pupils: 16
Special Needs: **EBD** SPLD
Approved Independent
52-week care

RIVERSIDE SCHOOL
Whassett, Milnthorpe, Cumbria
LA7 7DN
Tel: (01539) 562006
Head: Mr G Waterhouse
Type: Co-educational Boarding and
Day 10–16
No of pupils: B36 G36
Special Needs: ADD ADHD ASP DYS
EBD MLD SP&LD TOU W
Independent

WITHERSLACK HALL*
Grange-over-Sands, Witherslack,
Cumbria LA11 6SD
Tel: (01539) 552397
Head: Mr M A Barrow
Type: Boys Boarding and Day 11–16
No of pupils: 70 *No of Boarders:* F70
Special Needs: ADHD EBD SPLD
Approved Independent

DERBYSHIRE

ALDERWASLEY HALL SCHOOL
Alderwasley, Belper, Derbyshire
DE56 2SR
Tel: (01629) 822586
Head: Mr K P Hingorani
Type: Co-educational Boarding and
Day 5–19
No of pupils: 176 *No of Boarders:* F146
Special Needs: **ASP** DYP DYS SP&LD
Approved Independent

EASTWOOD GRANGE SCHOOL
Milken Lane, Ashover, Chesterfield,
Derbyshire S45 0BA
Tel: (01246) 590255
Head: Mr P J Brandt
Type: Boys Boarding
No of pupils: 36 *No of Boarders:* F36
Special Needs: **ADD EBD** MLD
SP&LD
Independent
52-week care

ROYAL SCHOOL FOR THE DEAF, DERBY*
Ashbourne Road, Derby, Derbyshire
DE22 3BH
Tel: (01332) 362512
Head: Mr T Silvester
Type: Co-educational Boarding and
Day 3–16
No of pupils: B46 G50
No of Boarders: W55
Special Needs: **HI**
Non-Maintained

TAXAL EDGE SCHOOL
Macclesfield Road, Whaley Bridge,
High Peak, Derbyshire SK23 7DR
Tel: (01663) 732122
Head: Ms S Wells
Type: Co-educational Day 11–16
No of pupils: 10
Special Needs: **EBD**
Independent

DEVON

BROOMHAYES SCHOOL
Kingsley House, Alverdiscott Road,
Bideford, Devon EX39 4PL
Tel: (01237) 473830
Head: Mrs B Dewar
Type: Co-educational Boarding 11–19
No of pupils: 25 *No of Boarders:* F25
Special Needs: AUT MLD PMLD SLD
SP&LD SPLD
Approved Independent
52-week care

CHELFHAM MILL SCHOOL
Chelfham, Barnstaple, Devon
EX32 7LA
Tel: (01271) 850448
Head: Mrs K Roberts
Type: Boys Boarding and Day 11–19
No of pupils: 58 *No of Boarders:* F48
Special Needs: ADD ADHD **ASP** EBD
EPI MLD TOU
Approved Independent
52-week care

CHELFHAM SENIOR SCHOOL*
Bere Alston, Yelverton, Devon
PL20 7EX
Tel: (01822) 840379
Head: Ms J Marks
Type: Boys Boarding 11–19
No of pupils: 63 *No of Boarders:* F63
Special Needs: ASP EBD MLD TOU
Approved Independent
52-week care

DAME HANNAH ROGERS SCHOOL*
Woodland Road, Ivybridge, Devon
PL21 9HQ
Tel: (01752) 892461
Head: Mr W R Evans
Type: Co-educational Boarding and
Day 8–19
No of pupils: B34 G21
No of Boarders: F30 W20
Special Needs: CP DEL EPI MLD **PH**
PMLD **SLD SP&LD** W
Non-Maintained

ROYAL WEST OF ENGLAND SCHOOL FOR THE DEAF
50 Topsham Road, Exeter, Devon
EX2 4NF
Tel: (01392) 272692
Head: Mr J F Shaw
Type: Co-educational Boarding and
Day 3–19
No of pupils: B57 G37
No of Boarders: F31 W33
Special Needs: **HI**
Non-Maintained

TRENGWEATH SCHOOL*
Hartley Road, Plymouth, Devon
PL3 5LW
Tel: (01752) 771975
Head: Mrs G Pratchett
Type: Co-educational Boarding and
Day 2–19
No of pupils: B8 G12
No of Boarders: F3 W3
Special Needs: CP EPI HI PH **PMLD**
SP&LD **VIS** W
Approved Independent

VRANCH HOUSE SCHOOL
Pinhoe Road, Exeter, Devon
EX4 8AD
Tel: (01392) 468333
Head: Miss M R Boon
Type: Co-educational Day 2–12
No of pupils: 20
Special Needs: **CP** MLD **PH** PMLD
SP&LD W
Approved Independent

THE WEST OF ENGLAND SCHOOL AND COLLEGE FOR PUPILS WITH LITTLE OR NO SIGHT
Countess Wear, Exeter, Devon
EX2 6HA
Tel: (01392) 454200
Head: Mr P Holland
Type: Co-educational Boarding and Day 2–16
No of pupils: B140 G40
No of Boarders: F40 W79
Special Needs: PH VIS W
Non-Maintained

WHITSTONE HEAD SCHOOL
Whitstone, Holsworthy, Devon
EX22 6TJ
Tel: (01288) 341251
Head: Mr D R McLean-Thorne
Type: Co-educational Boarding and Day 11–16
No of pupils: B30 G10
No of Boarders: F32
Special Needs: ADD ADHD DEL EBD HI MLD SPLD
Approved Independent

WYCHBURY HOUSE RESIDENTIAL SCHOOL
22 Cleveland Road, Torquay, Devon
TQ2 5BE
Tel: (01803) 293460
Head: Mr D Simpson
Type: Boys Boarding 9–16
No of pupils: 11 *No of Boarders:* F11
Special Needs: DYS EBD MLD SPLD
Independent
52-week care

DORSET

THE FORUM SCHOOL
Shillingstone, Dorset DT11 0QS
Tel: (01258) 860295
Head: Mrs G Waters
Type: Co-educational Boarding 7–14
No of pupils: B36 G5
No of Boarders: F41
Special Needs: **AUT**
Approved Independent

LANGSIDE SCHOOL
Langside Avenue, Parkstone, Poole,
Dorset BH12 5BN
Tel: (01202) 518635
Head: Mr J Ashby
Type: Co-educational Day 2–18
No of pupils: B28 G14
Special Needs: CP DEL EPI **PH PMLD SLD** VIS W
Independent

PHILIP GREEN MEMORIAL SCHOOL*
Boveridge House, Cranborne,
Wimborne, Dorset BH21 5RU
Tel: (01725) 517218
Head: Mrs L Walter
Type: Co-educational Boarding and Day 11–19
No of pupils: B16 G11
No of Boarders: F23 W3
Special Needs: ADD ASP AUT DEL DOW DYP **MLD SLD SP&LD**
Independent

PURBECK VIEW SCHOOL
Northbrook Road, Swanage, Dorset
BH19 1PR
Tel: (01929) 422760
Head: Mrs S Goulding
Type: Co-educational Boarding 11–19
No of pupils: B40 G4
No of Boarders: F44
Special Needs: **AUT**
Independent

THE SHEILING SCHOOL, RINGWOOD*
Horton Road, Ashley, Nr Ringwood,
Dorset BH24 2EB
Tel: (01425) 477488
Type: Co-educational Boarding and Day 6–19
No of pupils: 47
Special Needs: AUT **DOW** EBD EPI **MLD SLD** SP&LD
Independent

THE WESSEX AUTISTIC SOCIETY, PORTFIELD SCHOOL
4 Magdalen Lane, Christchurch,
Dorset BH23 1PH
Tel: (01202) 486626
Head: Mr P Gabony
Type: Co-educational Boarding and Day 2–19
No of pupils: 42 *No of Boarders:* W16
Special Needs: **AUT**
Independent

ESSEX

DOUCECROFT SCHOOL
163 High Street, Kelvedon,
Colchester, Essex CO5 9JA
Tel: (01376) 570060
Head: Mr K Cranmer
Type: Co-educational Boarding and
Day 2–19
No of pupils: B29 G5
No of Boarders: W20
Special Needs: ASP AUT
Approved Independent

ST JOHN'S RC SCHOOL
Turpins Lane, Woodford Green,
Essex IG8 8AX
Tel: (020) 8504 1818
Head: Mr B Sainsbury
Type: Co-educational Day 5–19
Special Needs: MLD SLD SP&LD
Non-Maintained

WOODCROFT SCHOOL*
Whitakers Way, Loughton, Essex
IG10 1SQ
Tel: (020) 8508 1369
Head: Mrs M Newton
Type: Co-educational Day 2–12
No of pupils: B20 G4
Special Needs: ADD ADHD ASP AUT
CP DEL DOW DYP DYS EBD EPI HI
MLD PH PMLD **SLD** SP&LD SPLD
VIS W
Approved Independent

GLOUCESTERSHIRE

**COTSWOLD CHINE
SCHOOL***
Box, Stroud, Gloucestershire
GL6 9AG
Tel: (01453) 837550
Head: Mr A Phipps
Type: Co-educational Boarding 10–16
No of pupils: 37
Special Needs: ADD **ADHD** ASP AUT
DYP **EBD** EPI MLD SLD SP&LD
SPLD TOU W
Approved Independent
52-week care

ST ROSE'S SCHOOL*
Stratford Lawn, Stroud,
Gloucestershire GL5 4AP
Tel: (01453) 763793
Head: Sister M Quentin
Type: Co-educational Boarding and
Day 2–18
No of pupils: B39 G31
No of Boarders: F17 W16
Special Needs: ASP CP DEL DYP EPI
MLD PH SP&LD SLD VIS W
Non-Maintained

HAMPSHIRE

COXLEASE SCHOOL
High Coxlease House, Clay Hill,
Lyndhurst, Hampshire SO43 7DE
Tel: (023) 8028 3633
Head: Mr S Cliffen
Type: Boys Boarding 9–17
No of pupils: 45 *No of Boarders:* F45
Special Needs: ADD ADHD ASP DYC
DYS DYP **EBD** EPI MLD SP&LD
SPLD TOU
Approved Independent

GRATELEY HOUSE SCHOOL
Grateley, Andover, Hampshire
SP11 8JR
Tel: (01264) 889751
Head: Mr A Sumner
Type: Co-educational Boarding 11–16
No of pupils: B31 G8
No of Boarders: F39
Special Needs: ADD **ADHD** ASP DYP
TOU
Approved Independent

HILL HOUSE SCHOOL
Rope Hill, Boldre, Lymington,
Hampshire SO41 8NE
Tel: (01590) 672147
Head: Ms J Wright
Type: Co-educational Boarding 11–19
No of pupils: B17 G5
No of Boarders: F22
Special Needs: AUT SLD
Approved Independent
52-week care

HOPE LODGE SCHOOL
22 Midanbury Lane, Bitterne Park,
Southampton, Hampshire SO18 4HP
Tel: (023) 8063 4346
Head: Mrs M Filley
Type: Co-educational Boarding and
Day 4–19
No of pupils: 46 *No of Boarders:* W27
Special Needs: **ASP AUT** SLD SP&LD
Approved Independent

LODDON SCHOOL
Wildmoor, Sherfield-on-Loddon,
Hook, Hampshire RG27 0JD
Tel: (01256) 882394
Head: Ms M Cornick
Type: Co-educational Boarding 8–18
No of pupils: 27 *No of Boarders:* F27
Special Needs: ADD ADHD AUT EPI
SLD SP&LD
Approved Independent
52-week care

MORDAUNT SCHOOL
Rose Road, Southampton,
Hampshire SO14 6TE
Tel: (023) 8022 9017
Head: Ms C M Spiller
Type: Co-educational Day 2–19
No of pupils: B15 G12
Special Needs: AUT CP EPI PH **PMLD**
SP&LD SPLD VIS W
Approved Independent

ST EDWARD'S SCHOOL*
Melchet Court, Sherfield English,
Romsey, Hampshire S051 6ZR
Tel: (01794) 884250
Head: Mr L P Bartel
Type: Boys Boarding 10–17
No of pupils: 68 *No of Boarders:* F64
Special Needs: ADD ADHD DYS EBD
MLD SPLD
Approved Independent

**SOUTHERN ENGLAND
PSYCHOLOGICAL SERVICES**
Fair Oak, Eastleigh, Hampshire
S05 7DE
Tel: (023) 8069 2621
Head: Dr L F Lowenstein
Type: Co-educational Boarding and
Day 10–16
No of pupils: B6 G6
Special Needs: ADD ADHD **ASP AUT**
DEL DOW DYS EBD EPI MLD PH
SPLD W
Independent
52-week care

SOUTHLANDS SCHOOL
Vicar's Hill, Boldre, Lymington,
Hampshire S041 8QB
Tel: (01590) 675350
Head: Ms S Gething
Type: Boys Boarding 8–16
No of pupils: 43 *No of Boarders:* F43
Special Needs: **ASP** AUT
Approved Independent

TRELOAR SCHOOL*
Upper Froyle, Alton, Hampshire
GU34 4LA
Tel: (01420) 526400
Head: Mr N Clark
Type: Co-educational Boarding and
Day 5–16
No of pupils: B81 G62
No of Boarders: F108
Special Needs: **CP** DEL DYP DYS EPI
HI **PH** SP&LD **SPLD** VIS W
Non-Maintained

HEREFORDSHIRE

**HILLCREST PENTWYN
SCHOOL**
Clyro, Hereford, Herefordshire
HR3 5SE
Tel: (01497) 821420
Head: Mrs E Hudson
Type: Boys Boarding 11–17
No of pupils: 12 *No of Boarders:* F12
Special Needs: ADD **ADHD** DYP DYS
EBD MLD SPLD
Independent
52-week care

ROWDEN HOUSE SCHOOL*
Winslow, Bromyard, Herefordshire
HR7 4LS
Tel: (01885) 488096
Head: Mrs H Hardy
Type: Co-educational Boarding 11–19
No of pupils: B22 G6
No of Boarders: F28
Special Needs: **AUT DOW** EPI PMLD
SLD TOU W
Approved Independent
52-week care

HERTFORDSHIRE

**MELDRETH MANOR
SCHOOL*.**
Fenny Lane, Meldreth, Royston,
Hertfordshire SG8 6LG
Tel: (01763) 268000
Head: Mr E Nash
Type: Co-educational Boarding and
Day 8–19
No of pupils: 62 *No of Boarders:* F56
Special Needs: AUT **CP** EPI HI **PH**
PMLD SLD SP&LD VIS W
Approved Independent

**RADLETT LODGE SCHOOL
FOR AUTISTIC CHILDREN**
Harper Lane, Radlett, Hertfordshire
WD7 9HW
Tel: (01923) 854922
Head: Mrs L Tucker
Type: Co-educational Day and
Boarding 3–11
No of pupils: B42 G7
No of Boarders: W16
Special Needs: ASP **AUT**
Approved Independent

ST ELIZABETH'S SCHOOL*
South End, Much Hadham,
Hertfordshire SG10 6EW
Tel: (01279) 844270
Head: Mrs C A Walker
Type: Co-educational Boarding and
Day 5–19
No of pupils: 80 *No of Boarders:* F68
Special Needs: **AUT EPI** MLD SLD
SP&LD
Non-Maintained

ISLE OF WIGHT

ST CATHERINE'S SCHOOL*
Grove Road, Ventnor, Isle of Wight
PO38 1TT
Tel: (01983) 852722
Head: Mr G E Shipley
Type: Co-educational Boarding and
Day 7–19
No of pupils: B65 G9
No of Boarders: F62 W6
Special Needs: **SP&LD**
Non-Maintained

KENT

BREWOOD EDUCATION CENTRE*
86 London Road, Deal, Kent
CT14 9TR
Tel: (01304) 363000
Head: Miss C Simcox
Type: Co-educational Day 7–14
No of pupils: B7 G2
Special Needs: ADD ADHD ASP DYC DYP DYS **EBD** HI **MLD** SP&LD TOU VIS
Independent

CALDECOTT COMMUNITY
Ashford, Kent TN25 5NH
Tel: (01233) 503954
Head: Mr D Marshall
Type: Co-educational Boarding 5–16
No of pupils: B34 G34
No of Boarders: F68
Special Needs: ADHD DYS **EBD** MLD
Non-Maintained
52-week care

CONEY HILL SCHOOL
Croydon Road, Hayes, Bromley, Kent
BR2 7AG
Tel: (020) 8462 2017
Head: Ms M Rimmer
Type: Co-educational Boarding and
Day 5–16
No of pupils: B15 G7
No of Boarders: W12
Special Needs: **CP** EPI PH **PMLD** VIS **W**
Non-Maintained

DON BUSS LEARNING CENTRE PRIMARY
The School, The Street,
Womenswold, Canterbury, Kent
CT4 6HE
Tel: (01227) 831236
Head: Miss L O'Keefe
Type: Boys Boarding and Day 7–12
No of pupils: 9
Special Needs: ADD ADHD ASP **EBD**
Approved Independent

DON BUSS LEARNING OPPORTUNITIES
Ringwould Road, Ringwould, Deal,
Kent DT14 8DW
Tel: (01304) 381906
Head: Ms D Ward
Type: Co-educational Boarding and
Day 11–16
No of pupils: B20 G1
Special Needs: ADD ADHD ASP **EBD**
Approved Independent

EAST COURT SCHOOL†
Victoria Parade, Ramsgate, Kent
CT11 8ED
Tel: (01843) 592077
Head: Dr M E Thomson
Type: Co-educational Boarding and
Day 7–13
No of pupils: B58 G11
No of Boarders: F12 W46
Special Needs: DYC DYP **DYS SPLD**
Independent

HELEN ALLISON SCHOOL
Longfield Road, Meopham, Kent
DA13 0EW
Tel: (01474) 814878
Head: Mrs J Ashton-Smith
Type: Co-educational Boarding and
Day 5–19
No of pupils: B65 G5
No of Boarders: W28
Special Needs: ASP **AUT**
Approved Independent

MEADOWS SCHOOL (BARNARDO'S)*
London Road, Southborough, Kent
TN4 0RJ
Tel: (01892) 529144
Head: Mrs S Paterson
Type: Co-educational Boarding and
Day 11–16
No of pupils: B45 G10
No of Boarders: W38
Special Needs: ADHD **EBD** MLD W
Non-Maintained

NCH WESTWOOD SCHOOL*
479 Margate Road, Broadstairs, Kent
CT10 2QA
Tel: (01843) 600820
Fax:: (01843) 600827
Head: Mr C L Walter
Type: Co-educational Day 11–16
No of pupils: B20 G3
Special Needs: ADHD **EBD** MLD
Independent

RIPPLEVALE SCHOOL
Ripple, Deal, Kent CT14 8JG
Tel: (01304) 373866
Head: Mr D Wilton
Type: Boys Boarding and Day 10–16
No of pupils: 45 *No of Boarders:* F24
Special Needs: **EBD**
Approved Independent

ROYAL LONDON SOCIETY FOR THE BLIND

Dorton House, Seal, Sevenoaks, Kent
TN15 OED
Tel: (01732) 592650
Head: Mr B Cooney
Type: Co-educational Boarding and
Day 5–16
No of pupils: B49 G33
No of Boarders: W48
Special Needs: VIS
Non-Maintained

THE ROYAL SCHOOL FOR DEAF CHILDREN MARGATE AND WESTGATE COLLEGE FOR DEAF PEOPLE

Victoria Road, Margate, Kent
CT9 1NB
Tel: (01843) 227561
Head: Mr D E Bond
Type: Co-educational Boarding and
Day 4–16
No of pupils: B60 G33
Special Needs: HI VIS
Non-Maintained
52-week care

LANCASHIRE

BEECH TREE SCHOOL

Meadow Lane, Bamber Bridge,
Preston, Lancashire PR5 8LN
Tel: (01772) 323131
Head: Ms L Bayliss
Type: Co-educational Boarding 7–16
No of pupils: B14 G1
No of Boarders: F15
Special Needs: AUT EBD EPI HI PH
SLD SP&LD VIS W
Approved Independent
52-week care

BIRTENSHAW HALL SCHOOL*

Darwen Road, Bromley Cross,
Bolton, Lancashire BL7 9AB
Tel: (01204) 304230
Head: Mr C D Jamieson
Type: Co-educational Boarding and
Day 3–19
No of pupils: 30 *No of Boarders:* F22
Special Needs: CP DEL EPI MLD PH
PMLD SLD SP&LD W
Non-Maintained
52-week care

CEDAR HOUSE SCHOOL

Kirkby Lonsdale, Via Carnforth,
Lancashire LA6 2HW
Tel: (01524) 271181
Head: Mr A W Cousins
Type: Co-educational Boarding and
Day 9–16
No of pupils: 70 *No of Boarders:* F56
Special Needs: ADHD EBD SPLD
Approved Independent

CROOKHEY HALL SCHOOL

Garstang Road, Cockerham,
Lancaster, Lancashire LA2 0HA
Tel: (01524) 792618
Head: Mr J Rider
Type: Boys Day 11–16
No of pupils: 64
Special Needs: EBD SPLD
Approved Independent

CROWTHORN SCHOOL (NCH ACTION FOR CHILDREN)

Broadhead Road, Edgworth, Bolton,
Lancashire BL7 0JS
Tel: (01204) 852143
Head: Mr S Forster
Type: Co-educational Day 8–16
No of pupils: 56
Special Needs: ADHD EBD MLD
Non-Maintained
52-week care

NUGENT HOUSE SCHOOL*

Carr Mill Road, Billinge, Wigan,
Lancashire WN5 7TT
Tel: (01744) 892551
Head: Mrs J L G Bienias
Type: Boys Boarding and Day 7–19
No of pupils: 89 *No of Boarders:* F59
Special Needs: ADD ADHD ASP DYS
EBD TOU
Approved Independent
52-week care

PONTVILLE SCHOOL*

Blackmoss Lane, Ormskirk,
Lancashire L39 4TW
Tel: (01695) 578734
Head: Mr R Farbon
Type: Co-educational Boarding and
Day 11–19
No of pupils: B39 G8
No of Boarders: F27
Special Needs: ADD ASP MLD TOU
Independent
52-week care

ROSSENDALE SPECIAL SCHOOL

Moorside Farm, Bamford Road,
Ramsbottom, Lancashire BL0 0RT
Tel: (01706) 822779
Head: Mr D G Duncan
Type: Co-educational Boarding and
Day
No of pupils: 56 *No of Boarders:* W15
Special Needs: ADHD ASP DYP DYS
EBD EPI TOU
Approved Independent

UNDERLEY GARDEN SCHOOL*

Kirkby Lonsdale, Carnforth,
Lancashire LA6 2DZ
Tel: (01524) 271569
Head: Mrs P Redican
Type: Co-educational Boarding 9–16
No of pupils: B21 G28
No of Boarders: F49
Special Needs: ADD ADHD ASP EBD
MLD SPLD
Approved Independent
52-week care

UNDERLEY HALL SCHOOL*
Kirkby Lonsdale, Carnforth,
Lancashire LA6 2HE
Tel: (01524) 271206
Head: Mr J Parkinson
Type: Boys Boarding 9–16
No of pupils: 70 *No of Boarders:* F70
Special Needs: **ADD ADHD** ASP **EBD**
MLD SPLD
Approved Independent
52-week care

WESTMORLAND SCHOOL*
Weldbank Lane, Chorley, Lancashire
PR7 3NQ
Tel: (01257) 278899
Head: Mr P Connor
Type: Co-educational Day 5–11
No of pupils: 30
Special Needs: EBD MLD PMLD SPLD
Independent

LINCOLNSHIRE

KISIMUL SCHOOL*
The Old Vicarage, Swinderby,
Lincoln, Lincolnshire LN6 9LU
Tel: (01522) 868279
Head: Mrs S Shaw
Type: Co-educational Boarding and
Day 10–19
No of pupils: 31 *No of Boarders:* F28
Special Needs: AUT DOW EPI **SLD**
SP&LD SPLD
Approved Independent
50-week care

LONDON

BLOSSOM HOUSE SCHOOL
8 The Drive, Wimbledon, London
SW20 8TG
Tel: (020) 8946 7348
Head: Mrs J Burgess
Type: Co-educational Day 3–12
No of pupils: 90
Special Needs: DYP **SP&LD** SPLD
Independent

CENTRE ACADEMY
92 St John's Hill, Battersea, London
SW11 1SH
Tel: (020) 7738 2344
Head: Mr F J O'Regan
Type: Co-educational Day 8–18
No of pupils: B40 G15
Special Needs: ADD ADHD DYC DYS
SP&LD SPLD
Independent

FAIRLEY HOUSE SCHOOL*†
30 Causton Street, London
SW1P 4AU
Tel: (020) 7976 5456
Head: Ms J Murray
Type: Co-educational Day 6–12
No of pupils: B100 G30
Special Needs: ADD ADHD **DYP DYS**
SPLD
Independent

**HOME SCHOOL OF STOKE
NEWINGTON**
46 Alkham Road, London N16 7AA
Tel: (020) 8806 6965
Head: Mrs C Allen
Type: Co-educational Day 11–16
No of pupils: B11
Special Needs: ASP DYC DYP DYS
SPLD
Independent

**HORNSEY CONDUCTIVE
EDUCATION CENTRE**
54 Muswell Hill, London N10 3ST
Tel: (020) 8444 7242
Head: Miss C Hewitt
Type: Co-educational Day 0–7
No of pupils: B15 G10
Special Needs: CP PH
Approved Independent

KISHARON DAY SCHOOL
1011 Finchley Road, London
NW11 7HB
Tel: (020) 8455 7483
Head: Mr G Lebrett
Type: Co-educational Day 3–16
(Jewish pupils only)
No of pupils: B12 G12
Special Needs: ADHD ASP **AUT** CP
DOW EBD **MLD** SP&LD
Approved Independent

THE MOAT SCHOOL*
Bishop's Avenue, Fulham, London
SW6 6EG
Tel: (020) 7610 9018
Head: Mr R M Carlysle
Type: Co-educational Day 11–17
No of pupils: B65 G15
Special Needs: **DYC** DYP **DYS**
Independent

THE NEW LEARNING CENTRE
211 Sumatra Road, London
NW6 1PF
Tel: (020) 7794 0321
Type: Co-educational Day 2–18
No of pupils: B7 G8
Special Needs: **ADHD** ASP DYC DYP
DYS **EBD** SP&LD **SPLD** TOU
Independent

PARAYHOUSE SCHOOL
Old Ellerslie Site, South Africa Road,
Shepherds Bush, London W12 7BP
Tel: (020) 8740 6333
Head: Mrs S L Jackson
Type: Co-educational Day 8–16
No of pupils: B31 G7
Special Needs: **DOW** EPI **MLD**
SP&LD W
Independent

THE SPEECH, LANGUAGE & HEARING CENTRE
Christopher Place, Chalton Street,
London NW1 1JF
Tel: (020) 7383 3834
Head: Ms A Harding
Type: Co-educational Day 0–5
No of pupils: 60
Special Needs: DYP HI SP&LD W
Independent

TREE HOUSE
49 Mecklenburgh Square, London
WC1N 2NY
Tel: (020) 7681 9982
Head: Mr S Eccles
Type: Co-educational Day 3–9
No of pupils: 80
Special Needs: **AUT**
Independent

WILLOUGHBY HALL DYSLEXIA CENTRE*
1 Willoughby Road, London
NW3 1RP
Tel: (020) 7794 3538
Head: Mrs J Hawkins
Type: Co-educational Day 6–12
No of pupils: B35 G6
Special Needs: **DYS** DYP
Independent

GREATER MANCHESTER

DIDSBURY SCHOOL
611 Wilmslow Road, Didsbury,
Manchester M20 6AD
Tel: (0161) 448 7022
Head: Mr H Millerman
Type: Co-educational Boarding and
Day
No of pupils: B14 G4
Special Needs: ADHD **EBD** MLD
Independent
52-week care

THE ST JOHN VIANNEY SCHOOL
(Upper School), Rye Bank Road,
Firswood, Stretford,
Greater Manchester M16 0EX
Tel: (0161) 881 7843
Head: Mr J Cusick
Type: Co-educational Day 11–16
No of pupils: 95
Special Needs: **MLD**
Non-Maintained

MERSEYSIDE

BIRKDALE SCHOOL FOR HEARING IMPAIRED CHILDREN*
40 Lancaster Road, Birkdale,
Southport, Merseyside PR8 2JY
Tel: (01704) 567220
Head: Mrs A Wood
Type: Co-educational Boarding and
Day 5–19
No of pupils: B16 G20
No of Boarders: F3 W14
Special Needs: ASP DYP DYS **HI MLD**
SP&LD
Non-Maintained

CLARENCE HOUSE SCHOOL
West Lane, Freshfield, Formby,
Merseyside L37 7AZ
Tel: (01704) 872151
Head: Ms M A Bird
Type: Co-educational Boarding and
Day 9–16
No of pupils: B58 G13
No of Boarders: F25
Special Needs: **EBD**
Approved Independent

LAKESIDE SCHOOL*
Naylor's Road, Liverpool L27 2YA
Tel: (0151) 487 7211
Head: Miss V E Shaw
Type: Co-educational Day 4–13
No of pupils: 24
Special Needs: SP&LD SPLD
Independent

PETERHOUSE SCHOOL FOR PUPILS WITH AUTISM
Preston New Road, Southport,
Merseyside PR9 8PA
Tel: (01704) 506682
Head: Ms B Matthews
Type: Co-educational Boarding and
Day 5–19
No of pupils: B37 G11
No of Boarders: F3 W15
Special Needs: **ASP AUT** W
Approved Independent
52-week care

ROYAL SCHOOL FOR THE BLIND
Church Road North, Wavertree,
Liverpool, Merseyside L15 6TQ
Tel: (0151) 733 1012
Head: Mr J P Byrne
Type: Co-educational Boarding and
Day 2–19
No of pupils: B39 G17
No of Boarders: W17
Special Needs: EBD HI MLD PH
PMLD SLD VIS W
Non-Maintained

ST VINCENT'S SCHOOL FOR BLIND AND PARTIALLY SIGHTED CHILDREN*
Yew Tree Lane, West Derby,
Liverpool, Merseyside L12 9HN
Tel: (0151) 228 9968
Head: Mr A MacQuarrie
Type: Co-educational Boarding and
Day 4–17
No of pupils: 100 *No of Boarders:* W36
Special Needs: ASP CP DEL EPI HI
MLD PH SP&LD SPLD **VIS** W
Non-Maintained

WARGRAVE HOUSE SCHOOL
449 Wargrave Road, Newton-le-
Willows, Merseyside WA12 8RS
Tel: (01925) 224899
Head: Mrs P M Maddock
Type: Co-educational Boarding and
Day 4–19
No of pupils: 62 *No of Boarders:* W20
Special Needs: ASP AUT
Approved Independent

WEST KIRBY RESIDENTIAL SCHOOL
Meols Drive, West Kirby, Wirral,
Merseyside L48 5DH
Tel: (0151) 632 3201
Head: Mr G W Williams
Type: Co-educational Boarding and
Day 6–16
No of pupils: B65 G30
No of Boarders: W35
Special Needs: ADD **ASP EBD** MLD
SP&LD TOU
Non-Maintained

MIDDLESEX

PIELD HEATH SCHOOL
Pield Heath Road, Uxbridge,
Middlesex UB8 3NW
Tel: (01895) 258507
Head: Sister J Rose
Type: Co-educational Boarding and
Day 7–19
No of pupils: B50 G50
No of Boarders: W30
Special Needs: ADD ASP AUT CP DEL
DOW DYP EPI **MLD** PMLD **SLD**
SP&LD SPLD VIS
Non-Maintained

RNIB SUNSHINE HOUSE SCHOOL
33 Dene Road, Northwood,
Middlesex HA6 2DD
Tel: (01923) 822538
Head: Mrs L Stewart
Type: Co-educational Boarding and
Day 2–11
No of pupils: 50 *No of Boarders:* W12
Special Needs: **VIS** W
Non-Maintained

THE SYBIL ELGAR SCHOOL
Havelock Court, Havelock Road,
Southall, Middlesex UB2 4NZ
Tel: (020) 8813 9168
Head: Ms C Phillips
Type: Co-educational Boarding and
Day 11–19
No of pupils: B76 G10
No of Boarders: W24
Special Needs: **AUT** SP&LD
Approved Independent

NORFOLK

BANHAM MARSHALLS COLLEGE
Mill Road, Banham, Norwich,
Norfolk NR16 2HU
Tel: (01953) 888656
Head: Mr R Wilson
Type: Co-educational Boarding and
Day 6–16
No of pupils: B80 G40
No of Boarders: F50 W40
Special Needs: ASP EBD SP&LD W
Approved Independent

CHURCH HILL SCHOOL
Banham, Norwich, Norfolk
NR16 2HN
Tel: (01953) 887815
Head: Mrs H Wilson
Type: Co-educational Boarding 8–16
No of pupils: B7 G8
Special Needs: ASP AUT
Independent

ST ANDREWS SCHOOL
Lower Common, East Runton,
Norfolk NR27 9PG
Tel: (01263) 511727
Head: Ms G Baker
Type: Co-educational Day 6–12
No of pupils: B8 G1
Special Needs: ASP DYP DYS MLD
SPLD
Independent

SHERIDAN HOUSE CHILD & FAMILY THERAPY UNIT*
Sheridan House, Southburgh,
Thetford, Norfolk IP25 7TJ
Tel: (01953) 850494
Head: Mrs S Sayer
Type: Boys Boarding 10–16
No of pupils: 12 *No of Boarders:* F12
Special Needs: **EBD**
Approved Independent
52-week care

NORTHAMPTONSHIRE

POTTERSPURY LODGE SCHOOL
Towcester, Northamptonshire
NN12 7LL
Tel: (01908) 542912
Head: Miss G Lietz
Type: Boys Boarding and Day 8–16
No of pupils: 49
No of Boarders: F15 W17
Special Needs: ADHD **ASP** DYP **EBD**
TOU
Approved Independent

RNIB RUSHTON HALL SCHOOL*
Rushton, Kettering,
Northamptonshire NN14 1RR
Tel: (01536) 710506
Head: Mrs R Kirkwood
Type: Co-educational Boarding and
Day 4–19
No of pupils: 45 *No of Boarders:* F35
Special Needs: CP EPI MLD PH **PMLD**
SLD SP&LD **VIS** W
Non-Maintained
52-week care

THORNBY HALL SCHOOL
Naseby Road, Thornby,
Northamptonshire NN6 8SW
Tel: (01604) 740001
Head: Mr R Barrett
Type: Co-educational Boarding 13–18
No of pupils: 17 *No of Boarders:* F17
Special Needs: DYS EBD EPI MLD
Independent

NORTHUMBERLAND

NUNNYKIRK CENTRE FOR DYSLEXIA†
Netherwitton, Morpeth,
Northumberland NE61 4PB
Tel: (01670) 772685
Head: Mr S Dalby-Ball
Type: Co-educational Boarding and
Day 7–16
No of pupils: B39 G6
No of Boarders: W20
Special Needs: **DYS** SPLD
Non-Maintained

NOTTINGHAMSHIRE

I CAN'S DAWN HOUSE SCHOOL*
Helmsley Road, Rainworth,
Mansfield, Nottinghamshire
NG21 0DQ
Tel: (01623) 795361
Head: Ms M Uden
Type: Co-educational Boarding and
Day 5–16
No of pupils: B60 G21
No of Boarders: W55
Special Needs: ASP DYP DYS SP&LD
Non-Maintained

RUTLAND HOUSE SCHOOL*
1 Elm Bank, Mapperley Road,
Nottingham NG5 3AJ
Tel: (0115) 962 1315
Head: Mrs C A Oviatt-Ham
Type: Co-educational Boarding and
Day 5–19
No of pupils: B17 G13
No of Boarders: F19 W6
Special Needs: CP EPI HI PH PMLD
SP&LD VIS W
Approved Independent

SUTHERLAND HOUSE SCHOOL (PRIMARY DEPARTMENT)
Sutherland Road, Nottingham
NG3 7AP
Tel: (0115) 987 3375
Head: Mrs M Allen
Type: Co-educational Day 7–11
No of pupils: B27 G3
Special Needs: AUT
Approved Independent

SUTHERLAND HOUSE SCHOOL (SECONDARY DEPARTMENT)
"Westward", 68 Cyprus Road,
Mapperley Park, Nottinghamshire
NG3 5ED
Tel: (0115) 969 1823
Head: Mrs C Byles
Type: Co-educational Day 11–16
No of pupils: 14
Special Needs: AUT
Approved Independent

OXFORDSHIRE

BESSELS LEIGH SCHOOL*
Bessels Leigh, Abingdon,
Oxfordshire OX13 5QB
Tel: (01865) 390436
Head: Mr J Boulton
Type: Boys Boarding 11–16
No of pupils: 38 *No of Boarders:* F38
Special Needs: ADHD DYS EBD SPLD
Non-Maintained
52-week care

BRUERN ABBEY SCHOOL
Chesterton Manor, Chesterton,
Oxfordshire OX26 1UY
Tel: (01869) 242448
Head: Mr J G Stover
Type: Boys Boarding and Day 8–13
No of pupils: 42
No of Boarders: F36 W36
Special Needs: DYP DYS SP&LD
SPLD
Independent

MULBERRY BUSH SCHOOL
Abingdon Road, Standlake, Witney,
Oxfordshire OX29 7RW
Tel: (01865) 300202
Head: Mr J Diamond
Type: Co-educational Boarding 5–12
No of pupils: B24 G12
No of Boarders: W36
Special Needs: EBD
Non-Maintained

PENHURST SCHOOL*
New Street, Chipping Norton,
Oxfordshire OX7 5LN
Tel: (01608) 647020
Head: Mr R Aird
Type: Co-educational Boarding 5–19
No of pupils: 24 *No of Boarders:* F21
Special Needs: CP EPI HI PH PMLD
SP&LD VIS W
Non-Maintained

SWALCLIFFE PARK SCHOOL*
Swalcliffe, Banbury, Oxfordshire
OX15 5EP
Tel: (01295) 780302
Head: Mr R Hooper
Type: Boys Boarding and Day 11–19
No of pupils: 62 *No of Boarders:* F57
Special Needs: ADD ADHD ASP EBD
MLD
Non-Maintained

THE UNICORN SCHOOL*†
Whitefield, Park Crescent,
Abingdon, Oxfordshire OX14 1DD
Tel: (01235) 530222
Head: Mrs E Christie
Type: Co-educational Day 6–12
No of pupils: B30 G2
Special Needs: ADD ADHD DYC DYP
DYS W
Independent

RUTLAND

THE GRANGE THERAPEUTIC SCHOOL
Knossington, Oakham, Rutland
LE15 8LY
Tel: (01664) 454264
Head: Mr D R Lee
Type: Boys Boarding 8–16
No of pupils: 60 *No of Boarders:* F60
Special Needs: **EBD**
Approved Independent

SHROPSHIRE

COTSBROOK COMMUNITY
Higford, Shifnal, Shropshire
TF11 9ET
Tel: (01952) 750 237
Head: Mr J Airth
Type: Co-educational Boarding 11–16
No of pupils: B13 G5
No of Boarders: F18
Special Needs: **EBD**
Approved Independent

CRUCKTON HALL
Cruckton, Shrewsbury, Shropshire
SY5 8PR
Tel: (01743) 860206
Head: Mr P D Mayhew
Type: Boys Boarding 8–19
No of pupils: 68 *No of Boarders:* F68
Special Needs: ADHD ASP AUT DYC
DYP DYS EBD EPI MLD SPLD
Approved Independent
52-week care

ORCHARD SCHOOL
Near Middleton, Shropshire
SY21 8EW
Tel: (01743) 884145
Head: Mr J W Kwaterski
Type: Co-educational Boarding 11–19
No of pupils: B6 G2 *No of Boarders:* F8
Special Needs: **AUT** DOW EBD EPI
SLD
Independent
52-week care

OVERLEY HALL SCHOOL
Wellington, Telford, Shropshire
TF6 5HE
Tel: (01952) 740262
Head: Mrs J Flannery
Type: Co-educational Boarding 9–19
No of pupils: B12 *No of Boarders:* F12
Special Needs: ADD ADHD ASP AUT
DOW DYC DYP DYS EBD **EPI** MLD
SLD SP&LD TOU
Independent

RNIB CONDOVER HALL SCHOOL*
Condover, nr Shrewsbury,
Shropshire SY5 7AH
Tel: (01743) 872320
Head: Mr H Dicks
Type: Co-educational Boarding and
Day 8–24
No of pupils: 60 *No of Boarders:* W38
Special Needs: ASP AUT CP EBD EPI
HI PH PMLD SLD SP&LD **VIS** W
Non-Maintained

SOMERSET

EDINGTON AND SHAPWICK SCHOOL†
Shapwick Manor, Shapwick,
Bridgwater, Somerset TA9 9NJ
Tel: (01278) 722012
Head: Mr D C Walker
and J P Whittock
Type: Co-educational Boarding and
Day 8–18
No of pupils: B132 G39
No of Boarders: F115 W15
Special Needs: DYC DYP **DYS** SPLD
Approved Independent

FARLEIGH COLLEGE*
Newbury, Near Mells, Frome,
Somerset BA11 3RG
Tel: (01373) 814980
Head: Mr D Walsh
Type: Co-educational Boarding and
Day 11–19
No of pupils: B35 G5
No of Boarders: F40
Special Needs: ASP
Independent

FARLEIGH SIXTH FORM COLLEGE*
19 Bath Road, Frome, Somerset
BA11 2HJ
Tel: (01373) 346 3172
Head: Mr A Chiffers
Type: Co-educational Boarding and
Day 16–19
Special Needs: ASP
Independent

THE MARCHANT-HOLLIDAY SCHOOL*
North Cheriton, Templecombe, Somerset BA8 0AH
Tel: (01963) 33234
Head: Mr J M Robertson
Type: Boys Boarding and Day 7–12
No of pupils: 38 *No of Boarders:* F34
Special Needs: ADD ADHD ASP DYS **EBD** SPLD
Approved Independent

MARK COLLEGE*†
Mark, Somerset TA9 4NP
Tel: (01278) 641632
Head: Dr S J Chinn
Type: Boys Boarding and Day 10–16
No of pupils: 80
No of Boarders: F55 W15
Special Needs: **DYC** DYP **DYS**
Approved Independent

NORTH HILL HOUSE*
North Parade, Frome, Somerset BA11 2AB
Tel: (01373) 466222
Head: Mr A Cobley
Type: Boys Boarding and Day 7–16
Special Needs: ASP
Independent

STAFFORDSHIRE

BLADON HOUSE SCHOOL
Newton Solney, Burton upon Trent, Staffordshire DE15 0TA
Tel: (01283) 563787
Head: Mrs B Murfin
Type: Co-educational Boarding and Day 5–19
No of pupils: B80 G34
Special Needs: AUT MLD SPLD
Approved Independent

HONORMEAD SCHOOL FOR CHILDREN WITH AUTISM
Blithbury Road, Blithbury, Rugeley, Staffordshire WS15 3JQ
Tel: 01889 504400
Head: Ms M Kehall
Type: Co-educational Boarding and Day 4–16
No of pupils: 36 *No of Boarders:* F36
Special Needs: AUT
Independent

MAPLE HAYES HALL DYSLEXIA SCHOOL*
Abnalls Lane, Lichfield, Staffordshire WS13 8BL
Tel: (01543) 264387
Head: Dr E Neville Brown
Type: Co-educational Boarding and Day 7–17 (Girls day only)
No of pupils: B111 G9
No of Boarders: W40
Special Needs: ADD ADHD DYS SPLD
Approved Independent

SUFFOLK

BRAMFIELD HOUSE
Walpole Road, Bramfield, Halesworth, Suffolk IP19 9AB
Tel: (01986) 784235
Head: Mr M G Read
Type: Boys Boarding and Day 10–16
No of pupils: 40 *No of Boarders:* F35
Special Needs: EBD MLD
Approved Independent

THE OLD RECTORY SCHOOL†
Brettenham, Ipswich, Suffolk IP7 7QR
Tel: (01449) 736404
Head: Miss A Furlong
Type: Co-educational Boarding and Day 7–13
No of pupils: B40 G16
No of Boarders: W45
Special Needs: DYP DYS SPLD
Independent

THE RYES SCHOOL
Little Henny, Sudbury, Suffolk CO10 7EA
Tel: (01787) 374998
Head: Mrs R Stamp
Type: Co-educational Boarding and Day 7–16
No of pupils: B22 G8
No of Boarders: F30
Special Needs: ADHD ASP AUT **EBD MLD** SLD TOU
Approved Independent
52-week care

SURREY

GRAFHAM GRANGE SCHOOL*
Grafham, Nr Bramley, Guildford, Surrey GU5 0LH
Tel: (01483) 892214
Head: Mr R Norman
Type: Boys Boarding 10–16
No of pupils: 40
Special Needs: **EBD**
Non-Maintained

I CAN'S MEATH SCHOOL*
Brox Road, Ottershaw, Surrey KT16 0LF
Tel: (01932) 872302
Head: Mr J Parrott
Type: Co-educational Boarding and Day 5–12
No of pupils: B54 G16
No of Boarders: W16
Special Needs: **SP&LD**
Non-Maintained

THE KNOWL HILL SCHOOL†
School Lane, Pirbright, Surrey GU24 0JN
Tel: (01483) 797032
Head: Mrs A J Bareford
Type: Co-educational Day 7–16
No of pupils: B38 G7
Special Needs: DYC DYP DYS SPLD
Approved Independent

THE LINK PRIMARY SCHOOL
138 Croydon Road, Beddington, Croydon, Surrey CR0 4PG
Tel: (020) 8688 5239
Head: Mr G Stewart
Type: Co-educational Day 6–12
No of pupils: B27 G10
Special Needs: **ASP AUT SP&LD** SPLD
Approved Independent

THE LINK SECONDARY SCHOOL
82–86 Croydon Road, Beddington, Surrey CRO 4PD
Tel: (020) 8688 7691
Head: Mr W E Fuller
Type: Co-educational Day 11–16
No of pupils: B29 G9
Special Needs: **ASP AUT SP&LD**
Approved Independent

MOON HALL SCHOOL*†
"Feldemore", Pasture Wood Lane, Holmbury St Mary, Dorking, Surrey RH5 6LQ
Tel: (01306) 731464
Head: Mrs J Lovett
Type: Co-educational Boarding and Day 7–13
No of pupils: B70 G24
No of Boarders: W17
Special Needs: **DYS**
Independent

MOOR HOUSE SCHOOL
Hurst Green, Oxted, Surrey RH8 9AQ
Tel: (01883) 712271
Head: Mr A A Robertson
Type: Co-educational Boarding 7–16
No of pupils: B64 G20
No of Boarders: F84
Special Needs: DYC DYP DYS **SP&LD**
Non-Maintained

MORE HOUSE SCHOOL†
Moons Hill, Frensham, Farnham, Surrey GU10 3AW
Tel: (01252) 792303
Head: Mr B G Huggett
Type: Boys Boarding and Day 9–16
No of pupils: 170
No of Boarders: F14 W40
Special Needs: DYS SPLD
Approved Independent

THE NATIONAL CENTRE FOR YOUNG PEOPLE WITH EPILEPSY (NCYPE) (FORMERLY ST. PIERS)*
St Piers Lane, Lingfield, Surrey RH7 6PW
Tel: (01342) 832243
Head: Mr R S Haughton
Type: Co-educational Boarding and Day 5–19+
No of pupils: 196 *No of Boarders:* 168
Special Needs: **EPI** MLD SLD SP&LD
Non-Maintained

RUTHERFORD SCHOOL
1A Melville Avenue, South Croydon, Surrey CR2 7HZ
Tel: (020) 8688 7560
Head: Mrs R G Hills
Type: Co-educational Day 2–12
No of pupils: 24
Special Needs: CP EPI HI PH **PMLD** SLD VIS **W**
Approved Independent

ST DOMINIC'S SCHOOL*
Hambledon, Godalming, Surrey GU8 4DX
Tel: (01428) 684693
Head: Mr G Chapman
Type: Co-educational Boarding and Day 7–16
No of pupils: B80 G10
No of Boarders: W59
Special Needs: ADD ADHD ASP **DEL** DYC DYP DYS EPI **SP&LD** SPLD
Non-Maintained

ST JOSEPH'S SCHOOL
Amlets Lane, Cranleigh, Surrey GU6 7DH
Tel: (01483) 272449
Head: Mr A Lowry
Type: Co-educational Boarding and Day 7–19
No of pupils: B50 G20
No of Boarders: F40
Special Needs: **AUT** DOW DYC DYP DYS **MLD SLD** SP&LD
Non-Maintained

ST MARGARET'S SCHOOL*
Tadworth Court, Tadworth, Surrey KT20 5RU
Tel: (01737) 365810
Head: Mrs J Cunningham
Type: Co-educational Boarding and Day 5–19
No of pupils: B14 G23
No of Boarders: F27
Special Needs: CP EPI HI **PMLD** VIS W
Approved Independent

EAST SUSSEX

CHAILEY HERITAGE SCHOOL*

Haywards Heath Road, North Chailey, East Sussex BN8 4EF
Tel: (01825) 724444
Head: Mr A C Bruce
Type: Co-educational Boarding and Day 3–19
No of pupils: B52 G43
No of Boarders: W26
Special Needs: CP MLD PH **SLD SP&LD VIS**
Non-Maintained

CORNERSTONES INDEPENDENT SCHOOL

110 Western Road, Brighton, East Sussex BN1 2AA
Tel: (01273) 734164
Head: Ms M Rees
Type: Co-educational Day 7–16
No of pupils: 12
Special Needs: **EBD**
Independent

FREWEN COLLEGE*†

Brickwall, Northiam, Rye, East Sussex TN31 6NB
Tel: (01797) 252494
Head: Mr S Horsley
Type: Boys Boarding and Day 9–17
No of pupils: 82 *No of Boarders:* W39
Special Needs: DYP **DYS**
Approved Independent

HAMILTON LODGE SCHOOL FOR DEAF CHILDREN

Walpole Road, Brighton, East Sussex BN2 2ET
Tel: (01273) 682362
Head: Mrs A K Duffy
Type: Co-educational Boarding and Day 5–18
No of pupils: B42 G33
No of Boarders: W59
Special Needs: **HI**
Non-Maintained

KINGS MANOR EDUCATION CENTRE

Southdown Road, Seaford, East Sussex BN25 4JS
Tel: (01323) 873400
Head: Mrs N Newman
Type: Co-educational Boarding 11–16
No of pupils: 42 *No of Boarders:* W6
Special Needs: ADD **ADHD** DEL **DYP** DYS EBD EPI MLD PH
Independent

NORTHEASE MANOR†

Rodmell, Lewes, East Sussex BN7 3EY
Tel: (01273) 472915
Head: Mr P Stanley
Type: Co-educational Boarding and Day 10–17
No of pupils: B61 G19
No of Boarders: W40
Special Needs: DYP **DYS SPLD**
Approved Independent

OVINGDEAN HALL SCHOOL

Greenways, Brighton, East Sussex BN2 7BJ
Tel: (01273) 301929
Head: Mr M Bown
Type: Co-educational Boarding and Day 10–19
No of pupils: B85 G50
No of Boarders: W115
Special Needs: ADHD CP DYS **HI** MLD **SP&LD** SPLD VIS
Non-Maintained

OWLSWICK SCHOOL

Newhaven Road, Kingston, Lewes, East Sussex BN7 3NF
Tel: (01273) 473078
Head: Mr & Mrs A K Harper
Type: Co-educational Boarding 10–18
No of pupils: B7 G4 *No of Boarders:* F11
Special Needs: ADD **ADHD** DYS **EBD MLD**
Approved Independent
52-week care

ST JOHN'S COLLEGE

Walpole Road, Brighton, East Sussex BN2 0AF
Tel: (01273) 244000
Head: Mr D Kent
Type: Co-educational Boarding and Day 6–19
No of pupils: 155 *No of Boarders:* F100
Special Needs: ADD ADHD ASP AUT DOW EPI **MLD SLD** SP&LD
Independent

ST MARY'S SCHOOL*

Wrestwood Road, Bexhill-on-Sea, East Sussex TN40 2LU
Tel: (01424) 730740
Head: Mr D Cassar
Type: Co-educational Boarding and Day 7–19
No of pupils: 138 *No of Boarders:* F118
Special Needs: ASP AUT CP DEL DOW DYP DYS EPI HI **MLD PH SP&LD** SPLD TOU VIS W
Approved Independent

WEST SUSSEX

FARNEY CLOSE SCHOOL
Bolney Court, Bolney, Haywards
Heath, West Sussex RH17 5RD
Tel: (01444) 881811
Head: Mr B Robinson
Type: Co-educational Boarding and
Day 11–16
No of pupils: B40 G25
No of Boarders: W65
Special Needs: ADD ADHD ASP **EBD**
MLD SPLD
Independent

**I CAN'S JOHN HORNIMAN
SCHOOL***
2 Park Road, Worthing, West Sussex
BN11 2AS
Tel: (01903) 200317
Head: Ms J Dunn
Type: Co-educational Boarding and
Day 4–11
No of pupils: B25 G4
No of Boarders: W9
Special Needs: **SP&LD**
Non-Maintained

INGFIELD MANOR SCHOOL*
Five Oaks, Billingshurst,
West Sussex RH14 9AX
Tel: (01403) 782294
Head: Mr C Jay
Type: Co-educational Boarding and
Day 3–11
No of pupils: 41
Special Needs: **CP**
Approved Independent

MUNTHAM HOUSE SCHOOL*
Barns Green, Horsham, West Sussex
RH13 7NJ
Tel: (01403) 730302
Head: Mr R Boyle
Type: Boys Boarding 8–18
No of pupils: 56 *No of Boarders:* F48
Special Needs: **ADHD EBD**
Non-Maintained

PHILPOTS MANOR SCHOOL*
West Hoathly, East Grinstead,
West Sussex RH19 4PR
Tel: (01342) 811382
Head: Mr S Blaxland-de Lange
Type: Co-educational Boarding and
Day 7–19
No of pupils: B47 G18
No of Boarders: F53
Special Needs: ADD ADHD ASP **AUT**
CP DEL DOW DYC DYP DYS **EBD**
EPI HI **MLD** SPLD SP&LD TOU
Approved Independent
52-week care

TYNE AND WEAR

**NORTHERN COUNTIES
SCHOOL FOR THE DEAF**
Great North Road, Newcastle-Upon-
Tyne, Tyne and Wear NE2 3BB
Tel: (0191) 281 5821
Head: Mr K J Lewis
Type: Co-educational Boarding and
Day 3–19
No of pupils: B55 G30
No of Boarders: W16
Special Needs: **HI** PH **PMLD VIS** W
Non-Maintained

PERCY HEDLEY SCHOOL
Station Road, Forest Hall,
Newcastle-upon-Tyne,
Tyne and Wear NE12 8YY
Tel: (0191) 266 5451
Head: Mr N Stromsoy
Type: Co-educational Boarding and
Day 3–18
No of pupils: B110 G54
No of Boarders: W18
Special Needs: CP SP&LD W
Non-Maintained

**TALBOT HOUSE
INDEPENDENT SPECIAL
SCHOOL**
Hexham Road, Walbottle,
Newcastle-upon-Tyne, Tyne and Wear
NE15 8HW
Tel: (0191) 229 0111
Head: Mr A P James
Type: Co-educational Day 11–16
No of pupils: 50
Special Needs: ADHD DYP **EBD**
Approved Independent

THORNHILL PARK SCHOOL
21 Thornhill Park, Sunderland,
Tyne and Wear SR2 7LA
Tel: (0191) 514 0659
Head: Mr D Walke
Type: Co-educational Boarding and
Day 2–19
No of pupils: 85 *No of Boarders:* F44
Special Needs: ASP AUT
Approved Independent

WEST MIDLANDS

NATIONAL INSTITUTE OF CONDUCTIVE EDUCATION
Cannon Hill House, Russell Road,
Moseley, Birmingham,
West Midlands B13 8RD
Tel: (0121) 449 1569
Head: Mr C McGuigan
Type: Co-educational Day 1–11
No of pupils: 26
Special Needs: CP DYP MLD
Independent

SUNFIELD
Clent Grove, Woodman Lane, Clent,
Stourbridge, West Midlands DY9 9PB
Tel: (01562) 882253
Head: Professor B R Carpenter
Type: Co-educational Boarding 6–19
No of pupils: B60 G15
No of Boarders: F70
Special Needs: ADD ADHD ASP AUT
DOW EBD PMLD SLD
Approved Independent

WILTSHIRE

APPLEFORD SCHOOL†
Shrewton, Salisbury, Wiltshire
SP3 4HL
Tel: (01980) 621020
Head: The Revd B Clarke
Type: Co-educational Boarding and
Day 7–13
No of pupils: B71 G18
No of Boarders: F10 W49
Special Needs: ADD ADHD **DYC** DYP
DYS SP&LD **SPLD**
Approved Independent

BELMONT SCHOOL
School Lane, Salisbury, Wiltshire
SP1 3YA
Tel: (01722) 421115
Head: Mr P T Kelly
Type: Co-educational Day
No of pupils: 25
Special Needs: **EBD**
Independent
52-week care

BURTON HILL SCHOOL
Malmesbury, Wiltshire SN16 0EG
Tel: (01666) 822685
Head: Mr P Drake
Type: Co-educational Boarding and
Day 8–19
No of pupils: B25 G13
No of Boarders: F17 W9
Special Needs: CP **MLD PH SLD** W
Non-Maintained

CALDER HOUSE SCHOOL†
Thickwood Lane, Colerne,
Chippenham, Wiltshire SN14 8BN
Tel: (01225) 742329
Head: Mrs S Agombar
Type: Co-educational Day 5–13
No of pupils: B30 G18
Special Needs: DEL DYC **DYP DYS
SPLD**
Approved Independent

WORCESTERSHIRE

RNIB NEW COLLEGE*
Whittington Road, Worcester,
Worcestershire WR5 2JX
Tel: (01905) 763933
Head: Mr N Ratcliffe
Type: Co-educational Boarding and
Day 11–19
No of pupils: B40 G51
No of Boarders: F89 W2
Special Needs: **VIS** W
Non-Maintained

NORTH YORKSHIRE

BRECKENBROUGH SCHOOL*
Thirsk, North Yorkshire YO7 4EN
Tel: (01845) 587238
Head: Mr T G Bennett
Type: Boys Boarding and Day 9–17
No of pupils: 42 *No of Boarders:* F16
Special Needs: ADD ADHD ASP DEL
DYS EBD
Non-Maintained

**SPRING HILL SCHOOL
(BARNARDO'S)***
Palace Road, Ripon, North Yorkshire
HG4 3HN
Tel: (01765) 603320
Head: Mrs J E Clarke
Type: Co-educational Boarding and
Day 8–19
No of pupils: B31 G8
No of Boarders: F34
Special Needs: ADD ASP AUT DEL
DOW EBD EPI MLD SLD W
Non-Maintained

SOUTH YORKSHIRE

**DONCASTER SCHOOL FOR
THE DEAF***
Leger Way, Doncaster,
South Yorkshire DN2 6AY
Tel: (01302) 386710
Head: Mr D A Gadd
Type: Co-educational Boarding and
Day 3–16
No of pupils: B26 G15
No of Boarders: F4 W18
Special Needs: DYS EBD HI MLD PH
SP&LD SPLD VIS W
Non-Maintained
52-week care

FULLERTON HOUSE SCHOOL
off Tickhill Square, Denaby,
Doncaster, South Yorkshire
DN12 4AR
Tel: (01709) 861663
Head: Mr D O'Connor
Type: Co-educational Boarding 8–19
No of pupils: B27 G9
No of Boarders: F36
Special Needs: AUT EPI SLD SP&LD
Approved Independent
52-week care

**THE ROBERT OGDEN
SCHOOL**
Clayton Lane, Thurnscoe,
Rotherham, South Yorkshire S63 0BE
Tel: (01709) 874443
Head: Mrs A Hull
Type: Co-educational Boarding and
Day 4–19
No of pupils: 132 *No of Boarders:* F40
Special Needs: ASP AUT MLD SLD
Approved Independent

WILSIC HALL SCHOOL
Wadworth, Doncaster,
South Yorkshire DN11 9AG
Tel: (01302) 856382
Head: Mr M V Henderson
Type: Co-educational Boarding and
Day 11–19
No of pupils: 33 *No of Boarders:* F33
Special Needs: **AUT** DOW SLD
SP&LD SPLD
Independent
52-week care

WEST YORKSHIRE

HOLLY BANK SCHOOL
Roe Head, Far Common Road,
Mirfield, West Yorkshire WF14 0DQ
Tel: (01924) 490833
Head: Mrs S Garland-Grimes
Type: Co-educational Boarding and
Day 5–19
No of pupils: 44
No of Boarders: F25 W18
Special Needs: CP EPI MLD **PH PMLD
SLD** SP&LD W
Non-Maintained
52-week care

**ST JOHN'S CATHOLIC
SCHOOL FOR THE DEAF***
Church Street, Boston Spa,
Wetherby, West Yorkshire LS23 6DF
Tel: (01937) 842144
Head: Mr T M Wrynne
Type: Co-educational Boarding and
Day 3–19
No of pupils: B37 G49
No of Boarders: F17 W31
Special Needs: DYP **HI SP&LD** W
Non-Maintained

**WILLIAM HENRY SMITH
SCHOOL**
Boothroyd, Brighouse,
West Yorkshire HD6 3JW
Tel: (01484) 710123
Head: Mr B J Heneghan
Type: Boys Boarding and Day 8–16
No of pupils: 64 *No of Boarders:* W56
Special Needs: **EBD**
Non-Maintained

NORTHERN IRELAND

COUNTY ANTRIM

JORDANSTOWN SCHOOLS
85 Jordanstown Road,
Newtownabbey, County Antrim
BT37 0QE
Tel: (028) 9086 3541
Head: Mr S L Clarke
Type: Co-educational Boarding and
Day 4–19
No of pupils: B53 G51
No of Boarders: W6
Special Needs: HI VIS W
Non-Maintained

SCOTLAND

ABERDEENSHIRE

THE CAMPHILL RUDOLF STEINER SCHOOLS
Central Office, Murtle Estate,
Bieldside, Aberdeenshire AB14 9EP
Tel: (01224) 867935
Head: Mr E Billet
Type: Co-educational Boarding and
Day 3–19
No of pupils: B61 G34
No of Boarders: F75 W10
Special Needs: ADD ADHD **ASP** AUT
CP DEL DOW DYP DYS EBD EPI HI
MLD PH PMLD SLD SP&LD SPLD
TOU VIS W
Independent

LINN MOOR RESIDENTIAL SCHOOL
Peterculter, Aberdeen,
Aberdeenshire AB31 5PB
Tel: (01224) 732246
Head: Mr J Davidson
Type: Co-educational Boarding 5–18
No of pupils: 30
Special Needs: ADD ADHD ASP AUT
EBD EPI MLD PMLD SLD
Independent

OAKBANK SCHOOL
Midstocket Road, Aberdeen,
Aberdeenshire AB15 5XP
Tel: (01224) 313347
Head: Mrs J C Arrowsmith
Type: Co-educational Boarding and
Day 12–18
No of pupils: B31 G10
No of Boarders: F41
Special Needs: ADHD **EBD**
Independent
52-week care

EAST AYRSHIRE

DALDORCH HOUSE SCHOOL
Thorn Road, Catrine, East Ayrshire
KA5 6NE
Tel: (01290) 551666
Head: Mrs S Pinkerton
Type: Co-educational Boarding and
Day 5–19
No of pupils: B35 G5
No of Boarders: F40
Special Needs: AUT
Independent
52-week care

NORTH AYRSHIRE

GEILSLAND SCHOOL
Beith, North Ayrshire KA15 1HD
Tel: (01505) 504044
Head: Mr R Mair
Type: Boys Boarding 15–18
No of pupils: 36 *No of Boarders:* F36
Special Needs: **EBD** MLD
Independent
52-week care

SEAFIELDS SCHOOL
86 Eglinton Road, Ardrossan,
North Ayrshire KA22 8NL
Tel: (01294) 470355
Head: Mrs M Moran
Type: Co-educational Boarding and
Day 5–16
No of pupils: B63 *No of Boarders:* F28
Special Needs: **EBD**
Independent

SOUTH AYRSHIRE

RED BRAE SCHOOL
24 Alloway Road, Maybole, South
Ayrshire KA19 8AA
Tel: (01655) 883104
Head: Dr R J Dalrymple
Type: Boys Day 10–16
No of pupils: 30
Special Needs: ADHD ASP **EBD**
Independent

CLACKMANNANSHIRE

STRUAN HOUSE SCHOOL
27 Claremont, Alloa,
Clackmannanshire FK10 2DF
Tel: (01259) 213435
Head: Mr J Taylor
Type: Co-educational Boarding and
Day 5–16
No of pupils: 30 *No of Boarders:* W22
Special Needs: **AUT**
Independent

DUMFRIES & GALLOWAY

WOODLANDS SCHOOL
Corsbie Road, Newton Stewart,
Dumfries & Galloway DG8 6JB
Tel: (01671) 402480
Head: Mr J White
Type: Boys Boarding 7–17
No of pupils: 24 *No of Boarders:* F24
Special Needs: ADD ADHD EBD MLD
SP&LD SPLD
Independent
52-week care

FIFE

HILLSIDE SCHOOL
Hillside, Aberdour, Fife KY3 0RH
Tel: (01383) 860731
Head: Mrs A Harvey
Type: Boys Boarding 11–16
No of pupils: 42 *No of Boarders:* F42
Special Needs: ADD ADHD DEL EBD
MLD SPLD
Independent

STARLEY HALL
Aberdour Road, Burntisland, Fife
KY3 0AG
Tel: (01383) 860314
Head: Mr A Pyle
Type: Co-educational Boarding and
Day 11–16
No of pupils: 44
No of Boarders: F32 W32
Special Needs: ADD ADHD ASP EBD
TOU
Independent

GLASGOW

ST FRANCIS DAY BOY UNIT
1190 Edinburgh Road, Springboig,
Glasgow G33 4EH
Tel: (0141) 774 4499
Head: Mrs L Johnson
Type: Boys Day 14–16
No of pupils: 34
Special Needs: EBD MLD
Independent

SPRINGBOIG ST JOHN'S
1190 Edinburgh Road, Glasgow
G32 4EH
Tel: (0141) 774 9791
Head: Mr W Fitzgerald
Type: Boys Boarding
No of pupils: 38 *No of Boarders:* F38
Special Needs: EBD
Independent
52-week care

HIGHLAND

RADDERY SCHOOL
Fortrose, Highland IV10 8SN
Tel: (01381) 620271
Head: Mr G Hurt
Type: Boys Boarding and Day
No of pupils: 28 *No of Boarders:* W22
Special Needs: ADD ADHD DYS **EBD**
Independent

NORTH LANARKSHIRE

ST PHILLIP'S SCHOOL
Plains, Airdrie, North Lanarkshire
ML6 7SF
Tel: (01236) 765407
Head: Mr P Hanrahan
Type: Boys Boarding and Day 10–16
No of pupils: 60 *No of Boarders:* F36
Special Needs: ADD ADHD **EBD** MLD
Independent
52-week care

SOUTH LANARKSHIRE

STANMORE HOUSE RESIDENTIAL SCHOOL
Lanark, South Lanarkshire
ML11 7RR
Tel: (01555) 665041
Head: Mrs P Donnelly
Type: Co-educational Boarding and Day 2–18
No of pupils: 76 *No of Boarders:* F31
Special Needs: **CP** EPI HI PH PMLD SLD SP&LD VIS
Independent

LOTHIAN

HARMENY SCHOOL
Balerno, Lothian EH14 7JY
Tel: (0131) 449 3938
Head: Mr P Webb
Type: Co-educational Boarding 6–13
No of pupils: 36
No of Boarders: F19 W7
Special Needs: ADD **ADHD** ASP DYC DYS **EBD** MLD SP&LD SPLD W
Independent
52-week care

MOORE HOUSE SCHOOL
Edinburgh Road, Bathgate, Lothian
EH48 1BX
Tel: (01506) 652312
Head: Mrs A Smith
Type: Co-educational Boarding
No of pupils: B20 G11
No of Boarders: F31
Special Needs: **EBD**
Independent
52-week care

ROYAL BLIND SCHOOL*
Craigmillar Park, Edinburgh, Lothian EH16 5NA
Tel: (0131) 667 1100
Head: Mr K Tansley
Type: Co-educational Boarding and Day 3–19
No of pupils: B60 G58
No of Boarders: W72
Special Needs: AUT CP DEL DYP EPI MLD PH PMLD SLD SPLD SP&LD TOU **VIS** W
Grant Aided

PERTHSHIRE

THE NEW SCHOOL
Dunkeld, Perthshire PH8 0HA
Tel: (01350) 724 216
Acting Head: Ms A Spouart
Type: Co-educational Boarding
No of pupils: 88
Special Needs: ADD ADHD ASP AUT DEL DYP DYS MLD SPLD TOU
Independent

OCHIL TOWER (RUDOLF STEINER) SCHOOL
140 High Street, Auchterarder, Perthshire PH3 1AD
Tel: (01764) 662416
Head: Mr U Ruprecht
Type: Co-educational Boarding and Day 6–18
No of pupils: B30 G10
No of Boarders: W28
Special Needs: **ADHD** ASP AUT DEL EBD EPI **MLD** PMLD **SLD**
Independent

PERTH AND KINROSS

BALNACRAIG SCHOOL
Fairmount Terrace, Perth, Perth and
Kinross PH2 7AR
Tel: (01738) 636456
Head: Mr E G Matthew
Type: Co-educational Boarding 12–16
No of pupils: B12 G12
No of Boarders: F24
Special Needs: **EBD**
Independent

SEAMAB HOUSE SCHOOL
Rumbling Bridge, Kinross, KY13 0PT
Tel: (01577) 840307
Head: Mrs A W Anderson
Type: Co-educational Boarding 7–12
No of pupils: 14 *No of Boarders:* W14
Special Needs: **EBD**
Independent

RENFREWSHIRE

GOOD SHEPHERD CENTRE
Greenock Road, Bishopton,
Renfrewshire PA7 5PF
Tel: (01505) 862814
Head: Mr F McCann
Type: Girls Boarding and Day 12–16
No of pupils: 60 *No of Boarders:* F30
Special Needs: **EBD** MLD
Independent
52-week care

KIBBLE SCHOOL
Goudie Street, Paisley, Renfrewshire
PA3 2LG
Tel: (0141) 889 0044
Head: Mr G Bell
Type: Boys Boarding and Day 12–17
No of pupils: 90 *No of Boarders:* F50
Special Needs: **EBD MLD** PMLD
SP&LD SPLD
Independent

STIRLING

BALLIKINRAIN RESIDENTIAL SCHOOL
Fintry Road, Balfron-by-Glasgow,
Stirling G63 0LL
Tel: (01360) 440244
Head: Mr C McKnott
Type: Boys Boarding and Day 8–16
No of pupils: 50 *No of Boarders:* F50
Special Needs: **EBD**
Independent

BARNARDO'S LECROPT PROJECT
Henderson Street, Bridge of Allan,
Stirling FK9 4NB
Tel: (01786) 834498
Head: Mr H Jones
Type: Co-educational Day 6–12
No of pupils: 18
Special Needs: **ADHD EBD** SP&LD
SPLD W
Independent

SNOWDON SCHOOL
31 Spittal Street, Stirling FK8 1DU
Tel: (01786) 464746
Head: Mr G Matthews
Type: Girls Boarding 12+
No of pupils: 18 *No of Boarders:* F18
Special Needs: **EBD** W
Independent
52-week care

STRATHCLYDE

CORSEFORD SCHOOL
Howwood Road, Milliken Park,
Kilbarchan, Strathclyde PA10 2NT
Tel: (01505) 702141
Head: Mrs M Boyle
Type: Co-educational Day and
Boarding 0–19
No of pupils: 50
No of Boarders: F9 W21
Special Needs: **PH**
Independent

WALES

CARDIFF

CRAIG-Y-PARC SCHOOL*
Pentyrch, Cardiff CF15 9NB
Tel: (029) 2089 0397
Head: Mr N Harvey
Type: Co-educational Boarding and
Day 3–19
No of pupils: 55 *No of Boarders:* F6 W7
Special Needs: CP **PH PMLD**
SP&LD W
Independent

GWYNEDD

ARAN HALL SCHOOL*
Rhydymain, Dolgellau, Gwynedd
LL40 2AR
Tel: (01341) 450641
Head: Mr M Ferguson
Type: Co-educational Boarding 11–19
No of pupils: B19 G6
No of Boarders: F25
Special Needs: ADD ADHD **ASP AUT**
EPI SLD
Independent
52-week care

PEMBROKESHIRE

PORTFIELD SCHOOL
Portfield, Haverfordwest,
Pembrokeshire SA61 1BS
Tel: (01437) 762701
Head: Mr P Brayshaw
Type: Co-educational Day 2–19
No of pupils: B39 G24
Special Needs: AUT CP EPI **PMLD**
SLD SP&LD VIS W
Approved Independent

POWYS

**MACINTYRE SCHOOL
WOMASTON***
Womaston House, Walton,
Presteigne, Powys LD8 2PT
Tel: (01544) 230308
Head: Mr M J Bertulis
Type: Co-educational Boarding 11–19
No of pupils: B13 G3
No of Boarders: F16
Special Needs: AUT MLD PMLD SLD
Approved Independent
52-week care

VALE OF GLAMORGAN

**NCH ACTION FOR
CHILDREN***
Headlands School, 2 St Augustines
Road, Penarth, Vale of Glamorgan
CF64 1YY
Tel: (029) 2070 9771
Head: Mr D Haswell
Type: Co-educational Boarding and
Day 11–16
No of pupils: 32 *No of Boarders:* F26
Special Needs: ADD ADHD ASP AUT
DYC DYP DYS EBD EPI MLD SPLD
TOU
Independent

2.2
Directory of Colleges and Other Provision at 16+

ENGLAND

BRISTOL

CINTRE COMMUNITY
54 St John's Road, Clifton, Bristol
BS8 2HG
Tel: (0117) 973 8546
Head: Ms C Twine
Type: Mixed Residential 16–35
No of pupils: B14 G7
No of Boarders: F13
Special Needs: AUT DOW DYS EBD
EPI MLD
Independent

CAMBRIDGESHIRE

THE PAPWORTH TRUST
Papworth Everard, Cambridge,
CB3 8RG
Tel: (01480) 830341
Head: Mr J Skipp
Type: Mixed Residential 19+
No of pupils: 50 *No of Boarders:* F40
Special Needs: CP DOW **EPI** HI **MLD**
PH W
52-week care

SENSE EAST
72 Church Street, Market Deeping,
Peterborough, Cambridgeshire
PE6 8AL
Tel: (01778) 344921
Head: Mrs J McNeill
Type: Mixed Residential 16+
No of pupils: B47 G39
No of Boarders: F86
Special Needs: CP EBD EPI **HI** MLD
PH **SLD VIS** W
52-week care

CHESHIRE

BRIDGE COLLEGE
Curzon Road, Offerton, Stockport,
Cheshire SK2 5DG
Tel: (0161) 487 4293
Head: Mrs S Preece
Type: Mixed Day
No of pupils: B46 G10
Special Needs: PH PMLD SLD

CORNWALL

PEREDUR TRUST
Altarnun, Launceston, Cornwall
PL15 7RF
Tel: (01566) 86575
Head: Mr S W Rudel and Mrs J Rudel
Type: Male Residential 19+
No of pupils: 11 *No of Boarders:* F11
Special Needs: AUT EBD

CUMBRIA

**LINDETH COLLEGE OF
FURTHER EDUCATION***
The Oaks, Lindeth, Bowness-on-
Windermere, Cumbria LA23 3NH
Tel: (01539) 446265
Head: Mrs N S Buckley
Type: Mixed Residential 16–25
No of pupils: 44 *No of Boarders:* F44
Special Needs: ADD ADHD ASP AUT
DOW DYS EPI HI **MLD** SP&LD
SPLD

DERBYSHIRE

**DERBY COLLEGE FOR DEAF
PEOPLE**
Ashbourne Road, Derby, Derbyshire
DE22 3BH
Tel: (01332) 297550
Head: Mr A Hendy
Type: Mixed Residential 16–25
No of pupils: B60 G40
No of Boarders: F94
Special Needs: **HI** MLD PH SLD SPLD
VIS W
Non-Maintained

GREEN LAUND F.E. CENTRE
The Grange, Hospital Lane,
Mickleover, Derby DE3 5DR
Tel: (01332) 512855
Head: Mrs V Parkes
Type: Mixed Residential 19+
No of pupils: 7 *No of Boarders:* F7
Special Needs: ASP AUT **MLD SLD
SP&LD** SPLD
Independent
52-week care

DEVON

EXETER COLLEGE
Hele Road, Exeter, Devon EX4 4JS
Tel: (01392) 205443
Head: Ms B Jansson
Type: Mixed Day 16+
No of pupils: 130
Special Needs: ADD ADHD ASP AUT
CP DOW DYC DYP DYS EBD EPI HI
MLD SLD SP&LD SPLD VIS W

OAKWOOD COURT
7–9 Oak Park Villas, Dawlish, Devon
EX7 0DE
Tel: (01626) 864066
Head: Mr J F Loft
Type: Mixed Residential 16–25
No of pupils: 30 *No of Boarders:* F30
Special Needs: ADHD ASP AUT CP
DOW DYP DYS EBD EPI MLD SLD
SP&LD SPLD TOU W
Independent
52-week care

RNIB MANOR HOUSE
Middle Lincombe Road, Torquay,
Devon TQ1 2NG
Tel: (01803) 214523
Head: Mrs J Read
Type: Mixed Residential and Day 16+
No of pupils: 25
Special Needs: PH VIS W

ROYAL SCHOOL FOR THE DEAF
Further Education College, 50
Topsham Road, Exeter, Devon
EX2 4NF
Tel: (01392) 215179
Head: Mr J F Shaw
Type: Mixed 16+
No of pupils: B18 G21
No of Boarders: F31
Special Needs: HI
Non-Maintained

ST LOYE'S COLLEGE
Fairfield House, Topsham Road,
Exeter, Devon EX2 6EP
Tel: (01392) 255428
Head: Miss M Peat
Type: Mixed Residential 18–63
No of pupils: 250 *No of Boarders:* F210
Special Needs: ASP DYS EPI HI PH
VIS W

THE WEST OF ENGLAND COLLEGE FOR STUDENTS WITH LITTLE OR NO SIGHT
Countess Wear, Exeter, Devon
EX2 6HA
Tel: (01392) 454245
Head: Mr R Ellis
Type: Mixed Residential and
Day 16–22
No of pupils: B20 G25
No of Boarders: W45
Special Needs: VIS
Non-Maintained

DORSET

FORTUNE CENTRE OF RIDING THERAPY
Avon Tyrrell, Bransgore,
Christchurch, Dorset BH23 8EE
Tel: (01425) 673297
Head: Mrs J Dixon-Clegg
Type: Mixed Residential 16–25
No of pupils: B15 G16
No of Boarders: F31
Special Needs: ADD ASP AUT CP
DOW DYC DYP DYS EBD EPI HI
MLD SLD SP&LD SPLD VIS
Independent

IVERS
Hains Lane, Marnhull, Sturminster
Newton, Dorset DT10 1JU
Tel: (01258) 820164
Head: Ms L Mathews
Type: Mixed Residential 16–25
No of pupils: 20 *No of Boarders:* F20
Special Needs: ASP AUT CP DOW
EBD EPI MLD SP&LD
Independent
52-week care

COUNTY DURHAM

FINCHALE TRAINING COLLEGE*
Durham, County Durham DH1 5RX
Tel: (0191) 386 2634
Head: Dr D T Etheridge
Type: Mixed Residential 18–63
No of pupils: 180 *No of Boarders:* F120
Special Needs: ADD ADHD ASP CP
DEL DYP DYS EPI HI MLD PH VIS W
Independent

GLOUCESTERSHIRE

**THE NATIONAL STAR
CENTRE'S COLLEGE OF
FURTHER EDUCATION**
Ullenwood Manor, Cheltenham,
Gloucestershire GL53 9QU
Tel: (01242) 527631
Head: Mrs H Sexton
Type: Mixed Residential and
Day 16–25
No of pupils: B79 G79
No of Boarders: F148
Special Needs: ASP **CP** DEL DYP EPI
PH PMLD SP&LD VIS **W**
Independent

STROUD COURT
Longfords, Minchinhampton,
Stroud, Gloucestershire GL6 9AN
Tel: (01453) 834020
Head: Mr C Atkins
Type: Mixed Residential and Day 19+
No of pupils: 37 *No of Boarders:* F37
Special Needs: AUT EBD EPI MLD
SLD SP&LD W

SOUTH GLOUCESTERSHIRE

THE HATCH
Camphill Community, St John's
House, Kington Lane, Thornbury,
South Gloucestershire BS35 1NA
Tel: (01454) 413010
Type: Mixed Residential 19–32
No of pupils: B12 G12
No of Boarders: F24
Special Needs: MLD SLD

HAMPSHIRE

ENHAM
Enham Alamein, Andover,
Hampshire SP11 6JS
Tel: (01264) 345800
Head: Mr D Fullerton and
Mr B Langfield
Type: Mixed Residential and Day 18+
Special Needs: DYS MLD PH W

**MINSTEAD TRAINING
PROJECT**
Minstead Lodge, Lyndhurst,
Minstead, Hampshire S043 7FU
Tel: (023) 8081 2254
Head: Mr M Lenaerts
Type: Mixed Residential and Day
18–30 (residential from 18)
No of pupils: B43 G6
No of Boarders: F14
Special Needs: ADD ASP **DOW MLD**
Independent

**YATELEY INDUSTRIES FOR
THE DISABLED LTD**
Mill Lane, Yateley, Hampshire
GU46 7TF
Tel: (01252) 872337
Head: Mrs L Robinson
Type: Mixed Residential and Day 18+
No of pupils: B26 G26
No of Boarders: F30
Special Needs: ADD ADHD ASP AUT
CP DOW DYP DYS EPI HI MLD PH
SP&LD SPLD W

HEREFORDSHIRE

**ROYAL NATIONAL COLLEGE
FOR THE BLIND**
College Road, Hereford,
Herefordshire HR1 1EB
Tel: (01432) 265725
Head: Mrs R Burge
Type: Mixed Residential and
Day 16–56
No of pupils: 200
Special Needs: DYS HI SPLD **VIS** W
Independent

HERTFORDSHIRE

DELROW COLLEGE
Hilfield Lane, Aldenham, Watford,
Hertfordshire WD25 8DJ
Tel: (01923) 856006
Head: Ms L Has
Type: Mixed Residential 20–65
No of pupils: 50
Special Needs: AUT CP HI **MLD**
Independent

KENT

**DORTON COLLEGE OF
FURTHER EDUCATION**
Seal Drive, Seal, Sevenoaks, Kent
TN15 0AH
Tel: (01732) 592602
Head: Mr M D Morris
Type: Mixed Residential and Day 16+
No of pupils: 65
Special Needs: MLD **VIS**
Independent

**NASH COLLEGE OF
FURTHER EDUCATION**
Croydon Road, Hayes, Bromley, Kent
BR2 7AG
Tel: (020) 8462 7419
Head: Mrs A Flynn
Type: Mixed Residential and Day 16+
No of pupils: B41 G37
No of Boarders: F48
Special Needs: CP DOW DYP EPI
MLD PH PMLD SLD SPLD VIS W

**WESTGATE COLLEGE FOR
DEAF PEOPLE***
Westcliff House, 37 Sea Road,
Westgate, Kent CT8 8QP
Tel: (01843) 836300
Head: Ms G Wills
Type: Mixed Residential and Day 16+
No of pupils: 70 *No of Boarders:* F70
Special Needs: ADD ASP AUT CP DEL
DOW DYC DYS DYP EBD EPI HI
MLD PH PMLD SLD SP&LD SPLD
VIS
Non-Maintained

LANCASHIRE

BEAUMONT COLLEGE OF FURTHER EDUCATION
Slyne Road, Lancaster, Lancashire
LA2 6AP
Tel: (01524) 541400
Head: Mr S Briggs
Type: Mixed Residential 16–25
No of pupils: B27 G50
No of Boarders: F77
Special Needs: CP EPI MLD PH SLD
SP&LD
Independent

LEICESTERSHIRE

HOMEFIELD RESIDENTIAL COLLEGE
42 St Mary's Road, Sileby,
Loughborough, Leicestershire
LE12 7TL
Tel: (01509) 814827
Head: Mr K O'Brien
Type: Mixed Residential and Day 16+
No of pupils: 32 *No of Boarders:* W30
Special Needs: AUT HI MLD SLD
Independent

RNIB VOCATIONAL COLLEGE*
Radmoor Road, Loughborough,
Leicestershire LE11 3BS
Tel: (01509) 611077
Head: Mr K Connell
Type: Mixed Residential and
Day 16–60
No of pupils: 80 *No of Boarders:* F74
Special Needs: DYC DYS EPI HI MLD
PH VIS W
Independent
52-week care

LINCOLNSHIRE

BROUGHTON HOUSE COLLEGE
Brant, Broughton, Lincolnshire
LN5 0SL
Tel: (01400) 272929
Head: Mr R Noble
Type: Mixed Residential 16–25
No of pupils: B15 G8
Special Needs: AUT SLD
52-week care

LINKAGE FURTHER EDUCATION COLLEGE
Toynton All Saints, Spilsby,
Lincolnshire PE23 5AE
Tel: (01790) 752499
Head: Mrs J Blakeley
Type: Mixed Residential 16–26
No of pupils: 216 *No of Boarders:* F216
Special Needs: ADD ADHD ASP AUT
CP DEL **DOW** DYP DYS EPI HI **MLD**
PH SLD **SP&LD** SPLD TOU VIS W
Independent

NORTH EAST LINCOLNSHIRE

WEELSBY HALL FURTHER EDUCATION COLLEGE
Weelsby Road, Grimsby, North East
Lincolnshire DN32 9RU
Tel: (01472) 361334
Head: Mrs G Gillings
Type: Mixed Residential 16+
No of pupils: B60 G40
No of Boarders: F100
Special Needs: ADHD ASP **AUT** CP
DEL **DOW** DYP DYS EPI HI MLD
SLD SP&LD SPLD
Independent

LONDON

LOVE WALK
10 Love Walk, Denmark Hill,
London SE5 8AE
Tel: (020) 7703 3632
Head: Mr P Baker
Type: Mixed Residential 16+
No of pupils: 22
No of Boarders: F22
Special Needs: PH

GREATER MANCHESTER

FOURWAYS ASSESSMENT UNIT
Cleworth Hall Lane, off Manchester
Lane, Tyldesley, Greater Manchester
M29 8NT
Tel: (01942) 870841
Head: Mr I Earnshaw
Type: Mixed Residential 18–65
No of pupils: 30
No of Boarders: F15 W15
Special Needs: CP PH

MERSEYSIDE

ARDEN COLLEGE*
40 Derby Road, Southport,
Merseyside PR9 0TZ
Tel: (01704) 534433
Head: Mr C Mayho
Type: Co-educational Boarding and
Day 16–25
Special Needs: ADD ADHD ASP AUT
DOW DYS EBD EPI HI MLD SPLD
SP&LD SLD
Independent

NORTHAMPTONSHIRE

**HINWICK HALL COLLEGE OF
FURTHER EDUCATION**
Hinwick, Wellingborough,
Northamptonshire NN29 7JD
Tel: (01933) 312470
Head: Mr E E Sinnott
Type: Mixed Residential and
Day 16–25
No of pupils: B29 G20
No of Boarders: F45
Special Needs: CP DOW EPI HI MLD
PH SLD SP&LD SPLD W
Independent
52-week care

SOLDEN HILL HOUSE
Banbury Road, Byfield, Daventry,
Northamptonshire NN11 6UA
Tel: (01327) 260234
Head: Ms A O'Hare
Type: Mixed Residential 19+
No of pupils: 30
No of Boarders: F30
Special Needs: **MLD**

NORTHUMBERLAND

**DILSTON COLLEGE OF
FURTHER EDUCATION**
Dilston Hall, Corbridge,
Northumberland NE45 5RJ
Tel: (01434) 632692
Head: Mr J A Jameson
Type: Mixed Residential and
Day 16–25
No of pupils: 60 *No of Boarders:* F50
Special Needs: ASP AUT DOW EPI HI
MLD SLD SP&LD SPLD
Independent

NOTTINGHAMSHIRE

PORTLAND COLLEGE*
Nottingham Road, Mansfield,
Nottinghamshire NG18 4TJ
Tel: (01623) 499111
Head: Mr M E A Syms
Type: Mixed Residential and
Day 16–25
No of pupils: 170
Special Needs: CP DYC DYP DYS EPI
HI MLD PH SP&LD W
Approved Independent

SHROPSHIRE

DERWEN COLLEGE
Oswestry, Shropshire SY11 3JA
Tel: (01691) 661234
Head: Mr D J Kendall
Type: Mixed Residential 16+
No of pupils: B111 G112
No of Boarders: F223
Special Needs: ASP CP DOW DYS EPI
HI MLD PH SLD SP&LD VIS W
Independent

**LOPPINGTON HOUSE
FURTHER EDUCATION &
ADULT CENTRE**
Loppington, Wem, Shropshire
SY4 5NF
Tel: (01939) 233926
Head: Mr P Harris
Type: Mixed Residential 16–25
No of pupils: B33 G10
No of Boarders: F43
Special Needs: AUT CP DOW EBD
EPI HI MLD SLD SP&LD SPLD VIS
52-week care

SOMERSET

LUFTON MANOR COLLEGE
Yeovil, Somerset BA22 8ST
Tel: (01935) 403120
Head: Mr R Elliott
Type: Mixed Residential 16–25
No of pupils: B37 G37
No of Boarders: F74
Special Needs: MLD PMLD SLD
Independent

NORTH EAST SOMERSET

RNID POOLEMEAD
Watery Lane, Twerton on Avon,
Bath, North East Somerset BA2 1RN
Tel: (01225) 332818
Head: Mr C Crowley
Type: Mixed Residential 18+
No of pupils: B18 G14
No of Boarders: F32
Special Needs: **HI** PH SP&LD VIS W
52-week care

STAFFORDSHIRE

STRATHMORE COLLEGE
High Cross, 107 Trewham Road,
Dresden, Stoke on Trent,
Staffordshire ST3 4EG
Tel: (01782) 333366
Head: Ms K Smith & Mr V A Heath
Type: Mixed Residential and Day 16+
No of pupils: 45 *No of Boarders:* F45
Special Needs: ASP **AUT** DOW EBD
EPI **MLD SLD** SPLD
Independent
52-week care

SURREY

**BANSTEAD PLACE BRAIN
INJURY REHABILITATION**
Brain Injury Centre, Park Road,
Banstead, Surrey SM7 3EE
Tel: (01737) 356222
Head: Ms E Jackman
Type: Mixed Residential 16–35
No of pupils: 28
Special Needs: EBD EPI MLD PH
SP&LD SPLD VIS W
Independent

**THE GRANGE CENTRE FOR
PEOPLE WITH DISABILITIES**
Rectory Lane, Bookham, Surrey
KT23 4DZ
Tel: (01372) 452608
Head: Mr P H Wood
Type: Mixed Residential and Day 19+
No of pupils: 48 *No of Boarders:* F48
Special Needs: CP DYS EPI HI MLD
PH W
Independent

**QUEEN ELIZABETH'S
TRAINING COLLEGE**
Leatherhead, Surrey KT22 0BN
Tel: (01372) 841100
Type: Mixed Residential and
Day 18–63
No of pupils: 205
Special Needs: CP DYS EBD EPI HI
MLD PH SPLD VIS W
52-week care

RNIB REDHILL COLLEGE*
Philanthropic Road, Redhill, Surrey
RH1 4DG
Tel: (01737) 768935
Head: Mrs J Foot
Type: Mixed Residential and
Day 16–60
No of pupils: B50 G50
No of Boarders: F90
Special Needs: ASP **AUT** CP DOW
DYS EBD EPI HI MLD PH **SLD VIS** W
Independent
52-week care

**SEEABILITY (FORMERLY
ROYAL SCHOOL FOR THE
BLIND)**
SeeABILITY House, Hook Road,
Epsom, Surrey KT19 8SQ
Tel: (01372) 755000
Head: Mr R M Perkins
Type: Mixed Residential and Day 18+
No of pupils: 200 *No of Boarders:* F150
Special Needs: CP EBD EPI HI MLD
PH PMLD SLD **VIS** W
Independent

EAST SUSSEX

THE MOUNT CAMPHILL COMMUNITY
Wadhurst, East Sussex TN5 6PT
Tel: (01892) 782025
Head: Mrs C Hart and Mrs G Brand
Type: Mixed Residential 16–25
No of pupils: 35
Special Needs: ASP AUT DOW EBD MLD

WEST MIDLANDS

HEREWARD COLLEGE
Bramston Crescent, Tile Hill Lane,
Coventry, West Midlands CV4 9SW
Tel: (024) 7646 1231
Head: Ms C Cole
Type: Mixed Residential and Day 16+
No of pupils: B200 G200
No of Boarders: F106
Special Needs: **ASP** CP DEL DOW
DYC DYP DYS EPI HI **MLD PH** SLD
SP&LD SPLD TOU VIS

QUEEN ALEXANDRA COLLEGE OF FURTHER EDUCATION
Court Oak Road, Harborne,
Birmingham, West Midlands
B17 9TG
Tel: (0121) 428 5050
Head: Ms S Wright
Type: Mixed Residential and
Day 16–63
No of pupils: B80 G40
No of Boarders: F100
Special Needs: **ASP** CP EPI HI MLD
PH VIS W
Independent

WILTSHIRE

FAIRFIELD OPPORTUNITY FARM
Dilton Marsh, Westbury, Wiltshire
BA13 4DL
Tel: (01373) 823028
Head: Ms J Kenward
Type: Mixed Residential and
Day 16–30
No of pupils: 27 *No of Boarders:* F25
Special Needs: ASP AUT DOW DYP
EPI HI MLD SLD SP&LD SPLD
Independent

NORTH YORKSHIRE

HENSHAW'S COLLEGE
Bogs Lane, Harrogate,
North Yorkshire HG1 4ED
Tel: (01423) 814508
Head: Mrs J Cole
Type: Mixed Residential 16+
No of pupils: B33 G32
No of Boarders: F65
Special Needs: ASP AUT CP DOW EPI
HI **MLD** PH **SLD VIS**

SOUTH YORKSHIRE

**DONCASTER COLLEGE FOR
THE DEAF**
Leger Way, Doncaster,
South Yorkshire DN2 6AY
Tel: (01302) 386710
Type: Mixed Residential and
Day 16–63
No of pupils: B101 G52
No of Boarders: F120
Special Needs: ASP CP DYP DYS **EBD**
HI MLD PH **SP&LD** SPLD VIS W
52-week care

HESLEY VILLAGE COLLEGE
Tickhill, Doncaster, South Yorkshire
DN11 9HH
Tel: (01302) 868313
Head: Mrs S Ekins
Type: Mixed Residential 16–25
No of pupils: B19 G3
No of Boarders: F22
Special Needs: AUT SLD
Approved Independent
52-week care

WEST YORKSHIRE

**PENNINE CAMPHILL
COMMUNITY**
Boyne Hill House, Chapelthorpe,
Wakefield, West Yorkshire WF4 3JH
Tel: (01924) 255281
Head: Mr S Hopewell
Type: Mixed Residential and
Day 16–25
No of pupils: B20 G18
No of Boarders: F38
Special Needs: AUT CP DEL DYS EBD
EPI HI MLD SLD SP&LD SPLD VIS
Independent

SCOTLAND

ABERDEENSHIRE

**EASTER AUGUSTON
TRAINING FARM**
Peterculter, Aberdeen AB14 0PJ
Tel: (01224) 733627
Head: Mr G Phillips
Type: Mixed Residential 16+
No of pupils: 18 *No of Boarders:* F16
Special Needs: **DOW MLD** SP&LD
Independent
52-week care

FIFE

RNIB ALWYN HOUSE
Alwyn House, 3 Wemysshall Road,
Ceres, Fife KY15 5LX
Tel: (01334) 828894
Head: Mr J Duncan
Type: Mixed Residential and
Day 16–65
No of pupils: 16
Special Needs: CP EBD **VIS**

STIRLING

**CAMPHILL BLAIR
DRUMMOND TRUST**
Blair Drummond House, Cuthil
Brae, Stirling FK9 4UT
Tel: (01786) 841573
Head: Mr G Allen
Type: Mixed Residential and
Day 16–30
No of pupils: 37 *No of Boarders:* F29
Special Needs: **AUT DOW** EBD EPI HI
MLD PMLD **SLD** SP&LD SPLD
52-week care

WALES

BRIDGEND

BRIDGEND COLLEGE*
Cowbridge Road, Bridgend
CF31 3DH
Tel: (01656) 302302
Head: Mr R Hampton
Type: Mixed Residential 16–25 (day age 16–40)
No of pupils: 23
Special Needs: DYS HI SPLD VIS

CARMARTHENSHIRE

COLEG ELIDYR*
Rhandirmwyn and Llangadog,
Llandovery, Carmarthenshire
SA20 0NL
Tel: (01550) 760400
Type: Mixed Residential 18+
No of pupils: B35 G30
No of Boarders: F65 W65
Special Needs: ADD ADHD ASP AUT
EBD EPI MLD **SLD**
Non-Maintained

CONWY

FURZE MOUNT
Copthorne Road, Upper Colwyn Bay,
Conwy LL28 5YP
Tel: (01492) 532679
Head: Miss S Edwards
Type: Mixed Residential 18+
No of pupils: 19 *No of Boarders:* W19
Special Needs: CP EPI PH W
Independent

DENBIGHSHIRE

PENGWERN COLLEGE
Rhuddlan, Denbighshire LL18 5UH
Tel: (01745) 590281
Head: Mr M Booker
Type: Mixed Residential 16–25
No of pupils: 52 *No of Boarders:* F52
Special Needs: AUT CP DOW EPI
MLD PMLD SLD SP&LD W
Independent

GWYNEDD

BRYN MELYN GROUP
Llandderfel, Bala, Gwynedd
LL23 7RA
Tel: (01678) 530330
Head: Mrs S Hamilton
Type: Mixed Residential 12–19
No of pupils: 18 *No of Boarders:* F18
Special Needs: ADD DYP EBD EPI
MLD

CERRIG CAMU
Old Barmouth Road, Dolgellau,
Gwynedd LL40 2SP
Tel: (01341) 423075
Head: Mrs N McGrail
Type: Mixed Residential 18+
No of pupils: 21 *No of Boarders:* F21
Special Needs: EBD MLD PH SLD
52-week care

2.3
Index of State Maintained Schools by Education Authority

State maintained schools are listed by Local Education Authority. Since 1996 a number of new unitary authorities have been created in addition to existing two-tier structures. The index below (for England) lists each local authority under the county of which it is deemed a part, and is designed to help you identify the local authorities responsible for schools in your area. Turn to the page number shown against each to find the schools within the authority. Schools in Northern Ireland, Scotland and Wales are listed by Local Education Authority only.

ENGLAND

NORTHERN IRELAND

SCOTLAND

WALES

2.4
Directory of State Maintained Schools by Education Authority

ENGLAND

BEDFORDSHIRE

Bedfordshire Education Authority

County Hall
Cauldwell Street
Bedford MK42 9AP
Tel: (01234) 363222

GLENWOOD SCHOOL
Beech Road, Dunstable,
Bedfordshire LU6 3LY
Tel: (01582) 667106
Head: Mrs S Crosbie
Type: Co-educational Day 2–11
No of pupils: 132
Special Needs: **AUT** DOW **PMLD SLD** W

GRANGE SCHOOL
Halsey Road, Kempston,
Bedfordshire MK42 8AU
Tel: (01234) 407100
Head: Mrs E Zapiec
Type: Co-educational Day 5–16
Special Needs: **AUT MLD**

HILLCREST SCHOOL
Ridgeway Avenue, Dunstable,
Bedfordshire LU5 4QL
Tel: (01582) 661983
Head: Mr P Skingley
Type: Co-educational Day 11–19
No of pupils: 89
Special Needs: **AUT PMLD SLD** W

OAK BANK SCHOOL
Sandy Lane, Leighton Buzzard,
Bedfordshire LU7 8BE
Tel: (01525) 374559
Head: Ms B Hales
Type: Boys Boarding 11–16
No of pupils: 40 *No of Boarders:* W24
Special Needs: **EBD**

RAINBOW SCHOOL
Chestnut Avenue, Bromham,
Bedford, Bedfordshire MK43 8HP
Tel: (01234) 822596
Head: Mrs J Mason
Type: Co-educational Day 2–19
No of pupils: 70
Special Needs: **AUT PMLD** SLD W

RIDGEWAY SCHOOL
Hill Rise, Kempston, Bedford,
Bedfordshire MK42 7EB
Tel: (01234) 402402
Head: Mr G Allard
Type: Co-educational Day 2–19
No of pupils: B46 G24
Special Needs: **PH** VIS

ST JOHNS SCHOOL
Austin Canons, Kempston, Bedford,
Bedfordshire MK42 8AA
Tel: (01234) 345565
Head: Mr R Babbage
Type: Co-educational Day 2–19
No of pupils: 130
Special Needs: **PMLD SLD** W

SUNNYSIDE SCHOOL
The Baulk, Biggleswade,
Bedfordshire SG18 0PT
Tel: (01767) 222662
Head: Mrs V G White
Type: Co-educational Day 2–19
No of pupils: B43 G19
Special Needs: **AUT PMLD SLD** W

WEATHERFIELD SCHOOL
Brewers Hill Road, Dunstable,
Bedfordshire LU6 1AF
Tel: (01582) 605632
Head: Mr C F Peters
Type: Co-educational Day
No of pupils: B82 G63
Special Needs: **MLD**

Luton Education Authority

Unity House
111 Stuart Street
Luton LU1 5NP
Tel: (01582) 548001

FIVE SPRINGS SCHOOL
Northwell Drive, Luton,
Bedfordshire LU3 3SP
Tel: (01582) 572880
Head: Mrs H Hardie
Type: Co-educational Day 11–19
No of pupils: 152
Special Needs: **ASP** AUT **MLD PMLD SLD**

LADY ZIA WERNER SCHOOL
Ashcroft Road, Luton, Bedfordshire
LU2 9AY
Tel: (01582) 28705
Head: Mrs J Jackson
Type: Co-educational Day 2–11
No of pupils: B41 G29
Special Needs: CP **DEL** DOW **PH PMLD** W

RICHMOND HILL SCHOOL
Sunridge Avenue, Luton,
Bedfordshire LU2 7JL
Tel: (01582) 721019
Head: Mr M W Love
Type: Co-educational Day 5–11
No of pupils: 105
Special Needs: **AUT PMLD SLD**

BERKSHIRE

Bracknell Forest Borough Council

Edward Elgar House
Skimped Hill Lane
Bracknell
Berkshire RG12 1LY
Tel: (01344) 354000

KENNEL LANE SCHOOL
Kennel Lane, Bracknell, Berkshire
RG42 2EX
Tel: (01344) 483872
Head: Ms J Calcroft
Type: Co-educational Day 2–19
No of pupils: 155
Special Needs: AUT MLD PMLD
SLD W

Reading Borough Council

PO Box 2623
Civic Centre
Reading RG1 7WA
Tel: (0118) 939 0923

THE AVENUE SCHOOL
Basingstoke Road, Reading,
Berkshire RG2 0EN
Tel: (0118) 901 5554
Head: Mrs V Brown
Type: Co-educational Day 2–19
No of pupils: 170
Special Needs: CP DEL EBD EPI MLD
PH PMLD SP&LD VIS W

READING ALTERNATIVE SCHOOL
40 Christchurch Road, Reading,
Berkshire RG2 7AY
Tel: (01734) 752095
Head: Ms J Kightley
Type: Co-educational Day 11–16
No of pupils: 84
Special Needs: EBD SPLD W

Slough Borough Council

Education Department
Town Hall
Bath Road
Slough SL1 3UQ
Tel: (01753) 522288

ARBOUR VALE SCHOOL
Stoke Road, Slough, Berkshire
SL2 5AY
Tel: (01753) 525291
Head: Mr J Mansfield
Type: Co-educational Day 2–19
No of pupils: 290
Special Needs: **AUT** EPI HI **MLD**
PMLD SLD SP&LD SPLD VIS W

CIPPENHAM MIDDLE SCHOOL
Elmshott Lane, Slough, Berkshire
SL1 5RB
Tel: (01628) 604665
Head: Mrs J Tidey
Type: Co-educational

LITTLEDOWN SCHOOL
Littledown Road, Slough, Berkshire
SL1 3QL
Tel: (01753) 521734
Head: Mrs V Goodwin
Type: Co-educational

WESTGATE SCHOOL
Cippenham Lane, Slough, Berkshire
SL1 5AH
Tel: (01628) 521320
Type: Co-educational Day
No of pupils: 650
Special Needs: DYS PH

West Berkshire Council

Education Offices
Avonbank House
West Street
Newbury
Berkshire RG14 1BZ
Tel: (01635) 42400

BROOKFIELDS SCHOOL
Sage Road, Tilehurst, Reading,
Berkshire RG31 6SW
Tel: (0118) 942 1382
Head: Mr J Byrne
Type: Co-educational Day
No of pupils: B148 G73
Special Needs: AUT **MLD PMLD**
SLD W

THE CASTLE SCHOOL
Love Lane, Donnington, Newbury,
Berkshire RG14 2JG
Tel: (01635) 42976
Head: Mrs K Gray
Type: Co-educational Day 2–19
No of pupils: 150
Special Needs: AUT **MLD PMLD** SLD

Windsor & Maidenhead Education Authority

Town Hall
St Ives Road
Maidenhead
Berkshire SL6 1RF
Tel: (01628) 798888

HOLYPORT MANOR SCHOOL
Ascot Road, Holyport, Maidenhead,
Berkshire SL6 3LE
Tel: (01628) 623196
Head: Mr P Donkersloot
Type: Co-educational Day and
Boarding 2–16
No of pupils: B134 G66
No of Boarders: W17
Special Needs: AUT CP EPI HI MLD
PH PMLD SLD SP&LD

Wokingham District Council

Education Department
PO Box 156
Shute End
Wokingham RG40 1WN
Tel: (0118) 974 6100

SOUTHFIELD SCHOOL
Gipsy Lane, Wokingham, Berkshire
RG40 2AR
Tel: (0118) 977 1293
Head: Mr K Bennett
Type: Co-educational 11–16
No of pupils: B69 *No of Boarders:* W20
Special Needs: EBD

BRISTOL

Bristol Education Authority

PO Box 57
Council House
College Green
Bristol BS99 7EB
Tel: (0117) 903 7961

BRIARWOOD SCHOOL
Briar Way, Fishponds, Bristol
BS16 4EA
Tel: (0117) 965 7536
Head: Mr D Hussey
Type: Co-educational Day 2–19
No of pupils: B44 G38
Special Needs: AUT PMLD SLD W

CLAREMONT SCHOOL
Henleaze Park, Henleaze, Bristol
BS9 4LR
Tel: (0117) 924 7527
Head: Mr B Coburn
Type: Co-educational Day 2–11
No of pupils: 94
Special Needs: PH PMLD SLD W

ELMFIELD SCHOOL
Greystoke Avenue, Westbury-on-
Trym, Bristol BS10 6AY
Tel: (0117) 903 0366
Head: Ms R Way
Type: Co-educational Day 3–16
No of pupils: 56
Special Needs: HI W

FLORENCE BROWN SCHOOL
Leinster Avenue, Knowle, Bristol
BS4 1NN
Tel: (0117) 966 8152
Head: Mr P Evans
Type: Co-educational Day 5–16
No of pupils: 200
Special Needs: EBD MLD PH
SP&LD W

KINGSDON MANOR SCHOOL
Kingsdon, Somerton, Somerset
TA11 3JZ
Tel: (01935) 840323
Head: Mr J Holliday
Type: Boys Boarding 10–16
No of pupils: 50
Special Needs: EBD MLD

KINGSWESTON SCHOOL
Napier Miles Road, Avonmouth,
Bristol BS11 0UT
Tel: (0117) 903 0400
Head: Mr D Capel
Type: Co-educational Day 3–19
No of pupils: B125 G65
Special Needs: ASP AUT MLD SLD

NEW FOSSEWAY SCHOOL
New Fosseway Road, Hengrove,
Bristol BS14 9LN
Tel: (01275) 839411
Head: Mr J Hiscox
Type: Co-educational Day 3–19
No of pupils: B52 G35
Special Needs: PMLD SLD W

NOTTON HOUSE
28 Notton, Lacock, Nr Chippenham,
Wiltshire SN15 2NP
Tel: (01249) 730407
Head: Mr G M Gamble
Type: Boys Boarding 9–16
No of pupils: 55 *No of Boarders:* F55
Special Needs: EBD

WARMLEY PARK SCHOOL
Tower Road North, Warmley, Bristol
BS15 2XL
Tel: (0117) 967 3422
Head: Mr S Morris
Type: Co-educational Day 2–19
No of pupils: 77

WOODSTOCK SCHOOL
Courtney Road, Kingswood, Bristol
BS15 9RL
Tel: (0117) 967 1832
Head: Mr G Parsons
Type: Co-educational Day 7–11
No of pupils: B54
Special Needs: EBD

BUCKINGHAMSHIRE

Buckinghamshire Education Authority

County Hall
Aylesbury
Buckinghamshire HP20 1UZ
Tel: (01296) 383104

ALFRISTON SCHOOL
Penn Road, Beaconsfield,
Buckinghamshire HP9 2TS
Tel: (01494) 673740
Head: Mrs V Gordon
Type: Girls Day and Boarding 11–18
No of pupils: 120 *No of Boarders:* W32
Special Needs: MLD

CHILTERN GATE SCHOOL

Verney Avenue, High Wycombe,
Buckinghamshire HP12 3NE
Tel: (01494) 532621
Head: Mr W Marshall
Type: Co-educational Day and
Boarding 4–11
No of pupils: 125
Special Needs: ADHD ASP **AUT** DOW
DYP **EBD** EPI HI **MLD** SP&LD TOU
VIS W

FURZE DOWN SCHOOL

Verney Road, Winslow,
Buckinghamshire MK18 3BL
Tel: (01296) 713385
Head: Mr N Ward
Type: Co-educational Day 5–18
No of pupils: 140
Special Needs: ADHD ASP AUT DYC
DYP DYS **EBD** EPI HI **MLD** SLD
SP&LD SPLD

HERITAGE HOUSE SCHOOL

Cameron Road, Chesham,
Buckinghamshire HP5 3BP
Tel: (01494) 771445
Head: Mr M Barrie
Type: Co-educational Day 2–19
No of pupils: B50 G40
Special Needs: AUT **PMLD SLD W**

KYNASTON SCHOOL

Stoke Leys Close, Kynaston Avenue,
Aylesbury, Buckinghamshire
HP21 9ET
Tel: (01296) 427221
Head: Mr R Westwood
Type: Co-educational Day 5–11
No of pupils: 50
Special Needs: **EBD**

MAPLEWOOD SCHOOL

Cressex Road, High Wycombe,
Buckinghamshire HP12 4PR
Tel: (01494) 525728
Head: Mrs J Appleyard
Type: Co-educational Day 3–19
No of pupils: 81
Special Needs: **PMLD SLD**

PARK SCHOOL

Stocklake, Aylesbury,
Buckinghamshire HP20 1DP
Tel: (01296) 23507
Head: Mrs R Cutler
Type: Co-educational Day 3–19
No of pupils: 85
Special Needs: **AUT** CP DOW PH
PMLD SLD W

PEBBLE BROOK SCHOOL

Churchill Avenue, Aylesbury,
Buckinghamshire HP21 8LZ
Tel: (01296) 415761
Head: Mrs J Lloyd
Type: Co-educational Day and
Boarding 11–16
No of pupils: 62
Special Needs: **MLD**

PRESTWOOD LODGE SCHOOL FOR BOYS

Nairdwood Lane, Prestwood, Great
Missenden, Buckinghamshire
HP16 0QQ
Tel: (01494) 863514
Head: Mr M Rosner
Type: Boys Boarding 11–16
No of pupils: 44
Special Needs: **EBD**

STOKE LEYS SCHOOL

Stoke Leys Close, Aylesbury,
Buckinghamshire HP21 9ET
Tel: (01296) 427441
Head: Mr R Westwood
Type: Co-educational Day 5–11
No of pupils: 77
Special Needs: ADD ADHD CP DOW
DYS EPI **MLD** PH SP&LD VIS

STONY DEAN SCHOOL

Orchard End Avenue, off Pineapple
Road, Amersham, Buckinghamshire
HP7 9JW
Tel: (01494) 762538
Head: Mr G Newsholme
Type: Co-educational Boarding and
Day 11–18
No of pupils: B103 G24
No of Boarders: W40
Special Needs: DYS **MLD** SP&LD
SPLD

VERNEY AVENUE SCHOOL

Verney Avenue, High Wycombe,
Buckinghamshire HP12 3NE
Tel: (01494) 530289
Head: Mr S Day
Type: Co-educational Day 11–18
No of pupils: 96
Special Needs: EBD **MLD** PH W

WENDOVER HOUSE SCHOOL

Church Lane, Wendover, Aylesbury,
Buckinghamshire HP22 6NL
Tel: (01296) 622157
Head: Mr N Morris
Type: Boys Boarding and Day 11–16
No of pupils: 64 *No of Boarders:* W30
Special Needs: EBD

Milton Keynes Education Authority

PO Box 106
Saxon Court
502 Avebury Boulevard
Milton Keynes MK9 3ZE
Tel: (01908) 253008

THE GATEHOUSE SCHOOL

Crosslands, Stantonbury, Milton
Keynes, Buckinghamshire MK14 6AX
Tel: (01908) 313903
Head: Mrs J Park
Type: Boys Boarding and Day 12–16
No of pupils: 21 *No of Boarders:* W10
Special Needs: **EBD** W

THE REDWAY

Farmborough, Netherfield, Milton
Keynes, Buckinghamshire MK6 4HG
Tel: (01908) 200000
Head: Mr R Fraser
Type: Co-educational Day 2–19
No of pupils: 120
Special Needs: AUT **PMLD SLD** W

ROMANS FIELD SCHOOL

Shenley Road, Bletchley,
Buckinghamshire MK3 7AW
Tel: (01908) 376011
Head: Mr J Thomas
Type: Co-educational Day and
Boarding 5–12
No of pupils: 50 *No of Boarders:* W25
Special Needs: **EBD**

SLATED ROW SCHOOL

Old Wolverton Road, Wolverton,
Milton Keynes, Buckinghamshire
MK12 5NJ
Tel: (01908) 316017
Head: Mr J O'Donnell
Type: Co-educational Day 5–19
No of pupils: B100 G55
Special Needs: **MLD**

THE WALNUTS SCHOOL

Simpson, Milton Keynes,
Buckinghamshire MK6 3AF
Tel: (01908) 670032
Head: Mr N Jackman
Type: Co-educational Boarding and
Day 4–12
No of pupils: B41 G4
No of Boarders: W11
Special Needs: **AUT** SP&LD

CAMBRIDGESHIRE

Cambridgeshire Education Authority

Castle Court
Castle Hill
Cambridge CB3 0AP
Tel: (01223) 717990

THE GREEN HEDGES SCHOOL
Bar Lane, Stapleford, Cambridge CB2 5BJ
Tel: (01223) 843872
Head: Mr G B Newell
Type: Co-educational Day 2–19
No of pupils: 70
Special Needs: AUT DOW PMLD SLD

HIGHFIELD SCHOOL
Downham Road, Ely,
Cambridgeshire CB6 1BD
Tel: (01353) 662085
Head: Mrs V M Ashton
Type: Co-educational Day 2–19
No of pupils: 89
Special Needs: ADD ASP AUT CP DOW DYP EPI HI MLD PH PMLD SLD SP&LD TOU VIS W

THE LADY ADRIAN SCHOOL
Courtney Way, Cambridge CB4 2EE
Tel: (01223) 508793
Head: Mrs K Taylor
Type: Co-educational Day 7–16
No of pupils: 135
Special Needs: MLD W

LITTLETON HOUSE SCHOOL
Girton, Cambridge CB3 0QL
Tel: (01223) 277191
Head: Mr D Sick
Type: Boys Boarding and Day 11–16
No of pupils: 85 *No of Boarders:* W32
Special Needs: EBD

THE MANOR SCHOOL
Station Road, Wilburton, Ely,
Cambridgeshire CB6 3RR
Tel: (01353) 740229
Head: Mr T G Moran
Type: Co-educational Boarding and Day 5–11
No of pupils: 55
Special Needs: AUT DYS EBD MLD

MARSHFIELDS SCHOOL
Eastern Close, Dogsthorpe,
Peterborough, Cambridgeshire PE1 4PP
Tel: (01733) 68058
Head: Mrs B S Berryman
Type: Co-educational

MEADOWGATE SCHOOL
Meadowgate Lane, Wisbech,
Cambridgeshire PE13 2JH
Tel: (01945) 461836
Head: Mrs R M Blunt
Type: Co-educational Day 2–19
No of pupils: 120
Special Needs: MLD PMLD SLD

REES THOMAS SCHOOL
Downhams Lane, Cambridge CB4 1YB
Tel: (01223) 712100
Head: Mrs J Gawlinski
Type: Co-educational Day 2–19
No of pupils: B40 G20
Special Needs: ADHD AUT CP DOW HI PMLD SLD VIS W

SAMUEL PEPYS SCHOOL
Pepys Road, St Neots,
Cambridgeshire PE19 2EW
Tel: (01480) 375012
Head: Mr D C Baldry
Type: Co-educational Day 2–19
No of pupils: 95
Special Needs: AUT MLD PMLD SLD

SPRING COMMON SCHOOL
American Lane, Huntingdon,
Cambridgeshire PE29 1TQ
Tel: (01480) 377403
Head: Mr N Parkinson
Type: Co-educational Day 2–19
No of pupils: B117 G50
Special Needs: AUT CP EPI HI MLD PMLD SLD VIS W

SPRINGFIELDS SCHOOL
Thames Road, Huntingdon,
Cambridgeshire PE18 7QW
Tel: (01480) 375106
Head: Mrs R S Keen
Type: Co-educational Day 2–11
No of pupils: 31
Special Needs: AUT MLD SLD SP&LD

THE WINDMILL SCHOOL
Fulbourn, Cambridge CB1 5EE
Tel: (01223) 880980
Head: Ms K Kemp
Type: Co-educational Day 2–19
No of pupils: 64
Special Needs: AUT CP DEL EPI HI PH PMLD SLD W

Peterborough Education Authority

Bayard Place
Broadway
Peterborough PE1 1FB
Tel: (01733) 748000

THE CAUSEWAY SCHOOL
Park Lane, Eastfield, Peterborough,
Cambridgeshire PE1 5GZ
Tel: (01733) 349438
Head: Mrs J Cleff
Type: Co-educational Day
No of pupils: B10 G2
Special Needs: ADD ADHD EBD

CLAYTON SCHOOL
Orton Goldhay, Peterborough,
Cambridgeshire PE2 5SD
Tel: (01733) 232346
Head: Mr R C Telfer
Type: Co-educational Day 2–19

HELTWATE SCHOOL
North Bretton, Peterborough,
Cambridgeshire PE3 8RL
Tel: (01733) 262878
Head: Mr D R Smith
Type: Co-educational Day 4–16
No of pupils: 110
Special Needs: AUT HI MLD PH SLD W

ST GEORGE'S SCHOOL
Lawn Avenue, Peterborough,
Cambridgeshire PE1 3RB
Tel: (01733) 62058
Head: Mr A B Rudgley
Type: Co-educational Day 2–19
No of pupils: B18 G23
Special Needs: PMLD SLD

CHANNEL ISLANDS

Guernsey Education Authority

Grange Road
St Peter Port
Guernsey GY1 1RQ
Tel: (01481) 710821

LONGFIELD CENTRE
Maurepas Road, St Peter Port,
Guernsey, Channel Islands GY1 2DS
Tel: (01481) 722339
Head: Mr R W Battye
Type: Co-educational Day 3–7
No of pupils: 35
Special Needs: MLD PH SP&LD W

MONT VAROUF SCHOOL
Le Neuf Chemin, St Saviours,
Guernsey, Channel Islands GY7 9FG
Tel: (01481) 63135
Head: Mr R W Battye
Type: Co-educational Day 3–19
No of pupils: B17 G19
Special Needs: AUT DOW EPI PMLD
SLD SP&LD VIS

OAKVALE SCHOOL
Collings Road, St Peter Port,
Guernsey, Channel Islands GY1 1FW
Tel: (01481) 723045
Head: Mr A T Brown
Type: Co-educational Day 7–16
No of pupils: B59 G40
Special Needs: EBD MLD W

Jersey Education Authority

PO Box 142
Jersey JE4 8QJ
Tel: (01534) 509500

D'HAUTREE HOUSE SCHOOL
St Saviour, Jersey, Channel Islands
JE2 4QP
Tel: (01534) 618042
Head: Mr R Matthews
Type: Co-educational Day 11–16
No of pupils: B19 G1
Special Needs: ADHD EBD MLD

MONT A L'ABBE SCHOOL
St Helier, Jersey, Channel Islands
JE2 3FN
Tel: (01534) 875801
Head: Ms S Eddie
Type: Co-educational Day 3–18
No of pupils: 95
Special Needs: AUT MLD PMLD
SLD W

CHESHIRE

Cheshire Education Authority

Education Department
County Hall
Chester CH1 1SQ
Tel: (01244) 602424

ADELAIDE SCHOOL
Adelaide Street, Crewe, Cheshire
CW1 3DT
Tel: (01270) 255661
Head: Mr L Willday
Type: Boys Day 11–16
No of pupils: 35
Special Needs: EBD

CAPENHURST GRANGE SCHOOL
Chester Road, Great Sutton,
Cheshire CH66 2NA
Tel: (0151) 339 5141
Head: Mrs C Creasy
Type: Co-educational Boarding 11–16
No of pupils: B59 G16
No of Boarders: F15 W35
Special Needs: EBD

CLOUGHWOOD SCHOOL
Stones Manor Lane, Hartford,
Northwich, Cheshire CW8 1NU
Tel: (01606) 76671
Head: Mr D H Smith
Type: Boys Boarding 9–18
No of pupils: 65
Special Needs: EBD

DEE BANKS SCHOOL
Sandy Lane, Chester, Cheshire
CH3 5UX
Tel: (01244) 324012
Head: Mrs J Pendry
Type: Co-educational Day 2–19
No of pupils: 85
Special Needs: AUT CP DOW EPI
PMLD SLD W

DORIN PARK SCHOOL
Wealstone Lane, Upton-by-Chester,
Cheshire CH2 1HP
Tel: (01244) 381951
Head: Mr P Kidman
Type: Co-educational Day 2–19
No of pupils: 90
Special Needs: PH PMLD

GREENBANK SCHOOL
off Green Bank Lane, Hartford,
Northwich, Cheshire CW8 1LD
Tel: (01606) 76521
Head: Mr K D Boyle
Type: Co-educational Boarding 6–18
No of pupils: B68 G24
No of Boarders: F65 W27
Special Needs: AUT DEL EPI MLD
SLD SP&LD

HEBDEN GREEN SCHOOL
Woodford Lane West, Winsford,
Cheshire CW7 4EJ
Tel: (01606) 594221/2
Head: Mr A W Farren
Type: Co-educational Day and
Boarding 2–19
No of pupils: B80 G32
No of Boarders: W33
Special Needs: PH

HINDERTON SCHOOL
Capenhurst Lane, Whitby, Ellesmere
Port, Cheshire CH65 7AQ
Tel: (0151) 355 2177
Head: Mr L McCallion
Type: Co-educational Day 3–7
No of pupils: 21
Special Needs: AUT SP&LD

MASSEY HALL SCHOOL
Half Acre Lane, Thelwall,
Warrington, Cheshire WA4 3JQ
Tel: (01925) 752016
Head: Mr C Gleave
Type: Co-educational Boarding 11–19
No of pupils: 64 *No of Boarders:* W64
Special Needs: EBD EPI MLD

OAKLANDS SCHOOL
Cheviot Square, Winsford, Cheshire
CW7 1NU
Tel: (01606) 551048
Head: Mr I G Hopkins
Type: Co-educational Day 11–16
No of pupils: 106
Special Needs: MLD

PARK LANE SCHOOL
Park Lane, Macclesfield, Cheshire
SK11 8JR
Tel: (01625) 423407
Head: Mr D Calvert
Type: Co-educational Day 2–19
No of pupils: B36 G34
Special Needs: PMLD SLD SPLD W

REDSANDS CHILDREN'S CENTRE
Crewe Road, Willaston, Nantwich,
Cheshire CW5 6NQ
Tel: (01270) 664116
Head: Mr R Grimwood
Type: Co-educational

ROSEBANK SCHOOL
Townfield Lane, Barnton,
Northwich, Cheshire CW8 4QP
Tel: (01606) 74975
Head: Mrs H Johnson
Type: Co-educational Day 3–11
No of pupils: 50
Special Needs: ADD ADHD ASP AUT
DYS MLD SP&LD

THE RUSSETT SCHOOL
Middlehurst Avenue, Weaverham,
Northwich, Cheshire CW8 3BW
Tel: (01606) 853005
Head: Mrs H M Watts
Type: Co-educational Day 2–19
No of pupils: 110
Special Needs: AUT DOW EPI HI
PMLD SLD VIS W

ST JOHN'S WOOD COMMUNITY SCHOOL
Longridge, Knutsford, Cheshire
WA16 8PA
Tel: (01565) 634578
Head: Mr A P Evans
Type: Co-educational Day
No of pupils: B31 G4
Special Needs: EBD

SPRINGFIELD SCHOOL
Crewe Green Road, Crewe, Cheshire
CW1 5HS
Tel: (01270) 582446
Head: Mr M Swaine
Type: Co-educational Day 3–19
No of pupils: B56 G50
Special Needs: AUT DOW PMLD SLD

Halton Borough Council

Education and Social Inclusion
Directorate
Grosvenor House
Halton Lea
Runcorn WA7 2WD
Tel: (0151) 424 2061

CAVENDISH SCHOOL
Lincoln Close, off Clifton Road,
Runcorn, Cheshire WA7 4YX
Tel: (01928) 561706
Head: Mrs B E Fowler
Type: Co-educational Day 2–19
No of pupils: 81
Special Needs: ADHD AUT CP DEL
DOW EPI PMLD SLD W

CHESNUT LODGE SCHOOL
Green Lane, Ditton, Widnes,
Cheshire WA8 7HF
Tel: (0151) 424 0679
Head: Mrs S R Lancaster
Type: Co-educational Day 2–16
No of pupils: B45 G43
Special Needs: PH W

Warrington Borough Council

Education Offices
New Town House
Buttermarket Street
Warrington WA1 2NJ
Tel: (01925) 442971

GRAPPENHALL RESIDENTIAL SCHOOL
Church Lane, Grappenhall,
Warrington, Cheshire WA4 3EU
Tel: (01925) 263895
Head: Mrs A Findlay
Type: Boys Boarding and Day 5–19
No of pupils: 121 *No of Boarders:* F25
Special Needs: ADD ADHD ASP AUT
DYP DYS EBD MLD SLD

GREEN LANE SCHOOL
Green Lane, Padgate, Warrington,
Cheshire WA1 4JL
Tel: (01925) 480128
Head: Mrs G Hunt
Type: Co-educational Day 4–16
No of pupils: 117
Special Needs: MLD SLD W

CORNWALL

Cornwall Education Authority

County Hall
Truro
Cornwall TR1 3AY
Tel: (01872) 322000

CURNOW SCHOOL
Drump Road, Redruth, Cornwall
TR15 1LU
Tel: (01209) 215432
Head: Mrs C Simpson
Type: Co-educational Day 2–19
No of pupils: B71 G48
Special Needs: PMLD SLD

DOUBLETREES SCHOOL
St Blazey Gate, St Blazey, Par,
Cornwall PL24 2DS
Tel: (01726) 812757
Head: Ms C McCarthy
Type: Co-educational Boarding and
Day 2–19
No of pupils: B57 G37
No of Boarders: W20
Special Needs: AUT HI PH PMLD SLD
VIS W

NANCEALVERNE SCHOOL
Madron Road, Penzance, Cornwall
TR20 8TP
Tel: (01736) 365039
Head: Mrs F J Cock
Type: Co-educational Day 2–19
No of pupils: 90
Special Needs: PMLD SLD W

PENCALENICK SCHOOL
Truro, Cornwall TR1 1TE
Tel: (01872) 520385
Head: Mr G Williams
Type: Co-educational Day 11–16

CUMBRIA

**Cumbria Education
Authority**

**Education Offices
5 Portland Square
Carlisle CA1 1PU**
Tel: (01228) 606877

**GEORGE HASTWELL
SCHOOL**
Moor Tarn Lane, Walney, Barrow in
Furness, Cumbria LA14 3LW
Tel: (01229) 475253
Head: Mr B J Gummett
Type: Co-educational Day 2–19
No of pupils: 50
Special Needs: AUT PMLD SLD W

JAMES RENNIE SCHOOL
Kingstown Road, Carlisle, Cumbria
CA3 0BU
Tel: (01228) 607559
Head: Mr S J Bowditch
Type: Co-educational Day 3–19
No of pupils: B100 G51
Special Needs: PMLD SLD W

MAYFIELD SCHOOL
Moresby, Whitehaven, Cumbria
CA28 8TU
Tel: (01946) 852676/7
Head: Ms S Leathers
Type: Co-educational Day 2–19
No of pupils: B57 G38
Special Needs: SLD

SANDGATE SCHOOL
Sandylands Road, Kendal, Cumbria
LA9 6JG
Tel: (01539) 773636
Head: Mrs W McManus
Type: Co-educational Day 2–19
No of pupils: B35 G15
Special Needs: AUT CP EBD EPI HI
MLD PH **PMLD SLD** SPLD VIS W

SANDSIDE LODGE SCHOOL
Sandside Road, Ulverston, Cumbria
LA12 9EF
Tel: (01229) 894180
Head: Mrs J Billingham
Type: Co-educational Day 2–19
No of pupils: B43 G17
Special Needs: AUT EPI HI PH **PMLD
SLD** SP&LD W

DERBYSHIRE

Derby City Council

**Education Offices
Middleton House
27 St. Mary's Gate
Derby DE1 3NN**
Tel: (01332) 293111

IVY HOUSE SCHOOL
249 Osmaston Road, Derby,
Derbyshire DE23 8LG
Tel: (01332) 344694
Head: Mrs P Sillitoe
Type: Co-educational Day 2–19
No of pupils: B48 G22
Special Needs: PMLD SLD W

ST ANDREW'S SCHOOL
St Andrew's View, Breadsall Hilltop,
Derby DE2 4ET
Tel: (01332) 832746
Head: Mr M Dawes
Type: Co-educational Day and
Boarding 2–19
No of pupils: 106 *No of Boarders:* W17
Special Needs: AUT PMLD **SLD**

ST CLARE'S SCHOOL
Rough Heanor Road, Mickleover,
Derby DE3 5AZ
Tel: (01332) 511757
Head: Mrs M C McKenna
Type: Co-educational Day 11–16
No of pupils: 110
Special Needs: AUT **EBD** HI **MLD** SLD
SP&LD

ST GILES SCHOOL
Hampshire Road, Chaddesden,
Derby DE21 6BT
Tel: (01332) 343039
Head: Mr P J Walsh
Type: Co-educational Day 5–11
No of pupils: 75
Special Needs: **AUT MLD SLD**
SP&LD

ST MARTIN'S SCHOOL
Wisgreaves Road, Alvaston, Derby
DE2 8RQ
Tel: (01332) 571151
Head: Mr W G Jepson
Type: Co-educational Day 11–16
No of pupils: B60 G26
Special Needs: ADD DOW EBD
MLD W

Derbyshire Education Authority

County Hall
Matlock
Derbyshire DE4 3AG
Tel: (01629) 580000

ASHGATE CROFT SCHOOL
Ashgate Road, Chesterfield,
Derbyshire S40 4BN
Tel: (01246) 275111/237200
Head: Mr M J Meaton
Type: Co-educational Day 2–19
No of pupils: 179
Special Needs: AUT CP DEL DYS EBD
EPI HI **MLD** PH **PMLD SLD** SP&LD
VIS **W**

BENNERLEY FIELDS SCHOOL
Stratford Street, Ilkeston, Derbyshire
DE7 8QZ
Tel: (0115) 932 6374
Head: Mrs M Stirling
Type: Co-educational Day 3–16
No of pupils: 75
Special Needs: ASP AUT CP DOW
DYP **EBD** HI **MLD** PH **SLD** SP&LD **W**

BRACKENFIELD SCHOOL
Bracken Road, Long Eaton,
Nottingham NG10 4DA
Tel: (0115) 973 3710
Head: Mrs S P Elkins
Type: Co-educational Day 5–16
No of pupils: B60 G18
Special Needs: EBD MLD

THE DELVES SCHOOL
Hayes Lane, Swanick, Derbyshire
DE55 1AR
Tel: (01773) 602198
Head: Mr I D Snodin
Type: Co-educational Day 5–16
No of pupils: 90
Special Needs: AUT EBD MLD SLD
SP&LD

HOLLY HOUSE SCHOOL
Church Street North, Old
Whittington, Chesterfield,
Derbyshire S41 9QR
Tel: (01246) 450530
Head: Mr G O'Neil
Type: Co-educational Day 4–11
No of pupils: 28
Special Needs: **EBD**

JOHN DUNCAN SCHOOL
Corbar Road, Buxton, Derbyshire
SK17 6RL
Tel: (01298) 23130
Head: Mrs S E Taylor
Type: Co-educational Boarding and
Day 11–16
No of pupils: B25 G15
No of Boarders: W10
Special Needs: DOW EPI MLD SLD
SP&LD

PARKWOOD COMMUNITY SPECIAL SCHOOL
Alfreton Park, Alfreton, Derbyshire
DE55 7AL
Tel: (01773) 832019
Head: Mrs R Mackenzie
Type: Co-educational Day 2–19
No of pupils: 60
Special Needs: PMLD **SLD** W

PEAK SCHOOL
Buxton Road, High Peak, Derbyshire
SK23 6ES
Tel: (01663) 751359
Head: Mrs L C Scowcroft
Type: Co-educational Boarding and
Day 2–19
No of pupils: 40 *No of Boarders:* W12
Special Needs: ASP **AUT** CP EPI PH
PMLD SLD W

STANTON VALE SCHOOL
Lower Stanton Road, Ilkeston,
Derbyshire DE7 4LR
Tel: (0115) 932 4783
Head: Mr M Emly
Type: Co-educational Day 2–19
No of pupils: B32 G33
Special Needs: **PMLD SLD** W

STUBBIN WOOD SCHOOL
Burlington Avenue, Langwith
Junction, Mansfield, Derbyshire
NG20 9AD
Tel: (01623) 742795
Head: Mr J M Youdan
Type: Co-educational Day 2–16
No of pupils: B94 G61
Special Needs: MLD PMLD SLD W

WESTBROOK SCHOOL
Thoresby Road, Long Eaton,
Nottingham NG10 3NP
Tel: (0115) 9729769
Head: Mr D J Ingham
Type: Co-educational Boarding and
Day 2–16
No of pupils: 92 *No of Boarders:* W20
Special Needs: CP **PH** W

DEVON

Devon Education Authority

County Hall
Topsham Road
Exeter EX2 4QG
Tel: (01392) 382000

BARLEY LANE SCHOOL
Barley Lane, St Thomas, Exeter,
Devon EX4 1TA
Tel: (01392) 430774
Head: Mr M S Davis
Type: Boys Day 10–16
No of pupils: 40
Special Needs: **EBD**

BARNSTAPLE TUTORIAL UNIT (PRU)
St Johns Lane, Barnstaple, Devon
EX32 9DD
Tel: (01271) 376641
Head: Mr P Bowrey
Type: Co-educational Day
No of pupils: 12
Special Needs: **EBD**

BIDWELL BROOK SCHOOL
Shinner's Bridge, Dartington, Devon
TQ9 6JU
Tel: (01803) 864120
Head: Mrs S M Love
Type: Co-educational Day 3–17
No of pupils: 86
Special Needs: **PMLD SLD** W

ELLEN TINKHAM SCHOOL
Hollow Lane, Exeter, Devon
EX1 3RW
Tel: (01392) 467168
Head: Dr M Megee
Type: Co-educational Day 3–19
No of pupils: B48 G26
Special Needs: AUT CP **DOW** EPI HI
MLD PMLD SLD VIS W

HILL CREST SCHOOL

St John's Road, Exmouth, Devon
EX8 4ED
Tel: (01395) 263480
Head: Mr G Adler
Type: Co-educational Boarding and
Day 10–16
No of pupils: B40 *No of Boarders:* W36
Special Needs: ADD ADHD DYS **EBD**

THE LAMPARD-VACHELL SCHOOL

St John's Lane, Barnstaple, Devon
EX32 9DD
Tel: (01271) 345416
Head: Mrs M T Buckland
Type: Co-educational Day 6–16
No of pupils: 65
Special Needs: **MLD**

MARLAND SCHOOL

Petersmarland, Torrington, Devon
EX3 8QQ
Tel: (01805) 601324
Head: Mr A Bates
Type: Boys Boarding 11–16
No of pupils: 36 *No of Boarders:* F36
Special Needs: ADD ADHD EBD
SP&LD SPLD

OAKLANDS PARK SCHOOL

John Nash Drive, Dawlish, Devon
EX7 9SF
Tel: (01626) 862363
Head: Mr R W Pugh
Type: Co-educational Boarding and
Day 3–19
No of pupils: B38 G12
No of Boarders: W25
Special Needs: AUT CP EPI PMLD
SLD

RATCLIFFE SCHOOL

John Nash Drive, Dawlish, Devon
EX7 9RL
Tel: (01626) 862939
Head: Mr C Hackett
Type: Co-educational Boarding
No of pupils: B50 G15
No of Boarders: W65
Special Needs: **EBD**

SOUTHBROOK SCHOOL

Bishop Westall Road, Exeter, Devon
EX2 6JB
Tel: (01392) 58373
Head: Mr N G Glover
Type: Co-educational Day 7–16
No of pupils: 157
Special Needs: **MLD**

Plymouth City Council

Department for Lifelong Learning
Windsor House
Tavistock Road
Plymouth PL1 2AA
Tel: (01752) 307400

COURTLANDS SCHOOL

Widey Court, Crownhill, Plymouth,
Devon PL6 5JS
Tel: (01752) 776848
Head: Mr G H J Dunkerley
Type: Co-educational Day 5–12
No of pupils: B81 G29
Special Needs: ADD ADHD ASP **MLD**
SP&LD

HILLSIDE SCHOOL

Bodmin Road, Whitleigh, Plymouth,
Devon PL5 4DZ
Tel: (01752) 773875
Head: Mr D Whitton
Type: Co-educational Day 11–19
No of pupils: 194
Special Needs: **MLD**

LONGCAUSE SCHOOL

Plympton, Plymouth, Devon PL7 3JB
Tel: (01752) 336881
Head: Mr M Jelly
Type: Co-educational Day 5–17
No of pupils: 92
Special Needs: **MLD**

MILL FORD SCHOOL

Rochford Crescent, Ernesettle,
Plymouth, Devon PL5 2PY
Tel: (01752) 300270
Head: Mr J Hill
Type: Co-educational Day 3–19
No of pupils: 115
Special Needs: AUT **PMLD SLD** W

MOUNT TAMAR SCHOOL

Row Lane, St Budeaux, Plymouth,
Devon PL5 2EF
Tel: (01752) 365128
Head: Mr I Weston
Type: Co-educational Day 5–16
No of pupils: 84
Special Needs: **EBD**

WOODLANDS SCHOOL

Bodmin Road, Whitleigh, Plymouth,
Devon PL5 4DZ
Tel: (01752) 778229
Head: Miss M A Vatcher
Type: Co-educational Day and
Boarding 2–17
No of pupils: B34 G39
No of Boarders: W12
Special Needs: **PH** W

Torbay Council

Education Services Directorate
Oldway Mansion
Torquay Road
Paignton
Devon TQ3 2TE
Tel: (01803) 208227

COMBE PAFFORD SCHOOL

Steps Lane, Watcombe, Torquay,
Devon TQ2 8NL
Tel: (01803) 327902
Head: Mr M E Lock
Type: Co-educational Day 5–16
No of pupils: B110 G57
Special Needs: **MLD**

MAYFIELD SCHOOL

Torquay Road, Paignton, Devon
TQ3 2AL
Tel: (01803) 557194
Head: Mrs J M Palmer
Type: Co-educational Day 2–19
No of pupils: 80
Special Needs: **PMLD SLD** W

DORSET

Bournemouth Borough Council

Education Offices
Dorset House
20–22 Christchurch Road
Bournemouth BH1 3NL
Tel: (01202) 456219

THE BICKNELL FOUNDATION SCHOOL
Petersfield Road, Bournemouth, Dorset BH7 6QP
Tel: (01202) 424361
Head: Mr B Hooper
Type: Boys Day and Boarding 7–16
No of pupils: 65
Special Needs: ADD ADHD ASP DYC DYP DYS **EBD** SP&LD SPLD TOU

LINWOOD SCHOOL
Alma Road, Bournemouth, Dorset BH9 1AJ
Tel: (01202) 525107
Head: Mr S D Brown
Type: Co-educational Day 3–19
No of pupils: 176
Special Needs: MLD PMLD SLD

Dorset Education Authority

County Hall
Dorchester DT1 1XJ
Tel: (01305) 251000

BEAUCROFT GRANT MAINTAINED SCHOOL
Wimborne Road, Colehill, Wimborne, Dorset BH21 2SS
Tel: (01202) 886083
Head: Mr A W Mears
Type: Co-educational Day 3–16
No of pupils: 127
Special Needs: AUT MLD

MOUNTJOY SCHOOL
Flood Lane, Bridport, Dorset DT6 3QG
Tel: (01308) 422250
Head: Mrs S G Hosking
Type: Co-educational Day 2–19
No of pupils: B29 G11
Special Needs: **AUT** CP DEL **DOW** EPI HI **PMLD** SLD SP&LD SPLD W

PENWITHEN SCHOOL
Winterborne Monkton, Dorchester, Dorset DT2 9PS
Tel: (01305) 266842
Head: Mr J R Burton
Type: Co-educational Boarding and Day 7–16
No of pupils: 55 *No of Boarders:* W25
Special Needs: **EBD**

THE PRINCE OF WALES UNIT
Maiden Castle Road, Dorchester, Dorset DT1 2HH
Tel: (01305) 257120
Head: Mr P Farrington
Type: Co-educational Day 2–9
No of pupils: 21
Special Needs: CP PH W

WESTFIELD TECHNOLOGY COLLEGE
Littlemoor Road, Preston, Weymouth, Dorset
Tel: (01305) 833518
Head: Mr P Silvester
Type: Co-educational Day 3–16
No of pupils: 174
Special Needs: AUT MLD W

WYVERN SCHOOL
307 Chickerell Road, Weymouth, Dorset DT4 0QU
Tel: (01305) 783660
Head: Miss H Mackenzie
Type: Co-educational Day
No of pupils: 60
Special Needs: AUT PMLD SLD W

YEWSTOCK SCHOOL
Honeymead Lane, Sturminster Newton, Dorset DT10 1EW
Tel: (01258) 472796
Head: Mrs J Davis
Type: Co-educational Day 2–19
No of pupils: 118
Special Needs: AUT MLD PMLD SLD W

Poole Borough Council

Education Offices
Room 159, Civic Centre
Poole BH15 2RU
Tel: (01202) 633202

LONGSPEE SCHOOL
Learoyd Road, Canford Heath, Poole, Dorset BH17 8PJ
Tel: (01202) 380266
Head: Mr M T Amos
Type: Co-educational Day 4–11
No of pupils: 62
Special Needs: **EBD**

MONTACUTE SCHOOL
3 Canford Heath Road, Poole, Dorset BH17 9NG
Tel: (01202) 693239
Head: Mrs M Sammons
Type: Co-educational Day 3–18
No of pupils: 75
Special Needs: AUT PMLD SLD

WINCHELSEA SCHOOL
Guernsey Road, Parkstone, Poole, Dorset BH12 4LL
Tel: (01202) 746240
Head: Mr R Barnsley
Type: Co-educational Day 3–16
No of pupils: 150
Special Needs: **MLD** W

COUNTY DURHAM

County Durham Education Authority

County Hall
Durham DH1 5UJ
Tel: (0191) 386 4411

DENE VIEW SCHOOL
Cotsford Park, Horden, Peterlee, County Durham SR8 4SZ
Tel: (0191) 586 4166
Head: Mr A Dawson
Type: Co-educational Day 5–16
No of pupils: B47 G17
Special Needs: **MLD** W

DURHAM TRINITY SCHOOL
Aykley Heads, Durham, County Durham DH1 5TS
Tel: (0191) 386 4612
Head: Miss J A Connolly
Type: Co-educational Day 2–19
No of pupils: B109 G68
Special Needs: **AUT** MLD **PMLD** SLD

ELEMORE HALL SCHOOL
Littletown, Sherburn, County
Durham DH6 1QD
Tel: (0191) 372 0275
Head: Mr M Davey
Type: Co-educational Boarding and
Day
No of pupils: B60 G10
No of Boarders: W40
Special Needs: **EBD**

GLEN DENE SCHOOL
Crawlaw Road, Easington Colliery,
Peterlee, County Durham SR8 3BQ
Tel: (0191) 527 0304
Head: Mr E Baker
Type: Co-educational Day 2–19
No of pupils: B86 G50
Special Needs: AUT DYC DYP DYS
MLD PMLD SLD W

HARE LAW SCHOOL
Catchgate, Annfield Plain, Stanley,
County Durham DH9 8DT
Tel: (01207) 234547
Head: Mr P H Eagle
Type: Co-educational Day 5–16
No of pupils: B80 G40
Special Needs: AUT MLD SLD W

MURPHY CRESCENT
SCHOOL
Murphy Crescent, Bishop Barrington
Campus, Woodhouse Lane, Bishop
Auckland, County Durham
DL14 6LA
Tel: (01388) 451199
Head: Mrs M Wilson
Type: Co-educational Day 2–19
No of pupils: B21 G15
Special Needs: PMLD **SLD** W

ROSEBANK SCHOOL
Rutherford Terrace, Broom,
Ferryhill, County Durham DL17 8AN
Tel: (01740) 651555
Head: Mrs S Stubbs
Type: Co-educational Day 4–19
No of pupils: B23 G14
Special Needs: PMLD SLD W

VILLA REAL SCHOOL
Villa Real Road, Consett, County
Durham DH8 6BH
Tel: (01207) 503651
Head: Mrs F Wood
Type: Co-educational Day 2–19
No of pupils: 75
Special Needs: AUT **PMLD SLD** W

WALWORTH SCHOOL
Bluebell Way, Newton Aycliffe,
County Durham DL5 7LP
Tel: (01325) 300194
Head: Mr A Dawson
Type: Co-educational Day and
Boarding 5–11
No of pupils: 60 *No of Boarders:* W30
Special Needs: **ADD ADHD** ASP **EBD**
MLD SP&LD SPLD

WARWICK ROAD SCHOOL
Warwick Road, Bishop Auckland,
County Durham DL14 6LS
Tel: (01388) 602683
Head: Mr G Price
Type: Co-educational Day
No of pupils: 100
Special Needs: DYP DYS **MLD**

WINDLESTONE HALL
SCHOOL
Rushyford, Chilton, Ferryhill,
County Durham DL17 0LX
Tel: (01388) 720337
Head: Mr P M Jonson
Type: Co-educational Boarding and
Day 11–16
No of pupils: 60 *No of Boarders:* F20
Special Needs: **EBD**

Darlington Education Authority

Town Hall
Darlington DL1 5QT
Tel: (01325) 388802

BEAUMONT HILL
TECHNOLOGY COLLEGE &
PRIMARY SCHOOL
Glebe Road, Darlington, County
Durham DL1 3EB
Tel: (01325) 254000
Head: Mrs D Smith
Type: Co-educational Day 2–19
No of pupils: B149 G76
Special Needs: ADD ADHD **AUT** CP
DOW **EBD** EPI HI MLD PH **PMLD**
SLD SP&LD

ESSEX

Essex Education Authority

PO Box 47
Chelmsford CM2 6WN
Tel: (01245) 436231

CASTLEDON SCHOOL
Bromfords Drive, Wickford, Essex
SS12 0PW
Tel: (01268) 761252
Head: Mr P B Webster
Type: Co-educational Day 4–16
No of pupils: B70 G29
Special Needs: AUT **MLD**

CEDAR HALL SCHOOL
Hart Road, Thundersley, Benfleet,
Essex SS7 3UQ
Tel: (01268) 774723
Head: Mr C Bent
Type: Co-educational Day 4–16
No of pupils: B74 G32
Special Needs: **HI MLD SP&LD**

THE EDITH BORTHWICK
SCHOOL
Fennes Road, Church Street,
Bocking, Braintree, Essex CM7 5LA
Tel: (01376) 326436
Head: Mr M Jelly
Type: Co-educational Day 3–19
No of pupils: 140
Special Needs: AUT MLD SLD

ELMBROOK SCHOOL
Church Road, Basildon, Essex
SS14 2EX
Tel: (01268) 521808
Head: Mr S Horsted
Type: Co-educational Day 3–19
No of pupils: B62 G25
Special Needs: AUT CP EPI HI PH
PMLD SLD W

THE ENDEAVOUR SCHOOL
Hogarth Avenue, Brentwood, Essex
CM15 8BE
Tel: (01277) 217330
Head: Mr P L Pryke
Type: Co-educational Day 4–16
No of pupils: B53 G21
Special Needs: **MLD** W

GLENWOOD SCHOOL
Rushbottom Lane, New Thundersley,
Benfleet, Essex SS7 4LW
Tel: (01268) 792575
Head: Mrs J Salter
Type: Co-educational Day 3–19
No of pupils: B60 G20
Special Needs: AUT PMLD SLD W

HARLOW FIELDS SCHOOL
Tendring Road, Harlow, Essex
CM18 6RN
Tel: (01279) 423670
Head: Dr B Thomas
Type: Co-educational Day 3–19
No of pupils: 125
Special Needs: **AUT** MLD **PMLD SLD**

THE HAYWARD SCHOOL
Maltese Road, Chelmsford, Essex
CM1 2PA
Tel: (01245) 258667
Head: Mr M B Reeve
Type: Co-educational Day 5–16
No of pupils: B82 G27
Special Needs: ADD ADHD AUT
DOW DYP DYS **MLD SP&LD**

THE HEATH SCHOOL
Winstree Road, Stanway, Colchester,
Essex CO3 5GE
Tel: (01206) 571379
Head: Mrs C F Creasy
Type: Boys Day and Boarding 11–16
No of pupils: 45 *No of Boarders:* W30
Special Needs: **EBD** W

HOMESTEAD SCHOOL
School Road, Langham, Colchester,
Essex CO4 5PA
Tel: (01206) 272303
Head: Mr W Campard
Type: Boys Boarding 11–18
No of pupils: 64
Special Needs: **EBD**

KINGSWODE HOE SCHOOL
Sussex Road, Colchester, Essex
CO3 3QJ
Tel: (01206) 576408
Head: Mrs E Drake
Type: Co-educational Day 5–16
No of pupils: B72 G30
Special Needs: **MLD**

THE LEAS SCHOOL
Leas Road, Clacton, Essex CO15 1DY
Tel: (01255) 426288
Head: Mr E A Barkley
Type: Co-educational Day 5–16
No of pupils: B64 G36
Special Needs: AUT MLD W

LEXDEN SPRINGS SCHOOL
Halstead Road, Colchester, Essex
CO3 5AB
Tel: (01206) 563321
Head: Mr S H Goldsmith
Type: Co-educational Day 3–19
No of pupils: B38 G27
Special Needs: AUT **PMLD SLD**

MARKET FIELD SCHOOL
School Road, Elmstead Market,
Colchester, Essex CO7 7ET
Tel: (01206) 825195
Head: Mr G R Smith
Type: Co-educational Day 5–16
No of pupils: B70 G40
Special Needs: **AUT DOW EBD** EPI
MLD SLD **SP&LD** SPLD W

MOAT HOUSE SCHOOL
Church Road, Basildon, Essex
SS14 2NQ
Tel: (01268) 522077
Head: Mr S Horsted
Type: Co-educational Day 5–16
No of pupils: 70
Special Needs: MLD

OAKVIEW SCHOOL
Whitehills Road, Loughton, Essex
IG10 1TS
Tel: (020) 8508 4293
Head: Mr S P Armstrong
Type: Co-educational Day 2–19
No of pupils: 90
Special Needs: AUT **MLD SLD** SPLD

THE RAMSDEN HALL SCHOOL
Ramsden Heath, Billericay, Essex
CM11 1HN
Tel: (01277) 624580
Head: Mr S Grant
Type: Boarding
No of pupils: 55 *No of Boarders:* W30
Special Needs: **EBD**

THRIFTWOOD SCHOOL
Slades Lane, Galleywood,
Chelmsford, Essex CM2 8RW
Tel: (01245) 266880
Head: Mrs S Davies
Type: Co-educational Day 5–16
No of pupils: 126
Special Needs: AUT **MLD** SP&LD

WELLS PARK SCHOOL
Lambourne Road, Chigwell, Essex
IG7 6NN
Tel: (020) 8502 6442
Head: Mr D Wood
Type: Co-educational Day and
Boarding 5–12
No of pupils: 40 *No of Boarders:* F40
Special Needs: **EBD** W

WINDSOR SPECIAL SCHOOL
Ogilvie House, 114 Holland Road,
Clacton, Essex CO15 6HF
Tel: (01255) 424412
Head: Mrs J Hodges
Type: Co-educational Day 3–19
No of pupils: B38 G24
Special Needs: PMLD SLD W

WOODLANDS SCHOOL
Patching Hall Lane, Chelmsford,
Essex CM1 4BX
Tel: (01245) 355854
Head: Mr O Caviglioli
Type: Co-educational Day 3–19
No of pupils: 110
Special Needs: **AUT DOW** PH **PMLD
SLD** W

Southend-on-Sea Borough Council

**Education and Library Services
5th Floor, Civic Centre
Victoria Avenue
Southend-on-Sea SS2 6ER
Tel:** (01702) 215921

KINGSDOWN SCHOOL
Snakes Lane, Southend-on-Sea,
Essex SS2 6XT
Tel: (01702) 527486
Head: Mr J F Hagyard
Type: Co-educational Day 3–19
No of pupils: B78 G37
Special Needs: CP DEL EPI PH W

LANCASTER SCHOOL
Prittlewell Chase, Westcliff-on-Sea,
Essex SS0 0RT
Tel: (01702) 342543
Head: Mrs A Farrow
Type: Co-educational Day 2–19
No of pupils: B65 G45
Special Needs: AUT CP **PMLD SLD**

PRIORY SCHOOL
Burr Hill Chase, Southend-on-Sea,
Essex SS2 6PE
Tel: (01702) 347490
Head: Mrs V S Wathen
Type: Co-educational Day 8–16
No of pupils: 46
Special Needs: **EBD**

THE ST CHRISTOPHER SCHOOL
Mountdale Gardens, Leigh-on-Sea,
Essex SS9 4AW
Tel: (01702) 524193
Head: Mr T G Wilson
Type: Co-educational Day 3–16
No of pupils: 110
Special Needs: **ADD ADHD ASP** AUT
DOW DYP **DYS EBD HI MLD SLD
SP&LD W**

ST NICHOLAS SCHOOL
Philpott Avenue, Southend-on-Sea,
Essex SS2 4RL
Tel: (01702) 462322
Head: Mrs G M Houghton
Type: Co-educational Day 4–16
No of pupils: 95
Special Needs: **MLD**

Thurrock Council

**Education Department
PO Box 118
Grays
Essex RM17 6GF
Tel: (01375) 652652**

KNIGHTSMEAD SCHOOL
Fortin Close, South Ockendon,
Essex RM15 5NH
Tel: (01708) 852956
Head: Ms J Thomas
Type: Co-educational Day 3–12
No of pupils: B27 G14
Special Needs: **AUT PMLD SLD** W

TREETOPS SCHOOL
Dell Road, Grays, Essex RM17 5LH
Tel: (01375) 372723
Head: Mr P Smith
Type: Co-educational Day 5–16
No of pupils: B70 G50
Special Needs: **AUT MLD**

WOODACRE SCHOOL
Erriff Drive, South Ockendon, Essex
RM15 5AY
Tel: (01708) 852006
Head: Mr J Stringer
Type: Co-educational Day 3–16
No of pupils: 100
Special Needs: **CP DYP EPI MLD PH
PMLD SLD SP&LD W**

GLOUCESTERSHIRE

Gloucestershire Education Authority

**Shire Hall
Gloucester GL1 2TP
Tel: (01452) 425322**

ALDERMAN KNIGHT SCHOOL
Ashchurch Road, Tewkesbury,
Gloucestershire GL20 8JJ
Tel: (01684) 295639
Head: Mr I T Walsh
Type: Co-educational Day 5–16
No of pupils: B60 G30
Special Needs: **ASP** AUT **CP** DEL DYS
EBD **EPI** HI MLD PH SLD SP&LD
SPLD VIS W

BATTLEDOWN CHILDREN'S CENTRE
Harp Hill, Battledown, Cheltenham,
Gloucestershire GL52 6PZ
Tel: (01242) 525472
Head: Mrs E M Rook
Type: Co-educational Day 2–7
No of pupils: 40
Special Needs: **ASP** AUT CP DOW EPI
HI **MLD PH** SLD SP&LD VIS W

BELMONT SCHOOL
Warden Hill Road, Cheltenham,
Gloucestershire GL51 5AT
Tel: (01242) 526919
Head: Mr M Bell
Type: Co-educational Day 5–16
No of pupils: 61
Special Needs: **DYS EBD MLD**

BETTRIDGE SCHOOL
Warden Hill Road, Cheltenham,
Gloucestershire GL51 5AT
Tel: (01242) 514934
Head: Mrs M Saunders
Type: Co-educational Day 2–19
No of pupils: 98
Special Needs: AUT PMLD SLD VIS W

CAM HOUSE SCHOOL
Drake Lane, Dursley, Gloucestershire
GL11 5HD
Tel: (01453) 542130
Head: Mrs B Turner
Type: Boys Boarding and Day 11–16
No of pupils: 61
Special Needs: **EBD**

COLN HOUSE SCHOOL
Horcott Road, Fairford,
Gloucestershire GL7 4DB
Tel: (01285) 712308
Head: Mr J W Davidson
Type: Co-educational Boarding and
Day 9–16
No of pupils: B45 G10
No of Boarders: W42
Special Needs: **EBD** MLD

DEAN HALL SCHOOL
Speech House Road, Coleford,
Gloucestershire GL16 7EJ
Tel: (01594) 822175
Head: Mr J N Haddock
Type: Co-educational Day 5–16
No of pupils: 90
Special Needs: EBD MLD

THE MILESTONE SCHOOL
Longford Lane, Gloucester GL2 9EU
Tel: (01452) 500499
Head: V W Stroud
Type: Co-educational Day 2–16

OAKDENE SCHOOL
Dockham Road, Cinderford,
Gloucestershire GL14 2AN
Tel: (01594) 822693
Head: Mrs E Oates
Type: Co-educational Day 3–19
No of pupils: B17 G5
Special Needs: PMLD SLD

PATERNOSTER SCHOOL
Watermoor Road, Cirencester,
Gloucestershire GL7 1JS
Tel: (01285) 652480
Head: Mr P Barton
Type: Co-educational Day 2–16
No of pupils: 50
Special Needs: PMLD SLD W

SANDFORD SCHOOL
Seven Springs, Cheltenham,
Gloucestershire GL53 9NG
Tel: (01242) 870224
Head: Mr S Jones
Type: Co-educational Day 5–16
No of pupils: B81 G10
Special Needs: EBD

THE SHRUBBERIES SCHOOL
Oldends Lane, Stonehouse,
Gloucestershire GL10 2DG
Tel: (01453) 822155
Head: Mr P J Morgan
Type: Co-educational Day 2–19
No of pupils: 90
Special Needs: AUT PMLD SLD
SP&LD

South Gloucestershire Education Authority
Bowling Hill
Chipping Sodbury
Bristol BS37 6JX
Tel: (01454) 868686

CULVERHILL SCHOOL
Kelston Close, Yate, South
Gloucestershire BS37 4SZ
Tel: (01454) 866930
Head: Miss A Binmore
Type: Co-educational Day 7–16

NEW SIBLANDS SCHOOL
Easton Hill Road, Thornbury, South
Gloucestershire BS12 1AU
Tel: (01454) 414188
Head: Mr P Casson
Type: Co-educational Day 2–19
No of pupils: 55
Special Needs: PMLD SLD

HAMPSHIRE

Hampshire Education Authority
The Castle
Winchester
Hampshire SO23 8UG
Tel: (01962) 841841

BAYCROFT SCHOOL
Gosport Road, Stubbington,
Fareham, Hampshire PO14 2AE
Tel: (01329) 664151
Head: Mr R A Hendry
Type: Co-educational Day 11–16
No of pupils: 170
Special Needs: ADD ADHD AUT DYP
DYS EBD EPI HI MLD

DOVE HOUSE SPECIAL SCHOOL
Sutton Road, Basingstoke,
Hampshire RG21 5SU
Tel: (01256) 351555
Head: Mr C House
Type: Co-educational Day 11–16
No of pupils: 110
Special Needs: MLD

FOREST EDGE SPECIAL SCHOOL
Lydlynch Road, Totton,
Southampton, Hampshire SO40 3DW
Tel: (023) 8086 4949
Head: Mr P Hodgson
Type: Co-educational Day 4–11
No of pupils: B42 G12
Special Needs: AUT MLD SP&LD

GLENWOOD SPECIAL SCHOOL
Washington Road, Evisworth,
Hampshire PO10 7NN
Tel: (01243) 373120
Head: Mrs C A Hill
Type: Co-educational Day 11–16
No of pupils: 92
Special Needs: MLD

GREENACRES SPECIAL SCHOOL
Andover Road, Winchester,
Hampshire SO22 6AU
Tel: (01962) 862450
Head: Mrs C Gayler
Type: Co-educational Day 3–19
No of pupils: B28 G15
Special Needs: AUT PMLD SLD

HAWTHORNS SPECIAL SCHOOL
Pack Lane, Kempshott, Basingstoke,
Hampshire RG22 5TH
Tel: (01256) 336601
Head: Mr A K Beavan
Type: Co-educational Day and
Boarding 10–16
No of pupils: B46 G6
No of Boarders: W10
Special Needs: EBD

HEATHFIELD SPECIAL SCHOOL
Oldbury Way, Peak Lane, Fareham,
Hampshire PO14 3BN
Tel: (01329) 845150
Head: Mrs E Muirhead
Type: Co-educational Day 3–11
No of pupils: B84 G39
Special Needs: ADHD ASP AUT CP
DYP EBD EPI HI MLD PH SP&LD
VIS W

HENRY TYNDALS SPECIAL SCHOOL
Croft Road, Church Lane East,
Aldershot, Hampshire GU11 3HR
Head: Mr C H Woodroffe
Type: Co-educational Day 5–16
Special Needs: ASP AUT MLD

ICKNIELD SPECIAL SCHOOL
River Way, Andover, Hampshire
SP11 6LT
Tel: (01264) 365297
Head: Mr S Steer-Smith
Type: Co-educational Day 2–19
No of pupils: B40 G32
Special Needs: **AUT PMLD SLD** W

LANKHILLS SPECIAL SCHOOL
Andover Road, Winchester,
Hampshire SO23 7BU
Tel: (01962) 854537
Head: Mr R J Wakelam
Type: Co-educational Boarding and
Day 11–19
No of pupils: 118 *No of Boarders:* W15
Special Needs: **MLD**

LIMINGTON HOUSE SPECIAL SCHOOL
St Andrew's Road, Basingstoke,
Hampshire RG22 6PS
Tel: (01256) 322148
Head: Mr M J C Balson
Type: Co-educational Day 2–19
No of pupils: 80
Special Needs: PMLD **SLD**

MAPLE RIDGE SPECIAL SCHOOL
Maple Crescent, Basingstoke,
Hampshire RG21 5SX
Tel: (01256) 323639
Head: Mrs J Martin
Type: Co-educational Day 4–11
No of pupils: B47 G15
Special Needs: AUT **MLD** W

THE MARK WAY SCHOOL
Bachelors Barn Road, Andover,
Hampshire SP10 1HR
Tel: (01264) 351835
Head: Mr T Oakley
Type: Co-educational Day 11–16
No of pupils: B40 G40
Special Needs: **ADHD** ASP **AUT** DYS
HI **MLD** SP&LD W

MEADOW SPECIAL SCHOOL
Mill Chase Road, Bordon,
Hampshire GU35 0HA
Tel: (01420) 474396
Head: Mr P Greenwood
Type: Co-educational Day 4–16
No of pupils: B70 G50
Special Needs: ADD ADHD **AUT**
DOW EPI **MLD** PH **SLD** SPLD
TOU W

NORMAN GATE SPECIAL SCHOOL
Vigo Road, Andover, Hampshire
SP10 1JZ
Tel: (01264) 323423
Head: Mrs J Sansome
Type: Co-educational Day 2–11
No of pupils: 58
Special Needs: AUT MLD W

OAK LODGE SCHOOL
Roman Road, Dibden Purlieu,
Southampton, Hampshire SO4 5RQ
Tel: (023) 8084 7213
Head: Mrs B A Hawker
Type: Co-educational Day 11–16
No of pupils: B78 G29
Special Needs: ASP AUT **MLD**

RACHEL MADOCKS
Eagle Avenue, Cowplain,
Portsmouth, Hampshire PO8 9XP
Tel: (023) 9224 1818
Head: Mrs C A Browne
Type: Co-educational Day 2–19
No of pupils: B44 G34
Special Needs: PMLD SLD

ST FRANCIS SPECIAL SCHOOL
Oldbury Way, Fareham, Hampshire
PO14 3BN
Tel: (01329) 845730
Head: Mrs S Chalmers
Type: Co-educational Day 2–19
No of pupils: 98
Special Needs: **AUT** CP EPI **PMLD**
SLD W

SALTERNS SPECIAL SCHOOL
Commercial Road, Totton,
Southampton, Hampshire SO40 3AF
Tel: (023) 8086 4211
Head: Mrs J Partridge
Type: Co-educational Day 4–19
No of pupils: 58
Special Needs: AUT CP EPI PMLD
SLD W

SAMUEL CODY SPECIAL SCHOOL
Lynchford Road, Farnborough,
Hampshire GU14 6BJ
Tel: (01252) 314720
Head: Mr L Bevan
Type: Co-educational Day 11–16
No of pupils: B45 G22
Special Needs: AUT **MLD**

SAXON WOOD SPECIAL SCHOOL
Rooksdown, Barron Place,
Basingstoke, Hampshire RG24 9NH
Tel: (01256) 356635
Head: Mr P B Skinner
Type: Co-educational Day 2–11
No of pupils: B25 G25
Special Needs: **CP** DEL **EPI** HI **PH** W

SHEPHERDS DOWN SCHOOL
Shepherds Lane, Compton,
Winchester, Hampshire SO21 2AJ
Tel: (01962) 713445
Head: Mr A Gazzard
Type: Co-educational Day 4–11
No of pupils: 105
Special Needs: AUT MLD SP&LD

WATERLOO SPECIAL SCHOOL
Warfield Avenue, Waterlooville,
Hampshire PO7 7JJ
Tel: (023) 9225 5956
Head: Mr J E M Cahill
Type: Co-educational Day and
Boarding 4–11
No of pupils: 42 *No of Boarders:* W10
Special Needs: **EBD**

WHITEDOWN SCHOOL
Albert Road, Alton, Hampshire
GU34 1LP
Tel: (01420) 82201
Head: Mrs B Livings
Type: Co-educational Day 2–19
No of pupils: 48
Special Needs: AUT PMLD **SLD**

Portsmouth City Council

4th Floor, Civic Offices
Guildhall Square
Portsmouth PO1 2EA
Tel: (023) 9284 1202

CLIFFDALE PRIMARY SCHOOL
Battenburg Avenue, North End,
Portsmouth, Hampshire PO2 0SN
Tel: (023) 9266 2601
Head: Mrs L Handford
Type: Co-educational Day 4–11
No of pupils: 124
Special Needs: AUT **MLD**

EAST SHORE SPECIAL SCHOOL
Eastern Road, Milton, Portsmouth, Hampshire PO3 6EP
Tel: (023) 9283 9331
Head: P Clarke
Type: Co-educational Day 2–19
No of pupils: 80
Special Needs: AUT DOW EPI **PMLD SLD** W

REDWOOD PARK SCHOOL
Wembley Grove, Highbury, Portsmouth, Hampshire PO6 2RY
Tel: (023) 9237 7500
Head: Mrs E A Nye
Type: Co-educational Day 11–16
No of pupils: B89 G39
Special Needs: AUT **MLD**

WATERSIDE SCHOOL & UNIT
Tipner Lane, Tipner, Portsmouth, Hampshire PO2 8RA
Tel: (023) 92 665664
Head: Mr T Stokes
Type: Co-educational Boarding and Day 11–16
No of pupils: B70 *No of Boarders:* W10
Special Needs: ADD ADHD **EBD** TOU W

THE WILLOWS NURSERY SPECIAL SCHOOL
Battenburg Avenue, North End, Portsmouth, Hampshire PO2 0SN
Tel: (023) 9266 6918
Head: Mrs A M Swann
Type: Co-educational Day 2–5
No of pupils: 36
Special Needs: ADD ADHD ASP **AUT** CP DEL DOW DYP DYS EBD EPI HI **MLD** PH SLD **SP&LD** VIS

Southampton City Council

5th Floor, Frobisher House
Nelson Gate
Southampton SO15 1BZ
Tel: (023) 8022 3855

NETLEY COURT SPECIAL SCHOOL
Victoria Road, Netley Abbey, Southampton, Hampshire SO3 5DR
Tel: (023) 8045 3259
Head: Mr W R Ferry
Type: Co-educational Day 4–11
No of pupils: 80
Special Needs: AUT SP&LD

THE POLYGON SPECIAL SCHOOL
Handel Terrace, The Polygon, Southampton, Hampshire SO1 2FH
Tel: (023) 8063 6776
Head: Mr L M Gent
Type: Boys Day 11–16
No of pupils: 56
Special Needs: EBD

RED LODGE SCHOOL
Vermont Close, Winchester Road, Southampton, Hampshire SO16 7LT
Tel: (023) 8076 7660
Head: Miss S P Mackie
Type: Co-educational Day 11–16
No of pupils: 155
Special Needs: **MLD**

RIDGEWAY HOUSE SPECIAL SCHOOL
Peartree Avenue, Bitterne, Southampton, Hampshire SO19 7JL
Tel: (023) 8044 8897
Head: Mrs S J Savage
Type: Co-educational Day 3–19
No of pupils: 90
Special Needs: **SLD**

VERMONT SPECIAL SCHOOL
Vermont Close, off Winchester Road, Southampton, Hampshire SO1 7LT
Tel: (023) 8076 7988
Head: Mr E Bell
Type: Boys Day 4–11
No of pupils: 28
Special Needs: **EBD** MLD SPLD

HARTLEPOOL

Hartlepool Education Authority

Level 4, Civic Centre
Hartlepool TS24 8AY
Tel: (01429) 523734

CATCOTE SCHOOL
Catcote Road, Hartlepool TS25 4EZ
Tel: (01429) 264036
Head: Mr N Carden
Type: Co-educational Day 11–19
No of pupils: 100
Special Needs: MLD PMLD SLD W

SPRINGWELL SCHOOL
Wiltshire Way, Hartlepool TS26 0TB
Tel: (01429) 280600
Head: Mr A J Lacey
Type: Co-educational Day 2–11
No of pupils: 66
Special Needs: ADD ADHD ASP AUT CP DOW EPI HI PMLD SLD SP&LD VIS W

HEREFORDSHIRE

Herefordshire Education Authority

PO Box 185
Hereford
HR4 9ZR
Tel: (01432) 260000

BARRS COURT SCHOOL
Barrs Court Road, Hereford,
Herefordshire HR1 1EQ
Tel: (01432) 265035
Head: Mrs S Ashley
Type: Co-educational Day 11–19
No of pupils: B24 G19
Special Needs: MLD PMLD SLD

BLACKMARSTON SCHOOL
Honddu Close, Hereford,
Herefordshire HR2 7NX
Tel: (01432) 272376
Head: Mrs S Bailey
Type: Co-educational Day 2–11
No of pupils: 45
Special Needs: PMLD SLD W

WESTFIELD SCHOOL & LEOMINSTER EARLY YEARS CENTRE
Westfield Walk, Leominster,
Herefordshire HR6 8HD
Tel: (01568) 613147
Head: Mrs P Chesters
Type: Co-educational Day 3–19
No of pupils: 60
Special Needs: PMLD SLD W

HERTFORDSHIRE

Hertfordshire Education Authority

Education Offices
County Hall
Hertford SG13 8DF
Tel: (01992) 555853

AMWELL VIEW SCHOOL
St Margarets, Stanstead Abbotts,
Hertfordshire SG12 8EH
Tel: (01920) 870027
Head: Mrs J S Liversage
Type: Co-educational Day 2–19
No of pupils: B66 G32
Special Needs: AUT CP DOW EPI PMLD SLD W

BATCHWOOD SCHOOL
Townsend Drive, St Albans,
Hertfordshire AL3 5RP
Tel: (01727) 765195
Head: Mr M E Hopkins
Type: Co-educational Day 11–16
No of pupils: 53
Special Needs: EBD

BOXMOOR HOUSE SCHOOL
Box Lane, Hemel Hempstead,
Hertfordshire HP3 0DF
Tel: (01442) 256915
Head: Mr J R Hooper
Type: Boys Day and Boarding 11–16
No of pupils: 62 No of Boarders: W37
Special Needs: EBD

THE COLLETT SCHOOL
Lockers Park Lane, Hemel
Hempstead, Hertfordshire HP1 1TQ
Tel: (01442) 398988
Head: Mrs M Lemarie
Type: Co-educational Day 5–16
No of pupils: B71 G52
Special Needs: MLD

COLNBROOK SCHOOL
Hayling Road, South Oxhey,
Watford, Hertfordshire WD19 7UY
Tel: (020) 8428 1281
Head: Mr R J Hill
Type: Co-educational Day 5–11
No of pupils: 88
Special Needs: AUT MLD W

FALCONER SCHOOL
Falconer Road, Bushey, Watford,
Hertfordshire WD2 3AT
Tel: (020) 8950 2505
Head: Mr J S B Page
Type: Boys Day and Boarding 11–16
No of pupils: 60 No of Boarders: W6
Special Needs: EBD

GARSTON MANOR SCHOOL
Horseshoe Lane, Garston, Watford,
Hertfordshire WD25 7HR
Tel: (01923) 673757
Head: Mr D N Harrison
Type: Co-educational Day 11–16
No of pupils: 115
Special Needs: MLD

GREENSIDE SCHOOL
Shephall Green, Stevenage,
Hertfordshire SG2 9XS
Tel: (01438) 315356
Head: Mr D Victor
Type: Co-educational Day 2–19
No of pupils: 100
Special Needs: AUT PMLD SLD W

HAILEY HALL SCHOOL
Hailey Lane, Hertford, Hertfordshire
SG13 7PB
Tel: (01992) 465208
Head: Mr B Evans
Type: Boys Boarding and Day 11–16
No of pupils: 55 No of Boarders: W30
Special Needs: EBD

HEATHLANDS SCHOOL
Heathlands Drive, St Albans,
Hertfordshire AL3 5AY
Tel: (01727) 868596
Head: Mr M Davis
Type: Co-educational Boarding and
Day 3–16
No of pupils: B58 G42
No of Boarders: W27
Special Needs: HI W

KNIGHTSFIELD SCHOOL
Knightsfield, Welwyn Garden City,
Hertfordshire AL8 7LW
Tel: (01707) 376874
Head: Mrs L M Leith
Type: Co-educational Day and
Boarding 11–18
No of pupils: 50 No of Boarders: W20
Special Needs: HI W

LAKESIDE SCHOOL
Lemsford Lane, Welwyn Garden City, Hertfordshire AL8 6YN
Tel: (01707) 327410
Head: Mrs J Chamberlain
Type: Co-educational Day 2–19
No of pupils: 63
Special Needs: PMLD SLD W

LARWOOD SCHOOL
Webb Rise, Stevenage, Hertfordshire SG1 5QU
Tel: (01438) 236333
Head: Mr A K Whittaker
Type: Co-educational Day and Boarding 4–11
No of pupils: B25 G26
Special Needs: EBD

LONSDALE SCHOOL
Webb Rise, Stevenage, Hertfordshire SG1 5QU
Tel: (01438) 357631
Head: Mrs P M Clark
Type: Co-educational Day and Boarding 3–18
No of pupils: 84 *No of Boarders:* W28
Special Needs: PH W

MEADOW WOOD SCHOOL
Coldharbour Lane, Bushey, Watford, Hertfordshire WD2 3NU
Tel: (020) 8420 4720
Head: Mr J Addison
Type: Co-educational Day 3–11
No of pupils: 32
Special Needs: PH W

MIDDLETON SCHOOL
Walnut Tree Walk, Ware, Hertfordshire SG12 9PD
Tel: (01920) 485152
Head: Mr A Staras
Type: Co-educational Day 4–11
Special Needs: MLD

ST LUKE'S SCHOOL
Crouch Hall Lane, Redbourn, Hertfordshire AL3 7ET
Tel: (01582) 626727
Head: Mr P Johnson
Type: Co-educational Day 9–16
No of pupils: 170
Special Needs: ASP AUT HI MLD

SOUTHFIELD SCHOOL
Travellers Lane, Hatfield, Hertfordshire AL10 8TJ
Tel: (01707) 258259
Head: Mr M B Philp
Type: Co-educational Day 4–11
No of pupils: B54 G26
Special Needs: MLD W

THE VALLEY SCHOOL
Valley Way, Stevenage, Hertfordshire SG2 9AB
Tel: (01438) 747274
Head: Mr R G Stabler
Type: Co-educational Day 11–16
No of pupils: B93 G79
Special Needs: MLD

WOODFIELD SCHOOL
Malmes Croft, Leverstock Green, Hemel Hempstead, Hertfordshire HP3 8RL
Tel: (01442) 253476
Head: Mrs J Johnson
Type: Co-educational Day 5–19
No of pupils: 78
Special Needs: AUT SLD W

WOOLGROVE SCHOOL
Pryor Way, Letchworth, Hertfordshire SG6 2PT
Tel: (01462) 622422
Head: Mrs R V Tutt
Type: Co-educational Day 5–11
No of pupils: 108
Special Needs: AUT MLD

ISLE OF WIGHT

Isle of Wight Education Authority

County Hall
Newport
Isle of Wight PO30 1UD
Tel: (01983) 821000

MEDINA HOUSE SCHOOL
School Lane, Newport, Isle of Wight PO30 2HS
Tel: (01983) 522917
Head: Mr D M Hughes
Type: Co-educational Day 2–19
No of pupils: 77
Special Needs: AUT CP DOW EPI PMLD SLD W

WATERGATE SCHOOL
Watergate Road, Newport, Isle of Wight PO30 1XW
Tel: (01983) 524634
Head: Mrs A E Munt-Davies
Type: Co-educational Day 3–18
No of pupils: 204
Special Needs: MLD W

KENT

Kent Education Authority

Sessions House
County Hall
Maidstone ME14 1XA
Tel: (01622) 696565

ASPEN 2
Archers Court School, Whitfield, Dover, Kent CT16 2EG
Tel: (01304) 825351
Head: Mr A Barwick
Type: Co-educational Day
No of pupils: B7 G9
Special Needs: PMLD SLD W

BOWER GROVE SCHOOL
Fant Lane, Maidstone, Kent ME16 8NL
Tel: (01622) 726773
Head: Mr T N Phipps
Type: Co-educational Day 5–16
No of pupils: B93 G62
Special Needs: AUT CP DOW DYP EBD EPI HI MLD PH SP&LD

BROOMHILL BANK SCHOOL
Broomhill Road, Rusthall, Tunbridge
Wells, Kent TN3 0TB
Tel: (01892) 522666
Head: Mr P Barnett
Type: Girls Boarding and Day 8–19
No of pupils: 90 *No of Boarders:* F28
Special Needs: **MLD** SP&LD

EK HOSPITAL SCHOOL
City View, Canterbury, Kent CT2 8PT
Tel: (01227) 781548
Type: Co-educational Day
No of pupils: 40

FIVE ACRE WOOD SCHOOL
Boughton Lane, Maidstone, Kent
ME15 9QL
Tel: (01622) 743925
Head: Ms J E Kratochvil
Type: Co-educational Day 5–19
No of pupils: 62
Special Needs: AUT **PMLD SLD** W

THE FORELAND SCHOOL
Lanthorne Road, Broadstairs, Kent
CT10 3NX
Tel: (01843) 863891
Head: Mr P S Hare
Type: Co-educational Day 2–19
No of pupils: 130
Special Needs: CP EPI HI PH **PMLD
SLD** VIS

FOXWOOD SCHOOL
Seabrook Road, Hythe, Kent
CT21 5QJ
Tel: (01303) 261155
Head: Mr C Soulsby
Type: Co-educational Boarding and
Day 2–19
No of pupils: B64 G30
No of Boarders: W26
Special Needs: AUT EBD PMLD SLD

FURNESS SCHOOL
Rowhill Road, Hextable, Swanley,
Kent BR8 7RP
Tel: (01322) 662937
Head: Mr R J Chapman
Type: Boys Day and Boarding 11–16
No of pupils: 72 *No of Boarders:* W52
Special Needs: ADHD EBD MLD

GAP HOUSE SCHOOL
South Cliffe Parade, Broadstairs,
Kent CT10 1TJ
Tel: (01843) 861679
Head: Mr I P Cooke
Type: Co-educational Boarding and
Day 3–11
No of pupils: B53 G15
No of Boarders: W26
Special Needs: ASP DYS SP&LD SPLD

GRANGE PARK
Birling Road, Leybourne, Maidstone,
Kent ME19 5QA
Tel: (01732) 842144
Head: Mrs J Hanley
Type: Co-educational Day 11–19
No of pupils: 40
Special Needs: ASP **AUT** CP EBD EPI
HI MLD PH PMLD SLD SP&LD
VIS W

HALSTEAD PLACE SCHOOL
Church Road, Halstead, Sevenoaks,
Kent TN14 7HQ
Tel: (01959) 533294
Head: Mr J Walden
Type: Co-educational Day and
Boarding 11–16
No of pupils: B60 *No of Boarders:* W24
Special Needs: ADD ADHD **EBD**

HARBOUR SCHOOL
Elms Vale Road, Dover, Kent
CT17 9PS
Tel: (01304) 201964
Head: Mr A Berresford
Type: Co-educational Day 5–16
No of pupils: B92 G46
Special Needs: **MLD** W

HIGHVIEW SCHOOL
Moat Farm Road, Folkestone, Kent
CT19 5DJ
Tel: (01303) 258755
Head: Mr C J Hurling
Type: Co-educational Day 5–16
No of pupils: 141
Special Needs: MLD SLD SP&LD

IFIELD SCHOOL
Cedar Avenue, Gravesend, Kent
DA12 5JT
Tel: (01474) 365485
Head: Mr S M Harrison
Type: Co-educational Day 5–16
No of pupils: B111 G56
Special Needs: ASP AUT DOW DYS
MLD PH SP&LD SPLD

LALEHAM SCHOOL†
Northdown Park Road, Margate,
Kent CT9 2TP
Tel: (01843) 221946
Head: Mr K Mileham
Type: Co-educational Boarding and
Day 11–16
No of pupils: B110 G15
No of Boarders: W60
Special Needs: DYC DYP **DYS** SP&LD
SPLD

MILESTONE SCHOOL
Ash Road, New Ash Green, Dartford,
Kent DA3 8JZ
Tel: (01474) 709420
Head: Miss E T Flanagan
Type: Co-educational Day 2–19
No of pupils: 160
Special Needs: **AUT PMLD SLD** VIS W

OAKLEY SCHOOL
Pembury Road, Tunbrige Wells, Kent
Tel: (01892) 823096
Head: M Absalom
Type: Co-educational Day 11–19

ORCHARD SCHOOL
Cambridge Road, Canterbury, Kent
CT1 3QQ
Tel: (01227) 769220
Head: Mr B S Shelley
Type: Co-educational Day 7–16
No of pupils: B80 G30
Special Needs: **MLD** W

PORTAL HOUSE SCHOOL
Sea Street, St Margaret's-at-Cliffe,
Dover, Kent CT15 6AR
Tel: (01304) 853033
Head: Mr L Sage
Type: Co-educational Boarding 6–11
No of pupils: 44 *No of Boarders:* W12
Special Needs: **EBD**

RIDGEVIEW SCHOOL
Cage Green Road, Tonbridge, Kent
TN10 4PT
Tel: (01732) 771384
Head: Mr A E Carver
Type: Co-educational Day 2–19
No of pupils: 95
Special Needs: **AUT** DOW **PMLD
SLD** W

ROWHILL SCHOOL
Stock Lane, Wilmington, Dartford,
Kent DA2 7BZ
Tel: (01322) 225490
Head: Mr M A Grimsby
Type: Co-educational Day 4–19

ST ANTHONY'S SCHOOL
St Anthony's Way, Margate, Kent
CT9 3RA
Tel: (01843) 292015
Head: Mr R A O'Dell
Type: Co-educational Day 3–16
No of pupils: 170
Special Needs: EBD **MLD**

ST BARTHOLOMEW'S SCHOOL
Attlee Way, North Street, Milton Regis, Sittingbourne, Kent ME10 2HE
Tel: (01795) 477888
Head: Ms G M Hurstfield
Type: Co-educational Day 4–16
No of pupils: 80
Special Needs: **AUT PMLD SLD** W

ST NICHOLAS' SCHOOL
Holme Oak Close, Nunnery Fields, Canterbury, Kent CT1 3JJ
Tel: (01227) 464316
Head: Mr D Lewis
Type: Co-educational Day 4–19
No of pupils: B57 G35
Special Needs: **AUT CP DOW PMLD SLD** W

ST THOMAS' SCHOOL
Swanstree Avenue, Sittingbourne, Kent ME10 4NL
Tel: (01795) 477788
Head: Mr P J Rankin
Type: Co-educational Day 5–19
No of pupils: B85 G55
Special Needs: **MLD SP&LD SPLD** W

STONE BAY SCHOOL
Stone Road, Broadstairs, Kent CT10 1EB
Tel: (01843) 863421
Head: Mr R Edey
Type: Boarding and Day 11–19
No of pupils: 58 *No of Boarders:* W39
Special Needs: **AUT MLD SLD**

SWINFORD MANOR SCHOOL
Great Chart, Ashford, Kent TN23 3BT
Tel: (01233) 622958
Head: Mr J L Davies
Type: Boys Day 11–16
No of pupils: 62 *No of Boarders:* W40
Special Needs: **EBD**

VALENCE SCHOOL
Westerham, Kent TN16 1QN
Tel: (01959) 562156
Head: Mr R Gooding
Type: Co-educational Boarding and Day 5–19
No of pupils: B69 G36
No of Boarders: W65
Special Needs: **CP EPI PH** W

WK HOSPITAL SCHOOL
Woodview Campus, Main Road, Longfield, Dartford, Kent DA3 7PW
Head: Mrs J Locke
Type: Co-educational Day
No of pupils: 42
Special Needs: **DEL EPI PH** W

WYVERN SCHOOL
Willesborough Site, Hythe Road, Ashford, Kent TN24 0QF
Tel: (01223) 621468
Head: Mr D Spencer
Type: Co-educational Day 5–19
Special Needs: **MLD SLD**

Medway Council

Civic Centre
Strood
Rochester ME2 4AU
Tel: (01634) 306000

ABBEY COURT SCHOOL
Rede Court Road, Strood, Rochester, Kent ME2 3SP
Tel: (01634) 718153/714600
Head: Ms K Joy
Type: Co-educational Day 5–19
No of pupils: B77 G38
Special Needs: **PMLD SLD**

BRADFIELDS SCHOOL
Churchill Avenue, Chatham, Kent ME5 0LB
Tel: (01634) 683990
Head: Mr P J Harris
Type: Co-educational Day 11–19
No of pupils: B142 G64
Special Needs: **AUT EBD MLD** PH

DANECOURT SCHOOL
Hotel Road, Gillingham, Kent ME8 6AA
Tel: (01634) 232589
Head: Mrs A Peters
Type: Co-educational Day 5–11
No of pupils: B67 G39
Special Needs: **ADD ADHD AUT DOW MLD** W

LANCASHIRE

Blackburn with Darwen Borough Council

Education Offices
Town Hall
Blackburn BB1 7DY
Tel: (01254) 585585

BANK HEY SCHOOL
Heys Lane, Blackburn, Lancashire BB2 4NW
Tel: (01254) 261655
Head: Mr T Feely
Type: Co-educational Day 11–16
No of pupils: 40
Special Needs: **ADD ADHD EBD**

BROADLANDS SCHOOL
Blackburn, Lancashire BB1 2LA
Tel: (01254) 56044
Head: Mrs D H Mitchell
Type: Co-educational Day 3–5

CROSSHILL SCHOOL
Shadsworth Road, Blackburn, Lancashire BB1 2HR
Tel: (01254) 667713
Head: Mr M J Hatch
Type: Co-educational Day 5–16
No of pupils: B105 G53
Special Needs: **MLD**

NEWFIELD SPECIAL SCHOOL
Roman Road, Blackburn, Lancashire BB1 2LA
Tel: (01254) 588600
Head: Mrs J B Barrie
Type: Co-educational Day 2–19

TULLYALLAN SCHOOL
Salisbury Road, Darwen, Lancashire BB3 1HZ
Tel: (01254) 702317
Head: Mrs J P Holman
Type: Co-educational Day 5–16
No of pupils: 50
Special Needs: **EBD**

Blackpool Borough Council

Education Offices
Progress House
Clifton Road
Blackpool FY4 4US
Tel: (01253) 477477

PARK SCHOOL
Whitegate Drive, Blackpool,
Lancashire FY3 9HF
Tel: (01253) 764130
Head: Mr E N M Parry
Type: Co-educational Day 4–16
No of pupils: 150
Special Needs: **MLD** W

WOODLANDS SCHOOL
Whitegate Drive, Blackpool,
Lancashire FY3 9HF
Tel: (01253) 316722
Head: Mr S J Forde
Type: Co-educational Day 2–19
No of pupils: B55 G26
Special Needs: PMLD SLD W

Lancashire Education Authority

PO Box 61
County Hall
Preston PR1 8RJ
Tel: (01772) 254868

ASTLEY PARK SCHOOL
Harrington Road, Chorley,
Lancashire PR7 1JZ
Tel: (01257) 262227
Head: Mr J McAndrew
Type: Co-educational Day 4–16
No of pupils: B80 G46
Special Needs: **MLD** W

BEACON SCHOOL
Tanhouse Road, Tanhouse,
Skelmersdale, Lancashire WN8 6BA
Tel: (01695) 721066
Head: Mr J H Taylor
Type: Co-educational Day 5–16
No of pupils: 72
Special Needs: EBD

BLACK MOSS SCHOOL
School Lane, Chapel House,
Skelmersdale, Lancashire WN8 8EH
Tel: (01695) 721487
Head: Mr P F Boycott
Type: Co-educational Day 4–18
No of pupils: 140
Special Needs: **MLD** PMLD

BLEASDALE HOUSE SCHOOL
Emesgate Lane, Silverdale,
Carnforth, Lancashire LA5 0RG
Tel: (01524) 701217
Head: Mrs L Ormrod
Type: Co-educational Boarding and
Day 2–19
No of pupils: 45 *No of Boarders:* F29
Special Needs: CP DEL EPI PH **PMLD**
SLD W

BROADFIELD SCHOOL
Fielding Lane, Oswaldtwistle,
Accrington, Lancashire BB5 3BE
Tel: (01254) 381782
Head: Mrs J White
Type: Co-educational Day 5–16
No of pupils: 115
Special Needs: AUT **MLD** SLD

BROOKFIELD SCHOOL
Poulton-le-Fylde, Lancashire
FY6 7HT
Tel: (01253) 886895
Head: I M Thomas
Type: Co-educational Day 11–16

CALDER VIEW SCHOOL
March Street, Burnley, Lancashire
BB12 0BU
Tel: (01282) 433946
Head: Mrs F Entwistle
Type: Co-educational Day 4–16
No of pupils: B90 G50
Special Needs: **MLD SLD** SP&LD W

THE COPPICE SCHOOL
Ash Grove, Bamber Bridge, Preston,
Lancashire PR5 6GY
Tel: (01772) 363342
Head: Mrs A Jenkins
Type: Co-educational Day 2–19
No of pupils: 58
Special Needs: PMLD SLD W

CRIBDEN HOUSE SCHOOL
Haslingden Road, Rawtenstall,
Rossendale, Lancashire BB4 6RX
Tel: (01706) 213048
Head: Mrs J Lord
Type: Co-educational Day 5–11
No of pupils: 50
Special Needs: EBD

ELMS SCHOOL
Moor Park, Blackpool Road, Preston,
Lancashire PR1 6AS
Tel: (01772) 792681
Head: Mr S Artis
Type: Co-educational Day 2–19
No of pupils: 70
Special Needs: PMLD SLD W

GIBFIELD SCHOOL
Gibfield Road, Colne, Lancashire
BB8 8JT
Tel: (01282) 865011
Head: Mr C I Cohen
Type: Co-educational Day 5–16

GREAT ARLEY SCHOOL
Holly Road, Thornton-Cleveleys,
Blackpool, Lancashire FY5 4HH
Tel: (01253) 821072
Head: Mrs J L Johns
Type: Co-educational Day 4–16
No of pupils: 90
Special Needs: **MLD**

HILLSIDE SCHOOL
Ribchester Road, Longridge, Preston,
Lancashire PR3 3XB
Tel: (01772) 782205
Head: Mr G J Fitzpatrick
Type: Co-educational Day 2–16
No of pupils: B50 G10
Special Needs: AUT

KINGSBURY SCHOOL
Skelmersdale, Lancashire WN8 8EL
Tel: (01695) 722991
Head: J Hajnrych
Type: Co-educational Day 2–19
No of pupils: B44 G15
Special Needs: SLD

THE LOYNE SCHOOL
Sefton Drive, Lancaster, Lancashire
LA1 2PZ
Tel: (01524) 64543
Head: Mrs C Murphy
Type: Co-educational Day 2–19
No of pupils: 53
Special Needs: AUT **PMLD** SLD W

MAYFIELD SCHOOL
Gloucester Road, Chorley,
Lancashire PR7 3HN
Tel: (01257) 263063
Head: Mr P Monk
Type: Co-educational Day 2–19
No of pupils: B34 G26
Special Needs: SLD W

MOOR HEY SCHOOL
Far Croft, Lostock Hall, Preston,
Lancashire PR5 5SU
Tel: (01772) 336976
Head: Mr C W T Wilson
Type: Co-educational Day 5–16
No of pupils: B70 G38
Special Needs: **MLD**

MOORBROOK SCHOOL
Ainslie Road, Preston, Lancashire
PR2 3DB
Tel: (01772) 774752
Head: Mr P Bardsley
Type: Co-educational Day 11–16

MOORFIELD SCHOOL
Preston, Lancashire PR1 6AA
Tel: (01772) 295378
Head: Mr P Johnson
Type: Co-educational Day 2–19
No of pupils: B31 G33
Special Needs: ADD AUT CP MLD **PH SLD SP&LD**

MORECAMBE ROAD SCHOOL
Morecambe Road, Morecambe,
Lancashire LA3 3AB
Tel: (01524) 414384/832074
Head: Mr T G Pickles
Type: Co-educational Day 3–16
No of pupils: 181
Special Needs: AUT DOW EBD HI **MLD** VIS

NORTH CLIFFE SCHOOL
Blackburn Old Road, Great
Harwood, Blackburn, Lancashire
BB6 7UW
Tel: (01254) 885245
Head: Mr R L Whitaker
Type: Co-educational Day 4–16
No of pupils: 110
Special Needs: **MLD**

PEAR TREE SCHOOL
29 Station Road, Kirkham,
Lancashire PR4 2HA
Tel: (01772) 683609
Head: Ms J Cook
Type: Co-educational Day 2–19
No of pupils: 60
Special Needs: PMLD **SLD** W

PRIMROSE HILL SCHOOL
Harrogate Crescent, Burnley,
Lancashire BB10 2NX
Tel: (01282) 424216
Head: Mr G McCabe
Type: Co-educational Day 3–16
No of pupils: B28 G19
Special Needs: CP DEL DYP DYS EBD **EPI** HI MLD **PH PMLD** SLD SP&LD SPLD VIS W

RED MARSH SCHOOL
Holly Road, Thornton Cleveleys,
Blackpool, Lancashire FY5 4HH
Tel: (01253) 868451
Head: Miss D Halpin
Type: Co-educational Day 2–19
No of pupils: 49
Special Needs: PMLD SLD

SHERBURN SCHOOL
Moor Park, Blackpool Road, Preston,
Lancashire PR1 6AA
Tel: (01772) 795749
Head: Mr M R Moss
Type: Co-educational Day 4–16
No of pupils: B58 G19
Special Needs: **MLD** W

TOR VIEW SCHOOL
Clod Lane, Haslingden, Lancashire
BB4 6LR
Tel: (01706) 214640
Head: Mr A J Squire
Type: Co-educational Day 4–19
No of pupils: 100
Special Needs: ASP **AUT** CP DOW DYC DYP DYS EPI HI **MLD** PH **PMLD** SLD VIS W

TOWNHOUSE SCHOOL
Townhouse Road, Nelson,
Lancashire BB9 8JT
Tel: (01282) 614013
Head: Mrs D E Morris
Type: Co-educational Day 2–19
No of pupils: B22 G19
Special Needs: **AUT** PH **PMLD SLD** W

WENNINGTON HALL
Wennington, Lancashire LA2 8NS
Tel: (01524) 221333
Head: Mr J W N Prendergast
Type: Boys Boarding and Day
No of pupils: 70 *No of Boarders:* W46
Special Needs: ADHD **EBD** SPLD

WESTWAY SCHOOL
March Street, Burnley, Lancashire
BB12 0BU
Tel: (01282) 704499
Head: Mrs A C Stafford
Type: Co-educational Day 3–19
No of pupils: 30
Special Needs: **PMLD SLD** W

WHITE ASH SCHOOL
Thwaites Road, Oswaldtwistle,
Accrington, Lancashire BB5 4QG
Tel: (01254) 235772
Head: Mr B D Frew
Type: Co-educational Day 3–19
No of pupils: B24 G13
Special Needs: **ASP** AUT CP DOW EPI **PMLD SLD** W

LEICESTERSHIRE

Leicester City Education Authority

Marlborough House
38 Welford Road
Leicester LE2 7AA
Tel: (0116) 252 7807

ASH FIELD SCHOOL
Broad Avenue, Leicester LE5 4PY
Tel: (0116) 273 7151
Head: Mr D Bateson
Type: Co-educational Day and
Boarding 4–19
No of pupils: B70 G50
No of Boarders: W18
Special Needs: **CP HI PH SP&LD** VIS W

ELLESMERE COLLEGE
Ellesmere Road, Leicester LE3 1BE
Tel: (0116) 289 4242
Head: Ms F Moir
Type: Co-educational Day 11–19
No of pupils: 250
Special Needs: MLD W

EMILY FORTEY SCHOOL
Glenfield Road, Leicester LE3 6DG
Tel: (0116) 285 7395
Head: Mr M W Thompson
Type: Co-educational Day 4–18
No of pupils: B48 G35
Special Needs: AUT CP EBD EPI HI PH **PMLD SLD** SP&LD SPLD VIS

MILLGATE CENTRE
18 Scott Street, Leicester LE2 6DW
Tel: (0116) 270 4922
Head: Mrs K M Howells
Type: Boys Boarding and Day 11–16
No of pupils: 45 *No of Boarders:* W10
Special Needs: EBD

NETHER HALL SCHOOL
Netherhall Road, Leicester LE5 1DT
Tel: (0116) 241 7258
Head: Mr P J Goodchild
Type: Co-educational Day 5–19
No of pupils: B43 G34
Special Needs: **PMLD SLD**

OAKLANDS SCHOOL
Whitehall Road, Evington, Leicester
LE5 6GJ
Tel: (0116) 241 5921/2
Head: Mr P C Rowlands
Type: Co-educational Day 5–11
No of pupils: 80
Special Needs: **MLD** W

PIPER WAY SCHOOL
Grenfield Road, Leicester LE3 6DN
Tel: (0116) 285 6181
Head: Mrs A Standley
Type: Co-educational Day 5–11
No of pupils: 80
Special Needs: AUT **MLD** W

WESTERN PARK SCHOOL
Western Park, Leicester LE3 6HX
Tel: (01274) 687236
Head: Mr R D Gordon
Type: Day
No of pupils: 60
Special Needs: CP DEL EPI SP&LD

Leicestershire Education Authority

County Hall
Glenfield
Leicester LE3 8RF
Tel: (0116) 232 3232

ASHMOUNT SCHOOL
Ashmount, Beacon Road,
Loughborough, Leicestershire
LE11 2BG
Tel: (01509) 268506
Head: Mrs K Waplington
Type: Co-educational Day 4–19
No of pupils: B35 G25
Special Needs: AUT CP DOW EPI PH
PMLD **SLD** W

CRAVEN LODGE SCHOOL
Burton Road, Melton Mowbray,
Leicestershire LE13 1DJ
Tel: (01664) 562246
Head: Mr P D Coopey
Type: Co-educational Day 4–11
No of pupils: 45
Special Needs: **AUT MLD** SP&LD

DOROTHY GOODMAN SCHOOL
Middlefield Lane, Hinckley,
Leicestershire LE10 0RB
Tel: (01455) 634582
Head: Mr T Smith
Type: Co-educational Day 3–19
No of pupils: 64
Special Needs: **AUT** DOW EPI **PMLD**
SLD W

FOREST WAY SCHOOL
Cropston Drive, Coalville, Leicester
LE67 4HS
Tel: (01530) 831899
Head: Ms L Slinger
Type: Co-educational Day 3–19
No of pupils: 86
Special Needs: AUT CP DEL DOW
EBD EPI HI PMLD **SLD** SP&LD
VIS W

MAPLEWELL HALL SCHOOL
Maplewell Road, Woodhouse Eaves,
Loughborough, Leicestershire
LE12 8QY
Tel: (01509) 890237
Head: Mrs P Jones
Type: Co-educational Day and
Boarding 11–16
No of pupils: B65 G50
No of Boarders: F17
Special Needs: AUT **MLD**

THE MOUNT SCHOOL
The Mount, Leicester Road, Melton
Mowbray, Leicestershire LE13 0DA
Tel: (01664) 562418
Head: Mr P Henshaw
Type: Co-educational Day 3–18
No of pupils: B19 G4
Special Needs: PMLD SLD

LINCOLNSHIRE

Lincolnshire Education Authority

County Offices
Newland
Lincoln LN1 1YQ
Tel: (01522) 552222

AMBERGATE SCHOOL
Dysart Road, Grantham,
Lincolnshire NG31 7LP
Tel: (01476) 564957
Head: Mr R McCrossen
Type: Co-educational Day 5–16
No of pupils: 70
Special Needs: **MLD** W

THE ASH VILLA SPECIAL SCHOOL
Rauceby Hospital, Willoughby Road,
Sleaford, Lincolnshire NG34 8PP
Tel: (01529) 416046
Head: Mr D Robinson
Type: Co-educational Boarding and
Day 8–16
No of pupils: B12 G8
No of Boarders: F16
Special Needs: ADD ADHD ASP DEL
DYP DYS EBD EPI MLD TOU W

THE BECKETT SCHOOL
White's Wood Lane, Gainsborough,
Lincolnshire DN21 1TW
Tel: (01427) 612139
Head: Mrs S Hayter
Type: Co-educational Day 2–19
No of pupils: B20 G13
Special Needs: PMLD SLD W

THE ERESBY SCHOOL
Eresby Avenue, Spilsby, Lincolnshire
PE23 5HU
Tel: (01790) 752441
Head: Mr D J Middlehurst
Type: Co-educational Day 2–19
No of pupils: 41
Special Needs: PMLD SLD W

GARTH SCHOOL
Pinchbeck Road, Spalding,
Lincolnshire PE11 1QF
Tel: (01775) 725566
Head: Mrs L Dowson
Type: Co-educational Day 2–19
No of pupils: 26
Special Needs: PMLD **SLD** W

GOSBERTON HOUSE SCHOOL
Westhorpe Road, Gosberton,
Spalding, Lincolnshire PE11 4EW
Tel: (01775) 840250
Head: Mr M R Allen
Type: Co-educational Day
No of pupils: 86
Special Needs: AUT MLD

JOHN FIELDING SCHOOL
Ashlawn Drive, Boston, Lincolnshire
PE21 9PX
Tel: (01205) 363395
Head: Mrs S M Meakin
Type: Co-educational Day 2–19
No of pupils: B21 G8
Special Needs: PMLD **SLD** W

PRIORY SCHOOL
Neville Avenue, Spalding,
Lincolnshire PE11 2EH
Tel: (01775) 724080
Head: Mr B J Howes
Type: Co-educational Day 11–16
No of pupils: 95
Special Needs: ADD **ADHD** ASP **AUT**
DOW EBD **MLD** W

ST FRANCIS SPECIAL SCHOOL
Wickenby Crescent, Lincoln LN1 3TJ
Tel: (01522) 526498
Head: Mrs A Hoffman
Type: Co-educational Day and
Boarding 2–19
No of pupils: 93 *No of Boarders:* W33
Special Needs: **CP** DEL **DOW** EPI
MLD **PH** W

ST LAWRENCE SCHOOL
Bowl Alley Lane, Horncastle,
Lincolnshire LN9 5EJ
Tel: (01507) 522563
Head: D Smith
Type: Co-educational Day and
Boarding 5–16
No of pupils: 120 *No of Boarders:* W40
Special Needs: **MLD** W

SANDON SCHOOL
Sandon Close, Sandon Road,
Grantham, Lincolnshire NG31 9AX
Tel: (01476) 564994
Head: Mrs S Gill
Type: Co-educational Day 2–19
No of pupils: B31 G22
Special Needs: AUT CP **DOW** EPI
PMLD SLD W

STUBTON HALL SCHOOL
Stubton, Newark, Lincolnshire
NG23 5DD
Tel: (01636) 626607
Head: Mr M Mihkelson
Type: Co-educational Boarding and
Day 6–16
No of pupils: B50 G4
No of Boarders: W46
Special Needs: **EBD**

WILLIAM HARRISON SPECIAL SCHOOL
Middlefield Lane, Gainsborough,
Lincolnshire DN21 1PU
Tel: (01427) 615498
Head: Dr M J Blackband
Type: Co-educational Day 3–16
No of pupils: B65 G35
Special Needs: ADD ADHD AUT
DOW EPI HI MLD SP&LD W

THE WILLOUGHBY SCHOOL
South Road, Bourne, Lincolnshire
PE10 9JE
Tel: (01778) 425203
Head: Mr P Pike
Type: Co-educational Day 2–19
No of pupils: 66
Special Needs: AUT CP DOW **PMLD**
SLD W

North Lincolnshire Education Authority
PO Box 35
Hewson House
Station Road
Brigg DN20 8XJ
Tel: (01724) 297240

ST LUKE'S SCHOOL
Burghley Road, Scunthorpe, North
Lincolnshire DN16 1JD
Tel: (01724) 844560
Head: Dr R W Ashdown
Type: Co-educational Day 3–16
No of pupils: 80
Special Needs: PMLD SLD W

North East Lincolnshire Education Authority
Eleanor Street
Grimsby
N. E. Lincolnshire DN32 9DU
Tel: (01472) 313131

CAMBRIDGE PARK SCHOOL
Cambridge Road, Grimsby, North
East Lincolnshire DN34 5EB
Tel: (01472) 230110
Head: Mrs G Kendall
Type: Co-educational Day 3–16
No of pupils: B108 G39
Special Needs: ADD **AUT** DOW DYP
EBD EPI HI **MLD SP&LD** VIS W

HUMBERSTON PARK SCHOOL
St Thomas Close, Humberston,
North East Lincolnshire DN36 4HS
Tel: (01472) 590645
Head: Mr A A Zielinski
Type: Co-educational Day 3–19
No of pupils: 80
Special Needs: PMLD SLD W

LONDON

Barnet Education Authority
The Old Town Hall
1 Friern Barnet Lane
London N11 3DL
Tel: (020) 8359 2000

MAPLEDOWN SCHOOL
Claremont Road, London NW2 1TR
Tel: (020) 8455 4111
Head: Mr J Feltham
Type: Co-educational Day 11–19
No of pupils: B29 G31
Special Needs: PMLD SLD

NORTHWAY SCHOOL
The Fairway, Mill Hill, London
NW7 3HS
Tel: (020) 8959 4232
Head: Mrs L Burgess
Type: Co-educational Day 5–11
No of pupils: B46 G19
Special Needs: **AUT MLD** W

OAK LODGE SCHOOL
Heath View, off East End Road,
London N2 0QY
Tel: (020) 8444 6711
Head: Mrs L Walker
Type: Co-educational Day 11–19
No of pupils: B90 G60
Special Needs: AUT MLD

OAKLEIGH SCHOOL
Oakleigh Road North, Whetstone,
London N20 0DH
Tel: (020) 8368 5336
Head: Mrs J L Charlesworth
Type: Co-educational Day 2–11
No of pupils: B30 G26
Special Needs: AUT PMLD W

Bexley Education Authority
Hill View Drive
Hill View
Welling
Kent DA16 3RY
Tel: (020) 8303 7777

MARLBOROUGH SCHOOL
Marlborough Park Avenue, Sidcup,
Kent DA15 9DP
Tel: (020) 8300 6896
Head: Mrs A Chamberlain
Type: Co-educational Day 11–19
No of pupils: B39 G25
Special Needs: PMLD SLD

OAKWOOD SCHOOL
Woodside Road, Bexleyheath, Kent
DA7 6LB
Tel: (01322) 529240
Head: Ms R Warner
Type: Co-educational Day 11–16
No of pupils: 56
Special Needs: EBD

SHENSTONE SCHOOL
Old Road, Crayford, Kent DA1 4DZ
Tel: (01322) 524145
Head: Mrs L Aldcroft
Type: Co-educational Day 2–11
No of pupils: B40 G20
Special Needs: AUT CP DOW EPI HI
PH PMLD SLD VIS W

WESTBROOKE SCHOOL
South Gipsy Road, Welling, Kent
DA16 1JP
Tel: (020) 8304 1320
Head: Mrs C A Hance
Type: Co-educational Day 4–11
No of pupils: 40
Special Needs: ASP EBD W

Brent Education Authority
PO Box 1
Chesterfield House
9 Park Lane
Wembley
Middlesex HA9 7RW
Tel: (020) 8937 3130

GROVE PARK SCHOOL
Grove Park, Kingsbury, London
NW9 0JY
Tel: (020) 8204 3293
Head: Ms J F Edwards
Type: Co-educational Day 2–19
No of pupils: B30 G30
Special Needs: CP DEL EPI PH W

HAY LANE SCHOOL
Grove Park, Kingsbury, London
NW9 0JY
Tel: (020) 8204 5396
Head: Mrs P M Theuma
Type: Co-educational Day 2–19
Special Needs: PMLD SLD W

MANOR SCHOOL
Chamberlayne Road, Kensal Rise,
London NW10 3NT
Tel: (020) 8968 3160
Head: Mrs J Drake
Type: Co-educational Day 4–11
No of pupils: 135
Special Needs: AUT DYP MLD SLD
SP&LD W

VERNON HOUSE SCHOOL
Drury Way, London NW10 0NQ
Tel: (020) 8451 6961
Head: Mr G S Davidson
Type: Co-educational Day 5–12
No of pupils: 50
Special Needs: EBD

WOODFIELD SCHOOL
Glenwood Avenue, Kingsbury,
London NW9 7LY
Tel: (020) 8205 1977
Head: Mr H Williams
Type: Co-educational Day 11–16
No of pupils: 100
Special Needs: MLD SP&LD

Bromley Education Authority
Civic Centre
Stockwell Close
Bromley BR1 3UH
Tel: (020) 8464 3333

GLEBE SCHOOL
Hawes Lane, West Wickham, Kent
BR4 9AE
Tel: (020) 8777 4540
Head: Mr K Seed
Type: Co-educational Day 11–16
No of pupils: 180
Special Needs: MLD

MARJORIE MCCLURE SCHOOL
Hawkwood Lane, Chislehurst, Kent
BR7 5PS
Tel: (020) 8467 0174
Head: Dr J W Wardle
Type: Co-educational Day 3–19
No of pupils: 80
Special Needs: CP DEL EPI PH W

RECTORY PADDOCK SCHOOL & RESEARCH UNIT
Main Road, Orpington, Kent
BR5 3HS
Tel: (01689) 870519
Head: Dr V I Hinchcliffe
Type: Co-educational Day 4–19
No of pupils: 75
Special Needs: PMLD SLD W

WOODBROOK SCHOOL
2 Hayne Road, Beckenham, Kent
BR3 4HY
Tel: (020) 8650 7205
Head: Mr S Gillow
Type: Co-educational Day 4–19
No of pupils: 67
Special Needs: PMLD SLD W

Camden Education Authority
Crowndale Centre
218–220 Eversholt Street
London NW1 1BD
Tel: (020) 7974 1525

CHALCOT SCHOOL
Harmood Street, London NW1 8DP
Tel: (020) 7485 2147
Head: Ms E Hales
Type: Boys Day 9–16
No of pupils: 54
Special Needs: EBD

FRANK BARNES SCHOOL
Harley Road, London NW3 3BY
Tel: (020) 7586 4665
Head: Ms K Simpson
Type: Co-educational Day 2–11
No of pupils: 45
Special Needs: **HI**

PENN SCHOOL
Church Road, Penn, High Wycombe,
Buckinghamshire HP10 8LZ
Tel: (01494) 812139
Head: Mr A Jones
Type: Boarding and Day
No of pupils: 22 *No of Boarders:* W13
Special Needs: **HI SP&LD** W

SWISS COTTAGE SCHOOL
Avenue Road, London NW8 6HX
Tel: (020) 7681 8080
Head: Ms K Bedford
Type: Co-educational Day 2–16
No of pupils: 136
Special Needs: **MLD PH** PMLD SLD
SP&LD W

Croydon Education Authority

Taberner House
Park Lane
Croydon CR9 1TP
Tel: (020) 8686 4433

BENSHAM MANOR SCHOOL
Ecclesbourne Road, Thornton
Heath, Surrey CR7 7BR
Tel: (020) 8684 0116
Head: Mrs E J Green
Type: Co-educational Day 11–16
No of pupils: B110 G51
Special Needs: AUT **MLD**

PRIORY SCHOOL
Tennison Road, South Norwood,
London SE25 5RR
Tel: (020) 8653 8222
Head: Ms J Thomas
Type: Co-educational Day 12–19
No of pupils: B35 G20
Special Needs: AUT **PMLD SLD** W

RED GATES SCHOOL
489 Purley Way, Croydon, Surrey
CR9 4RG
Tel: (020) 8688 1761
Head: Miss B A Fox
Type: Co-educational Day 3–14
No of pupils: 62
Special Needs: AUT **PMLD SLD** W

REDGATES
489 Purley Way, Croydon, Surrey
CR0 4RG
Tel: (020) 8688 8222
Head: Ms S Beaman
Type: Co-educational Day 3–12
Special Needs: AUT SLD

ST GILES' SCHOOL
Pampisford Road, Croydon, Surrey
CR2 6DF
Tel: (020) 8680 2141
Head: Mrs J Thomas
Type: Co-educational Day 3–16
No of pupils: 108
Special Needs: **PH** W

ST NICHOLAS SCHOOL
Old Lodge Lane, Purley, Surrey
CR8 4DN
Tel: (020) 8660 4861
Head: Mrs J Melton
Type: Co-educational Day 4–11
No of pupils: 101
Special Needs: AUT MLD SP&LD

SOUTH NORWOOD PRIMARY
34 Crowther Road, London
SE25 5QP
Tel: (020) 8654 2983
Head: Mr A Rydzewski
Type: Co-educational Day
No of pupils: B11 G1
Special Needs: **MLD**

Ealing Education Authority

Percival House
14–16 Uxbridge Road
Ealing
London W5 2HL
Tel: (020) 8579 2424

BELVUE SCHOOL
Rowdell Road, Northolt, Middlesex
UB5 6AG
Tel: (020) 8845 5766
Head: Mr D Whitton
Type: Co-educational Day 12–19
No of pupils: 124
Special Needs: **MLD**

CASTLEBAR SCHOOL
Hathaway Gardens, Ealing, London
W13 0DH
Tel: (020) 8998 3135
Head: Mr D J Perkins
Type: Co-educational Day 4–12
No of pupils: 118
Special Needs: **MLD** W

CAVENDISH SCHOOL
Compton Close, Cavendish Avenue,
Ealing, London W13 0JG
Tel: (020) 8998 6940
Head: Ms M Byrne
Type: Co-educational Day 7–12
No of pupils: 22
Special Needs: **ADHD EBD MLD** W

JOHN CHILTON SCHOOL
Compton Crescent, Northolt,
Middlesex UB5 5LD
Tel: (020) 8842 1329
Head: Mrs B A Cursi
Type: Co-educational Day 2–18

MANDEVILLE SCHOOL
Eastcote Lane, Northolt, Middlesex
UB5 4HW
Tel: (020) 8864 4921
Head: Mrs C Marks
Type: Co-educational Day 2–12
No of pupils: B50 G30
Special Needs: **PMLD SLD** W

ST ANN'S SCHOOL
Springfield Road, Hanwell, London
W7 3JP
Tel: (020) 8567 6291
Head: Mrs M Hughes
Type: Co-educational Day 12–19
No of pupils: 59
Special Needs: PMLD **SLD** W

SPRINGHALLOW SCHOOL
Compton Close, Cavendish Avenue,
Ealing, London W13 0JG
Tel: (020) 8998 2700
Head: Miss J E Birch
Type: Co-educational Day 3–16
No of pupils: B38 G12
Special Needs: AUT W

Enfield Education Authority

PO Box 56
Civic Centre
Enfield EN1 3XQ
Tel: (020) 8366 6565

DURANTS SCHOOL
4 Pitfield Way, Enfield, Middlesex
EN3 5BY
Tel: (020) 8804 1980
Head: Mr K G Bovair
Type: Co-educational Day 5–19
No of pupils: 120
Special Needs: **MLD** W

OAKTREE SCHOOL
Chase Side, Southgate, London
N14 4HN
Tel: (020) 8440 3100
Head: Mr J H Harrison
Type: Co-educational Day 5–19
No of pupils: 120
Special Needs: **MLD**

RUSSET HOUSE
11 Autumn Close, Enfield,
Middlesex EN1 4JA
Tel: (020) 8350 0650
Head: Ms J Foster
Type: Co-educational Day 3–11
No of pupils: 66
Special Needs: ASP **AUT** SPLD

WAVERLEY SCHOOL
105 The Ride, Enfield, Middlesex
EN3 7DL
Tel: (020) 8805 1858
Head: Mrs L C Gibbs
Type: Co-educational Day 3–19
No of pupils: 115
Special Needs: PMLD SLD W

WEST LEA SCHOOL
Haslebury Road, Edmonton, London
N9 9TU
Tel: (020) 8807 2656
Head: Mrs A S Fox
Type: Co-educational Day 5–17
No of pupils: 120
Special Needs: ADD **ASP** CP **DEL** EPI
HI PH **SP&LD** W

Greenwich Education Authority

Riverside House
Woolwich High Street
London SE18 6DF
Tel: (020) 8854 8888

BRANTRIDGE SCHOOL
Staplefield Place, Staplefield,
Haywards Heath, West Sussex
RH17 6EQ
Tel: (01444) 400228
Head: Mr R Winn
Type: Boys Boarding 6–12
No of pupils: 36 *No of Boarders:* F36
Special Needs: ADHD DYS **EBD**

CHARLTON SCHOOL
Charlton Park Road, London
SE7 8HX
Tel: (020) 8854 6259
Head: Mr M Dale-Emberton
Type: Co-educational Boarding and
Day 10–19
No of pupils: B50 G35
Special Needs: **CP** EPI **PH PMLD** SLD
SP&LD W

CHURCHFIELD SCHOOL
Church Manorway, London SE2 0HY
Tel: (020) 8854 3739
Head: Mr P Goulden
Type: Co-educational Day 11–17
No of pupils: 202
Special Needs: DEL MLD SPLD

WILLOW DENE SCHOOL
Swingate Lane, Plumstead, London
SE18 2JD
Tel: (020) 8854 9841
Head: Mr P Hardakor
Type: Co-educational Day 2–11
No of pupils: B110 G70
Special Needs: AUT MLD PMLD
SLD W

Hackney Education Authority

Edith Cavell Building
Enfield Road
London N1 5BA
Tel: (020) 8356 8401

CRUSOE HOUSE SCHOOL
Nile Street, London N1 7DR
Tel: (020) 7251 3932
Head: Mrs I Flynn
Type: Boys Day 11–16
No of pupils: 50
Special Needs: EBD

DOWNSVIEW SCHOOL
Tiger Way, Downs Road, London
E5 8QP
Tel: (020) 8985 6833
Head: Mr W R Bulman
Type: Co-educational Day 5–16
No of pupils: 100
Special Needs: MLD

HORIZON SCHOOL
Wordsworth Road, London N16 8BZ
Tel: (020) 7254 8096
Head: Ms A Uhart
Type: Co-educational Day 5–16
No of pupils: 92
Special Needs: SPLD

ICKBURGH SCHOOL
Ickburgh Road, London E5 8AD
Tel: (020) 8806 4638
Head: Mr P Goss
Type: Co-educational Day 2–19
No of pupils: B59 G31
Special Needs: PMLD SLD

STORMONT HOUSE SCHOOL
Downs Park Road, London E5 8NP
Tel: (020) 8985 4245
Head: Ms A Murphy
Type: Co-educational Day 11–16
No of pupils: 100
Special Needs: DEL SP&LD

Hammersmith and Fulham Education Authority

Cambridge House
Cambridge Grove
London W6 0LE
Tel: (020) 8753 3621

CAMBRIDGE SCHOOL
Cambridge Grove, London W6 0LB
Tel: (020) 8748 7585
Head: Ms J Barton
Type: Co-educational Day 11–16
No of pupils: 100
Special Needs: MLD

GIBBS GREEN SCHOOL
Mund Street, North End Road,
London W14 9LY
Tel: (020) 7385 3908
Head: Mr R Davies
Type: Co-educational Day 4–11
No of pupils: 30
Special Needs: EBD

HEATHERMOUNT SCHOOL
Devenish Road, Ascot, Berkshire
SL5 9PG
Tel: (01344) 875101
Head: Ms S Lord
Type: Co-educational Boarding and
Day 5–19
No of pupils: 36 *No of Boarders:* W11
Special Needs: **ASP** AUT

JACK TIZARD SCHOOL
Finlay Street, London SW6 6HB
Tel: (020) 7736 7949
Head: Mr T Baker
Type: Co-educational Day 2–19
No of pupils: 75
Special Needs: PMLD SLD W

QUEENSMILL SCHOOL

Clancarty Road, London SW6 3AA
Tel: (020) 7384 2330
Head: Mrs J Page
Type: Co-educational Day 3–11
No of pupils: B50 G12
Special Needs: AUT

WOODLANE HIGH SCHOOL

Du Cane Road, London W12 0TN
Tel: (020) 8743 5668
Head: Mr N Holt
Type: Co-educational Day 11–16
No of pupils: 40
Special Needs: DEL VIS W

Haringey Education Authority

48 Station Road
Wood Green
London N22 7TY
Tel: (020) 8489 0000

BLANCHE NEVILE SCHOOL AND SERVICE

(Admin & Resources Centre),
Williams Grove, Wood Green,
London N22 5NR
Tel: (020) 8352 2100
Head: Mr P Makey
Type: Co-educational Day 3–19
No of pupils: B53 G44
Special Needs: HI

GREENFIELDS SCHOOL

Coppetts Road, London N10 1JP
Tel: (020) 8444 5366
Head: Ms S Wood
Type: Boys Day 7–16
No of pupils: 40
Special Needs: ADD ADHD **EBD**

MOSELLE SPECIAL SCHOOL

Adams Road, London N17 6HW
Tel: (020) 8808 8869
Head: Mr A Redpath
Type: Co-educational Day 4–19
No of pupils: 123
Special Needs: AUT DOW EPI MLD
SP&LD

VALE SPECIAL SCHOOL

c/o Northumberland Park
Community School, Trulock Road,
London N17 0PY
Tel: (020) 8801 6111
Head: Mr G Hill
Type: Co-educational Day 2–19
No of pupils: 80
Special Needs: CP PH W

WILLIAM C HARVEY SPECIAL SCHOOL

Adams Road, London N17 6HW
Tel: (020) 8808 7120
Head: Ms M Sumner
Type: Co-educational Day 3–19
No of pupils: 75
Special Needs: PMLD SLD W

Harrow Education Authority

PO Box 22
Civic Centre
Harrow HA1 2UW
Tel: (020) 8863 5611

WOODLANDS FIRST & MIDDLESCHOOL

Whittlesea Road, Weald, Harrow
HA3 6ND
Tel: (020) 8421 3637
Head: Mrs M Jarvis
Type: Co-educational Day
No of pupils: B19 G16
Special Needs: PMLD SLD

Havering Education Authority

The Broxhill Centre
Broxhill Road
Harold Hill
Romford RM4 1XN
Tel: (01708) 434343

CORBETS TEY SCHOOL

Harwood Hall Lane, Corbets Tey,
Upminster, Essex RM14 2YQ
Tel: (01708) 225888
Head: Mrs S D Gardiner
Type: Co-educational Day 4–16
No of pupils: 90
Special Needs: AUT **MLD** SLD

DYCORTS SCHOOL

Settle Road, Harold Hill, Romford,
Essex RM3 9YA
Tel: (01708) 343649
Head: Mr G Wroe
Type: Co-educational Day 3–16
No of pupils: 75
Special Needs: DYS EPI MLD PH
SP&LD SPLD W

RAVENSBOURNE SCHOOL

Neave Crescent, Farringdon Avenue,
Harold Hill, Romford, Essex
RM3 8HN
Tel: (01708) 341800
Head: Mrs M Cameron
Type: Co-educational Day 2–19
No of pupils: 75
Special Needs: AUT CP DEL DOW
DYS EBD VIS W

Hillingdon Education Authority

Civic Centre
Uxbridge UB8 1UW
Tel: (01895) 250529

CHANTRY SCHOOL

Falling Lane, Yiewsley, West
Drayton, Middlesex UB7 8AB
Tel: (01895) 446747
Head: Mr R Warnes
Type: Co-educational Day 11–18
No of pupils: B56 G4
Special Needs: ADD ADHD EBD

HEDGEWOOD SCHOOL

Weymouth Road, Hayes, Middlesex
UB4 8NF
Tel: (020) 8845 6756
Head: Mr M J Goddard
Type: Co-educational Day 5–11
No of pupils: 95
Special Needs: ASP **AUT** CP DOW
DYP HI MLD **SP&LD** SPLD VIS W

MEADOW SCHOOL

Royal Lane, Hillingdon, Uxbridge,
Middlesex UB8 3QU
Tel: (01895) 443310
Head: Mr R Payne
Type: Co-educational Day 11–18
No of pupils: B124 G65
Special Needs: **MLD** W

MOORCROFT SCHOOL

Harlington Road, Hillingdon,
Uxbridge, Middlesex UB8 3HD
Tel: (01895) 236430
Head: Ms M J Geddes
Type: Co-educational Day 11–19
No of pupils: 67
Special Needs: AUT SLD W

THE WILLOWS SCHOOL

Stipularis Drive, Off Glencoe Road,
Hayes, Middlesex UB4 9QB
Tel: (020) 8841 7176
Head: Mrs F King
Type: Co-educational Day 5–11
No of pupils: 30
Special Needs: EBD

Hounslow Education Authority

Civic Centre
Lampton Road
Hounslow TW3 4DN
Tel: (020) 8583 2600

THE CEDARS PRIMARY SCHOOL
High Street, Cranford, Middlesex TW5 9RU
Tel: (020) 8230 0015
Head: Mr A Costello
Type: Co-educational Day 4–11
No of pupils: 50
Special Needs: EBD

MARJORY KINNON SPECIAL SCHOOL
Hatton Road, Bedfont, Middlesex TW14 9QZ
Tel: (020) 8890 2032
Head: Mr D J Harris
Type: Co-educational Day 5–16
No of pupils: 171
Special Needs: AUT MLD W

OAKLANDS SCHOOL
Woodlands Road, Isleworth, Middlesex TW7 6HD
Tel: (020) 8560 3569
Head: Mrs E Felstead
Type: Co-educational Day 11–19
No of pupils: 72
Special Needs: PMLD SLD W

SYON PARK SCHOOL
Twickenham Road, Isleworth, Middlesex TW7 6AU
Tel: (020) 8560 4300
Head: Mr K Nowobilski
Type: Co-educational Day 11–16
No of pupils: 50
Special Needs: EBD

Islington Education Authority

Laycock Street
London N1 1TH
Tel: (020) 7527 5666

HARBOROUGH SCHOOL
Elthorne Road, London N19 4AB
Tel: (020) 7272 5739
Head: Mrs Earnshaw
Type: Co-educational Day 2–19
No of pupils: B35 G8
Special Needs: AUT

RICHARD CLOUDESLEY SCHOOL
Golden Lane, London EC1Y 0TJ
Tel: (020) 7251 1161
Head: Ms A Corbett
Type: Co-educational Day 2–18
No of pupils: B35 G13
Special Needs: CP EPI PH SP&LD W

ROSEMARY SCHOOL
75 Prebend Street, London N1 8PW
Tel: (020) 7226 8223
Head: Mr J Wolger
Type: Co-educational Day 2–11
No of pupils: 76
Special Needs: AUT PMLD SLD

SAMUEL RHODES SCHOOL
Richmond Avenue, London N1
Tel: (020) 7837 9075
Head: Ms J Blount
Type: Co-educational Day 5–16
No of pupils: 100
Special Needs: MLD

Kensington and Chelsea Education Authority

The Town Hall
Hornton Street
London W8 7NX
Tel: (020) 7361 3334

PARKWOOD HALL SCHOOL
Beechenlea Lane, Swanley, Kent BR8 8DR
Tel: (01322) 664441
Head: Mrs H Dando
Type: Co-educational Boarding and Day 8–17
No of pupils: B44 G35
Special Needs: EPI MLD SLD SP&LD

Kingston Upon Thames Education Authority

Guildhall 2
Kingston upon Thames KT1 1EU
Tel: (020) 8546 2121

BEDELSFORD SCHOOL
Grange Road, Kingston upon Thames, Surrey KT1 2QZ
Tel: (020) 8546 9838
Head: Mr J Murfitt
Type: Co-educational Day 2–16
No of pupils: B40 G21
Special Needs: CP DEL EPI HI MLD PH VIS W

DYSART SPECIAL SCHOOL
Dukes Avenue, Kingston upon Thames, Surrey KT2 5QY
Tel: (020) 8546 0610
Head: Ms P Smillie
Type: Co-educational Day 2–19
No of pupils: 65
Special Needs: ADHD AUT CP DOW PH PMLD SLD TOU VIS

ST PHILIP'S SPECIAL SCHOOL
Harrow Close, Leatherhead Road, Chessington, Surrey KT9 2HP
Tel: (020) 8397 2672
Head: Mrs H J Goodall
Type: Co-educational Day 5–16
No of pupils: B90 G54
Special Needs: DOW MLD SPLD

Lambeth Education Authority

5th Floor, International House
Canterbury Crescent
London SW9 7QE
Tel: (020) 7926 9658

ELM COURT SCHOOL
Elmcourt Road, West Norwood, London SE27 9BZ
Tel: (020) 8670 6577
Head: Mr W Hutcheson
Type: Co-educational Day
No of pupils: 100
Special Needs: ADD CP DEL DOW DYS EBD EPI MLD SP&LD SPLD W

LANSDOWNE SCHOOL
Argyll Close, Dalyell Road, London SW9 9QL
Tel: (020) 7737 3713
Head: Mrs G Bealing
Type: Co-educational Day 5–16
No of pupils: B47 G28
Special Needs: MLD

THE LIVITY SCHOOL
Mandrell Road, London SW2 5DW
Tel: (020) 7733 0681
Head: Ms G Lee
Type: Co-educational Day 2–11

THE MICHAEL TIPPETT SCHOOL
Oakden Street, London SE11 4UG
Tel: (020) 7735 5050
Head: Mr M L Lozano-Luoma
Type: Co-educational Day
No of pupils: 80
Special Needs: AUT PMLD SLD W

TURNEY SCHOOL
Turney Road, West Dulwich, London
SE21 8LX
Tel: (020) 8670 7220
Head: Ms J Davis
Type: Co-educational Day 5–16
No of pupils: 164
Special Needs: ADD ADHD ASP **AUT
DOW MLD SP&LD**

WILLOWFIELD SCHOOL
Heron Road, Milkwood Road,
London SE24 0HY
Tel: (020) 7274 4372
Head: Ms J Loy
Type: Boys Day and Boarding 11–16
No of pupils: 48
Special Needs: **EBD**

Lewisham Education Authority

3rd Floor, Laurence House
1 Catford Road
Catford
London SE6 4RU
Tel: (020) 8314 6301

ANERLEY SCHOOL
Versailles Road, London SE20 8AX
Tel: (020) 8402 2929
Head: Mr E B Milner
Type: Boys Day and Boarding 11–16
No of pupils: 40
Special Needs: **EBD**

GREENVALE SCHOOL
69 Perry Rise, Forest Hill, London
SE23 2QU
Tel: (020) 8699 6515
Head: Mr P A Munro
Type: Co-educational Day 11–19
No of pupils: 60
Special Needs: **PMLD SLD W**

MEADOWGATE SCHOOL
Revelon Road, Brockley, London
SE4 2PR
Tel: (020) 7635 9022
Head: Mr R Leszczynski
Type: Co-educational Day 4–11
Special Needs: **MLD**

NEW WOODLANDS SCHOOL (JMI)
49 Shroffold Road, Bromley, Kent
BR1 5PD
Tel: (020) 8314 9911
Head: Mr D H Harper
Type: Co-educational Day 5–11
No of pupils: 40
Special Needs: **ADD ADHD EBD**

PENDRAGON SECONDARY SCHOOL
Pendragon Road, Downham,
Bromley, Kent BR1 5LD
Tel: (020) 8698 9738
Head: Mr H Calthrop
Type: Co-educational Day 11–19
No of pupils: 132
Special Needs: **MLD**

WATERGATE SCHOOL
Church Grove, London SE13 7UU
Tel: (020) 8314 1751
Head: Ms A Youd
Type: Co-educational Day 2–11
No of pupils: 65
Special Needs: PMLD **SLD** W

Merton Education Authority

Civic Centre
London Road
Morden
Surrey SM4 5DX
Tel: (020) 8545 3268

CRICKET GREEN SCHOOL
Lower Green West, Mitcham, Surrey
CR4 3AF
Tel: (020) 8640 1177
Head: Ms H Gannaway
Type: Co-educational Day 5–16
No of pupils: 120
Special Needs: **MLD** W

MELROSE SCHOOL
Church Road, Mitcham, Surrey
CR4 3BE
Tel: (020) 8646 2620
Head: Mr D Eglin
Type: Co-educational Day 9–16
No of pupils: 60
Special Needs: **EBD**

ST ANN'S SCHOOL
Bordesley Road, Morden, Surrey
SM4 5LT
Tel: (020) 8648 9737
Head: Ms T Harvey
Type: Co-educational Day 2–19
No of pupils: 81
Special Needs: AUT PMLD SLD

Newham Education Authority

Broadway House
322 High Street
Stratford
London E15 1AJ
Tel: (020) 8430 5066

ELEANOR SMITH SCHOOL & PRIMARY SUPPORT SERVICE
North Street, London E13 9HN
Tel: (020) 8471 0018/9
Head: Mr M R Leaman
Type: Co-educational Day 5–11
No of pupils: 120
Special Needs: **EBD**

JOHN F. KENNEDY SCHOOL
Pitchford Street, London E15 9HN
Tel: (020) 8534 8544
Head: Mrs G Goldsmith
Type: Co-educational Day 2–19

Redbridge Education Authority

Lynton House
255–259 High Road
Ilford
Essex IG1 1NN
Tel: (020) 8478 3020

ETHEL DAVIS SCHOOL
258 Barley Lane, Goodmayes, Ilford,
Essex IG3 8XS
Tel: (020) 8599 1768
Head: Mr P Bouldstridge
Type: Co-educational Day 2–19
No of pupils: B30 G25
Special Needs: CP MLD **PH PMLD
SLD** VIS W

HATTON SCHOOL
Roding Lane South, Woodford
Green, Essex IG8 8EU
Tel: (020) 8551 4131
Head: Miss L Richardson
Type: Co-educational Day 5–11
No of pupils: 142
Special Needs: **ASP AUT** DOW DYP
MLD **SP&LD** W

HYLEFORD SCHOOL
Loxford Lane, Ilford, Essex IG3 9AR
Tel: (020) 8590 7272
Head: Mrs G D Morgan
Type: Co-educational Day 3–19
No of pupils: 85
Special Needs: PMLD **SLD** W

NEW RUSH HALL SCHOOL
Fencepiece Road, Hainault, Essex
IG6 2LJ
Tel: (020) 8501 3951
Head: Mr J V d'Abbro
Type: Co-educational Day 5–16
No of pupils: 60
Special Needs: EBD

Richmond upon Thames Education Authority

Regal House
London Road
Twickenham TW1 3QB
Tel: (020) 8891 7500

CLARENDON SCHOOL
Hanworth Road, Hampton,
Middlesex TW12 3DH
Tel: (020) 8979 1165
Head: Mrs A Coward
Type: Co-educational Day 7–16
No of pupils: 100
Special Needs: MLD W

RICHMOND HOUSE SCHOOL
Buckingham Road, Hampton,
Middlesex TW12 3LT
Tel: (020) 8941 2623
Head: Mr A Mitchell
Type: Co-educational Day
No of pupils: 20
Special Needs: EBD

STRATHMORE SCHOOL
Meadlands Drive, Petersham, Surrey
TW10 7ED
Tel: (020) 8948 0047
Head: Mr S Rosenberg
Type: Co-educational Day 7–19
No of pupils: 47
Special Needs: PMLD SLD W

Southwark Education Authority

John Smith House
144–152 Walworth Road
London SE17 1JL
Tel: (020) 7525 5001

BEORMUND PRIMARY SCHOOL
Crosby Row, Long Lane, London
SE1 3PS
Tel: (020) 7525 9027
Head: Ms S Gray
Type: Co-educational Day 5–11
No of pupils: 35
Special Needs: EBD W

BREDINGHURST SCHOOL
Stuart Road, London SE15 3AZ
Tel: (020) 7639 2541
Head: Ms J Anderson
Type: Boys Boarding and Day 11–16
No of pupils: 49 *No of Boarders:* W15
Special Needs: ADD ADHD EBD

CHERRY GARDEN SPECIAL PRIMARY SCHOOL
Macks Road, London SE16 3XU
Tel: (020) 7237 4050
Head: Ms M Trembath
Type: Co-educational Day 2–11
No of pupils: 46
Special Needs: AUT CP EPI HI PH
PMLD SLD SP&LD VIS W

HAYMERLE'S SCHOOL
Haymerle Road, London SE15 6SY
Tel: (020) 7639 6080
Head: Mr E M Nolan
Type: Co-educational Day 4–11
No of pupils: B57 G29
Special Needs: ADD ADHD AUT CP
DEL DOW DYP DYS EBD EPI MLD
PH SP&LD W

HIGHSHORE SPECIAL SCHOOL
Bellenden Road, London SE15 5BB
Tel: (020) 7639 7211
Head: Mrs Y Conlon
Type: Co-educational Day 11–17
No of pupils: 128
Special Needs: ADD ADHD DYC DYP
DYS MLD SP&LD

MAUDSLEY & BETHLEM SPECIAL SCHOOL
Royal Hospital School, Monks
Orchard Road, Beckenham, Kent
BR3 3BX
Tel: (020) 8777 1897
Head: Ms W French
Type: Co-educational Boarding
No of pupils: 25
Special Needs: ADD ADHD ASP AUT
EBD EPI MLD TOU

SPA SCHOOL
Monnow Road, London SE1 5RN
Tel: (020) 7237 3714
Head: Ms A Crispin
Type: Co-educational Day 11–16
No of pupils: 83
Special Needs: ASP AUT MLD

TUKE SCHOOL
4 Woods Road, London SE15 2PX
Tel: (020) 7639 5584
Head: Miss H Tully
Type: Co-educational Day 11–19
No of pupils: B38 G15
Special Needs: AUT PMLD SLD W

Sutton Education Authority

The Grove
Carshalton
Surrey SM5 3AL
Tel: (020) 8770 6568

CAREW MANOR SCHOOL
Church Road, Wallington, Surrey
SM6 7NH
Tel: (020) 8647 8349
Head: Mr M Midgley
Type: Co-educational Day 7–16
No of pupils: 125
Special Needs: ADD ADHD ASP AUT
CP DEL DOW DYP DYS EBD EPI HI
MLD SLD SP&LD SPLD VIS W

SHERWOOD PARK SCHOOL
Streeters Lane, Wallington, Surrey
SM6 7NP
Tel: (020) 8773 9930
Head: Mrs R Bezant
Type: Co-educational Day 2–19
No of pupils: 80
Special Needs: PMLD SLD W

WANDLE VALLEY SCHOOL
Welbeck Road, Carshalton, Surrey
SM5 1LP
Tel: (020) 8648 1365
Head: Mr D L Bone
Type: Co-educational Day 5–16
No of pupils: 80
Special Needs: EBD

Tower Hamlets Education Authority

Town Hall
Mulberry Place
5 Clove Crescent
London E14 2BG
Tel: (020) 7364 5000

BEATRICE TATE SCHOOL
St Jude's Road, London E2 9RW
Tel: (020) 7739 6249
Head: Mr A Black
Type: Co-educational Day 11–19
No of pupils: 75
Special Needs: PMLD SLD W

BOWDEN HOUSE
Firle Road, Seaford, East Sussex
BN25 2JB
Tel: (01323) 893138
Head: Mr M Price
Type: Boys Boarding 9–16
No of pupils: 47 *No of Boarders:* F47
Special Needs: EBD

BROMLEY HALL SCHOOL
Bromley Hall Road, London E14 0LF
Tel: (020) 7987 2563
Head: Mr J Earnshaw
Type: Co-educational Day 3–19
No of pupils: B13 G13
Special Needs: CP DEL EPI HI MLD
PH PMLD SLD SP&LD VIS W

GRENFELL SCHOOL
Myrdle Street, London E1 1HL
Tel: (020) 7247 9475
Head: Mr S Quilter
Type: Co-educational Day 3–11
No of pupils: 120
Special Needs: MLD SP&LD

HARPLEY SCHOOL
Globe Road, London E1 4DZ
Tel: (020) 7790 5170
Head: Mr A M Finch
Type: Co-educational Day 11–16
No of pupils: B44 G25
Special Needs: EBD MLD

PHOENIX SCHOOL
49 Bow Road, London E3 2AD
Tel: (020) 8980 4740
Head: Mr S Harris
Type: Co-educational Day 2–16
No of pupils: B84 G48
Special Needs: AUT MLD SP&LD

STEPHEN HAWKING SCHOOL
Brunton Place, London E14 7LL
Tel: (020) 7423 9848
Head: Ms C Sibley
Type: Co-educational Day 2–11
No of pupils: 90
Special Needs: PMLD SLD

Waltham Forest Education Authority

Municipal Offices
High Road
Leyton
London E10 5QJ
Tel: (020) 8527 5544

BROOKFIELD HOUSE SCHOOL
Alders Avenue, Woodford Green,
Essex IG8 9PY
Tel: (020) 8527 2464
Head: Ms H Clasper
Type: Co-educational Day 2–16
No of pupils: 82
Special Needs: DEL PH

HAWKSWOOD SCHOOL AND CENTRE
Antlers Hill, London E4 7RT
Tel: (020) 8529 2561
Head: Ms K Khan
Type: Co-educational Day 2–16
No of pupils: 47
Special Needs: HI MLD SLD

JOSEPH CLARKE SCHOOL
Vincent Road, London E4 9PP
Tel: (020) 8527 8818
Head: Mr F Smith
Type: Co-educational Day 2–19
No of pupils: 120
Special Needs: VIS W

WHITEFIELD SCHOOL AND CENTRE
Macdonald Road, London E17 4AZ
Tel: (020) 8531 3426
Head: Mr N Chapman
Type: Co-educational Day and
Boarding 2–19
No of pupils: 310
Special Needs: ASP AUT CP DOW
DYP EPI HI MLD PMLD SLD SP&LD
SPLD VIS W

WILLIAM MORRIS SCHOOL
Folly Lane, London E17 5NT
Tel: (020) 8503 2225
Head: Mr I Johnston
Type: Co-educational Day 11–19
No of pupils: 135
Special Needs: MLD PMLD SLD W

Wandsworth Education Authority

Town Hall
Wandsworth High Street
London SW18 2PU
Tel: (020) 8871 8013

BRADSTOW SCHOOL
34 Dumpton Park Drive, Broadstairs,
Kent CT10 1RG
Tel: (01843) 862123
Head: Mr B Furze
Type: Co-educational Boarding 6–19
No of pupils: 50 *No of Boarders:* W50
Special Needs: AUT EBD EPI SLD

CHARTFIELD DELICATE SCHOOL
St Margaret's Crescent, London
SW15 6HL
Tel: (020) 8788 7471
Head: Ms V Hand-Armitage
Type: Co-educational Day 11–16
No of pupils: B75 G25
Special Needs: ADD ADHD ASP DEL
DYC DYP DYS EBD SP&LD SPLD

ELSLEY SCHOOL
Elsely Road, London SW11 5TZ
Tel: (020) 7738 2968
Head: Ms L D King
Type: Co-educational Day 5–11

GARRATT PARK SCHOOL
Waldron Road, London SW18 3SY
Tel: (020) 8946 5769
Head: Ms J Price
Type: Co-educational Day 11–17
No of pupils: B83 G42
Special Needs: ADHD AUT DYC DYS
MLD SP&LD

GREENMEAD SCHOOL
St Margaret's Crescent, London
SW15 6HL
Tel: (020) 8789 1466
Head: Miss A Laxton
Type: Co-educational Day 3–11
No of pupils: B22 G18
Special Needs: CP MLD PH PMLD
SLD SP&LD

LINDEN LODGE SCHOOL
61 Princes Way, London SW19 6JB
Tel: (020) 8788 0107
Head: Mr A Hudson
Type: Co-educational Day and
Boarding 5–18
No of pupils: 80
Special Needs: VIS

NIGHTINGALE BOYS SCHOOL
Beechcroft Road, Tooting, London
SW17 7DF
Tel: (020) 8874 9096
Head: Mr R Hughes
Type: Boys Day 11–18

OAK LODGE SCHOOL
101 Nightingale Lane, London
SW12 8NA
Tel: (020) 8673 3453
Head: Mr P Merrifield
Type: Co-educational Boarding and
Day 11–19
No of pupils: B46 G32
No of Boarders: W20
Special Needs: HI

PADDOCK SCHOOL
Priory Lane, London SW15 5RT
Tel: (020) 8878 1521
Head: Mrs N Evans
Type: Co-educational Day 3–19
No of pupils: 92
Special Needs: PMLD SLD W

THE VINES
Forthbridge Road, London
SW11 5NX
Tel: (020) 7228 0602
Head: Ms J Hilary
Type: Co-educational 4–11
No of pupils: 100
Special Needs: **MLD** W

City of Westminster Education Authority

13th Floor, Westminster City Hall
64 Victoria Street
London SW1E 6QP
Tel: (020) 7641 6000

COLLEGE PARK SCHOOL
Monmouth Road, London W2 4UT
Tel: (020) 7641 4460
Head: Ms A Anderson
Type: Co-educational Day 5–16
No of pupils: 80
Special Needs: **MLD**

QUEEN ELIZABETH II SCHOOL
Kennet Road, London W9 3LG
Tel: (020) 7641 5825
Head: Ms M Loughnan
Type: Co-educational Day 5–19
No of pupils: B33 G33
Special Needs: PMLD SLD W

GREATER MANCHESTER

Bolton Education Authority

PO Box 53
Paderborn House
Civic Centre
Bolton BL1 1JW
Tel: (01204) 333333

FIRWOOD SCHOOL
Crompton Way, Bolton, Greater
Manchester BL2 3AF
Tel: (01204) 303499
Head: Dr J Steele
Type: Co-educational Day 11–19
No of pupils: 82
Special Needs: PMLD SLD W

GREEN FOLD SCHOOL
Highfield Road, Farnworth, Greater
Manchester BL4 0RA
Tel: (01204) 572524
Head: Mrs C Chapman
Type: Co-educational Day 3–11
No of pupils: 70
Special Needs: CP EPI **PMLD** SLD W

LADYWOOD SCHOOL
Masefield Road, Little Lever, Bolton,
Greater Manchester BL3 1NG
Tel: (01204) 840709
Head: Mrs S McFarlane
Type: Co-educational Day 4–11
No of pupils: B49 G23
Special Needs: AUT MLD

LEVER PARK SCHOOL
Stocks Park Drive, Horwick, Bolton,
Greater Manchester BL6 6DE
Tel: (01204) 840321
Head: Mrs C A Hargreaves
Type: Co-educational Day 8–16
No of pupils: 50
Special Needs: ADD ADHD **EBD** W

RUMWORTH SCHOOL
Armadale Road, Bolton, Greater
Manchester BL3 4UN
Tel: (01204) 333600
Head: Mr B Bradbury
Type: Co-educational Day
No of pupils: B94 G47
Special Needs: **MLD SLD** W

THOMASSON MEMORIAL SCHOOL
Devonshire Road, Bolton, Greater
Manchester BL1 4PJ
Tel: (01204) 843063
Head: Mr W Wilson
Type: Co-educational Day 3–11
No of pupils: B25 G19
Special Needs: HI

Bury Education Authority

Athenaeum House
Market Street
Bury BL9 0BN
Tel: (0161) 253 5000

ELMS BANK HIGH SCHOOL
Ripon Avenue, Whitefield, Greater
Manchester M45 8PJ
Tel: (0161) 766 1597
Head: Ms L Lines
Type: Co-educational Day 11–19
No of pupils: B77 G56
Special Needs: AUT **MLD** PH **PMLD**
SLD W

MILLWOOD PRIMARY SPECIAL SCHOOL
Fletcher Fold Road, Bury, Greater
Manchester BL9 9RX
Tel: (0161) 253 6083
Head: Mr B J Emblem
Type: Co-educational Day 2–11
No of pupils: 86
Special Needs: MLD PMLD SLD W

Manchester Education Authority

Overseas House
Quay Street
Manchester M3 3BB
Tel: (0161) 234 7125

BIRCHES SCHOOL
New Holme Road, West Didsbury,
Manchester, M20 2XZ
Tel: (0161) 448 8895
Head: Ms Morgan
Type: Co-educational Day 2–11

CAMBERWELL PARK SCHOOL
Bank House Road, Blakeley,
Manchester M9 8LT
Tel: (0161) 740 1897
Head: Mrs P Vermes
Type: Co-educational Day 5–11
Special Needs: AUT PMLD SLD

CASTLEFIELD SCHOOL
Jackson Crescent, Hulme,
Manchester M15 5AL
Tel: (0161) 226 2289
Head: Ms J Rose
Type: Co-educational Day
No of pupils: B40 G5
Special Needs: EBD

EWING SCHOOL
Central Road, Manchester, M20 4ZA
Tel: (0161) 445 0745
Head: Ms P Derbyshire
Type: Co-educational Day 5–16
No of pupils: 78
Special Needs: SP&LD

GORTON BROOK FIRST SCHOOL
Belle Vue Street, Manchester,
M12 5PW
Tel: (0161) 223 1822
Head: Mr I John
Type: Co-educational Day 5–11
No of pupils: 100
Special Needs: MLD W

GRANGE SCHOOL
77 Dickenson Road, Rusholme,
Manchester, M14 5AZ
Tel: (0161) 248 4841
Head: Mrs Fitzpatrick
Type: Co-educational Day 4–19
No of pupils: B42 G6
Special Needs: AUT

LANCASTERIAN SCHOOL
Elizabeth Slinger Road, West
Didsbury, Manchester M20 2XA
Tel: (0169) 445 0123
Head: Mr R Billinge
Type: Co-educational Day 2–16
No of pupils: 95
Special Needs: PH W

MEADE HILL SCHOOL
Middleton Road, Crumpsall,
Manchester M8 4NB
Tel: (0161) 795 8445
Head: Mr J Lancester
Type: Co-educational Day 11–16
No of pupils: B43 G2
Special Needs: ADD ADHD ASP DYP
DYS EBD HI MLD SP&LD TOU

MEDLOCK VALLEY HIGH SCHOOL
Palmestone Street, Ancotes,
Manchester M12 6PT
Tel: (0161) 274 4667
Head: D Norton
Type: Co-educational Day 11–16

MELLAND HIGH SCHOOL
Holmcroft Road, Gorton,
Manchester M18 7NG
Tel: (0161) 223 9915
Head: Mrs J D O'Kane
Type: Co-educational Day 11–19
No of pupils: B51 G51
Special Needs: PMLD SLD W

NEWBROOK SCHOOL
Newholme Road, West Didsbury,
Manchester M20 2XZ
Tel: (0161) 445 0745
Head: Mrs S Parsons
Type: Co-educational Day 2–16

NORTH MANCHESTER SUPPORT SERVICE
Meade Hill Centre, Middleton Road,
Manchester M8 6NB
Tel: (0161) 795 8445
Head: Mr A J Farrell
Type: Co-educational Day 11–16
No of pupils: 70
Special Needs: ADD ADHD EBD W

PIPER HILL SPECIAL SCHOOL
200 Yew Tree Lane, Manchester
M23 0FF
Tel: (0161) 998 4068
Head: Ms J Andrews
Type: Co-educational Day 11–19
No of pupils: B40 G45
Special Needs: PMLD SLD W

RICHMOND PARK SCHOOL
Cochrane Avenue, Longsight,
Manchester M12 4FA
Tel: (0161) 273 4894
Head: Mrs J Holt
Type: Co-educational Day 5–11
No of pupils: B71 G39
Special Needs: MLD

RODNEY HOUSE SPECIAL SCHOOL
388 Slade Lane, Burnage,
Manchester M19 2HT
Tel: (0161) 224 2774
Head: Ms P H Stanier
Type: Co-educational Day 2–7
No of pupils: 48
Special Needs: ASP AUT CP DEL
DOW EBD EPI HI MLD PH PMLD
SLD SP&LD SPLD TOU VIS W

ROUNDWOOD SCHOOL
Roundwood Road, Northenden,
Manchester M22 4AB
Tel: (0161) 998 4138
Head: Ms S L Hibbert
Type: Co-educational Day 11–16
No of pupils: 230
Special Needs: MLD

SHAWGROVE SCHOOL
Cavendish Road, Manchester
M20 1QB
Tel: (0161) 445 9435
Head: Mr H S Taylor
Type: Co-educational Day 3–11
No of pupils: 18
Special Needs: VIS W

WOODSIDE SPECIAL SCHOOL
Crossacres Road, Manchester
M22 5DR
Tel: (0161) 437 5697
Head: Mrs A M Stuart
Type: Co-educational Day 5–11
No of pupils: 76
Special Needs: MLD

Oldham Education Authority

Level 5, Civic Centre
West Street
Oldham OL1 1XJ
Tel: (0161) 911 4260

HARDMAN FOLD SCHOOL
Dean Street, Failsworth, Greater
Manchester M35 0DQ
Tel: (0161) 688 7114
Head: Mr R Maycock
Type: Co-educational Boarding and
Day 11–16
No of pupils: 71 *No of Boarders:* W14
Special Needs: EBD

HILL TOP SCHOOL
Arncliffe Rise, Pennine Meadow,
Oldham, Greater Manchester
OL4 2LZ
Tel: (0161) 620 6070
Head: Mr G Quinn
Type: Co-educational Day 11–19
No of pupils: 75
Special Needs: ASP AUT DOW SLD W

KINGFISHER COMMUNITY SPECIAL SCHOOL
Chadderton, Oldham, Manchester
OL9 9QR
Tel: (0161) 284 5335
Head: Mr D Wall
Type: Co-educational Day 2–11
No of pupils: 130
Special Needs: AUT MLD PMLD SLD

PARK DEAN SCHOOL

St Martin's Road, Oldham, Greater
Manchester OL8 2PZ
Tel: (0161) 620 0231
Head: Mrs A Higgins
Type: Co-educational Day 2–19
No of pupils: 95
Special Needs: CP DEL HI PH VIS W

SPRING BROOK SCHOOL

Chadderton, Oldham, Manchester
OL9 0LS
Tel: (0161) 911 5007
Head: D Wall
Type: Co-educational Day 7–11

Rochdale Education Authority

PO Box 70
Municipal Offices
Smith Street
Rochdale OL16 1YD
Tel: (01706) 647474

ALDERMAN KAY SPECIAL SCHOOL

Tintern Road, Hollin, Middleton,
Greater Manchester M24 6TQ
Tel: (0161) 643 4917
Head: Mrs J Clark
Type: Co-educational Day 5–16
No of pupils: 115
Special Needs: DOW DYS EBD EPI HI
MLD SLD SP&LD

ALF KAUFMAN SPECIAL SCHOOL

Highwood, Norden, Rochdale,
Greater Manchester OC11 5PX
Tel: (01706) 359153
Head: Mr P D Geldeart
Type: Co-educational Day 3–11
No of pupils: 37
Special Needs: PH W

INNES SPECIAL SCHOOL

Ings Lane, Rochdale, Greater
Manchester OL12 7AL
Tel: (01706) 646605
Head: Mrs A Wilson
Type: Co-educational Day 3–19
No of pupils: B35 G29
Special Needs: CP EPI PMLD SLD
VIS W

RYDINGS SPECIAL SCHOOL

Great Howarth, Wardle Road,
Rochdale, Greater Manchester
OL12 9HJ
Tel: (01706) 57993
Head: Mr R A Jazwinski
Type: Co-educational Day 3–16
No of pupils: 100
Special Needs: EBD MLD SLD W

Salford Education Authority

Minerva House
Pendlebury Road
Swinton
Manchester M27
Tel: (0161) 832 9751

IRWELL PARK SCHOOL

Britannia Street, Salford, Greater
Manchester M6 6FX
Tel: (0161) 737 0024
Head: M M Ironmonger
Type: Co-educational Day 11–16
No of pupils: 53

NEW CROFT HIGH SCHOOL

Seedley Road, Salford, Greater
Manchester M6 5NQ
Tel: (0161) 736 6415
Head: Mr J S Chapman
Type: Co-educational Day 11–19
No of pupils: 78
Special Needs: PMLD SLD W

NORTHUMBERLAND HIGH SCHOOL

Northumberland Street, Salford,
Greater Manchester M7 4RP
Tel: (0161) 792 8504
Head: Mrs A Kennedy
Type: Co-educational Day 11–16
No of pupils: 35
Special Needs: EBD

Stockport Education Authority

3rd Floor, Stopford House
Town Hall
Stockport SK1 3XE
Tel: (0161) 480 4949

CASTLE HILL SCHOOL

Lapwing Lane, Brinnington,
Stockport, Greater Manchester
SK5 8LF
Tel: (01472) 879282
Head: Mr M Marra
Type: Co-educational Day 11–16
No of pupils: 168
Special Needs: MLD

HEATON SCHOOL

St James Road, Heaton Moor,
Stockport, Greater Manchester
SK4 4RE
Tel: (0161) 432 1931
Head: Ms E A Seers
Type: Co-educational Day 11–19
No of pupils: 50
Special Needs: AUT PMLD SLD

LISBURNE SCHOOL

Half Moon Lane, Offerton,
Stockport, Greater Manchester
SK2 5LB
Tel: (0161) 483 5045
Head: Mrs S Reid
Type: Co-educational Day 5–11
No of pupils: B33 G16
Special Needs: DYP MLD PH SLD
SP&LD

TAXAL LODGE SCHOOL

Linglongs Road, Whaley Bridge,
Greater Manchester SK12 7DU
Tel: (01663) 732613
Head: Mr M R Douglass
No of pupils: 30
Special Needs: EBD

VALLEY SCHOOL

Whitehaven Road, Bramhall,
Stockport, Greater Manchester
SK7 1EN
Tel: (0161) 439 7343
Head: Mrs C M Goodlet
Type: Co-educational Day 2–11
No of pupils: 70
Special Needs: AUT CP PH PMLD
SLD W

WINDLEHURST

Windlehurst Lane, Hawk Green,
Marple, Stockport, Cheshire
SK6 7HZ
Tel: (0161) 427 4788
Head: Mr S G Woodgate
Type: Co-educational Day 11–16
No of pupils: 42
Special Needs: EBD

Thameside Education Authority

Council Offices
Wellington Road
Ashton-under-Lyne
Lancashire OL6 6DL
Tel: (0161) 342 8355

CROMWELL SECONDARY SCHOOL
Thornley Lane South, Reddish, Stockport, Greater Manchester SK5 6QW
Tel: (0161) 320 8728
Head: Mrs S Cooper
Type: Co-educational Day 11–16
No of pupils: B25 G25
Special Needs: PMLD **SLD** W

HAWTHORNS SCHOOL
Corporation Road, Audenshaw, Greater Manchester M34 5LZ
Tel: (0161) 336 3389
Head: Mr J M Shore
Type: Co-educational Day 4–11
No of pupils: 80
Special Needs: **MLD**

OAKDALE SCHOOL & ACORN NURSERY
Cheetham Hill Road, Dukinfield, Greater Manchester SK16 5LD
Tel: (0161) 367 9299
Head: Mrs I Howard
Type: Co-educational Day 2–11
No of pupils: 105
Special Needs: AUT **PMLD SLD** W

SAMUEL LAYCOCK SCHOOL
Mereside, Stalybridge, Cheshire SK15 1JF
Tel: (0161) 303 1321
Head: Mr S Andrew
Type: Co-educational Day 11–16
No of pupils: B77 G46
Special Needs: **MLD**

Trafford Education Authority

PO Box 40
Talbot Road
Stretford
Manchester M32 0EL
Tel: (0161) 912 1212

BRENTWOOD SCHOOL
Brentwood Avenue, Timperley, Altrincham, Greater Manchester WA14 1SR
Tel: (0161) 928 8109
Head: Mr C Oxley
Type: Co-educational Day 11–19
No of pupils: 70
Special Needs: PMLD SLD W

DELAMERE SCHOOL
Irlam Road, Flixton, Urmston, Greater Manchester M41 6AP
Tel: (0161) 747 5893
Head: Ms S M Huddart
Type: Co-educational Day
No of pupils: 64
Special Needs: AUT PMLD SLD W

LONGFORD PARK SCHOOL
Longford Park, Stretford, Greater Manchester M32 8PR
Tel: (0161) 881 2341
Head: Mr M G Coxe
Type: Co-educational Day 5–11
No of pupils: 56
Special Needs: ADD ADHD EBD **MLD** SPLD

PICTOR SCHOOL
Harboro Road, Sale, Greater Manchester M33 5AH
Tel: (0161) 962 5432
Head: Mrs J Spruce
Type: Co-educational Day 2–11
No of pupils: 79
Special Needs: ADD ADHD ASP **AUT** CP DOW DYC DYS EBD EPI HI MLD **PH** SP&LD **SPLD**

Wigan Education Authority

Gateway House
Standishgate
Wigan WN1 1AE
Tel: (01942) 828891

BROOKFIELD HIGH
Park Road, Hindley, Wigan, Greater Manchester WN2 3RY
Tel: (01942) 776142
Head: Mr J H Young
Type: Co-educational Day 11–16
No of pupils: B105 G42
Special Needs: **MLD**

GREEN HALL PRIMARY SCHOOL
Green Hall Close, Atherton, Greater Manchester M46 9HP
Tel: (01942) 883928
Head: Mr Triska
Type: Co-educational Day 4–11
No of pupils: B66 G33
Special Needs: **MLD**

HIGHLEA SECONDARY SHOOL
294 Mosley Common Road, Worsley, Greater Manchester M28 1DA
Tel: (0161) 790 2698
Head: Mr J Leamon
Type: Co-educational Boarding
No of pupils: B41 G2
No of Boarders: W12
Special Needs: EBD

HINDLEY TANFIELD
Borsdane Avenue, Hindley, Wigan, Greater Manchester WN2 3QB
Tel: (01942) 255682
Head: Mrs E M Edge
Type: Co-educational Day 2–19

WIGAN HOPE SCHOOL
Kelvin Grove, Marus Bridge, Wigan, Greater Manchester WN3 6SP
Tel: (01942) 824150
Head: Mr J P Dahlstrom
Type: Co-educational Day 2–19
No of pupils: 120
Special Needs: AUT PMLD SLD W

KINGSHILL SCHOOL
Elliot Street, Tyldesley, Greater Manchester M29 8JE
Tel: (01942) 892104
Head: M J Myerslough
Type: Co-educational Day 11–16
No of pupils: B53 G6
Special Needs: EBD

MERE OAKS SCHOOL
Boars Head, Standish, Wigan,
Greater Manchester WN1 2RF
Tel: (01942) 243481
Head: Mrs J Leach
Type: Co-educational Day 2–19
No of pupils: B58 G50
Special Needs: **PH** W

MONTROSE SCHOOL
Montrose Avenue, Pemberton,
Wigan, Greater Manchester
WN5 9XN
Tel: (01942) 223431
Head: Mr A Farmer
Type: Co-educational Day 7–16
No of pupils: 126
Special Needs: **MLD** W

WILLOW GROVE PRIMARY
Willow Grove, Ashton-in-Makefield,
Wigan, Greater Manchester
WN4 9HP
Tel: (01942) 727717
Head: Mr V Pearson
Type: Co-educational Day
No of pupils: 56
Special Needs: **EBD**

MERSEYSIDE

Knowsley Education Authority
Huyton Hey Road
Huyton
Liverpool L36 5YH
Tel: (0151) 443 3232

ALT BRIDGE SECONDARY SUPPORT CENTRE
Wellcroft Road, Huyton, Knowsley,
Merseyside L36 7TA
Tel: (0151) 489 1050
Head: Mr I Chisnall
Type: Co-educational Day 11–16
No of pupils: 172
Special Needs: ASP EBD HI **MLD**
SP&LD **SPLD**

THE ELMS SPECIAL SCHOOL
Whitethorn Drive, Stockbridge
Village, Merseyside L28 1RX
Tel: (0151) 489 6517
Head: Mrs L Lowe
Type: Co-educational Day 2–19
No of pupils: 115
Special Needs: **AUT** DOW **PMLD**
SLD W

HIGHFIELD SCHOOL
Baileys Lane, Halewood, Merseyside
L26 0TY
Tel: (0151) 486 4787
Head: Mr A Macquarrie
Type: Co-educational Day 6–16
No of pupils: 48
Special Needs: **EBD**

KNOWSLEY CENTRAL PRIMARY SUPPORT CENTRE
Huyton, Knowsley, Merseyside
L36 7SY
Tel: (0151) 489 5024
Head: Mrs P Thomas
Type: Co-educational Day 2–12

KNOWSLEY NORTHERN PRIMARY SUPPORT CENTRE
Bramcote Walk, Northwood, Kirkby,
Merseyside L33 9UR
Tel: (0151) 546 2156
Head: Mrs B Twiss
Type: Co-educational Day 2–12
No of pupils: B43 G20
Special Needs: DYS **MLD** SP&LD
SPLD

KNOWSLEY SOUTHERN PRIMARY SUPPORT CENTRE
Arncliffe Road, Halewood,
Liverpool, Merseyside L25 9QE
Tel: (0151) 486 5514
Head: Mr E Smith
Type: Co-educational Day 2–11
No of pupils: 50
Special Needs: **MLD** W

PARKFIELD SCHOOL
Bracknell Avenue, Southdene,
Kirkby, Merseyside L32 9PW
Tel: (0151) 546 6355
Head: Ms J L Schofield-King
Type: Co-educational Day 5–16
No of pupils: 72
Special Needs: EBD SPLD

SPRINGFIELD SPECIAL SCHOOL
Cawthorne Close, Kirkby,
Merseyside L32 3XG
Tel: (0151) 549 1425
Head: Mr I Cordingley
Type: Co-educational Day 2–19
No of pupils: B45 G35
Special Needs: PH PMLD W

Liverpool Education Authority
4 Renshaw Street
Liverpool L1 4NX
Tel: (0151) 233 8207

ABBOTS LEA SCHOOL
Beaconsfield Road, Liverpool,
Merseyside L25 6EE
Tel: (0151) 428 1161
Head: Mrs C A Boycott
Type: Co-educational Boarding and
Day 4–19
No of pupils: B46 G12
No of Boarders: W16
Special Needs: ASP **AUT**

ACORN NURSERY SCHOOL
Lowerson Road, Liverpool,
Merseyside L11 8LW
Tel: (0151) 226 0309
Head: Mrs L Wright
Type: Co-educational Day 2–5
No of pupils: 30
Special Needs: ASP **AUT** PMLD
SLD W

ASHFIELD SCHOOL
Childwall Abbey Road, Childwall,
Liverpool, Merseyside L16 5EY
Tel: (0151) 228 9500
Head: Mr J Ashley
Type: Co-educational Day 5–16
No of pupils: 150
Special Needs: ADD ASP AUT DYP
DYS **EBD** EPI **MLD** SP&LD **SPLD**

CLIFFORD HOLROYDE SPECIAL SCHOOL
Thingwall Lane, Liverpool,
Merseyside L14 7NX
Tel: (0151) 525 6943
Head: Mr M J Rees
Type: Co-educational Day 5–16
No of pupils: 55
Special Needs: **EBD**

ERNEST COOKSON SPECIAL SCHOOL

Mill Lane, Liverpool, Merseyside
L12 7JA
Tel: (0151) 220 1874
Head: Mr S W Roberts
Type: Co-educational Day 5–16
No of pupils: 50
Special Needs: **EBD**

FINCHLEA SCHOOL

Mill Lane, Old Swan, Liverpool,
Merseyside L13 5TF
Tel: (0151) 228 2578
Head: Mrs D Newman
Type: Co-educational 4–19
No of pupils: 36
Special Needs: **AUT DOW EPI SLD**

GRANTSIDE SPECIAL SCHOOL

Mill Road, Everton, Liverpool,
Merseyside L6 2AS
Tel: (0151) 263 6417
Head: Mr M H Horne
Type: Boys Day
No of pupils: 45
Special Needs: **EBD**

HAROLD MAGNAY SCHOOL

Woolton Hill Road, Liverpool,
Merseyside L25 6JA
Tel: (0151) 428 6305
Head: Mr M Little
Type: Co-educational Day and
Boarding 2–11
No of pupils: 70 *No of Boarders:* W24
Special Needs: **PH** W

LOWER LEE SPECIAL SCHOOL

Beaconsfield Road, Liverpool,
Merseyside L25 6EF
Tel: (0151) 428 4071
Head: Mr P Wright
Type: Boys Boarding 8–16
No of pupils: 45 *No of Boarders:* F36
Special Needs: **EBD**

MARGARET BEAVAN SCHOOL

Almonds Green, West Derby,
Liverpool, Merseyside L12 5HP
Tel: (0151) 226 1306
Head: Mr T B Flynn
Type: Co-educational Day 5–16
No of pupils: B80 G60
Special Needs: **MLD**

MEADOW BANK SPECIAL SCHOOL

Sherwoods Lane, Liverpool,
Merseyside L10 1LW
Tel: (0151) 525 3451
Head: Mrs C Clancy
Type: Co-educational Day 5–17
No of pupils: 145
Special Needs: **ADD** ASP **AUT** EPI
MLD SP&LD SPLD

MERSEY VIEW SCHOOL

Minehead Road, Liverpool,
Merseyside L17 6AX
Tel: (0151) 427 1863
Head: Mr C J Muscatelli
Type: Co-educational Day 5–16
No of pupils: B70 G20
Special Needs: **MLD**

MILLSTEAD SPECIAL NEEDS PRIMARY SCHOOL

Old Mill Lane, Wavertree, Liverpool,
Merseyside L15 8LW
Tel: (0151) 722 0974
Head: Mrs M Lucas
Type: Co-educational Day 2–11
No of pupils: B32 G18
Special Needs: **AUT PMLD SLD** W

PALMERSTON SCHOOL

Beaconsfield Road, Woolton,
Liverpool, Merseyside L25 6EE
Tel: (0151) 428 2128
Head: Mr J F Wright
Type: Co-educational Day 11–19
No of pupils: B51 G23
Special Needs: **ADD ADHD ASP AUT
CP** DEL DOW DYP **EPI** HI PH **PMLD**
SLD SP&LD VIS W

PRINCES SCHOOL

Selborne Street, Liverpool,
Merseyside L8 1YQ
Tel: (0151) 709 2602
Head: Mrs V Healy
Type: Co-educational Day 2–11
No of pupils: 50
Special Needs: **AUT** CP DOW HI
PMLD SLD SP&LD W

REDBRIDGE HIGH SCHOOL

Sherwoods Lane, Liverpool,
Merseyside L10 1LW
Tel: (0151) 525 5733
Head: Mrs S Coates
Type: Co-educational Day 11–19
No of pupils: 89
Special Needs: **AUT PMLD SLD** W

SANDFIELD PARK SCHOOL

Sandfield Walk, Liverpool,
Merseyside L12 1LH
Tel: (0151) 228 0324
Head: Mr J Hudson
Type: Co-educational Day 11–19
No of pupils: B53 G26
Special Needs: **CP EPI MLD** PH
PMLD W

WATERGATE SCHOOL

Speke Road, Liverpool, Merseyside
L25 8QA
Tel: (0151) 428 5812
Head: Mr P J Richardson
Type: Co-educational Day
No of pupils: 130
Special Needs: **MLD SP&LD**

WHEATHILL SCHOOL

Naylorsfield Drive, Liverpool,
Merseyside L27 0YD
Tel: (0151) 498 4811
Head: Mr D R Wade
Type: Co-educational Day 5–11
No of pupils: 30
Special Needs: ADHD **EBD** W

WHITE THORN SCHOOL (ASSESSMENT)

Ranworth Square, Liverpool,
Merseyside L11 3DQ
Tel: (0151) 233 4094
Head: Miss J Roberts
Type: Co-educational Day 3–7
No of pupils: 30
Special Needs: **EBD MLD** SLD
SP&LD W

St Helens Education Authority

**The Rivington Centre
Rivington Road
St Helens
Merseyside WA10 4ND
Tel: (01744) 455328**

HAMBLETT SCHOOL

Rainford Road, St Helens,
Merseyside WA10 6BX
Tel: (01744) 678770
Head: Mr R Brownlow
Type: Co-educational Day 3–16
No of pupils: 60
Special Needs: **AUT CP** DEL DYP **EPI**
PH PMLD W

HURST SCHOOL
Hard Lane, St Helens, Merseyside
WA10 6PN
Tel: (01744) 25643
Head: Mr M J Carolan
Type: Co-educational Day 5–16
No of pupils: 170
Special Needs: MLD SP&LD

MILL GREEN SCHOOL
Mill Lane, Newton-le-Willows,
Merseyside WA12 8BG
Tel: (01925) 226213
Head: Mr G C Brown
Type: Co-educational Day 2–19
No of pupils: 88
Special Needs: PMLD SLD

PENKFORD SCHOOL
Wharf Road, Newton-le-Willows,
Merseyside WA12 9XZ
Tel: (01925) 224195
Head: Mr D N Hartley
Type: Co-educational Day 5–16
No of pupils: B85 G40
Special Needs: EBD MLD W

Sefton Education Authority

Town Hall
Oriel Road
Bootle
Merseyside L20 7AE
Tel: (0151) 934 3201

MEREFIELD SPECIAL SCHOOL
Westminster Drive, Southport,
Merseyside PR8 2QZ
Tel: (01704) 577163
Head: Ms A Foster
Type: Co-educational Day 2–19
No of pupils: 44
Special Needs: AUT PMLD SLD W

NEWFIELD SPECIAL SCHOOL
Edge Lane, Liverpool, Merseyside
L23 4TG
Tel: (0151) 931 3030
Head: Mr J Taylor
Type: Co-educational Day 5–16
No of pupils: B71 G3
Special Needs: ADD ADHD ASP DYP DYS EBD EPI

PRESFIELD SPECIAL SCHOOL
Preston New Road, Southport,
Merseyside PR9 8PA
Tel: (01704) 227831
Head: Mr E T Powell
Type: Co-educational Day 8–16
No of pupils: 80
Special Needs: MLD

RONALD HOUSE SCHOOL
De Villiers Avenue, Crosby,
Merseyside L23 2TH
Tel: (0151) 924 3671
Head: Mrs B M Dornan
Type: Co-educational Day 5–16
No of pupils: B73 G52
Special Needs: ADHD ASP EBD MLD

ROWAN PARK SCHOOL
Onell Road, Bootle, Merseyside
L20 6DU
Tel: (0151) 330 0528
Head: Mrs J A Kelly
Type: Co-educational Day
No of pupils: 110
Special Needs: AUT DOW PMLD SLD SP&LD VIS W

THE SCHOOL OF THE GOOD SHEPHERD
Sterrix Lane, Ford, Liverpool,
Merseyside L21 0DA
Tel: (0151) 928 6165
Head: Mr A M Sullivan
Type: Co-educational Day 2–16
No of pupils: 50
Special Needs: CP DEL EPI PH W

Wirral Education Authority

Hamilton Building
Conway Street
Birkenhead
Merseyside CH41 4FD
Tel: (0151) 666 2121

CLARE MOUNT SCHOOL
Fender Lane, Moreton, Wirral,
Merseyside CH46 9PA
Tel: (0151) 606 0274/9440
Head: Mrs L C Clare
Type: Co-educational 11–19
No of pupils: B145 G75
Special Needs: MLD

ELLERAY PARK SCHOOL
Elleray Park Road, Wallasey,
Merseyside CH45 0LH
Tel: (0151) 639 3594
Head: Mr D Quaife
Type: Co-educational Day 2–11
No of pupils: 80
Special Needs: ASP AUT CP DEL DOW DYP DYS EPI HI MLD PH PMLD SLD SP&LD SPLD VIS W

FOXFIELD SCHOOL
Douglas Drive, Moreton, Wirral,
Merseyside CH46 6BT
Tel: (0151) 677 8555
Head: Mr A M Baird
Type: Co-educational Day 11–19
No of pupils: B50 G40
Special Needs: AUT PMLD SLD W

GILBROOK SCHOOL
Pilgrim Street, Birkenhead,
Merseyside CH41 5EH
Tel: (0151) 647 8411
Head: Mr K E Jackson
Type: Co-educational Day 5–11
No of pupils: 50
Special Needs: ADD ADHD EBD W

HAYFIELD SCHOOL
Manor Drive, Upton, Wirral,
Merseyside CH49 4PJ
Tel: (0151) 677 9303
Head: Ms S A Lowy
Type: Co-educational Day 4–11
No of pupils: 120
Special Needs: AUT MLD SP&LD

KILGARTH SCHOOL
Cavendish Street, Birkenhead,
Merseyside CH41 8BA
Tel: (0151) 652 8071
Head: Miss J M Dawson
Type: Boys Day 11–16
No of pupils: 50
Special Needs: EBD

THE LYNDALE SCHOOL
Wirral, Merseyside CH63 4JY
Tel: (0151) 334 6120
Head: Mrs P Stewart
Type: Co-educational Day 2–11
No of pupils: 59

MEADOWSIDE SCHOOL
Pool Lane, Woodchurch,
Birkenhead, Merseyside CH49 5LA
Tel: (0151) 6787711
Head: Ms L Kane
Type: Co-educational Day 11–19
No of pupils: B45 G25
Special Needs: AUT CP DYP EPI MLD PH PMLD SLD SP&LD W

ORRETS MEADOW SCHOOL
Chapelhill Road, Moreton,
Birkenhead, Merseyside CH46 9QQ
Tel: (0151) 678 8070
Head: Mrs S E Blythe
Type: Co-educational Day 7–11
No of pupils: 66
Special Needs: DYS SPLD

STANLEY SCHOOL
Pensby Road, Thingwall, Heswall,
Merseyside CH61 7UG
Tel: (0151) 648 3171
Head: Mr A Newman
Type: Co-educational Day 2–11
No of pupils: 90
Special Needs: AUT **SLD**

MIDDLESBROUGH

Middlesbrough Borough Council

Education Service
PO Box 69
Vancouver House
Gurney Street
Middlesbrough TS1 1EL

BEVERLEY SCHOOL FOR CHILDREN WITH AUTISM
Beverley Road, Middlesbrough
TS4 3LQ
Tel: (01642) 815500
Head: Mr N Carden
Type: Co-educational Day 4–19
No of pupils: B50 G10
Special Needs: AUT

HOLMWOOD SCHOOL
Saltersgill Avenue, Middlesbrough
TS4 3JS
Tel: (01642) 819157
Head: Mr D Johnson
Type: Co-educational Day 5–11
No of pupils: B60 G40
Special Needs: **MLD**

PRIORY WOODS SCHOOL
Tothill Avenue, Netherfields,
Middlesbrough TS3 0RH
Tel: (01642) 321212
Head: Mrs B Knill
Type: Co-educational Day 4–19
No of pupils: B88 G59
Special Needs: PMLD **SLD** W

TOLLESBY SCHOOL
Saltersgill Avenue, Middlesbrough
TS4 3JS
Tel: (01642) 815765
Head: Mr J Whittingham
Type: Co-educational Day 11–16
No of pupils: B100 G40
Special Needs: EBD **MLD**

NORFOLK

Norfolk Education Authority

County Hall
Norwich NR1 2DL
Tel: (01603) 222146

ALDERMAN JACKSON SPECIAL SCHOOL
Marsh Lane, Gaywood, King's Lynn,
Norfolk PE30 3AE
Tel: (01553) 672779/674281
Head: Mrs L F Tolfree
Type: Co-educational Day 2–19
No of pupils: B35 G28
Special Needs: **AUT CP PMLD** SLD W

THE CLARE SCHOOL
South Park Avenue, Norwich,
Norfolk NR4 7AU
Tel: (01603) 54199
Head: Mr C R Hocking
Type: Co-educational Day 4–19
No of pupils: 110
Special Needs: CP DYP EPI HI PH
SP&LD VIS W

EATON HALL SPECIAL SCHOOL
Pettus Road, Norwich, Norfolk
NR4 7BU
Tel: (01603) 457480
Head: Mr S T Lord
Type: Boys Boarding and Day 8–16
No of pupils: 48
Special Needs: **EBD**

EDINBURGH ROAD SPECIAL SCHOOL
Norwich Road, Holt, Norfolk
NR25 6SL
Tel: (01263) 713358
Head: Mrs D Whitham
Type: Co-educational Day 2–19
No of pupils: 34
Special Needs: PMLD SLD W

FRED NICHOLSON SPECIAL SCHOOL
Westfield Road, Dereham, Norfolk
NR19 1BJ
Tel: (01362) 693915
Head: Mr M Clayton
Type: Co-educational Day and
Boarding 7–16
No of pupils: B60 G35
No of Boarders: W25
Special Needs: **MLD** W

HALL SPECIAL SCHOOL
St Faith's Road, Old Catton,
Norwich, Norfolk NR6 7AD
Tel: (01603) 466467
Head: Mrs A M Ruthven
Type: Co-educational Day 3–19
No of pupils: 80
Special Needs: AUT CP DEL DOW
EPI HI PH **PMLD SLD** VIS W

HARFORD MANOR SPECIAL SCHOOL
43 Ipswich Road, Norwich, Norfolk
NR2 2LN
Tel: (01603) 451809
Head: Mr G Kitchen
Type: Co-educational Day 3–19
No of pupils: 75
Special Needs: AUT PMLD SLD

JOHN GRANT SPECIAL SCHOOL
St George's Drive, Caistor-on-Sea,
Great Yarmouth, Norfolk NR30 5QW
Tel: (01493) 720158
Head: Mr G A Hampson
Type: Co-educational Day 4–19
No of pupils: B56 G37
Special Needs: PMLD **SLD** W

PARKSIDE SPECIAL SCHOOL
College Road, Norwich, Norfolk
NR2 3JA
Tel: (01603) 441126
Head: Mr B Payne
Type: Co-educational Day 7–16
No of pupils: 145
Special Needs: **MLD**

SIDESTRAND HALL SPECIAL SCHOOL
Cromer Road, Sidestrand, Cromer,
Norfolk NR27 0NH
Tel: (01263) 578144
Head: Mr G R Scott
Type: Co-educational Boarding and
Day 7–16
No of pupils: 110 *No of Boarders:* W25
Special Needs: **MLD**

NORTHAMPTONSHIRE

Northamptonshire Education Authority

PO Box 216
John Dryden House
8–10 The Lakes
Northampton NN4 7DD
Tel: (01604) 236236

BILLING BROOK SCHOOL
Penistone Road, Lumbertubs,
Northampton NN3 8EZ
Tel: (01604) 773910
Head: Mr D Scott
Type: Co-educational Day 2–16
No of pupils: B95 G55
Special Needs: AUT **MLD SLD**

FAIRFIELDS SCHOOL
Trinity Avenue, Northampton
NN2 6JN
Tel: (01604) 714777
Head: Mrs C Murray
Type: Co-educational Day 3–11
No of pupils: 70
Special Needs: EPI **PH** PMLD SLD W

FRIARS SCHOOL
Friar's Close, Wellingborough,
Northamptonshire NN8 2LA
Tel: (01933) 304950
Head: Mrs P A Norton
Type: Co-educational Day 11–16
No of pupils: B98 G47
Special Needs: ASP AUT CP DEL
DOW DYS **MLD** SLD W

GREENFIELDS SCHOOL
Harborough Road, Northampton
NN2 8LR
Tel: (01604) 843657
Head: Mrs J Moralee
Type: Co-educational Day 11–19
No of pupils: 70
Special Needs: AUT **PMLD SLD** W

ISEBROOK SCHOOL
Eastleigh Road, Kettering,
Northamptonshire NN15 6PT
Tel: (01536) 81606
Head: Mr K McHenry
Type: Co-educational Day 11–16
No of pupils: B63 G15
Special Needs: ASP AUT AUT MLD
PH W

KINGS MEADOW
273 Welford Road, Northampton
NN2 8PW
Tel: (01604) 846018
Head: Mr B Kettleborough
Type: Co-educational Day 4–11

KINGSLEY SCHOOL
Churchill Way, Kettering,
Northamptonshire NN15 5DP
Tel: (01536) 316880
Head: Ms J C Thompson
Type: Co-educational Day 3–11
No of pupils: 104
Special Needs: ASP AUT MLD PMLD
SLD W

MAPLEFIELDS SCHOOL
School Place, Gainsborough Road,
Corby, Northamptonshire NN18 0QP
Tel: (01536) 409040
Head: Mrs L Morgan
Type: Co-educational Day 4–11
No of pupils: B36 G4
Special Needs: ADD ADHD EBD

NORTHGATE SCHOOL
Queens Park Parade, Northampton
NN2 6LR
Tel: (01604) 714098
Head: Mr R Conway
Type: Co-educational Day 11–16
No of pupils: 120
Special Needs: ADD ADHD ASP DOW
DYP MLD SLD W

ORCHARD SCHOOL
Beatrice Road, Kettering,
Northamptonshire NN16 9QR
Tel: (01536) 513726
Head: Mrs V Payne
Type: Co-educational Day 11–16
No of pupils: 45
Special Needs: EBD W

RAEBURN SCHOOL
Raeburn Road, Northampton
NN2 7EU
Tel: (01604) 460017
Head: Mr D R Lloyd
Type: Co-educational Day 11–16
No of pupils: B45 G5
Special Needs: EBD

ROWANGATE PRIMARY SCHOOL
Finedon Road, Wellingborough,
Northamptonshire NN8 4NS
Tel: (01933) 304970
Head: Mrs F Sutton
Type: Co-educational Day 3–11
No of pupils: B54 G33
Special Needs: ADD ADHD ASP **AUT**
CP DEL DOW DYP DYS EPI **MLD** PH
PMLD SLD SP&LD SPLD VIS W

WREN SPINNEY SCHOOL
Westover Road, off Westhill Drive,
Kettering, Northamptonshire
NN16 0AP
Tel: (01536) 481 939
Head: Ms D Withers
Type: Co-educational Day 11–19
No of pupils: 60
Special Needs: AUT PMLD SLD

NORTHUMBERLAND

Northumberland Education Authority

County Hall
Morpeth
Northumberland NE61 2EF
Tel: (01670) 533000

ATKINSON HOUSE SCHOOL
North Terrace, Seghill, Cramlington,
Northumberland NE23 7EB
Tel: (0191) 2980838
Head: R McGlashan
Type: Boys Day
No of pupils: 40
Special Needs: ADD ADHD **EBD**

BARNDALE HOUSE SCHOOL
Barndale House, Howling Lane,
Alnwick, Northumberland
NE66 1DQ
Tel: (01665) 602541
Head: Mr J P Chappells
Type: Co-educational Day and
Boarding 3–19
No of pupils: 35
Special Needs: **SLD**

CLEASWELL HILL SCHOOL
Guide Post, Choppington,
Northumberland NE62 5DJ
Tel: (01670) 823182
Head: Mr R J Hope
Type: Co-educational Day 4–16
No of pupils: B70 G35
Special Needs: **MLD**

COLLINGWOOD SCHOOL
Thingwall Lane, Morpeth,
Northumberland L14 7NX
Tel: (01670) 56374
Head: Ms C Hetherington
Type: Co-educational Day
No of pupils: 120
Special Needs: **MLD**

EAST HARTFORD SCHOOL
East Hartford, Cramlington,
Northumberland NE23 9AR
Tel: (01670) 713881
Head: Mr W K Telfer
Type: Co-educational 4–11
No of pupils: 53
Special Needs: **MLD**

THE GROVE SCHOOL
Grove Gardens, Tweedmouth,
Berwick Upon Tweed,
Northumberland TD15 2EN
Tel: (01289) 360390
Head: Mrs E E Brown
Type: Co-educational Day 3–19
No of pupils: 23
Special Needs: AUT DOW PMLD
SLD W

HACKWOOD PARK SCHOOL
Gallows Bank, Hexham,
Northumberland NE46 1AU
Tel: (01434) 604039
Head: Mr J Wells
Type: Co-educational Day
No of pupils: 86 *No of Boarders:* W12
Special Needs: **MLD**

PRIORY SCHOOL
Dene Park, Hexham,
Northumberland NE46 1HN
Tel: (01434) 605021
Head: Mr M Thompson
Type: Co-educational Day 3–18
No of pupils: B26 G14
Special Needs: **PMLD SLD** W

NOTTINGHAMSHIRE

Nottingham City Council

Sandfield Centre
Sandfield Road
Lenton
Nottingham NG7 1QH
Tel: (0115) 915 0600

ASPLEY WOOD SCHOOL
Robins Wood Road, Aspley,
Nottingham NG8 3LD
Tel: (0115) 913 1400
Head: Mrs B Mole
Type: Co-educational Day 3–16
No of pupils: B25 G20
Special Needs: **CP PH VIS** W

NETHERGATE SCHOOL
Swansdowne Drive, Clifton Estate,
Nottingham NG11 8HX
Tel: (0115) 915 2959
Head: Mr S Johnson-Marshall
Type: Co-educational Day 5–16
No of pupils: B43 G22
Special Needs: ADHD **AUT DOW**
DYP DYS EBD EPI **MLD** SP&LD
SPLD VIS W

ROSEHILL SCHOOL

St Matthias Road, Nottingham
NG3 2FE
Tel: (0115) 9502038
Head: Mr J Pearson
Type: Co-educational Day 3–19
No of pupils: B55 G15
Special Needs: ASP AUT

SHEPHERD SCHOOL

Harvey Road, Off Beechdale Road,
Bilborough, Nottingham NG8 3BB
Tel: (0115) 929 1011
Head: Mr D S Stewart
Type: Co-educational 3–19
No of pupils: B69 G41
Special Needs: AUT EPI MLD PMLD
SLD W

WESTBURY SCHOOL

Chingford Road, Billingborough,
Nottingham NG8 3BT
Tel: (0115) 913 8005
Head: Mr J Haw
Type: Co-educational Day 10–16
No of pupils: B19
Special Needs: EBD

WOODLANDS SCHOOL

Beechdale Road, Aspley, Nottingham
NG8 3EZ
Tel: (0115) 929 5947
Head: S D Fee
Type: Co-educational Day 3–16
No of pupils: 120
Special Needs: AUT EBD MLD SLD W

Nottinghamshire Education Authority

County Hall
West Bridgford
Nottingham NG2 7QP
Tel: (0115) 982 3823

ASH LEA SCHOOL

Owthorpe Road, Cotgrave,
Nottingham NG12 3PA
Tel: (0115) 9892744
Head: Mrs L Skillington
Type: Co-educational Day 3–19
No of pupils: B32 G31
Special Needs: SLD

BEECH HILL SCHOOL

Fairholme Drive, Mansfield,
Nottinghamshire NG19 6DX
Tel: (01623) 26008
Head: Mr M Sutton
Type: Co-educational Day 11–16
No of pupils: 70
Special Needs: AUT EBD **MLD**

BRACKEN HILL SCHOOL

Chartwell Road, Kirkby-in-Ashfield,
Nottinghamshire NG17 7HZ
Tel: (01623) 753068
Head: Mr A M Kawalek
Type: Co-educational Day 3–19
No of pupils: B45 G15
Special Needs: ADD ADHD ASP AUT
DEL MLD SLD SP&LD W

CARLTON DIGBY SCHOOL

Digby Avenue, Mapperley,
Nottinghamshire NG3 6DS
Tel: (0115) 956 8289
Head: Mrs G Clifton
Type: Co-educational Day 3–19
No of pupils: B42 G21
Special Needs: AUT PMLD SLD W

DERRYMOUNT SCHOOL

Churchmoor Lane, Arnold,
Nottinghamshire NG5 8HN
Tel: (0115) 953 4015
Head: Mr E Thompson
Type: Co-educational Day 3–16
No of pupils: 60
Special Needs: **AUT** CP EBD EPI **HI**
MLD PH SLD SP&LD VIS

FOUNTAINDALE SCHOOL

Nottingham Road, Mansfield,
Nottinghamshire NG18 5BA
Tel: (01623) 792671
Head: Mr M Dengel
Type: Co-educational Boarding and
Day 3–19
No of pupils: B38 G40
No of Boarders: W8
Special Needs: CP DEL EPI PH
SP&LD VIS W

FOXWOOD SCHOOL

Derby Road, Bramcote Hills,
Beeston, Nottinghamshire NG9 3GE
Tel: (0115) 9177202
Head: Ms J Baker
Type: Co-educational Day 3–19
No of pupils: B63 G32
Special Needs: ASP AUT MLD SPLD W

REDGATE SCHOOL

Somersall Street, Mansfield,
Nottinghamshire NG19 6EL
Tel: (01623) 455955
Head: Mr K G Fallows
Type: Co-educational Day 3–11
No of pupils: B40 G10

ST GILES SCHOOL

North Road, Retford,
Nottinghamshire DN22 7XN
Tel: (01777) 703683
Head: Mrs C M Kirk
Type: Co-educational Day 3–19
No of pupils: 86
Special Needs: ADD ADHD ASP AUT
CP DOW EBD EPI HI MLD PH PMLD
SLD VIS W

YEOMAN PARK SCHOOL

Park Hall Road, Mansfield
Woodhouse, Mansfield,
Nottinghamshire NG19 8PS
Tel: (01204) 840709
Head: Mr P Betts
Type: Co-educational Day 3–19
No of pupils: 73
Special Needs: SLD W

OXFORDSHIRE

Oxfordshire Education Authority

Macclesfield House
New Road
Oxford OX1 1NA
Tel: (01865) 792422

BARDWELL SCHOOL

Hendon Place, Sunderland Drive,
Bicester, Oxfordshire OX26 4RZ
Tel: (01869) 242182
Head: Mrs C Hughes
Type: Co-educational Day 2–16
No of pupils: 56
Special Needs: AUT CP PMLD SLD SP&LD W

FITZWARYN SPECIAL SCHOOL

Denchworth Road, Wantage,
Oxfordshire OX12 9ET
Tel: (01235) 764504
Head: Mrs M Tighe
Type: Co-educational Day 3–16
No of pupils: B54 G22
Special Needs: MLD PMLD SLD W

FRANK WISE SCHOOL

Hornbeam Close, Banbury,
Oxfordshire OX16 9RL
Tel: (01295) 263520
Head: Mr K Griffiths
Type: Co-educational Day 2–16
No of pupils: 92
Special Needs: PMLD SLD W

IFFLEY MEAD SPECIAL SCHOOL

Iffley Turn, Oxford OX4 4DU
Tel: (01865) 747606
Head: Mr J Knox
Type: Co-educational Day 5–16
No of pupils: 111
Special Needs: MLD

JOHN WATSON SPECIAL SCHOOL

Littleworth Road, Wheatley, Oxford
OX33 1NN
Tel: (01865) 872515
Head: Ms S Cook
Type: Co-educational Day 2–16
No of pupils: 68
Special Needs: PMLD SLD W

KINGFISHER SCHOOL

Radley Road, Abingdon, Oxfordshire
OX14 3RR
Tel: (01235) 523843
Head: Mrs A O'Meara
Type: Co-educational Day 2–16
No of pupils: 115
Special Needs: MLD PMLD SLD W

MABEL PRICHARD SPECIAL SCHOOL

St Nicholas Road, Littlemore,
Oxfordshire OX4 4PN
Tel: (01865) 777878
Head: Miss J Wallington
Type: Co-educational Day 2–16
No of pupils: 63
Special Needs: PMLD SLD W

NORTHERN HOUSE SPECIAL SCHOOL

South Parade, Summertown, Oxford
OX2 7JN
Tel: (01865) 557004
Head: Mrs A J Battersby
Type: Co-educational Day 5–13
No of pupils: B73 G5
Special Needs: EBD

NORTHFIELD SPECIAL SCHOOL

Knights Road, Blackbird Leys,
Oxford OX4 5HN
Tel: (01865) 771703
Head: Mr P Sheldon
Type: Co-educational Day 11–16
No of pupils: B88 No of Boarders: F7 W12
Special Needs: EBD

ORMEROD SPECIAL SCHOOL

Waynflete Road, Headington, Oxford
OX3 8DD
Tel: (01865) 744173
Head: Mr C Peters
Type: Co-educational Day 2–16
No of pupils: 42
Special Needs: PH

SPRINGFIELD SPECIAL SCHOOL

9 Moorland Close, Witney,
Oxfordshire OX28 6NA
Tel: (01993) 703963
Head: Mrs C Niner
Type: Co-educational Day 2–16
No of pupils: B66 G83
Special Needs: PMLD SLD W

WOODEATON MANOR SCHOOL

Woodeaton, Oxford OX3 9TS
Tel: (01865) 58722
Head: Miss C Greenhow
Type: Co-educational Boarding and Day 7–16
No of pupils: 63 No of Boarders: W24
Special Needs: EBD EPI HI MLD VIS

REDCAR AND CLEVELAND

**Redcar & Cleveland
Education Authority**

PO Box 83
Council Offices
Kirkleatham Street
Redcar
Cleveland TS10 1YA
Tel: (01642) 444000

KILTON THORPE SCHOOL
Marshall Drive, Brotton, Redcar and
Cleveland TS12 2UW
Tel: (01287) 677265
Head: Ms N Robinson
Type: Co-educational Day 3–19
No of pupils: B71 G49
Special Needs: ADD ADHD **AUT** CP
DOW DYP EBD EPI HI **MLD** PH
PMLD SLD SP&LD SPLD VIS W

**KIRKLEATHAM HALL
SCHOOL**
Kirkleatham, Redcar, Redcar and
Cleveland TS10 4QR
Tel: (01642) 483009
Head: Mrs A G Naylor
Type: Co-educational Day 2–19
No of pupils: B75 G55
Special Needs: CP DOW EPI **MLD**
PMLD SLD SP&LD W

RUTLAND

Rutland Education Authority

Catmose
Oakham
Rutland LE15 6HP
Tel: (01572) 758489

THE PARKS SCHOOL
Barleythorpe Road, Oakham,
Rutland LE15 6NR
Tel: (01572) 756747
Head: Mrs B Marchant
Type: Co-educational Day 2–6
No of pupils: 26
Special Needs: ASP AUT CP DEL
DOW EBD EPI HI MLD PH PMLD
SLD SP&LD SPLD VIS W

SHROPSHIRE

**Shropshire Education
Authority**

Shirehall
Abbey Foregate
Shrewsbury SY2 6ND
Tel: (01743) 251000

**THE CHARLES DARWIN
SCHOOL**
North Road, Wellington, Telford,
Shropshire TF1 3ET
Tel: (01952) 242229
Head: Mr I Crawshaw
Type: Boys Day 13–16
No of pupils: 25
Special Needs: EBD

SEVERNDALE SCHOOL
Hearne Way, Monkmoor,
Shrewsbury, Shropshire SY2 5SL
Tel: (01743) 281600
Head: Mr C Davies
Type: Co-educational Day 2–19
Special Needs: AUT CP DEL **DOW**
DYC DYP EPI HI MLD PH PMLD
SLD SP&LD SPLD VIS

TRENCH HALL SCHOOL
Tilley Green, Wem, Shrewsbury,
Shropshire SY4 5PJ
Tel: (01939) 232372
Head: Mr B M Blakemore
Type: Co-educational Day 13–16
No of pupils: 35
Special Needs: **ADD** ADHD ASP **EBD**
SPLD

**Telford and Wrekin
Education Authority**

Civic Offices
PO Box 440
Telford TF3 4WF
Tel: (01952) 202121

MOUNT GILBERT SCHOOL
North Road, Wellington, Telford,
Shropshire TF1 3ET
Head: Ms J Bampton
Type: Boys Day 13–16
No of pupils: 43
Special Needs: EBD

SOUTHALL SCHOOL
off Rowan Road, Dawley, Telford,
Shropshire TF4 3PN
Tel: (01952) 592485
Head: Mr A J Day
Type: Co-educational Day 5–16
No of pupils: B103 G52
Special Needs: MLD

SOMERSET

Bath & North East Somerset Education Authority

PO Box 25
Riverside
Temple Street
Keynsham
Bristol BS31 1DN
Tel: (01225) 394200

BARTLETT'S ELM SCHOOL
Field Road, Langport, Somerset
TA10 9SP
Tel: (01458) 252852
Head: Mr J P Lowe
Type: Boys Day 10–16
No of pupils: 56
Special Needs: **EBD**

FOSSE WAY SCHOOL
Longfellow Road, Radstock, Bath,
North East Somerset BA3 3AL
Tel: (01761) 412198
Head: Mr D Gregory
Type: Co-educational Boarding and
Day 3–19
No of pupils: B77 G29
No of Boarders: W14
Special Needs: **AUT MLD** PMLD **SLD**

LIME GROVE SCHOOL
Pulteney Road, Bath, North East
Somerset BA2 4HE
Tel: (01225) 424732
Head: Mrs J Pulham
Type: Co-educational Day 2–19
No of pupils: B21 G24
Special Needs: PMLD **SLD** W

ROYAL UNITED HOSPITAL SCHOOL
Cynthia Mossman House, Combe
Park, Bath, North East Somerset
BA1 3NJ
Tel: (01225) 824223
Head: Mrs L Harris
Type: Co-educational Day 4–11
No of pupils: 27
Special Needs: MLD **PH** SLD

SUMMERFIELD SCHOOL
Weston Park East, Bath, North East
Somerset BA1 2UY
Tel: (01225) 423607
Head: Mr G Williams
Type: Co-educational Day 7–16
No of pupils: B60 G30
Special Needs: EBD **MLD** SP&LD

WANSDYKE SCHOOL
Frome Road, Odd Down, Bath,
North East Somerset BA2 5RF
Tel: (01225) 832212
Head: Mr J Ward
Type: Co-educational Day 11–16
No of pupils: 64 *No of Boarders:* W11
Special Needs: **EBD**

North Somerset Education Authority

PO Box 51
Town Hall
Weston-Super-Mare
North Somerset BS23 1ZZ
Tel: (01934) 888888

BAYTREE SCHOOL
Baytree Road, Weston-Super-Mare,
North Somerset BS22 8HG
Tel: (01934) 625567
Head: Mrs C Penney
Type: Co-educational Day 3–19
No of pupils: 67
Special Needs: **PMLD SLD** W

RAVENSWOOD SCHOOL
Pound Lane, Nailsea, North
Somerset BS48 2NN
Tel: (01275) 854134
Head: Mrs G A Sawyer
Type: Co-educational Day 3–19
No of pupils: B76 G40
Special Needs: ASP **AUT** DYC DYP
DYS **MLD SLD** W

WESTHAVEN SCHOOL
Ellesmere Road, Uphill, Weston-
Super-Mare, North Somerset
BS23 4UT
Tel: (01934) 632171
Head: Mrs J Moss
Type: Co-educational Day 7–16
No of pupils: B54 G21
Special Needs: **MLD**

Somerset Education Authority

County Hall
Taunton TA1 4DY
Tel: (01823) 355455

AVALON SPECIAL SCHOOL
Brooks Road, Street, Somerset
BA16 0PS
Tel: (01458) 43081
Head: Mrs J M King
Type: Co-educational Day 3–16
No of pupils: B46 G32
Special Needs: ASP AUT CP DOW
DYP EPI MLD PH **PMLD SLD**
SP&LD VIS W

CRITCHILL SCHOOL & LEARNING SUPPORT CENTRE
Nunney Road, Frome, Somerset
BA11 4LB
Tel: (01373) 464148
Head: Mr L Rowsell
Type: Co-educational Day 4–16
No of pupils: B35 G23
Special Needs: ASP AUT MLD PMLD
SLD W

ELMWOOD SPECIAL SCHOOL
Hamp Avenue, Bridgwater, Somerset
TA6 6AP
Tel: (01278) 422866
Head: Mrs J Tobin
Type: Co-educational Day 4–16
No of pupils: B60 G30
Special Needs: **MLD**

FAIRMEAD COMMUNITY SPECIAL SCHOOL
Mudford Road, Yeovil, Somerset
BA21 4NZ
Tel: (01935) 421295
Head: Mr R Hatt
Type: Co-educational Day 4–16
No of pupils: B66 G29
Special Needs: **MLD** W

FIVEWAYS SPECIAL SCHOOL
Victoria Road, Yeovil, Somerset
BA21 5AZ
Tel: (01935) 476227
Head: Mr M Collis
Type: Co-educational Day 4–19
No of pupils: B45 G22
Special Needs: PMLD SLD W

PENROSE SPECIAL SCHOOL

Albert Street, Bridgwater, Somerset
TA6 7ET
Tel: (01278) 423660
Head: Mrs S J Neale
Type: Co-educational Day 2–19
No of pupils: B28 G15
Special Needs: AUT CP DOW EPI
PMLD **SLD** W

THE PRIORY SCHOOL

Pickeridge Close, Taunton, Somerset
TA2 7HW
Tel: (01823) 275569
Head: Mr G Toller
Type: Boys Boarding and Day 11–16
No of pupils: 56 *No of Boarders:* W7
Special Needs: EBD

SELWORTHY SPECIAL SCHOOL

Selworthy Road, Taunton, Somerset
TA2 8HD
Tel: (01823) 284970
Head: Mr D J Machell
Type: Co-educational Day 2–19
No of pupils: 65
Special Needs: ADD ADHD **AUT** CP
DOW EPI HI MLD PH **PMLD SLD**
VIS

STAFFORDSHIRE

Staffordshire Education Authority

Tipping Street
Stafford ST16 2DH
Tel: (01785) 223121

BITHAM SPECIAL SCHOOL

Bitham Lane, Stretton, Burton upon
Trent, Staffordshire DE13 0HB
Tel: (01283) 566988
Head: Ms P M Bullen
Type: Co-educational Day 4–18
No of pupils: 110
Special Needs: **MLD**

BLACKFRIARS SPECIAL SCHOOL

Priory Road, Newcastle under Lyme,
Staffordshire ST5 2TF
Tel: (01782) 297780
Head: Mr C E Lilley
Type: Co-educational Day 2–19
No of pupils: B95 G85
Special Needs: **CP DEL** DOW DYP
EPI **PH** SP&LD W

CHERRY TREES SPECIAL SCHOOL

Giggetty Lane, Wombourne,
Wolverhampton, West Midlands
WV5 0AX
Tel: (01902) 894484
Head: Mrs L J Allman
Type: Co-educational Day 2–19
No of pupils: B26 G10
Special Needs: PMLD SLD W

CICELY HAUGHTON SCHOOL

Westwood Manor, Westley Rocks,
Stoke on Trent, Staffordshire
ST9 0BX
Tel: (01782) 550202
Head: Mr N Phillips
Type: Boys Boarding and Day 5–11
No of pupils: 54 *No of Boarders:* F10
W45
Special Needs: EBD

COPPICE SPECIAL SCHOOL

Abbots Way, Westlands, Newcastle
under Lyme, Staffordshire ST5 2EY
Tel: (01782) 857030
Head: Mr J M Bevan
Type: Co-educational Day 3–16
No of pupils: 130
Special Needs: ASP MLD

CROWN SPECIAL SCHOOL

Bitham Lane, Stretton, Burton upon
Trent, Staffordshire DE13 0HB
Tel: (01283) 239700
Head: Mrs J M Harris
Type: Co-educational Day 2–19
No of pupils: B67 G28
Special Needs: AUT PMLD **SLD** W

GREENHALL COMMUNITY SPECIAL SCHOOL

Second Avenue, Holmcroft,
Staffordshire ST16 IPS
Tel: (01785) 246159
Head: Mrs S I Barlow
Type: Co-educational Day 2–5
No of pupils: 49
Special Needs: AUT CP EPI HI **PH**
PMLD SLD VIS

HORTON LODGE SPECIAL SCHOOL

Rudyard, Leek, Staffordshire
ST13 8RB
Tel: (01538) 306214
Head: Ms C Coles
Type: Co-educational Day and
Boarding 2–11
No of pupils: 61 *No of Boarders:* W16
Special Needs: CP **PH** SP&LD VIS W

MARSHLANDS SPECIAL SCHOOL

Lansdowne Way, Wildwood, Stafford
ST17 4RD
Tel: (01785) 664475
Head: Mr J P Kirkby
Type: Co-educational Day 2–19
No of pupils: 49
Special Needs: PMLD SLD

MEADOWS SPECIAL SCHOOL

Tunstall Road, Biddulph, Stoke on
Trent, Staffordshire ST8 7AB
Tel: (01782) 297920
Head: Mr C Fielding
Type: Co-educational Day 3–18
No of pupils: 120
Special Needs: ASP DOW **MLD** TOU

MERRYFIELDS SPECIAL SCHOOL

Hoon Avenue, Newcastle under
Lyme, Staffordshire ST5 9NY
Tel: (01782) 296076
Head: Mrs A E Bird
Type: Co-educational Day 2–19
No of pupils: 84
Special Needs: PMLD SLD W

PARK SPECIAL SCHOOL
Solway Close, Wiggington Park,
Tamworth, Staffordshire B79 8EB
Tel: (01827) 475690
Head: Mr F Bartlett
Type: Co-educational Day 4–16
No of pupils: 130
Special Needs: **MLD**

QUEEN'S CROFT COMMUNITY SCHOOL
Birmingham Road, Lichfield,
Staffordshire WS13 6PJ
Tel: (01543) 510669
Head: Mrs A Hardman
Type: Co-educational Day 4–16
No of pupils: 150
Special Needs: **MLD** W

QUINCE TREE SPECIAL SCHOOL
Quince, Amington Heath,
Tamworth, Staffordshire B77 4EN
Tel: (01827) 475740
Head: Mrs V A Vernon
Type: Co-educational Day 2–19
No of pupils: 84
Special Needs: PMLD **SLD** W

ROCKLANDS SPECIAL SCHOOL
Wissage Road, Lichfield,
Staffordshire WS13 6SW
Tel: (01543) 510760
Head: Mr A Dooley
Type: Co-educational Day 2–19
No of pupils: 84
Special Needs: ASP AUT PMLD SLD

SAXON HILL SPECIAL SCHOOL
Kings Hill Road, Lichfield,
Staffordshire WS14 9DE
Tel: (01543) 263231
Head: Mr D J Butcher
Type: Co-educational Day and
Boarding 2–18
No of pupils: 112 *No of Boarders:* W16
Special Needs: **PH** W

SPRINGFIELD SPECIAL SCHOOL
Springfield Road, Leek, Staffordshire
ST13 6LQ
Tel: (01538) 383558
Head: Ms I Corden
Type: Co-educational Day 2–19
No of pupils: 38
Special Needs: PMLD **SLD** W

WALTON HALL SPECIAL SCHOOL
Stafford Road, Eccleshall, Stafford
ST21 6JR
Tel: (01785) 850420
Head: Mr R B Goldthorpe
Type: Co-educational Day 5–19
No of pupils: 130 *No of Boarders:* W40
Special Needs: **MLD** W

WIGHTWICK HALL SPECIAL SCHOOL
Tinacre Hill, Wightwick,
Wolverhampton, West Midlands
WV6 8DA
Tel: (01902) 761889
Head: Mr P H Archer
Type: Co-educational Day and
Boarding 2–16
No of pupils: 90 *No of Boarders:* F10
Special Needs: AUT MLD SP&LD W

WILLIAM BAXTER SPECIAL SCHOOL
Stanley Road, Hednesford, Cannock,
Staffordshire WS12 4JS
Tel: (01543) 423714
Head: Mrs C M Allsop
Type: Co-educational Day 5–16
No of pupils: 130
Special Needs: **MLD**

Stoke-on-Trent Education Authority

Swann House
Boothen Road
Stoke-on-Trent ST4 4SY
Tel: (01782) 232014

ABBEY HILL SPECIAL SCHOOL
Greasley Road, Bucknall, Stoke on
Trent, Staffordshire ST2 8LG
Tel: (01782) 534727
Head: Mrs M Coutouvidis
Type: Co-educational Day 2–19
No of pupils: B165 G57
Special Needs: AUT MLD SLD

AYNSLEY SPECIAL SCHOOL
Aynsley's Drive, Blythe Bridge,
Staffordshire ST11 9HJ
Tel: (01782) 392071
Head: Mrs S Addis
Type: Co-educational Day 5–16
No of pupils: 120
Special Needs: EBD **MLD**

HEATHFIELD SPECIAL SCHOOL
Chell Heath Road, Chell Heath,
Stoke on Trent, Staffordshire
ST6 6PD
Tel: (01782) 838938
Head: Mrs J Colesby
Type: Co-educational Day 2–19
No of pupils: 56
Special Needs: PH PMLD SLD

KEMBALL SPECIAL SCHOOL
Duke Street, Fenton, Stoke on Trent,
Staffordshire ST4 3NR
Tel: (01782) 234879
Head: Mrs E Spooner
Type: Co-educational Day 2–19
No of pupils: 77
Special Needs: PMLD SLD

MIDDLEHURST SPECIAL SCHOOL
Turnhurst Road, Chell, Stoke on
Trent, Staffordshire ST6 6NQ
Tel: (01782) 234612
Head: Mrs M Dutton
Type: Co-educational Day 5–16
No of pupils: B65 G35
Special Needs: EBD MLD SP&LD

MOUNT SPECIAL SCHOOL
The Mount, Penkhull, Stoke on
Trent, Staffordshire ST4 7JU
Tel: (01782) 44313
Head: Mr B J Richards
Type: Co-educational Day 2–16
Special Needs: HI

STOCKTON-ON-TEES

Stockton-on-Tees Borough Council

PO Box 228
Church Road
Stockton-on-Tees
TS18 1XE
Tel: (01642) 393440

ABBEY HILL SCHOOL, TECHNOLOGY COLLEGE
Ketton Road, Hardwick, Stockton-on-Tees TS19 8BU
Tel: (01642) 677113
Head: Mr C M Vening
Type: Co-educational Day 11–19
No of pupils: 220
Special Needs: AUT MLD PMLD SLD

SUFFOLK

Suffolk Education Authority

St Andrew House
County Hall
Ipswich IP4 1LJ
Tel: (01473) 583000

THE ASHLEY SCHOOL
Ashley Downs, Lowestoft, Suffolk
NR32 4EU
Tel: (01502) 574847
Head: Mr D Field
Type: Co-educational Day and
Boarding 7–16
No of pupils: 115 *No of Boarders:* W29
Special Needs: MLD

BEACON HILL SCHOOL
Stone Lodge Lane West, Ipswich,
Suffolk IP2 9HW
Tel: (01473) 601175
Head: Mr D Stewart
Type: Co-educational Day 5–16
No of pupils: B87 G68
Special Needs: MLD W

BELSTEAD SCHOOL
Sprites Lane, Belstead, Ipswich,
Suffolk IP8 3ND
Tel: (01473) 556200
Head: Ms D Margerison
Type: Co-educational Day 11–19
No of pupils: B50 G26
Special Needs: PMLD SLD W

HEATHSIDE SCHOOL
Heath Road, Ipswich, Suffolk
IP4 5SN
Tel: (01473) 725508
Head: Mr O Doran
Type: Co-educational Day
No of pupils: B39 G21
Special Needs: AUT PMLD SLD W

HILLSIDE SCHOOL
Hitchcock Place, Sudbury, Suffolk
CO10 1NN
Tel: (01787) 372808
Head: Miss J Freeman
Type: Co-educational Day 3–19
No of pupils: 68
Special Needs: AUT PMLD SLD W

PRIORY SCHOOL
Mount Road, Bury St Edmunds,
Suffolk 1P32 3JZ
Tel: (01284) 761934
Head: Mr P Spencer
Type: Co-educational Day 7–16

RIVERWALK SCHOOL
South Close, Bury St Edmunds,
Suffolk IP33 3JZ
Tel: (01284) 764280
Head: Mr B Ellis
Type: Co-educational Day
No of pupils: 88
Special Needs: PMLD SLD W

THOMAS WOLSEY SCHOOL
Ipswich, Suffolk IP1 6LA
Tel: (01473) 467600
Head: Mrs N McArdie
Type: Co-educational Day 3–19

WARREN SCHOOL
Clarkes Lane, Oulton Broad,
Lowestoft, Suffolk NR33 8HT
Tel: (01502) 561893
Head: Mr C Moore
Type: Co-educational 3–19
No of pupils: B65 G42
Special Needs: PMLD SLD W

SURREY

Surrey Education Authority

County Hall
Kingston upon Thames
KT1 2DJ
Tel: (020) 8541 8800

THE ABBEY SCHOOL
Menin Way, Farnham, Surrey
GU9 8DY
Tel: (01252) 725059
Head: Ms A Scott
Type: Co-educational Day 7–16
No of pupils: 100
Special Needs: MLD

BROOKLANDS SCHOOL
27 Wray Park Road, Reigate, Surrey
RH2 0DF
Tel: (01737) 249941
Head: Mrs S Wakenell
Type: Co-educational Day 2–10
No of pupils: 80
Special Needs: PMLD SLD W

CARWARDEN HOUSE COMMUNITY SCHOOL
118 Upper Chobham Road, Camberley, Surrey GU15 1EJ
Tel: (01276) 709080
Head: Mr J G Cope
Type: Co-educational Day 7–19
No of pupils: 140
Special Needs: **MLD**

CLIFTON HILL SCHOOL
Chaldon Road, Caterham, Surrey CR3 5PH
Tel: (01883) 347740
Head: Mr M Unsworth
Type: Co-educational Day 10–19
No of pupils: B46 G38
Special Needs: **SLD** W

FREEMANTLES SCHOOL
Pycroft Road, Chertsey, Surrey KT16 9ER
Tel: (01932) 563460
Head: Mrs R Buchan
Type: Co-educational Day 4–11
No of pupils: 66
Special Needs: **AUT** SP&LD W

GOSDEN HOUSE SCHOOL
Bramley, Guildford, Surrey GU5 0AH
Tel: (01483) 892008
Head: Mr J David
Type: Co-educational Boarding Boys 5–11 Girls 5–16
No of pupils: B30 G90
No of Boarders: W55
Special Needs: MLD SP&LD

LIMPSFIELD GRANGE SCHOOL
89 Blue House Lane, Limpsfield, Oxted, Surrey RH8 0RZ
Tel: (01883) 713928
Head: Mrs J A Humphreys
Type: Girls Boarding and Day 11–16
No of pupils: 56 *No of Boarders:* W36
Special Needs: DEL DYP DYS SP&LD SPLD

LINDEN BRIDGE SCHOOL
Grafton Road, Worcester Park, Surrey KT4 7JW
Tel: (020) 8330 3009
Head: Mrs R Smith
Type: Co-educational Boarding and Day 4–19
No of pupils: 107 *No of Boarders:* F33
Special Needs: AUT

MANOR MEAD SCHOOL
Laleham Road, Shepperton, Surrey TW17 8EL
Tel: (01932) 241834
Head: Mrs F Neal
Type: Co-educational Day 2–11
No of pupils: 63
Special Needs: CP EPI PMLD **SLD** W

THE PARK SCHOOL
Onslow Crescent, Woking, Surrey GU22 7AT
Tel: (01483) 772057
Head: Mrs K Eastwood
Type: Co-educational Day 8–16
No of pupils: 93
Special Needs: **MLD** SP&LD W

PHILIP SOUTHCOTE SCHOOL
Addlestonemoor, Addlestone, Surrey KT15 2QH
Tel: (01932) 562326
Head: Mr G L Rogers
Type: Co-educational Day 8–16
No of pupils: 110
Special Needs: HI **MLD**

POND MEADOW SCHOOL
Pond Meadow, Park Barn Estate, Guildford, Surrey GU2 6LG
Tel: (01483) 532239
Head: Miss A E Brighty
Type: Co-educational Day 2–19
Special Needs: PMLD SLD W

PORTESBERY SCHOOL
Portesbery Road, Camberley, Surrey GU15 3SZ
Tel: (01276) 63078
Head: Mrs J Nuthall
Type: Co-educational Day 2–19
No of pupils: B35 G30
Special Needs: PMLD **SLD**

THE RIDGEWAY SCHOOL
14 Frensham Road, Farnham, Surrey GU9 8HB
Tel: (01252) 724562
Head: Mrs M Hattey
Type: Co-educational Day 2–19
No of pupils: B50 G27
Special Needs: PMLD SLD

ST NICHOLAS SCHOOL
Taynton Drive, Merstham, Redhill, Surrey RH1 3PU
Tel: (01737) 215488
Head: Mr R Edey
Type: Co-educational Boarding and Day 11–16
No of pupils: 58 *No of Boarders:* W40
Special Needs: ADD EBD MLD

SIDLOW BRIDGE CENTRE
Ironsbottom Lane, Reigate, Surrey RH2 8PP
Tel: (01737) 249079
Head: Mr D Davies
Type: Co-educational Day 14–16
No of pupils: 30
Special Needs: EBD

STARHURST SCHOOL
Chart Lane South, Dorking, Surrey RH5 4DB
Tel: (01306) 883763
Head: Mr H J Kiernan
Type: Boys Boarding and Day 11–16
No of pupils: 56 *No of Boarders:* W36
Special Needs: EBD

SUNNYDOWN SCHOOL†
Portley House, 152 Whyteleafe Road, Caterham, Surrey CR3 5ED
Tel: (01883) 342281/346502
Head: Mr T M Armstrong
Type: Boys Boarding and Day 11–16
No of pupils: 74 *No of Boarders:* W44
Special Needs: DYS SPLD

THORNCHACE SPECIAL SCHOOL
Grove Road, Merrow, Guildford, Surrey GU1 2HL
Tel: (01483) 573859
Head: Mr C Lodge
Type: Girls Boarding and Day 11–16
No of pupils: 24
Special Needs: EBD

WALTON LEIGH SCHOOL
Queens Road, Walton-on-Thames, Surrey KT12 5AB
Tel: (01932) 223243
Head: Mrs L Curtis
Type: Co-educational 12–19
No of pupils: 60
Special Needs: AUT **PMLD SLD** W

WEST HILL SCHOOL
Kingston Road, Leatherhead, Surrey KT22 7PW
Tel: (01372) 814714
Head: Ms M Goldie
Type: Co-educational Day 7–16
No of pupils: 140
Special Needs: MLD

WEY HOUSE SCHOOL
Bramley, Guildford, Surrey GU5 0BJ
Tel: (01483) 898130
Head: Mr M Keane
Type: Boys Day and Boarding 7–11
No of pupils: 48 *No of Boarders:* W21
Special Needs: EBD

WISHMORE CROSS SCHOOL
Alpha Road, Chobham, Surrey
GU24 8NE
Tel: (01276) 857555
Head: Mr J A Orr
Type: Boys Boarding 10–16
No of pupils: 60
Special Needs: **EBD**

WOODFIELD SCHOOL
Sunstone Grove, Merstham, Redhill,
Surrey RH1 3PR
Tel: (01737) 642623
Head: Miss S M Plant
Type: Co-educational Day 8–16
No of pupils: 140
Special Needs: **MLD** W

WOODLANDS SCHOOL
Fortyfoot Road, Leatherhead, Surrey
KT22 8RY
Tel: (01372) 377922
Head: Mrs H D J Taylor
Type: Co-educational Day 2–19
No of pupils: B35 G50
Special Needs: **AUT PMLD SLD** W

EAST SUSSEX

Brighton & Hove Council

PO Box 2503
Kings House
Grand Avenue
Hove
East Sussex BN3 2SU
Tel: (01273) 290000

ALTERNATIVE CENTRE FOR EDUCATION
St George's House, 43 Dyke Road,
Brighton, East Sussex BN1 3JA
Tel: (01273) 327389
Head: M Whitby
Type: Co-educational Day 5–16
No of pupils: 124
Special Needs: EBD

CASTLEDEAN SCHOOL
Lynchet Close, Brighton, East Sussex
BN1 7FP
Tel: (01273) 702121
Head: S Furdas
Type: Co-educational Day 4–11
No of pupils: 64
Special Needs: **MLD** SP&LD

DOWNS PARK SCHOOL
Foredown Road, Portslade, Brighton,
East Sussex BN41 2FU
Tel: (01273) 417448
Head: Mr A S Jedras
Type: Co-educational Day 5–16
No of pupils: B90 G32
Special Needs: **AUT EBD MLD**

DOWNS VIEW SCHOOL
Warren Road, Brighton, East Sussex
BN2 6BB
Tel: (01273) 601680
Head: Mrs J Reed
Type: Co-educational Day 2–19
No of pupils: B76 G31
Special Needs: **AUT MLD PMLD
SLD** W

HILLSIDE SCHOOL
Foredown Road, Portslade, Brighton,
East Sussex BN41 2FU
Tel: (01273) 416979
Head: Mr R Wall
Type: Co-educational Day 3–19
No of pupils: B46 G26
Special Needs: **PMLD SLD** W

PATCHAM HOUSE SCHOOL
7 Old London Road, Patcham,
Brighton, East Sussex BN1 8XR
Tel: (01273) 551028
Head: Mr R L Humphrey
Type: Co-educational Day 3–16
No of pupils: 70
Special Needs: ASP **CP** DEL DYP EPI
EPI **PH** SP&LD SPLD W

UPLANDS SCHOOL
Lynchet Road, Brighton, East Sussex
BN1 7FP
Tel: (01273) 558622/3
Head: Mr P Atkins
Type: Co-educational Day
No of pupils: 110
Special Needs: **MLD**

East Sussex Education Authority

PO Box 4
County Hall
St Anne's Crescent
Lewes
East Sussex BN7 1SG
Tel: (01273) 481000

CUCKMERE HOUSE
Eastbourne Road, Seaford, East
Sussex BN25 4BA
Tel: (01323) 893319
Head: Mr F Stanford
Type: Boys Boarding and Day 9–16
No of pupils: 60 *No of Boarders:* W12
Special Needs: ADHD DYS **EBD**

THE DOWNS SCHOOL
Beechy Avenue, Eastbourne, East
Sussex BN20 8NU
Tel: (01323) 730302
Head: Mrs E D Gidlow
Type: Co-educational Day 4–11
No of pupils: 88
Special Needs: ADHD ASP **AUT** CP
DOW DYP EBD EPI **MLD** SP&LD

GLYNE GAP SCHOOL
School Place, Hastings Road, Bexhill-
on-Sea, East Sussex TN40 2PU
Tel: (01424) 217720
Head: Mr J A Hassell
Type: Co-educational Day 2–19
No of pupils: 97
Special Needs: AUT PMLD SLD

GROVE PARK SCHOOL
Church Road, Crowborough, East
Sussex TN6 1BN
Tel: (01892) 663018
Head: Ms C A Moody
Type: Co-educational Day 2–19
No of pupils: 56
Special Needs: AUT PMLD **SLD** W

HAZEL COURT SCHOOL
Shinewater Lane, Milfoil Drive,
Eastbourne, East Sussex BN23 8AT
Tel: (01323) 761061
Head: Mr P Gordon
Type: Co-educational Day 2–19
No of pupils: 106
Special Needs: PMLD SLD W

INGLESEA SCHOOL
2 Tile Barn Road, St Leonards-on-
Sea, East Sussex TN38 9QU
Tel: (01424) 853232
Head: Mr L E Bush
Type: Boys Day 6–16
No of pupils: 42
Special Needs: **EBD**

THE LINDFIELD SCHOOL
Lindfield Road, Eastbourne, East
Sussex BN22 0BQ
Tel: (01323) 502988
Head: Ms J Oatey
Type: Co-educational Day 10–16
No of pupils: 78
Special Needs: ADD ADHD **ASP AUT**
DEL DOW DYC DYS **EBD** EPI HI
MLD PH SP&LD SPLD VIS

ST ANNE'S SCHOOL
Rotten Row, Lewes, East Sussex
BN7 1LJ
Tel: (01273) 473018
Head: Ms G Ingold
Type: Co-educational Day 4–16
No of pupils: B67 G30
Special Needs: **ADHD MLD SPLD**

ST MARY'S SCHOOL
Horam, Heathfield, East Sussex
TN21 0BT
Tel: (01435) 812278
Head: Mr D F Bashford
Type: Co-educational Boarding and
Day 11–19
No of pupils: 61
Special Needs: EBD MLD

SAXON MOUNT SCHOOL
Edinburgh Road, St Leonards-on-
Sea, East Sussex TN38 8DA
Tel: (01424) 426303
Head: Mrs S Furey
Type: Co-educational Day 11–16
No of pupils: 120
Special Needs: AUT **MLD** SP&LD

TORFIELD SCHOOL
Croft Road, Hastings, East Sussex
TN34 3JT
Tel: (01424) 428228
Head: Mr C D Owen
Type: Co-educational Day 3–11
No of pupils: 120
Special Needs: **AUT** EBD MLD
SP&LD

WEST SUSSEX

West Sussex Education Authority
County Hall
West Street
Chichester
West Sussex PO19 1RF
Tel: (01243) 777100

ABBOTSFORD SPECIAL SCHOOL
Cuckfield Road, Burgess Hill, West
Sussex RH15 8RE
Tel: (01444) 235848
Head: Mr P Moxton
Type: Boys Boarding and Day 8–16
No of pupils: 68 *No of Boarders:* W24
Special Needs: ADD ADHD ASP AUT
DYS **EBD**

CATHERINGTON SCHOOL
Crawley, West Sussex RH11 7SF
Tel: (01293) 526873
Head: D L Reid
Type: Co-educational Day 3–19

CORNFIELD
Cornfield Close, Littlehampton,
West Sussex BN17 6HY
Tel: (01903) 731277
Head: Mrs S Roberts
Type: Co-educational 10–16
No of pupils: 50
Special Needs: EBD

COURT MEADOW SPECIAL SCHOOL
Hanlye Lane, Cuckfield, Haywards
Heath, West Sussex RH17 5HN
Tel: (01444) 454535
Head: Mrs J Hedges
Type: Co-educational Day 2–19
No of pupils: B52 G41
Special Needs: PMLD **SLD** W

DEERSWOOD SCHOOL
Ifield Green, Crawley, West Sussex
RH11 0GH
Tel: (01293) 520351
Head: Mr M R Turney
Type: Co-educational Day 5–16
No of pupils: 163
Special Needs: AUT MLD

FORDWATER SPECIAL SCHOOL
Summersdale Road, Chichester,
West Sussex PO19 4PL
Tel: (01243) 782475
Head: Mr R Rendall
Type: Co-educational Day 2–19
No of pupils: B66 G41
Special Needs: **AUT** DOW HI **MLD**
PMLD SLD **SP&LD** VIS W

HERONS DALE SPECIAL SCHOOL
Hawkins Crescent, Shoreham-by-
Sea, West Sussex BN43 6TN
Tel: (01273) 596904
Head: Mrs S A Pritchard
Type: Co-educational Day 4–16
No of pupils: 116
Special Needs: ASP **MLD**

HIGHDOWN SCHOOL
Durrington Lane, Worthing, West
Sussex BN13 2QQ
Tel: (01903) 249611
Head: Mr G Elliker
Type: Co-educational Day 3–19
No of pupils: 106
Special Needs: PMLD SLD

LITTLEGREEN SPECIAL SCHOOL
Compton, Chichester, West Sussex
PO18 9NW
Tel: (023) 9263 1259
Head: Mr A R Bicknell
Type: Boys Boarding and Day 7–14
No of pupils: 42 *No of Boarders:* W12
Special Needs: ADD ADHD ASP **EBD**
MLD TOU

NEWICK HOUSE SPECIAL SCHOOL
Birchwood Grove Road, Burgess Hill,
West Sussex RH15 0DP
Tel: (01444) 233550
Head: Mr A M Roberts
Type: Co-educational 5–16
No of pupils: 135
Special Needs: ADD ADHD DEL
DOW DYP DYS EBD EPI HI **MLD** PH
SLD SP&LD SPLD W

PALATINE SCHOOL
Palatine Road, Worthing, West
Sussex BN12 6JP
Tel: (01903) 242835
Head: Mr J D Clough
Type: Co-educational Day 4–16
No of pupils: B102 G50
Special Needs: **MLD** W

QUEEN ELIZABETH II SILVER JUBILEE SCHOOL
Comptons Lane, Horsham, West Sussex RH13 5NW
Tel: (01403) 266215
Head: Mrs L K Dyer
Type: Co-educational Day 2–19
No of pupils: 42
Special Needs: PMLD SLD W

ST ANTHONY'S SCHOOL
Woodlands Lane, off St Paul's Road, Chichester, West Sussex PO19 3PA
Tel: (01243) 785965
Head: Mr T Salt and Mr B Griffin
Type: Co-educational Day 5–16
No of pupils: B110 G54
Special Needs: ASP MLD SP&LD

ST CUTHMAN'S SPECIAL SCHOOL
Stedham, Midhurst, West Sussex GU29 0QJ
Tel: (01730) 812331/2
Head: Mr H L Rooks
Type: Co-educational Day and Boarding 7–16
No of pupils: B44 G26
No of Boarders: W16
Special Needs: MLD

TYNE AND WEAR

Gateshead Education Authority

Civic Centre
Regent Street
Gateshead NE8 1HH
Tel: (0191) 433 3000

THE CEDARS SPECIAL SCHOOL
Ivy Lane, Low Fell, Gateshead, Tyne and Wear NE9 6QD
Tel: (0191) 487 7591/482 2993
Head: Mr E D Bartley
Type: Co-educational Day 2–16
No of pupils: 90
Special Needs: PH SP&LD W

DRYDEN SCHOOL
Shotley Gardens, Gateshead, Tyne and Wear NE9 5UR
Tel: (0191) 420 3811
Head: Mr G J Foster
Type: Co-educational Day 11–19
No of pupils: B34 G16
Special Needs: SLD

FURROWFIELD SCHOOL
Senior Site, Whitehills Drive, Felling, Gateshead, Tyne and Wear NE10 9RZ
Tel: (0191) 469 9499
Head: Mr S Roberts
Type: Co-educational Day 7–11 (boys 11–16)
No of pupils: 79 *No of Boarders:* W14
Special Needs: EBD W

HILL TOP SCHOOL
Wealcroft, Felling, Gateshead, Tyne and Wear NE10 8LT
Tel: (0191) 4692 462
Head: E M Colquhoun
Type: Co-educational Day 11–16
No of pupils: B61 G38
Special Needs: AUT MLD SLD

Newcastle upon Tyne Education Authority

Civic Centre
Barras Bridge
Newcastle upon Tyne NE1 8PU
Tel: (0191) 232 8520

DENEVIEW SCHOOL
Freeman Road, Gosforth, Newcastle upon Tyne, Tyne and Wear NE3 4PD
Tel: (0191) 284 3533
Head: Mrs M Kiernan

HADRIAN SCHOOL
Bertram Crescent, Newcastle upon Tyne, Tyne and Wear NE15 6PY
Tel: (0191) 273 4440
Head: Mrs E Turnbull
Type: Co-educational Day 2–11
No of pupils: B76 G47
Special Needs: PMLD SLD W

KENTON LODGE SCHOOL
Kenton Road, Newcastle Upon Tyne, Tyne and Wear NE3 4PD
Tel: (0191) 285 5392
Head: Mr D Tait
Type: Boys Boarding and Day 7–13
Special Needs: EBD

SIR CHARLES PARSONS SCHOOL
Westbourne Avenue, Newcastle Upon Tyne, Tyne and Wear NE6 4HQ
Tel: (0191) 263 0261
Head: Mr J C Preston
Type: Co-educational
No of pupils: 140
Special Needs: EBD MLD PMLD SLD SP&LD W

THOMAS BEWICK SCHOOL
Hillhead Parkway, Newcastle upon Tyne, Tyne and Wear NE15 IDS
Tel: (0191) 267 5435
Head: Mr R Heard
Type: Co-educational Day 5–19

THOMAS BEWICK SCHOOL
(Residential Provision), Bertram Crescent, Newcastle upon Tyne, Tyne and Wear NE15 6PY
Tel: (0191) 273 4440
Head: Mr R Heard

TRINITY SCHOOL
Cental Administration, Condercum Road, Newcastle upon Tyne, Tyne and Wear NE4 8JX
Tel: (0191) 226 1500
Head: Mr D Edmondson
Type: Co-educational Day 5–16

North Tyneside Education Authority

Stephenson House
Stephenson Street
North Shields
Tyne & Wear NE30 1QA
Tel: (0191) 200 5022

ASHLEIGH SCHOOL
Charlotte Street, North Shields, Tyne and Wear NE30 1BP
Tel: (0191) 200 6339
Head: Mrs S Gibbon
Type: Co-educational Day 2–19
No of pupils: 66
Special Needs: AUT PMLD SLD W

OAKFIELD COLLEGE
Condercum Road, Newcastle-upon-Tyne, Tyne and Wear NE4 8XJ
Tel: (0191) 273 5558
Head: Mr I Galletley

PARKSIDE SCHOOL
Mullen Road, High Farm, Wallsend,
Tyne and Wear NE28 9HA
Tel: (0191) 262 3846
Head: Mrs H Jones
Type: Co-educational Day 2–19
No of pupils: B55 G45
Special Needs: AUT **SLD**

SOUTHLANDS SCHOOL
Beach Road, Tynemouth, North
Shields, Tyne and Wear NE30 2QR
Tel: (0191) 200 6348
Head: Mr D J Erskine
Type: Co-educational Day 11–17
No of pupils: B79 G51
Special Needs: EBD **MLD**

WOODLAWN SCHOOL
Langley Avenue, Monkseaton,
Whitley Bay, Tyne and Wear
NE25 9DF
Tel: (0191) 200 8729
Head: Mr B Hickman
Type: Co-educational Day 2–16
No of pupils: B69 G25
Special Needs: CP DEL DYP HI PH
SPLD W

South Tyneside Education Authority

Town Hall and Civic Offices
South Shields
Tyne & Wear NE33 2RL
Tel: (0191) 427 1717

BAMBURGH SCHOOL
Cautley Road, South Shields, Tyne
and Wear NE34 7TD
Tel: (0191) 454 0671
Head: Mrs J M Fawcett
Type: Co-educational Day 2–17
No of pupils: 140
Special Needs: ASP CP DEL DYP EPI
HI PH W

EPINAY SCHOOL
Clervaux Terrace, Jarrow, Tyne and
Wear NE32 5UP
Tel: (0191) 489 8949
Head: Mrs H Harrison
Type: Co-educational Day 5–17
No of pupils: B64 G40
Special Needs: **MLD**

GREENFIELDS SCHOOL
Victoria Road East, Hebburn, Tyne
and Wear NE31 1YQ
Tel: (0191) 489 7480
Head: Miss M C Conway
Type: Co-educational Day 2–19
No of pupils: 47
Special Needs: CP DOW EPI HI PH
PMLD SLD VIS W

MARGARET SUTTON SCHOOL
Ashley Road, South Shields, Tyne
and Wear NE34 0PF
Tel: (0191) 455 3309
Head: Miss A Godfrey
Type: Co-educational Day 5–17
No of pupils: B59 G34
Special Needs: **MLD**

OAKLEIGH GARDENS SCHOOL
Oakleigh Gardens, Cleadon, Nr.
Sunderland, Tyne and Wear SR6 7PT
Tel: (0191) 536 2590
Head: Mrs M J Lockney
Type: Co-educational Day 2–19
No of pupils: B36 G19
Special Needs: **PMLD SLD** W

Sunderland Education Authority

Box 101 Civic Centre
Sunderland SR2 7DN
Tel: (0191)553 1000

BARBARA PRIESTMAN SCHOOL
Meadowside, Sunderland, Tyne and
Wear SR2 7QN
Tel: (0191) 553 6000
Head: Mr W F Hitchcock
Type: Co-educational Day 3–19
No of pupils: 140
Special Needs: EPI MLD PH SP&LD
SPLD W

DAVENPORT SCHOOL
Durham Road, Houghton-le-Spring,
Tyne and Wear DH5 8NF
Tel: (0191) 553 6572
Head: Mrs K Elliot
Type: Co-educational Day 3–13
No of pupils: B55 G26
Special Needs: AUT MLD PMLD **SLD**

FELSTEAD SCHOOL
Fordfield Road (North Side),
Sunderland, Tyne and Wear SR4 0DA
Tel: (0191) 567 4258
Head: Mr I Reed
Type: Co-educational Day 13–25
No of pupils: B182 G36
Special Needs: EBD MLD

MAPLEWOOD SCHOOL
Redcar Road, Sunderland, Tyne and
Wear SR5 5PA
Tel: (0191) 553 5587
Head: Mrs J Wilson
Type: Co-educational 5–13
No of pupils: B88 G2
Special Needs: ADD ADHD EBD W

PORTLAND SCHOOL
Weymouth Road, Chapel Garth,
Sunderland, Tyne and Wear SR3 2NQ
Tel: (0191) 553 6050
Head: Mrs J Chart
Type: Co-educational Day 13–19
No of pupils: B67 G40
Special Needs: **PMLD SLD** W

SPRINGWELL DENE SCHOOL
Swindon Road, Sunderland, Tyne
and Wear SR3 4EE
Tel: (0191) 553 6067
Head: Mrs M D Mitchell
Type: Co-educational Day 13–16
No of pupils: B62 G3
Special Needs: EBD

SUNNINGDALE SCHOOL
Shaftoe Road, Sunderland, Tyne and
Wear SR3 4HA
Tel: (0191) 553 5880
Head: Mr J McKnight
Type: Co-educational Day 3–13
No of pupils: 175
Special Needs: MLD PMLD SLD W

WELLBANK SCHOOL
Wellbank Road, Washington, Tyne
and Wear NE37 1NL
Tel: (0191) 416 2514
Head: Mrs J Macleod
Type: Co-educational Day 3–13
No of pupils: 60
Special Needs: **MLD PMLD SLD** W

WARWICKSHIRE

Warwickshire Education Authority

22 Northgate Street
Warwick CV34 4SP
Tel: (01926) 410410

BROOKE SCHOOL
Merttens Drive, Rugby,
Warwickshire CV22 7AE
Tel: (01788) 576145
Head: Mrs S Cowen
Type: Co-educational Day 2–19
No of pupils: B93 G41
Special Needs: MLD PMLD SLD W

CORLEY (COVENTRY) SCHOOL
Church Lane, Corley, Warwickshire
CV7 8AZ
Tel: (01676) 540218
Head: Mr R Nason
Type: Co-educational Day and
Boarding
No of pupils: 74 No of Boarders: F55
Special Needs: AUT MLD

THE GRIFF SCHOOL
Coventry Road, Nuneaton,
Warwickshire CV10 7AX
Tel: (024) 7638 3315
Head: Mrs R M Scott
Type: Co-educational Day 5–16
No of pupils: 139
Special Needs: MLD

LAMBERT SCHOOL
Blue Cap Road, Stratford upon Avon,
Warwickshire CV37 6TQ
Tel: (01789) 266845
Head: Mrs S Franklin
Type: Co-educational Day 2–19
No of pupils: B54 G30
Special Needs: AUT DOW EPI PH
PMLD SLD W

MARIE CORELLI SCHOOL & SUPPORT SERVICE
Drayton Avenue, Stratford upon
Avon, Warwickshire CV37 9PT
Tel: (01789) 205992
Head: Mrs H Cobb
Type: Co-educational Day 5–16
No of pupils: 71
Special Needs: MLD

RIDGEWAY SCHOOL
Montague Road, Warwick CV34 5LW
Tel: (01926) 491987
Head: Mrs P A Flynn
Type: Co-educational Day 2–19
No of pupils: B62 G30
Special Needs: PMLD SLD W

RIVER HOUSE SCHOOL
Stratford Road, Henley-in-Arden,
Solihull, West Midlands B95 6AD
Tel: (01564) 792514
Head: Mr M J Turner
Type: Boys Day 11–16
No of pupils: 35
Special Needs: EBD

THE ROUND OAK SCHOOL
Pound Lane, Lillington, Leamington
Spa, Warwickshire CV32 7RT
Tel: (01926) 335566
Head: Mrs S Read
Type: Co-educational Day 5–16
No of pupils: B48 G32
Special Needs: AUT EBD MLD

SPARROWDALE SCHOOL
Spon Lane, Grendon, Atherstone,
Warwickshire CV9 2PD
Tel: (01827) 713436
Head: Mr B R Fitter
Type: Co-educational 4–16
No of pupils: 116
Special Needs: ASP AUT CP DOW
EBD EPI MLD

WELCOMBE HILLS SCHOOL
Blue Cap Road, Stratford-upon-
Avon, Warwickshire CV37 6TQ
Tel: (01789) 266845
Head: Ms M Cobb
Type: Co-educational Day 2–19
No of pupils: 115
Special Needs: MLD PMLD SLD

WEST MIDLANDS

Birmingham Education Authority

Margaret Street
Birmingham B3 3BU
Tel: (0121) 3032590

BASKERVILLE SCHOOL
Fellows Lane, Birmingham, West
Midlands B17 9TS
Tel: (0121) 427 3191
Head: Mr G J Thornett
Type: Co-educational Boarding 11–19
No of pupils: B30 G6
No of Boarders: W20
Special Needs: ASP AUT

BEAUFORT SCHOOL
16 Coleshill Road, Birmingham,
West Midlands B36 8AA
Tel: (0121) 783 3886
Head: Ms S B Allen
Type: Co-educational 3–11
No of pupils: B20 G20
Special Needs: AUT PMLD SLD W

BLYTHE SCHOOL
Packington Lane, Coleshill,
Birmingham, West Midlands B46 3JE
Tel: (01675) 463590
Head: Mrs G Simpson
Type: Co-educational Day 2–19
No of pupils: B44 G38
Special Needs: AUT EBD PMLD SLD

BRAIDWOOD SCHOOL
Perry Common Road, Birmingham,
West Midlands B23 7AT
Tel: (0121) 373 5558
Head: Mrs F Ison-Jacques
Type: Co-educational Day 11–18
No of pupils: B36 G33
Special Needs: HI

BRIDGE SCHOOL
290 Reservoir Road, Birmingham,
West Midlands B23 6DE
Tel: (0121) 373 8265
Head: Mr S White
Type: Co-educational 2–11
No of pupils: 37
Special Needs: PMLD SLD

CALTHORPE SCHOOL
Darwin Street, Birmingham, West
Midlands B12 0JJ
Tel: (0121) 773 4637
Head: Mr G Hardy
Type: Co-educational Day 2–19
No of pupils: B146 G98
Special Needs: ASP **AUT** CP DOW
EBD EPI HI PH **PMLD SLD** W

CHERRY OAK SCHOOL
60 Frederick Road, Birmingham,
West Midlands B29 6PB
Tel: (0121) 472 1263
Head: Mrs L Fowler
Type: Co-educational Day 2–11
No of pupils: B37 G11
Special Needs: PMLD **SLD** W

DAME ELLEN PINSENT
SCHOOL
Ardencote Road, Birmingham, West
Midlands B13 0RW
Tel: (0121) 444 2487
Head: Mrs S Rodgers
Type: Co-educational 4–11
No of pupils: B108 G37
Special Needs: AUT DOW DYP **MLD**
SLD

FOX HOLLIES SCHOOL AND
PERFORMING ARTS
COLLEGE
419 Fox Hollies Road, Birmingham,
West Midlands B27 7QA
Tel: (0121) 777 6566
Head: Ms K O'Leary
Type: Co-educational Day 11–19
No of pupils: 67
Special Needs: PMLD **SLD** W

HALLMOOR SCHOOL
Hallmoor Road, Birmingham, West
Midlands B33 9QY
Tel: (0121) 783 3972
Head: Mrs S Charvis
Type: Co-educational Day 4–19
No of pupils: 240
Special Needs: **MLD**

HAMILTON SCHOOL
Hamilton Road, Birmingham, West
Midlands B21 8AH
Tel: (0121) 554 1676
Head: Mr N P Carter
Type: Co-educational Day 4–11
No of pupils: 70
Special Needs: ADHD DOW DYP HI
MLD SLD SP&LD

KINGSTANDING SCHOOL
Old Oscott Hill, Birmingham, West
Midlands B44 9SP
Tel: (0121) 360 8222
Head: Ms M C Pipe
Type: Co-educational Day 11–19
No of pupils: 83
Special Needs: AUT **PMLD SLD**
SP&LD W

LANGLEY SCHOOL
Lindridge Road, Sutton Coldfield,
West Midlands B75 7HU
Tel: (0121) 329 2929
Head: Mr A Reid
Type: Co-educational Day 3–11
No of pupils: 120
Special Needs: DOW **MLD** SP&LD

LONGMOOR SCHOOL
Coppice View Road, Sutton
Coldfield, West Midlands B7 6UE
Tel: (0121) 353 7833
Head: Mrs V Jenkins
Type: Co-educational Day and
Boarding 2–11
No of pupils: 40 *No of Boarders:* F12
W12
Special Needs: AUT PMLD **SLD**

LONGWILL SCHOOL
Bell Hill, Birmingham, West
Midlands B31 1LD
Tel: (0121) 475 3923
Head: Mr P Plant
Type: Co-educational Day 2–11
No of pupils: B37 G21
Special Needs: **HI**

MAYFIELD SCHOOL
Finch Road, Birmingham, West
Midlands B19 1HP
Tel: (0121) 554 3354
Head: Mr P Jenkins
Type: Co-educational Day 2–19
No of pupils: B65 G46
Special Needs: ADHD **AUT** CP DOW
EBD EPI HI **PMLD SLD** W

PINES SCHOOL
Dreghorn Road, Birmingham, West
Midlands B36 8LL
Tel: (0121) 747 6136
Head: Mr S G Tuft
Type: Co-educational Day 3–11
No of pupils: 100
Special Needs: AUT DEL **SP&LD** W

PRIESTLEY SMITH SCHOOL
Perry Common Road, Erdington,
Birmingham, West Midlands B23 7AT
Tel: (0121) 373 5493
Head: Mr C G Lewis
Type: Co-educational Day 2–17
No of pupils: B31 G30
Special Needs: DYS MLD **VIS** W

QUEENSBURY SCHOOL
Wood End Road, Birmingham, West
Midlands B24 8BL
Tel: (0121) 373 5731
Head: Mr W Warriner
Type: co-educational Day 11–19
No of pupils: 240
Special Needs: **MLD**

SKILTS (RESIDENTIAL)
SCHOOL
Gorcott Hill, Redditch, West
Midlands B98 9ET
Tel: (0152) 785 3851
Head: Miss M K Probert
Type: Boys Boarding and Day 4–12
No of pupils: 50 *No of Boarders:* W46
Special Needs: ADD **ADHD ASP** DYS
EBD MLD SPLD

SPRINGFIELD HOUSE
SCHOOL
Kenilworth Road, Knowle, Solihull,
West Midlands B93 0AJ
Tel: (01564) 775696
Head: Mrs P A Jacques
Type: Co-educational Day 4–11
No of pupils: B38 G12
No of Boarders: W40
Special Needs: ASP **EBD** MLD

UFFCULME SCHOOL
Queensbridge Road, Birmingham,
West Midlands B13 8QB
Tel: (0121) 449 1081
Head: Mr A MacDonald
Type: Co-educational Day 3–11
No of pupils: 116
Special Needs: ASP AUT SP&LD

UNDERWOOD SCHOOL
Rowden Drive, Birmingham, West
Midlands B23 5UL
Tel: (0121) 373 5742
Head: Mr G Barratt
Type: Co-educational Day 11–16
No of pupils: 57
Special Needs: **EBD**

VICTORIA SCHOOL
Bell Hill, Birmingham, West
Midlands B31 1LD
Tel: (0121) 476 9478
Head: Mr J Kane
Type: Co-educational Day 2–19
No of pupils: B116 G100
Special Needs: CP EPI HI MLD **PH**
PMLD SLD VIS W

WILSON STUART SCHOOL
Perry Common Road, Birmingham,
West Midlands B23 7AT
Tel: (0121) 373 4475
Head: Mrs A Tomkinson
Type: Co-educational Day 3–19
No of pupils: 144
Special Needs: PH W

Coventry Education Authority

New Council Offices
Earl Street
Coventry CV1 5RS
Tel: (024) 7683 1511

ALICE STEVENS SCHOOL
Ashington Grove, Coventry, West
Midlands CV3 4DE
Tel: (024) 7630 3776
Head: Mr R I McAllister
Type: Co-educational Day 11–18
No of pupils: 200
Special Needs: MLD W

BAGINTON FIELDS
Sedgemoor Road, Coventry, West
Midlands CV3 4EA
Tel: (024) 7630 3854
Head: Mr S Grant
Type: Co-educational 11–19
No of pupils: B60 G35
Special Needs: ADD ADHD ASP AUT
CP DOW DYP EBD EPI MLD PH
PMLD SLD SP&LD VIS W

DARTMOUTH SPECIAL SCHOOL
Tiverton Road, Coventry, West
Midlands CV2 3DN
Tel: (024) 7644 4141
Head: Mr P Davies
Type: Boys Day 11–16
No of pupils: 65
Special Needs: ADD ADHD AUT EBD
TOU W

DEEDMORE SPECIAL SCHOOL
Petitor Crescent, Coventry, West
Midlands CV2 1EW
Tel: (024) 7661 2271
Head: Mr G L Wilkinson
Type: Co-educational Day3–11
No of pupils: 80
Special Needs: MLD

HAWKESBURY FIELDS SCHOOL
176/178 Aldermans Green Road,
Coventry, West Midlands CV2 1PL
Tel: (024) 7636 7075
Head: Ms H Bishton
Type: Co-educational Day 2–11
No of pupils: 58
Special Needs: PMLD SLD W

THE MEADOWS
Hawthorn Lane, Coventry, West
Midlands CV4 9PB
Tel: (024) 7646 2355/6
Head: Mr Robinson
Type: Boys Day and Boarding 11–16
No of pupils: 33
Special Needs: EBD

SHERBOURNE FIELDS SCHOOL
Rowington Close, off Kingsbury
Road, Coventry, West Midlands
CV6 1PS
Tel: (024) 7659 1501/2
Head: Mr D Southeard
Type: Co-educational Day 2–19
No of pupils: B80 G40
Special Needs: PH W

THREE SPIRES SCHOOL
Kingsbury Road, Coventry, West
Midlands CV6 1PJ
Tel: (024) 7659 4952
Head: Mr C Worrall
Type: Co-educational Day 3–11
No of pupils: B43 G25
Special Needs: MLD

TIVERTON SPECIAL SCHOOL
Rowington Close, off Kingsbury
Road, Coventry, West Midlands
CV6 1PS
Tel: (024) 7659 4954
Head: Mr A Chave
Type: Co-educational 3–11
No of pupils: 45
Special Needs: SLD W

WAINBODY WOOD SPECIAL SCHOOL
Stoneleigh Road, Coventry, West
Midlands CV4 7AB
Tel: (024) 7641 8755
Head: Mr J McGinty
Type: Co-educational Day 5–11
No of pupils: 55
Special Needs: EBD

Dudley Education Authority

Westox House
1 Trinity Road
Dudley DY1 1JQ
Tel: (01384) 814225

THE BRIER SPECIAL SCHOOL
Cottage Street, Brierley Hill, West
Midlands DY5 1RE
Tel: (01384) 816000
Head: Mr D K Postlethwaite
Type: Co-educational Day 5–16
No of pupils: B84 G47
Special Needs: MLD SP&LD

HALESBURY SPECIAL SCHOOL
Feldon Lane, Halesowen, West
Midlands B62 9DR
Tel: (01384) 818630
Head: Mr J Hackett
Type: Co-educational Day 5–16
No of pupils: 120
Special Needs: ASP MLD

PENS MEADOW SCHOOL
Ridge Hill, Brierley Hill Road,
Stourbridge, West Midlands DY8 5ST
Tel: (01384) 818945
Head: Mrs K Grew
Type: Co-educational Day 3–19
No of pupils: 70
Special Needs: SLD

ROSEWOOD SCHOOL
Overfield Road, Russells Hall Estate,
Dudley, West Midlands DY1 2NX
Tel: (01384) 816800
Head: Mrs E M Williams
Type: Boys Day 11–16
No of pupils: 40
Special Needs: EBD W

THE WOODSETTON SPECIAL SCHOOL
Tipton Road, Woodsetton, Dudley,
West Midlands DY3 1BY
Tel: (01384) 818265
Head: Mr P A Rhind-Tutt
Type: Co-educational Day 4–11
No of pupils: B80 G20
Special Needs: MLD

Sandwell Education Authority

PO Box 41
Shaftesbury House
402 High Street
West Bromwich
West Midlands B70 9LT
Tel: (0121) 525 7366

THE MEADOWS SCHOOL
Red Lion Close, Tividale, Oldbury,
West Midlands B69 3BU
Tel: (0121) 525 2873
Head: Mr R Meredith
Type: Co-educational Day 2–19
No of pupils: 55

THE ORCHARD SCHOOL
Coopers Lane, Smethwick, West
Midlands B67 1QN
Tel: (0121) 558 1069
Head: Mrs H Atkins
Type: Co-educational Day 2–11
No of pupils: B54 G33
Special Needs: AUT PMLD SLD

SHENSTONE LODGE SCHOOL
Shenstone, Lichfield, Staffordshire
WS14 0LB
Tel: (01543) 263231
Head: Mr S P Butt
Type: Boys Boarding and Day 7–11
No of pupils: 28
Special Needs: AUT **EBD**

THE WESTMINSTER SCHOOL
Upper Church Lane, Tipton, West
Midlands DY4 9PF
Tel: (0121) 5572528
Head: Mrs C Willetts
Type: Co-educational 5–16
No of pupils: 96

THE WESTMINSTER SCHOOL
Westminster Road, West Bromwich,
West Midlands B71 2JN
Tel: (0121) 588 2421
Head: Mrs D Williams
Type: Co-educational Day
No of pupils: B162 G71
Special Needs: AUT EBD MLD

WHITTINGTON GRANGE SCHOOL
Burton Road, Whittington, Lichfield,
Staffordshire WS14 9NU
Tel: (01543) 432296
Head: Mr D J Winzor
Type: Boys Boarding and Day 11–16
No of pupils: 30 *No of Boarders:* F5
W25
Special Needs: EBD

Solihull Education Authority

PO Box 20
Council House
Solihull B91 3QU
Tel: (0121) 704 6656

FOREST OAK SCHOOL
Lanchester Way, Castle Bromwich,
Birmingham, West Midlands B36 9LF
Tel: (0121) 748 3411
Head: Mrs P L Sankey
Type: Co-educational Day 4–16
No of pupils: B65 G32
Special Needs: **MLD** W

HAZEL OAK SCHOOL
Hazel Oak Road, Shirley, Solihull,
West Midlands B90 2AZ
Tel: (0121) 744 4162
Head: Mr P Wright
Type: Co-educational Day 5–16
No of pupils: 100
Special Needs: ASP AUT **MLD**

MERSTONE SCHOOL
Exeter Drive, Marston Green,
Birmingham, West Midlands
B37 5NX
Tel: (0121) 788 8122
Head: Mrs A R Mordey
Type: Co-educational Day 2–19
No of pupils: B43 G24
Special Needs: **AUT CP DOW EPI PH
PMLD SLD** W

REYNALDS CROSS SCHOOL
Kineton Green Road, Olton, Solihull,
West Midlands B92 7ER
Tel: (0121) 707 3012
Head: Ms M Daniels
Type: Co-educational Day 2–19
Special Needs: PMLD SLD W

Walsall Education Authority

Civic Centre
Darwall Street
Walsall WS1 1DQ
Tel: (01922) 650000

CASTLE SPECIAL SCHOOL
Odell Road, Leamore, Walsall, West
Midlands WS3 2ED
Tel: (01922) 710129
Head: Mrs H J Whitehouse
Type: Co-educational Day 4–19
No of pupils: B79 G21
Special Needs: ASP **AUT** DOW DYP
MLD SLD SP&LD

DAW END SPECIAL SCHOOL
Floyds Lane, Rushall, Walsall, West
Midlands WS3 2ED
Tel: (01922) 721081
Head: Mr R Wilson
Type: Co-educational Day and
Boarding 5–16
No of pupils: B65 *No of Boarders:* W10
Special Needs: **EBD**

JANE LANE SCHOOL
Churchill Road, Bentley, Walsall,
West Midlands WS2 0JH
Tel: (01922) 721161
Head: Mrs H Lomas
Type: Co-educational Day 4–19
No of pupils: 135
Special Needs: **MLD** W

MARY ELLIOT SPECIAL SCHOOL
Brewer Street, Walsall, West
Midlands WS2 8BA
Tel: (01922) 720706
Head: Mrs E A Jordan
Type: Co-educational Day 13–19
No of pupils: B29 G23
Special Needs: **PMLD SLD** W

OAKWOOD SPECIAL SCHOOL
Druids Walk, Walsall Wood, Walsall,
West Midlands WS9 9JS
Tel: (01543) 452040
Head: Mrs K E Mills
Type: Co-educational Day 2–14
No of pupils: 60
Special Needs: AUT CP EPI HI PH
PMLD SLD VIS W

OLD HALL SPECIAL SCHOOL
Bentley Lane, Walsall, West
Midlands WS2 7LU
Tel: (01902) 368045
Head: Mr S W Jones-Eddie
Type: Co-educational Day 2–14
No of pupils: B55 G35
Special Needs: AUT PMLD SLD W

THREE CROWNS SPECIAL SCHOOL
Skip Lane, Walsall, West Midlands
WS5 3NB
Tel: (01922) 721119
Head: Mr P Nickless
Type: Co-educational Day 2–19
No of pupils: 57
Special Needs: PH

Wolverhampton Education Authority

Civic Centre
St Peter's Square
Wolverhampton WV1 1RR
Tel: (01902) 556556

BROADMEADOW NURSERY SPECIAL SCHOOL
Lansdowne Road, Wolverhampton, West Midlands WV1 4AL
Tel: (01902) 558330
Head: Mrs A R Coates
Type: Co-educational Day 2–6
No of pupils: 40
Special Needs: AUT PMLD SLD W

GREEN PARK SPECIAL SCHOOL
Green Park Avenue, Lumbertubs, Bilston, West Midlands WV14 6EH
Tel: (01902) 556429
Head: Mr M Partington
Type: Co-educational Day 5–19
No of pupils: 66
Special Needs: PMLD SLD W

PENN FIELDS SCHOOL
Birches Barn Road, Penn Fields, Wolverhampton, West Midlands WV3 7BJ
Tel: (01902) 831910
Head: Miss I C Turner
Type: Co-educational Day 5–16
No of pupils: 160
Special Needs: AUT **EBD** HI **MLD** SP&LD VIS W

PENN HALL SCHOOL
Vicarage Road, Penn, Wolverhampton, West Midlands WV4 5HP
Tel: (01902) 558355
Head: Mr A J Stoll
Type: Co-educational Day 3–19
No of pupils: B50 G30
No of Boarders: W6
Special Needs: PH VIS W

TETTENHALL WOOD SCHOOL
School Road, Tettenhall Wood, Wolverhampton, West Midlands WV6 8EJ
Tel: (01902) 758545
Head: Mr M Mahoney
Type: Co-educational Day 5–19
No of pupils: 54
Special Needs: ADD ADHD AUT CP DOW DYP EBD EPI HI **SLD** SP&LD SPLD VIS W

WESTCROFT SCHOOL
Greenacres Avenue, Underhill, Wolverhampton, West Midlands WV10 8NZ
Tel: (01902) 558350
Head: Mr A M Chilvers
Type: Co-educational Day 4–16
No of pupils: 180
Special Needs: **MLD SLD SP&LD** W

WILTSHIRE

Wiltshire Education Authority

County Hall
Bythesea Road
Trowbridge
Wiltshire BA14 8JB
Tel: (01225) 713000

DOWNLANDS SCHOOL
Downlands Road, Devizes, Wiltshire SN10 5EF
Tel: (01380) 724193
Head: Mr D Walsh
Type: Boys Boarding 10–16
No of pupils: 56
Special Needs: EBD SPLD

EXETER HOUSE SPECIAL SCHOOL
Somerset Road, Salisbury, Wiltshire SP1 3BL
Tel: (010722) 334168
Head: Mrs G Heather
Type: Co-educational Day 2–19
No of pupils: 69
Special Needs: AUT PMLD SLD W

LARKRISE SPECIAL SCHOOL
Ashton Street, Trowbridge, Wiltshire BA14 7EB
Tel: (01225) 761434
Head: Mr M Hull
Type: Co-educational Day 3–19
No of pupils: 53
Special Needs: PMLD SLD

ROWDEFORD SPECIAL SCHOOL
Rowde, Devizes, Wiltshire SN10 2QQ
Tel: (01380) 850309
Head: Mr G R Darnell
Type: Co-educational Day and Boarding 11–16
No of pupils: 90 No of Boarders: W25
Special Needs: AUT MLD

ST NICHOLAS SCHOOL
Malmesbury Road, Chippenham, Wiltshire SN15 1QF
Tel: (01249) 650435
Head: Mr C Riches
Type: Co-educational Day 2–19
No of pupils: 63
Special Needs: PMLD SLD

SPRINGFIELDS SPECIAL SCHOOL
Curzon Street, Calne, Wiltshire SN11 0DS
Tel: (01249) 814125
Head: Mr R Nethercott
Type: Co-educational Boarding 10–17
No of pupils: 60
Special Needs: EBD

Swindon Borough Council

Sanford House
Sanford Street
Swindon SN1 1QH
Tel: (01793)463902

THE CHALET SPECIAL SCHOOL
Queens Drive, Swindon, Wiltshire SN3 1AR
Tel: (01793) 534537
Head: Mrs M Topping
Type: Co-educational Day 2–7
No of pupils: 30
Special Needs: **AUT CP** EPI HI MLD SLD **SP&LD**

CROWDYS HILL SPECIAL SCHOOL
Jefferies Avenue, Cricklade Road, Swindon, Wiltshire SN2 6HJ
Tel: (01793) 332400
Head: Mr K Smith
Type: Co-educational Day 11–16
No of pupils: 160
Special Needs: ASP **MLD** W

NYLAND SPECIAL SCHOOL
Nyland Road, Nythe, Swindon, Wiltshire SN3 3RD
Tel: (01793) 535023
Head: Mr P Sunners
Type: Co-educational Day 5–11
No of pupils: 60
Special Needs: AUT EBD EPI MLD SP&LD

ST LUKE'S SPECIAL SCHOOL
Cricklade Road, Swindon, Wiltshire SN2 5AH
Tel: (01793) 705566
Head: Mr J Truscello
Type: Co-educational Day 11–16
No of pupils: 64
Special Needs: **EBD** W

UPLANDS SPECIAL SCHOOL
Leigh Road, Penhill, Swindon, Wiltshire SN2 5DE
Tel: (01793) 724751
Head: Miss M E Bishop
Type: Co-educational Day 11–19
No of pupils: 75
Special Needs: **AUT** CP DOW **PMLD SLD** W

WORCESTERSHIRE

Worcestershire Education Authority

PO Box 73
County Hall
Spetchley Road
Worcester WR5 2NP
Tel: (01906) 763763

THE ALEXANDER PATTERSON SCHOOL
Park Gate Road, Wolverley, Kidderminster, Worcestershire DY10 3PU
Tel: (01562) 851396
Head: Mrs M E Calvert
Type: Co-educational Day 2–19
No of pupils: 73
Special Needs: AUT EBD **MLD PMLD** SP&LD W

BLAKEBROOK SCHOOL
Bewdley Road, Kidderminster, Worcestershire DY11 6RL
Tel: (01562) 753066
Head: Mr M O G Russell
Type: Co-educational Day
No of pupils: B33 G19
Special Needs: ADD ADHD AUT CP DOW DYP EPI HI PH PMLD SLD VIS W

CHADSGROVE SCHOOL
Meadow Road, Catshill, Bromsgrove, Worcestershire B61 0JW
Tel: (01527) 871511
Head: Mr R Aust
Type: Co-educational Day 2–19
No of pupils: 110
Special Needs: CP DEL EPI **PH** PMLD VIS W

CLIFFEY HOUSE SCHOOL
Hanley Castle, Worcester WR8 0AD
Tel: (01684) 310336
Head: Mr D Bishop-Rave
Type: Co-educational Day 11–16
No of pupils: B90 G42
Special Needs: ASP AUT **MLD**

MANOR PARK SCHOOL
Turnpike Close, Oldbury Road, Worcester WR2 6AB
Tel: (01905) 423403
Head: Mr D C Palmer
Type: Co-educational Day 4–19
No of pupils: 75
Special Needs: PMLD **SLD** W

PITCHEROAK SCHOOL
Willow Way, Redditch, Worcestershire B97 6PQ
Tel: (01527) 65576
Head: Ms K Earle
Type: Co-educational Day 2–18
No of pupils: 180
Special Needs: AUT **MLD** PMLD **SLD**

REDGROVE UPPER SCHOOL
Shaw Lane, Stoke Prior, Bromsgrove, Worcestershire B60 4EL
Tel: (01527) 878888
Head: Mrs S Nash
Type: Co-educational Day 11–16
No of pupils: 60
Special Needs: EBD

RIGBY HALL SCHOOL
Rigby Lane, Bromsgrove, Worcestershire B60 2EP
Tel: (01527) 875475
Head: Mrs P A Griffiths
Type: Co-educational Day
No of pupils: 110
Special Needs: MLD SLD

RIVERSIDE UPPER SCHOOL
Thornloe Road, Worcester WR1 3HZ
Tel: (01905) 21261
Head: Mrs B Scott
Type: Co-educational Day 11–16
Special Needs: EBD

ROSE HILL SCHOOL
Windermere Drive, Warndon, Worcester WR4 9JL
Tel: (01905) 454828
Head: Mr F W Steel
Type: Co-educational Day 2–19
No of pupils: B46 G33
Special Needs: **CP DEL PH** PMLD W

STOURMINSTER SCHOOL
Comberton Road, Kidderminster,
Worcestershire DY10 3DX
Tel: (01562) 823156
Head: Mr I D Hardicker
Type: Co-educational 7–16
No of pupils: B104 G53
Special Needs: AUT **MLD** W

THORNTON HOUSE SCHOOL
Radley Road, Worcester WR5 1DR
Tel: (01905) 523843
Head: Mr H B Thomas
Type: Co-educational Day 2–11
No of pupils: 122
Special Needs: AUT MLD

VALE OF EVESHAM SCHOOL
Four Pools Lane, Evesham,
Worcestershire WR11 6DH
Tel: (01386) 443367
Head: Mr E P Matthews
Type: Co-educational Boarding and
Day 4–19
No of pupils: 148 *No of Boarders:* W15
Special Needs: ADD ADHD ASP **AUT**
CP DEL DOW DYP DYS EBD EPI HI
MLD PH **PMLD** SLD SP&LD SPLD
VIS W

EAST RIDING OF YORKSHIRE

East Riding of Yorkshire Education Authority

County Hall
Beverley
East Riding of Yorkshire HU17 9BA
Tel: (01482) 392000

GANTON SCHOOL
Springhead Lane, Willerby Road,
Hull, East Riding of Yorkshire
HU5 6YJ
Tel: (01482) 564646
Head: Mrs P J Glover
Type: Co-educational Day 3–19
No of pupils: 120
Special Needs: AUT CP DOW EPI
PMLD SLD W

KING'S MILL SCHOOL
Victoria Road, Driffield, East Riding
of Yorkshire YO25 7UG
Tel: (01377) 253375
Head: Ms S Young
Type: Co-educational Day and
Boarding 2–16
No of pupils: 64 *No of Boarders:* W16
Special Needs: PMLD SLD W

ST ANNE'S SCHOOL
St Helen's Drive, Welton, Brough,
East Riding of Yorkshire HU15 1NR
Tel: (01482) 667379
Head: Mr M Stubbins
Type: Co-educational Boarding and
Day 3–16
No of pupils: 75
Special Needs: SLD

SOUTH WOLDS SCHOOL
Dalton Holme, Beverley, East Riding
of Yorkshire HU17 7PB
Tel: (0191) 200 6348
Head: Mr L M Powell
Type: Co-educational Boarding and
Day 8–16
No of pupils: 80 *No of Boarders:* W60
Special Needs: **EBD** W

Kingston upon Hull Education Authority

Essex House
Manor Street
Hull HU1 1YD
Tel: (01482) 613161

FREDERICK HOLMES SCHOOL
Inglemire Lane, Kingston upon Hull,
East Riding of Yorkshire HU6 8JJ
Tel: (01482) 804766
Head: Mr D Boyes
Type: Co-educational 2–19
No of pupils: 97
Special Needs: **PH** W

NORTHCOTT SCHOOL
Dulverton Close, Bransholme,
Kingston upon Hull, East Riding of
Yorkshire HU7 4EL
Tel: (01482) 825311
Head: Mr M Johnson
Type: Co-educational Day 3–16
No of pupils: 108
Special Needs: AUT DEL EBD EPI
SP&LD

TWEENDYKES SCHOOL
Tweendykes Road, Sutton, Kingston
upon Hull, East Riding of Yorkshire
HU7 4XJ
Tel: (01482) 826508
Head: Mr K J Ogilvie
Type: Co-educational Day 3–16
No of pupils: 79
Special Needs: PMLD SLD W

NORTH YORKSHIRE

North Yorkshire Education Authority

County Hall
Northallerton
North Yorkshire DL7 8AE
Tel: (01609) 780780

AIREVILLE SCHOOL
Gargrave Road, Skipton,
North Yorkshire BD23 1UQ
Tel: (01756) 792965
Head: Mr D Croll
Type: Co-educational Day 11–16

BALIOL SCHOOL
Sedbergh, North Yorkshire LA10 5LQ
Tel: (015396) 20232
Head: Mr D Anderson
Type: Boys Boarding 10–16
No of pupils: 48 *No of Boarders:* F48
Special Needs: ADHD **EBD** MLD

BRAYTON HIGH SCHOOL
Doncaster Road, Selby,
North Yorkshire YO8 9QS
Tel: (01757) 707731
Head: Mr P A Beever

BROMPTON HALL SCHOOL
Brompton-by-Sawdon, Scarborough,
North Yorkshire YO13 9BD
Tel: (01723) 859121
Head: Mr M Mihkelson
Type: Boys Boarding 8–16
No of pupils: 46 *No of Boarders:* W40
Special Needs: ADHD **EBD** MLD

BROOKLANDS SCHOOL
Burnside Avenue, Skipton,
North Yorkshire BD23 2LX
Tel: (01756) 794028
Head: Mr K Shorrock
Type: Co-educational Day 2–19

DALES SCHOOL
Moreton-on-Swale, Northallerton,
North Yorkshire DL7 9QW
Tel: (01609) 772932
Head: Mr W F Rab
Type: Co-educational Day 2–19
No of pupils: 65
Special Needs: AUT PMLD SLD VIS

FOREST SCHOOL
Park Lane, Knaresborough,
North Yorkshire HG5 0DG
Tel: (01423) 864586
Head: Mrs S M Wootton
Type: Co-educational Day 2–16
No of pupils: 133
Special Needs: MLD SP&LD W

HOOKSTONE CHASE SCHOOL
Hookstone, Harrogate,
North Yorkshire HG2 7DJ
Tel: (01423) 886026
Head: Ms A Fairman

MOWBRAY SCHOOL
Masham Road, Bedale,
North Yorkshire DL8 2DS
Tel: (01677) 422446
Head: Mr A Burnett
Type: Co-educational Day 2–16
No of pupils: 150
Special Needs: AUT EBD **MLD** SLD SP&LD

NETHERSIDE HALL SCHOOL
Threshfield, Skipton,
North Yorkshire BD23 5PP
Tel: (01756) 752324
Head: Mr M E Hopkins
Type: Boys Boarding and Day 10–16
No of pupils: 45 *No of Boarders:* W37
Special Needs: **DYS** SPLD

NEW PARK SCHOOL
Skipton Road, Harrogate,
North Yorkshire HG1 3HF
Tel: (01423) 503011
Head: Mr J R Prydderch

NEWBY CP SCHOOL
Highfield Estate, Newby,
Scarborough, North Yorkshire
YO12 5JA
Tel: (01723) 365686
Head: Mrs C Hanby

SCALBY SCHOOL
Newby, Scarborough,
North Yorkshire YO12 6TH
Tel: (01723) 362301
Head: Mr D C Pynn

SELBY ABBEY CE SCHOOL
New Lane, Selby, North Yorkshire
YO8 4QB
Tel: (01757) 703817
Head: Mrs S Tite

SPRINGHEAD SCHOOL
Barry's Lane, Scarborough,
North Yorkshire YO11 4HA
Tel: (01723) 367829
Head: Mrs C D Wilson
Type: Co-educational Day 2–19
No of pupils: 46
Special Needs: PMLD SLD W

SPRINGWATER SCHOOL
High Street, Starbeck, Harrogate,
North Yorkshire HG2 7LW
Tel: (01423) 883214
Head: Mrs G M Cook
Type: Co-educational Day 2–19
No of pupils: 45
Special Needs: AUT PMLD SLD

WELBURN HALL SCHOOL
Kirbymoorside, York,
North Yorkshire YO62 7HQ
Tel: (01751) 431218
Head: Mr J V Hall
Type: Co-educational Boarding and Day 8–19
No of pupils: 70 *No of Boarders:* W35
Special Needs: CP EPI HI MLD PH SLD SP&LD W

THE WOODLANDS SCHOOL
Woodlands Drive, Scarborough,
North Yorkshire YO12 6QN
Tel: (01723) 373260
Head: Mr C J Webley
Type: Co-educational Day 2–16
No of pupils: 79 *No of Boarders:* F15
Special Needs: AUT MLD SLD W

York Education Authority

PO Box 404
10–12 George Hudson Street
York YO1 6ZG
Tel: (01904) 613161

FULFORD CROSS SCHOOL
Fulford Cross, York, North Yorkshire
YO1 4PB
Tel: (01904) 653219
Head: Mrs J Lock
Type: Co-educational Day 8–16
No of pupils: 140
Special Needs: **MLD**

GALTRES SCHOOL
Bad Bargain Lane, York,
North Yorkshire YO31 0LW
Tel: (01904) 415924
Head: Mr G Gilmore
Type: Co-educational Day 11–19
No of pupils: B37 G28
Special Needs: PMLD SLD W

LIDGETT GROVE SCHOOL
Wheatlands Grove, Acomb, York,
North Yorkshire YO2 5NH
Tel: (01904) 791437
Head: Mr R Nicholls
Type: Co-educational Day 2–11
No of pupils: 70
Special Needs: AUT PMLD SLD

SOUTH YORKSHIRE

Doncaster Education Authority

PO Box 266
The Council House
College Road
Doncaster DN1 3AD
Tel: (01302) 737222

ANCHORAGE LOWER SCHOOL
Cusworth Lane, York Road,
Doncaster, South Yorkshire DN5 8JL
Tel: (01302) 391007
Head: Mr J Taylor
Type: Co-educational Day 4–12
No of pupils: B49 G21
Special Needs: EBD MLD

ANCHORAGE UPPER SCHOOL
Barnsley Road, Scawsby, Doncaster,
South Yorkshire DN5 7UB
Tel: (01302) 391006
Head: Mr J Taylor
Type: Co-educational Day 13–16
Special Needs: MLD

ATHELSTANE SCHOOL
Old Road, Conisbrough, Doncaster,
South Yorkshire DN12 3LR
Tel: (01709) 864978
Head: Mr G Davies
Type: Co-educational Day 4–16
No of pupils: 130
Special Needs: EBD MLD

CEDAR SCHOOL
Cedar Road, Balby, Doncaster,
South Yorkshire DN4 9HT
Tel: (01302) 853361
Head: Mr T M Kellett
Type: Co-educational 3–19
Special Needs: SLD

CHASE SCHOOL
Ash Hill, Hatfield, Doncaster,
South Yorkshire DN7 6JH
Tel: (01302) 844883
Head: Mr W J Evans
Type: Co-educational Day 3–19
No of pupils: 106
Special Needs: AUT PMLD SLD W

FERNBANK SCHOOL
Village Street, Adwick-le-Street,
Doncaster, South Yorkshire DN6 7AA
Tel: (01302) 723571
Head: Mr A R Bickerton
Type: Co-educational Day 2–19
No of pupils: 75
Special Needs: PMLD SLD

SANDALL WOOD SCHOOL
Leger Way, Doncaster,
South Yorkshire DN2 6HQ
Tel: (01302) 322044
Head: Mrs C M Ray
Type: Co-educational Day 3–19
No of pupils: 101
Special Needs: CP EPI PH PMLD SP&LD W

Rotherham Education Authority

Norfolk House
Walker Place
Rotherham S65 1AR
Tel: (01709) 382121

ABBEY SCHOOL
Little Common Lane, Kimberworth,
Rotherham, South Yorkshire S61 2RA
Tel: (01709) 740074
Head: Mr J S Swain
Type: Co-educational Day 5–16
No of pupils: 143
Special Needs: MLD

GREEN ARBOUR SCHOOL
Locksley Drive, Thurcroft,
Rotherham, South Yorkshire S66 9NT
Tel: (01709) 542539
Head: Mr P Gawthorpe
Type: Co-educational Day 5–16
No of pupils: 140
Special Needs: AUT MLD SP&LD

HILLTOP SCHOOL
Larch Road, Maltby, Rotherham,
South Yorkshire S66 8AZ
Tel: (01709) 813386
Head: Mr P Leach
Type: Co-educational Day 2–19
No of pupils: 90
Special Needs: AUT CP DOW PMLD
SLD W

KELFORD SCHOOL
Oakdale Road, Kimberworth,
Rotherham, South Yorkshire
S61 2NU
Tel: (01709) 512088
Head: Mrs S Greenhough
Type: Co-educational Day 2–19
No of pupils: 108
Special Needs: PMLD SLD W

MILTON SCHOOL
Storey Street, Swinton, Mexborough,
South Yorkshire S64 8QG
Tel: (01709) 570246
Head: Mr C D Garford
Type: Co-educational Day 4–16
No of pupils: B83 G24
Special Needs: ASP AUT MLD W

NEWMAN SCHOOL
East Bawtry Road, Whiston,
Rotherham, South Yorkshire S60 2LX
Tel: (01709) 828262
Head: Mrs J Richards
Type: Co-educational Day 2–19
No of pupils: 90
Special Needs: CP PH W

WHISTON GRANGE SCHOOL
East Bawtry Road, Whiston,
Rotherham, South Yorkshire S60 3LX
Tel: (01709) 828838
Head: Mr B Wilcock
Type: Co-educational Day 11–14
No of pupils: B43
Special Needs: **EBD** W

Sheffield Education Authority

Leopold Street
Sheffield S1 1RJ
Tel: (0114) 272 6444

BENTS GREEN SECONDARY SCHOOL
Ringinglow Road, Sheffield,
South Yorkshire S11 7TB
Tel: (0114) 236 3545
Head: Mr R J Ellks
Type: Co-educational Day and Boarding 11–16
No of pupils: 96 *No of Boarders:* F30
Special Needs: **AUT** DEL EBD HI **MLD** VIS

BROAD ELMS SCHOOL
Broad Elms Lane, Sheffield,
South Yorkshire S11 9RQ
Tel: (0114) 2368277
Head: Mr N Elliot
Type: Co-educational Day 4–11

DEERLANDS SCHOOL
Lindsay Road, Sheffield,
South Yorkshire S5 7WE
Tel: (0114) 2400271
Head: Mr C Trainor
Type: Co-educational Day 10–16

DR JOHN WORRALL SCHOOL
Maltby Street, Sheffield,
South Yorkshire S9 2QA
Tel: (0114) 2441762
Head: Mrs B M Burdon
Type: Co-educational Day 5–16

EAST HILL PRIMARY SCHOOL
East Bank Road, Sheffield,
South Yorkshire S2 3PX
Tel: (0114) 272 9897
Head: Mr T Johnson
Type: Co-educational Day 4–11
No of pupils: 56
Special Needs: **MLD**

EAST HILL SECONDARY SCHOOL
East Bank Road, Sheffield,
South Yorkshire S2 3PX
Tel: (0114) 276 0245
Head: Mr K Jenkins
Type: Co-educational 11–16
No of pupils: 110
Special Needs: **MLD**

MOSSBROOK SCHOOL
Bochum Parkway, Sheffield,
South Yorkshire S8 8JR
Tel: (0114) 237 2768
Head: Mrs M Brough
Type: Co-educational Day and Boarding 5–11
No of pupils: B54 G22
No of Boarders: W15
Special Needs: **AUT** DEL DOW EBD EPI MLD **SLD** SP&LD **SPLD** W

NORFOLK PARK PRIMARY SCHOOL
Park Grange Road, Sheffield,
South Yorkshire S2 3QF
Tel: (0114) 272 6165
Head: Mrs G M Croston
Type: Co-educational Day 2–11

OAKES PARK SCHOOL
Hemsworth Road, Sheffield,
South Yorkshire S8 8LN
Tel: (0114) 255 6754
Head: Mrs P Johnson
Type: Co-educational Day 2–19
No of pupils: 55
Special Needs: **PH** W

THE ROWAN SCHOOL
4 Durvale Court, Sheffield,
South Yorkshire S17 3PT
Tel: (0114) 235 0479
Head: Mr D R Quayle
Type: Co-educational Day 4–10
No of pupils: 60
Special Needs: ASP AUT SP&LD

WOOLLEY WOOD SCHOOL
Oaks Fold Road, Sheffield,
South Yorkshire S5 0TG
Tel: (0114) 245 6885
Head: Ms M J Holly
Type: Co-educational Day 3–10
No of pupils: 58
Special Needs: PMLD SLD W

WEST YORKSHIRE

Bradford Education Authority

Flockton House
Flockton Road
Bradford BD4 7RY
Tel: (01274) 751840

BOLLING SCHOOL
Bradford, West Yorkshire BD4 7S4
Tel: (01274) 721962
Head: A Moore
Type: Co-educational Day 11–19

BRAITHWAITE SCHOOL
Braithwaite Road, Keighley,
West Yorkshire BD22 6PR
Tel: (01535) 603041
Head: Mrs P A Pearson
Type: Co-educational Day 2–19
Special Needs: MLD

BRANSHAW SCHOOL
Keighley, West Yorkshire BD21 1QX
Tel: (01535) 662739
Head: J E Graveson
Type: Co-educational Day 2–19
No of pupils: B26 G13
Special Needs: **PMLD SLD**

CHAPEL GRANGE SCHOOL
Rhodesway, Bradford, West Yorkshire BD8 0DQ
Tel: (01274) 773307
Head: Mrs H Morrison
Type: Co-educational Day 11–19
No of pupils: 102
Special Needs: AUT MLD **SLD**

GREENFIELD SCHOOL
Bradford, West Yorkshire BD10 8LU
Tel: (01274) 614092
Head: Ms J Taylor
Type: Co-educational Day 2–11
No of pupils: 50
Special Needs: AUT SLD

HAYCLIFFE SCHOOL
Haycliffe Lane, Bradford,
West Yorkshire BD5 9ET
Tel: (01274) 576123
Head: Mr K G Fair
Type: Co-educational Day 11–19
No of pupils: 120
Special Needs: **MLD** SLD W

HEATON ROYDS SCHOOL
Redburn Drive, Shipley,
West Yorkshire BD18 3AZ
Tel: (01274) 583759
Head: Mrs M Fowler
Type: Co-educational Day 2–11
No of pupils: B28 G17
Special Needs: EPI MLD **SLD** SP&LD

LISTER LANE SCHOOL
Lister Lane, Bradford, West Yorkshire
BD2 4LL
Tel: (01274) 777107/777108
Head: Mr W G Freeth
Type: Co-educational Day 2–13
No of pupils: 70
Special Needs: **PH** W

NETHERLANDS AVENUE SCHOOL
Netherlands Avenue, Bradford,
West Yorkshire BD6 1EA
Tel: (01274) 677711
Head: Mr G Bowden
Type: Co-educational Day 2–11
No of pupils: B45 G30
Special Needs: AUT CP EBD EPI HI
MLD PH **SLD SP&LD**

TEMPLE BANK SCHOOL
Daisy Hill Lane, Bradford,
West Yorkshire BD9 6BN
Tel: (01274) 776566/776588
Head: Mr R C Neal
Type: Co-educational Day 2–19
No of pupils: B31 G19
Special Needs: **VIS** W

THORN PARK SCHOOL
Thorn Lane, Bingley Road, Bradford,
West Yorkshire BD9 6RY
Tel: (01274) 773770
Head: Mr D Muir
Type: Co-educational Day 2–19
No of pupils: 85
Special Needs: **HI**

WEDGWOOD SCHOOL & COMMUNITY NURSERY
Landscove Avenue, Holmewood,
Bradford, West Yorkshire BD4 0NQ
Tel: (01274) 687236
Head: Mrs J Godward
Type: Co-educational Day 2–11
No of pupils: 81
Special Needs: CP MLD PH **PMLD**
SLD W

Calderdale Education Authority

PO Box 33
Northgate House
Halifax HX1 1UN
Tel: (01422) 357257

HIGHBURY SCHOOL
Lower Edge Road, Rastrick,
Brighouse, West Yorkshire HD6 3LD
Tel: (01484) 716319
Head: Miss P J Sellers
Type: Co-educational Day 2–11
No of pupils: 40
Special Needs: ADD ADHD ASP AUT
CP DEL DOW DYC DYP DYS EBD
EPI HI MLD PH **PMLD SLD** SP&LD
SPLD TOU VIS W

RAVENSCLIFFE HIGH SCHOOL
Skircoat Green, Halifax,
West Yorkshire HX3 0RZ
Tel: (01422) 358621
Head: Mr M D Hirst
Type: Co-educational Day 11–19
No of pupils: 115
Special Needs: AUT CP DYP DYS EPI
HI MLD PH PMLD SLD SP&LD
VIS W

WOOD BANK SPECIAL SCHOOL
Dene View, Luddendenfoot, Halifax,
West Yorkshire HX2 6PB
Tel: (01422) 884170
Head: Mrs J Ingham
Type: Co-educational Day 2–11
No of pupils: 40
Special Needs: **AUT** CP **PMLD SLD** W

Kirklees Education Authority

Oldgate House
2 Oldgate
Huddersfield HD1 6QW
Tel: (01484) 225242

FAIRFIELD SCHOOL
Dale Lane, Heckmondwike,
West Yorkshire WF16 9PA
Tel: (01924) 325700
Head: Mrs S L Williams
Type: Co-educational Day 3–19
No of pupils: B51 G36
Special Needs: PMLD SLD W

HIGHFIELDS SCHOOL
Cemetery Road, Edgerton,
Huddersfield, West Yorkshire
HD1 5NF
Tel: (01484) 226659
Head: Mr R T Ware
Type: Co-educational Day 3–19
No of pupils: B50 G27
Special Needs: PMLD SLD W

LONGLEY SCHOOL
Smithy Lane, Huddersfield,
West Yorkshire HD5 8JE
Tel: (01484) 223937
Head: Mr M Hogarth
Type: Co-educational Day 5–16
No of pupils: 135
Special Needs: ADD ADHD ASP **AUT**
CP DEL DOW DYP DYS **EBD** EPI HI
MLD SP&LD VIS W

LYDGATE SCHOOL
Kirkroyds Lane, New Mill,
Huddersfield, West Yorkshire
HD7 7LS
Tel: (01484) 222484
Head: Mr W Goler
Type: Co-educational Day 5–16
No of pupils: B52 G35
Special Needs: **MLD** W

NORTONTHORPE HALL SCHOOL
Busker Lane, Scissett, Huddersfield,
West Yorkshire HD8 9JU
Tel: (01484) 222921
Head: Mr M Ironmonger
Type: Co-educational Boarding and
Day 7–16
No of pupils: 70
Special Needs: **EBD**

RAVENSHALL SCHOOL
Ravensthorpe Road, Dewsbury,
West Yorkshire WF12 9EE
Tel: (01924) 325234
Head: Mr C Newby
Type: Co-educational Day 11–16
No of pupils: 87
Special Needs: **MLD** W

TURNSHAWS SCHOOL
Turnshaws Avenue, Kirkburton,
Huddersfield, West Yorkshire
HD8 0TJ
Tel: (01484) 222760
Head: Ms G Taylor
Type: Co-educational Day 3–19
No of pupils: 50
Special Needs: PMLD SLD W

Leeds Education Authority

3rd Floor East
Civic Hall
Leeds LS1 1UR
Tel: (0113) 247 5590

BROOMFIELD SCHOOL
Broom Place, Leeds, West Yorkshire
LS10 3JP
Tel: (0113) 277 1603
Head: Mr D M Dewhirst
Type: Co-educational Day 2–19
No of pupils: B71 G28
Special Needs: AUT CP EBD EPI HI
MLD PH **PMLD SLD** VIS W

ELMETE WOOD SCHOOL
Elmete Lane, Leeds, West Yorkshire
LS8 2LJ
Tel: (0113) 265 5457
Head: Mr W J Chatwin
Type: Co-educational Day 11–19
No of pupils: 120
Special Needs: **MLD**

GRAFTON SCHOOL
Craven Road, Leeds, West Yorkshire
LS6 2PW
Tel: (0113) 293 0323
Head: Mr K Purches
Type: Co-educational 3–11
No of pupils: 74
Special Needs: HI MLD

GREEN MEADOWS SCHOOL
Bradford Road, Guiseley,
West Yorkshire LS20 8PP
Tel: (01943) 878536
Head: Mrs D Seed
Type: Co-educational Day 2–19
No of pupils: B77 G40
Special Needs: ADHD ASP AUT CP
DEL DOW DYP DYS EPI HI **MLD** PH
PMLD SLD SP&LD SPLD TOU VIS W

JOHN JAMIESON SCHOOL
Hollin Hill Drive, Leeds,
West Yorkshire LS8 2PW
Tel: (0113) 293 0236
Head: Mr P Hutchinson
Type: Co-educational Day 2–19
No of pupils: 100
Special Needs: CP DEL **MLD PH** W

MILESTONE SCHOOL
4 Town Street, Stanningley,
West Yorkshire LS28 6HL
Tel: (0113) 214 6107
Head: Mr J C Tearle
Type: Co-educational Day 2–19
No of pupils: 64
Special Needs: **ADHD AUT** PMLD
SLD W

NORTHWAYS SCHOOL
Willow Lane, Clifford, Wetherby,
West Yorkshire LS23 6JN
Tel: (01937) 843766
Head: Mr J Boulton
Type: Boys Boarding and Day
No of pupils: 57
Special Needs: EBD

PENNY FIELD SCHOOL
Tongue Lane, Leeds, West Yorkshire
LS6 4QE
Tel: (0113) 278 3577
Head: Mrs H M Barrett
Type: Co-educational Day 2–19
No of pupils: 75
Special Needs: CP EPI HI PH **PMLD**
SLD VIS W

STONEGATE SCHOOL
Stonegate Road, Leeds,
West Yorkshire LS6 4QJ
Tel: (0113) 278 6464
Head: Mr P Bailey
Type: Co-educational Day 11–16
No of pupils: 75
Special Needs: EBD

VICTORIA PARK SCHOOL
Victoria Park Grove, Leeds,
West Yorkshire LS13 2RD
Tel: (0113) 278 3957
Head: Mr P J Miller
Type: Co-educational Day 11–19
No of pupils: 130
Special Needs: **MLD**

Wakefield Education Authority

County Hall
Wakefield WF1 2QL
Tel: (01924) 306090

THE FELKIRK SCHOOL
Highwell Hill Lane, South Hiendley,
Barnsley, South Yorkshire S72 9DL
Tel: (01226) 718613
Head: Mr T R Howe
Type: Boys Boarding and Day 5–16
No of pupils: 80 *No of Boarders:* F30
Special Needs: EBD

HIGHFIELD SCHOOL
Gawthorpe Lane, Ossett,
West Yorkshire WF5 9BS
Tel: (01924) 302980
Head: Mrs M Smith
Type: Co-educational Day 11–16
No of pupils: 120
Special Needs: ADD ADHD ASP AUT
MLD PH SLD W

OAKTREE SCHOOL
Barnsley Road, Ackworth,
Pontefract, Wakefield,
West Yorkshire WF7 7DT
Tel: (01977) 723145
Head: Mrs W Fereday
Type: Co-educational Day 2–19

WAKEFIELD PATHWAYS SCHOOL
Poplar Avenue, Townville,
Castleford, Wakefield,
West Yorkshire WF10 3QJ
Tel: (01977) 723085
Head: Miss Y Limb
Type: Co-educational Day 5–11

NORTHERN IRELAND

BELFAST

Belfast Area Education & Library Board

40 Academy Street
Belfast BT1 2NO
Tel: (028) 9056 4000

BELFAST HOSPITAL SCHOOL
Belfast, County Antrim BT12 6BE
Tel: (02890) 346407
Head: Mr E A Swallow
Type: Co-educational Day 3–19 (Hospital)
Special Needs: ADD ADHD ASP AUT CP DEL DOW DYC DYP DYS EBD EPI HI MLD PH PMLD SLD SP&LD SPLD TOU VIS W

CEDAR LODGE SPECIAL SCHOOL
Gray's Lane, Newtownabbey, Belfast, County Antrim BT36 7EB
Tel: (01232) 777292
Head: Mrs E G Bunting
Type: Co-educational Day 4–16
No of pupils: B100 G50
Special Needs: ADHD ASP DEL EPI MLD SP&LD W

CLARAWOOD SCHOOL
Clarawood Park, Belfast, County Antrim BT5 6FR
Tel: (01232) 472736
Head: Mr S McIntaggart
Type: Co-educational Day 8–13
No of pupils: 35
Special Needs: EBD

FLEMING FULTON SCHOOL
Upper Malone Road, Belfast, County Antrim BT9 6TY
Tel: (01232) 613877
Head: Dr D Mehaffey
Type: Co-educational Day and Boarding 2–19
No of pupils: B99 G65
No of Boarders: W6
Special Needs: PH SP&LD W

GLENVEAGH SPECIAL SCHOOL
Harberton Park, Belfast, County Antrim BT9 6TX
Tel: (01232) 669907
Head: Mrs K Murphy
Type: Co-educational Day 8–19
No of pupils: B100 G70
Special Needs: AUT PMLD SLD

GREENWOOD HOUSE ASSESSMENT CENTRE
Greenwood Avenue, Belfast, County Antrim BT4 3JJ
Tel: (01232) 471000
Head: Mrs P E Scott
Type: Co-educational Day 4–7
No of pupils: 54
Special Needs: ADD ADHD ASP AUT DEL DOW DYP DYS EBD HI MLD PH SLD SP&LD SPLD VIS

JAFFE CENTRE
Craft Annex, Carolan Road, Belfast, County Antrim BT15 4HS
Tel: (01232) 492601
Head: Mr D McConnell
Type: Co-educational Day 11–16
No of pupils: 45
Special Needs: EBD

MITCHELL HOUSE SPECIAL SCHOOL
Marmont, 405 Holywood Road, Belfast, County Antrim BT4 2GU
Tel: (01232) 768407
Head: Mrs P Grindle
Type: Co-educational Day 2–19
No of pupils: 75
Special Needs: CP PH W

OAKWOOD SCHOOL ASSESSMENT CENTRE
Harberton Park, Belfast, County Antrim BT9 6TX
Tel: (01232) 605116
Head: Mrs M E Watson
Type: Co-educational 3–8
No of pupils: 77
Special Needs: AUT CP DEL DOW EBD EPI HI PH PMLD SLD SP&LD VIS W

PARK EDUCATION RESOURCE CENTRE
145 Ravenhill Road, Belfast, County Antrim BT6 8GH
Tel: (01232) 450513
Head: Mr F Mitchell
Type: Co-educational Day 11–16
Special Needs: MLD

ST FRANCIS DE SALES SPECIAL SCHOOL
Beechmount Drive, Belfast, County Antrim BT12 7LU
Tel: (01232) 245599
Head: Sister M Byrne
Type: Co-educational Day 3–7

ST GERARD'S EDUCATION RESOURCE CENTRE
Upper Springfield Road, Belfast, County Antrim BT12 7QP
Tel: (01232) 245593
Head: Mr A McGlone
Type: Co-educational Day 4–16
No of pupils: B160 G85
Special Needs: MLD

NORTH EASTERN AREA

North Eastern Area Education & Library Board

County Hall
182 Galgorm Road
Ballymena
County Antrim BT42 1HN
Tel: (028) 2565 3333

BEECHGROVE SCHOOL
91 Fry's Road, Ballymena, County
Antrim BT43 7EN
Tel: (0282) 564 8264
Head: Mrs A Pinches
Type: Co-educational Day 3–11
No of pupils: 24
Special Needs: ADHD CP DEL EPI **PH**
VIS **W**

DUNFANE SCHOOL
91 Fry's Road, Ballymena, County
Antrim BT43 7EN
Tel: (01266) 48263
Head: Mr J Dixon
Type: Co-educational 3–16
No of pupils: B89 G53
Special Needs: ADD DOW DYP EBD
EPI MLD PH SP&LD VIS W

HILL CROFT SCHOOL
Abbot's Road, Newtownabbey,
County Antrim BT37 9RB
Tel: (01232) 863262
Head: Mr T Howard
Type: Co-educational Day 3–19
Special Needs: SLD W

KILRONAN SCHOOL
46 Ballyronan Road, Magherafelt,
County Londonderry BT45 6EN
Tel: (01648) 32168
Head: Mrs J Clarke
Type: Co-educational Day 3–19
No of pupils: 80
Special Needs: AUT CP DOW PMLD
SLD W

LOUGHAN SCHOOL
22 Old Ballymoney Road, Ballymena,
County Antrim BT43 6LX
Tel: (028) 2565 2944
Head: Miss M H Norris
Type: Co-educational Day 3–19
No of pupils: B48 G27
Special Needs: **SLD** W

RIVERSIDE SCHOOL
Fennel Road, Antrim, County
Antrim BT41 4PB
Tel: (028) 9442 8946
Head: Mrs R A Rankin
Type: Co-educational Day 3–19
No of pupils: B27 G18
Special Needs: AUT EPI PMLD **SLD**
SP&LD

RODDENSVALE SCHOOL
The Roddens, Larne, County Antrim
BT40 1PU
Tel: (01574) 272802
Head: Miss M Lynas
Type: Co-educational Day 3–19
No of pupils: 56
Special Needs: AUT CP DEL DOW
EBD EPI HI PH PMLD SLD SP&LD
SPLD VIS W

ROSSTULLA SCHOOL
2–6 Jordanstown Road,
Newtownabbey, County Antrim
BT37 0QF
Tel: (01232) 862743
Head: Mrs F Burke
Type: Co-educational 4–16
No of pupils: B99 G64
Special Needs: EBD EPI **MLD**

SANDELFORD SCHOOL
8 Rugby Avenue, Coleraine, County
Londonderry BT52 1JL
Tel: (028) 70343062
Head: Mrs M C McElhinney
Type: Co-educational Day 3–19

THORNFIELD SPECIAL SCHOOL
8–12 Jordanstown Road,
Newtownabbey, County Antrim
BT37 0QF
Tel: (01232) 851089
Head: Mrs A Ingram
Type: Co-educational Day 5–16
No of pupils: B68 G11
Special Needs: **SP&LD**

SOUTH EASTERN AREA

South Eastern Area Education & Library Board

Grahamsbridge Road
Dundonald
Belfast BT16 2HS
Tel: (028) 9056 6200

ARDMORE HOUSE SCHOOL & SUPPORT SERVICE
95a Saul Street, Downpatrick,
County Down BT30 6NJ
Tel: (01396) 614881
Head: Mr W Dale
Type: Co-educational Day 11–16
No of pupils: 28
Special Needs: EBD

BEECHLAWN SCHOOL
3 Dromore Road, Hillsborough,
County Down BT26 6HY
Tel: (01846) 682302/682283
Head: Mr E S Gamble
Type: Boys Day 10–16
No of pupils: 250
Special Needs: DYP **DYS MLD SPLD**

BROOKFIELD SCHOOL
6 Halfpenny Gate Road, Moira,
Craigavon, County Armagh
BT67 0HN
Tel: (01846) 611498
Head: Mr A F Sturgeon
Type: Co-educational Day 5–11

CLIFTON SCHOOL
15 Ballyholme Road, Bangor, County Down BT20 5JH
Tel: (01247) 270210
Head: Mrs J H Crowther
Type: Co-educational 3–19
No of pupils: 102
Special Needs: **AUT CP DOW EBD EPI HI PH PMLD SLD** SP&LD VIS W

KILLARD HOUSE SCHOOL
North Road, Newtownards, County Down NT23 3AN
Tel: (01247) 813613
Head: Mr W J Haddick
Type: Girls Day and Boarding 4–16 (co-educational 4–11)
No of pupils: 205
Special Needs: MLD SP&LD

KNOCKEVIN SCHOOL
29 Racecourse Hill, Killough Road, Downpatrick, County Down BT30 6PU
Tel: (01396) 612167
Head: Mrs I E McBride
Type: Co-educational Day 3–19

LINDSAY SPECIAL SCHOOL
Foster Green Hospital, 110 Saintfield Road, Belfast, South Eastern Area BT8 4HD
Tel: (02890) 793681
Head: Mr P W Doherty
Type: Co-educational Day and Boarding 3–15
No of pupils: 25 *No of Boarders:* W15
Special Needs: **ADHD ASP** AUT DYP DYS **EBD** MLD SPLD

LONGSTONE SCHOOL
Millar's Lane, Dundonald, Belfast, County Antrim BT16 0DA
Tel: (01232) 480071/484660
Head: Mr W J McLaughlin
Type: Co-educational Day 4–16
No of pupils: 200
Special Needs: **EBD MLD SPLD** W

PARKVIEW SCHOOL
2 Brokerstown Road, Lisburn, County Antrim BT28 2EE
Tel: (02892) 601197
Head: Ms M A Martin
Type: Co-educational Day 3–19
No of pupils: 135
Special Needs: **AUT PMLD SLD** W

SOUTHERN AREA

Southern Area Education & Library Board
3 Charlemont Place
The Mail
Armagh BT61 9AX
Tel: (028) 3751 2200

CEARA SPECIAL SCHOOL
Sloan Street, Lurgan, Craigavon, County Armagh BT61 8NY
Tel: (01762) 323312
Head: Mrs A Blakely

LISANALLY SPECIAL SCHOOL
85 Lisanally Lane, Armagh, County Armagh BT61 7HF
Tel: (01861) 523563
Head: Mrs M T Williams
Type: Co-educational Day 4–19

RATHFRILAND HILL SPECIAL SCHOOL
Rathfriland Hill, Newry, County Down BT34 1HU
Tel: (01693) 63068
Head: Mr R Cassidy
Type: Co-educational Day 3–19
No of pupils: B55 G34
Special Needs: **AUT PMLD SLD**

SPERRINVIEW SPECIAL SCHOOL
8 Coalisland Road, Dungannon, County Tyrone BT71 4AA
Tel: (028) 8772 2467
Head: Mr O Sherry
Type: Co-educational Day 2–19
No of pupils: B46 G18
Special Needs: **PMLD SLD** W

WESTERN AREA

Western Area Education and Library Board
Headquarters Office
1 Hospital Road
Omagh
County Tyrone BT79 0AW
Tel: (028) 8241 1411

BELMONT HOUSE SCHOOL
Racecourse Road, Londonderry, County Londonderry BT48 7RE
Tel: (01504) 351266
Head: Mr T McCully
Type: Co-educational Day 3–19
No of pupils: 219
Special Needs: EBD MLD SP&LD

CRANNY SPECIAL SCHOOL
4a Deverney Road, Cranny, Omagh, County Tyrone BT79 0JJ
Tel: (01662) 242939
Head: Mrs K McGerty
Type: Co-educational Day 3–19
No of pupils: B18 G11
Special Needs: AUT CP DOW EPI HI PH **PMLD SLD SPLD** VIS W

ELMBROOK
Derrygonnelly, Enniskillen, County
Fermanagh BT7 4AY
Tel: (01365) 329947
Head: Mrs H Lendrum
Type: Co-educational Day 4–19
No of pupils: 54
Special Needs: AUT CP DEL EBD EPI
PMLD SLD W

ENNISKILLEN MODEL PRIMARY SCHOOL
Special Unit (Language),
Enniskillen, Western Area BT74 6HZ
Tel: (01365) 324865
Head: Mrs S W Glass
Type: Co-educational 4–11
No of pupils: B13 G5
Special Needs: SP&LD W

ERNE SPECIAL SCHOOL
Derrygonnelly Road, Enniskillen,
County Fermanagh BT74 7EX
Tel: (01365) 323942
Head: Mrs K Turnbull
Type: Co-educational Day 4–16
No of pupils: 134
Special Needs: MLD W

FOYLE VIEW SCHOOL
15 Racecourse Road, Londonderry,
County Londonderry BT48 7RB
Tel: (02871) 263270
Head: Mr M Dobbins
Type: Co-educational Day 3–19
No of pupils: 108
Special Needs: AUT PMLD SLD W

GLASVEY SPECIAL SCHOOL
15 Loughermore Road, Ballykelly,
Limavady, County Londonderry
BT49 9PB
Tel: (01504) 762462
Head: Mrs L Wilson
Type: Co-educational Day 3–19
No of pupils: B28 G12
Special Needs: AUT CP DEL DYS EBD
EPI HI PH PMLD SLD SP&LD VIS W

GLENSIDE SCHOOL
45a Derry Road, Strabane, County
Tyrone BT82 8DY
Tel: (01504) 883319
Head: Ms C McCauley
Type: Co-educational Day 3–19
No of pupils: B21 G20
Special Needs: AUT CP DEL DOW
EBD EPI HI PH PMLD SLD SP&LD
SPLD VIS W

HEATHERBANK SCHOOL
17 Deverney Road, Omagh, County
Tyrone BT79 0ND
Tel: (01662) 249182
Head: Mr H McAteer
Type: Co-educational Day 4–19
No of pupils: 140
Special Needs: MLD

LIMEGROVE SCHOOL
2 Ballyquin Road, Limavady, County
Londonderry BT49 9ET
Tel: (028) 7776 2351
Head: Ms C O' Neil
Type: Co-educational Day 3–16
No of pupils: B68 G22
Special Needs: EBD MLD

SCOTLAND

ABERDEENSHIRE

Aberdeen City Education Authority

Summerhill Education Centre
Stronsay Drive
Aberdeen
AB15 6JA
Tel: (01224) 346101

ABERDEEN SCHOOL FOR THE DEAF
Regent Walk, Aberdeen AB24 1SX
Tel: (01224) 480303
Head: Mrs M Falconer
Type: Co-educational Day 2–12
No of pupils: B10 G8
Special Needs: HI SP&LD W

BEECHWOOD SCHOOL
Raeden Park Road, Aberdeen
AB15 5PD
Tel: (01224) 323405
Head: Mr A Young
Type: Co-educational Day 5–18
No of pupils: 145
Special Needs: MLD SLD SP&LD W

BRIDGE OF DON ACADEMY SEN BASE
Braehead Way, Bridge of Don,
Aberdeen AB22 8RR
Tel: (01224) 707583
Head: Mr R McClymont

BUCKSBURN SCHOOL SEN BASE
Iverurie Road, Bucksburn, Aberdeen
AB21 9LL
Tel: (01224) 712862
Head: Mr M Robertson
Type: Co-educational Day
No of pupils: B4 G3
Special Needs: ASP MLD SP&LD

CARDEN SCHOOL
Gordon Terrace, Dyce, Aberdeen
AB21 7BD
Tel: (01224) 770362
Head: Mr P Inglis
Type: Co-educational Day 5–12

CORDYCE RESIDENTIAL SCHOOL
Riverview Drive, Dyce, Aberdeen
AB21 7NF
Tel: (01224) 724215
Head: Mr N C Brown
Type: Co-educational Day 11–16
No of pupils: 42
Special Needs: EBD

CULTS SCHOOL SEN BASE
Earlswells Road, Cults, Aberdeen
AB15 9RG
Tel: (01224) 869221
Head: Mr I Smithers
Type: Co-educational Day
No of pupils: B9 G4
Special Needs: AUT CP DOW

DONBANK SCHOOL SEN BASE
Dill Road, Tillydrone, Aberdeen
AB24 2XL
Tel: (01224) 483217
Head: Ms M Bolton

DYCE ACADEMY AUTISM UNIT
Riverview Drive, Dyce, Aberdeen
AB21 7NF
Tel: (01224) 725118
Head: Mr M Taylor
Type: Co-educational Day 11–18
No of pupils: 8
Special Needs: ASP AUT

DYCE SCHOOL LANGUAGE UNIT
Gordon Terrace, Dyce, Aberdeen
AB21 7BD
Tel: (01224) 772220
Head: Ms J E Fenton

EAL SERVICE
Linksfield Academy, 520 King Street,
Aberdeen AB24 5SS
Tel: (01224) 494272
Head: Mr M McDowall

EDUCATIONAL SERVICE FOR THE HEARING
Impaired and Aberdeen, School for
the Deaf, Regent Walk, Aberdeen
AB24 1SX
Tel: (01224) 480303
Head: Mr M Kell

FERNIELEA SCHOOL SEN BASE
Stronsay Place, Aberdeen AB15 6HD
Tel: (01224) 318533
Head: Mr E Pike
Type: Co-educational Day
No of pupils: B8 G5
Special Needs: AUT DOW DYP EBD
EPI HI MLD SLD SP&LD W

GILCOMSTOUN SCHOOL SEN BASE
Skene Street, Aberdeen AB10 1PG
Tel: (01224) 642722
Head: Mr S Duncan

HARLAW ACADEMY SEN BASE
18/20 Albyn Place, Aberdeen
AB10 1RG
Tel: (01224) 589251
Head: Mr J Murray

HAZLEHEAD ACADEMY SEN BASE
Groat's Road, Aberdeen AB15 8BE
Tel: (01224) 310184
Head: Mr B J Wood

HAZLEWOOD SCHOOL
Fernielea Road, Aberdeen AB15 6JU
Tel: (01224) 321363
Head: Mrs R Jarvis
Type: Co-educational Day 4–18
No of pupils: 80
Special Needs: MLD PMLD SLD

HOLY FAMILY RC SCHOOL SEN BASE
Summerhill Terrace, Aberdeen
AB15 6HE
Tel: (01224) 316446
Head: Mr G McKnight

HOSPITAL AND HOME TUITION SERVICE
Lowit Unit, RACH, Cornhill Road,
Aberdeen AB25 2ZG
Tel: (01224) 404438/840978
Head: Ms M Allan

KAIMHILL PRIMARY SCHOOL
Pitmeddon Terrace, Aberdeen
AB10 7HR
Tel: (01224) 316356
Head: Mr A Baxter
Type: Co-educational

KINCORTH ACADEMY
Kincorth Circle, Aberdeen AB12 5NL
Tel: (01224) 872881
Head: Mr D Milne
Type: Co-educational

KIRKHILL SCHOOL
Cairngorm Gardens, Aberdeen
AB12 5BS
Tel: (01224) 874439
Head: Ms L Brodie
Type: Co-educational

LINKSFIELD ACADEMY
520 King Street, Aberdeen AB24 5SS
Tel: (01224) 481343
Head: Mr R Erridge
Type: Co-educational
Special Needs: ADD ADHD AUT CP
DEL DYC DYS EBD EPI **MLD** SLD
SPLD

LOIRSTON PRIMARY S.E.N BASE
Loirston Avenue, Cove Bay,
Aberdeen AB12 3HE
Tel: (01224) 897686
Head: Mrs M Thom
Type: Co-educational Day
No of pupils: B4 G3
Special Needs: ADD ADHD ASP CP
DOW DYS EPI HI MLD PH SLD
SP&LD SPLD W

MARLPOOL SCHOOL
Cloverfield Gardens, Bucksburn,
Aberdeen AB21 9QN
Tel: (01224) 712735
Head: Mrs H Gordon
Type: Co-educational Day
No of pupils: B40 G30
Special Needs: ADD ADHD ASP **AUT**
CP DEL DOW DYS EBD EPI HI **MLD**
PH PMLD **SLD** SP&LD TOU W

MUIRFIELD SCHOOL
Mastrick Drive, Aberdeen AB16 6UE
Tel: (01224) 694958
Head: Ms A Sleven
Type: Co-educational Day

NORTHFIELD ACADEMY
Granitehill Place, Aberdeen
AB16 7AU
Tel: (01224) 699715
Head: Mr T Robertson
Type: Co-educational

OLDMACHER ACADEMY
Jesmond Drive, Bridge of Don,
Aberdeen AB22 8UR
Tel: (01224) 820887
Head: Mr J Leiper
Type: Co-educational

RAEDEN CENTRE
Mid-stocket Road, Aberdeen,
Grampian AB15 5PD
Tel: (01224) 321381
Head: Miss R Murray
Type: Co-educational 3–5

REDCRAIGS
14 Polmuir Road, Aberdeen
AB11 7SY
Tel: (01224) 581977
Head: Ms E Milbank
Type: Boys Day 13–16
No of pupils: 10

SCOTSTOWN SCHOOL
Scotstown Road, Bridge of Don,
Aberdeen AB22 8HH
Tel: (01224) 703331
Head: Ms C Bain

SEATON SCHOOL
Seaton Place East, Aberdeen
AB24 1XE
Tel: (01224) 483414
Head: Ms C Harkess
Type: Co-educational Day
No of pupils: B6 G4
Special Needs: AUT MLD SPLD

SMITHFIELD SCHOOL
Clarke Street, Aberdeen AB16 7XJ
Tel: (01224) 696952
Head: Ms A Walker

ST MACHAR ACADEMY
St Machar Drive, Aberdeen AB24 3YZ
Tel: (01224) 492855
Head: Mr L A Taylor

ST MACHAR SCHOOL
Harris Drive, Tillydrone, Aberdeen
AB24 2TF
Tel: (01224) 644540
Head: Ms L McIntosh

SUNNYBANK HEARING IMPAIRED UNIT SCHOOL
Sunnybank Road, Aberdeen
AB24 3NJ
Tel: (01224) 633363
Head: Mr A May
Type: Co-educational Day 3–11
No of pupils: 9
Special Needs: HI

TORRY ACADEMY
Tullos Circle, Aberdeen AB11 8HD
Tel: (01224) 876733
Head: Mr Robert

TULLOS SCHOOL
Girdleness Road, Aberdeen AB11 8FJ
Tel: (01224) 876621
Head: Ms L Martin
Type: Co-educational Day

VISUAL IMPAIRMENT PROVISION
Newhills School, Wagley Parade,
Bucksburn, Aberdeen AB21 9UB
Tel: (01224) 715648
Head: Ms P Dowds
Type: Co-educational Day

WALKER ROAD
Walker Road, Aberdeen AB11 8DL
Tel: (01224) 879720
Head: Ms M Robertson
Type: Co-educational

WOODLANDS SCHOOL
Craigton Road, Cults, Aberdeen
AB15 9PR
Tel: (01224) 868814
Head: Mr M Johnston
Type: Co-educational Day 5–18
No of pupils: 55
Special Needs: **PMLD** W

Aberdeenshire Education Authority

Woodhill House
Westburn Road
Aberdeen AB15 6JA
Tel: (01224) 346101

CARRONHILL SCHOOL
Mill of Forest Road, Stonehaven,
Kincardineshire AB59 2GZ
Tel: (01569) 763886
Head: Mrs L Hawksfield
Type: Co-educational Day 3–17
No of pupils: B30 G12
Special Needs: AUT MLD PMLD SLD

CENTRAL PRIMARY SCHOOL
St Peter Street, Peterhead,
Aberdeenshire AB42 6QD
Tel: (01779) 72211
Head: Mr S Paul
Type: Co-educational Day
No of pupils: B7
Special Needs: **SP&LD**

CRIMOND SCHOOL
Logie Road, Crimond, Fraserburgh,
Aberdeenshire AB43 8QL
Tel: (01346) 532251
Head: Mrs H Ross
Type: Co-educational Day
No of pupils: 6
Special Needs: **DYS**

DALES PARK SCHOOL
Berryden Road, Peterhead,
Aberdeenshire AB42 6GD
Tel: (01779) 477133
Head: Miss D Mair
Type: Co-educational Day
No of pupils: B154 G131
Special Needs: HI SP&LD VIS W

ELLON PRIMARY SCHOOL
SEN Base, Modley Place, Ellon,
Aberdeenshire AB41 9BB
Tel: (01358) 720692
Head: Mrs J Buchan
Type: Co-educational Day
No of pupils: B18 G15
Special Needs: **AUT** CP DOW EBD
EPI **MLD** PMLD **SLD** SP&LD VIS W

KEMNAY ACADEMY
Bremner Way, Kemnay, Inverurie,
Aberdeenshire AB51 5FW
Tel: (01467) 643535
Type: Co-educational Day
No of pupils: 550
Special Needs: ADD ASP AUT CP DEL
DOW DYC DYP DYS EBD EPI HI
MLD PH SP&LD SPLD TOU VIS W

ST ANDREW'S SCHOOL
St Andrew's Gardens, Inverurie,
Aberdeenshire AB51 3XT
Tel: (01467) 621215
Head: Mrs J Burnett
Type: Co-educational Day 3–16
No of pupils: 100
Special Needs: AUT CP EBD EPI HI
MLD PH PMLD SLD SP&LD VIS

THE STEVENSON CENTRE
Victoria Street, Fraserburgh,
Aberdeenshire AB43 9PJ
Tel: (01346) 510187
Head: Ms J A Kinnon
Type: Co-educational Day 12–16
No of pupils: B10 G8
Special Needs: ADD ADHD DYS **EBD**
EPI W

WESTFIELD SCHOOL
Argyll Road, Fraserburgh,
Aberdeenshire AB43 9BL
Tel: (01346) 28699
Head: Mr J Anderson
Type: Co-educational Day 3–18
No of pupils: B44 G16
Special Needs: AUT CP DEL DOW
DYS EBD EBD EPI HI MLD PH PMLD
SLD SP&LD VIS W

ARGYLL AND BUTE

Argyll and Bute Education Authority

Argyll House
Alexandra Parade
Dunoon
Argyll PA23 8AJ
Tel: (01369) 704000

BOWMER PRIMARY SCHOOL
Flora Street, Bowmore, Isle of Islay,
Argyll and Bute PA43 7JX
Tel: (01496) 810522
Head: Mr F MacDougall
Type: Co-educational Day
No of pupils: B1
Special Needs: AUT DYS EPI PMLD W

PARKLANDS SCHOOL
27 Charlotte Street, Helensburgh,
Argyll and Bute G84 7EZ
Tel: (01436) 673714
Head: Mrs L Downie
Type: Co-educational Day 5–18
No of pupils: 32
Special Needs: ASP AUT DOW **MLD**
PMLD SLD W

EAST AYRSHIRE

East Ayrshire Education Authority

Council Headquarters
London Road
Kilmarnock KA3 7BU
Tel: (01563) 576017

HILLSIDE SCHOOL
Dalgleish Avenue, Cumnock, East
Ayrshire KA18 1QQ
Tel: (01290) 423239
Head: Mr M McCaffrey
Type: Co-educational Day 3–18
No of pupils: B20 G14
Special Needs: AUT CP DOW DYP
PMLD SLD W

PARK SCHOOL
Grassyards Road, Kilmarnock, East
Ayrshire KA3 7BB
Tel: (01563) 25316
Head: Mr G M Donnell
Type: Co-educational Day 5–18
Special Needs: AUT CP DOW DYP
EBD EPI MLD PH SP&LD W

WITCHHILL SCHOOL
Witch Road, Kilmarnock, East
Ayrshire KA3 1JF
Tel: (01563) 33863
Head: Mrs N Lauchlan
Type: Co-educational Day 3–18
No of pupils: 20
Special Needs: **PMLD** W

WOODSTOCK SCHOOL
30 North Hamilton Street,
Kilmarnock, East Ayrshire KA1 2QJ
Tel: (01563) 533550
Head: Mrs L MacPhee
Type: Co-educational Day 5–18
No of pupils: B21 G9
Special Needs: **SLD** W

NORTH AYRSHIRE

North Ayrshire Education Authority

4th Floor, Cunninghame House
Irvine
Ayrshire KA12 8EE
Tel: (01294) 324400

HAYSHOLM SCHOOL

Bank Street, Irvine, North Ayrshire
KA12 0NE
Tel: (01294) 72481
Head: Mrs M O'Brien
Type: Co-educational Day 5–16

JAMES MACFARLANE SCHOOL

Dalry Road, Ardrossan, North
Ayrshire KA22 7DQ
Tel: (01294) 61370
Head: Mrs J Calvert
Type: Co-educational Day 2–18
No of pupils: B15 G11
Special Needs: **AUT** CP EPI PH **PMLD**
SLD W

JAMES REID SCHOOL

Primrose Place, Saltcoats, North
Ayrshire KA21 6LH
Tel: (01294) 67105
Head: Mrs V Balatine
Type: Co-educational Day 5–18
No of pupils: 55
Special Needs: **ADD** ADHD ASP AUT
CP DEL DOW DYP DYS **EBD** EPI HI
MLD PH SP&LD SPLD VIS W

STANECASTLE SCHOOL

Burns Crescent, Girdle Toll, Irvine,
North Ayrshire KA11 1AQ
Tel: (01294) 211914
Head: Mrs D Heron
Type: Co-educational Day 5–18

SOUTH AYRSHIRE

South Ayrshire Education Authority

County Buildings
Ayr KA17 1DR
Tel: (01292) 612201

CRAIGPARK SCHOOL

Belmont Avenue, Ayr, South Ayrshire
KA7 2ND
Tel: (01292) 288982
Head: Miss L Stoddart
Type: Co-educational Day 2–19
No of pupils: B13 G10
Special Needs: CP DOW EPI **PMLD**
VIS W

CLACKMANNANSHIRE

Clackmannanshire Education Authority

Lime Tree House
Alloa
Clackmannanshire FK10 1EX
Tel: (01259) 450000

CLACKMANNANSHIRE SECONDARY SCHOOL SUPPORT SERVICE

South School, Bedford Place, Alloa,
Clackmannanshire FK10 1LJ
Tel: (01259) 724345
Head: Mr S Barrett
Type: Co-educational Day
No of pupils: 30
Special Needs: EBD

FAIRFIELD SCHOOL

Pompee Road, Sauchie, Alloa,
Clackmannanshire FK10 3BX
Tel: (01259) 721660
Head: Mrs A H Morgan
Type: Co-educational Day 12–18
No of pupils: B13 G6
Special Needs: **SLD** W

LOCHIES SCHOOL

Gartmorn Road, Sauchie,
Clackmannanshire FK10 3PB
Tel: (01259) 216928
Head: Mrs A H Morgan
Type: Co-educational Day 5–12
No of pupils: B24 G12
Special Needs: ADHD ASP **AUT** CP
DOW **SLD SP&LD**

DUMFRIES & GALLOWAY

Dumfries and Galloway Education Authority

30 Edinburgh Road
Dumfries DG1 1NW
Tel: (01387) 260427

CALSIDE SCHOOL
Calside Road, Dumfries, Dumfries & Galloway DG1 4HB
Tel: (01387) 68567
Head: Mr C R Ferguson
Type: Co-educational Day 5–12
No of pupils: 353
Special Needs: ASP AUT DOW MLD SP&LD

ELM BANK SCHOOL
Lovers Walk, Dumfries, Dumfries & Galloway DG1 1DP
Tel: (01387) 254438
Head: Mr W Maxwell
Type: Co-educational Day 12–16
No of pupils: B16 G4
Special Needs: EBD

LANGLANDS SCHOOL
Loreburn Park, Dumfries, Dumfries & Galloway DG1 1LS
Tel: (01387) 267834
Head: Mrs E Rae
Type: Co-educational Day 5–18
No of pupils: B13 G12
Special Needs: AUT CP PMLD SLD SP&LD VIS W

LOCHSIDE SCHOOL
Lochside Road, Dumfries, Dumfries & Galloway DG2 0NF
Tel: (01387) 720318
Head: Mrs M Farrell
Type: Co-educational Day
No of pupils: B131 G127
Special Needs: ADHD AUT CP DOW DYP DYS EBD HI MLD PH SP&LD SPLD VIS W

PENNINGHAME SCHOOL
Learning Centre, Auchendoon Road, Newton Stewart, Dumfries & Galloway DG8 6HD
Tel: (01671) 402386
Type: Co-educational Day 5–11
No of pupils: 7
Special Needs: AUT CP MLD W

STRANRAER ACADEMY
McMaster's Road, Stranraer, Dumfries & Galloway DG9 8BW
Tel: (01776) 706484
Type: Co-educational Day
No of pupils: B569 G579
Special Needs: ADHD ASP CP DEL DOW DYP DYS EBD EPI HI MLD PH PMLD SLD SP&LD VIS W

EAST DUNBARTONSHIRE

East Dunbartonshire Education Authority

Boclair House
100 Milngavie Road
Bearsden
Glasgow G61 2TQ
Tel: (0141) 578 8000

CAMPSIE VIEW SCHOOL
Boghead Road, Lenzie, East Dunbartonshire G66 4DR
Tel: (0141) 777 6269
Head: Mrs C P Bowie
Type: Co-educational Day 2–18
No of pupils: B31 G25
Special Needs: AUT CP DOW EPI PH PMLD SLD SP&LD VIS W

MERKLAND SCHOOL
Langmuir Road, Kirkintilloch, East Dunbartonshire G66 2QF
Tel: (0141) 776 3454
Head: Mr J Simmons
Type: Co-educational Day 3–19
No of pupils: B54 G40
Special Needs: MLD W

WEST DUNBARTONSHIRE

West Dunbartonshire Education Authority

Garshake Road
Dumbarton G82 3PU
Tel: (01389) 737301

CUNARD SCHOOL
Whitecrook, Cochno Street,
Clydebank, West Dunbartonshire
G81 1RQ
Tel: (0141) 952 6614
Head: Mrs E Divers
Type: Co-educational Day 6–12
No of pupils: 27
Special Needs: **EBD**

KILPATRIC SCHOOL
Mountblow Road, Dalmuir,
Clydebank, West Dunbartonshire
G81 4SW
Tel: (01389) 872171
Head: Ms M Radcliffe
Type: Co-educational Day 5–18
No of pupils: B60 G30
Special Needs: MLD PMLD SLD W

DUNDEE

Dundee Education Authority

Floor 8
Tayside House
Dundee DD1 3RJ
Tel: (01382) 434000

KINGSPARK SCHOOL
Gillburn Road, Dundee DD3 0AB
Tel: (01382) 436284
Head: Mr S H Johnston
Type: Co-educational Day 5–18
No of pupils: B91 G74
Special Needs: AUT CP EPI MLD PH
PMLD SLD SP&LD W

EDINBURGH

Edinburgh Education Authority

Wellington Court
8–10 Waterloo Place
Edinburgh EH1 3BY
Tel: (0131) 469 3000

CAIRNPARK SCHOOL
Redhall House Drive, Edinburgh
EH14 1JE
Tel: (0131) 443 0903
Head: Mrs H Heslop
Type: Co-educational Day 14–16
No of pupils: 35
Special Needs: **EBD**

CANNONMILLS SCHOOL
Rodney Street, Edinburgh, Lothian
EH7 4EL
Tel: (0131) 556 6000
Head: Ms M Wilson
Type: Co-educational Day 12–16
No of pupils: B41 G13
Special Needs: **EBD**

DONALDSON'S COLLEGE FOR THE DEAF
West Coates, Edinburgh, Lothian
EH12 5JJ
Tel: (0131) 337 9911
Head: Mrs J L Allan
Type: Co-educational Boarding and
Day 3–19
No of pupils: B53 G22
No of Boarders: W16
Special Needs: HI SP&LD W

DRYLAW SPECIAL SCHOOL
Easter Drylaw Drive, Edinburgh,
Lothian EH4 2RY
Tel: (0131) 343 6116
Head: Mrs J Perry
Type: Co-educational Day 5–12
No of pupils: B54 G6
Special Needs: EBD W

GRAYSMILL SCHOOL
1 Redhall House Drive, Edinburgh,
Lothian EH14 1JE
Tel: (0131) 443 8096
Head: Mr I H Elfick
Type: Co-educational Day 3–18
No of pupils: B45 G40
Special Needs: PH W

KAIMES SPECIAL SCHOOL
140 Lasswade Road, Edinburgh,
Lothian EH16 6RT
Tel: (0131) 664 8241
Head: Mrs C Mumford
Type: Co-educational Day 5–18
No of pupils: B70 G13
Special Needs: **ASP** AUT DYS EBD
SP&LD W

KINGSINCH SPECIAL SCHOOL
233 Gilmerton Road, Edinburgh,
Lothian EH16 5UD
Tel: (0131) 664 1911
Head: Mrs M Price
Type: Co-educational Day 5–18
No of pupils: 106
Special Needs: ADHD AUT DOW
MLD SP&LD SPLD

OAKLANDS SPECIAL SCHOOL
Broomhouse Crescent, Edinburgh,
Lothian EH11 3UB
Tel: (0131) 455 7311
Head: Mrs S Harland
Type: Co-educational Day 5–18
No of pupils: 33
Special Needs: **PMLD**

PILRIG PARK SCHOOL
Balfour Place, Edinburgh, Lothian
EH6 5DW
Tel: (0131) 467 7960
Head: Mrs J H Mudie
Type: Co-educational Day 11–18
No of pupils: 80
Special Needs: ADD ADHD CP DOW
DYP DYS EBD EPI HI **MLD** SP&LD

PROSPECT BANK
81 Restalrig Road, Edinburgh,
Lothian EH6 8BQ
Tel: (0131) 553 2239
Head: Mrs M E Donaldson
Type: Co-educational Day 5–12
No of pupils: B35 G25
Special Needs: **MLD** SP&LD

ST CRISPIN'S SCHOOL
Watertoun Road, Edinburgh
EH9 3HZ
Tel: (0131) 667 4831
Head: Mr S Pinkerton
Type: Co-educational Day 5–18
No of pupils: B47 G17
Special Needs: **AUT** CP DOW EBD
EPI PH **SLD** SP&LD W

ST NICHOLAS SPECIAL SCHOOL
Gorgie Road, Edinburgh, Lothian
EH11 2RG
Tel: (0131) 337 6077
Head: Mrs C McLaren
Type: Co-educational Day
No of pupils: B49 G31
Special Needs: **MLD**

WILLOWPARK SPECIAL SCHOOL
Gorgie Road, Edinburgh, Lothian
EH11 2RG
Tel: (0131) 337 1622
Head: Mr D J Strathdee
Type: Co-educational Day 5–17
No of pupils: 84
Special Needs: DYP EPI PH SP&LD
SPLD

FALKIRK

Falkirk Education Authority
McLaren House
Marchmont Avenue
Polmont
Falkirk FK2 0NZ
Tel: (01324) 506600

CARRONGRANGE SCHOOL
Corrongrange Avenue,
Stenhousemuir, Larbert, Falkirk
FK5 3BH
Tel: (01324) 555266
Head: Mr K O'Hagan
Type: Co-educational Day 5–18
No of pupils: 230
Special Needs: **MLD** SLD

ROSSVAIL SCHOOL
108 Glasgow Road, Camelon,
Falkirk FK1 4HS
Tel: (01324) 508660
Head: Mrs H Fitzpatrick
Type: Co-educational Day 11–18
No of pupils: B19 G11
Special Needs: PMLD SLD W

TORWOOD SCHOOL
Stirling Road, Larbert, Falkirk
FK5 4SR
Tel: (01324) 503970
Head: Ms J Stewart
Type: Co-educational Day 0–12
No of pupils: B13 G12
Special Needs: AUT CP DEL DOW
EPI PH SLD SP&LD W

WEEDINGSHALL EDUCATION UNIT
Polmont, Falkirk FK2 0XS
Tel: (01324) 506770
Head: Mrs M Kydd
Type: Co-educational Day 12–16
No of pupils: 30
Special Needs: **EBD**

WINDSOR PARK SCHOOL
Bantaskine Road, Falkirk FK1 5HT
Tel: (01324) 508640
Head: Mrs C Finestone
Type: Co-educational Day 4–18
No of pupils: B7 G8
Special Needs: **HI** VIS

FIFE

Fife Education Authority
Council Headquarters
Fife House
North Street
Glenrothes
Fife KY7 5LT
Tel: (01592) 414141

HEADWELL SPECIAL SCHOOL
Headwell Avenue, Dunfermline, Fife
KY12 0JU
Tel: (01383) 721589
Head: Mrs J Lopez
Type: Co-educational 5–18
No of pupils: B23 G11
Special Needs: **AUT** EBD **EPI** HI SLD
SP&LD VIS

HYNDHEAD SCHOOL
Barncraig Street, Buckhaven, Leven,
Fife KY8 1JE
Tel: (01592) 414499
Head: Mrs M Bendex
Type: Co-educational Day 3–19
No of pupils: B15 G10
Special Needs: PMLD SLD W

JOHN FERGUS SCHOOL

Erskine Place, Glenrothes, Fife
KY7 4EF
Tel: (01592) 415335
Head: Mrs M A Sankey
Type: Co-educational Day 3–18
No of pupils: B8 G4
Special Needs: ADD ASP **AUT** CP
DOW EBD EPI HI PH **PMLD** SLD
VIS W

KILMARON SPECIAL SCHOOL

Balgarvie Road, Cupar, Fife
KY15 4PE
Tel: (01334) 53125
Head: Ms W Lawson
Type: Co-educational Day 3–19
Special Needs: ASP DOW PMLD
SLD W

LOCHGELLY NORTH SPECIAL SCHOOL

McGregor Avenue, Lochgelly, Fife
KY5 9PE
Tel: (01592) 418110
Head: Mrs H Farmer
Type: Co-educational Day 4–19
No of pupils: 22
Special Needs: MLD PMLD SLD W

ROBERT HENRYSON SCHOOL

Linburn Road, Dunfermline Road,
Fife KY11 4LD
Tel: (01383) 728004
Head: Ms M Lorimer
Type: Co-educational Day 2–19
No of pupils: B25 G26
Special Needs: AUT CP EPI PMLD
SLD VIS W

ROSSLYN SCHOOL

Viewforth Terrace, Kirkcaldy, Fife
KY1 3BP
Tel: (01592) 415930
Head: Mrs G Macfarlane
Type: Co-educational Day 3–16
No of pupils: B11 G9
Special Needs: PMLD SLD W

GLASGOW

Glasgow City Education Authority

Nye Bevan House
20 India Steet
Glasgow G2 4PF
Tel: (0141) 287 2000

ABERCORN SCHOOL

195 Garscube Road, Glasgow
G4 9QH
Tel: (0141) 332 6212
Head: Mrs P Smith
Type: Co-educational Day 11–18
No of pupils: B98 G34
Special Needs: **MLD**

ASHCRAIG SCHOOL

100 Avenue End Road, Glasgow
G33 3SW
Tel: (0141) 774 3428
Head: Ms M McGeever
Type: Co-educational Day 12–19
No of pupils: B91 G53
Special Needs: CP EPI PH VIS W

BANNERMAN COMMUNICATION DISORDER UNIT

C/o Bannerman High, Glasgow
Road, Glasgow G69 7NS
Tel: (0141) 771 8770
Head: Ms M Wheeler
Type: Boys Day
No of pupils: 8
Special Needs: ASP AUT

BROOMLEA SCHOOL

168 Broomhill Drive, Glasgow
G11 7NH
Tel: (0141) 339 6494
Head: Mrs L Rankin
Type: Co-educational Day 2–12
No of pupils: 36
Special Needs: PMLD

CALEDONIA LANGUAGE UNIT

C/o Caledonia Primary, Calderwood
Drive, Baillieston, Glasgow G69 7DJ
Tel: (0141) 781 4239
Head: Ms J Ferguson
Type: Co-educational

CARNBOOTH SCHOOL

Carnbooth House, Carmunnock,
Glasgow G76 9EG
Tel: (0141) 644 2773
Head: Ms C Clark
Type: Co-educational Boarding and
Day
No of pupils: B10 G4
No of Boarders: F1 W5
Special Needs: W

CARTVALE SCHOOL

80 Vicarfield Street, Glasgow
G51 2DF
Tel: (0141) 445 5272
Head: Miss M Castle
Type: Boys Day 11–16
No of pupils: 30
Special Needs: EBD

CROFTCROIGHN SCHOOL

180 Findochty Street, Glasgow
G33 5EP
Tel: (0141) 774 7777
Head: Mrs W Craig
Type: Co-educational Day 2–11
No of pupils: 65
Special Needs: AUT CP **DOW** EPI
PMLD SLD W

CROOKSTON LANGUAGE UNIT

C/o St Monica's Primary, 30
Kempsthorn Road, Glasgow G53 5SR
Tel: (0141) 892 0813
Head: Ms R Garside
Type: Co-educational

DARNLEY VISUAL IMPAIRMENT UNIT

C/o Darnley Primary, 169 Glen
Morriston Road, Glasgow G53 7HT
Tel: (0141) 621 2919
Head: Ms M McGeever
Type: Co-educational Day
No of pupils: B5 G10
Special Needs: VIS

DRUMCHAPEL LEARNING CENTRE

77 Hecla Avenue, Glasgow G15 8LX
Tel: (0141) 944 8517
Head: Ms Evelyn Hill

DRUMMORE SCHOOL
129 Drummore Road, Glasgow
G15 7NH
Tel: (0141) 944 1323
Head: Mrs M Wallace
Type: Co-educational Day 5–12
No of pupils: 68
Special Needs: **MLD**

DUNTARVIE PRE-SCHOOL
C/o Cadder Primary, 60 Herma
Primary, Glasgow G23 5AR
Tel: (0141) 946 3835
Head: Mrs P Campbell
Type: Co-educational Day
No of pupils: 20
Special Needs:

EASTMUIR SCHOOL
211 Hallhill Road, Glasgow G33 4QL
Tel: (0141) 771 3464
Head: Mrs S Conway
Type: Co-educational Day 4–11
No of pupils: B53 G21
Special Needs: AUT **MLD**

EDUCATION AUDIOLOGY UNIT
Paediatric Centre, Old Rutherglen
Road, Glasgow G5 0RA
Tel: (0141) 201 0930
Head: Ms M McFarlane
Type: Co-educational

GADBURN SCHOOL
70 Rockfield Road, Glasgow
G21 3DZ
Tel: (0141) 558 5373
Head: Mr G Hercus
Type: Co-educational Day 5–12
No of pupils: B50 G10
Special Needs: **MLD** W

GREENVIEW SCHOOL
Buckley Street, Glasgow G22 6DJ
Tel: (0141) 336 8391
Head: Mr D McGrorry
Type: Co-educational Day 5–13

HAMPDEN SCHOOL
80 Ardnahoe Avenue, Glasgow
G42 0DL
Tel: (0141) 647 7720
Head: Mrs M Cloughley
Type: Co-educational Day 2–12
No of pupils: 35
Special Needs: AUT DOW EPI PMLD
SLD SP&LD W

HILLPARK COMMUNICATION DISORDER UNIT
C/o Hillpark Secondary, 36
Cairngorm Road, Glasgow G43 2XB
Tel: (0141) 637 2949
Head: Ms N Barber
Type: Co-educational Day
No of pupils: B11 G1
Special Needs: ASP AUT

HOLLYBROOK SCHOOL
135 Hollybrook Street, Glasgow
G42 7HU
Tel: (0141) 423 5937
Head: Mrs M Horn
Type: Co-educational Day 12–19
No of pupils: 128
Special Needs: **MLD**

HOWFORD SCHOOL
487 Crookston Road, Pollok,
Glasgow, Strathclyde G53 7TX
Tel: (0141) 882 2605
Head: Mrs M Barwell
Type: Co-educational Day
No of pupils: B42 G36
Special Needs: AUT MLD W

KELBOURNE SCHOOL
109 Hotspur Street, Glasgow
G20 8LH
Tel: (0141) 946 1405
Head: Mrs M McIntosh
Type: Co-educational Day 2–12
No of pupils: B25 G27
Special Needs: **CP EPI MLD PH**
SP&LD SPLD VIS W

KELVIN SCHOOL
69 Nairn Street, Glasgow, Strathclyde
G3 8SE
Tel: (0141) 339 5835
Head: Sister P Gribben
Type: Co-educational Day 3–16
No of pupils: 41
Special Needs: AUT CP DEL EBD EPI
HI MLD PH PMLD SLD SP&LD
VIS W

KENNYHILL SCHOOL
375 Cumbernauld Road, Glasgow
G31 3LP
Tel: (0141) 554 2765
Head: Miss I Orr
Type: Co-educational Day 12–19
No of pupils: 120
Special Needs: **MLD**

KIRKRIGGS SCHOOL
500 Croftfoot Road, Glasgow
G45 0NJ
Tel: (0141) 634 7158
Head: Mr F Muldoon
Type: Co-educational Day 5–12
No of pupils: B38 G23
Special Needs: AUT MLD SLD

LADYWELL SCHOOL
12A Victoria Park Drive South,
Glasgow G14 9RU
Tel: (0141) 959 6665
Head: Ms A Bombelli
Type: Co-educational Day 12–16

LANGLANDS SCHOOL
100 Mallaig Road, Glasgow G51 4PE
Tel: (0141) 445 1132
Head: Mrs W Crawford
Type: Co-educational

LINBURN SCHOOL
77 Linburn Road, Penilee, Glasgow
G52 4EX
Tel: (0141) 883 2082
Head: Mrs M Hardie
Type: Co-educational Day 12–18
No of pupils: B28 G16
Special Needs: PMLD SLD W

MIDDLEFIELD SCHOOL
26 Partickhill Road, Glasgow
G11 5BP
Tel: (0141) 334 0159
Head: Ms L McKenna
Type: Co-educational Day and
Boarding 5–16
No of pupils: 24
Special Needs: ASP AUT

MILTON SCHOOL
6 Liddesdale Terrace, Glasgow
G51 4PE
Tel: (0141) 762 2102
Head: Mrs E McCallum
Type: Co-educational

NEWHILLS SCHOOL
Newhills Road, Glasgow G33 4HJ
Tel: (0141) 773 1296
Head: Mrs M Mimnagh
Type: Co-educational Day 12–18
No of pupils: B26 G24
Special Needs: PMLD SLD W

PARKHEAD PRE-SCHOOL
1346 Gallowgate, Glasgow G31 4DJ
Tel: (0141) 551 9591
Head: Mrs M Morris

PENILEE SECONDARY SCHOOL
11 Craigmuir Road, Glasgow
G52 4DW
Tel: (0141) 883 8878
Head: Ms J Leeming
Type: Co-educational
No of pupils: 7

RICHMOND PARK SCHOOL
30 Logan Street, Glasgow G5 0HP
Tel: (0141) 429 6095
Head: Mrs M Pollard
Type: Co-educational Day 4–11
No of pupils: 100
Special Needs: CP EPI MLD PH SP&LD

ROSEPARK TUTORIAL CENTRE
Floor 2, Room 9, C/o Thornwood
Primary, 11 Thornwood Avenue,
Glasgow G11 7QZ
Tel: (0141) 334 5700
Head: Miss M Brown

ROSEVALE SCHOOL
48 Scalpay Street, Glasgow G22 7DD
Tel: (0141) 772 1756
Head: Ms C Fraser
Type: Co-educational

ROYSTON LANGUAGE UNIT
C/o Royston Primary, 102 Royston
Road, Glasgow G21 2NU
Tel: (0141) 552 1673
Head: Ms M McArthur
Type: Co-educational Day
No of pupils: 24
Special Needs: SP&LD

RUCHILL COMMUNICATION UNIT
C/o St Charles' Primary, 13
Kelvinside Gardens, Glasgow
G20 9HW
Tel: (0141) 948 0073
Head: Ms H Barr

ST AIDAN'S SCHOOL
255 Rigby Street, Glasgow G32 6DJ
Tel: (0141) 556 6276
Head: Mr A G McDonald
Type: Co-educational

ST CHARLES' LANGUAGE UNIT
C/o St Charles' Primary, 13
Kelvinside Gardens, Glasgow
G20 6BG
Tel: (0141) 945 2121
Head: Ms J Ross
Type: Co-educational

ST JOAN OF ARC SCHOOL
722 Balmore Road, Glasgow G22 6QS
Tel: (0141) 336 6885
Head: Miss M McCusker
Type: Co-educational Day 12–19
No of pupils: B44 G56
Special Needs: **MLD** SPLD

ST JOSEPH'S HEARING IMPAIRED UNIT
C/o St Joseph's Primary, 39 Raglan
Street, Glasgow G4 9QX
Tel: (0141) 353 6136
Head: Ms V O'Hagan
Type: Co-educational

ST KEVIN'S SCHOOL
25 Fountainwell Road, Glasgow
G21 1TN
Tel: (0141) 557 3722
Head: Miss M T Gallagher
Type: Co-educational Day 5–12
No of pupils: 70
Special Needs: **EBD MLD SP&LD** W

ST OSWALD'S SCHOOL
83 Brunton Street, Glasgow G44 3NF
Tel: (0141) 637 3952
Head: Mr G McDonnell
Type: Co-educational Day 12–16
No of pupils: B76 G60
Special Needs: AUT DYS **MLD**

ST RAYMOND'S SCHOOL
384 Drakemire Drive, Glasgow
G45 9SR
Tel: (0141) 634 1551
Head: Mrs E Muchan
Type: Co-educational Day 5–11
No of pupils: B26 G15
Special Needs: ADD ADHD AUT
DOW DYP DYS EBD EPI HI MLD PH
SP&LD SPLD W

ST ROCH'S SECONDARY SCHOOL
Hearing Impairment Unit, 40
Royston Road, Glasgow G21 2NF
Tel: (0141) 582 0270
Head: Mrs E Orr
Type: Co-educational Day
No of pupils: 25
Special Needs: HI

ST THOMAS AQUINAS UNIT
C/o St Thomas Aquinas Secondary,
80 Westland Drive, Glasgow
G14 9PG
Tel: (0141) 958 0774
Head: Mr D Swann and Mr David
Swann
Type: Co-educational Day
No of pupils: B17 G6
Special Needs: SP&LD

ST VINCENT'S (TOLLCROSS) SCHOOL
30 Fullarton Avenue, Tollcross,
Glasgow G32 8NJ
Tel: (0141) 778 2254
Head: Mrs A Crilly
Type: Co-educational Day 2–16
No of pupils: 40
Special Needs: HI W

ST VINCENT'S UNIT
C/o St Vincent's Primary, 40 Crebar
Street, Glasgow G46 8EQ
Tel: (0141) 621 1968
Head: Ms I McAllister
Type: Co-educational

TORYGLEN COMMUNICATION DISORDER UNIT
6 Drummreoch Place, Glasgow
G42 0ER
Tel: (0141) 613 3840
Head: Ms R Russell
Type: Co-educational Day
No of pupils: 24
Special Needs: ASP AUT

UDDINGSTON GRAMMAR SCHOOL
Station Road, Uddingston, Glasgow
G71 7BS
Tel: (01698) 327400
Head: Mr D Greenshields
Type: Co-educational Day
No of pupils: B605 G645
Special Needs: SPLD VIS

HIGHLAND

Highland Education Authority

Glenurquhart Road
Inverness IV3 5NX
Tel: (01463) 702000

DRUMMOND SCHOOL
Drummond Road, Inverness,
Highland IV2 4NZ
Tel: (01463) 233091
Head: Mr M Butler
Type: Co-educational Day 2–19
No of pupils: 122
Special Needs: AUT MLD PMLD
SLD W

ST CLEMENT'S SCHOOL
Tulloch Street, Dingwall, Highland
IV15 9JZ
Tel: (01349) 863284
Head: Mrs J Livingstone
Type: Co-educational Day Boys 5–16
Girls 3–17
No of pupils: B11 G13

ST CLEMENT'S SCHOOL
Old Academy, Dingwall, Highland
IV15 9JZ
Tel: (01349) 63284
Head: Mrs J Livingstone
Type: Co-educational Day 3–19
No of pupils: 40
Special Needs: AUT SLD W

ST DUTHUS SCHOOL
Old Academy, Tain, Highland
IV19 1ED
Tel: (01862) 894407
Head: Mrs M MacKenzie
Type: Co-educational Day 3–19
No of pupils: B11 G5
Special Needs: ASP AUT DOW EBD
PMLD SLD W

INVERCLYDE

Inverclyde Education Authority

105 Dalrymple Street
Greenock
Renfrewshire PA15 1HT
Tel: (01475) 712850

GARVEL SCHOOL
Chester Road, Larkfield, Greenock,
Inverclyde PA16 0TT
Tel: (01475) 635477
Head: Ms C Tulloch
Type: Co-educational Day 2–11
No of pupils: B3 G5
Special Needs: HI W

GLENBURN SCHOOL
Inverkip Road, Greenock, Inverclyde
PA16 0QG
Tel: (01475) 715400
Head: Mrs E McGeer
Type: Co-educational Day
No of pupils: B59 G32
Special Needs: MLD SP&LD W

HIGHLANDERS ACADEMY PRIMARY SCHOOL
24 Mount Pleasant Street, Greenock,
Inverclyde PA15 4DP
Tel: (01475) 745121
Head: Mr C McConnachie
Type: Co-educational Day 5–11
No of pupils: 12
Special Needs: SP&LD

LILYBANK SCHOOL
Birkmyre Avenue, Port Glasgow,
Inverclyde PA14 5AN
Tel: (01475) 715703
Head: Ms E Stewart
Type: Co-educational Day 5–18
No of pupils: B40 G13
Special Needs: AUT CP DOW EPI
PMLD SLD W

NORTH LANARKSHIRE

North Lanarkshire Education Authority

Municipal Buildings
Kildonan Street
Coatbridge
Lanarkshire ML5 3BT
Tel: (01236) 812222

BOTHWELL PARK SCHOOL
Annan Street, Motherwell, North
Lanarkshire ML1 2DL
Tel: (01698) 230700
Head: Mrs B McFarlane
Type: Co-educational Day 12–18
No of pupils: 23

CLYDEVIEW SCHOOL
Magna Street, Motherwell, North
Lanarkshire ML1 3QZ
Tel: (01698) 264843
Head: Mrs A D Donaldson
Type: Co-educational Day 3–12
No of pupils: B22 G9
Special Needs: SLD SP&LD

DRUMPARK SCHOOL
Coatbridge Road, Bargeddie, North
Lanarkshire G69 7TW
Tel: (01236) 423955
Head: Mrs M Sutherland
Type: Co-educational Day 4–19
No of pupils: B92 G80
Special Needs: ASP DOW **MLD** SLD
SP&LD W

FALLSIDE SCHOOL
Sanderson Avenue, View Park,
Uddington, North Lanarkshire
G71 6JZ
Tel: (01698) 747721
Head: C McGarvey
Type: Co-educational Day 12–18
No of pupils: 30

FIRPARK SCHOOL
Firpark Street, Motherwell, North
Lanarkshire ML1 2PR
Tel: (01698) 251313
Head: Mr J Connelly
Type: Co-educational Day 3–18
No of pupils: 210
Special Needs: AUT CP DOW DYP
DYS EBD EPI HI MLD PH **SLD**
SP&LD SPLD VIS W

GLENCRYAN SCHOOL
Greenfaulds Ring Road,
Cumbernauld, North Lanarkshire
G67 2XJ
Tel: (01236) 724125
Head: Mrs A B Irvine
Type: Co-educational Day 3–18
No of pupils: 142
Special Needs: ADD ASP DEL DOW
DYC DYP DYS HI MLD PH SP&LD
SPLD TOU VIS W

MAVISBANK SCHOOL
Mitchell Street, Airdrie, North
Lanarkshire ML6 0EB
Tel: (01236) 752725
Head: Mrs M J McGurl
Type: Co-educational 2–19
No of pupils: B18 G15
Special Needs: **PMLD** W

PENTLAND SCHOOL
Pentland Road, Coatbridge, North
Lanarkshire ML5 2NA
Tel: (0141) 779 3351
Head: Mr I Porteous
Type: Co-educational Day 5–12
No of pupils: B13 G2
Special Needs: EBD

PORTLAND HIGH SCHOOL
31 - 33 Kildonan Street, Coatbridge,
North Lanarkshire ML5 3LG
Tel: (01236) 440634
Head: L Innes
Type: Co-educational 12–16
No of pupils: 30

REDBURN
Mossknowe Building, Kildrum Ring
Road, Cumbernauld, North
Lanarkshire G67 2EL
Tel: (01236) 736904
Head: Ms M H O'Brien
Type: Co-educational Day 2–19
No of pupils: B34 G18
Special Needs: AUT CP DOW EBD
EPI PH PMLD SLD SP&LD VIS W

VIEWPARK SUPPORT CENTRE
Viewpark Community Centre, Old
Edinburgh Road, Uddingston,
Lanarkshire G71 6HL
Tel: (01698) 811215
Head: Mr V Jack
Type: Co-educational Day
No of pupils: 25
Special Needs: EBD

WILLOWBANK SCHOOL
299 Bank Street, Coatbridge, North
Lanarkshire ML5 1EG
Tel: (01236) 421911
Head: Mr V Jack
Type: Co-educational Day 11–17
No of pupils: 55
Special Needs: EBD

SOUTH LANARKSHIRE

South Lanarkshire Education Authority

Council Offices
Almada Street
Hamilton
Lanarkshire ML3 0AE
Tel: (01698) 454379

CRAIGHEAD SCHOOL
Whistleberry Road, Hamilton, South
Lanarkshire ML3 0EG
Tel: (01698) 285678
Head: Mr J McEnaney
Type: Co-educational Day 5–18
No of pupils: B156 G74
Special Needs: ASP AUT DYP **MLD PH**
SLD W

EARLY LEARNING UNIT
Avon School, Carlisle Road,
Hamilton, South Lanarkshire
ML3 7EW
Tel: (01698) 281228
Head: Mrs C Young
Type: Co-educational Day 3–5
No of pupils: B22 G8
Special Needs: ADD ASP AUT CP
DOW EPI HI MLD PH SP&LD VIS W

HAMILTON SCHOOL FOR THE DEAF
Wellhall Road, Hamilton, South
Lanarkshire ML3 9UE
Tel: (01698) 286618
Head: Ms J Gorman
Type: Co-educational Day 3–11
No of pupils: B13 G6
Special Needs: **HI** W

NERSTON RESIDENTIAL SCHOOL
Nerston, East Kilbride, South
Lanarkshire G74 4PD
Tel: (01355) 279 242
Head: Mrs M Roberts
Type: Co-educational

SANDERSON HIGH SCHOOL
High Common Road, St Leonards's,
East Kilbride, South Lanarkshire
G74 2LX
Tel: (01355) 249073
Head: Ms M McLullich
Type: Co-educational Day 11–18
No of pupils: B34 G19
Special Needs: ADHD ASP AUT CP
DOW DYP EPI HI MLD PMLD SLD
SP&LD VIS W

VICTORIA PARK SCHOOL
Market Road, Carluke, South
Lanarkshire ML8 4BE
Tel: (01555) 750591
Head: Mrs M Constable
Type: Co-educational Day 3–18
No of pupils: 65
Special Needs: AUT CP DOW EBD
EPI PH PMLD SLD SP&LD SPLD
VIS W

WEST MAINS SCHOOL
Logie Park, East Kilbride, South
Lanarkshire G74 4BU
Tel: (013552) 49938
Head: Mrs M Campbell
Type: Co-educational Day 5–9
No of pupils: B23 G3
Special Needs: SP&LD

MIDLOTHIAN

**Midlothian Education
Authority**

Fairfield House
8 Lothian Road
Dalkeith
Midlothian EH22 3ZG
Tel: (0131) 271 3718

SALTERSGATE SCHOOL
Lugton Brae, Dalkeith, Midlothian
EH22 1JX
Tel: (0131) 663 7146
Head: Mrs L Walker
Type: Co-educational Day 5–18
No of pupils: B89 G40
Special Needs: ADD AUT DEL DOW
DYS EBD EPI MLD SLD SP&LD
SPLD W

WEST LOTHIAN

**West Lothian Education
Authority**

Lindsay House
South Bridge Street
Bathgate
West Lothian EH48 1TS
Tel: (01506) 776000

BEATLIE SPECIAL SCHOOL
The Mall, Craigshill, Livingston,
Lothian EH54 5EJ
Tel: (01506) 777598
Head: Ms K E White
Type: Co-educational Day 3–16
No of pupils: 34

BURNHOUSE SCHOOL
The Avenue, Whitburn, West
Lothian EH47 0BX
Tel: (01501) 678100
Head: Ms K McNairney
Type: Co-educational Day 10–16

**CEDARBANK SPECIAL
SCHOOL**
Cedarbank, Ladywell East,
Livingston, Lothian EH54 6DR
Tel: (01506) 442172
Head: Mrs D McPhail
Type: Co-educational Day 3–16
No of pupils: 50

**PINEWOOD SPECIAL
SCHOOL**
Elm Grove, Blackburn, Bathgate,
West Lothian EH47 7OX
Tel: (01506) 56374
Head: Mrs R Bayne
Type: Co-educational Day 5–18

MORAYSHIRE

Moray Education Authority

The Moray Council
High Street
Elgin
Morayshire IV30 1BX
Tel: (01343) 563267

KINLOSS SCHOOL
Burghead Road, Kinloss, Morayshire
IV36 3SX
Tel: (01309) 690376
Head: Mr I Brodie
Type: Co-educational Day
No of pupils: B2 G1
Special Needs: ASP AUT

ORKNEY

Orkney Education Authority

Council Offices
Kirkwall
Orkney KW15 1NY
Tel: (01856) 873535

GLAITNESS AURRIDA SPECIAL SCHOOL
Pickaquoy Road, Kirkwall, Orkney
KW15 1RP
Tel: (01856) 870330
Head: Mr T Delaney
Type: Co-educational Day and
Boarding 2–18
No of pupils: B14 G7
Special Needs: MLD PMLD SLD W

PERTH AND KINROSS

Perth and Kinross Education Authority

Pullar House
35 Kinnoull Street
Perth PH1 5GD
Tel: (01738) 476200

CHERRYBANK SCHOOL
Viewlands Terrace, Perth, Perth and
Kinross PH2 0LZ
Tel: (01738) 622147
Head: Mr G Hutchison
Type: Co-educational Day 2–11
No of pupils: 25
Special Needs: AUT PMLD SLD W

THE GLEBE SCHOOL
Abbey Road, Scone, Perth, Perth and
Kinross PH2 6LW
Tel: (01738) 551493
Head: Mrs N Guthrie
Type: Co-educational Day and
Boarding 10–18
No of pupils: B15 G6
No of Boarders: W12
Special Needs: CP EPI MLD PMLD
SP&LD VIS

ROBERT DOUGLAS MEMORIAL P.S (AUTISTIC UNIT)
Spoutwells Road, Scone, Perth, Perth
and Kinross PH2 6RS
Tel: (01738) 551136
Head: Mr D F Campbell
Type: Co-educational Day
No of pupils: B10 G2
Special Needs: AUT

RENFREWSHIRE

Renfrewshire Education Authority

South Building
Cotton Street
Paisley PA1 1LE
Tel: (0141) 842 5663

CLIPPENS SCHOOL
Brediland Road, Linwood,
Renfrewshire PA3 3RX
Tel: (01505) 325333
Head: Mrs O Clark
Type: Co-educational Day 5–19
No of pupils: 46
Special Needs: AUT PMLD SLD W

GATESIDE SCHOOL SENSORY IMPAIRMENT SERVICE
Craigelinn Avenue, Paisley,
Renfrewshire PA2 8RH
Tel: (0141) 884 2090
Head: Mrs E Quinn
Type: Co-educational Day 5–18
No of pupils: B65 G56
Special Needs: HI VIS

HUNTERHILL TUTORIAL CENTRE
Cartha Crescent, Paisley,
Renfrewshire PA2 7EL
Tel: (0141) 889 6876
Head: Mrs R Campbell
Type: Boys Day 5–11
No of pupils: 21
Special Needs: ADD ADHD DYS EBD

KERSLAND SCHOOL
Ben Nevis Road, Paisley,
Renfrewshire PA2 7BU
Tel: (0141) 889 8251
Head: Mrs C Jackson
Type: Co-educational Day 5–18
No of pupils: B33 G30
Special Needs: AUT SLD W

SCOTTISH BORDERS

Scottish Borders Education Authority

Council Headquarters
Newtown St Boswells
Melrose
Roxburghshire TD6 0SA
Tel: (01835) 824000

BERWICKSHIRE HIGH SCHOOL SPECIAL UNIT

Duns, Scottish Borders TD11 3QQ
Tel: (01361) 883710
Head: Mr R F Kelly
Type: Co-educational Day
Special Needs: DOW MLD PH SLD SPLD W

COLDSTREAM PRIMARY SCHOOL

Coldstream, Berwickshire, Scottish Borders TD12 4DT
Tel: (01890) 882189
Head: Mr M Kerr
Type: Co-educational Day
No of pupils: B92 G92
Special Needs: SP&LD

EARLSTON PRIMARY SCHOOL

Earlston, Berwickshire, Scottish Borders TD4 6JQ
Tel: (01896) 848851
Head: Mr C Maclean
Type: Co-educational Day
No of pupils: B105 G100
Special Needs: HI W

KELSO HIGH SCHOOL SPECIAL UNIT

Bowmont Street, Kelso, Scottish Borders TD5 7EG
Tel: (01573) 224444
Head: Mr A Johnston
Type: Co-educational Day
Special Needs: ADHD CP DYS EBD EPI MLD SP&LD SPLD

PHILLIPHAUGH COMMUNITY SCHOOL

2 Linglie Road, Selkirk, Scottish Borders TD7 5JJ
Tel: (01750) 21774
Head: Mr S Vannan
Type: Co-educational Day
No of pupils: 18
Special Needs: SP&LD W

WILTON PRIMARY SCHOOL SPECIAL SCHOOL

Wellfield Road, Hawick, Scottish Borders TD9 7EN
Tel: (01450) 272075
Head: Mr I Topping
Type: Co-educational Day 5–13
No of pupils: 27
Special Needs: CP DYS EBD EPI MLD PH PMLD SLD W

STIRLING

Stirling Education Authority

Viewforth
Stirling FK8 2ET
Tel: (01786) 443322

CALLANDER PRIMARY SCHOOL

Bridgend, Callander, Stirling FK17 8AG
Tel: (01877) 331576
Type: Co-educational Day
No of pupils: B12 G2
Special Needs: ADD AUT DOW DYP DYS EBD MLD SP&LD SPLD

CHARLES BROWN SCHOOL

Fallin Primary School, Lamont Crescent, Fallin, Stirling FK7 7EJ
Tel: (01786) 816756
Head: Mrs J Smith
Type: Co-educational Day
No of pupils: B6 G5
Special Needs: PH W

WESTERN ISLES

Western Isles Education Authority

Stornoway
Isle of Lewis HS1 2BW
Tel: (01851) 703773

STORNOWAY PRIMARY SCHOOL SPECIAL CLASS

Stornoway, Western Isles HS1 2LF
Tel: (01851) 704700
Head: Mrs G L Veals
Type: Co-educational Day
No of pupils: B6 G2
Special Needs: AUT DOW PMLD SLD W

WALES

ANGLESEY

Isle of Anglesey City Council

Ffordd Glanhwfa
Llangefni
Anglesey LL77 7EY
Tel: (01248) 752900

YSGOL Y BONT
The Industrial Estate, Llangefni,
Anglesey LL77 7JA
Tel: (01248) 750151
Head: Mr D Hughes
Type: Co-educational Day 3–19
Special Needs: MLD PMLD SLD

GWENT

Blaenau Gwent County Borough

Education Department
Victoria House
Victoria Business Park
Victoria
Ebbw Vale NP23 8ER
Tel: (01495) 355437

PEN Y CWM SCHOOL
Beaufort Hill, Ebbw Vale, Gwent
NP23 5QG
Tel: (01495) 304031
Head: Mr R Dickenson
Type: Co-educational Day
No of pupils: B35 G25
Special Needs: PMLD SLD W

BRIDGEND

Bridgend County Borough

Education Services
Sunnyside
Bridgend CF31 4AR
Tel: (01656) 642610

HERONSBRIDGE SCHOOL
Ewenny Road, Bridgend CF31 3HT
Tel: (01656) 653974
Head: Mr C D Major
Type: Co-educational Boarding and
Day 3–19
No of pupils: B110 G55
No of Boarders: W7
Special Needs: ASP AUT CP DOW EPI
PMLD SLD VIS W

YSGOL BRYN CASTELL
Llangewydd Road, Cefn Glas,
Bridgend CF31 4JP
Tel: (01656) 767517
Head: Mr G Le Page
Type: Co-educational Boarding and
Day 8–16
No of pupils: 187 *No of Boarders:* W26
Special Needs: ADHD ASP **EBD** MLD
SLD SP&LD

CAERPHILLY

Caerphilly County Borough

Education Offices
Caerphilly Road
Ystrad Mynach
Hengoed CF82 7EP
Tel: (01443) 864956

**TRINITY FIELDS SCHOOL &
RESOURCE CENTRE**
Caerphilly Road, Ystrad Mynach,
Hengoed, Caerphilly CF82 7XW
Tel: (01443) 866000
Head: Mr M Hughes
Type: Co-educational Day 3–19
No of pupils: 133
Special Needs: PMLD SLD

CARDIFF

Cardiff Education Authority

County Hall
Atlantic Wharf
Cardiff CF10 4UW
Tel: (029) 2087 2000

THE COURT SCHOOL
96a Station Road, Llanishen, Cardiff
CF4 5UX
Tel: (029) 2075 2713
Head: Mrs G Unwin
Type: Co-educational Day 5–11
No of pupils: 35
Special Needs: ADD ADHD DYP **EBD**
MLD

GREENHILL SCHOOL
Heol Brynglas, Rhiwbina, Cardiff
CF4 6UJ
Tel: (029) 2069 3786
Head: Mr A R Lewis
Type: Co-educational Day 11–16
No of pupils: B55 G1
Special Needs: **EBD**

THE HOLLIES SCHOOL
Pentwyn Drive, Pentwyn, Cardiff
CF2 7XG
Tel: (029) 2073 4411
Head: Mrs C M Matthews
Type: Co-educational Day 3–11
No of pupils: 92
Special Needs: ADD ADHD ASP AUT
CP **PH SP&LD** SPLD W

MEADOWBANK SCHOOL
Colwill Road, Gabalfa, Cardiff
CF14 2QQ
Tel: (029) 2061 6018
Head: Mrs C Arthurs
Type: Co-educational Day 5–11
No of pupils: B31 G7
Special Needs: **SP&LD**

RIVERBANK SCHOOL
Vincent Road, Ely, Cardiff CF5 5AQ
Tel: (029) 2056 3860
Head: Mrs G A Evans
Type: Co-educational Day 4–11
No of pupils: 70
Special Needs: ADHD AUT CP DOW
DYP EBD EPI HI **MLD** PH **SLD**
SP&LD

TY GWYN SCHOOL
Ty Gwyn Road, Penylan, Cardiff
CF23 5JG
Tel: (029) 2048 5570
Head: Mr D Dwyer
Type: Co-educational Day 3–19
No of pupils: B41 G41
Special Needs: **PMLD** SLD W

WOODLANDS SCHOOL
Vincent Road, Ely, Cardiff CF5 5AQ
Tel: (029) 2056 1279
Head: Mrs E Dunne
Type: Co-educational Day 11–19

CARMARTHENSHIRE

Carmarthenshire County Council

Education Services Department
Pibwrlwyd
Carmarthen SA31 2NH
Tel: (01267) 224532

YSGOL HEOL GOFFA
Heol Goffa, Llanelli,
Carmarthenshire SA15 3LS
Tel: (01554) 759465
Head: Mr R A Davies
Type: Co-educational Day 2–19
No of pupils: 73
Special Needs: CP EPI **PMLD SLD** W

CONWY

Conwy County Borough

Government Buildings
Dinerth Road
Colwyn Bay
Conwy LL28 4UL
Tel: (01492) 575001

CANOLFAN ADDYSG Y GOGARTH
Ffordd Nant y Gamar, Llandudno,
Conwy LL30 1YF
Tel: (01492) 860077
Head: Mr I G Jones
Type: Co-educational Boarding and
Day 3–19
No of pupils: B73 G48
No of Boarders: F17 W11
Special Needs: ADHD ASP AUT CP
DOW EPI HI **MLD PH** PMLD SLD
SP&LD VIS W

CEDAR COURT SCHOOL
65 Victoria Park, Colwyn Bay,
Conwy LL29 7AJ
Tel: (01492) 533199
Head: Mrs P M Stanley
Type: Co-educational Boarding and
Day 11–18
No of pupils: B12 G6
No of Boarders: W12
Special Needs: **EBD**

YSGOL Y GRAIG
Penrhos Avenue, Colwyn Bay,
Conwy LL29 9HW
Tel: (01492) 516838
Head: Mr J Hewitt
Type: Co-educational Boarding 3–19
Special Needs: AUT CP EBD EPI HI
PH PMLD SLD SP&LD SPLD VIS

DENBIGHSHIRE

Denbighshire Education Authority

Caledfryn
Smithfield Road
Denbigh LL16 3RJ
Tel: (01824) 706777

RHUALLT PUPIL REFERRAL UNIT
Rhuallt, St Asaph, Denbighshire
LL18 0TD
Tel: (01745) 583375
Head: Mr D H O Messum
Type: Co-educational Day
No of pupils: B54 G15
Special Needs: ADD ADHD DEL **EBD**
MLD

YSGOL PLAS BRONDYFFRYN
Ystrad Road, Denbigh, Denbighshire
LL11 4RH
Tel: (01745) 813841
Head: Dr M Toman
Type: Co-educational Boarding and
Day 3–19
No of pupils: B79 G16
No of Boarders: W30
Special Needs: **ASP AUT** EPI SP&LD

YSGOL TIRMORFA
Ffordd Derwen, Rhyl, Denbighshire
LL18 2RN
Tel: (01745) 350388
Head: Mr S Murphy
Type: Co-educational Day 3–19
No of pupils: 175
Special Needs: ADD DOW **EBD** EPI
HI **MLD** PH **SLD** SP&LD VIS W

FLINTSHIRE

Flintshire Education Authority

County Hall
Mold
Flintshire CH7 6ND
Tel: (01352) 704010

YSGOL BELMONT
Windmill Road, Buckley, Flintshire
CH7 3HA
Tel: (01244) 543971/546358
Head: Mr D G Jones
Type: Co-educational Day 2–19
No of pupils: B100 G56
Special Needs: CP EPI MLD PH SLD

YSGOL DELYN
Alexandra Road, Mold, Flintshire
CH7 1HJ
Tel: (01352) 755701
Head: Mrs V Newman
Type: Co-educational Day 2–19
No of pupils: 55
Special Needs: ADD ADHD ASP AUT
CP DEL DEL DOW DYP DYS EBD
EPI EPI HI MLD PH **PMLD SLD**
SP&LD SPLD VIS W

YSGOL Y BRYN
King George Street, Shotton,
Flintshire CH5 1EA
Tel: (01244) 830281
Head: Mrs S A Taylor
Type: Co-educational Day 2–19
No of pupils: B41 G18
Special Needs: AUT PMLD **SLD** W

GWYNEDD

Gwynedd Education Authority

County Offices
Shirehall Street
Caernarfon
Gwynedd LL55 1SH
Tel: (01286) 672255

YSGOL COEDMENAI

Bangor, Gwynedd LL57 2RX
Tel: (01248) 353527
Head: Mr J O Grisdale
Type: Co-educational Boarding 9–16
No of pupils: 45 *No of Boarders:* W23
Special Needs: **EBD**

YSGOL HAFOD LON

Y Ffor, Pwllheli, Gwynedd LL53 6UD
Tel: (01766) 810626
Head: Mrs D R Davies
Type: Co-educational Day 4–19
No of pupils: 25
Special Needs: ADHD AUT **CP DOW**
EPI PH **PMLD** SLD SP&LD SPLD W

YSGOL PENDALAR

Victoria Road, Caernarfon, Gwynedd
LL55 2RN
Tel: (01286) 672141
Head: Mr E Jones
Type: Co-educational Day 2–19
No of pupils: 72
Special Needs: **AUT** EPI MLD **PMLD**
SLD SP&LD SPLD W

MERTHYR TYDFIL

Merthyr Tydfil Education Authority

Ty Keir Hardie
Riverside Court
Avenue De Clichy
Merthyr Tydfil CF47 8XD
Tel: (01685 724600

GREENFIELD SPECIAL SCHOOL

Duffryn Road, Pentrebach, Merthyr
Tydfil CF48 4BJ
Tel: (01443) 690468
Head: Mr A Blake
Type: Co-educational Day 2–19
No of pupils: 145
Special Needs: **MLD** PH **PMLD SLD**
SP&LD W

MONMOUTHSHIRE

Monmouthshire County Council

County Hall
Cwmbran
Torfaen NP44 2XH
Tel: (01633) 644498

MOUNTON HOUSE SCHOOL

Pwyllmeyric, Chepstow,
Monmouthshire NP6 6LA
Tel: (01291) 622014
Head: Mr R A Hughes
Type: Boys Day and Boarding
No of pupils: 58 *No of Boarders:* W30
Special Needs: EBD MLD

NEATH PORT TALBOT

Neath Port Talbot

Civic Centre
Port Talbot SA13 1PJ
Tel: (01639) 763298

BRITON FERRY SPECIAL SCHOOL
Ynysmaerdy Road, Briton Ferry,
Neath Port Talbot SA11 2TL
Tel: (01639) 813100
Head: Mrs M Scales
Type: Co-educational Day 2–19
No of pupils: B14 G14
Special Needs: PMLD SLD W

YSGOL HENDRE SPECIAL SCHOOL
Main Road, Bryncoch, Neath, Neath
Port Talbot SA10 7TY
Tel: (01639) 642786
Head: Mr P H Smith
Type: Co-educational Boarding
No of pupils: B70 G20
No of Boarders: W10
Special Needs: ADD ADHD DOW DYS
EBD EPI **MLD** SLD

NEWPORT

Newport Education Authority

Civic Centre
Newport NP20 4UR
Tel: (01633) 233473

MAES EBBW SCHOOL
Maesglas Road, Malpas, South
Wales, Newport NP20 3DG
Tel: (01633) 855170
Head: Mrs L Meyrick
Type: Co-educational Day 3–19
No of pupils: 84
Special Needs: PMLD SLD SPLD W

POWYS

Powys City Council

County Hall
Llandrindod Wells LD1 5LG
Tel: (01597) 826000

BRYNLLYWARCH HALL SCHOOL
Kerry, Newtown, Powys SY16 4PB
Tel: (01686) 670276
Head: Mr D C Williams
Type: Co-educational Boarding and
Day
No of pupils: B35 G19
No of Boarders: W28
Special Needs: ADD ASP **EBD MLD**

YSGOL CEDEWAIN
Maesyrhandir, Newtown, Powys
SY16 1LH
Tel: (01686) 627454
Head: Mr P A Tudor
Type: Co-educational Day 2–19
No of pupils: 40
Special Needs: PMLD **SLD** SP&LD
VIS W

YSGOL PENMAES
Canal Road, Brecon, Powys LD3 7HL
Tel: (01874) 623508
Head: Mr I Elliott
Type: Co-educational Day 2–19
No of pupils: 48
Special Needs: AUT PMLD SLD W

RHONDDA CYNON TAFF

Rhondda Cynon Taff Education Authority

The Education Centre
Grawen Street
Porth CF39 0BU
Tel: (01443) 687666

PARK LANE SPECIAL SCHOOL

Park Lane, Trecynon, Aberdare,
Rhondda Cynon Taff CF44 8HN
Tel: (01685) 874489
Head: Mr C R Jones
Type: Co-educational
No of pupils: 53
Special Needs: AUT CP DOW EBD
EPI HI PMLD **SLD** SP&LD VIS W

RHONDDA SPECIAL SCHOOL

Brithweunydd Road, Trealaw,
Tonypandy, Rhondda Cynon Taff
CF40 2UH
Tel: (01443) 433046
Head: Mrs H Dando
Type: Co-educational
No of pupils: B47 G21
Special Needs: PMLD SLD W

YSGOL TY COCH

Lansdale Drive, Tonteg, Pontypridd,
Rhondda Cynon Taff CF38 1PG
Tel: (01443) 203471
Head: Mr H Hodges
Type: Co-educational Boarding 3–19
No of pupils: B47 G31
No of Boarders: W11
Special Needs: ASP AUT CP DOW
EBD EPI HI PMLD SLD VIS W

SWANSEA

Swansea City & County Council

County Hall
Swansea SA1 3SN
Tel: (01792) 636000

PENBRYN SPECIAL SCHOOL

Glasbury Road, Morriston, Swansea
SA6 7PA
Tel: (01792) 799064
Head: Mr A Williams
Type: Co-educational Day and
Boarding 4–19
No of pupils: 115 *No of Boarders:* W13
Special Needs: AUT **MLD** SLD

YSGOL CRUG GLAS

Croft Street, Swansea SA1 1QA
Tel: (01792) 652388
Head: Mrs E Jones
Type: Co-educational 2–19
No of pupils: B27 G23
Special Needs: **PMLD** W

TORFAEN

Torfaen County Borough

County Hall
Cwmbran
Torfaen NP44 2WN
Tel: (01633) 648610

CROWNBRIDGE SCHOOL

Greenhill Road, Sebastopol,
Pontypool, Torfaen NP4 5YW
Tel: (01782) 857030
Head: Mr R Phillips
Type: Co-educational Day 3–19
No of pupils: B47 G28
Special Needs: AUT DOW PMLD SLD
SP&LD W

VALE OF GLAMORGAN

Vale of Glamorgan Education Authority

Civic offices
Holton Road
Barry CF63 4RU
Tel: (01446) 709146

ASHGROVE SCHOOL

Sully Road, Penarth, Vale of
Glamorgan CF64 2TP
Tel: (029) 2070 4212
Head: Mr B Brayford
Type: Day and Boarding
No of pupils: 88 *No of Boarders:* W8
Special Needs: ADD **ASP AUT HI** W

YSGOL ERW'R DELYN

St Cyres Road, Penarth, Vale of
Glamorgan CF64 1WR
Tel: (029) 2070 7225
Head: Mr M Farrell
Type: Co-educational Boarding and
Day 3–19
No of pupils: B35 G22
No of Boarders: W6
Special Needs: PH PMLD

YSGOL MAES DYFAN

Gibbonsdown Rise, Barry, Vale of
Glamorgan CF6 7QZ
Tel: (01446) 732112
Head: Mr J A Aubrey
Type: Co-educational Day
No of pupils: 98
Special Needs: AUT CP DOW EPI HI
MLD SLD VIS W

WREXHAM

Wrexham Education Authority

Ty Henblas
Queen's Square
Wrexham LL13 8AZ
Tel: (01978) 297400

ST CHRISTOPHER SCHOOL

Stockwell Grove, Wrexham
LL13 7BW
Tel: (01978) 346910
Head: Mrs M P Grant
Type: Co-educational Day 5–19
No of pupils: 238
Special Needs: ADD ADHD ASP AUT
CP DEL DOW DYC DYP DYS **EBD** HI
MLD PH PMLD **SLD** SP&LD SPLD
VIS W

SPECIAL EDUCATION CENTRE

Park Avenue, Wrexham LL12 7AQ
Tel: (01978) 290101
Head: Mrs P A Pumford
Type: Co-educational Day 3–11
No of pupils: 113
Special Needs: ADD ADHD ASP AUT
CP DOW DYP EBD EPI HI MLD PH
SP&LD VIS VIS

YSGOL POWYS

Dodd's Lane, Gwersyllt, Wrexham
LL11 4PA
Tel: (01978) 755921
Head: Mr R Williams
Type: Co-educational Day 2–19
No of pupils: 42
Special Needs: AUT CP DEL DOW
EPI HI PH **PMLD SLD** SP&LD VIS

PART THREE: PROFILES OF SPECIAL SCHOOLS AND COLLEGES

3.1
Profiles of Independent and Non-maintained Special Schools

Annie Lawson School

Ravenswood Village, Nine Mile Ride, Crowthorne, Berkshire RG45 6BQ
Tel: 01344 755508   Fax: 01344 762317
E-mail: lynnemorris@annielawson.org.uk   Website: www.nwrw.org   www.gabbitas.net

Founded 1954
Religious denomination Jewish faith, students also welcome from all cultural and ethnical backgrounds
School status DfES approved independent co-educational boarding and day
Special needs provision PMLD, SLD
Other needs catered for Complex learning difficulties
Age range 11–19
Boarding from 11
No of pupils 23
Boarders (full) 20 (some day pupils)

Set in 126 acres of Berkshire countryside, the Annie Lawson School offers freedom of movement within a safe and varied natural environment.

The School aims to meet the needs of students with severe and profound learning difficulties. Many of our students have additional physical disabilities or sensory impairments or have difficulties understanding and managing their own behaviour, which gives rise to problems accessing the wider curriculum.

The Annie Lawson School is committed to meeting the individual needs of students, through a holistic approach, with priority being given to their physical and emotional well-being, communication skills and access to motivating learning experiences. Individual development is the focus of our school. Access to the National Curriculum is supported by a programme of Personal, Social and Health Education (PSHE) which puts an emphasis on individual self-esteem and personal communication.

We aim to make students feel valued by engaging them in interaction at their level, by entering into their world if they are unable or unwilling to enter ours.

Students benefit from a wide range of facilities:

- Three sensory rooms offering activities ranging from relaxation and aromatherapy to choice making and interactive environmental control
- A wide variety of IT equipment, access devices and software to support the curriculum
- Gym, with integral trampoline
- Wheelchair accessible adventure playground
- Access to onsite swimming/hydrotherapy pool and to horse riding and carting

Therapists are an integral part of our team including speech, language, music and physiotherapy.

Aran Hall School

Rhydymain, Dolgellau, Gwynedd LL40 2AR
Tel: 01341 450641   Fax: 01341 450637
E-mail: Mferguson@aranhall.demon.com
Website: www.aranhall.demon.co.uk   www.gabbitas.net

Head M Ferguson BEd, DipSpEd
Founded 1980
School status Co-educational independent boarding
Accredited by DfEE and National Assembly for Wales
Special needs provision ADD, ADHD, ASP, AUT, EPI, SLD
Other needs catered for Challenging behaviour
Age range 11–19 *boarding from* 11
No of pupils 25
Girls 6 *boys* 19

Aran Hall benefits from being within the picturesque and relaxing environment of Snowdonia National Park. It is situated within easy reach of the sea, mountains and Bala Lake. Full use is made of all these natural resources in addition to local libraries, leisure centres, riding clubs, shops and cafes to encourage integration within the community.

Individual programmes, based upon each pupil's statement of special educational needs, are implemented consistently within educational and care environments. Each pupil is a member of a small family group with a high staff ratio. There is a homely environment for twenty-five pupils.

The quality of relationships between pupils and staff is central to all our work.

Teachers and care staff work in close partnership to realise individual objectives for each pupil. These individual plans are agreed with the pupil, parents, carers, local education, health and social services departments.

Recent, very positive Ofsted inspection report is available, together with Social Services and Investors in People reports.

Barnardo's

High Close School

Wiltshire Road, Wokingham, Berkshire RG40 1TT   Tel: 0118 978 5767
Fax: 0118 989 4220   Email: high.close@barnardos.org.uk   Website: www.gabbitas.net

Principal Rose Mahony
Founded 1939
School status Co-educational non-maintained
boarding and day DfES approved independent
Special needs provision EBD, MLD, W
Age range 6–16   *boarding from* 10
No of pupils 64
Girls 26 *boys* 38
Fees per annum (boarding) £51,975 *(day)*
£25,988

High Close is a co-educational, non-maintained special school for pupils with emotional, social, behavioural and associated learning difficulties. The school has purpose-built education facilities with four on-site residential units. There are places for 44 boarders (aged 10–16) and 24 day pupils (aged 6–16). There is also a field social work team, which supports families and provides after-care to pupils when they leave at age 16.

Meadows School

London Road, Southborough, Kent TN4 0RJ   Tel: 01892 529144
Fax: 01892 527787   Email: meadows@barnardos.org   Website: www.gabbitas.net

Principal Sandy Paterson
Founded 1950
School status Co-educational non-maintained
boarding and day
Special needs provision EBD, ADHD, MLD
Age range 11–16   *boarding from* 11
No of pupils 55   *No of boarders* 38
Girls 10 *boys* 45
Fees per annum (boarding) £59,000 *(day)*
£24,500

Meadows is a co-educational, non-maintained special school for pupils with severe social, emotional, behavioural and associated learning difficulties. The school has purpose-built education facilities with two on-site and two off-site residential units. There are places for 48 boarders and 17 day pupils. Meadows has one separate residential unit for girls and three for boys.

Spring Hill School

Palace Road, Ripon, North Yorkshire HG4 3HN
Tel: 01765 603320   Website: www.gabbitas.net

Principal Janet Clarke
Founded 1950
School status Co-educational non-maintained
boarding and day
Special needs provision DEL, DOW, EBD, EPI,
MLD, SLD, W
Other needs catered for AUT, ADD
Age range 8–19   *boarding from* 10
No of pupils 39
Girls 8 *boys* 31
Fees per annum (boarding) £48,950

Spring Hill is a residential co-educational, non-maintained special school for pupils aged 8–19 who have moderate to severe learning difficulties and challenging behaviour. Some pupils have medical, emotional and psychiatric conditions with mild sensory deficits. Accommodation is for 44 pupils in four purpose-built cottages around an administrative and teaching resource block. The post-16 curriculum follows EQUALS, ASDAN, OCR key skills as well as NPTC accreditation in horticulture, catering and retail.

Bessels Leigh School

Bessels Leigh, Abingdon, Oxfordshire OX13 5QB
Tel: 01865 390436   Fax: 01865 390688   Website: www.gabbitas.net

Principal Mr J Boulton DipPsych, BEd (Hons), MEd
Founded 1962
Special needs provision ADHD, DYS, EBD, SPLD
School status Boys DfES registered non-maintained boarding
Religious denomination All
Age range 11–16
No of pupils 38
Fees per annum £48,300 (*38 weeks*); £82,950 (*52 weeks*); £43,950 (*weekly*)

Curriculum: the school aims to provide a warm, caring and supportive environment so that each boy can develop to his full potential. The school follows a curriculum which is sympathetic to the needs of the boys and is closely allied to the National Curriculum.
Entry requirements: all boys have a specific statement of special educational needs and are generally referred to the school by local education authorities or social service departments.
Examinations offered: GCSE, City and Guilds, AEB Basic Tests and Achievement tests are offered as well as vocational courses including TRIDENT, work experience and Duke of Edinburgh Awards.
Academic and leisure facilities: there are four general-purpose classrooms as well as rooms for art, science, home economics and workshop crafts. A sports hall and swimming pool complement the 23-acre site.
Special approaches: an SPLD department is growing and the school caters for dyslexic children with associated behaviour problems. An increasing number of boys have been diagnosed as being ADD/ADHD.

Birkdale School for Hearing Impaired Children

40 Lancaster Road, Birkdale, Southport, Merseyside PR8 2JY
Tel: 01704 567220   Fax: 01704 568342
E-mail: admin@birkdale-school.merseyside.org   Website: www.bshic.co.uk   www.gabbitas.net

Principal Mrs Anne Wood BA (Hons)
Founded 1825
Special needs provision ASP, DYS, DYP, HI, MLD. SP&LD
School status Non-maintained co-educational boarding and day
Religious denomination Non-denominational
Member of NASS
Age range 5–19 *boarding from* 5
No of pupils 36
Junior school 2; *Senior school* 23; *FE dept* 11
Boys 16; *girls* 20
No of boarders (termly) 3; *(weekly)* 14
Fees per annum on application

Birkdale School for Hearing Impaired Children is a non-maintained school which provides an oral education for primary and secondary aged children who have a moderate, severe or profound hearing-impairment. The school provides a broad and balanced curriculum, giving the pupils the opportunity to achieve excellent results in a wide range of GCSEs, Certificates of Achievement and GNVQ. Students are achieving 100% pass rates at A–G. Pupils are taught by qualified Teachers of the Deaf in acoustically treated classrooms. We also cater for hearing-impaired children who may have additional special needs. The audiological needs of pupils are reviewed regularly in a well-resourced Audiology Department. The Language Department works in conjunction with a Speech and Language Therapist to enhance pupils' language development. Our Further Education Support Service supports post 16 hearing-impaired students in local mainstream colleges of Further Education. Resident pupils are looked after by dedicated Care Officers.

Birtenshaw Hall School

Darwen Road, Bromley Cross, Bolton, Lancashire BL7 9AB
Tel: 01204 304230   Fax: 01204 597995   E-mail: enquiries@birtenshawhall.bolton.sch.uk
Website: www.birtenshawhall.bolton.sch.uk   www.gabbitas.net

Principal Mr C D Jamieson
School status Co-educational non-maintained
boarding and day
Member of NAIMS, NASS   *Accredited by* DfES
Special needs provision Physical disabilities with
associated learning difficulties including PMLD.
CP, DEL, EPI, MLD, PH, SLD, SP&LD, W *Other
needs catered for* unusual medical conditions
Age range 3–19   *boarding from* 7
No of pupils (boarding) (weekly) 15
Fees per annum (boarding) (full) £67,275–
£82,800; *(weekly)* £30,710–£43,143; *(day)*
£20,273–£28,853

A high staff/pupil ratio is provided by our
multi-disciplinary team of teaching, physiotherapy, occupational therapy, speech and language therapy, nursing and care staff.
Specialist facilities include swimming/hydro-
therapy pool, dark room, multi-sensory room,
MOVE groups and a wide variety of extra-
curricular activities. Our accommodation
provides a variety of recreational, dining and
bedroom facilities. Some bedrooms are
equipped with overhead tracking giving direct
access to purpose designed en-suite bathrooms.

Birtenshaw Hall offers day and residential education for pupils with physical disabilities and
associated learning difficulties. Individual programmes provide a full, varied, balanced and
relevant curriculum, including access to the
National Curriculum, suitably differentiated
to meet individual needs.

Breckenbrough School

Thirsk, North Yorkshire YO7 4EN
Tel: 01845 587238   Fax: 01845 587385

Head Mr T G Bennett
Founded 1934
School status DfES approved independent Boys
boarding and day
Religious denomination Society of Friends
Special needs provision ADD, ADHD, ASP, DEL,
DYS, EBD
Other needs catered for Emotional and
behavioural difficulties
Age range 9–17   *boarding from* 9
No of pupils 42   *boarding* 16
Fees per annum Available on request

The school has small teaching groups (up to a
maximum of seven) and has enjoyed much
success in achieving very good public examination results and re-socialisation of pupils to
take an equal place in society.
The school has an individual approach to help
each pupil build strong foundations upon
which to base their future. We offer all National
Curriculum subjects and a range of up to 12
different GCSE options.

Breckenbrough is a residential special school,
which specialises in the care and education of
boys of high academic potential who have emotional and behavioural difficulties (EBD).

Brewood Education Centre

86 London Road, Deal, Kent CT14 9TR
Tel: 01304 363000   Fax: 01304 363099   Website: www.gabbitas.net

Head Miss Chris Simcox BSc, PGCE
Founded 1995
School status Co-educational independent day
only DfES registered
Religious denomination Non-denominational
Special needs provision EBD, MLD, ADD,
ADHD, ASP, DYC, DYP, DYS, HI, SP&LD,
TOU, VIS
Age range 7–14 (Key stages 2 & 3)
No of pupils 9; *Senior* 5; *Junior* 4
Boys 7 *girls* 2
Fees per annum (day) £20,567

The school offers provision for children being
looked after either in residential settings or in
foster care, but we are also willing to consider
other children, for whom mainstream education is not immediately appropriate. The ethos
of the school is that although the children have
been assessed as EBD/MLD, they can achieve
and ultimately be considered for inclusion into
mainstream schools. The school is proud that
several of its pupils have not only been reinte-
grated into mainstream schools but have gone
on to be successful. Emphasis is placed on
praising the success of the individual and therefore promoting self-esteem. Children in the
school experience full National Curriculum
with use of a science laboratory, ICT equipment
and DT studio. The average class size is four or
less and the ratio for staff to pupils is 2:1; in
some instances 1:1 provision is offered. All the
staff are aware of the nature of problems experienced by the children and are able to provide
the therapeutic atmosphere required to achieve
positive outcomes.

Chailey Heritage School

Haywards Heath Road, North Chailey, East Sussex BN8 4EF
Tel: 01825 724444   Fax: 01825 723773
E-mail: chschool@btopenworld.com   Website: www.chs.org.uk   www.gabbitas.net

Head A C Bruce MA
Founded 1903
School status Non-maintained co-educational
boarding and day
Member of NAIMS, NASS
Accredited by DfES
Special needs provision CP, PH, MLD, SLD,
SP&LD, VIS
Age range 3–19   *Boarding from* 8
No of pupils 95
Fees per annum (boarding) (weekly) £20,034–
£30,465; *(day)* £15,642–£20,136

Chailey Heritage School is a nationally
recognised non-maintained residential special
school catering for children of all ages, who
have a wide range of physical and learning
difficulties.

The children we cater for may have:
- severe, complex, and multiple physical
  disabilities
- speech and language impairment
- communication difficulties
- a range of learning difficulties

The provision includes:
- health cover, provided by South Downs
  Health (NHS) Trust, working in close
  conjunction with school staff
- on-site Rehabilitation and Engineering Unit,
  making and maintaining special postural
  equipment.

The Charmandean Dyslexia Centre

Lillingstone Dayrell, Buckingham MK18 5AN
Tel: 01280 860182   Website: www.gabbitas.net

Head June Hawkins
Founded 1998
School status Co-educational independent day
Religious denomination Non-denominational
Age range 8–16
Girls 25 *boys* 74
Fees per annum Tuition fees £8,268

The Charmandean Dyslexia Centre, which opened in September 1998, offers a comprehensive education for pupils aged from 8 to 16 who are held back by Dyslexia and certain other learning difficulties.

Curriculum: All pupils have an Individual Education Plan outlining their needs and targets for each term. Teaching is in small classes with additional periods of intensive specialised tuition directed at overcoming specific difficulties. The main emphasis for the younger children is on English and Mathematics, using a multi-sensory approach. Science, French (mainly oral), History, Geography, Scripture, Art, Design, Music, Drama, Computing (including keyboard skills) and Study Skills all feature in the curriculum. The mainstream curriculum is followed wherever possible, but it is presented in ways best suited to individual learning patterns.

Physical education: Pupils are able to take part in a varied programme of Physical Education and Games. In the winter term the main sports for boys are rugby and football; in the summer term the main sports are cricket and athletics. For girls the winter sports are netball and hockey, with rounders, athletics and tennis in the summer. Charmandean has its own covered and heated swimming pool for use throughout the year. There is a full programme of competitive fixtures with other schools.

Drama and Music: Both Drama and Music are an integral part of the Dyslexia Centre curriculum. In addition, individual tuition can be arranged with our peripatetic teachers on a wide variety of musical instruments.

Computing: Benefiting from an up-to-date facility, the pupils are taught keyboard skills and basic computing. Those pupils for whom a laptop computer is an essential classroom aid are thus able to use it to best advantage.

Mrs Hawkins is the Head Teacher and in charge of organising and supervising the work. Every term there is a more formal parents' evening to review pupils' achievements and a detailed written report is sent home.

Entry is by interview, test and a psychological assessment arranged by the school.

Chelfham Senior School

Bere Alston, Yelverton, Devon PL20 7EX   Tel: 01822 840379   Fax: 01822 841489
Kilworthy House, Tavistock, Devon PL19 0JN   Tel: 01822 618515   Fax: 01822 618703
Website: www.gabbitas.net

Principal Ms Julia Marks
School status Boys residential DfES approved independent
Religious denomination Multi-faith
Special needs provision ASP, EBD, MLD, TOU
Age range 11–16 (Bere Alston site) 15–19 (Tavistock site)
No of pupils 37 (Bere Alston site) 26 (Tavistock site)
Fees per annum From £17,000 per term

The students who attend Chelfham Senior School have a range of emotional and behavioural difficulties with associated learning difficulties. Many of the students will have experienced failure, disappointment and criticism, resulting in feelings of inadequacy and poor self-image. They require a consistent and supportive environment in which they can gain confidence and enhance their self-esteem. The school specialises in working with emotionally vulnerable students who have difficulty with acquiring appropriate social communication skills.

Some of our young people will also have other complicating conditions and syndromes, eg, Asperger's Syndrome, Gilles de la Tourette's Syndrome and Obsessive Compulsive Disorder often exhibiting bizarre and obsessive behaviours. We do not admit pupils exhibiting streetwise or delinquent behaviour or those with criminal tendencies. We offer either 38 or 52-week provision, a broad and balanced 24-hour curriculum including the National Curriculum for 11–16, and courses which focus on communication skills, social competence, and vocational awareness for 15–19. High staff/pupil ratio, individual bedrooms and a keyworker system. The main therapeutic approach is the use of positive behavioural techniques, eg token economy and individual programmes. Please telephone for a prospectus. Informal visits welcome.

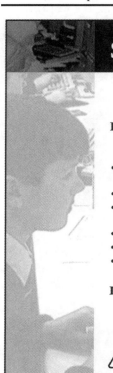

Cotswold Chine School

Box, Near Stroud, Gloucestershire GL6 9AG
Tel: 01453 837550   Fax: 01453 837555
E-mail: mail@cotswold-chine.org.uk   Website: www.gabbitas.net

Head Mr A Phipps
Founded 1953
School status Co-educational DfES approved
independent boarding
Religious denomination Non-denominational
Christian
Special needs provision EBD, ADD, ADHD, ASP,
AUT, DYP, EPI, MLD, SLD, SP&LD, SPLD,
TOU, Emotional and behavioural
Age range 10–16 (and exceptionally 8–18
years)   *boarding from* 10
No of pupils 37
Fees per annum £38,000–£55,000 per term

The school's November 2000 OFSTED Inspection said 'Teamwork is of a very high standard.

The quality of the residential care is high and the ethos of the school is distinctive and very positive. The pupils trust and respect adults in the school and turn to them readily if they need support. The quality of teaching has improved greatly since the last inspection: 69% of the lessons seen were good or very good. This high quality of teaching is reflected in the good quality of learning across the school. The School's procedures for ensuring pupils' welfare and support are excellent. The pupils are happy and feel safe and secure: they enjoy the education, the care and the therapies provided.'

The school caters for children who need a high staff ratio and also pupils with a wide range of learning difficulties. Specific medical needs

can be catered for. The placements are available for term and holiday time. Respite care is also available.

The school offers a modern approach to Rudolf Steiner curriculum linked to the National Curriculum where appropriate. The children are taught in small groups and all have access to individual tuition in certain areas. The therapeutic curriculum includes pottery, music, horse riding, drama, woodwork, sailing, biking and computer skills. Children are encouraged to develop their full potential through many varied activities with a strong emphasis on arts, crafts and sciences.

Teaching staff meet DfES requirements and many are Rudolf Steiner trained or experts in their own fields. All pupils study for examinations in numeracy and literacy. The school also offers Certificate of Education and GCSE courses.

The children have eurythmy movement therapy, art and speech therapy. Informal counselling is offered and the school has access to the county's psychiatric advisors.

The houses operate upon the therapeutic guidelines taken from the caring insights of Rudolf Steiner, and are situated on the main school site and in detached houses close by. Its February 2001 welfare inspection praised, in particular, the non-institutionalised atmosphere of the school and the housegroups.

The school is set amidst rolling hills and is adjacent to National Trust common land in the heart of the Cotswolds. Parents/carers can visit any time by arrangement. Regular interviews are held where parents/carers and other professionals connected to the child discuss the child's progress with school staff.

Coxlease School

High Coxlease House, Clay Hill, Lyndhurst, Hampshire SQ43 7DF
Tel: 023 8028 3633   Fax: 023 8028 2515
E-mail: mail@coxleaseschool.co.uk   Website: www.coxleaseschool.co.uk   www.gabbitas.net

Head Mr S Cliffen
Founded 1982
School status DfES approved independent
boys only boarding
Religious denomination Non-denominational
Primary needs catered for EBD
Special needs provision ADD ADHD ASP DYC
DYS DYP EPI MLD SP&LD SPLD TOU
Other needs catered for victim/victimised
Age range 9–16+   *boarding from* 9
No of pupils 49; *(Junior)* 8; *(Senior)* 40;
(boarding) (full) 49
Fees per annum On application

Coxlease School delivers high quality Education, Therapy and Care to a total of 49 severely challenging EBD Keystage 2, 3 and 4 boys. There are six residential units on site and two in Southampton. We offer termly boarding and up to 70 days respite during school holidays.

The National Curriculum is fully delivered together with ASDAN, college links and work experience at Key Stage 4. Main stream inclusion is pursued as appropriate.

On site therapy provides Child Psychiatry, Psychotherapy, Art Therapy, Speech and Language Therapy.

Pupils are encouraged to pursue their physical, intellectual, emotional and spiritual development in order to enable them to enter society as contributing adults.

In October 2001, the school received an outstanding OFSTED report. Comments included:

- 'one of the best schools of its kind, a delightful school'
- 'the school gives very good value for money'
- 'leadership is exceptional'
- 'high quality teaching and learning'

Dame Hannah Rogers School

Woodland Road, Ivybridge, Devon PL21 9HQ
Tel: 01752 892461   Fax: 01752 898101
E-mail: dhrs@iname.com   Website: www.damehannah.com

Principal Mr W R Evans
Founded 1787
School status Co-educational non-maintained boarding and day
Religious denomination Multi-faith
Member of NAIMS, NASS
Accredited by DfES (878/7082)
Special needs provision CP, DEL, EPI, MLD, PH, PMLD, SLD, SP&LD, W
Age range 8–19   *boarding from* 8
No of pupils 55; *(boarding) (full)* 30; *(weekly)* 20; *(day)* 5
Girls 21 *boys* 34
Fees per annum (boarding) £32,345–£62,514

'This is a highly effective school in which there is exceptional leadership, very good teaching and very good provision of therapy within a multi-disciplinary environment. There is a very high quality of residential care ... The school gives very good value for money.' (OFSTED 2001).

Dame Hannah Rogers School is a recognised centre of excellence, meeting the needs of young people with physical disabilities and learning difficulties. Its duty is to ensure the young people in its care are valued as individuals and treated with dignity and respect. It encourages self-esteem and develops individual's self-dependence in a variety of settings.

Independence training and augmentative communication are, along with therapeutic aims, reinforced throughout each students waking hours so that skills can become an integral part of each student's life. Independence bungalows enable students in the Further Education department to develop their own quality of life.

Doncaster School for the Deaf

Leger Way, Doncaster, South Yorkshire DN2 6AY
Tel: 01302 386710   Fax: 01302 361808
E-mail: enquiries@ddt-deaf.org.uk   Website: www.ddt-dsd.org.uk   www.gabbitas.net

Director Mr D A Gadd BA
Founded 1828
School status Non-maintained DfES approved
Special needs provision HI, PH, EBD, MLD, SP&LD, SPLD, DYS, VIS and 52-week provision
Age range 3–16
No of pupils (day) 24; *(weekly boarders)* 18; *(52-week boarders)* 4
Pupils considered for admission throughout the year
Fees per annum Available on request

Doncaster School for the Deaf, provides high quality education and care for Deaf and Hearing Impaired resident or day pupils, some of whom have other special needs. A broad and balanced curriculum, including the National Curriculum and Work-Related Curriculum ensure that each pupil has the opportunity to reach his/her potential.

Pupils are entered for appropriate examinations including GCSE and Certificate of Achievement. The experienced staff includes Teachers of the Deaf, many of whom are subject specialists, an Educational Audiologist, a Speech and Language Therapist and a team of experienced Learning Support Assistants. The school has an Educational Management Unit for pupils with significant behavioural difficulties and an Additional Needs Unit.

The excellent sporting facilities include a multi-faceted Sports Hall, an indoor heated swimming pool and extensive playing fields. **We welcome visitors throughout the year, please contact the School for a prospectus or to arrange a suitable time to visit us.**

Eden Grove School

Bolton, Appleby, Cumbria CA16 6AJ
Tel: 017683 61346   Fax: 017683 61356   E-mail: ianmcready@prioryhealthcare.co.uk
Website: www.prioryhealthcare.co.uk   www.gabbitas.net

Head Mr I G McCready
Founded 1955
School status Boys DfES approved independent boarding and day
Religious denomination Non-denominational
Member of Priory Services for Young People
Special needs provision ADD, ADHD, ASP, AUT, EBD, EPI, HI, MLD, SP&LD, TOU
Age range 8–19
Boarding from 8
No of pupils 78
Fees per annum (boarding) (38 week) £32,271; *(51 week)* £43,837; *(day)* £23,642

Eden Grove is situated two miles from the A66 at the edge of a small village called Bolton, in the heart of the Eden Valley. It is two hours from Glasgow, Manchester, Liverpool and Newcastle-upon-Tyne by road via the A66 or the M6. The nearest mainline rail station is Penrith, 20 minutes from the school.

The school offers flexible placement packages to local authorities for young people aged between 8 and 19. Current placement facilities are as follows:

- 51 week placements
- 38 week placements
- day pupil placements
- 16+ placements
- 38 week placements with holiday care
- 1:1 placements

Most of the young people referred to Eden Grove have a Statement of Special Educational Needs which has been prepared by their placing authority. Some also come with the label of having Learning Difficulties. A significant amount of these children are diagnosed as having a 'syndrome' such as Attention Deficit Disorder, Tourettes, Language Delay, Fragile X and Autistic Spectrum Disorder.

The school has a full comprehensive education package which is regularly inspected by OFSTED. The subjects on the curriculum include: English, Maths, Science, History, Geography, Art, IT, Home Economics, PE, Religious and Moral Education, Outdoor Pursuits and Careers. In terms of nationally accredited courses, the school operates the National Curriculum, ASDAN Award Scheme, Certificate of Achievement, CLAIT and COA Unit awards and GCSE. All of the above are supported by the school Learning Support Department. There is also an extensive Work Experience and College Placement Programme in operation. In addition the school operates a Complex Developmental Needs Programme for nine young people whose needs can best be met in a smaller setting.

Eden Grove was founded on the principles of family values and the ethos of structure, content and purpose. This remains the case to this day. All of our young people are part of a particular Unit, which is age-associated. Within this Unit there are routines and expectations which would apply to any household. There is also an opportunity for young people to engage with adults in a positive/trusting way and an opportunity to participate in a wide range of activities. An opportunity is also there to address any specific difficulty.

All young people have a Care Plan, which is addressed through their own Unit staff.

The school has a thriving Cadets Programme, which has been described by a Senior Army Officer as 'the best Detachment in Cumbria'. All young people involved participate in a variety of activities/skill-training exercises. These include an annual skiing trip, hillcraft and Army-Base related activities at the Warcop camp.

The 16+ Initiative is based in a completely refurbished Unit that can accommodate, in single bedrooms, up to seven young people. These young people still require a great deal of support.

The Unit provides Life-Skills, Work Experience, College Placements, Careers Advice and many other individual packages that suit the needs and aspirations of the young people involved.

The school employs the services of a counsellor, an educational psychologist, a speech/language therapist and a play therapist. These services allow the school to address specific difficulties with young people in a very personal way.

Fairley House School

30 Causton Street, London SW1P 4AU
Tel: 020 7976 5456   Fax: 020 7976 5905
E-mail: office@fairleyhouse.westminster.sch.uk   Website: www.gabbitas.net

Principal Ms J Murray and Mr N Rees
Founded 1982
School status Co-educational independent day
Religious denomination Inter-denominational
Special needs provision ADD, ADHD, DYS, DYP, SPLD
Age range 6–11 Upper School 11–14
No of pupils 130
Girls 30 *boys* 100
Fees per annum £16,875 *Upper School* £14,250

Curriculum: the prime aim is to improve the basic literacy, numeracy and self-confidence of dyslexic children. There is a 1:3.5 staff-pupil ratio with small group and individual teaching, and a structured, multi-sensory approach. The National Curriculum is followed throughout the school with emphasis on ICT, Science, and DT. Most children normally remain for two to three years and are carefully prepared for appropriate onward placement, which since September 2001 could include Fairley House Upper School.

The multi-disciplinary team includes full-time speech and language and occupational therapists. The School's Principal is a fully qualified educational psychologist. All class teachers and special provision staff are experienced in teaching SPLD children and the majority hold a recognised SPLD qualification.

Entry requirements: Fairley House School assessment.

Farleigh Education Group

Swallow Barn, Buckland Dinham, Frome, Somerset, BA11 2QS   Tel/Fax: 01373 463 172
Email: brads@zetnet.co.uk   Website: www.nhh4as.co.uk   www.gabbitas.net

Farleigh Education Group are highly structured schools for students with Asperger's Syndrome with high expectations for academic achievement, specialising in developing communication and social skills. We aim to provide the highest quality of teaching. Our educational ethos is based on the belief that children require an education programme specifically tailored to their unique needs. We utilise a team approach of specialist speech and language therapists, occupational therapist, educational psychologist and specially trained, experienced teachers to ensure the individual development of each pupil 24 hours a day. All staff have specific qualifications and experience. Our philosophy is one of partnership with parents. Parents receive regular written and verbal reports. Each child has a key person who acts to facilitate home/college contact.
Farleigh Education Group promotes the fostering of a responsible outlook on life and achievement through the provision of an appropriate and stimulating educational environment. To develop and enhance a wide variety of abilities, giving appropriate guidance with realistic expectations.

Farleigh College

Newbury, Nr Mells, Frome, Somerset, BA11 3RG
Tel: 01373 814980   Fax: 01373 814984

Head Desmond Walsh
School status Residential & day co-educational
Accredited by DfES   *Member of* NASEN, NAS
Special needs provision ASP
Age range 11–19

Farleigh College is a boarding and day school set in an impressive Grade II listed Queen Anne house located in the small hamlet of Newbury, approximately 14 miles south of Bath. The college has a staff/student ratio of 2:1.

North Hill House

North Parade, Frome, Somerset, BA11 2AB
Tel: 01373 466222   Fax: 01373 300374
E-mail: andyc@nhh4as.co.uk   Website: www.nhh4as.co.uk

Head Andy Cobley
School Status Residential & day boys only
Accredited by DfES   *Member of* NASEN, NAS
Age range 7–16
Special Needs Provision ASP
Other needs catered for Pervasive development disorder, Semantic/Pragmatic disorder, social/communication difficulties

North Hill House is a boys only, boarding and day school set in a large, recently refurbished Georgian property with its own secure and spacious grounds. These afford the opportunity for students to enjoy freedom and space while ensuring safety. The rear of the property adjoins a recently landscaped park.

Farleigh Sixth Form College

19 Bath Road, Frome, Somerset, BA11 2HJ
Tel/Fax: 01373 3463172   Email: brads@zetnet.co.uk   Website: www.nhh4as.co.uk

Head Andrew Chiffers
School Status Residential & day co-educational college
Accredited by LSC
Member of NASEN, NAS, NATSPEC
Age Range 16–19
Special Needs Provision ASP
Other Needs Catered for Pervasive development disorder, Semantic/Pragmatic disorder, social/communication difficulties

Farleigh Sixth Form College is for students aged over 16 years with Asperger's Syndrome who aspire to function effectively in a mainstream education and working environment. Students are encouraged to develop self-reliance and confidence in the domestic environment.

To give support in a mainstream academic and social situation. To prepare students for life as fulfilled and self-reliant adults by teaching strategies to minimise the difficulties associated with Asperger's Syndrome and to celebrate and develop the gifts they have been given.

The college is situated in the town of Frome approximately 25 minutes from Bath. It is a large, well-equipped house, close to the town centre and other local amenities. Students are encouraged to join clubs, attend evening classes, visit restaurants and use the shops.

Frewen College

Brickwall, Northiam, Near Rye, East Sussex, TN31 6NB
Tel: 01797 252494   Fax: 01797 252567
E-mail: post@frewcoll.demon.co.uk   Website: www.frewcoll.demon.co.uk   www.gabbitas.net

Head S C Horsley B.A. (Hons)
Founded 1947
School status Boys DfES approved independent weekly boarding and day
Religious denomination Non-denominational
Supporting Corporate member of British Dyslexia Association
Accredited by CReSTeD Category A(SP); ISA
Special needs provision DYS
Other needs catered for DYP
Age range 9–17 *weekly boarding from* 9
No of pupils 82; *(boarding) (weekly)* 39
Junior 10; *Senior* 72
Fees per annum (weekly boarding) from £16,599 *(day)* from £9,444

Frewen College is a specialist school for the education of dyslexic boys. We believe not only in tackling the difficulties which each boy has but also in establishing the strengths and talents of each individual so that success is experienced at every level.

There are 82 boys and 22 teaching staff. All boys go on to further and/or higher education. The full National Curriculum is offered within a small class environment which allows for a whole school approach to the problems of specific learning difficulites. Each boy has an individual education plan which allows for the tackling of his dyslexic problems and for the development of his strengths. Literacy problems are tackled using a range of programmes including THRASS and the Dyslexic Institute Literacy Programme. A wide range of GCSEs are offered.

There is a particular emphasis on Technology, Art and Design with fully equipped Design and Technology workshops, Motor Mechanics workshop, pottery, art studio and food technology area. Music facilities allow for teaching up to GCSE as well as individual lessons in instruments of the pupil's choice.

Information Technology is at the heart of our educational programmes. A 'state of the art' computer network runs through the main teaching areas with a pupil computer ratio of 1:4. Pupils have access to the network throughout the working day and during prep sessions both in classrooms and in the open access study centre.

Our unique sixth form offers City and Guilds courses in Professional Cookery and Motor Vehicle Repair and Maintenance as well as GCSE retakes and a structured introduction to the adult world.

Dyspraxia provision includes specialist tuition within a fully equipped fitness studio. All programmes are developed in consultation with our visiting Occupational Therapist. There is also a Speech and Language Therapist on the staff.

Boarding provision features en-suite bedrooms, a full range of supervised recreational activities and transport to and from London on Friday and Sunday evenings. Day placements are also available.

Grafham Grange School

Grafham Grange, Bramley, Guildford, Surrey GU5 0LH
Tel: 01483 892214   Fax: 01483 894297
E-mail: dggrafham@aol.com   Website: www.gabbitas.net

Head Mr R Norman
Founded 1946
School status Boys non-maintained boarding
Special needs provision EBD
Age range 10–16   *boarding from* 10
No of pupils 40
Fees per annum £37,000

Grafham Grange provides residential education for boys aged 10–16 within the average range of cognitive ability, who may be under-functioning as a result of emotional and behavioural disorder.

Set in 40 acres with four self-contained living groups and an independence living group, the school provides a wide range of facilities. We offer an intensive programme of remediation, high staff to pupil ratio, external examinations in Years 10 and 11, independence training, FE links and post-16 support.

We use a range of adaptable techniques to achieve each pupil's potential; a keyworker provides individual support and counselling, and monitors progress. The school provides expert support to pupils and their families, recognising the importance of the family unit whilst allowing pupils to develop towards independence at their own pace.

We also offer specialist family support work which is carried out by our own Social Work Department, consultant psychiatrist and specialist counsellors.

Headlands School

(NCH) 2 Augustine's Road, Penarth, Vale of Glamorgan CF64 1YY
Tel: 029 2070 9771   Fax: 029 2070 0515
E-mail: wahs@mail.nch.org.uk   Website: www.nch.org.uk   www.gabbitas.net

Head Mr David Haswell
Founded 1918
School status Independent co-educational boarding and day
Special needs provision EBD, ADD, ADHD, ASP, AUT, CP, DYC, DYS, DYP, EPI, MLD, SPLD, TOU
Age range 11–16
No of pupils 32   *boarding* 26   *day* 6
Fees per annum (boarding) (38 week) £67,248; *(52 week)* £92,022; *(day)* £28,001 (reviewed April 2003)

Headlands School specialises in unlocking the potential of young people otherwise disengaged from their educational entitlement as the result of their challenging behaviour.

The most recent inspection found that Headlands is an improving school with good features in pastoral and welfare arrangements. Curriculum, external examinations and specialist input including Clinical Psychology are particular strengths of the school's provision.

Residential Care is of a very high quality with a strong emphasis placed upon improving standards through quality assurance and staff training and development.

Headland's commitment to staff development has been recognised by the award of Investors in People status. User participation is important and is developed through the school's council, residents meetings and regular consultation. An Independent Advocacy Service bolsters the NCH complaints procedure in safeguarding young people's rights.

Class groups are typically made up of 6 pupils with a qualified teacher and two Learning Support Assistants. Links with other schools and work placements are particularly strong with the school gaining benefits from its location.

I CAN

Helps Children Communicate
registered charity 210031

4 Dyer's Buildings, Holborn, London EC1N 2QP
Tel: 0870 010 4066   Fax: 0870 010 4067
E-mail: ican@ican.org.uk   Website: www.ican.org.uk   www.gabbitas.net

I CAN is the national educational charity for children with speech and language difficulties. In addition to three special schools (Dawn House, John Horniman and Meath) the charity runs other programmes for Early Years, Training and Information and Mainstream Support for mainstream schools via partnership projects.

I CAN's Dawn House School

Helps Children Communicate
registered charity 210031

Helmsley Road, Rainworth, Nottinghamshire NG21 0DQ
Tel: 01623 795361   Fax: 01623 491173   E-mail: dawnhouse@ican.org.uk

Head Ms M Uden
Founded 1974
School status Co-educational non-maintained boarding and day
Special needs provision Speech and language impairment
Age range 5–16   *boarding from* 6
No of pupils (day) 34; *(boarding)* 47
Girls 21 *boys* 60
Fees per annum (boarding) £30,366; *(day)* £18,684

Dawn House School is known nationally as a centre of excellence, which specialises in meeting the needs of pupils with speech and language problems from 5–16. The OFSTED Inspection Team praised Dawn House for providing "high quality teaching and good value for money". The pupils are offered access to the National Curriculum through courses leading to external accreditation at the end of Key Stage 4. The school aims to support the pupil's development in speech and language, thinking and reasoning, self-confidence and independence. Integrated education, therapy and care programmes are tailored to meet the needs of each pupil. Joint planning by our highly qualified and experienced staff ensures that the school provides a fully integrated language environment. Teaching and therapy are supported by up-to-date technology and Paget Gorman Signed Speech.
Pupils are encouraged to develop their independence throughout the 24-hour curriculum the school works in close partnership with parents.

I CAN's John Horniman School

Helps Children Communicate
registered charity 210031

2 Park Road, Worthing, West Sussex BN11 2AS
Tel: 01903 200317   Fax: 01903 214151   E-mail: johnhorniman@ican.org.uk

Head Ms J Dunn
School status Co-educational non-maintained boarding and day
Accredited by DfES
Age range 4–11   *boarding from* 4
No of pupils (day) 20; *(boarding) (weekly)* 9
Girls 4 *boys* 25
Fees per annum (boarding) £29,616; *(day)* £19,158

John Horniman School works with children where speech and language impairment is their primary area of need. Multi-disciplinary teams of teaching staff, care workers and speech and language therapists work together to provide a specialised and innovative approach to teaching and learning, integrating education and therapy. OFSTED inspectors noted the school offers "a wealth of expertise in speech and language disorders".
Intensive individual and small group speech and language therapy programmes are delivered flexibly in order to meet each child's specific needs. Key Stages 1 and 2 of the National Curriculum including the National Literacy and Numeracy Strategies are followed at the appropriate level for each child and Paget Gorman Signing is incorporated into the learning environment.

I CAN's Meath School

Brox Road, Ottershaw, Surrey KT16 0LF
Tel: 01932 872302   Fax: 01932 875180   E-mail: meath@ican.org.uk

Helps Children Communicate
registered charity 210031

Head Mr John Parrott
School status Co-educational non-maintained
boarding and day
Age range 5–12   *boarding from* 5
No of Pupils (day) 54; *(boarding) (weekly)* 16
Girls 16 *boys* 54
Fees per annum (boarding) £28,460–£33,497;
day £17,410–£19,508

Pupils at Meath School show language impairment which severely affects their communication and learning; many also have speech, literacy and co-ordination difficulties.

Children within the average or below average range of non-verbal ability benefit from the school's integrated multi-professional approach to delivering a curriculum, which includes many practical and experience based activities. Meath School is cited as being "particularly successful in developing pupils' self confidence and self esteem and in securing their good progress in English" and the pupils' levels of attainment in this area is the "result of skilled teaching and management ... and the effective work of teams of teachers, therapists and support staff".

The National Curriculum is adapted to the specific needs of the children and delivered through subject specific teaching and cross curricular topic work. Individual programmes of speech and language therapy are integrated into the curriculum leading to a strong emphasis on the development of the children's communication skills throughout class and residential groups. Augmentative communication systems are used as appropriate, eg Paget Gorman Signing, Cued Articulation and individual communication aids.

Ingfield Manor School

Five Oaks, Billingshurst, West Sussex RH14 9AX
Tel: 01403 782294   Fax: 01403 785066   Website: www.gabbitas.net

Head Mr Christopher Jay
Founded 1961
School status DfES approved independent
(supported by Scope)
Special needs provision CP
Age range 3–11   *boarding from* 3
No of pupils (day) 29   *(boarding) (weekly)* 12
Girls 22 *boys* 19
Fees per annum On application

Ingfield Manor is a day and weekly boarding school for children with cerebral palsy with learning abilities in the average range. The school is at the forefront of the development of Conductive Education in the UK and is advised and supported by the Peto Institute in Budapest. Staff work in inter-disciplinary teams responsible for the needs of the children throughout the day.

OFSTED concluded that, 'The work in Conductive Education by pupils and staff is outstanding. This is a centre of excellence for an alternative approach to the education of children with cerebral palsy'.

Children follow National Curriculum core and foundation subjects. The curriculum is based on a holistic view of children and their intellectual, emotional and social needs. Information technology features strongly and is used to support the children as they extend their repertoire of skills. The school has a national reputation for the development of computer assisted communication.

Kisimul School

The Old Vicarage, High Street, Swinderby, Lincolnshire LN6 9LU
Tel: 01522 868279   Fax: 01522 866000
E-mail: sueshaw@kisimul.co.uk   Website: www.kisimul.co.uk   www.gabbitas.net

Head Mrs S J Shaw
Founded 1977
School status Co-educational DfES approved boarding and day
Religious denomination Non-denominational
Special needs provision SLD, AUT, DOW, EPI, SP&LD, SPLD
Age range 10–19   *boarding from* 10
No of pupils 31
Girls 6 boys 25
Junior 0; Senior 13; Sixth Form 18
Fees per annum On application

Access to both the National Curriculum and our own developmental curriculum based upon individual needs. We aim to provide a warm, caring environment in which a child can flourish and be able to develop skills to his or her full potential. We provide a consistent 24-hour approach with house and school staff working together as a team. Each child has an individual programme based on an assessment of his or her needs in which parental views are considered to be an important contribution.

We have a very high staff/pupil ratio that enables us to fully utilise facilities within the community. The school has its own soft play, adventure playground, heated indoor swimming pool and multi-sensory room. Speech and music therapy are provided, occupational and physiotherapy are available together with external support agencies. The school also has a consultant educational psychologist.

MACINTYRE CARE

602 South Seventh Street, Milton Keynes, Buckinghamshire, MK9 2JA
Tel: 01908 230100   Fax: 01908 234379   Website: www.gabbitas.net

MacIntyre Care is a national charity which has been providing support to children and adults with learning disabilities across the UK for the last thirty years. Current services include residential accommodation, supported living, and adult education and training opportunities, as well as its schools at Wingrave and Womaston.

MacIntyre School Wingrave

MACINTYRE CARE

Leighton Road, Wingrave, Nr Aylesbury, Buckinghamshire HP22 4PD
Tel: 01296 681274   Fax: 01296 681091
E-mail: wingrave@macintyre-care.org   Website: www.macintyre-care.org

Head Mr S Smith – Acting Principal
School status Co-educational independent boarding only
Special needs provision SLD
Other needs catered for Complex learning difficulties, AUT, EPI, PMLD, SLD, SP&LD, SPLD; *Member of* NASS
Age range 10–19 *boarding from* 10
No of boarders (full) 34   Girls 12 boys 22
Junior 22; *Sixth Form* 12
Fees per annum (boarding) (full) £77,775

MacIntyre School Wingrave is located in rural Buckinghamshire five miles from the towns of Aylesbury and Leighton Buzzard. Students live in purpose-built houses and are taught in small classes by specialist staff. Our Individual Education and Care Plans are based on Person Centred Planning and reflect the needs and aspirations of each person in a caring and supportive environment.

We work in partnership with parents and other professionals to support the young people to acquire the skills and experience to enable them to take their rightful place as valued and contributing members of society.

MacIntyre School Womaston

Walton, Presteigne, Powys LD8 2PT   Tel: 01544 230308   Fax: 01544 231317
E-mail: womaston@macintyre-care.org   Website: www.macintyre-care.org

MACINTYRE CARE

Head Mr M J Bertulis
Founded 1986
School status DfES approved independent co-educational voluntary boarding only
Special needs provision SLD, AUT, MLD, PMLD
Age range 11–19 *boarding from* 11
No of boarders (full) 16
Girls 3 boys 13
Fees per annum (boarding) (full) £81,030

A 52 week boarding school providing education and care for children who need a '24 hour approach'. The school has consistently provided good quality education for young people who have suffered exclusion from schools and/or have found it difficult to live at home. The school has recently achieved a successful ESTYN inspection report. The school is set in 20 acres of grounds.

Philosophy and Approaches: The school employs an empathetic, person-centred approach aiming to understand, develop and extend each student. Positive behavioural standards are set whilst maintaining an understanding of the communication intended by the behaviour.

Curriculum and Resources: Students follow individual curricula with an emphasis on physical, creative and environmental activities to complement and aid delivery of the key skills. Students are expected to play an active part in the choice of activities and programmes selected. Womaston has positive links with Coleg Powys. Specialist support is available to the school in psychiatry, psychology, sexuality, speech therapy and physiotherapy.

Well equipped residential houses and classrooms for up to five students, pottery, craft workshop, training kitchen, multisensory room and individual session rooms.

Maple Hayes School

Abnall's Lane, Lichfield, Staffordshire WS13 8BL
Tel: 01543 264387   Fax: 01543 262022
Website: www.dyslexia.gb.com   www.gabbitas.net

Principal Dr E N Brown
Founded 1982
School status Co-educational DfES approved
independent boarding and day
Religious denomination Church of England
Member of ISIS, ISA, ISC, ECIS
Special needs provision ADD, ADHD, DYS,
SPLD
Age range 7–17   *Boarding (Boys) from* 7
No of pupils (day) 80; *(weekly boarding)* 40
Girls day only
Fees per annum (weekly boarding) £11,880–
£15,210 *(day)* £9,375–£12,705

Maple Hayes School is one of the select few
schools for dyslexics and underachievers which
is inspected and approved by the Department
for Education. The school is set in extensive
grounds near Lichfield and caters for up to 120
children from 7 to 17 years. We have a world-
wide reputation for our unique and effective
teaching methods and for our examination
results. After taking GCSEs with us, most
students go on to higher education at college
or university. Excellent OFSTED report.
We provide a good all-round education without
the stigma of withdrawal to a special unit and
our youngsters compete well in the Midland
and National Independent School sports
championships. Children's learning is under
the supervision of a chartered psychologist
and an assessment service is available. Private
and LEA placements are welcome. In addition
to bursaries for private placements, there is a
bursary scheme for children of very high
intelligence. Admission is by interview and
psychologist's report.

The Marchant-Holliday School

North Cheriton, Templecombe, Somerset BA8 0AH
Tel: 01963 33234   Fax: 01963 33432
E-mail: mhs@ncheriton.freeserve.co.uk

Head Mr J M Robertson BEd (Hons), DipEd
Founded 1950
School status Boys DfES approved independent
boarding and day
Religious denomination Non-denominational
Member of AWCEBD, NASEN, NASS
Special needs provision EBD, ADD, ADHD, ASP,
DYS, SP&LD
Age range 7–12   *boarding from* 7
No of pupils 36; *(day)* 1; *(boarding)* 35
Junior 36
Fees per annum (boarding) £33,120; *(day)*
£16,301

This is a charity-based independent residential
school for junior aged boys who have emotional and behavioural difficulties. Associated
learning difficulties and dyslexia can also be
catered for. Pupils follow the National Curriculum, but at a level appropriate to their needs.
Classes are of no more than eight pupils and
facilities and resources are of the highest standard. Children are encouraged to fulfil their
potential for social and academic growth and
often make sufficient progress to allow a return
to mainstream schooling. We are accredited by
Somerset Social Services and had a very successful OFSTED inspection in February 1998.

Mark College

Blackford Road, Mark, Highbridge, Somerset TA9 4NP
Tel: 01278 641632   Fax: 01278 641426
E-mail: post@markcollege.somerset.sch.uk
Website: www.markcollege.somerset.sch.uk   www.gabbitas.net

Principal Dr S J Chinn
Founded 1986
School status Boys DfES approved independent boarding and day
Religious denomination Non affiliated
Member of ISA; *Accredited by* ISC, DfES, (CReSTeD)
Special needs provision DYS, DYC
Age range 10–16   *boarding from* 10
No of pupils 80; *boarders* 55; *(weekly)* 15; *(day)* 10
Senior 80
Fees per annum (boarding) £15,162–£16,668 *(full)*; £14,934–£16,326 *(weekly)*; £10,527–£11,691 *(day)*

Mark College is a specialist secondary school for dyslexic boys. Founded in 1986, it has established an international reputation for its expertise. Its success has been recognised in the UK by achieving approval from the DfES followed by an outstanding Ofsted report, which led to Beacon status. The college offers superb facilities for sport, boarding and academic work. It has been at the forefront of using ITC for English and for teaching mathematics to dyslexics. The college runs teacher-training courses for both these areas. GCSE results in 2001 were excellent. These results were achieved by boys whose dyslexic problems were at the severe end of the spectrum. The second Ofsted report (2001) is now available from the college.

The Moat School

Bishop's Avenue, Fulham, London SW6 6EG
Tel: 0207 610 9018   Fax: 0207 610 9098
E-mail: office@moatschool.org.uk   Website: www.moatschool.org.uk   www.gabbitas.net

Head Mr R M Carlysle
Founded 1998
School status Independent co-educational day only
Religious denomination Non-denominational
Member of BDA
Special needs provision DYS, DYC, DYP
Age range 11–17
No of pupils 80; *Senior* 80
Girls 15 *boys* 65
Fees per annum £16,050

The Moat's site is within the historic conservation area associated with Fulham Palace, and is easily accessible by road, rail and tube. The school is kept deliberately small, with classes of no more than 10 in number. Each form group has the support of a Learning Support Assistant. Extensive use is made of ICT and each pupil is issued with a laptop by the school.

The structure, high level of resourcing and academic expectations are all designed to produce an educational experience for our pupils that is mainstream in structure but specialist in nature.

The Moat runs a substantial enrichment programme of activities that are built into the day for the first three years, as well as a range of extra-curricular activities, such as the Duke of Edinburgh's Award Scheme, and performing arts productions. The PE Department runs a full fixture programme, and rowing is a particular strength.

Moon Hall School for Dyslexic Children

Feldemore, Holmbury St Mary, Nr Dorking, Surrey RH5 6LQ
Tel: 01306 731464   Fax: 01306 731504
E-mail: enquiries@moonhall.surrey.sch.uk   Website: www.moonhall.surrey.sch.uk

Head Mrs J Lovett
Founded 1985
School status Co-educational independent boarding and day
Religious denomination Church of England
Member of BDA, IAPS   *Accredited by* CReSTeD "A"   *Special needs provision* DYS
Age range 7–13   *boarding from* 7
No of pupils (day) 74 *(boarding at Belmont)* 20
Girls 24 *boys* 70
Fees per annum (boarding) (weekly) £14,658; *(day)* £11,475 (2001–2002)

Moon Hall has a special relationship with Belmont Preparatory (3–13 year olds). Together they provide unrivalled opportunities for intelligent dyslexic children:

- Purpose-built Moon Hall school house
- Full-time specialist teaching (7–11 year olds)
- English and Maths groups: normal maximum six pupils
- Other subjects: normal maximum – 12 pupils
- One-to-one as needed
- Vast array of materials/equipment
- Well-equipped computer room – additional machines in form rooms
- Every child taught touch-typing. OCR examinations taken where appropriate
- 60-acre site – heated swimming pool, all-weather pitches, Sports Hall etc
- Games/PE – taught by Preparatory School – pupils play in joint school teams
- Regular cross-site dramatic/musical productions
- Uniform common to both schools. Assemblies/lunches/playtimes together
- Dyslexic pupils move into Belmont classes when ready – returning for ongoing support as required up to age 13
- Personal tutors for all.

Muntham House School

Barns Green, Horsham, West Sussex RH13 7NJ
Tel: 01403 730302   Fax: 01403 730510
Website: www.munthamhouse.w-sussex.sch.uk   www.gabbitas.net

Principal Mr R Boyle
Founded 1953
School status Non-maintained
Special needs provision EBD, ADHD
Age range 8–18   *boarding from* 8
No of boys in total 56 *Junior* 10 *Senior* 38
Sixth Form 8
No of boarders (full) 46 *(weekly)* 10
Fees per annum On application

Aims and Philosophy: Muntham House School is a safe, caring and positive environment dedicated to supporting individual needs and seeking effective change in order to send our students forward into society.
Specialist Facilities: Small class sizes, specialist primary and post 16 facilities. Full National Curriculum access. Specialist Literacy support and Vocational Development.

Support Services: Consultant GP. The school has access to the services of the Local Health Authority. We also have our own Consultant Paediatric Psychiatrist and Educational Psychologist plus specific support through a bank of consultants.
Home School Links: Muntham House determines admission by whether the Parents or Carers are willing to enter a partnership in developing their child's education and behaviour. The school has a Family Support and Pupil Induction Team dedicated to maintaining links with parents and supporting families through visits, counselling and advocacy.

The National Centre for Young People with Epilepsy (NCYPE)

St Piers Lane, Lingfield, Surrey RH7 6PW   Tel: 01342 832243   Fax: 01342 834639
E-mail: mail@ncype.org.uk   Website: www.ncype.org.uk   www.gabbitas.net

Chief Executive Mr R S Haughton BA(psych), BSW
Founded 1895
School status DfES approved independent co-educational non-maintained boarding and day
Special needs provision EPI, MLD, SLD, SP&LD
Member of NAIMS, NASS, NASAN, BILD, NATSPEC, ADC, EQUALS; *Accredited by* OCR, City and Guilds, SRCON, British Trampoline Federation, Amateur Swimming Association
Age range 5–19+   *Boarding from* 5
No of students 196; *Junior* 71; *Senior* 125
Boys 129; *girls* 67; *boarding* 168; *day* 28
Fees per annum at January 2002 (full boarding) £37,923–£92,442; *(day)* £24,648–£60,087

NCYPE is the major provider of specialised services for young people with epilepsy in the UK. NCYPE provides integrated education and care with residential and day attendance at the St Piers School for Children up to the age of 16 and at the NCYPE Further Education College for young people from 16 - 19+.
Medical Consultant posts shared with Great Ormond Street Hospital for Children NHS Trust. A National Assessment Service, including outreach support and rehabilitation for young people from across the UK.
An on-site Epilepsy Resource Centre offering a programme of seminars and study days for parents, carers and professionals.

NCH Westwood School

479 Margate Road, Broadstairs, Kent CT10 2QA
Tel: 01843 600820   Fax: 01843 600827
E-mail: sews@mail.nch.org.uk   Website: www.gabbitas.net

Head Mr C L Walter
Founded 1995
School status Co-educational independent day
Religious denomination Methodist
Member of NCH
Special needs provision EBD, ADHD, MLD
Age range 11–16
No of pupils 23
Girls 3 *boys* 20
Junior 13; *Senior* 10
Fees per annum £19,570–£20,900

Westwood School is situated on the outskirts of Broadstairs – one of Kent's premier seaside towns. The School is managed by NCH, one of Britain's leading child care charities.
Westwood School currently caters for up to 30 young people between the ages of 11 and 16, whose primary special needs are concerned with Emotional and Behavioural Difficulties (EBD). Pupils may also experience delay with their academic progress and consequently require additional classsroom support.
Children benefit from an excellent teacher-pupil ratio, enabling us to deliver a tailored curriculum to meet the needs of the individual. Our team of experienced staff is able to offer pastoral care, in addition to delivering the National Curriculum up to GCSE level in a number of subjects. A discrete Vocational Programme also provides vital independence skills and knowledge for later life. This programme includes units on citizenship, careers education, and work experience.
"We wish to be a special, happy and caring school, expecting all users to be valued and expecting them to value the school."

Nugent House

Carr Mill Road, Billinge, Wigan, St Helens WN5 7TT
Tel: 01744 892551   Fax: 01744 895697
E-mail: HEAD@NugentWiganSch.uk   Website: www.gabbitas.net

Head Mrs J L G Bienias
Founded 1983
School status Boys DfES approved independent boarding and day
Religious denomination Catholic, although referrals are accepted of all faiths
Special needs provision EBD, ADD, ADHD, DYS, ASP, TOU
Age range 7–19   *boarding from* 7
No of pupils 89 *(day)* 30 *(boarding)* 59
Fees per annum (boarding) from £27,657 *(day) from* £20,742

Nugent House is a residential special school catering for the needs of boys who are experiencing behavioural and emotional problems. It seeks to meet the educational, spiritual, social and welfare needs of its children in a supportive, caring environment. Where possible, the school encourages and promotes the facilitation of a reintegration into mainstream education.

A range of educational ability exists therefore specialised support is available. A full public examination programme is offered and children are grouped and educated according to National Curriculum guidelines. A modified or differentiated curriculum is offered where appropriate.

Provision is made for both primary and secondary aged pupils. Education is provided in specialist departments including ICT, Science and Art. The school has a large Sports Hall accommodating PE, gymnastics and indoor games.

The school employs a team of therapists including Art, Play, Drama and Horticulture under the direction of a consultant psychiatrist. Independent counsellors are also available working with young people on an individual or group basis.

Close contact with home is maintained via telephone, visits and home leave on a regular, planned basis. The residential part of the school is made up of nine separate houses varying in size and staffing levels, dependent upon the needs of the children. The school offers provision for children with a variety of complex needs.

The school is situated in a pleasant semi-rural district of south-west Lancashire, midway between Liverpool and Manchester and with easy access to motorway and rail links.

The teaching staff are expected to pursue programmes of advanced qualification in special education. All staff have access to the training department of the Nugent Care Society. The school has a full-time training officer who is responsible for the implementation of the NVQ scheme throughout the school. Large proportions of the care staff are already qualified at NVQ Level 3 in line with the requirements of the National Care Standards.

The school provides a balanced, broadly based curriculum which seeks to promote spiritual, moral, cultural, mental and physical development and prepares them for the opportunities and responsibilities of adult life. A varied activity programme throughout the day, evening and at weekends provides an opportunity for young people to experience and develop skill in a variety of sporting and cultural recreational activities.

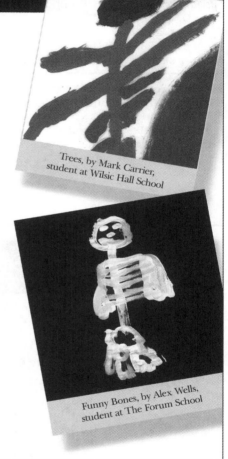

Penhurst School

New Street, Chipping Norton, Oxfordshire OX7 5LN
Tel: 01608 647020   Fax: 01608 647029   Website: www.gabbitas.net

Head Richard Aird
Founded 1903
School status Non-maintained DfES approved independent
Religious denomination Methodist
Member of NASEN, NAIMS, NASS
Special needs provision CP, EPI, HI, PH, PMLD, SP&LD, VIS, W
Age range 5–19
No of pupils 24
Fees per annum available on request

Pupils at Penhurst School have full access to the National Curriculum, but delivery and coverage is differentiated to match pupils' individual abilities. Teaching and learning is further enhanced by the provision of a specialist curriculum that relates directly to the special educational needs of the children on roll. This specialist curriculum, together with priorities taken from the care plans of individual pupils, is used to help minimise the handicapping effects of profound and multiple disability and enable pupils to reach their full potential.

Penhurst School is a residential, multi-agency school in which professionals from different disciplines work together in partnership with parents. The work of teachers, care workers, therapists, nurses and classroom assistants is fully integrated to ensure that the holistic needs of pupils are fully accommodated and that their education, care and treatment is delivered in a dynamic, caring environment over a 24 hour period.

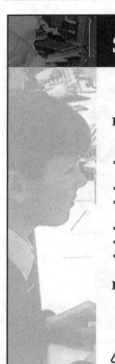

Penn School

Church Road, Penn, High Wycombe, Buckinghamshire HP10 8LZ
Tel: 01494 812139   Fax: 01494 811400
E-mail: office@pennschool.bucks.sch.uk   Website: www.gabbitas.net

Head Mary-Nêst Richardson BA(Hons), PGCE, M.Ed, Ad.Dip, B.Phil
Founded 1921
School status Non-maintained co-educational boarding and day
Religious denomination Non-denominational
Primary needs catered for Deafness (severe/profound) or Speech and Language difficulties, with additional learning or physical problems
Special needs provision AUT, CP, DEL, DYC, DYS, DYP, EPI, HI, MLD, PH, SLD, SP&LD, SPLD, TOU, VIS, W
Other needs catered for XP Syndrome (UV filtered windows), Social interaction difficulties
Age range Secondary school   *boarders from* 11
No of pupils 26 *girls* 12 *boys* 14
No of boarders (weekly full-time) 12
(weekly part-time) 6
Fees per annum (boarding weekly) £41,748; *(day)* £19,458

Penn School exists to provide a rich and stimulating environment in which the pupils develop and work towards achieving their full potential in academic and social terms. Penn School is a small school with a family atmosphere and many children feel secure in this type of environment and are able to learn and succeed. WE BELIEVE THAT HAPPY CHILDREN LEARN.

The pupils follow the broader National Curriculum and obtain examination certificates in a range of subjects. Each child has an Individual Education Plan addressing their SEN, which is jointly devised by the specialist teacher and the speech and language therapist.

Philip Green Memorial School

Boveridge House, Cranborne, Wimborne, Dorset BH21 5RU
Tel: 01725 517218   Fax: 01725 517968   E-mail: pgmschool@hotmail.com

Head Mrs L M Walter
Founded 1964
School status Co-educational independent
boarding and day
Religious denomination Non-denominational
Member of NASEN
Accredited by OCR, WGEC, SEG
Special needs provision Principal: MLD, SLD,
SP&LD. Other: ADD, ASP, AUT, DOW, DYP
Age range 11–19   *boarding from* 11
No of pupils 28; *(day)* 4; *(boarding) (full)* 22;
(weekly) 2
Girls 11 *boys* 16   *Senior* 15 *Sixth Form* 13
Fees per annum (boarding) (full) £21,750;
(weekly) £19,500; *(day)* £9,000

The students follow the National Curriculum prior to a modified GCSE or equivalent curriculum. Older pupils follow a life skills programme in addition to the academic curriculum. Extra-curricular activities include sports, drama, craft, visits etc.

The Philip Green Memorial School (formerly Boveridge House) is a school which caters for children with moderate/severe learning difficulties and/or speech and language disorders. The school's age range for boarding students is 11-19 years.

The Philip Green Memorial School is an elegant Georgian mansion offering the highest standards of education, care and accommodation to students.

Philpots Manor School and Further Training Centre

West Hoathly, East Grinstead, West Sussex RH19 4PR
Tel: 01342 811382/810268   Fax: 01342 811363   Website: www.gabbitas.net

Administrator Simon Blaxland-de Lange
Founded 1959
School status Co-educational DfES approved
independent boarding and day
Religious denomination Christian
(non-denominational)
Member of Committee for Steiner Special
Schools. Affiliated to Steiner Waldorf Schools
Fellowship
Accredited by OFSTED, DfES
Special needs provision ADD, ADHD, ASP, AUT,
CP(mild), DEL, DOW, DYC, DYS, DYP, EBD,
EPI(mild), HI(mild), MLD, SP&LD, SPLD, TOU
Age range 7–19   *boarding from* 7
No of pupils (day) 12; *(boarding) (full)* 53
Girls 18 *boys* 47
Junior 33   *Senior* 19   *Training Course* 13
Fees per annum (boarding) £34,587;
(day) £25,941

Philpots Manor School is a residential school and training centre based on the education

principles of Rudolf Steiner. It was founded in 1959 to offer care and education to children with special needs who, because of their particular difficulties, have been unable to learn and develop in an ordinary school.

The school admits children who present a broad range of emotional and behavioural difficulties. Most, but not all, are of below average ability and have moderate learning difficulties. These may stem from social deprivation, abuse and a recognised clinical condition such as epilepsy, a developmental disorder or mild autism. Children are eligible providing they have the potential to function in a classroom situation where children are helped to reach their full potential within the Steiner curriculum. It is our aim that by the time pupils leave, they have acquired a sense of self-respect, self-control and personal responsibility in order to give them confidence to go out into the community.

Prior's Court School

Hermitage, Thatcham, Berkshire RG18 9NU
Tel: 01635 247202   Fax: 01635 247203
Email: mail@priorscourt.org.uk   Website: www.priorscourt.org.uk   www.gabbitas.net

Principal Mr R G Hubbard
Founded 1999
Chair of Governors Sir Derek Hornby
School status Co-educational independent
boarding and day DfES approved independent
(boarding 38 weeks/weekly)
Registered Charity Number 1070227
Religious denomination Multi-denominational
Special needs provision AUT, Autism with
moderate to severe learning difficulties
DfES Number 869/6014; *Accredited by* IIP
Age range 5–16   *boarders from* 5
No of students 41   *boys* 34 *girls* 7
No of boarders (full) 14; *(weekly)* 22; *(day)* 5
Fees per annum available on request

Prior's Court School is a specialist residential
school for children diagnosed as Autistic who
have moderate to severe learning difficulties.
Prior's Court School is particularly appropriate
for pupils who require a coordinated
programme of education and care.
The strengths of Daily Life Therapy, TEACCH
and the best practices from other approaches
have been adapted, incorporated with a clear
contemporary knowledge of Autism.
The Curriculum includes the National
Curriculum, sensory curriculum and Informa-
tion-Communication Technology. There is
strong emphasis on physical activities, music
and the arts.
Staff are available to discuss the school with
parents, Local Authorities and visits can be
arranged.

RNIB Condover Hall School

Condover, Shrewsbury, Shropshire SY5 7AH
Tel: 01743 872320   Fax: 01743 873310
E-mail: condover.office@rnib.org.uk   Website: www.gabbitas.net

Principal Mr H Dicks
Special needs provision Visual impairment and
additional disabilities, including deafblind/
multi-sensory impaired, ASP, AUT, CP, EBD,
EPI, HI, PH, PMLD, SLD, SP&LD, VIS, W
Age range 8–24
No of pupils 60
Fees per annum 38 week boarding from
£40,357

We provide education, care and support for
children and young people who are visually
impaired and have additional disabilities.
Students' individual needs are met by a multi-
professional team of specialist teachers, classroom assistants, care staff, physiotherapists,
speech and language therapists, an occupational therapist, a mobility teacher and an
educational psychologist, all of whom regularly
work with students on a one-to-one basis.
Students follow the National Curriculum,
adapted in content and delivery, and are also
encouraged to develop personal care, living and
social skills.
Students live in small groups in modern,
purpose-built flats and are cared for and
supported by fully qualified residential care
staff. We aim to provide a home-from-home
and to give our students the best possible
opportunities for learning, thereby enabling
them to reach their full potential.
The School is situated in extensive grounds in
the pretty village of Condover. We welcome
visits from parents, LEAs and Social Services.

RNIB New College Worcester

Whittington Road, Worcester, Worcestershire WR5 2JX
Tel: 01905 763933   Fax: 01905 763277
E-mail: hodgetts@rnibncw.demon.co.uk   Website: www.gabbitas.net

Head Mr N Ratcliffe MA JP
Founded 1866
School status Independent co-educational
boarding and day
Religious denomination All denominations
Member of HMC
Special needs provision VIS, W
Age range 11–19   *boarding from* 11
No of pupils in total 91 *Senior* 50 *Sixth Form* 41
Girls 40 *boys* 51
No of boarders (full) 89 *(weekly)* 2
Fees per annum (full boarding)
Standard £29,967 6th £31,614
(weekly) Standard £27,066 6th £28,548
(day) Standard £20,295 6th £21,942

RNIB New College Worcester is a co-educational residential special school. Our aim is to provide a broad and balanced curriculum for blind and partially sighted students aged 11–19 years. Students study for 8 or 9 GCSE subjects, AS and A2 levels. 98% of students go on to university.

All teaching staff are experienced specialists in their subject and are additionally qualified to teach visually impaired students. Special attention is paid to Mobility, Living Skills and Braille and the wide range of teaching facilities includes a new Learning Resources Centre, science laboratories, a drama studio, computer rooms, a gymnasium and a swimming pool.

RNIB Rushton Hall School

Rushton, Kettering, Northamptonshire NN14 1RR
Tel: 01536 710506   Fax: 01536 418506   Website: www.gabbitas.net
From July 2002: Wheelwright Lane, Coventry CV9 9RA Tel: 02476 369500

Head Mrs R Kirkwood
Founded 1961
Needs for which school offers provision Children
with visual impairment and multiple
disabilities (MDVI)
School status Non-maintained – DfES
Registered No. 928/7004
Registered Charity No. 226227
Age range 4–19
No of pupils (boarding) 35 *(day)* 10
Fees per annum Available on request

Rushton provides education and care for pupils who are aged 4–19 years with visual impairment and additional disabilities of a learning, physical, medical, social or emotional nature. Rushton aims to give each young person a high quality of life and the opportunity to maximise their independence.

The National Curriculum aims to help pupils and students to acquire the knowledge and skills to be as independent as possible and provides a wide range of learning opportunities. In addition, access to specialist resources and the multi-disciplinary team approach provide the focus on individual learning. Older students currently follow the EQUALS 'Moving On' curriculum which combines life experience with basic skills training.

Residential care enables the school to provide a rich PSHE curriculum. Boarding can be on a weekly, termly or 52 week basis. Respite is also provided. The school is registered as a Children's Home and is planning to relocate to Warwickshire in June 2002.

Rowden House School

Rowden, Bromyard, Herefordshire HR7 4LS
Tel: 01885 488096   Fax: 01885 483361
E-mail: info@rowden.co.uk   Website: www.rowden.co.uk

Head Mrs H Hardy
Founded 1986
School status Co-educational DfES approved
independent boarding
Member of BILD, SCA
Special needs provision SLD, AUT, DOW, EPI,
PMLD, TOU, W
Other needs catered for Severe learning
difficulties, challenging behaviour
Age range 11–19 *boarding from* 11
No of pupils (boarding) (full) 28
Girls 6   *Boys* 22
Fees per annum £75,000–£115,000

Rowden House School is pleased to announce the completion of the final phase of a £1.5m redevelopment programme which now enables the school to offer all its residents single bedrooms in purpose-built, single-storey accommodation.

The Coppice, The Glade, The Spinney and The Grove are high-specification homes each offering single-occupancy rooms for seven residents in a courtyard setting. Each unit has generously proportioned communal living spaces with fully equipped kitchen, dining room and lounge. Each private room has built-in bedroom furniture and has facilities to enable residents to use TV, sound systems and computers as appropriate. There are washrooms, bathrooms and showers on each wing of the buildings.

Each home has a Unit Manager with a dedicated team of fifteen Support Staff. Waking night staff are available to the children throughout the night, supported by sleep-in staff with whom they are connected by radio handset.

The homes have been designed within a courtyard setting at the edge of the woodland which borders the Rowden site. These units therefore offer an unrivalled situation within an outstanding natural environment. New purpose-built play facilities adjoin the homes.

We believe these new facilities will enable each of our client youngsters to develop skills towards independence in an appropriate domestic and social setting.

For further information regarding these developments and our education offer, visit our website at www.rowden.co.uk

The Royal Blind School, Edinburgh

Craigmillar Park, Edinburgh EH16 5NA
Tel: 0131 667 1100 Fax: 0131 662 9700 E-mail: office@royalblindschool.org.uk
Website: www.royalblindschool.org.uk www.gabbitas.net

Head Mr K Tansley
Religious denomination Non-denominational
School status Grant aided co-educational
boarding and day
Member of Scottish Council of Independent
Schools (SCIS) Headteachers' Association of
Scotland (HAS)
Accredited by Scottish Executive
Special needs provision AUT, CP, DEL, DYP, EPI,
MLD, PH, PMLD, SLD, SP&LD, SPLD, TOU,
VIS, W
Age range 3–19
No of pupils 126 *Junior* 30 *Senior* 42
Nursery 7 *PMLD* 47
Fees per annum On application

The Royal Blind School is a national centre of
expertise, providing high quality education and
care, for blind and partially sighted young
people. Throughout this day/residential school
the children are provided with individual
programmes of study and guidance, they have
access to the latest technology, small classes,
mobility training and the availability of
physiotherapists, speech & language therapists
and OT.
The school is organised into four departments:
Nursery – consists of the Pre School Unit, play
group and toy library. Primary & Secondary
Departments – follow the full 5–14 programme,
Standard Grade, Higher Still courses and work
experience. Canaan Lane caters for visually
impaired pupils in the 5–19 age range who have
severe additional disabilities.
The school has been completely refurbished
and provides a wide range of additional services
for parents and professionals, these include: a
multi-professional assessment service, outreach
support for children in mainstream school, in
service training, advice and support for families
provided by our parent counsellor.

Royal School for the Deaf Derby

Ashbourne Road, Derby DE22 3BH
Tel/Minicom: 01332 362512 Fax: 01332 299708
E-mail: admin.rsdd@virgin.net Website: www.rsd-derby.org.uk

Head Mr T Silvester
Founded 1893
School status Co-educational non-maintained
boarding and day
Religious denomination Non-denominational
Member of NASS *Special needs provision* HI
Age range 3–16 *Boarding from* 5
No of pupils (day) 41; *(boarding) (weekly)* 55
Girls 50 *boys* 46
Junior 29; *Senior* 67
Fees per annum (boarding) (weekly) £22,224;
(day) £15,657

RSD Derby meets the communicative, academic and social needs of deaf children within
a bilingual environment.
Weekly boarders and day pupils access a curriculum best suited to their needs. The school's
bilingual approach using British Sign Language,
written and spoken English aims to produce
independent individuals confident of their ability to integrate into the community. Dedicated
staff, both deaf and hearing ensure that pupils
fulfil their potential in a supportive environment. Commitment to academic achievement is
combined with excellent facilities for sport and
outdoor education.
The nursery offers free places to deaf children
from the ages of three to five. Primary curriculum is designed to develop skills at every level
and follows the framework and guidelines of
the National Curriculum. In secondary school
all National Curriculum subjects are taught by
specialist teachers and offered for GCSE. The
Certificate of Achievement is offered for pupils
who may not achieve GCSE.

Royal Schools for the Deaf (Manchester)

Stanley Road, Cheadle Hulme, Cheadle, Cheshire SK8 6RQ
Tel: 0161 610 0100   Fax: 0161 610 0101
E-mail: info@rsdmanchester.org
Website: www.rsdmanchester.org   www.gabbitas.net

INVESTOR IN PEOPLE

Head Mrs H Ward
Founded 1823
School status Independent non-maintained
co-educational boarding and day
Accredited by DfES
Special needs provision AUT, CP, EPI, HI, MLD,
PH, PMLD, SLD, SP&LD, SPLD, TOU, VIS, W
Other needs catered for severe/complex learning
difficulties
Age range 5–19+   *boarding from* 5
Fees per annum On application

Specialist provision for pupils/students with
complex communication difficulties arising
from sensory loss, severe learning difficulties,
autistic spectrum disorders or behaviours that
challenge services.
High staff/pupil ratio (1:1 in our deafblind
department) ensure learning opportunities are
appropriately constructed and are supported by
our specialist assessment centre staff.
Our curriculum takes account of the individual's communication difficulties and encompasses needs-related teaching/care programmes
designed to meet present and future needs.
Our total communication approach includes
the use of B.S.L. and sign-supported English,
together with pictorial system creating and
communicating environment across both the
school and residential care.
Leisure and recreational activities support the
pupils needs and include a swimming and
hydrotherapy pool, outdoor sensory gardens,
recreational areas, multi-sensory rooms,
together with a variety of youth clubs.

Rutland House School

Elm Bank, Mapperley Road, Nottingham NG5 3AJ
Tel: 0115 962 1315   Fax: 0115 962 2867
E-mail: caroleoviatt-ham113674.2000@compuserve.com   Website: www.gabbitas.net

Head Mrs C Oviatt-Ham
Founded 1979
School status DfEE approved independent
Special needs provision CP, EPI, HI, PH, PMLD,
SP&LD, VIS, W
Age range 5–19   *boarding from* 5
No of pupils (day) 6 *(boarding) (full)* 18 *(weekly)* 6
Girls 13 *boys* 17
Junior 16 *Senior* 10 *Sixth Form* 4
Fees per annum £31,112–£65,057

Rutland House School is managed by Scope. This
school is staffed with specialist teachers, therapists, conductors, nurses, qualified support staff
and access to a qualified advocate. A comprehensive team of medical specialists oversees the
medical and health needs of the children.
The education philosophy of the school is
founded on the teaching and principles of
Conductive Education. The school has successfully combined the Conductive Education
system with the National Curriculum. The curriculum is designed to promote the child's
physical, cognitive, communication, social,
emotional and independence skills.
The school has four departments:
The School For Parents is designed for parents
of pre-school children to provide support,
information and a comprehensive education
programme. The primary school curriculum is
designed to promote the child's physical skills,
social awareness, communication and growing
independence.
The Secondary School and 16–19 Unit occupy a
separate site. All students live in specially
adapted and resourced bungalows in the local
community. The aim of the secondary school is
to consolidate skills and knowledge in a wider
environment. The aim of the 16–19 programme
is to prepare the students for adult life by
maintaining, developing and transferring skills
in a range of settings.

Sheiling School, Camphill Community Thornbury

Thornbury Park, Park Road, Thornbury, Bristol BS35 1HP
Tel: 01454 412194   Fax: 01454 411860
E-mail: mail@sheilingschool.org.uk   Website: www.sheilingschool.org.uk

Contact Point Admissions Co-ordinator
Founded 1952
School status Independent co-educational
boarding and day
Member of Association of Camphill
Communities
Special needs provision MLD, SLD, AUT, DOW,
EBD, EPI, PMLD, SP&LD
Age range 6–19+
No of pupils (boarding) (full) 28; *(weekly)* 4
(day) 3; *(boarding)* 35
Girls 12 *boys* 23
Fees per annum on request

A caring, residential environment in a beautiful
parkland close to the historic town of
Thornbury is offered for pupils with a wide
range of learning difficulties. The school curriculum is based on Rudolf Steiner's Waldorf
Curriculum. There are small classes where the
needs of each child are assessed. Swimming,
eurythmy, weaving, pottery, woodwork, gymnastics, gardening and farming are available.
Individual therapies are prescribed where
needed, including speech therapy, eurythmy
therapy and art therapy. The home life in family
settings provides education and life skills to
enhance individual development.
A varied social life is provided both within the
school setting and in the locality.
There is high staff:pupil ratio.
Recent HMI and Social Services inspection
reports available on request.

The Sheiling School, Ringwood

Horton Road, Ashley, Near Ringwood, Dorset BH24 2EB
Tel: 01425 477488   Fax: 01425 479536
E-mail: enquiries@sheilingschool.co.uk   Website: www.sheilingschool.co.uk

Contact point Admissions co-ordinator
Founded 1951
School status Independent co-educational
boarding and day
Religious denomination Christian (non-
denominational)
Special needs provision MLD/SLD, FragileX,
Williams Syndrome, AUT, DOW, EBD, EPI,
MLD, SLD, SP&LD
Member of Association of Camphill
Communities
Age range 6–19
No of students 47; *Junior* 30; *Senior* 17
Boys 29; *girls* 18
Residential fees from £22,620. Full details on
application

The Sheiling School is an independent
Camphill Rudolf Steiner School for children
from 6 to 19 years.

The school is situated close to Ringwood in the
New Forest. A 58 acre semi-rural site of fields,
gardens and woodlands surround family sized
houses, classrooms, gymnasium, swimming
pool, therapy centre, workshops, chapel, hall
and play areas.
The Sheiling provides a fully integrated school
and house life in a community village setting. It
offers residential care (38 weeks), education
(based on the Waldorf curriculum) and special
therapies for up to 55 children/students with
severe and moderate learning difficulties. A
three-year Upper School Programme (16–19)
is available for up to 25 students. The
programme offers training, education and
workshops, onsite integrated activities with
other organisations, and a strong, round-the-
clock social and cultural programme. Outward
bound activities take a central role within this
programme.

Sheridan House

Southburgh, Thetford, Norfolk
Tel: 01953 850494   Fax: 01953 851498   E-mail: sheridanhouse@prioryhealthcare.co.uk
Website: www.prioryhealthcare.co.uk   www.gabbitas.net

Head Mrs S J Sayer
Founded 1979
School status DfES approved independent boys boarding only
Member of Charterhouse Group of Therapeutic Communities, NASEN AWCEBD
Special needs provision EBD, pupils may also present ADD, ADHD, DYS, SPLD
Age range 10–16   *boarding from* 10
No of boys (boarding) (full) 12
Fees per annum £115,705

Sheridan House is a residential therapeutic community approved as a special school by the DfES. It provides an integrated programme of care, education and psychotherapy for 12 boys, aged 10 to 16 years, who experience emotional conflicts, who present with challenging behaviour and who have disrupted educational experiences. Many of the pupils will have experienced trauma, inconsistent and confusing care and emotional rejection and will lack self-esteem. Placements, which are drawn from a national catchment area, are long term and for 52 weeks a year.

Sheridan House seeks to provide a warm and caring environment with firm and consistent boundaries and is concerned with the establishment of positive relationships based on mutual respect. A multi-disciplinary approach is taken in the creation of a community that allows each young person to gain a sense of personal worth. The aim is to guide each of our young people towards more personal and enriching relationships as well as aiding them in the development of social and educational skills. Cause and effect are emphasised so that the pupils are assisted in making positive change and accepting increasing responsibility for their actions. Regular contact is maintained with families and carers.

Education is provided on site in a designated purpose built school. Teaching groups are small (on average 4 pupils) providing for a high level of adult support. A broad and balanced curriculum is provided by experienced special needs teachers with a wide range of National Curriculum work differentiated for individual needs and abilities. Pupils are encouraged to achieve success through a wide range of nationally recognised external accreditation including GCSE, Entry Level Certificates and the ASDAN awards. Links have been developed with local providers of vocational education leading to the possibility of NVQ accreditation and a work related curriculum.

Following initial assessment of each young person's needs, regular monitoring, evaluation and assessment of progress takes place with the pupils fully involved in identifying and reviewing their educational targets which form part of a comprehensive Individual Education, Care and Therapy Plan. Education is not seen in isolation and there are close links between education, care and therapy.

All young people have the opportunity of receiving individual psychotherapy on a regular basis from the resident psychotherapist. The psychotherapist is also able to work with parents and carers in their own homes and is able to offer individual, marital and family psychotherapy.

Pupils are encouraged to take an active part in a wide range of purposeful activities both within Sheridan House and the wider community.

The qualifications of professional staff include teaching, social work, counselling and group work. Supervision, support and training of staff are given a high priority and both psycho-therapeutic and practice supervision is provided for staff.

Sheridan House is situated in rural Norfolk 15 miles to the west of Norwich and within easy range of a number of small market towns. Mainline train links are available in Norwich and equally accessible are the trunk road links of the A11, A47, A14 and A1.

St Catherine's School

Grove Road, Ventnor, Isle of Wight PO38 1TT
Tel: 01983 852722   Fax: 01983 857219
E-mail: general@stcatherines.org.uk   Website: www.stcatherines.org.uk   www.gabbitas.net

Principal Mr G E Shipley
Founded 1879
School status Co-educational non-maintained boarding and day
Religious denomination Church of England
Member of NASS   DfES No. 921 7000
Accredited by Investors in People, Basic Skills Agency
Special needs provision SP&LD
Age range 7–19   boarding from 7
No of pupils 74; (boarding) (full) 62; (weekly) 6
Girls 9 boys 65
Junior 8; *Senior* 49; *Sixth Form* 17
Fees per annum (boarding) (full) £25,902; (weekly) £24,053; (day) £19,427

Special needs catered for: Specific speech and language disorder plus associated learning difficulties.
Specialist facilities: Speech and language therapy delivered across the curriculum with teachers and therapists working together.
Education: The curriculum is broad, balanced and relevant to the needs of each student. Our basic skills curriculum has been awarded a quality mark by the Basic Skills Agency. Students have access to mainstream education and work experience.
Support services: School nurse, occupational therapy.
Home/school links: Frequent communication by letter and telephone. Parents always encouraged to visit. Regular annual review other events.
General environment: Residentially divided into five separate Houses. Access to many local community activities.
Aims and philosophy: To provide, through a multi-disciplinary approach, a programme of education and language remediation that meets the individual needs of each student.

St Christopher's School

Carisbrooke Lodge, Westbury Park, Bristol BS6 7JE
Tel: 0117 973 3301/ 973 6875   Fax: 0117 974 3665   Website: www.gabbitas.net

Head Ms Orna Matz
Founded 1945
School status Co-educational independent boarding
Religious denomination Christian non-denominational
Special needs provision AUT, CP, EPI, PMLD, SLD, SP&LD, W
Age range 6–19   Boarding from 6
No of pupils 48–50
Girls 15 boys 33
Fees per annum Available on request

St Christopher's is a residential school for pupils aged 6–19 with severe and complex, profound and multiple learning difficulties and associated conditions. The curriculum is guided by the educational principles of Rudolf Steiner and includes relevant aspects of the National Curriculum. Emphasis on developing skills is done through individual care and education plans for each pupil. Residential provision is available for up to 52 weeks.

Therapeutic support is provided from an occupational therapist, physiotherapist, speech and language therapist, educational psychologist, Steiner-trained therapists and regular qualified nursing support. Staff in houses and classes work with no more than two pupils; some pupils have one-to-one support. Each house has waking night staff.

The school is situated in spacious, attractive grounds, with a heated indoor swimming pool and other facilities on site.

For further information contact the Educational Registrar.

St Dominic's School

Hambledon, Godalming, Surrey GU8 4DX
Tel: 01428 684693   Fax: 01428 685018   Website: www.gabbitas.net

Head Mr G Chapman
Founded 1929
School status Co-educational non-maintained boarding and day
Religious denomination Roman Catholic
Special needs provision Speech and language difficulties, SPLD, Medical conditions, ADD, ADHD, ASP, DEL, DYC, DYS, DYP, EPI, SP&LD
Other needs catered for Social communication difficulties
Age range 7–16 *boarding from* 8
No of pupils 90 *no of boarders (weekly)* 59
Girls 10 *boys* 80
Fees per annum (boarding) (weekly) £24,981–£27,948; *(day)* £16,653–£19,620

St Dominic's provides residential and day placements for pupils of average intelligence but with special needs. These include impaired physical health, specific learning, speech and language and social communication difficulties. Pupils may also be emotionally vulnerable and have motor planning, co-ordination and perceptual difficulties.

The School offers a caring environment where pupils do not miss out on educational opportunities as they are given access to a curriculum similar to that found in mainstream schools leading to GCSE examinations.

Pupils are taught in small class groups with help from learning support teachers. A modern and customised therapy suite meets the needs of physiotherapy, sensory integration therapy, occupational and speech and language therapy. There is a fully equipped surgery with 24-hour nursing cover to meet the needs of children with medical problems, including asthma and epilepsy.

Admission is usually arranged through the Local Education Authority in whose area the child's family reside.

St Edward's School

Melchet Court, Sherfield English, Romsey, Hampshire SO51 6ZR
Tel: 01794 884271   Fax: 01794 884903   Website: www.gabbitas.net

Headteacher Mr L P Bartel BEd (Hons)
Founded 1963
School status Boys independent boarding only, DfES approved independent
Religious denomination Non-denominational
Special needs provision EBD, ADD, ADHD, DYS, MLD, SPLD
Age range 10–17   *boarding from* 10
No of pupils (boarding) (full) 64
Junior 32; *Senior* 32
Fees per annum (boarding) £44,352

Special needs catered for: A residential special school for emotionally and behaviourally disturbed boys, including those whose condition may be complicated by mild, moderate and specific learning difficulties.

Specialist facilities: The full National Curriculum is followed at all levels. Specialist learning support for a wide range of learning difficulties. Emphasis upon vocational preparation in Years 10 and 11. Options are matched to individual interests and aptitudes. The school is organised into three year groups for education and care. Separate accommodation allows distinct arrangements reflecting the age and maturity of the pupils. Lower school (ages 10–14) Year 6–9 have a very wide variety of learning experiences covering 11 subjects. Emphasis is placed on core subjects with specialist assistance for boys with learning difficulties. Middle school (ages 14–15) Year 10 are taught within a broad curriculum including Science, Information Communication Technology, Physical Education, Personal and Social Education, Design Technology, Games, Geography and History. Mathematics and English are given very full and specialist treatment. Senior school (ages 15–16) Year 11. Within the National Curriculum framework GCSE courses are followed in English, Mathematics, Science, Art, Physical Education, Information Communication Technology, Religious Studies and Design Technology. Vocational courses are followed in building craft, painting and decorating, and horticulture, taken to pre-NVQ level (i.e. LCCI courses).

Support services provided: A comprehensive educational and personality assessment can be offered by our consultant child and educational psychologist.

General environment: The school offers a wide range of sporting and social activities, which take place at weekends and evenings throughout the year. The activities are too numerous to list in full, but they include: motorcycling, quad biking, motor mechanics, sub-aqua club, horse riding, canoeing, food technology, judo, weight training, computers, swimming, roller hockey, archery, football, badminton, basketball, art and multigym. An extensive summer expedition programme complements the leisure activities. The week long expeditions include outward bound activities in Devon; cycling, canoeing and hiking in the Yorkshire Dales; pony riding in the New Forest; and fishing on our own lakes.

Aims and philosophy: St Edward's School Charitable Trust aims to foster each boy's personal and social growth.

St Elizabeth's School

South End, Much Hadham, Hertfordshire SG10 6EW
Tel: 01279 844270   Fax: 01279 843903   Website: www.stelizabeths.org.uk   www.gabbitas.net

Principal Mrs Clare-Ann Walker
School status Non-maintained boarding and day co-educational
Religious denomination Roman Catholic
Special needs provision EPI, MLD, SLD, SP&LD, AUT
Age range 5–19+
Registered (boarders) 68; *(day)* 12
Fees per annum (boarding) £49,508–£72,212; *(day)* £29,705–£45,727

Curriculum: St Elizabeth's offers a 24-hour curriculum, which embraces all areas of the National Curriculum. French is the modern foreign language. A high ratio of teaching and support staff alongside well-resourced specialist subject rooms support truly differentiated programmes of study. Senior pupils and students have the opportunity to take part in enterprise projects, work experience and community service. There is a stress on self-help and independence training at all levels. Link programmes of study are available in local colleges.

Entry requirements: Pupils are formally referred through their LEA – possible joint funding with social services and health. Students 16–19 are placed through their specialist careers service. The options of informal visits, interview, overnight stays are all possible. Admission forms to be completed before formal interview. The school welcomes children from all or no faiths.

External Accreditation: All school leavers and students, work towards their achievements being accredited by one or more of the following national schemes: OCR Accreditation for Life and Living or the National Skills profile; WJEC First Skills Award; ASDAN Towards Independence, alternatively the Bronze and Silver (NVQ Level II) Youth Award Schemes; City and Guild; Numberpower, Wordpower or Communication Skills; Young Enterprise – Team Enterprise award and the Duke of Edinburgh Award. Every young person has their own individual programme and full review meetings are held annually.

Academic and leisure facilities: Academic and residential areas are light, airy, comfortably furnished and well equipped. Situated within a 68-acre site, there are many areas for sport and leisure. Excellent use is made of local leisure facilities. The school has on-site medical/nursing support with staff on nightly duty. Speech and language, physiotherapy and occupational therapy are available on site. The school's educational psychologist and counsellor are available in both residential and academic settings. Families may stay in self-catering accommodation on site.

Religious activities: St Elizabeth's is administered by the Congregation of the Daughters of The Cross of Liege (RC). It admits children of any or no faith. Dignity and privacy are key words in helping each child and family to a better quality of life through improved seizure control and independence. St Elizabeth's is committed to an equal opportunities policy and welcomes the opportunity to work with families. There is parental representation on the governing body and regular parent/staff contact to guarantee the degree of contact, commitment and service. Daughters of The Cross (St Elizabeth's), a registered charity, exists to provide education, training and care for children and students who have epilepsy and associated disabilities.

Our 1998 OFSTED Inspection said:

- "Teaching is very good or better in one out of every three lessons"
- "The Curriculum is broad and highly relevant to pupils"
- "Provision for pupils' spiritual development is outstanding"
- "Particular strengths of teaching are the management of pupils and the quality of lesson planning"
- "The school provides good value for money"
- "The good team work between teachers, learning support assistants and care staff ensures that pupils and students are actively and meaningfully involved in all areas of school life"
- "Parents ... speak highly of the patience of care staff and the quality of medical support available to pupils".

St John's Catholic School for the Deaf

Church Street, Boston Spa, West Yorkshire LS23 6DF
Tel: 01937 842144   Fax: 01937 541471
E-mail: info@stjohns.org.uk   Website: www.stjohns.org.uk

Head Mr T M Wrynne, BEd (Hons), MA, TOD
Founded 1870
School status Co-educational non-maintained boarding and day
Religious denomination Roman Catholic catering for pupils of all denominations
Special needs provision DYP, HI, SP&LD, W
Age range 3–19   *boarding from* 5
No of pupils (boarding) (full) 17; *(weekly)* 31
Girls 49 *boys* 37
Junior 23; *Senior* 55; *Sixth Form* 8
Fees per annum On application

St John's is a non-maintained residential and day school offering a first class oral education for children aged from 3 to 19 years of age. A strong Christian ethos permeates all aspects of school life and children of all denominations are welcomed. The curriculum is broad and balanced and provides the opportunity for pupils to take GCSEs, Certificates of Achievement and a wide range of vocationally oriented courses. In addition to 20 qualified teachers of the deaf, support is available from our speech and language therapists, audiologist, and school nurse. The OFSTED inspectors who visited our school said, *St John's is an excellent school for pupils and students who have a hearing impairment and gives them an excellent quality of education, supported by a high level of commitment and care from all staff.*

St Margaret's School

The Children's Trust, Tadworth Court, Tadworth, Surrey KT20 5RU
Tel: 01737 365810   Fax: 01737 365819

Head Mrs J E Cunningham
Founded 1985
School status Co-educational DfES approved
independent boarding and day
Member of NAIMS, NASS
Special needs provision CP, EPI, HI, PMLD, VIS
Other needs catered for Complex care and
medical needs
Age range 5–19
No of pupils 37 (capacity 40)
Girls 23 *boys* 14
Fees per annum On application

Curriculum: St Margaret's School provides education and care and therapy, and accesses for all pupils a broad, balanced curriculum designed to be relevant to individual needs, which is delivered to a 24-hour model. The curriculum emphasises sensory awareness, the importance of developing precursors to learning, intentional communication and interactions. It also promotes the integration of all therapy procedures in order to facilitate a holistic delivery.

Entry requirements: Informal visits, followed by request for assessment to establish individual special needs. LEA sponsorship.

Open for 48 weeks a year, the school has its own doctor, small team of nurses and provides 24 hour medical cover.

The Children's Trust, a registered charity, exists to offer care, treatment and education to children with exceptional needs and profound disabilities, and to give support to their families.

St Mary's School

Wrestwood Road, Bexhill-on-Sea, East Sussex TN40 2LU   Website: www.gabbitas.net
Tel: 01424 730740   Fax: 01424 733575   E-mail: stmarys@wrestwood.freeserve.co.uk

Principal and C.E.O. Mr David Cassar MA,
MIMgt, FRSA
Founded 1922
School status Co-educational non-maintained
voluntary boarding and day
Religious denomination Christian Foundation
Member of NASS
Special needs provision Primary – Speech/
Language and Autism. ASP, AUT, CP, DEL,
DOW, DYP, DYS, EPI, HI, MLD, PH, SP&LD,
SPLD, TOU, VIS, W
Other needs catered for Complex medical
conditions
Age range 7–19 *boarding from* 7
No of pupils (day) 20; *(boarding)* 118
Fees per annum Contact head of administration
for information

Curriculum: We follow the National Curriculum, differentiated where necessary, plus individual learning programmes and a comprehensive life skills programme. We have a team of speech and language therapists, an art therapist, physiotherapists, occupational therapists, specialist teacher for the hearing impaired and a high ratio of qualified and experienced care and nursing staff.

Entry requirements: Formal assessments and interview. Referrals are normally made through local education departments. Private referrals are also considered.

St Mary's is a DfES non-maintained special school, situated in a semi-rural location in Sussex near the sea. It is set in attractive buildings in woodland on the outskirts of Bexhill. Children are referred from all parts of the country and abroad.

St Mary's Wrestwood Educational Trust is a registered charity which exists to provide high quality education, therapy and care in a residential setting, for boys and girls with special educational needs, which can include quite complex and unique conditions and syndromes.

St Rose's School

Stratford Lawn, Stroud, Gloucestershire GL5 4AP
Tel: 01453 763793   Fax: 01453 752617
Website: www.stroses.gloucs.sch.uk   www.gabbitas.net

Head Sister M Quentin OP, BA
Founded 1912
School status Non-maintained boarding and day
Religious denomination Catholic
Member of NAIMS, NASS, NCSE
Special needs provision ASP, CP, DEL, DYP, EPI, MLD, PH, SLD, SP&LD, VIS, W
Age range 2–18   *boarding from* 5
No of pupils 70 (day) 37 (boarding) (full) 33
Girls 31 *boys* 39
Fees per annum Available on request

Curriculum: The curriculum includes all National Curriculum subjects, and GCSE is available for those who are able. For the less able a broad-based curriculum is available with accreditation through ASDAN, C&G and the Basic Skills Agency. To suit the needs of the children, this would include social skills, therapy, creative skills etc.

Entry requirements: All children have a physical disabilities and other associated impairments. St Rose's School exists to provide high quality education and care for children with special needs, and is part of the English Dominican Sisters of St Catherine of Siena Charitable Trust.

St Vincent's School for Blind and Partially Sighted Children (Founded 1849)

Yew Tree Lane, West Derby, Liverpool L12 9HN   Tel: 0151 228 9968   Fax: 0151 252 0216
Website: www.ourworld.compuserve.com/homepages/STVINCENTS/   www.gabbitas.net

Head Mr A MacQuarrie
School status Co-educational non-maintained weekly boarding and day
Member of OPSIS, NASS, CES
Accredited by DfES   Charity No. 526756
Special needs provision VIS
Age range 4–17 *Boarding from* 4 *No of pupils* 100

What we provide:
- Academic, vocational, personal and social education. Access to National Curriculum, tailored to individual need, leading to GCSE, NVQ, AEB, Basic and Certificates of Education, Youth Award Scheme.
- High staff to pupil ratio. Specialist staff supported by a qualified team of learning support assistants and nursery nurses.
- Independence training by mobility officers and care staff.
- Access to physiotherapist, speech therapist, optician, ophthalmologist, dentist, doctor and Educational Psychologist.

Facilities at St Vincent's:
- Well-equipped classrooms with appropriate lighting and blinds, computers with speech synthesizers, large print facility and low vision resources.
- Specialist rooms for science, art, IT, DT, food technology and music studio.
- Multi-gym, indoor swimming pool, canoes, all-weather pitch and soft play room.

Extra-curricular activities include:
- Educational visits and field trips, Duke of Edinburgh Awards.
- Tandem riding, cricket, football, snooker, karaoke, make-up and beauty.

The staff are committed to serving the needs of the pupils.
Applications should be made to the Head by the LEA, who are also responsible for the fees.

Sunfield School

Clent Grove, Woodman Lane, Clent, Stourbridge, West Midlands DY9 9PB
Tel: 01562 882253   Fax: 01562 883856   E-mail: sunfield@sunfield.worcs.sch.uk
Website: www.sunfield-school.org.uk   www.gabbitas.net

Head Professor B Carpenter OBE
Founded 1930
School status DfES approved independent co-educational boarding, registered charity
Religious denomination Non-denominational
Member of NAIMS, NASS, Association of West Midlands and Non-maintained Special Schools
Accredited by DfES
Special needs provision ADD, ADHD, ASP, AUT, DOW, EBD, PMLD, SLD
Other needs catered for Severe and complex learning needs and challenging behaviour
Age range 6–19   *Boarding from* 6
No of pupils 75
girls 15 *boys* 60
Fees per annum Available on application

Sunfield offers education and 52-week residential care for children with severe and complex learning needs. There is also specialist provision for children with severe autistic spectrum disorders. Our integrated care and education based curriculum encompasses National Curriculum and individual needs. Students are supported by a variety of therapists and psychologists.

Eleven houses each provide homes for 6–9 children. The school buildings comprise classrooms, theatre, games, craft, soft play and sensory rooms, kitchen, library and shop.

In preparation for citizenship, we use community facilities, eg, swimming pools, leisure centres, local clubs and shops. Our grounds, shop and farm offer meaningful accredited work experience for older students.

At Sunfield we recognise each child as a learner and communicator with a unique contribution to make. The principles of dignity and respect inform all aspects of our practice.

Swalcliffe Park School

Swalcliffe, nr. Banbury, Oxfordshire OX15 5EP
Tel: 01295 780302   Fax: 01295 780006
E-mail: admin@swalcliffepark.co.uk   Website: www.gabbitas.net

Principal Ray Hooper
Founded 1965
School status DfES approved non-maintained 931/7007 boys only, boarding and day
Religious denomination Non-denominational
Member of NAES, NAS(Corp), NASS, SERSS
Special needs provision EBD, ASP, ADHD, ADD, MLD
Age range 11–19   *boarding from* 11
No of pupils Boys 62; *(boarding)* 57; *(day)* 5
Fees per annum from £30,540 *(day)* to £47,265

Facilities include purpose-built educational and residential accommodation, set in 20 acres with lake, adventure playground, motorbikes, go-karts and swimming pool.

High quality education and care is offered to young people who have previously failed in a variety of educational establishments. We offer provision for a range of developmental, learning, behavioural and emotional difficulties.

A wide range of recreational activities are available. There is special provision for young people with Asperger Syndrome. Pupils follow the National Curriculum with emphasis on literacy, numeracy, practical curriculum (where appropriate) and a range of external examinations including GCSEs, City & Guilds and Certificates of Achievement.

A well qualified co-ordinator gives individual help with severe literacy difficulties. Support is provided by an Educational Psychologist and a Psychiatrist. Counselling can be facilitated at an additional cost.

Treloar School

Upper Froyle, Alton, Hampshire GU34 4LA
Tel: 01420 526400   Fax: 01420 526426
E-mail: admissions@treloar.org.uk   Website: www.treloar.org.uk   www.gabbitas.net

Head Mr Neil Clark
Founded 1908
School status Co-educational non-maintained boarding and day
Religious denomination Non-denominational
Member of NAIMS, NASS
Accredited by OFSTED
Special needs provision PH, CP, DEL, DYP, DYS, EPI, HI, SP&LD, SPLD, VIS, W
Other needs catered for The school has experience of managing and supporting young people with degenerative conditions
Age range 5–16+   *boarding from* 7
No of pupils 144
No of boarders (full) 71 *(weekly)* 37 *(day)* 35
Girls 62 *boys* 81
Fees per annum (boarding full) £21,537–£55,272

Treloar School provides education, independence training and care for young people with physical disabilities. Our teaching, care, therapy and counselling staff work together to develop a detailed 24-hour curriculum for each student providing each individual with the support, confidence and skills to achieve in all aspects of daily living. Emphasis is on independence.

The school provides a curriculum based on the individual needs and abilities of each student. We offer all National Curriculum subjects and a range of certificated courses at Key Stage 4, including 12 subjects at GCSE.

The school has its own medical centre with full night cover. The medical team consists of a doctor and over 30 nurses and physio-, occupational and speech and language therapists.

The school has three boarding houses. Day-to-day responsibility falls to the care co-ordinator working with other house staff and the wider school community to develop a warm, supportive environment.

Trengweath School

Hartley Road, Plymouth, Devon PL3 5LW
Tel: 01752 771975   Fax: 01752 793388   Website: www.gabbitas.net

Head Mrs G B Pratchett MEd, BA
School status Co-educational DfES approved independent boarding and day
Religious denomination Non-denominational
Member of Scope
Special needs provision PMLD, CP, SLD
Other needs catered for Multiply-disabled visually impaired, multi-sensory impairment
Age range 2–19
No of pupils 30
Girls 12 *boys* 8
Junior 12 *Senior* 8
Fees per annum On application

Trengweath is set in a residential district within easy reach of Plymouth City. It is a centre of advice and help for the community, keeping close links with local families.

School: Day and boarding pupils aged 2–19 years, including a nursery. Mainstream children learn alongside those with special needs in our Integrated Nursery. Opportunities for integration in mainstream are available.

Therapy: We provide physiotherapy, music, occupational and speech and language therapy. Facilities include a gym, hydrotherapy pool, sensory room, soft play area and sensory garden.

Family Support: Working directly with parent and child in-group sessions. Children attend from three years old or from their first diagnosis. There is an Outreach Service in Cornwall.

Respite care: Operates in partnership with local authorities. Open seven days a week, fifty weeks of the year, on a 24-hour basis with an Emergency Service available.

Underley Garden School

Kirkby Lonsdale, Carnforth, Lancashire LA6 2DZ
Tel: 01524 271569   Fax: 01524 272581
E-mail: underleyes@hotmail.com   Website: www.gabbitas.net

Head Mrs Pam Redican
Founded 1990
School status Co-educational DfES approved independent boarding
Religious denomination Non-denominational
Special needs provision ADD, ADHD, ASP, EBD, MLD, SPLD
Age range 9–16   *boarding from* 9
No of pupils 49
Girls 28; *boys* 21
Currently undergoing expansion to cater for an additional 36 pupils.
Fees per annum Available on application

Curriculum: 24-hour care and education curriculum for boys and girls who have special educational needs that leave them vulnerable and troubled, and need help to develop confidence and relationships.
Entry requirements and procedures: Referrals by local education authorities and/or social services, resident and consultant staff available for assessment.
Examinations offered: GCSEs, Certificates of Achievement, AEB Basic Tests, AQA Units of Accreditation, CLAIT.
Academic and leisure facilities: Classrooms, residential accommodation, vocational workshops, laboratory, sports hall and playing fields, permanent camp site.
Special approaches: Small classes (7–8 pupils), individual education programmes of study, specialist and class teachers with a learning support assistant, special needs department (educational psychologist and learning support co-ordinator), consultant child psychiatrist, careers programme and work experience.
Boarding facilities: Residence in purpose built bungalows with domestic routines for seven pupils. Progression towards independence.

Underley Hall School

Kirkby Lonsdale, Carnforth, Lancashire LA6 2HE
Tel: 01524 271206   Fax: 01524 272581
E-mail: underleyes@hotmail.com   Website: www.gabbitas.net

Head Mr John Parkinson
Founded 1976
School status Boys DfES approved independent boarding
Religious denomination Non-denominational
Special needs provision ADD, ADHD, EBD, MLD, SPLD
Age range 9–16   *boarding from* 9
No of pupils 70
Fees per annum Available on application

Curriculum: 24-hour care and education curriculum for boys who are unable to make or hold good relationships, may have learning difficulties and who often cause problems or anxiety at home.
Entry requirements and procedures: Referrals by local education authorities and/or social services, resident and consultant staff available for assessment.
Examinations offered: GCSEs, Certificates of Achievement, AEB Basic Tests, AQA Units of Accreditation.
Academic and leisure facilities: Classrooms, residential accommodation, vocational workshops, laboratory, sports hall and playing fields, permanent camp site.
Special approaches: Small classes (7–8 pupils), individual education programmes of study, specialist and class teachers with a learning support assistant, special needs department (educational psychologist and learning support co-ordinator), consultant child psychiatrist, careers programme and work experience.
Boarding facilities: Residence in living areas with domestic routines. Progression towards independence with a town house for school leavers.

The Unicorn School

Whitefield, 18 Park Crescent, Abingdon, Oxfordshire OX14 1DD
Tel: 01235 530222   Fax: 01235 530222   E-mail: unicorndyslexia@hotmail.com
Website: www.unicorndyslexia.co.uk   www.gabbitas.net

Head Mrs E Christie
Founded 1991
School status Co-educational independent day
Religious denomination Non-denominational
Special needs provision DYS, ADD, ADHD, DYC, DYP, W
Member of BDA; *Accredited by* CReSTeD
Age range 6–12
No of pupils 32
Boys 30; *girls* 1
Fees per annum £8,400

Aims and philosophy
To provide specialist education for dyslexic children, from both independent and maintained sector, and to teach strategies and skills to enable them to return to mainstream education as soon as possible.

The Unicorn caters for dyslexic children who often also have difficulties stemming from ADD, ADHD, dyspraxia and dyscalculia. Pupils are taught by specialist teachers in small classes of 8–10, with a daily half-hour of individual tuition, including Phonographix.

A structured, multi-sensory programme, including an appropriately differentiated national curriculum is followed with extensive use of word processors and encouragement to develop creative talents.

Educational and emotional needs are met on an individual basis as well as through a friendly atmosphere and community spirit.

Close liaison is maintained with the local education authority; parents are supported throughout the time they are associated with the Unicorn and helped to find suitable schools for their children to move on to.

Willoughby Hall Dyslexia Centre

1 Willoughby Road, London NW3 1RP
Tel: 020 7794 3538   Fax: 020 7435 2872   Website: www.gabbitas.net

Head June Hawkins
Founded September 1998
School status Co-educational independent day
Religious denomination Non-denominational
Age range 6–12
Girls 6 boys 35
Fees per annum £13,029

Willoughby Hall Dyslexia Centre offers a complete course of education for pupils aged from 6 to 12 years, who are held back by dyslexia and other learning difficulties. The Centre is a development of work done over the last twenty years at North Bridge House School, culminating in the opening of this special facility, itself based on a pilot scheme at our Parkway premises.

The teaching is based on a three year full-time course which aims to provide the pupils with a thorough knowledge of the skills required in Secondary Education, enabling pupils to return to the mainstream. As dyslexic children can have a very limited span of concentration, the intensive work in therapy can only be maintained for very short periods. This means that other activities such as Art, Music and CDT must be simultaneously available so that they can relax, whenever necessary. The children are taught in a small group from which individuals are drawn out to concentrate on building the

skills they have failed to develop earlier and overcoming their specific difficulties.

Each pupil works to an Individual Education Plan. The main emphasis is on English and Mathematics, using a multi-sensory approach. Science, History, Geography, Scripture, Art, Design, Music, Drama, Computing (including keyboarding skills) and Study Skills all feature in the curriculum. We keep as close as possible to the mainstream syllabus.

Pupils are able to take part in a varied programme of Physical education at Willoughby Hall.

Dyslexia Centre pupils are taught keyboard skills and basic computing. Those pupils for whom a laptop computer is an essential classroom aid will thus be able to use it to best advantage.

At the Dyslexia Centre it is understood that parents will want to be very closely involved with their child's education and the Head Teacher and the teacher in charge will always make time to see parents, even at short notice. Should you wish to discuss the work of the Willoughby Hall Dyslexia Centre further, please telephone the secretary on 020 7794 3538. Entry to the centre is by interview and test. The parent is also required to arrange for an assessment by an Educational Psychologist recommended by the school.

Witherslack Group of Schools

Group Aim and Philosophy

The six schools, which comprise the Witherslack Group of Schools, are specialist communities working with and for children with emotional, behavioural and learning difficulties. A range of associated needs are also provided for including specific learning difficulties. The Group is committed to respecting and valuing all individual pupils and staff, to providing the highest standards of care and to ensuring safety, security and opportunities for success.

Witherslack Hall School

Witherslack, Grange-over-Sands, Cumbria LA11 6SD
Tel: 015395 52397   Fax: 015395 52419   Website: www.gabbitas.net

Head Mr M Barrow B.Ed, PGCE, Man
Boys only
Age Range 11–16
Boarding from 11
No of pupils 70
Special Needs provision EBD, SPLD, ADHD
Fees available on application

The school has a range of specialist facilities including provision for science, art and craft, CDT, information technology, domestic science and rural studies.

There is a variety of residential provision, including semi-independent living provision for older pupils in nearby cottages.

Cedar House School

Kirkby Lonsdale, via Carnforth, Lancashire LA6 2HW
Tel: 015242 71181   Fax: 015242 71910   Website: www.gabbitas.net

Head Mr A W Cousins BEd (Hons) MSc
Age range 9–16
Boarding from 9
No of pupils 70 Boys and girls
Special Needs provision EBD, SPLD, ADHD
Fees available on application

The school has excellent facilities, including a separate primary teaching base. There are well-equipped specialist facilities for science, information technology, and art and craft.

Residential accommodation is maintained to the highest standard, and a range of designated leisure areas are provided. There are well-established links with the local community maintained in a variety of ways.

The school was originally a small mansion house to which purpose-built dining, assembly, residential and two separate teaching blocks have been added.

Lowgate House School

Levens, Kendal, Cumbria LA8 8NJ
Tel: 015395 60124   Fax: 015395 60648   Website: www.gabbitas.net

Head Mrs J Richardson
Boys only
Age range 7–13 *Boarding from* 7
No of pupils 16
38/52 week provision
Special Needs provision EDB, SPLD
Fees available on request

The school provides for small class groupings, coupled with opportunities for individual teaching where appropriate. The school has a semi-independent living provision for children nearing reintegration to mainstream education and home.

Lowgate is a small school where all staff are committed to providing an intimate and homely environment. Extensive grounds provide generous recreational areas. Residential accommodation is maintained to a high standard of furnishing, decoration and comfort.

Pontville School

Black Moss lane, Ormskirk, Lancashire L39 4TW
Tel: 01695 578 734   Fax: 01695 579 224   Website: www.gabbitas.net

Head Mr R Farbon
Age range 11–19
Boarding from 11
No of pupils 70
Special Needs provision ADD, ASP, MLD, TOU

The school caters for young people aged 11–19 years with moderate learning difficulties and social, emotional problems. The full National

Curriculum is offered by specialist teachers in specialised accommodation.
Pontville also has a Transition Unit offering a vocational curriculum for students aged 16–19. Courses include basic education, social and life skills, woodwork, ceramics, catering, vehicle maintenance, animal husbandry, horticulture studies and IT.

Lakeside School

Naylor's Road, Liverpool L27 2YA
Tel: 0151 487 7211   Fax: 0151 487 7214   Website: www.gabbitas.net

Head Miss V E Shaw Cert Ed, Dip Ed
Age range 4–13
No of pupils 24
Fees available on application

Lakeside is a co-educational day, with residential provision off site, special school catering for 24 Early Years, Key Stage 1 and Key Stage 2 pupils who exhibit complex patterns of learning and communication difficulties. In some circumstances children may continue their schooling into Key Stage 3. A continuation of

provision is available at KS3, KS4 and post 16 at our sister school Pontville.
Lakeside has a residential clinical team under the leadership of Mr Colin Critchley, Director of Clinical Services. The school also has access to additional therapeutic services via local Child and Adolescent Mental Health Provision – Occupational Play, Art, Horticultural, Music, Speech and Language, Psychological, Psychiatric, Family Therapy, Sexual/Physical/Emotional abuse counselling.

Westmorland School

Weldbank Lane, Chorley, Lancashire PR7 3NQ
Tel: 01257 278 899   Fax: 01257 266 5505   Website: www.gabbitas.net

Head Mr P Connor
Special Needs provision EBD, SPLD, MLD, LD, PLD
Age range 5–11
No of pupils 30 Boys and girls
Fees available on application

Westmorland School was opened in May 2000 as part of the Witherslack Group's continuing commitment to offer services in areas of identified local authority need. Thus the school was

established to cover the age range from Reception to Key Stage 2.
The school is supported by Mr Colin Critchley, Director of Clinical Services. The school also has access to additional therapeutic services via local Child and Adolescent Mental Health Provision – Occupational Play, Art, Horticultural, Music, Speech and Language, Psychological, Psychiatric, Family Therapy, Sexual/Physical/Emotional abuse counselling.

Woodcroft School

Whitakers Way, Loughton, Essex IG10 1SQ
Tel: 020 8508 1369   Fax: 020 8502 4855   Website: www.gabbitas.net

Head Mrs Margaret Newton
Founded 1963
School status DfES approved independent
Special needs provision ADD, ADHD, ASP, AUT, CP, DEL, DOW, DYS, DYP, EBD, EPI, HI, MLD, PH, PMLD, SLD, SPLD, SP&LD, VIS, W
Age range 2–11   *No of pupils (day)* 24
Fees per annum On application

Woodcroft School provides child-centred educational and therapeutic interventions for children who have been referred from local education authorities for a variety of reasons. These include uneven developmental progress; 'failing in school'; being under educational, emotional or social stress; and having varying degrees of communication, sensory and physical disorders. A broad and balanced curriculum, including the National Curriculum, is fostered by providing a high ratio of qualified and experienced staff to pupils; a flexible structure, which can adapt to the pupils' abilities and aptitudes; and a setting which is secure, friendly and pleasant. Close co-operation is maintained with sending authorities and parents. Our on-site mainstream nursery for children from the local area provides a unique resource for children to integrate appropriately with others, and links with local mainstream schools offer similar opportunities. Our aim is to help children to make the most of their abilities and to prepare them to enter or to continue their schooling under their LEA's statutory provision.

3.2
Profiles of Colleges and Other Provision at 16+

Arden College

40 Derby Road, Southport, Merseyside PR9 0TZ   Tel: 01704 534433   Fax: 01704 549711
E-mail: info@ardencollege.com   Website: www.gabbitas.net

Principal Mr C A Mayho
Religious denomination non-denominational
College status Independent co-educational
boarding and day
Special needs provision SLD, SP&LD, ADHD,
ADD, ASP, AUT, DOW, DYS, EBD, EPI, HI,
MLD, SPLD
Member of NATSPEC, ARC
Age range 16–25   *boarders from* 16
No of boarders (full) 60; *(day)* 16
Fees per annum (full boarding) £28,000–
£55,000

The primary aim of the College is to provide
our students with an inclusive quality
educational and social care service provision
that enables them to achieve their potential and
supports their social, behavioural and
emotional development.

All programmes are inclusive, focused as they
are on enabling the student to access the
community, live a more independent life and,
where appropriate, engage in further education,
training or employment.

Courses include community and vocational
skills, literacy, numeracy, information communication technology, independent living and
social and recreational activities.

The students are supported by a high ratio of
staff (1:3 and, where required, 1:1) who offer
guidance, support and encouragement across
the 24 hour curriculum.

The students reside in well-maintained and
colourfully decorated homes in Southport thus
facilitating their access to the community and
all amenities. Long-term living opportunities
exist for students wishing to continue to live
in the area.

Bridgend College

Cowbridge Road, Bridgend, CF31 3DH
Tel: 01656 302302   Fax: 01656 663912
E-mail: KMjones@bridgend.ac.uk   Website: www.bridgend.ac.uk   www.gabbitas.net

Principal Mr Roger Hampton
Founded 1929
College Status Co-educational, FEFCW
maintained
Special needs provision DYS, HI, SPLD, VIS
Member of NFAC
Accredited by National Federation of Access
Centres
Age range 16–25
No of resident places 23

The College has a long established provision for
students with special needs and this continues
to evolve to meet the needs of our students. The
college's SEN provision has two modes of attendance. Students may attend specialist and
mainstream courses on a day or residential
basis.

School of Pre-Vocational Education
Classroom accommodation is at the centre of
the college with safe and easy access to the main
college facilities. The department has an Access
Centre for technical assessment and support
as well as specialist service for students with
Dyslexia, hearing and visual impairments.
Weston House
This purpose-built facility has been developed
to provide opportunities for young people
with learning difficulties and/or disabilities to
access further education, enhancing their
career prospects and quality of life. The students are offered a 24-hour curriculum, which
is individually negotiated in conjunction with
the student's chosen college course. The residential unit operates from Sunday to Friday
afternoons.

Coleg Elidyr

Rhandirmwyn, Llandovery, Carmarthenshire SA20 0NL
Tel: 01550 760400   Fax: 01550 760331   E-mail: colegrhan@aol.com

Contact Admissions Group
Founded 1973
College of Further Education status Co-educational independent boarding
Special needs provision ADD, ADHD, ASP, AUT, EBD, EPI, MLD, SLD and developmental delay.
Age range 18+
No of pupils (boarding) 65
Fees per annum (boarding) in line with L.S.C. Funding Matrix (reviewed every August)

Coleg Elidyr is a Camphill Community College and a registered charity for further education and training for young people with learning difficulties. It is set on three sites, in the beautiful Towy Valley. The residential houses are run as family units, for up to 10 students.

We offer a 3-year residential programme of learning for the post-18 age group, which includes opportunities to develop and improve the following: independent living skills, basic/key skills (literacy, numeracy and IT), arts/crafts, personal and social skills, as well as work experience in a range of vocational areas. The extended curriculum allows for learning throughout a student's individual programme. Where relevant, students can continue with a 2-year vocational apprenticeship. Nationally recognised courses are accredited through LCCIEB, NPTC and SWWOCN. Students may also have the opportunity of progressing to our more adult setting at Glasallt Fawr, or to the more independent household in the village of Llangadog.

Finchale Training College

Durham, DH1 5RX
Tel: 0191 386 2634   Fax: 0191 386 4962
E-mail: finchale.college@mailbox.as   Website: www.finchalecollege.co.uk   www.gabbitas.net

Head Dr D T Etheridge
Founded 1943
School status N/A
Religious denomination Non-denominational
Member of NCVO   *Accredited by* ISO9002; lip
Special needs provision ADD, ADHD, ASP, CP, DEL, DYS, DYP, EPI, HI (limited provision), MLD, PH, VIS (limited provision), W
Age range 18+
No of students (boarding) approx. 120
(day) approx. 60
Fees per annum N/A

Finchale Training College offers integrated programmes of vocational training and individual specialist support to disabled adults who have a wide range of impairments, ranging from physical to stress-related conditions. Our students come to us having shared experiences of unemployment and the barriers, as a result of their condition, faced in gaining employment. It is our aim and focus to enable the individual to gain the skills necessary to make the transition from welfare dependency to work. This is achieved through varied means, for some it involves short courses that build confidence and personal skills and others undertake full time vocational training programmes leading to employment in the related industry.

Personal support, including counselling, is tailored to meet individual needs with qualified nursing staff and wardens on duty 24 hours a day. Finchale also has a Learning Support Unit, which enables the development of literacy, communication and numerical skills. It also provides dyslexia support.

At Finchale We actively promote Equal Opportunities for All

Lindeth College of Further Education

The Oaks, Lindeth, Bowness-on-Windermere, Cumbria LA23 3NH
Tel: 015394 46265   Fax: 015394 88840

Head Mrs N S Buckley
Founded 1985
School status Co-educational independent
boarding only
Religious denomination Non-denominational
Member of NATSPEC, ARC
Special needs provision ADD, ADHD, ASP, AUT,
DOW, DYS, EPI, HI, MLD, SP&LD, SPLD
Age range 16–25   *boarding from* 16
No of boarders (full) 44
Fees per annum (boarding) (full) £14,000–
£30,000 (L.S.T. Fees Matrix)

The College provides residential education
courses for up to a 3-year period within a
caring, supportive and inclusive learning residential environment. Individual Programmes
are negotiated and formulated according to
student needs.

The 24-hour curriculum offers courses in
independent living and community skills, vocational training, IT, literacy and numeracy and
work placement opportunities. The aim is that
on leaving the College the student will be able
to live more independently, and access the local
community, further education, training or
employment opportunities as appropriate.

The atmosphere is happy and purposeful,
within a structured and disciplined framework.
Initial accommodation is provided in the main
house, which is homely, colourfully decorated
and well maintained. When confident and
ready for further independence, students are
able to move to the training cottages.

The students are supported by a high ratio of
staff who offer guidance and encouragement in
their continued development in academic,
social and recreational skills.

Portland College

Nottingham Road, Mansfield, Nottinghamshire NG18 4TJ
Tel: 01623 499111   Fax: 01623 499134
E-mail: ykerr@portland.org.uk   Website: www.portland.org.uk   www.gabbitas.net

Head M E A Syms OBE
Founded 1950
School status Co-educational boarding and day
independent
Religious denomination Non-denominational
Member of NATSPEC; *Accredited by* Ofsted
Inspected by Ofsted
Special needs provision CP, DYC, DYS, DYP, EPI,
HI, MLD, PH, SP&LD, W
Age range 16–25 *boarding from* 16
No of pupils (boarding) (full) 130; *(weekly)* 38
Fees per annum (boarding) £14,000–£52,000

Portland College provides first class education
and training in a caring residential environment
for students with disabilities age 16–25. Portland is able to offer individual customised programmes of education and training, allowing
each student to develop their potential. A wide
programme of activity and learning takes place

throughout the day placing great emphasis on a
complete 'living' experience for all students.

Vocational programmes lead to occupation in
the fields of business and information technology, electronics, engineering and horticulture,
and to the achievement of National Vocational
Qualifications.

Accommodation on campus is purpose built
with easy access for those with mobility problems. Students live in comfortable residences,
each with single study bedrooms. All meals are
provided and the catering service is able to offer
any type of diet.

Experienced care and welfare staff, together
with 24 hour medical cover and the disciplines
of physiotherapy, occupational and speech and
language therapy, provide a comprehensive
student support service.

The recreation and leisure facilities are excellent providing a wide range of activity.

RNIB Redhill College

Philanthropic Road, Redhill, Surrey RH1 4DG
Tel: 01737 768935   Fax: 01737 778776
E-mail: liliffe@rnib-redhill.ac.uk   Website: www.rnib.org.uk/services/redhill   www.gabbitas.net

Head Mrs Judith Foot
Founded 1958
School status Co-educational independent voluntary
Member of NATSPEC
Accredited by LSC, TSC
Special needs provision VIS, SLD, AUT, ASP, CP, DOW, DYS, EBD, EPI, HI, MLD, PH, W
Age range 16–60   *boarding from* 16
No of pupils 100   *boys* 50 *girls* 50
Fees per annum Various

RNIB Redhill College provides further education and vocational training courses for people with sight difficulties between the ages of 16 and 60. Programmes range from a course to develop skills for independent living through to vocational training courses. The College fosters a holistic and developmental approach to learning, with programmes tailored to meet the learning needs of each student.

The College has a wide range of specialist equipment designed to meet the needs of students of differing abilities and needs, supported by staff with appropriate specialist qualifications. The Fitness Centre has a wide range of adapted equipment as well as an exercise pool. Redhill College has close links with local mainstream FE colleges, as well as providing link courses for some schools. Students are encouraged, if appropriate, to access mainstream courses on a part-time basis, and are supported by experienced staff from Redhill College.
A range of specialist support staff, including a physiotherapist and speech therapist, provide a comprehensive student support service.
The College is situated on a 13-acre campus close to Redhill with good rail links with London, Reading and the south coast. It is also close to the M25, M23 and Gatwick Airport.

RNIB Vocational College

Radmoor Road, Loughborough, Leicestershire LE11 3SB
Tel: 01509 611077   Fax: 01509 232013
E-mail: enquiries@rnibvocoll.ac.uk   Website: www.rnibvcoll.ac.uk

Head Mr K Connell
Founded 1989
Status Co-educational boarding and day DfES approved independent
Member of NATSPEC, National Federation of Access Centres
Special needs provision VIS-primarily, DYC, DYS, EPI, HI, MLD, PH, VIS, W
Age range 16–60   *boarding from* 16
No of students 80   *no of boarders* 74
Fees per annum Upon application

RNIB Vocational College Loughborough is a residential college for people who are blind or partially sighted, sometimes with additional disabilities or moderate learning difficulties. The college is situated on the same campus and works in close partnership with Loughborough College to provide students with an unrivalled range of specialist and mainstream courses, in a superb location with all the support they need.
Staff are experienced at supporting students. A wide range of adapted materials and specialist equipment can be provided, based upon the student's particular needs. The Residential Support team provides counselling and training in a variety of independent living skills. A dedicated Employment Placement Officer helps students to prepare for work or continuing education upon leaving.
New on-campus, 60 room residential centre opened in September 2001. All study bedrooms are en-suite and have computer network links and private phone line.
Students have access to all the clubs and facilities provided by Loughborough Students Union and the college has a busy social life.

Westgate College for Deaf People

Westcliff House, 37 Sea Road, Westgate on Sea, Kent CT8 8QP
Tel: 01843 836300   Fax: 01843 830001
E-mail: enquiries@westgatecollegeadmin.co.uk   Website: www.westgate-college.org.uk

Head Gillian Wills
School status Non-maintained co-educational
boarding and day
Religious denomination All welcome
Member of NATSPEC, ACC
Primary needs catered for Deaf, Deaf/Blind 16+
Special needs provision ADD, ASP, AUT,
CP(mild/moderate), DEL, DOW, DYC, DYS,
DYP, EBD, EPI, HI, MLD, PH(mild/moderate),
PMLD, SLD, SP&LD, SPLD, VIS, W(parts of
college fully accessible, some residential areas
currently inaccessible
Age range 16+   *boarding from* 16
No of pupils 70
Fees per annum Matched to individual
assessment of needs

Westgate College provides further education
and training programmes for deaf people and
those with communication needs.
Westgate College is located within the local
community and include single bedrooms,
shared bedrooms and self-contained flats.
The college provides individual learning
programmes for students aged 16 to 25 and
vocational training for trainees aged 16 to 60.
Successful collaboration with sector colleges
enables students to achieve nationally
recognised qualifications in a wide range of
vocational areas or to access elements of
courses matched to individual needs and
learning styles.
On site, Westgate College runs vocational
programmes using real work environments
including college kitchens, farm and gardens.
The college provides a functional learning
environment for deaf students with additional
needs, preparing for their future through
maximising independence.
Qualified and experienced Teachers of the Deaf;
learning support staff, residential staff and
therapists support students.

PART FOUR: INDEPENDENT MAINSTREAM SCHOOLS WITH SPECIALIST PROVISION

4.1
Provision for special educational needs in independent mainstream schools: An Introduction

As a parent, you have the best knowledge of your child's individual needs. You will want to consider whether he or she would be happy and able to thrive with appropriate help in a mainstream school, or whether a special school, with highly specialist facilities and resources, is more appropriate. You may feel that a special school will be best able to meet his or her needs. Alternatively, you may prefer your child to learn in a mainstream school environment if the right support is available.

Many independent mainstream schools offer help for pupils with SEN, most often with specific learning difficulties such as dyslexia. However, most will not accept children with Statements of SEN and the vast majority are unlikely to be able to cater for children with severe emotional and behavioural difficulties. The specialist teaching expertise and facilities in school, and the extent of help available, varies widely from one school to another. Some have extensive experience in providing SEN support. A few have a significant proportion of students with SEN and a dedicated unit in school staffed by qualified specialist teachers. Pupils may be withdrawn from certain lessons during the school day, during which time they receive specialist support. Some may offer differentiated work within the normal classroom. Others may be sympathetic to special needs but may not have the facilities to make any special provision. It is important to remember that in most cases schools will expect your child to meet the normal entry requirements for the school and to be able to cope in an ordinary school setting.

If you are considering mainstream schools, it is important to find out exactly how these would meet your child's individual needs. To help you find out which schools in the directory are appropriate for your child, the help available at each school for each type of need listed is shown in one of three different categories (see page 415). If you are looking for schools which make provision for dyslexia, you may also find it helpful to consult the register of schools produced by CReSTeD (Council for the Registration of Schools Teaching Dyslexic pupils) on page 495.

When contacting or visiting schools which interest you, you may wish to ask about the following points to help you make an assessment of the school's suitability:

Academic pace
Finding the right academic environment for your child is every bit as essential as finding a school that will provide the right level of SEN support. Ask to see examples of children's work. Where do leavers go? Is the school's overall thrust and ethos suitable for your child?

Experience and expertise in managing SEN
- How much experience has the school had of teaching children with needs or a spectrum of needs similar to your child's?
- How many such students are currently enrolled? What help do these students receive?
- What proportion of pupils in the school have SEN?
- Are staff qualified in SEN teaching?
- Does the school have full-time SEN teaching specialists or is teaching done on a part-time basis?
- What have been the destinations of recent leavers with SEN?

Meeting the needs of your child
- What strategy would the school suggest for meeting your child's needs? How many special lessons would your child have per week? How big are the groups for these lessons? Will your child have to give up another subject in order to have special lessons or will these be given outside normal lesson times? What will the lessons cover? Will there be additional support in class? If so, from whom?
- If Information Technology facilities are an important resource for your child, what can the school offer? Is there a dedicated area available? Are computers and laptops freely available for use?
- Will the school arrange for special arrangements during GCSE and/or A Level examinations, if appropriate?

Communication with teachers and parents
- How will those in school, who are responsible for teaching and caring for your child, be kept informed of his or her needs and progress by the Special Needs department?
- How, and how often, will parents be kept in touch with progress and plans?

Wider needs
- It is equally important to check that your child's strengths and interests outside the classroom can be catered for. If he or she is good at music, sport, drama or has a special interest in, for example, outdoor pursuits or debating, will the school offer the right levels of encouragement and opportunities to develop these, either now or at a later stage?
- Similarly, what help and advice is given to senior school pupils about university entry and careers?
- Does your child have particular medical or dietary needs that must be provided for in school?
- Are there any religious considerations? If your family is of a faith different from that of the school, how will your child's faith be accommodated? Will he/she find it difficult to play a full part in school life?
- Does the school share your values as a parent? What are its policies with reference to discipline, bullying and drugs and the extent of guidance given on Personal & Social Education (PSE)?

For information on individual schools, see the profiles in this section (pages 410–414). If you would like more personal help to find suitable mainstream schools for your child, contact Gabbitas, who can assist with independent educational assessment and make a personal selection of schools.

Gabbitas Educational Consultants
Carrington House, 126–130 Regent Street, London W1B 5EE
Tel: 020 7734 0161   Fax: 020 7437 1764
Email: admin@gabbitas.co.uk   Website: www.gabbitas.co.uk

Independent Mainstream Schools with Specialist Provision
Note on information given in the directory section

Type of school

This directory comprises schools listed within the Department for Education and Skills Register of Independent Schools which replied to our request for information. These schools offer varying levels of help for students with special needs, from additional tuition on a limited withdrawal basis, to specialist units and teaching programmes (see below). For specific details parents should contact individual schools direct.

Each school is given a brief description, which explains whether the school is single-sex or co-educational. In some cases schools take small numbers of the opposite sex within a specified age range. These are indicated where appropriate, eg: Boys boarding and day 3–18 (Day girls 16–18).

Schools are described as 'boarding' (which indicates boarding pupils only), 'boarding and day', 'day and boarding' (indicating a predominance of day pupils) or 'day' only.

Number of boarders

Where necessary these are divided into full boarders (F) and weekly boarders (W). Weekly boarding arrangements vary according to individual school policy.

Fees

All fees are given annually from September 2001 unless otherwise stated. It should be remembered, however, that some schools increase fees during the year and the figures shown may therefore be subject to change after September 2001. Where the date is other than September 2001, the information provided is the latest available from the school. Figures are shown for full boarding (FB), weekly boarding (WB) and day fees. In some instances the fees for full and weekly boarding are the same (F/WB). A minimum and a maximum fee are given for each range. These figures are intended as a guide only. For more precise information schools should be contacted direct.

Symbols

* denotes that the school has a profile later in this section
† denotes that the school is registered with CReSTeD (see Part 5.2)

Levels of Provision

The schools in this section are mainstream independent schools which offer levels of varying provision for students with special needs. In some cases help may be extensive; in others it may be more limited. In order to offer a guide to the level of provision, each school is asked to classify its provision for each type of need at one of three levels:

Level 1

The school has a dedicated special needs unit with suitably qualified staff to provide for this type of special need or provides teaching by suitably qualified staff in special classes for pupils with this type of need.

Level 2

Pupils with this type of special need are withdrawn from certain lessons during the school day, during which time they receive extra support from suitably qualified staff, or are given differentiated work within the normal classroom environment.

Level 3

Pupils with this type of special need are treated sympathetically but there is no specialist support available.

Unspecified

Special needs for which the school makes provision but has not given a classification are listed as 'Unspecified'.

Key to abbreviations

Abbreviations used to denote Special Needs provision in this section are as follows:

ADD	Attention Deficit Disorder	EPI	Epilepsy
ADHD	Attention Deficit/Hyperactivity Disorder	HI	Hearing Impairment
		MLD	Moderate Learning Difficulties
ASP	Asperger Syndrome	PH	Physical Impairment
AUT	Autism	PMLD	Profound and Multiple Learning Difficulties
CP	Cerebral Palsy		
DEL	Delicate	SLD	Severe Learning Difficulties
DOW	Down's Syndrome	SP&LD	Speech and Language Difficulties
DYC	Dyscalculia		
DYP	Dyspraxia	SPLD	Specific Learning Difficulties
DYS	Dyslexia	TOU	Tourette's Syndrome
EBD	Emotional and Behavioural Difficulties	VIS	Visual Impairment
		W	Wheelchair access

4.2
Directory of Independent Mainstream Schools with Specialist Provision

ENGLAND

BEDFORDSHIRE

BEDFORD MODERN SCHOOL
Manton Lane, Bedford MK41 7NT
Tel: (01234) 332500
Head: Mr S Smith
Type: Boys Day and Boarding 7–18
No of pupils: B1090
No of Boarders: F50
Fees: (September 01) FB £10605 –
£12570 Day £4995 – £6960
Special Needs: Level 2: DYP DYS

BROADMEAD SCHOOL
Tennyson Road, Luton, Bedfordshire
LU1 3RR
Tel: (01582) 722570
Head: Mr A F Compton
Type: Co-educational Day 2–11
No of pupils: B65 G65
Fees: (September 01) Day £3213
Special Needs: Level 2: DYC DYS
SP&LD

PHOENIX SCHOOL
Flitwick Road, Westoning,
Bedfordshire MK45 5AA
Tel: (01525) 718241
Head: Mrs S Harral
Type: Co-educational Day 2–6
No of pupils: 49
Fees: (September 01) Day £3735 –
£3795
Special Needs: Level 3: ADD ADHD
ASP AUT CP DEL DOW DYP DYS
EBD EPI HI PH PMLD SLD SP&LD
SPLD TOU VIS Unspecified: W

BERKSHIRE

CHEAM SCHOOL
Headley, Newbury, Berkshire
RG19 8LD
Tel: (01635) 268381
Head: Mr M R Johnson
Type: Co-educational Boarding and
Day 3–13
No of pupils: B210 G143
No of Boarders: F58 W35
Fees: (September 01) FB £13050 Day
£5520 – £9660
Special Needs: Level 2: DYP DYS
SPLD

CLAIRES COURT SCHOOL
Ray Mill Road East, Maidenhead,
Berkshire SL6 8TE
Tel: (01628) 411470
Head: Mr J T Wilding
Type: Boys Day 11–18 (Co-ed VIth
Form)
No of pupils: B356 G31
Fees: (September 01) Day £6165 –
£7290
Special Needs: Level 2: DYC DYP DYS
SPLD Level 3: ADD ADHD HI VIS
Unspecified: SP&LD

FOXLEY PNEU SCHOOL
Manor Drive, Shurlock Row,
Reading, Berkshire RG10 0PX
Tel: (0118) 934 3578
Head: Miss M J Fallon
Type: Co-educational Day 3–5
No of pupils: B15 G15
Fees: (September 01) Day £1750 –
£3000
Special Needs: Unspecified: DYS EBD
MLD SP&LD

HEATHFIELD SCHOOL
London Road, Ascot, Berkshire
SL5 8BQ
Tel: (01344) 898343
Head: Mrs H M Wright
Type: Girls Boarding 11–18
No of pupils: 220 *No of Boarders:* F220
Fees: (September 01) FB £17325
Special Needs: Level 2: DYS
Level 3: DYP

HOLME GRANGE SCHOOL
Heathlands Road, Wokingham,
Berkshire RG40 3AL
Tel: (0118) 978 1566
Head: Mr N J Brodrick
Type: Co-educational Day 3–13
No of pupils: B180 G142
Fees: (September 01) Day £2484 –
£6324
Special Needs: Level 2: DYS SP&LD
SPLD Level 3: ADD ADHD DYP

LAMBROOK HAILEYBURY
Winkfield Row, Bracknell, Berkshire
RG42 6LU
Tel: (01344) 882717
Head: Mr R J G Deighton
Type: Co-educational Boarding and
Day 4–13
No of pupils: B268 G80
No of Boarders: F13 W22
Fees: (September 01) FB £10200 –
£11925 Day £5100 – £8550
Special Needs: Level 1: DYP DYS

LONG CLOSE SCHOOL
Upton Court Road, Slough,
Berkshire SL3 7LU
Tel: (01753) 520095
Head: Mr N Murray
Type: Co-educational Day 2–13
No of pupils: B172 G64
Fees: (September 01) Day £3486 –
£6750
Special Needs: Level 2: DYS
Level 3: DYP Unspecified: W

MARIST CONVENT SENIOR SCHOOL
Kings Road, Sunninghill, Ascot,
Berkshire SL5 7PS
Tel: (01344) 624291
Head: Mr K McCloskey
Type: Girls Day 11–18
No of pupils: G335
Fees: (September 01) On application
Special Needs: Level 2: DYC DYP DYS
MLD Level 3: ADD ADHD
Unspecified: W

MARLSTON HOUSE SCHOOL
Hermitage, Newbury, Berkshire
RG18 9UL
Tel: (01635) 200293
Head: Mrs C Riley
Type: Girls Boarding and Day 6–13
No of pupils: G85
No of Boarders: F8 W12
Fees: (September 01) FB £10260
Day £5160 – £7770
Special Needs: Level 2: DYS SPLD

THE ORATORY PREPARATORY SCHOOL
Goring Heath, Reading, Berkshire
RG8 7SF
Tel: (0118) 984 4511
Head: Mr D L Sexon
Type: Co-educational Day and
Boarding 3–13
No of pupils: B271 G96
No of Boarders: F43
Fees: (September 01) FB £10695 Day
£2175 – £7725
Special Needs: Level 2: DYP DYS MLD
SPLD

THE ORATORY SCHOOL
Woodcote, Reading, Berkshire
RG8 0PJ
Tel: (01491) 680207
Head: Mr C I Dytor
Type: Boys Boarding and Day 11–18
No of pupils: 400 *No of Boarders:* F250
Fees: (September 01) FB £13185 –
£16755 Day £9615 – £13185
Special Needs: Unspecified: DYP DYS
SPLD

PAPPLEWICK
Windsor Road, Ascot, Berkshire
SL5 7LH
Tel: (01344) 621488
Head: Mr D R Llewellyn
Type: Boys Boarding and Day 7–13
No of pupils: B209 *No of Boarders:* F134
Fees: (September 01) FB £13200
Day £10140
Special Needs: Level 2: DYP DYS
Level 3: ADHD ASP

READING BLUE COAT SCHOOL
Holme Park, Sonning, Reading,
Berkshire RG4 6SU
Tel: (0118) 944 1005
Head: Mr S J W McArthur
Type: Boys Day 11–18 (Co-ed VIth
Form)
No of pupils: 613
Fees: (September 01) Day £7530
Special Needs: Level 3: ADD ADHD
DYP DYS EBD EPI HI MLD SPLD

ST BERNARD'S PREPARATORY SCHOOL
Hawtrey Close, Slough, Berkshire
SL1 1TB
Tel: (01753) 521821
Head: Mrs M F Casey
Type: Co-educational Day 3–11
No of pupils: B120 G90
Fees: (September 01) Day £4050 –
£4485
Special Needs: Level 2: DYS

ST GEORGE'S SCHOOL
Ascot, Berkshire SL5 7DZ
Tel: (01344) 629900
Head: Mrs J Grant Peterkin
Type: Girls Boarding and Day 11–18
No of pupils: G300
No of Boarders: F140
Fees: (September 01) FB £16050 Day
£10275
Special Needs: Unspecified: DYC DYP
DYS

ST GEORGE'S SCHOOL
Windsor Castle, Windsor, Berkshire
SL4 1QF
Tel: (01753) 865553
Head: Mr J R Jones
Type: Co-educational Boarding and
Day 3–13
No of pupils: B186 G76
No of Boarders: F23 W12
Fees: (September 01) FB £11460
WB £11190 Day £2400 – £8505
Special Needs: Level 2: DYC DYS
Unspecified: MLD

ST MARY'S SCHOOL, ASCOT
St Mary's Road, Ascot, Berkshire
SL5 9JF
Tel: (01344) 623721
Head: Mrs M Breen
Type: Girls Boarding 11–18
No of pupils: G351
No of Boarders: F336
Fees: (September 01) FB £16440
Day £11040
Special Needs: Level 2: DYS

ST PIRAN'S PREPARATORY SCHOOL
Gringer Hill, Maidenhead, Berkshire
SL6 7LZ
Tel: (01628) 627316
Head: Mr J Carroll
Type: Co-educational Day 3–13
No of pupils: B260 G103
Fees: (September 01) Day £3780 –
£6870
Special Needs: Level 2: DYP DYS
SPLD

SILCHESTER HOUSE SCHOOL
Silchester House, Bath Road, Taplow,
Maidenhead, Berkshire SL6 0AP
Tel: (01628) 620549
Head: Mrs D J Austen
Type: Co-educational Day 2–12
No of pupils: B92 G78
Fees: (September 01) Day £1825 –
£5770
Special Needs: Level 2: DYS

SUNNINGDALE SCHOOL
Sunningdale, Berkshire SL5 9PY
Tel: (01344) 620159
Head: Mr T M E Dawson and
Mr A J N Dawson
Type: Boys Boarding 8–13
No of pupils: B100 *No of Boarders:* F100
Fees: (September 01) FB £10650
Special Needs: Level 2: DYP DYS
SPLD

THORNGROVE SCHOOL
The Mount, Highclere, Newbury,
Berkshire RG20 9PS
Tel: (01635) 253172
Head: Mr & Mrs N J Broughton
Type: Co-educational Day 2–13
No of pupils: B114 G86
Fees: (September 01) Day £4575 –
£6210
Special Needs: Level 2: DYS

UPTON HOUSE SCHOOL
115 St Leonard's Road, Windsor,
Berkshire SL4 3DF
Tel: (01753) 862610
Head: Mrs M Collins
Type: Girls Day 3–11 (Boys 3–7)
No of pupils: B50 G148
Fees: (September 01) Day £2265 –
£5475
Special Needs: Level 2: DEL DYC DYP
DYS EBD EPI HI MLD PH SPLD
Level 3: ADD ADHD ASP CP DOW
TOU VIS W

WAVERLEY SCHOOL
Waverley Way, Finchampstead,
Wokingham, Berkshire RG40 4YD
Tel: (0118) 973 1121
Head: Mr S G Melton
Type: Co-educational Day 3–11
No of pupils: B78 G78
Fees: (September 01) Day £1920 –
£5361
Special Needs: Level 2: DYP DYS
SPLD

WHITE HOUSE PREPARATORY SCHOOL
Finchampstead Road, Wokingham,
Berkshire RG40 3HD
Tel: (0118) 978 5151
Head: Mrs M L Blake
Type: Girls Day 3–11 (Boys 3–4)
No of pupils: B2 G135
Fees: (September 01) Day £4785 –
£5385
Special Needs: Level 2: DYS

BRISTOL

BRISTOL GRAMMAR SCHOOL
University Road, Bristol BS8 1SR
Tel: (0117) 973 6006
Head: Dr D J Mascord
Type: Co-educational Day 7–18
No of pupils: B856 G397
Fees: (September 01) Day £3318 –
£5649
Special Needs: Level 2: DYS
Level 3: ADD ADHD ASP DYC DYP
EPI

CLEVE HOUSE SCHOOL
254 Wells Road, Bristol BS4 2PN
Tel: (0117) 977 7218
Head: Mr D Lawson and Mrs E
Lawson
Type: Co-educational Day 3–11
No of pupils: B66 G76
Fees: (September 01) Day £2685
Special Needs: Level 2: DYS

CLIFTON COLLEGE
32 College Road, Clifton, Bristol
BS8 3JH
Tel: (0117) 3157 000
Head: Dr M S Spurr
Type: Co-educational Boarding and
Day 13–18
No of pupils: B430 G240
No of Boarders: F430
Fees: (September 01) FB £16770 –
£18030 Day £11170
Special Needs: Level 1: DYC DYP DYS
Level 2: MLD Level 3: ADD

CLIFTON COLLEGE PREPARATORY SCHOOL†
The Avenue, Clifton, Bristol BS8 3HE
Tel: (0117) 315 7502
Head: Dr R J Acheson
Type: Co-educational Boarding and
Day 3–13
No of pupils: B398 G189
No of Boarders: F54 W17
Fees: (September 01)
FB £11925 – £12406
WB £11400 – £11893
Day £3795 – £8265
Special Needs: Unspecified: DYP DYS

COLSTON'S GIRLS' SCHOOL
Cheltenham Road, Bristol BS6 5RD
Tel: (0117) 942 4328
Head: Mrs J P Franklin
Type: Girls Day 10–18
No of pupils: G450
Fees: (September 01) Day £3675 –
£5400
Special Needs: Level 3: DYP DYS HI
VIS

QUEEN ELIZABETH'S HOSPITAL
Berkeley Place, Bristol BS8 1JX
Tel: (0117) 929 1856
Head: Mr S W Holliday
Type: Boys Day and Boarding 11–18
No of pupils: B550
No of Boarders: F40 W15
Fees: (September 01) FB £10299
WB £9369 Day £5589
Special Needs: Level 2: DYS

SACRED HEART PREPARATORY SCHOOL
Winford Road, Chew Magna, Bristol
BS40 8QY
Tel: (01275) 332470
Head: Mrs B Huntley
Type: Co-educational Day 3–11
No of pupils: B55 G60
Fees: (September 01) Day £750 –
£900
Special Needs: Level 2: DYC DYP DYS
MLD SPLD

ST URSULA'S HIGH SCHOOL
Brecon Road, Westbury-on-Trym,
Bristol BS9 4DT
Tel: (01179) 622616
Head: Mrs M A Macnaughton
Type: Co-educational Day 3–16
No of pupils: B185 G138
Fees: (September 01) Day £3225 –
£4920
Special Needs: Level 2: ADD ADHD
ASP CP DYC DYP DYS EPI MLD
SPLD TOU VIS Level 3: HI

TOCKINGTON MANOR SCHOOL
Tockington, Bristol BS32 4NY
Tel: (01454) 613229
Head: Mr R G Tovey
Type: Co-educational Day and
Boarding 2–14
No of pupils: B168 G87
No of Boarders: F32
Fees: (September 01)
FB £9960 – £11085
Day £4320 – £7470
Special Needs: Level 1: DYS
Level 2: DYP

BUCKINGHAMSHIRE

AKELEY WOOD JUNIOR SCHOOL
Wicken Park, Wicken, Milton
Keynes, Buckinghamshire
MK19 6DA
Tel: (01908) 571231
Head: Mrs S R Chaplin
Type: Co-educational Day 2–8
No of pupils: B150 G138
Fees: (September 01) Day £2199 –
£5490
Special Needs: Level 1: DYP DYS

AKELEY WOOD SCHOOL*
Buckingham, Buckinghamshire
MK18 5AE
Tel: (01280) 814110
Head: Mr J C Lovelock
Type: Co-educational Day 2–18
No of pupils: B502 G341
Fees: (September 01) Day £4398 –
£6450
Special Needs: Level 2: DYS

BURY LAWN SCHOOL
Soskin Drive, Stantonbury Fields,
Milton Keynes, Buckinghamshire
MK14 6DP
Tel: (01404) 881702
Head: Mrs H Kiff
Type: Co-educational Day 1–18
No of pupils: B260 G170
Fees: (September 01) Day £4440 –
£6180
Special Needs: Unspecified: ADD CP
DYP DYS EBD EPI MLD SP&LD

CHESHAM PREPARATORY SCHOOL
Orchard Leigh, Chesham,
Buckinghamshire HP5 3QF
Tel: (01494) 782619
Head: Mr J Marjoribanks
Type: Co-educational Day 4–13
No of pupils: B208 G162
Fees: (September 01) Day £4875 –
£5790
Special Needs: Level 2: DYC DYP DYS

FILGRAVE SCHOOL
Filgrave, Newport Pagnell,
Buckinghamshire MK16 9ET
Tel: (01234) 711534
Head: Mrs S Marriott
Type: Co-educational Day 2–11
No of pupils: B20 G21
Fees: (September 01) Day £3936
Special Needs: Level 2: ADD ADHD
ASP AUT DYC DYP DYS SPLD

GODSTOWE PREPARATORY SCHOOL
Shrubbery Road, High Wycombe,
Buckinghamshire HP13 6PR
Tel: (01494) 529273
Head: Mrs F J Henson
Type: Girls Day and Boarding 3–13
(Boys 3–8)
No of pupils: B15 G446
No of Boarders: F101 W35
Fees: (September 01) F/WB £12750
Day £5835 – £8880
Special Needs: Level 2: DYP DYS
SPLD

GROVE INDEPENDENT SCHOOL
Redland Drive, Loughton, Milton
Keynes, Buckinghamshire MK5 8HD
Tel: (01908) 664336
Head: Mrs D M Berkin
Type: Co-educational Day 2–13
No of pupils: B116 G111
Fees: (September 01) Day £6300
Special Needs: Level 2: ADD ADHD
ASP DYP DYS EBD MLD PH SP&LD

HIGH MARCH SCHOOL
23 Ledborough Lane, Beaconsfield,
Buckinghamshire HP9 2PZ
Tel: (01494) 675186
Head: Mrs P A Forsyth
Type: Girls Day 3–12 (Boys 3–5)
No of pupils: B16 G290
Fees: (September 01) Day £1980 –
£6180
Special Needs: Level 2: DYP DYS
SPLD Level 3: HI SP&LD
Unspecified: PH

ST MARY'S SCHOOL
Packhorse Road, Gerrards Cross,
Buckinghamshire SL9 8JQ
Tel: (01753) 883370
Head: Mrs F Balcombe
Type: Girls Day 3–18
No of pupils: G302
Fees: (September 01) Day £3495 –
£6695
Special Needs: Level 3: DYS

ST TERESA'S SCHOOL
Aylesbury Road, Princes Risborough,
Buckinghamshire HP27 0JW
Tel: (01844) 345005
Head: Mrs C M Sparkes
Type: Co-educational Day 3–11
No of pupils: B92 G66
Fees: (September 01) Day £1110 –
£3855
Special Needs: Level 2: DYC DYS
SP&LD SPLD Level 3: ADD ADHD
ASP AUT DYP EBD PH Unspecified:
MLD

THORPE HOUSE SCHOOL
Oval Way, Gerrards Cross,
Buckinghamshire SL9 8PZ
Tel: (01753) 882474
Head: Mr A F Lock
Type: Boys Day 3–13
No of pupils: B280
Fees: (September 01) Day £3522 –
£6690
Special Needs: Level 2: DYP DYS MLD
SPLD Level 3: ADD ASP HI VIS

CAMBRIDGESHIRE

CAMBRIDGE ARTS & SCIENCES (CATS)
Round Church Street, Cambridge
CB5 8AD
Tel: (01223) 314431
Head: Miss E R Armstrong and
Mr P McLaughlin
Type: Co-educational Day and
Boarding 14–19
No of pupils: B100 G90
No of Boarders: F170 W5
Fees: (September 01)
FB/WB £7500 – £18000
Day £3600 – £10500
Special Needs: Unspecified: ADD
ADHD DYC DYP DYS EBD EPI MLD

HORLERS PRE-PREPARATORY SCHOOL
20 Green End, Comberton,
Cambridge CB3 7DY
Tel: (01223) 264564
Head: Mrs A Horler
Type: Co-educational Day 4–8
No of pupils: B15 G15
Fees: (September 01) Day £1670
Special Needs: Level 2: ADD DYC
DYP DYS HI MLD Unspecified: EBD
PH SP&LD SPLD VIS

KIMBOLTON SCHOOL
Kimbolton, Huntingdon,
Cambridgeshire PE28 0EA
Tel: (01480) 860505
Head: Mr R V Peel
Type: Co-educational Boarding and
Day 4–18 (Boarders from 11)
No of pupils: B418 G368
No of Boarders: F60
Fees: (September 01) FB £12810
Day £3990 – £7710
Special Needs: Level 2: ADD ADHD
DYC DYP DYS

KIRKSTONE HOUSE SCHOOL
Main Street, Baston, Peterborough,
Cambridgeshire PE6 9PA
Tel: (01778) 560350
Head: Mr M J Clifford
Type: Co-educational Day 3–16
No of pupils: B122 G104
Fees: (September 01) Day £3300 –
£5880
Special Needs: Level 2: ADD ADHD
DYC DYP DYS MLD SP&LD SPLD

THE LEYS SCHOOL
Cambridge, Cambridgeshire
CB2 2AD
Tel: (01223) 508900
Head: Rev Dr J C A Barrett
Type: Co-educational Boarding and
Day 11–18
No of pupils: B325 G195
No of Boarders: F280
Fees: (September 01)
FB £11400 – £15900
Day £7200 – £11850
Special Needs: Level 1: ADHD ASP
DYP DYS EBD EPI HI Level 2: ADD
SPLD

MANDER PORTMAN WOODWARD
3/4 Brookside, Cambridge CB2 1JE
Tel: (01223) 350158
Head: Dr N Marriott and P Hill
Type: Co-educational Day 15–19
No of pupils: B50 G50
No of Boarders: F20 W20
Fees: (September 01)
F/WB £6129 – £14406
Day £2529 – £10806
Special Needs: Level 2: ADD ADHD
DYC DYP DYS

OUNDLE SCHOOL LAXTON JUNIOR
North Street, Oundle, Peterborough,
Cambridgeshire PE8 4AL
Tel: (01832) 273673
Head: Miss S C Thomas
Type: Co-educational Day 4–11
No of pupils: B71 G72
Fees: (September 01) Day £5544
Special Needs: Unspecified: ADD
ADHD DYP DYS SPLD

PETERBOROUGH HIGH SCHOOL
Thorpe Road, Peterborough,
Cambridgeshire PE3 6JF
Tel: (01733) 343357
Head: Mrs S A Dixon
Type: Girls Day and Boarding 3–18
(Boys 3–11)
No of pupils: B72 G274
No of Boarders: F7 W11
Fees: (September 01)
FB £11583 – £12342
WB £9795 – £10554
Day £3558 – £6150
Special Needs: Level 2: DYP DYS

ST COLETTE'S SCHOOL
Tenison Road, Cambridge CB1 2DP
Tel: (01223) 353696
Head: Mrs A C Wilson
Type: Co-educational Day 2–7
No of pupils: B80 G80
Fees: (September 01) Day £3870 –
£4440
Special Needs: Level 3: DYP DYS
SPLD

ST JOHN'S COLLEGE SCHOOL
The Garden House, 75 Grange Road, Cambridge CB3 9AA
Tel: (01223) 353532
Head: Mr K L Jones
Type: Co-educational Day and Boarding 4–13
No of pupils: 451 *No of Boarders:* F39
Fees: (September 01) F/WB £11679 Day £5454 – £7395
Special Needs: Level 2: ADD ADHD ASP DYC DYP DYS EBD SPLD Unspecified: SP&LD

ST MARY'S SCHOOL
Bateman Street, Cambridge CB2 1LY
Tel: (01223) 353253
Head: Mrs J Triffitt
Type: Girls Day and Boarding 11–18
No of pupils: G464
No of Boarders: F14 W23
Fees: (September 01)
FB £13650 – £14550
WB £11070 – £12150
Day £6180 – £6780
Special Needs: Level 3: ASP CP DEL DYS EPI SPLD

SANCTON WOOD SCHOOL
2 St Paul's Road, Cambridge CB1 2EZ
Tel: (01223) 359488
Head: Mrs J Avis
Type: Co-educational Day 1–16
No of pupils: B105 G69
Fees: (September 01) Day £4350 – £5355
Special Needs: Level 2: DYS HI SP&LD SPLD Level 3: ADD DEL DYP PH

WHITEHALL SCHOOL
117 High Street, Somersham, Huntingdon, Cambridgeshire PE28 3EH
Tel: (01487) 840966
Head: Mrs D Hutley
Type: Co-educational Day 3–11
No of pupils: B52 G57
Fees: (September 01) Day £3165 – £3906
Special Needs: Level 2: DYP DYS MLD SPLD Level 3: EBD

CHANNEL ISLANDS

VICTORIA COLLEGE
Jersey, Channel Islands JE1 4HT
Tel: (01534) 638200
Head: Mr R Cook
Type: Boys Day 11–19 (VIth Form with Jersey Girls College)
No of pupils: B625
Fees: (September 01) Day £2640
Special Needs: Level 3: DYS

VICTORIA COLLEGE PREPARATORY SCHOOL
Pleasant Street, St Helier, Jersey, Channel Islands
Tel: (01534) 723468
Head: Mr P Stevenson
Type: Boys Day 7–11
No of pupils: 270
Fees: (September 01) Day £2478
Special Needs: Level 2: MLD

CHESHIRE

ABBEY GATE COLLEGE
Saighton Grange, Saighton, Chester, Cheshire CH3 6EG
Tel: (01244) 332077
Head: Mr E W Mitchell
Type: Co-educational Day 4–18
No of pupils: B191 G156
Fees: (September 01) Day £3321 – £5874
Special Needs: Level 3: ADD ADHD ASP AUT CP DEL DOW DYC DYP DYS EBD EPI HI MLD PH PMLD SLD SP&LD SPLD TOU VIS

ABBEY GATE SCHOOL
Victoria Road, Chester, Cheshire CH2 2AY
Tel: (01244) 380552
Head: Mrs S Fisher
Type: Co-educational Day 3–11
No of pupils: B60 G60
Fees: (September 01) Day £2445 – £2625
Special Needs: Level 2: DYP DYS

BEECH HALL SCHOOL
Beech Hall Drive, Tytherington, Macclesfield, Cheshire SK10 2EG
Tel: (01625) 422192
Head: Mr J S Fitz-Gerald
Type: Co-educational Day 4–13 (Kindergarten 1–5)
No of pupils: B130 G62
Fees: (September 01) Day £3495 – £5490
Special Needs: Level 2: ADD ASP DYC DYP DYS EBD HI MLD PH SLD SP&LD SPLD VIS

BRABYNS SCHOOL
34–36 Arkwright Road, Marple, Stockport, Cheshire SK6 7DB
Tel: (0161) 427 2395
Head: Mrs P Turner
Type: Co-educational Day 2–11
No of pupils: B75 G90
Fees: (September 01) Day £1995 – £3246
Special Needs: Level 2: DYS SLD

CRANSLEY SCHOOL
Belmont Hall, Great Budworth, Northwich, Cheshire CW9 6HN
Tel: (01606) 891747
Head: Mrs H P Laidler
Type: Girls Day 3–16 (Boys 3–11)
No of pupils: B32 G171
Fees: (September 01) Day £3591 – £5682
Special Needs: Unspecified: ASP DYC DYS

THE FIRS SCHOOL
45 Newton Lane, Chester, Cheshire CH2 2HJ
Tel: (01244) 322443
Head: Mrs M Denton
Type: Co-educational Day 4–11
No of pupils: B118 G97
Fees: (September 01) Day £3465
Special Needs: Level 2: DYC DYP DYS PH SP&LD SPLD

GREENBANK
Heathbank Road, Cheadle Hulme, Cheadle, Cheshire SK8 6HU
Tel: (0161) 485 3724
Head: Mr K Phillips
Type: Co-educational Day 3–11
No of pupils: B102 G73
Fees: (September 01) Day £2235 – £3900
Special Needs: Level 2: DYC DYP DYS SPLD

HILLCREST GRAMMAR SCHOOL
Beech Avenue, Stockport, Cheshire SK3 8HB
Tel: (0161) 480 0329
Head: Mr D K Blackburn
Type: Co-educational Day 3–16
No of pupils: B180 G100
Fees: (September 01) Day £4380
Special Needs: Level 2: DYP DYS Unspecified: MLD SPLD W

THE KING'S SCHOOL
Macclesfield, Cheshire SK10 1DA
Tel: (01625) 260000
Head: Dr S Coyne
Type: Co-educational Day 3–18 (Single sex education 11–16)
No of pupils: B800 G600
Fees: (September 01) Day £3840 – £5745
Special Needs: Level 2: ADD ADHD DYP DYS Level 3: ASP EPI

LORETO PREPARATORY SCHOOL
Dunham Road, Altrincham, Cheshire WA14 4AH
Tel: (0161) 928 8310
Head: Mrs R A Hedger
Type: Girls Day 4–11 (Boys 4–7)
No of pupils: B2 G168
Fees: (September 01) Day £2475
Special Needs: Level 2: CP DEL DYP DYS EPI MLD PH SP&LD SPLD

MOSTYN HOUSE SCHOOL
Parkgate, South Wirral, Cheshire CH64 6SG
Tel: (0151) 336 1010
Head: Mr A D J Grenfell
Type: Co-educational Day 4–18
No of pupils: B191 G114
Fees: (September 01) Day £2696 – £6554
Special Needs: Level 1: DYP DYS Level 3: ADD ADHD DOW DYC SPLD

ORIEL BANK
Devonshire Park Road, Davenport, Stockport, Cheshire SK2 6JP
Tel: (0161) 483 2935
Head: Mr R A Bye
Type: Girls Day 3–16
No of pupils: 180
Fees: (September 01) Day £2100 – £4890
Special Needs: Level 2: DYP DYS MLD SP&LD SPLD Level 3: EBD PH

RAMILLIES HALL SCHOOL
Cheadle Hulme, Cheadle, Cheshire SK8 7AJ
Tel: (0161) 485 3804
Head: Mrs A L Poole & Miss D M Patterson
Type: Co-educational Boarding and Day 0–13
No of pupils: B114 G71
No of Boarders: F11 W4
Fees: (September 01) FB £9180 WB £8130 Day £3780 – £4935
Special Needs: Level 2: DYC DYP DYS SPLD Level 3: ADD ADHD

THE RYLEYS
Ryleys Lane, Alderley Edge, Cheshire SK9 7UY
Tel: (01625) 583241
Head: Mr P G Barrett
Type: Boys Day 3–13
No of pupils: B291
Fees: (September 01) Day £5004 – £5565
Special Needs: Level 2: DYC DYP DYS SPLD Level 3: ADD DEL EBD EPI HI PH SP&LD TOU VIS

CORNWALL

ROSELYON PREPARATORY SCHOOL
St Blazey Road, Par, Cornwall
PL24 2HZ
Tel: (01726) 812110
Head: Mr S C Bradley
Type: Co-educational Day 2–11
No of pupils: B33 G37
Fees: (September 01) Day £3741
Special Needs: Level 3: DYP DYS PH
SPLD

ST IA SCHOOL
St Ives Road, Carbis Bay, St Ives,
Cornwall TR26 2SF
Tel: (01736) 796963
Head: Mr D M P Bennett
Type: Co-educational Day 4–12
No of pupils: B25 G15
Fees: (September 01) Day £975 –
£1155
Special Needs: Level 2: DYP MLD

ST JOSEPH'S SCHOOL
15 St Stephen's Hill, Launceston,
Cornwall PL15 8HN
Tel: (01566) 772580
Head: Mr A R Doe
Type: Girls Day 3–16 (Boys 3–11)
No of pupils: B24 G146
Fees: (September 01) Day £3945 –
£5730
Special Needs: Level 2: DYS MLD
SPLD

ST PETROC'S SCHOOL
Ocean View Road, Bude, Cornwall
EX23 8NJ
Tel: (01288) 352876
Head: Mr B P Dare
Type: Co-educational Day 3–11
(Nursery from 3 mths)
No of pupils: B48 G42
Fees: (September 01) Day £2940 –
£4845
Special Needs: Level 1: ASP
Level 2: DYS SPLD Level 3: ADD
ADHD EBD MLD

TRELISKE SCHOOL
Truro, Cornwall TR1 3QN
Tel: (01872) 272616
Head: Mr R L Hollins
Type: Co-educational Day and
Boarding 3–11
No of pupils: B134 G86
No of Boarders: W6
Fees: (September 01)
F/WB £8763 – £10695
Day £2304 – £5778
Special Needs: Level 2: DYC DYP DYS
MLD SPLD Unspecified: W

TRURO SCHOOL
Trennick Lane, Truro, Cornwall
TR1 1TH
Tel: (01872) 272763
Head: Mr P K Smith
Type: Co-educational Day and
Boarding 11–18
No of pupils: B481 G283
No of Boarders: F96
Fees: (September 01)
F/WB £11520 – £12327
Day £5961 – £6318
Special Needs: Level 2: DYS
Level 3: ADD ADHD DYP EPI HI

CUMBRIA

AUSTIN FRIARS
Etterby Scaur, Carlisle, Cumbria
CA3 9PB
Tel: (01228) 528042
Head: Mr N J B O'Sullivan
Type: Co-educational Day 3–18
No of pupils: B218 G212
Fees: (September 01) Day £3100 –
£6045
Special Needs: Level 1: DYS

HARECROFT HALL SCHOOL
Gosforth, Seascale, Cumbria
CA20 1HS
Tel: (01946) 725220
Head: Mr P Block
Type: Co-educational Boarding and
Day 4–16
No of pupils: B49 G47
Fees: (September 01)
FB £8895 – £9747 WB £8490 – £9375
Day £4395 – £6195
Special Needs: Level 2: DYP DYS MLD

ST BEES SCHOOL
St Bees, Cumbria CA27 0DS
Tel: (01946) 822263
Head: Mr P J Capes
Type: Co-educational Boarding and
Day 11–18
No of pupils: B184 G112
No of Boarders: F92 W46
Fees: (September 01)
FB £11355 – £15513
WB £9840 – £13974
Day £7800 – £9909
Special Needs: Level 1: DYC DYS
SPLD Level 2: DYP VIS Level 3: ADD
ASP HI

SEDBERGH SCHOOL
Sedbergh, Cumbria LA10 5HG
Tel: (01539) 620535
Head: Mr C H Hirst
Type: Co-educational Boarding and
Day 8–18
No of pupils: B342 G40
No of Boarders: F362
Fees: (September 01)
FB £10320 – £16500
Day £7020 – £12195
Special Needs: Level 1: DYS
Level 3: ADD ADHD ASP DYC DYP
EPI HI PH

DERBYSHIRE

ASHBOURNE PNEU SCHOOL
St Monica's House, Windmill Lane,
Ashbourne, Derbyshire DE6 1EY
Tel: (01335) 343294
Head: Mrs M A Broadbent
Type: Co-educational Day 0–13
No of pupils: 60
Fees: (September 01) On application
Special Needs: Level 2: ADD ADHD
ASP AUT CP DEL DOW DYC DYP
DYS EBD EPI HI MLD PH PMLD SLD
SP&LD SPLD VIS

DERBY GRAMMAR SCHOOL
FOR BOYS
Rykneld Road, Littleover, Derby
DE23 7BH
Tel: (01332) 523027
Head: Mr R D Waller
Type: Boys Day 7–18
No of pupils: B300
Fees: (September 01) Day £4620 –
£5775
Special Needs: Level 2: DYS PH
Level 3: ADD ADHD ASP DYC DYP
EBD EPI HI MLD VIS

MOUNT ST MARY'S COLLEGE†
Spinkhill, Derbyshire S21 3YL
Tel: (01246) 433388
Head: Mr P G MacDonald
Type: Co-educational Boarding and
Day 11–18
No of pupils: B190 G100
No of Boarders: F80 W25
Fees: (September 01)
FB £9195 – £12510
WB £8130 – £11085
Day £6045 – £6990
Special Needs: Level 1: DYS
Level 2: ADD DYP

ST ANSELM'S
Bakewell, Derbyshire DE45 1DP
Tel: (01629) 812734
Head: Mr R J Foster
Type: Co-educational Boarding and
Day 7–13
No of pupils: B110 G83
No of Boarders: F85
Fees: (September 01) FB £10950
Day £7380 – £9300
Special Needs: Level 2: DYC DYP DYS
SPLD Level 3: ADD ADHD ASP

ST JOSEPH'S CONVENT
42 Newbold Road, Chesterfield,
Derbyshire S41 7PL
Tel: (01246) 232392
Head: Mrs B Deane
Type: Co-educational Day 2–11
No of pupils: B69 G66
Fees: (September 01) Day £2600 –
£3500
Special Needs: Level 1: CP
Level 2: ADD ADHD DYC DYP DYS

ST PETER & ST PAUL
SCHOOL
Brambling House, Hady Hill,
Chesterfield, Derbyshire S41 0EF
Tel: (01246) 278522
Head: Mrs B Beet
Type: Co-educational Day 2–11
No of pupils: B82 G91
Fees: (September 01) Day £3276
Special Needs: Level 1: W Level 2: ASP
DYS MLD SPLD Level 3: ADD ADHD
DYP EBD Unspecified: SP&LD

DEVON

BLUNDELL'S SCHOOL
Tiverton, Devon EX16 4DN
Tel: (01884) 252543
Head: Mr J Leigh
Type: Co-educational Boarding and
Day 11–18
No of pupils: B320 G190
No of Boarders: F115 W255
Fees: (September 01)
FB £10515 – £15810
WB £6645 – £14290
Day £5685 – £9825
Special Needs: Level 2: DYS

ELM GROVE SCHOOL
Elm Grove Road, Topsham, Exeter,
Devon EX3 0EQ
Tel: (01392) 873031
Head: Mrs K M Parsons and
Mr B E Parsons
Type: Co-educational Day 2–8
No of pupils: B30 G30
Fees: (September 01) Day £2400
Special Needs: Level 2: ADD ADHD
DYC DYP DYS EBD HI MLD PH
SP&LD Level 3: ASP AUT DEL

EXETER CATHEDRAL
SCHOOL
The Chantry, Palace Gate, Exeter,
Devon EX1 1HX
Tel: (01392) 255298
Head: Mr C I S Dickinson
Type: Co-educational Day and
Boarding 3–13
No of pupils: B119 G57
No of Boarders: F25 W5
Fees: (September 01)
FB £8835 – £9000
WB £8460 – £8625
Day £3195 – £5505
Special Needs: Level 2: DYS
Unspecified: SPLD

EXETER TUTORIAL COLLEGE
44/46 Magdalen Road, Exeter, Devon
EX2 4TE
Tel: (01392) 278101
Head: Mr K D Jack
Type: Co-educational Day 15+
No of pupils: B30 G35
Fees: (September 01) Day £3400 –
£7000
Special Needs: Unspecified: DYS

GRAMERCY HALL SCHOOL
Churston Ferrers, Torbay, Devon
TQ5 0HR
Tel: (01803) 844338
Head: Mr N Thomas
Type: Co-educational Day 3–16
No of pupils: B112 G75
No of Boarders: F15 W3
Fees: (September 01) FB £8950
WB £7590 Day £3600 – £4350
Special Needs: Level 3: ASP DYP DYS
EPI HI MLD PH TOU

GRENVILLE COLLEGE*†
Bideford, Devon EX39 3JR
Tel: (01237) 472212
Head: Mr D M Cane
Type: Co-educational Day and
Boarding 2–19
No of pupils: B235 G170
No of Boarders: F105
Fees: (September 01)
FB £10860 – £13986
WB £8142 – £10485
Day £2904 – £6924
Special Needs: Unspecified: DYS

KELLY COLLEGE
Tavistock, Devon PL19 0HZ
Tel: (01822) 813127
Head: M S Steed
Type: Co-educational Boarding and
Day 11–18
No of pupils: B220 G150
No of Boarders: F105 W80
Fees: (September 01)
FB £13050 – £15600
WB £1200 – £15000
Day £6600 – £9900
Special Needs: Level 2: DYC DYP DYS
Level 3: ADD ADHD

KING'S SCHOOL
Hartley Road, Mannamead,
Plymouth, Devon PL3 5LW
Tel: (01752) 771789
Head: Mrs J Lee
Type: Co-educational Day 3–11
No of pupils: B98 G74
Fees: (September 01) Day £2655 –
£2985
Special Needs: Level 2: DYS MLD
SP&LD SPLD Level 3: ADD
Unspecified: DYP

MANOR HOUSE SCHOOL
Springfield House, Honiton, Devon
EX14 9TL
Tel: (01404) 42026
Head: Mr S J Bage
Type: Co-educational Day 3–11
No of pupils: B65 G65
Fees: (September 01) Day £2940 –
£4050
Special Needs: Level 2: DYP DYS MLD
SP&LD SPLD

NEW SCHOOL
Exe Vale, Exminster, Exeter, Devon
EX6 8AT
Tel: (01392) 496122
Head: Mrs G Redman
Type: Co-educational Day 4–8
No of pupils: B32 G31
Fees: (September 01) Day £2235 –
£2835
Special Needs: Level 2: DYS
Level 3: DYP HI PH SP&LD
Unspecified: W

OSHO KO HSUAN SCHOOL
Chawleigh, Chulmleigh, Devon
EX18 7EX
Tel: (01769) 580896
Head: Mr K Bartlam
Type: Co-educational Boarding 7–16
No of pupils: B14 G15
No of Boarders: F26 W3
Fees: (September 01) FB £7200
WB £5850 Day £4050
Special Needs: Level 2: DYP DYS

RUDOLF STEINER SCHOOL
Hood Manor, Buckfastleigh Road,
Dartington, Totnes, Devon TQ9 6AB
Tel: (01803) 762528
Head: Mr C Cooper
Type: Co-educational Day 3–16
No of pupils: B145 G149
No of Boarders: F4 W4
Fees: (September 01) Day £2517 –
£4179
Special Needs: Level 3: DEL

ST AUBYN'S SCHOOL
Milestones House, Blundell's Road,
Tiverton, Devon EX16 4NA
Tel: (01884) 252393
Head: Mr N A Folland
Type: Co-educational Day 0–11
No of pupils: B171 G133
No of Boarders: W3
Fees: (September 01) Day £1044 –
£5640
Special Needs: Level 1: DYP
Level 2: DYC DYS HI SPLD
Level 3: MLD

ST CHRISTOPHERS SCHOOL
Mount Barton, Staverton, Totnes,
Devon TQ9 6PF
Tel: (01803) 762202
Head: Mrs J E Kenyon
Type: Co-educational Day 2–11
No of pupils: B45 G35
Fees: (September 01) Day £2340 –
£3591
Special Needs: Level 2: ASP AUT CP
DOW DYS HI MLD PH Unspecified:
DEL DYC EBD SP&LD W

ST JOHN'S SCHOOL
Broadway, Sidmouth, Devon
EX10 8RG
Tel: (01395) 513984
Head: Mr N R Pockett
Type: Co-educational Day and
Boarding 2–13
No of pupils: B127 G123
No of Boarders: F50 W10
Fees: (September 01) FB £10212
WB £9561 Day £1611 – £5670
Special Needs: Level 1: DYC DYP
Level 2: DYS MLD

ST MICHAEL'S
Tawstock Court, Barnstaple, Devon
EX31 3HY
Tel: (01271) 343242
Head: Mr J W Pratt
Type: Co-educational Day and
Boarding 0–13
No of pupils: B133 G83
No of Boarders: W4
Fees: (September 01)
WB £10380 – £10695
Day £3225 – £7011
Special Needs: Level 2: ADD ADHD
DYC DYP DYS MLD SP&LD SPLD

SANDS SCHOOL
Greylands, 48 East Street,
Ashburton, Devon TQ13 7AX
Tel: (01364) 653666
Head: Mr S Bellamy
Type: Co-educational Day 10–16
No of pupils: B36 G34
Fees: (September 01) Day £4500
Special Needs: Level 3: DYS

DORSET

HOMEFIELD SCHOOL
SENIOR & PREPARATORY
Salisbury Road, Winkton,
Christchurch, Dorset BH23 7AR
Tel: (01202) 479781/476644
Head: Mr A C Partridge
Type: Co-educational Boarding and
Day 3–18
No of pupils: B250 G100
No of Boarders: F50 W3
Fees: (September 01) F/WB £11475
Day £2775 – £4755
Special Needs: Unspecified: ADD
ADHD DYC DYP DYS W

KNIGHTON HOUSE
Durweston, Blandford Forum,
Dorset DT11 0PY
Tel: (01258) 452065
Head: Mrs E A Heath
Type: Girls Day and Boarding 3–13
(Day boys 3–7)
No of pupils: B14 G138
No of Boarders: F26 W27
Fees: (September 01) F/WB £11670
Day £1800 – £8520
Special Needs: Level 2: DYS MLD
SPLD

MILTON ABBEY SCHOOL
Blandford Forum, Dorset DT11 0BZ
Tel: (01258) 880484
Head: Mr J Hughes-D'Aeth
Type: Boys Boarding and Day 13–18
No of pupils: 224 *No of Boarders:* F190
Fees: (September 01) FB £16455
Day £12345
Special Needs: Unspecified: ADD
ADHD ASP DYC DYP DYS

PORT REGIS
Motcombe Park, Shaftesbury, Dorset
SP7 9QA
Tel: (01747) 852566
Head: Mr P A E Dix
Type: Co-educational Boarding and
Day 3–13
No of pupils: B230 G170
No of Boarders: F152 W105
Fees: (September 01) F/WB £13980
Day £4650 – £10485
Special Needs: Level 2: DYC DYP DYS
SP&LD SPLD Level 3: HI PH

SUNNINGHILL
PREPARATORY SCHOOL
South Court, South Walks,
Dorchester, Dorset DT1 1EB
Tel: (01305) 262306
Head: Mr C Pring
Type: Co-educational Day 3–13
No of pupils: B92 G93
Fees: (September 01) Day £2175 –
£4800
Special Needs: Unspecified: DYC DYP
DYS

TALBOT HEATH
Rothesay Road, Bournemouth,
Dorset BH4 9NJ
Tel: (01202) 761881
Head: Mrs C Dipple
Type: Girls Day and Boarding 3–18
(Boys 3–7)
No of pupils: B6 G652
No of Boarders: F29 W5
Fees: (January 02) FB £12420
WB £12090 Day £2310 – £7290
Special Needs: Level 2: DYS
Level 3: ADD ADHD DEL DYC DYP
EPI HI PH SPLD

THORNLOW PREPARATORY
SCHOOL†
Connaught Road, Weymouth, Dorset
DT4 0SA
Tel: (01305) 785703
Head: Mr R A Fowke
Type: Co-educational Day 3–13
No of pupils: B43 G35
Fees: (September 01) Day £1395
Special Needs: Level 1: DYC DYS
SPLD

UPLANDS SCHOOL
40 St Osmund's Road, Parkstone,
Poole, Dorset BH14 9JY
Tel: (01202) 742626
Head: Mrs P M Malden
Type: Co-educational Day 2–16
No of pupils: B199 G165
Fees: (September 01) Day £2700 –
£5925
Special Needs: Level 1: DYS

WENTWORTH COLLEGE
College Road, Bournemouth, Dorset
BH5 2DY
Tel: (01202) 423266
Head: Miss S Coe
Type: Girls Boarding and Day 11–18
No of pupils: G225
No of Boarders: F40 W20
Fees: (September 01) F/WB £11550
Day £7275
Special Needs: Level 2: DYS SPLD
Level 3: DYC DYP

YARRELLS SCHOOL
Yarrells House, Upton, Poole, Dorset
BH16 5EU
Tel: (01202) 622229
Head: Mrs Covell
Type: Co-educational Day 2–13
No of pupils: B114 G149
Fees: (September 01) Day £1175 –
£6075
Special Needs: Level 2: ADHD ASP
DYP DYS SP&LD Level 3: ADD EPI
HI

COUNTY DURHAM

BOW SCHOOL
South Road, Durham, County
Durham DH1 3LS
Tel: (0191) 384 8233
Head: Mr R N Baird
Type: Boys Day 3–13
No of pupils: 159
Fees: (September 01) Day £3372 –
£6309
Special Needs: Level 2: DYS MLD
Level 3: ADD ADHD ASP

THE CHORISTER SCHOOL
Durham, County Durham DH1 3EL
Tel: (0191) 384 2935
Head: Mr C S S Drew
Type: Co-educational Day and
Boarding 4–13
No of pupils: B143 G46
No of Boarders: F20 W10
Fees: (September 01)
F/WB £4761 – £8952
Day £4272 – £6120
Special Needs: Level 2: DYP DYS
Level 3: ADD ADHD ASP AUT DEL

DURHAM HIGH SCHOOL FOR GIRLS
Farewell Hall, Durham, County
Durham DH1 3TB
Tel: (0191) 384 3226
Head: Mrs A J Templeman
Type: Girls Day 3–18
No of pupils: 530
Fees: (September 01) Day £4080 –
£6135
Special Needs: Level 2: DYS

DURHAM SCHOOL
Durham, County Durham DH1 4SZ
Tel: (0191) 384 7977
Head: Mr M N G Kern
Type: Co-educational Boarding and
Day 11–18
No of pupils: B256 G83
No of Boarders: F78
Fees: (September 01) FB £14295
Day £6465 – £9357
Special Needs: Level 2: ADD DYS
Level 3: PH

POLAM HALL
Darlington, County Durham
DL1 5PA
Tel: (01325) 463383
Head: Mrs H C Hamilton
Type: Girls Boarding and Day 4–18
No of pupils: G470
No of Boarders: F40 W5
Fees: (September 01)
FB £10095 – £13155
WB £9795 – £12855
Day £2895 – £6120
Special Needs: Level 1: MLD
Level 2: ASP CP DEL DYC DYP DYS
EPI PH SPLD VIS Level 3: HI SP&LD

ESSEX

BANCROFT'S SCHOOL
Woodford Green, Essex IG8 0RF
Tel: (020) 8505 4821
Head: Dr P R Scott
Type: Co-educational Day 7–18
No of pupils: B461 G520
Fees: (September 01) Day £6057 –
£7989
Special Needs: Level 3: DYC DYP DYS
EBD EPI PH

BRENTWOOD SCHOOL
Ingrave Road, Brentwood, Essex
CM15 8AS
Tel: (01277) 243243
Head: Mr J A B Kelsall
Type: Co-educational Boarding and
Day 3–18
No of pupils: B854 G546
No of Boarders: F75 W20
Fees: (September 01) FB £14621
Day £8406
Special Needs: Level 2: ADD DYP DYS

COLCHESTER HIGH SCHOOL
Wellesley Road, Colchester, Essex
CO3 3HD
Tel: (01206) 573389
Head: Mr A T Moore
Type: Boys Day 3–16 (Girls 3–11)
No of pupils: B340 G35
Fees: (September 01) Day £1380 –
£5085
Special Needs: Level 2: DYC DYP DYS
SPLD Level 3: PH

DAME JOHANE BRADBURY'S SCHOOL
Ashdon Road, Saffron Walden, Essex
CB10 2AL
Tel: (01799) 522348
Head: Mrs R M Rainey
Type: Co-educational Day 3–11
No of pupils: B158 G158
Fees: (September 01) Day £3828 –
£5073
Special Needs: Level 2: DYS

FELSTED SCHOOL
Felsted, Dunmow, Essex CM6 3LL
Tel: (01371) 822 600
Head: Mr S C Roberts
Type: Co-educational Boarding and
Day 13–18
No of pupils: B254 G151
No of Boarders: F278
Fees: (September 01) FB £15720
Day £11490 – £12390
Special Needs: Level 2: DYS SPLD
Level 3: ADD DYC DYP EBD EPI HI
PH VIS

FRIENDS' SCHOOL
Mount Pleasant Road, Saffron
Walden, Essex CB11 3EB
Tel: 01799 525 351
Head: Mr A Waters
Type: Co-educational Boarding and
Day 3–18
No of pupils: B183 G143
No of Boarders: F81 W5
Fees: (September 01)
F/WB £8919 – £13674
Day £4542 – £8205
Special Needs: Level 1: DYS SPLD
Level 2: ASP DEL DYP SP&LD
Level 3: CP EBD EPI HI PH VIS

GLENARM COLLEGE
20 Coventry Road, Ilford, Essex
IG1 4QR
Tel: (020) 8554 1760
Head: Mrs V Mullooly
Type: Co-educational Day 3–11
No of pupils: B54 G86
Fees: (September 01) Day £4005 –
£4305
Special Needs: Unspecified: ADD DEL
DYS MLD

HEATHCOTE SCHOOL
Eves Corner, Danbury, Chelmsford,
Essex CM3 4QB
Tel: (01245) 223131
Head: Mrs L Mitchell-Hall
Type: Co-educational Day 2–11
No of pupils: B96 G88
Fees: (September 01) Day £4200
Special Needs: Level 2: ADD ADHD
ASP DEL DYP DYS MLD SPLD TOU
Level 3: PH VIS Unspecified: W

HOLMWOOD HOUSE†
Chitts Hill, Lexden, Colchester,
Essex CO3 5ST
Tel: (01206) 574305
Head: Mr H S Thackrah
Type: Co-educational Day and
Boarding 4–14
No of pupils: B229 G138
Fees: (September 01)
WB £10386 – £11625
Day £5049 – £8991
Special Needs: Level 2: DYC DYP DYS

LITTLEGARTH SCHOOL
Horkesley Park, Nayland,
Colchester, Essex CO6 4JR
Tel: (01206) 262332
Head: Mrs E P Coley
Type: Co-educational Day 2–11
No of pupils: B153 G140
Fees: (September 01) Day £990 –
£4485
Special Needs: Level 2: DYP DYS
SPLD

MALDON COURT PREPARATORY SCHOOL
Silver Street, Maldon, Essex
CM9 4QE
Tel: (01621) 853529
Head: Mr A G Webb
Type: Co-educational Day 4–11
No of pupils: B66 G57
Fees: (September 01) Day £3840 –
£3990
Special Needs: Level 2: DYS

ST AUBYN'S SCHOOL
Bunces Lane, Woodford Green,
Essex IG8 9DU
Tel: (020) 8504 1577
Head: Mr G James
Type: Co-educational Day 3–13
No of pupils: B280 G180
Fees: (September 01) Day £2040 –
£5709
Special Needs: Level 3: DYC DYP DYS
PH

ST HILDA'S SCHOOL
15 Imperial Avenue, Westcliff-on-
Sea, Essex SSO 8NE
Tel: (01702) 344542
Head: Mrs S O'Riordan
Type: Girls Day 2–16 (Boys 2–7)
No of pupils: B1 G180
Fees: (September 01) On application
Special Needs: Level 2: DYS
Level 3: ADD ASP DYC DYP SPLD

ST JOHN'S SCHOOL
Stock Road, Billericay, Essex
CM12 0AR
Tel: (01277) 623070
Head: Mrs S Hillier and
Mrs F S Armour
Type: Co-educational Day 3–16
No of pupils: B238 G164
Fees: (September 01) Day £2775 –
£5250
Special Needs: Level 2: ASP DYS
Level 3: ADD ADHD DYC

ST MARGARET'S SCHOOL
Gosfield Hall Park, Gosfield,
Halstead, Essex CO9 1SE
Tel: (01787) 472134
Head: Mrs B Y Boyton
Type: Co-educational Day 2–11
No of pupils: B98 G102
Fees: (September 01) Day £3375 –
£5100
Special Needs: Level 2: ADD ADHD
ASP DEL DYP DYS HI MLD PH
SP&LD SPLD Unspecified: W

ST PHILOMENA'S PREPARATORY SCHOOL
Hadleigh Road, Frinton-on-Sea,
Essex CO13 9HQ
Tel: (01255) 674492
Head: Mrs B Buck
Type: Co-educational Day 3–11
No of pupils: 169
Fees: (September 01) Day £2400
Special Needs: Unspecified: ASP DYS
MLD TOU

WIDFORD LODGE
Widford Road, Chelmsford, Essex
CM2 9AN
Tel: (01245) 352581
Head: Mr S C Trowell
Type: Co-educational Day 2–11
No of pupils: B130 G65
Fees: (September 01) Day £4020 –
£5250
Special Needs: Level 3: ADD ADHD
ASP AUT CP DEL DOW DYC DYP
DYS EBD HI MLD PH SPLD VIS

GLOUCESTERSHIRE

THE ABBEY SCHOOL
Church Street, Tewkesbury,
Gloucestershire GL20 5PD
Tel: (01684) 294460
Head: Mr I R Griffin and Mrs J Wilson
Type: Co-educational Day and
Boarding 2–13
No of pupils: B67 G38
No of Boarders: W10
Fees: (September 01)
WB £7284 – £9714
Day £1170 – £7014
Special Needs: Level 2: DYC DYP DYS
SPLD Level 3: ADD DEL MLD
SP&LD

AIRTHRIE SCHOOL
29 Christ Church Road,
Cheltenham, Gloucestershire
GL50 2NY
Tel: (01242) 512837
Head: Mrs A E Sullivan
Type: Co-educational Day 3–11
No of pupils: B90 G90
Fees: (September 01) Day £3210 –
£4140
Special Needs: Level 1: DYC DYS
SPLD Level 3: CP EPI Unspecified:
DYP

BEAUDESERT PARK
Minchinhampton, Stroud,
Gloucestershire GL6 9AF
Tel: (01453) 832072
Head: Mr J P R Womersley
Type: Co-educational Boarding and
Day 4–13
No of pupils: B212 G144
No of Boarders: F10 W45
Fees: (September 01) F/WB £12210
Day £4515 – £8985
Special Needs: Level 2: DYP DYS
SPLD Unspecified: SP&LD W

BERKHAMPSTEAD SCHOOL
Pittville Circus Road, Cheltenham,
Gloucestershire GL52 2QA
Tel: (01242) 523263
Head: Mr T R Owen
Type: Co-educational Day 3–11
No of pupils: B115 G135
Fees: (September 01) Day £2475 –
£4275
Special Needs: Level 2: DYC DYP DYS

BREDON SCHOOL*†
Pull Court, Bushley, Tewkesbury,
Gloucestershire GL20 6AH
Tel: (01684) 293156
Head: Mr M Newby
Type: Co-educational Boarding and
Day 7–18
No of pupils: B140 G60
No of Boarders: F83 W45
Fees: (September 01)
FB £10995 – £15690
WB £10710 – £14775
Day £5595 – £10695
Special Needs: Level 1: ADD DYC
DYP DYS MLD SPLD Level 2: SP&LD

DEAN CLOSE PREPARATORY SCHOOL
Lansdown Road, Cheltenham,
Gloucestershire GL51 6QS
Tel: (01242) 512217
Head: Mr S W Baird
Type: Co-educational Boarding and
Day 2–13
No of pupils: B190 G170
No of Boarders: F58
Fees: (September 01) FB £12300
Day £3960 – £8415
Special Needs: Level 2: ADD DYP DYS

DEAN CLOSE SCHOOL
Shelburne Road, Cheltenham,
Gloucestershire GL51 6HE
Tel: (01242) 522640
Head: The Revd T M Hastie-Smith
Type: Co-educational Boarding and
Day 13–18
No of pupils: B253 G207
No of Boarders: F267
Fees: (September 01) FB £16800
Day £11790
Special Needs: Level 2: DYP DYS
SPLD

HATHEROP CASTLE SCHOOL
Hatherop, Cirencester,
Gloucestershire GL7 3NB
Tel: (01285) 750206
Head: Mr P Easterbrook
Type: Co-educational Boarding and
Day 4–13
No of pupils: B115 G98
No of Boarders: F24
Fees: (September 01)
F/WB £9510 – £10020
Day £3900 – £6480
Special Needs: Level 2: ADD DYC
DYP DYS EBD MLD SP&LD
Unspecified: ADHD

HOPELANDS SCHOOL
38 Regent Street, Stonehouse,
Gloucestershire GL10 2AD
Tel: (01453) 822164
Head: Mrs B J Janes
Type: Co-educational Day 3–11
No of pupils: B14 G55
Fees: (September 01) Day £2775 –
£3510
Special Needs: Level 1: DYS MLD

THE KING'S SCHOOL
Pitt Street, Gloucester GL1 2BG
Tel: (01452) 337337
Head: Mr P R Lacey
Type: Co-educational Boarding and
Day 3–18
No of pupils: B286 G185
No of Boarders: F3 W10
Fees: (September 01)
WB £13290 – £14535
Day £3945 – £9390
Special Needs: Level 2: DYP DYS
SPLD

THE RICHARD PATE SCHOOL
Southern Road, Cheltenham,
Gloucestershire GL53 9RP
Tel: (01242) 522086
Head: Mr E L Rowland
Type: Co-educational Day 3–11
No of pupils: B159 G137
Fees: (September 01) Day £1650 –
£4950
Special Needs: Level 2: DYS
Unspecified: W

WESTONBIRT SCHOOL
Tetbury, Gloucestershire GL8 8QG
Tel: (01666) 880333
Head: Mrs M Henderson
Type: Girls Boarding and Day 11–18
No of pupils: G200
No of Boarders: F105 W20
Fees: (September 01) FB £15720
Day £10956
Special Needs: Level 2: DYS
Level 3: DEL PH

WYCLIFFE COLLEGE*
Stonehouse, Gloucestershire
GL10 2JQ
Tel: (01453) 822432
Head: Dr R A Collins
Type: Co-educational Boarding and
Day 13–18
No of pupils: B271 G149
No of Boarders: F273
Fees: (September 01)
FB £16515 – £18600
Day £10755 – £11160
Special Needs: Level 2: DYP DYS

HAMPSHIRE

THE ATHERLEY SCHOOL
Grove Place, Upton Lane, Nursling,
Southampton, Hampshire SO16 0AB
Tel: (023) 8074 1629
Head: Mrs M Bradley
Type: Girls Day 3–18 (Boys 3–11)
No of pupils: B60 G340
Fees: (September 01) Day £1498 –
£2098
Special Needs: Level 2: DYS
Level 3: ASP CP DEL EPI PH
Unspecified: W

BEDALES SCHOOL
Petersfield, Hampshire GU32 2DG
Tel: (01730) 300100
Head: Mr K Budge
Type: Co-educational Boarding and
Day 13–18
No of pupils: B182 G222
No of Boarders: F307
Fees: (September 01) FB £17814
Day £13620
Special Needs: Level 2: DYP DYS

BOUNDARY OAK SCHOOL
Roche Court, Fareham, Hampshire
PO17 5BL
Tel: (01329) 280955
Head: Mr R B Bliss
Type: Co-educational Boarding and
Day 3–13
No of pupils: B166 G49
No of Boarders: W25
Fees: (September 01)
F/WB £7725 – £10335
Day £2190 – £7125
Special Needs: Level 2: DYC DYP DYS
EPI HI PH SP&LD SPLD Level 3: ADD
ADHD ASP AUT CP DEL DOW

CHILTERN TUTORIAL UNIT
c/o Otterbourne Village Hall,
Cranbourne Drive, Otterbourne,
Winchester, Hampshire SO21 2ET
Tel: (01962) 860482
Head: Mrs J Gaudie
Type: Co-educational Day 8–11
No of pupils: B12 G4
Fees: (September 01) Day £4920
Special Needs: Level 1: DYS

CHURCHERS COLLEGE
Portsmouth Road, Petersfield,
Hampshire GU31 4AS
Tel: (01730) 263033
Head: Mr G W Buttle
Type: Co-educational Day 4–18
No of pupils: B452 G292
Fees: (September 01) Day £3705 –
£6915
Special Needs: Level 2: DYS SPLD
Level 3: ADD ADHD DYC DYP EBD
EPI HI PH VIS Unspecified: W

DITCHAM PARK SCHOOL
Ditcham Park, Petersfield,
Hampshire GU31 5RN
Tel: (01730) 825659
Head: Mrs K S Morton
Type: Co-educational Day 4–16
No of pupils: B198 G119
Fees: (September 01) Day £4185 –
£6990
Special Needs: Level 2: DYS

**DUNHURST (BEDALES
JUNIOR SCHOOL)**
Alton Road, Steep, Petersfield,
Hampshire GU32 2DP
Tel: (01730) 300200
Head: Mr R Hancock
Type: Co-educational Boarding and
Day 8–13
No of pupils: B104 G90
No of Boarders: F68
Fees: (September 01) FB £12243
Day £8976
Special Needs: Level 2: DYP DYS
SPLD

DURLSTON COURT
Becton Lane, Barton-on-Sea, New
Milton, Hampshire BH25 7AQ
Tel: (01425) 610010
Head: Mr D C Wansey
Type: Co-educational Day 2–13
No of pupils: B125 G93
Fees: (September 01) Day £2175 –
£7650
Special Needs: Level 2: ADD ADHD
ASP DYC DYP DYS SPLD Level 3: EBD
EPI HI

GLENHURST SCHOOL
16 Beechworth Road, Havant,
Hampshire PO9 1AX
Tel: (023) 9248 4054
Head: Mrs E Haines
Type: Co-educational Day 3–9
No of pupils: B43 G38
Fees: (September 01) Day £2170 –
£2910
Special Needs: Level 2: ASP DEL DYP
DYS

GREY HOUSE PREPARATORY SCHOOL
Mount Pleasant Road, Hartley
Wintney, Basingstoke, Hampshire
RG27 8PW
Tel: (01252) 842353
Head: Mrs E M Purse
Type: Co-educational Day 4–11
No of pupils: B83 G69
Fees: (September 01) Day £4128 –
£5082
Special Needs: Level 2: DYS

HIGHFIELD SCHOOL
Liphook, Hampshire GU30 7LQ
Tel: (01428) 728000
Head: Mr P G S Evitt
Type: Co-educational Boarding and
Day 7–13
No of pupils: B111 G84
No of Boarders: F94
Fees: (September 01)
FB £10800 – £12375
Day £8325 – £10875
Special Needs: Level 2: DYP DYS

HORDLE WALHAMPTON SCHOOL
Walhampton, Lymington,
Hampshire SO41 5ZG
Tel: (01590) 672013
Head: Mr R H C Phillips
Type: Co-educational Boarding and
Day 2–13
No of pupils: B183 G163
No of Boarders: F35 W34
Fees: (September 01) F/WB £11250
Day £4170 – £8580
Special Needs: Level 2: ADD ADHD
CP DYC DYP DYS MLD Level 3: HI

LORD WANDSWORTH COLLEGE
Long Sutton, Hook, Hampshire
RG29 1TB
Tel: (01256) 862201
Head: Mr I G Power
Type: Co-educational Boarding and
Day 11–18
No of pupils: B365 G135
No of Boarders: F52 W300
Fees: (September 01)
F/WB £13845 – £14610
Day £10425 – £10980
Special Needs: Level 2: DYS
Unspecified: W

MAYVILLE HIGH SCHOOL†
35 St Simon's Road, Southsea,
Hampshire PO5 2PE
Tel: (023) 9273 4847
Head: Mrs L Owens
Type: Co-educational Day 2–16
No of pupils: B114 G218
Fees: (September 01) Day £3225 –
£4800
Special Needs: Level 1: DYS SPLD

NETHERCLIFFE SCHOOL
Hatherley Road, Winchester,
Hampshire SO22 6RS
Tel: (01962) 854570
Head: Mr R F Whitfield
Type: Co-educational Day 3–11
No of pupils: B88 G60
Fees: (September 01) Day £2130 –
£4380
Special Needs: Level 2: ADD ADHD
DYS SP&LD

ST ANNE'S NURSERY & PRE-PREPARATORY SCHOOL
13 Milvil Road, Lee-on-the-Solent,
Hampshire PO13 9LU
Tel: (023) 9255 0820
Head: Mrs A M Whitting
Type: Co-educational Day 3–8
No of pupils: B15 G15
Fees: (September 01) Day £2370
Special Needs: Level 1: DYC DYP DYS
Level 3: ADD ADHD EBD EPI MLD
PH SP&LD Unspecified: W

STANBRIDGE EARLS SCHOOL*†
Stanbridge Lane, Romsey, Hampshire
SO51 0ZS
Tel: (01794) 516777
Head: Mr N R Hall
Type: Co-educational Boarding and
Day 11–18
No of pupils: B149 G39
No of Boarders: F160
Fees: (September 01)
FB £14700 – £16170
Day £10980 – £12000
Special Needs: Level 1: DYC DYS
Level 2: ADD ADHD ASP DEL DYP
SP&LD

STOCKTON HOUSE SCHOOL
Stockton Avenue, Fleet, Aldershot,
Hampshire GU51 4NS
Tel: (01252) 616323
Head: Mrs C Tweedie-Smith
Type: Co-educational Day 2–8
No of pupils: B30 G30
Fees: (September 01) Day £240 –
£3150
Special Needs: Unspecified: DYS

THE STROUD SCHOOL
Highwood House, Romsey,
Hampshire SO51 9ZH
Tel: (01794) 513231
Head: Mr A J Dodds
Type: Co-educational Day 3–13
No of pupils: B201 G110
Fees: (September 01) Day £2175 –
£7725
Special Needs: Unspecified: DYS

TWYFORD SCHOOL
Winchester, Hampshire SO21 1NW
Tel: (01962) 712269
Head: Mr P Fawkes
Type: Co-educational Day and
Boarding 3–13
No of pupils: B212 G100
No of Boarders: F20 W45
Fees: (September 01) FB £12450
Day £2535 – £9150
Special Needs: Level 2: DYS

YATELEY MANOR PREPARATORY SCHOOL
51 Reading Road, Yateley, Hampshire
GU46 7UQ
Tel: (01252) 405500
Head: Mr F G Howard
Type: Co-educational Day 3–13
No of pupils: B344 G189
Fees: (September 01) Day £4250 –
£7062
Special Needs: Unspecified: CP DYS
HI W

HERTFORDSHIRE

ABBOT'S HILL
Bunkers Lane, Hemel Hempstead,
Hertfordshire HP3 8RP
Tel: (01442) 240333
Head: Mrs K Lewis
Type: Girls Boarding and Day 11–16
No of pupils: 190
No of Boarders: W30
Fees: (September 01) WB £14400
Day £8700
Special Needs: Level 2: ASP CP DYC
DYP DYS HI SPLD Unspecified: DEL
EPI SP&LD VIS

DUNCOMBE SCHOOL
4 Warren Park Road, Bengeo,
Hertford SG14 3JA
Tel: (01992) 414100
Head: Mr D Baldwin
Type: Co-educational Day 2–11
No of pupils: B174 G170
Fees: (September 01) Day £392 –
£6228
Special Needs: Level 2: ASP DYC DYP
DYS HI MLD SP&LD SPLD VIS
Level 3: ADD AUT EPI

EGERTON-ROTHESAY
SCHOOL
Durrants Lane, Berkhamsted,
Hertfordshire HP4 3UJ
Tel: (01442) 865275
Head: Mrs N Boddam-Whetham
Type: Co-educational Day 2–18
No of pupils: B344 G176
Fees: (September 01) Day £4800 –
£10950
Special Needs: Level 1: MLD
Level 2: DYC DYP DYS HI PH SP&LD
SPLD

HABERDASHERS' ASKE'S
BOYS' SCHOOL
Butterfly Lane, Elstree, Hertfordshire
WD6 3AF
Tel: (020) 8266 1700
Head: Mr P B Hamilton
Type: Boys Day 7–18
No of pupils: 1300
Fees: (September 01) Day £7650 –
£8250
Special Needs: Level 3: DYP DYS

HAILEYBURY
Hertford, Hertfordshire SG13 7NU
Tel: (01992) 463353
Head: Mr S A Westley
Type: Co-educational Boarding and
Day 11–18
No of pupils: B400 G280
No of Boarders: F400
Fees: (September 01) FB £11160 –
£17505 Day £8505 – £12750
Special Needs: Level 2: DYP DYS
SPLD Level 3: ADD DYC

HARESFOOT PREPARATORY
SCHOOL
Chesham Road, Berkhamsted,
Hertfordshire HP4 2SZ
Tel: (01442) 872742
Head: Mrs G R Waterhouse
Type: Co-educational Day 3–11
No of pupils: B98 G90
Fees: (September 01) Day £1125 –
£4620
Special Needs: Level 2: DYP DYS
SP&LD SPLD

HEATH MOUNT SCHOOL
Woodhall Park, Watton-at-Stone,
Hertford SG14 3NG
Tel: (01920) 830230
Head: Rev H J Matthews
Type: Co-educational Boarding and
Day 3–13
No of pupils: B218 G143
Fees: (September 01)
WB £9762 – £11325
Day £2385 – £8130
Special Needs: Level 2: DYS

CKHR IMMANUEL COLLEGE
87/91 Elstree Road, Bushey,
Hertfordshire WD23 4EB
Tel: (020) 8950 0604
Head: Mr P Skelker
Type: Co-educational Day 11–18
No of pupils: B220 G170
Fees: (September 01) Day £7800
Special Needs: Level 2: DYC DYP DYS
SPLD Level 3: ADD ADHD ASP

KINGSHOTT
St Ippolyts, Hitchin, Hertfordshire
SG4 7JX
Tel: (01462) 432009
Head: Mr P R Ilott
Type: Co-educational Day 4–13
No of pupils: B215 G116
Fees: (September 01) Day £4560 –
£5880
Special Needs: Level 2: DYS

LITTLE ACORNS
MONTESSORI SCHOOL
Lincolnsfields Centre, Bushey Hall
Drive, Bushey, Hertfordshire
WD2 2ER
Tel: (01923) 230705
Head: Ms J Nugent and Ms R Lau
Type: Co-educational Day 2–7
No of pupils: 24
Fees: (September 01) On application
Special Needs: Level 2: ASP AUT DYS
EPI HI PH SP&LD Level 3: ADD
ADHD DOW EBD MLD

LONGWOOD SCHOOL
Bushey Hall Drive, Bushey,
Hertfordshire WD23 2QG
Tel: (01923) 253715
Head: Mr M Livesey
Type: Co-educational Day 3–9
No of pupils: B49 G47
Fees: (September 01) Day £2250 –
£3450
Special Needs: Level 3: DYC DYP DYS
EBD EPI HI MLD PH SP&LD SPLD
VIS Unspecified: W

MARLIN MONTESSORI
SCHOOL
1 Park View Road, Berkhamsted,
Hertfordshire HP4 3EY
Tel: (01442) 866290
Head: Mrs J Harrison-Sills
Type: Co-educational Day 0–5
No of pupils: B24 G24
Fees: (September 01) Day £924 –
£4734
Special Needs: Unspecified: ADD ASP
CP DEL DOW DYP DYS MLD
SP&LD

NORFOLK LODGE NURSERY
& PREPARATORY SCHOOL
Dancers Hill Road, Barnet,
Hertfordshire EN5 4RP
Tel: (020) 8447 1565
Head: Mrs L Beirne
Type: Day
No of pupils: B90 G80
Fees: (September 01) Day £930 –
£4650
Special Needs: Level 2: DYP DYS EBD
Level 3: ADD ADHD AUT EPI
Unspecified: ASP DEL DOW SP&LD

THE PRINCESS HELENA COLLEGE
Preston, Hitchin, Hertfordshire
SG4 7RT
Tel: (01462) 432100
Head: Mrs A M Hodgkiss
Type: Girls Boarding and Day 11–18
No of pupils: 156
No of Boarders: F60 W25
Fees: (September 01)
F/WB £11280 – £14175
Day £7620 – £9585
Special Needs: Level 2: ADD ADHD
ASP DYP DYS HI TOU

RICKMANSWORTH PNEU SCHOOL
88 The Drive, Rickmansworth,
Hertfordshire WD3 4DU
Tel: (01923) 772101
Head: Mrs S K Marshall-Taylor
Type: Girls Day 3–11
No of pupils: G140
Fees: (September 01) Day £1686 –
£4812
Special Needs: Level 2: DYC DYP DYS
SPLD

ST ANDREW'S MONTESSORI SCHOOL
Garston Manor, High Elms Lane,
Watford, Hertfordshire WD2 0JX
Tel: (01923) 663875
Head: Mrs S O'Neill
Type: Co-educational Day 0–12
No of pupils: B29 G31
Fees: (September 01) Day £381 –
£4962
Special Needs: Level 2: ASP DOW DYS
MLD SP&LD SPLD Level 3: DEL DYP
HI PH VIS Unspecified: W

ST COLUMBA'S COLLEGE
King Harry Lane, St Albans,
Hertfordshire AL3 4AW
Tel: (01727) 855185
Head: Dom S Darlington
Type: Boys Day 4–18
No of pupils: B800
Fees: (September 01) Day £4710 –
£6120
Special Needs: Level 1: ADD ADHD
DYC DYP DYS EBD SPLD Level 3: ASP
EPI HI PH SP&LD TOU

ST HILDA'S SCHOOL
High Street, Bushey, Hertfordshire
WD23 3DA
Tel: (020) 8950 1751
Head: Mrs L Cavanagh
Type: Girls Day 3–11
No of pupils: B6 G164
Fees: (September 01) Day £3000 –
£5625
Special Needs: Unspecified: DYS HI

ST JOSEPH'S IN THE PARK*
St Mary's, Hertingfordbury, Hertford
SG14 2LX
Tel: (01992) 581378
Head: Mrs J King
Type: Co-educational Day 3–11
No of pupils: B90 G90
Fees: (September 01) Day £1700
Special Needs: Level 1: MLD PH VIS
Level 2: DYC DYP DYS SP&LD SPLD
Level 3: DEL

ST NICHOLAS HOUSE
Bunkers Lane, Hemel Hempstead,
Hertfordshire HP3 8RP
Tel: (01442) 839107
Head: Mrs B B Vaughan
Type: Girls Day 3–11 (Boys 3–7)
No of pupils: B29 G183
Fees: (September 01) Day £1630 –
£2020
Special Needs: Level 2: DYC DYP DYS
Unspecified: DEL

STANBOROUGH SCHOOL
Stanborough Park, Garston,
Watford, Hertfordshire WD25 9JT
Tel: (01923) 673268
Head: Mr S Rivers
Type: Co-educational Day and
Boarding 3–16
No of pupils: B146 G124
No of Boarders: F19 W10
Fees: (September 01)
FB £10470 – £12012
WB £9030 – £9300
Day £2970 – £4290
Special Needs: Unspecified: DYP DYS

YORK HOUSE SCHOOL
Redheath, Croxley Green,
Rickmansworth, Hertfordshire
WD3 4LW
Tel: (01923) 772395
Head: Mr P B Moore
Type: Boys Day 4–13 (Co-ed 2–5)
No of pupils: B261 G12
Fees: (September 01) Day £6078
Special Needs: Level 2: DYP DYS
Level 3: HI VIS

KENT

ASHFORD SCHOOL
East Hill, Ashford, Kent TN24 8PB
Tel: (01233) 625171
Head: Mrs P Holloway
Type: Girls Day and Boarding 3–18
No of pupils: G510 *No of Boarders:* F60
Fees: (September 01)
FB £13200 – £15150
WB £11895 – £13650
Day £4320 – £8700
Special Needs: Level 3: DYC DYS EPI
HI PH

ASHGROVE SCHOOL
116 Widmore Road, Bromley, Kent
BR1 3BE
Tel: (020) 8460 4143
Head: Dr P Ash
Type: Co-educational Day 3–11
No of pupils: 118
Fees: (September 01) Day £4791
Special Needs: Level 3: ADD DYC
DYP DYS

BABINGTON HOUSE SCHOOL
Grange Drive, Chislehurst, Kent
BR7 5ES
Tel: (020) 8467 5537
Head: Miss D Odysseas
Type: Girls Day 3–16 (Boys 3–7)
No of pupils: B60 G160
Fees: (September 01) Day £1875 –
£6300
Special Needs: Level 2: DYC DYP
DYS SPLD Level 3: ADD HI PH
SP&LD VIS

BASTON SCHOOL
Baston Road, Hayes, Bromley, Kent
BR2 7AB
Tel: (020) 8462 1010
Head: Mr C R C Wimble
Type: Girls Day 2–18
No of pupils: 157
Fees: (September 01) Day £1377 –
£6420
Special Needs: Level 2: DYS
Level 3: ADD ADHD HI

BEDGEBURY SCHOOL
Bedgebury Park, Goudhurst,
Cranbrook, Kent TN17 2SH
Tel: (01580) 211221
Head: Mrs H Moriarty
Type: Girls Boarding and Day 2–18
(Boys Day 2–7)
No of pupils: B18 G375
No of Boarders: F57 W74
Fees: (September 01)
F/WB £9960 – £15120
Day £2280 – £9390
Special Needs: Level 1: SPLD
Level 2: DYC DYP DYS HI
Level 3: ADD ADHD SP&LD

BENEDICT HOUSE
PREPARATORY SCHOOL
1–5 Victoria Road, Sidcup, Kent
DA15 7HD
Tel: (020) 8300 7206
Head: Mrs A Brown
Type: Co-educational Day 3–11
No of pupils: B70 G70
Fees: (September 01) Day £1995 –
£4290
Special Needs: Level 3: ADD ADHD
ASP AUT CP DEL DOW DYC DYP
DYS EBD EPI HI MLD PH PMLD SLD
SP&LD SPLD TOU VIS

BETHANY SCHOOL†
Goudhurst, Cranbrook, Kent
TN17 1LB
Tel: (01580) 211273
Head: Mr N Dorey
Type: Co-educational Boarding and
Day 11–18
No of pupils: B250 G65
No of Boarders: F145
Fees: (September 01)
F/WB £13452 – £14367
Day £8646 – £9102
Special Needs: Level 1: DYS
Level 3: ADD DYP HI

BISHOP CHALLONER RC
SCHOOL
Bromley Road, Shortlands, Bromley,
Kent BR2 0BS
Tel: (020) 8460 3546
Head: Mr J A de Waal
Type: Co-educational Day 3–18
No of pupils: B307 G93
Fees: (September 01) Day £3600 –
£5430
Special Needs: Level 2: DYP DYS
Level 3: ADD ADHD ASP AUT DEL
DYC EPI HI

COBHAM HALL†
Cobham, Gravesend, Kent DA12 3BL
Tel: (01474) 823371
Head: Mrs R McCarthy
Type: Girls Boarding and Day 11–18
No of pupils: G200
No of Boarders: F104 W16
Fees: (September 01)
F/WB £14100 – £16200
Day £8850 – £10950
Special Needs: Level 2: DYC DYP DYS
Unspecified: SP&LD

CRANBROOK SCHOOL
Cranbrook, Kent TN17 3JD
Tel: (01580) 711800
Head: Mrs A Daly
Type: Co-educational Day and
Boarding 13–18
No of pupils: B403 G312
No of Boarders: F245
Fees: (September 01) FB £6450
Special Needs: Level 2: DYS SLD

DOVER COLLEGE
Effingham Crescent, Dover, Kent
CT17 9RH
Tel: (01304) 205969
Head: Mr H W Blackett
Type: Co-educational Boarding and
Day 7–18
No of pupils: B166 G116
No of Boarders: F100 W3
Fees: (September 01)
FB £11178 – £14250
WB £10440 – £11220
Day £4050 – £8328
Special Needs: Level 2: ADD ADHD
DYC DYP DYS

DUKE OF YORK'S ROYAL
MILITARY SCHOOL
Dover, Kent CT15 5EQ
Tel: (01304) 245029
Head: Mr J A Cummings
Type: Co-educational Boarding 11–18
No of pupils: B348 G152
No of Boarders: F500
Fees: (September 01) FB £1200
Special Needs: Level 2: DYS
Level 3: ADD

DULWICH PREPARATORY
SCHOOL, CRANBROOK
Coursehorn, Cranbrook, Kent
TN17 3NP
Tel: (01580) 712179
Head: Mr M C Wagstaffe
Type: Co-educational Day and
Boarding 3–13
No of pupils: B306 G237
No of Boarders: F7 W37
Fees: (September 01) FB £12300
WB £11985 Day £2805 – £8160
Special Needs: Level 1: DYP DYS
Level 3: EPI

ELLIOTT PARK SCHOOL
Marina Drive, Minster, Isle of
Sheppey, Sheerness, Kent ME12 2DP
Tel: (01795) 873372
Head: Mr R E Fielder
Type: Co-educational Day 4–11
No of pupils: 79
Fees: (September 01) Day £2700 –
£3000
Special Needs: Level 2: DYC DYS

FARRINGTONS &
STRATFORD HOUSE
Perry Street, Chislehurst, Kent
BR7 6LR
Tel: (020) 8467 0256
Head: Mrs C James
Type: Girls Boarding and Day 2–18
No of pupils: 480
No of Boarders: F70 W10
Fees: (September 01)
FB £12990 – £14340
WB £12450 – £13860
Day £5100 – £7290
Special Needs: Unspecified: DYS

HOLMEWOOD HOUSE
Langton Green, Tunbridge Wells,
Kent TN3 0EB
Tel: (01892) 860000
Head: Mr A S R Corbett
Type: Co-educational Boarding and
Day 3–13
No of pupils: B293 G211
No of Boarders: W26
Fees: (September 01) WB £14265
Day £2670 – £9900
Special Needs: Level 2: ADD ADHD
DYP DYS SPLD Level 3: HI

THE JUNIOR SCHOOL, ST LAWRENCE COLLEGE
Ramsgate, Kent CT11 7AF
Tel: (01843) 591788
Head: Mr R Tunnicliffe
Type: Co-educational Boarding and Day 3–13
No of pupils: B113 G93
No of Boarders: F61 W2
Fees: (September 01)
FB £12480 – £16560
Day £3654 – £10632
Special Needs: Level 2: ADD ADHD ASP AUT DYC DYP DYS EBD HI MLD SP&LD SPLD

KENT COLLEGE
Canterbury, Kent CT2 9DT
Tel: (01227) 763231
Head: Mr E B Halse
Type: Co-educational Boarding and Day 3–18
No of pupils: B399 G295
No of Boarders: F150
Fees: (September 01) FB £15300
Day £8790
Special Needs: Unspecified: DYS

KING'S PREPARATORY SCHOOL, ROCHESTER
King Edward Road, Rochester, Kent ME1 1UB
Tel: (01634) 843657
Head: Mr R Overend
Type: Co-educational Day and Boarding 8–13
No of pupils: B165 G80
No of Boarders: F12 W6
Fees: (September 01)
F/WB £11505 – £12405
Day £6870 – £7770
Special Needs: Level 2: DYC DYP DYS

KING'S SCHOOL ROCHESTER†
Satis House, Boley Hill, Rochester, Kent ME1 1TE
Tel: (01634) 843913
Head: Dr I R Walker
Type: Co-educational Day and Boarding 4–18
No of pupils: B497 G207
No of Boarders: F37 W20
Fees: (September 01) F/WB £11505 – £17385 Day £5250 – £10125
Special Needs: Level 2: DYP DYS

THE MEAD SCHOOL
16 Frant Road, Tunbridge Wells, Kent TN2 5SN
Tel: (01892) 525837
Head: Mrs A Culley
Type: Co-educational Day 3–11
No of pupils: B85 G85
Fees: (September 01) Day £2460 – £5670
Special Needs: Level 3: DYP DYS HI

NORTHBOURNE PARK SCHOOL
Betteshanger, Deal, Kent CT14 0NW
Tel: (01304) 611215/8
Head: Mr S Sides
Type: Co-educational Day and Boarding 3–13
No of pupils: B128 G100
No of Boarders: F49 W10
Fees: (September 01)
FB £10260 – £12555
Day £4740 – £8040
Special Needs: Level 2: ADD ASP DYC DYP DYS SPLD Level 3: ADHD HI

ROCHESTER INDEPENDENT COLLEGE
Star Hill, Rochester, Kent ME1 1XF
Tel: (01634) 828115
Head: Mr S de Belder and Mr B Pain
Type: Co-educational Day and Boarding 14–18
No of pupils: B100 G100
No of Boarders: F66
Fees: (September 01)
FB £14340 – £15270
Day £9300 – £10800
Special Needs: Level 3: ADD ASP DYC DYP DYS EPI SPLD

ROSE HILL SCHOOL
Culverden Down, Tunbridge Wells, Kent TN4 9SY
Tel: (01892) 525591
Head: Mr P D Westcombe
Type: Co-educational Day 2–13
No of pupils: 305
Fees: (September 01) Day £2400 – £7560
Special Needs: Level 2: DYP DYS

ST ANDREW'S SCHOOL
24–28 Watts Avenue, Rochester, Kent ME1 1SA
Tel: (01634) 843479
Head: Mr N D Kynaston
Type: Co-educational Day 4–11
No of pupils: B150 G160
Fees: (September 01) Day £2646 – £2820
Special Needs: Level 1: ADD DYS Level 2: DYP SPLD Level 3: ADHD ASP AUT CP DEL DOW DYC EBD EPI HI MLD PH PMLD SLD SP&LD TOU VIS

ST CHRISTOPHER'S SCHOOL
New Dover Road, Canterbury, Kent CT1 3DT
Tel: (01227) 462960
Head: Mr D Evans
Type: Co-educational Day 2–11
No of pupils: B60 G70
Fees: (September 01) Day £3075 – £3750
Special Needs: Level 2: ADD ADHD ASP AUT DEL DOW DYC DYP DYS EBD EPI HI MLD SP&LD

ST EDMUND'S JUNIOR SCHOOL
Canterbury, Kent CT2 8HU
Tel: (01227) 475600
Head: Mr R G Bacon
Type: Co-educational Day and Boarding 3–13
No of pupils: B181 G106
No of Boarders: F49
Fees: (September 01)
FB £11562 – £11754
Day £1800 – £8274
Special Needs: Level 1: EPI Level 2: ADD ASP DYC DYP DYS SPLD

ST FAITH'S AT ASH SCHOOL
5 The Street, Ash, Canterbury, Kent CT3 2HH
Tel: (01304) 813409
Head: Mr S G I Kerruish
Type: Co-educational Day 3–11
No of pupils: B120 G112
Fees: (September 01) Day £1560 – £3765
Special Needs: Level 2: ADD DYS Unspecified: DYP

ST MARY'S WESTBROOK
Ravenlea Road, Folkestone, Kent
CT20 2JU
Tel: (01303) 854006
Head: Mrs L A Watson
Type: Co-educational Boarding and
Day 2–16
No of pupils: B165 G119
No of Boarders: F43
Fees: (September 01)
FB £10473 – £11544
Day £4347 – £7686
Special Needs: Level 1: ASP AUT DYS
Level 2: ADD ADHD DYP SPLD
Level 3: SP&LD

ST MICHAEL'S SCHOOL
Otford Court, Otford, Sevenoaks,
Kent TN14 5SA
Tel: (01959) 522137
Head: Dr P Roots
Type: Co-educational Day 2–13
No of pupils: B223 G196
Fees: (September 01) Day £850 –
£2256
Special Needs: Level 1: HI SP&LD
Level 2: DYC DYP DYS

SEVENOAKS SCHOOL
Sevenoaks, Kent TN13 1HU
Tel: (01732) 455133
Head: Mr T R Cookson
Type: Co-educational Day and
Boarding 11–18
No of pupils: B505 G456
No of Boarders: F333
Fees: (September 01)
FB £16194 – £17535
Day £9873 – £11214
Special Needs: Level 2: DYC DYP DYS
Unspecified: VIS

STEEPHILL SCHOOL
Castle Hill, Fawkham, Longfield,
Kent DA3 7BG
Tel: (01474) 702107
Head: Mrs C Birtwell
Type: Co-educational Day 3–11
No of pupils: B50 G49
Fees: (September 01) Day £3400
Special Needs: Level 2: ADD ADHD
DYC DYP DYS EBD MLD SP&LD

WALTHAMSTOW HALL
Hollybush Lane, Sevenoaks, Kent
TN13 3UL
Tel: (01732) 451334
Head: Mrs J S Lang
Type: Girls Day 3–18
No of pupils: G435
Fees: (September 01) Day £3650 –
£9105
Special Needs: Level 2: DYS PH SPLD
Unspecified: W

LANCASHIRE

BOLTON SCHOOL (GIRLS' DIVISION)
Chorley New Road, Bolton,
Lancashire BL1 4PB
Tel: (01204) 840201
Head: Miss E J Panton
Type: Girls Day 4–18 (Boys 4–8)
No of pupils: B110 G1087
Fees: (September 01) Day £4566 –
£6090
Special Needs: Level 3: DYP DYS EPI
HI PH VIS

BURY GRAMMAR SCHOOL (GIRLS')
Bridge Road, Bury, Lancashire
BL9 0HH
Tel: (0161) 797 2808
Head: Miss C H Thompson
Type: Girls Day 4–18 (Boys 4–7)
No of pupils: B82 G991
Fees: (September 01) Day £3660 –
£5130
Special Needs: Level 3: DYS HI VIS

CHORCLIFFE SCHOOL
The Old Manse, Park Street, Chorley,
Lancashire PR7 1ER
Tel: (01257) 268807
Head: Ms H Mayer
Type: Co-educational Day 4–16
No of pupils: 18
Fees: (September 01) Day £4500
Special Needs: Level 3: ADD ASP DYC
DYP DYS EBD SPLD

KING EDWARD VII AND QUEEN MARY SCHOOL
Clifton Drive South, Lytham St
Annes, Lancashire FY8 1DT
Tel: (01253) 736459
Head: Mr P J Wilde
Type: Co-educational Day 3–18
No of pupils: B488 G423
Fees: (September 01) Day £5040
Special Needs: Level 2: DYP DYS
SPLD Level 3: HI PH

KINGSWOOD COLLEGE AT SCARISBRICK HALL†
Southport Road, Ormskirk,
Lancashire L40 9RQ
Tel: (01704) 880200
Head: Mr E J Borowski
Type: Co-educational Day 2–18
No of pupils: B274 G233
Fees: (September 01) Day £2100 –
£4425
Special Needs: Level 2: ADD DYC
DYP DYS SPLD

MOORLAND SCHOOL
Ribblesdale Avenue, Clitheroe,
Lancashire BB7 2JA
Tel: (01200) 423833
Head: Mrs J E Harrison
Type: Co-educational Boarding and
Day 2–16
No of pupils: B73 G77
No of Boarders: F30 W1
Fees: (September 01)
FB £9609 – £10095
WB £9500 – £9850
Day £3786 – £4533
Special Needs: Level 2: DYP DYS MLD
Unspecified: EPI

OAKHILL COLLEGE
Wiswell Lane, Whalley, Clitheroe,
Lancashire BB7 9AF
Tel: (01254) 823546
Head: Mr P S Mahon
Type: Co-educational Day 2–16
No of pupils: B136 G89
Fees: (September 01) Day £3762 –
£5850
Special Needs: Level 1: EPI PH
Level 2: ADD DYC DYP DYS SP&LD
SPLD

ROSSALL SCHOOL
Fleetwood, Lancashire FY7 8JW
Tel: (01253) 774201
Head: Mr T J Wilbur
Type: Co-educational Boarding and
Day 11–18
No of pupils: B247 G173
No of Boarders: F167
Fees: (September 01)
FB £10485 – £16485
Day £5460 – £7485
Special Needs: Level 1: ADD ADHD
DYP DYS

STONYHURST COLLEGE
Stonyhurst, Clitheroe, Lancashire
BB7 9PZ
Tel: (01254) 826345
Head: Mr A J F Aylward
Type: Co-educational Boarding and
Day 13–18
No of pupils: B300 G85
No of Boarders: F300 W10
Fees: (September 01) FB £15912
WB £14334 Day £9666
Special Needs: Level 1: ADD DYC
DYP DYS EBD EPI

LEICESTERSHIRE

THE DIXIE GRAMMAR SCHOOL
Market Bosworth, Leicestershire
CV13 0LE
Tel: (01455) 292244
Head: Mr R S Willmott
Type: Co-educational Day 10–18
No of pupils: B144 G174
Fees: (September 01) Day £5055
Special Needs: Level 3: DYS SPLD

FAIRFIELD SCHOOL
Leicester Road, Loughborough,
Leicestershire LE11 2AE
Tel: (01509) 215172
Head: Mr T A Eadon
Type: Co-educational Day 4–11
No of pupils: B245 G213
Fees: (September 01) On application
Special Needs: Level 2: DYS

LEICESTER GRAMMAR SCHOOL
8 Peacock Lane, Leicester LE1 5PX
Tel: (0116) 222 0400
Head: Mr C P M King
Type: Co-educational Day 10–18
No of pupils: B400 G294
Fees: (September 01) Day £5985
Special Needs: Level 3: DYS

LOUGHBOROUGH GRAMMAR SCHOOL
Burton Walks, Loughborough,
Leicestershire LE11 2DU
Tel: (01509) 233233
Head: Mr P B Fisher
Type: Boys Day and Boarding 10–18
No of pupils: 970
No of Boarders: F45 W20
Fees: (September 01) FB £10989
WB £9747 Day £6354
Special Needs: Level 3: DYP DYS

MANOR HOUSE SCHOOL
South Street, Ashby-de-la-Zouch,
Leicestershire LE65 1BR
Tel: (01530) 412932
Head: Mr I R Clews
Type: Co-educational Day 3–14
No of pupils: B112 G113
Fees: (September 01) Day £3387 –
£4380
Special Needs: Level 2: DYP DYS MLD

OUR LADY'S CONVENT SCHOOL
Burton Street, Loughborough,
Leicestershire LE11 2DT
Tel: (01509) 263901
Head: Sister S Fynn
Type: Girls Day 3–18 (Boys 3–5)
No of pupils: 540
Fees: (September 01) Day £3066 –
£5178
Special Needs: Level 2: DYP DYS

ST CRISPIN'S SCHOOL (LEICESTER) LTD.
6 St Mary's Road, Leicester LE2 1XA
Tel: (0116) 270 7648
Head: Mrs D Lofthouse
Type: Co-educational Day 2–16
No of pupils: B100 G20
Fees: (September 01) Day £1743 –
£5145
Special Needs: Level 2: ADD ADHD
DYC DYP DYS MLD SP&LD SPLD

LINCOLNSHIRE

CONWAY PREPARATORY SCHOOL
Tunnard Street, Boston, Lincolnshire
PE21 6PL
Tel: (01205) 363150/355539
Head: Mr S P McElwain
Type: Co-educational Day 2–11
No of pupils: B70 G70
Fees: (September 01) Day £273 –
£2895
Special Needs: Level 2: DYS

COPTHILL SCHOOL
Barnack Road, Uffington, Stamford,
Lincolnshire PE9 4TD
Tel: (01780) 757506
Head: Mr J A Teesdale
Type: Co-educational Day 2–11
No of pupils: B152 G187
Fees: (September 01) Day £810 –
£4380
Special Needs: Level 2: DYS
Level 3: ASP DYC DYP HI MLD PH
SP&LD SPLD VIS

LINCOLN MINSTER SCHOOL
Hillside, Lindum Terrace, Lincoln
LN2 5RW
Tel: (01522) 543764/523769
Head: Mr C Rickart
Type: Co-educational Day and
Boarding 2–18
No of pupils: B311 G306
No of Boarders: F42 W40
Fees: (September 01)
FB £10575 – £12270
WB £9810 – £11340
Day £4440 – £6480
Special Needs: Level 2: DYC DYP DYS
SPLD Level 3: EPI PH VIS

ST HUGH'S SCHOOL
Cromwell Avenue, Woodhall Spa,
Lincolnshire LN10 6TQ
Tel: (01526) 352169
Head: Mr S G Greenish
Type: Co-educational Boarding and
Day 2–13
No of pupils: B90 G75
No of Boarders: F20 W40
Fees: (September 01) F/WB £9618 –
£9843 Day £3936 – £7278
Special Needs: Level 2: DYC DYP DYS
Level 3: ADD ADHD EPI

ST MARY'S PREPARATORY SCHOOL
5 Pottergate, Lincoln LN2 1PH
Tel: (01522) 524622
Head: Mr M Upton
Type: Co-educational Day 2–11
No of pupils: B150 G141
Fees: (September 01) Day £4560 –
£5610
Special Needs: Level 2: DYS SPLD

STAMFORD SCHOOL
St Paul's Street, Stamford,
Lincolnshire PE9 2BQ
Tel: (01780) 750300/1
Head: Dr P R Mason
Type: Boys Day and Boarding 11–18
No of pupils: 640
No of Boarders: F75 W10
Fees: (September 01) FB £12444
WB £12396 Day £6396
Special Needs: Unspecified: DYS

NORTH EAST LINCOLNSHIRE

ST MARTIN'S PREPARATORY SCHOOL
63 Bargate, Grimsby, North East
Lincolnshire DN34 5AA
Tel: (01472) 878907
Head: Mrs M Preston
Type: Co-educational Day 3–11
No of pupils: B109 G125
Fees: (September 01) Day £2760 –
£3150
Special Needs: Level 2: DYC DYP DYS

LONDON

E2

GATEHOUSE SCHOOL
Sewardstone Road, Victoria Park,
London E2 9JG
Tel: (020) 8980 2978
Head: Miss A Eversole
Type: Co-educational Day 2–11
No of pupils: B72 G88
Fees: (September 01) Day £3750 –
£5600
Special Needs: Unspecified: AUT
DOW DYP DYS EBD HI MLD

E18

SNARESBROOK COLLEGE PREPARATORY SCHOOL
75 Woodford Road, South
Woodford, London E18 2EA
Tel: (020) 8989 2394
Head: Mrs L J Chiverrell
Type: Co-educational Day 3–11
No of pupils: B76 G84
Fees: (September 01) Day £3849 –
£5154
Special Needs: Level 2: DYS
Level 3: ASP CP DYP EPI PH SP&LD

EC1V

DALLINGTON SCHOOL
8 Dallington Street, London
EC1V 0BW
Tel: (020) 7251 2284
Head: Mrs M C Hercules
Type: Co-educational Day 3–11
No of pupils: B102 G110
Fees: (September 01) Day £4249 –
£5763
Special Needs: Level 2: DYP DYS
SPLD Level 3: SP&LD

EC2A

THE LYCEUM
6 Paul Street, London EC2A 4JH
Tel: (020) 7247 1588
Head: Mr J Rowe and Mrs L Mannay
Type: Co-educational Day 3–11
No of pupils: 128
Fees: (September 01) Day £5550
Special Needs: Level 2: DYC DYP DYS
HI SP&LD SPLD VIS Level 3: CP

N2

ANNEMOUNT SCHOOL
18 Holne Chase, London N2 0QN
Tel: (020) 8455 2132
Head: Mrs G Maidment
Type: Co-educational Day 2–7
No of pupils: B50 G50
Fees: (September 01) Day £3600 –
£5850
Special Needs: Level 2: DYC DYP DYS
EBD HI SP&LD Unspecified: ADD
ADHD ASP MLD PH

THE KEREM SCHOOL
Norrice Lea, London N2 0RE
Tel: (020) 8455 0909
Head: Mrs R Goulden
Type: Co-educational Day 4–11
No of pupils: B79 G81
Fees: (September 01) Day £4830
Special Needs: Unspecified: DYP DYS

N6

HIGHGATE JUNIOR SCHOOL
Cholmeley House, 3 Bishopswood
Road, Highgate, London N6 4PL
Tel: (020) 8340 9193
Head: Mr H S Evers
Type: Boys Day 7–13
No of pupils: B365
Fees: (September 01) Day £8880
Special Needs: Level 3: ADD ADHD
DYP DYS EBD SPLD

HIGHGATE SCHOOL
North Road, London N6 4AY
Tel: (020) 8340 1524
Head: Mr R P Kennedy
Type: Boys Day 13–18
No of pupils: 550
Fees: (September 01) Day £9750
Special Needs: Level 2: DYC DYP DYS
Level 3: ADD ADHD EBD EPI HI
Unspecified: ASP AUT CP DEL DOW
MLD PH PMLD SLD SP&LD SPLD
TOU VIS

N10

THE MONTESSORI HOUSE
5 Princes Avenue, Muswell Hill,
London N10 3LS
Tel: (020) 8444 4399
Head: Mrs L Christoforou
Type: Co-educational Day 2–5
No of pupils: B30 G30
Fees: (September 01) Day £2190 –
£5700
Special Needs: Level 3: ASP AUT CP
DOW DYS MLD SPLD

PRINCES AVENUE SCHOOL
5 Princes Avenue, Muswell Hill,
London N10 3LS
Tel: (020) 8444 4399
Head: Mrs L Christoforou
Type: Co-educational Day 5–7
No of pupils: B12 G12
Fees: (September 01) Day £6900
Special Needs: Level 3: DOW DYS
MLD SPLD

N11

WOODSIDE PARK INTERNATIONAL SCHOOL
Friern Barnet Road, London
N11 3DR
Tel: (020) 8368 3777
Head: Mr S D Anson
Type: Co-educational Day 2–18
No of pupils: B376 G184
Fees: (September 01) Day £2730 –
£9000
Special Needs: Level 1: ADD ASP AUT
DYC DYP MLD SP&LD SPLD
Level 3: DYS

N14

SALCOMBE SCHOOL
224–226 Chase Side, Southgate,
London N14 4PL
Tel: (020) 8441 5282
Head: Mr A Guha
Type: Co-educational Day 2–11
No of pupils: B255 G175
Fees: (September 01) Day £4730
Special Needs: Level 2: DYS MLD
SP&LD

N21

KEBLE PREPARATORY SCHOOL
Wades Hill, Winchmore Hill, London N21 1BG
Tel: (020) 8360 3359
Head: Mr V W P Thomas
Type: Boys Day 4–13
No of pupils: 200
Fees: (September 01) Day £5550 – £6975
Special Needs: Level 2: DYC DYP DYS SPLD Level 3: ADD EPI PH

NW1

INTERNATIONAL COMMUNITY SCHOOL
4 York Terrace East, Regent's Park, London NW1 4PT
Tel: (020) 7935 1206
Head: Mr P Hurd
Type: Co-educational Day 3–18
No of pupils: B100 G100
Fees: (September 01) Day £6951 – £9861
Special Needs: Level 2: ADD ADHD ASP AUT DYP DYS MLD SP&LD SPLD Unspecified: EBD

NORTH BRIDGE HOUSE SCHOOL*
1 Gloucester Avenue, London NW1 7AB
Tel: (020) 7267 6266
Head: Mr H Richardson
Type: Co-educational Day 2–18
No of pupils: 893
Fees: (September 01) Day £7425
Special Needs: Unspecified: DYS

NW2

THE MULBERRY HOUSE SCHOOL
7 Minster Road, West Hampstead, London NW2 3SD
Tel: (020) 8452 7340
Head: Ms B Lewis-Powell
Type: Co-educational Day 2–8
No of pupils: B114 G98
Fees: (September 01) Day £4700 – £8648
Special Needs: Level 1: DEL DYS Level 2: SP&LD Unspecified: HI

NW3

SOUTHBANK INTERNATIONAL SCHOOL, HAMPSTEAD
16 Netherhall Gardens, Hampstead, London NW3 5TH
Tel: (020) 7431 1200
Head: Mrs J Treftz
Type: Co-educational Day 3–14
No of pupils: B90 G86
Fees: (September 01) Day £6150 – £12900
Special Needs: Level 2: DYP DYS SPLD

UNIVERSITY COLLEGE SCHOOL
Frognal, Hampstead, London NW3 6XH
Tel: (020) 7435 2215
Head: Mr K J Durham
Type: Boys Day 11–18
No of pupils: 720
Fees: (September 01) Day £9000 – £9750
Special Needs: Level 2: DYP DYS

NW4

HENDON PREPARATORY SCHOOL
20 Tenterden Grove, Hendon, London NW4 1TD
Tel: (020) 8203 7727
Head: Mr J Gear
Type: Co-educational Day 2–13
No of pupils: B184 G88
Fees: (September 01) Day £6090 – £7635
Special Needs: Level 2: DYP DYS

NW7

THE MOUNT SCHOOL
Milespit Hill, Mill Hill, London NW7 2RX
Tel: (020) 8959 3403
Head: Mrs J K Jackson
Type: Girls Day 4–18
No of pupils: G400
Fees: (September 01) Day £4920 – £5820
Special Needs: Level 3: ADD ADHD ASP CP DEL DYP DYS HI PH SPLD VIS

NW10

WELSH SCHOOL OF LONDON
Welsh School of London, c/o Stonebridge Primary School, Shakespeare Avenue, London NW10 8NG
Tel: (020) 8965 3585
Head: Miss S Edwards
Type: Co-educational Day 4–11
No of pupils: 28
Fees: (September 01) Day £1500
Special Needs: Unspecified: MLD

SE1

THE SCHILLER INTERNATIONAL SCHOOL
Royal Waterloo House, 51–55 Waterloo Road, London SE1 8TX
Tel: (020) 7928 1372
Head: Mr G Selby
Type: Co-educational Day 14–18
No of pupils: 40
Fees: (September 01) Day £9635 – £9670
Special Needs: Level 2: ADD ADHD DYC DYS SPLD Level 3: DYP

SE9

ELTHAM COLLEGE
Grove Park Road, Mottingham, London SE9 4QF
Tel: (020) 8857 1455
Head: Mr P J Henderson
Type: Boys Day and Boarding 7–18 (Co-ed VIth Form)
No of pupils: B735 G52
No of Boarders: F5 W5
Fees: (September 01) FB £16659 WB £16609 Day £8064
Special Needs: Level 3: DYP DYS

ST OLAVE'S PREPARATORY SCHOOL
106–110 Southwood Road, New Eltham, London SE9 3QS
Tel: (020) 8294 8930
Head: Miss M P Taylor
Type: Co-educational Day 3–11
No of pupils: B137 G74
Fees: (September 01) Day £2208 – £5208
Special Needs: Level 2: DYS

SE12

COLFE'S SCHOOL
Horn Park Lane, London SE12 8AW
Tel: (020) 8852 2283
Head: Mr A H Chicken
Type: Co-educational Day 3–18
No of pupils: B830 G223
Fees: (September 01) Day £5112 –
£7632
Special Needs: Unspecified: DYP DYS

SW1

WESTMINSTER SCHOOL
17 Dean's Yard, Westminster,
London SW1P 3PB
Tel: (020) 7963 1003
Head: Mr T Jones-Parry
Type: Boys Boarding and Day 13–18
(Co-ed VIth Form)
No of pupils: B581 G104
No of Boarders: F190
Fees: (September 01) FB £17712
Day £12267
Special Needs: Level 2: DYC DYP DYS
Level 3: ADD EPI HI PH

FRANCIS HOLLAND SCHOOL
39 Graham Terrace, London
SW1W 8JF
Tel: (020) 7730 2971
Head: Miss S Pattenden
Type: Girls Day 4–18
No of pupils: 440
Fees: (September 01) Day £8700
Special Needs: Level 3: DYS HI

HELLENIC COLLEGE OF LONDON
67 Pont Street, London SW1X 0BD
Tel: (020) 7581 5044
Head: Mr J Wardrobe
Type: Co-educational Day 2–18
No of pupils: B95 G95
Fees: (September 01) Day £6099 –
£7632
Special Needs: Unspecified: DYP DYS
HI

MORE HOUSE
22–24 Pont Street, Chelsea, London
SW1X 0AA
Tel: (020) 7235 2855
Head: Mrs L Falconer
Type: Girls Day 11–18
No of pupils: G220
Fees: (September 02) Day £8340
Special Needs: Level 3: DYS

SW3

CAMERON HOUSE
4 The Vale, Chelsea, London
SW3 6AH
Tel: (020) 7352 4040
Head: Miss F N Stack
Type: Co-educational Day 4–11
No of pupils: B53 G63
Fees: (September 01) Day £7605 –
£8025
Special Needs: Level 2: DYP DYS
SPLD

SW4

EATON HOUSE THE MANOR
58 Clapham Common Northside,
London SW4 9RU
Tel: (020) 7924 6000
Head: Mr S Hepher and Mrs S Segrave
Type: Boys Day 2–13 (Girls 2–4)
No of pupils: B360 G30
Fees: (September 01) Day £1545 –
£7950
Special Needs: Unspecified: DYP DYS
SPLD

SW5

COLLINGHAM
23 Collingham Gardens, London
SW5 0HL
Tel: (020) 7244 7414
Head: Mr G Hattee
Type: Co-educational Day 14–20
No of pupils: B125 G115
Fees: (September 01) Day £9780 –
£12240
Special Needs: Level 2: DYC DYP DYS
VIS Level 3: ADD ASP DEL EPI HI

SW7

FALKNER HOUSE
19 Brechin Place, London SW7 4QB
Tel: (020) 7373 4501
Head: Mrs A Griggs
Type: Girls Day 3–11 (Co-ed 3–4)
No of pupils: B10 G170
Fees: (September 01) Day £8250
Special Needs: Level 3: DYC DYP DYS
HI

THE HAMPSHIRE SCHOOLS (KNIGHTSBRIDGE UNDER SCHOOL)
5 Wetherby Place, London SW7 4NX
Tel: (020) 7584 3297
Head: Mr A G Bray
Type: Co-educational Day 3–6
No of pupils: B45 G45
Fees: (September 01) Day £3075 –
£6285
Special Needs: Level 2: DYP DYS
Level 3: ADD ADHD

THE HAMPSHIRE SCHOOLS (KNIGHTSBRIDGE UPPER SCHOOL)
63 Ennismore Gardens, London
SW7 1NH
Tel: (020) 7584 3297
Head: Mr A G Bray
Type: Co-educational Day 6–11
No of pupils: B56 G56
Fees: (September 01) Day £6615 –
£8520
Special Needs: Level 2: DYP DYS
Level 3: ADD ADHD Unspecified:
DYC

MANDER PORTMAN WOODWARD
24 Elvaston Place, London SW7 5NL
Tel: (020) 7584 8555
Head: Mr S D Boyes
Type: Co-educational Day 14+
No of pupils: B230 G210
Fees: (September 01) On application
Special Needs: Level 3: DYP DYS EPI
HI

ST PHILIP'S SCHOOL
6 Wetherby Place, London SW7 4ND
Tel: (020) 7373 3944
Head: Mr H Biggs-Davison
Type: Boys Day 7–13
No of pupils: B111
Fees: (September 01) Day £6900
Special Needs: Level 2: DYS

SW11

DOLPHIN SCHOOL
Northcote Road Baptist Church, 106
Northcote Road, London SW11 6QP
Tel: (020) 7924 3472
Head: Mrs S Rogers
Type: Co-educational Day 4–11
No of pupils: B46 G40
Fees: (September 01) Day £4950 –
£5250
Special Needs: Level 1: AUT
Unspecified: DYS

THE DOMINIE
142 Battersea Park Road, London
SW11 4NB
Tel: (020) 7720 8783
Head: Mrs L Robertson
Type: Co-educational Day 6–13
No of pupils: B22 G10
Fees: (September 01) Day £11400
Special Needs: Level 1: DYP DYS
SP&LD SPLD

EMANUEL SCHOOL
Battersea Rise, London SW11 1HS
Tel: (020) 8870 4171
Head: Mrs A Sutcliffe
Type: Co-educational Day 10–18
No of pupils: B579 G161
Fees: (September 01) Day £7743 –
£8073
Special Needs: Level 3: DYC DYP DYS

NORTHCOTE LODGE
26 Bolingbroke Grove, London
SW11 6EL
Tel: (020) 7924 7170
Head: Mr P Cheeseman
Type: Boys Day 8–13
No of pupils: 150
Fees: (September 01) Day £8055 –
£8460
Special Needs: Level 2: ADD ADHD
DYC DYP DYS

SW12

BROOMWOOD HALL
SCHOOL
74 Nightingale Lane, London
SW12 8NR
Tel: (020) 8673 1616
Head: Mrs K A H Colquhoun
Type: Co-educational Day Boys 4–8
Girls 4–13
No of pupils: B200 G280
Fees: (September 01) On application
Special Needs: Unspecified: DYS
MLD W

HORNSBY HOUSE SCHOOL
Hearnville Road, London SW12 8RS
Tel: (020) 8673 7573
Head: Mrs J Strong
Type: Co-educational Day 3–11
No of pupils: B142 G115
Fees: (September 01) Day £2625 –
£6933
Special Needs: Level 2: DYC DYP DYS
SPLD Level 3: ADD ADHD CP EBD
EPI HI PH VIS Unspecified: W

SW14

TOWER HOUSE SCHOOL
188 Sheen Lane, London SW14 8LF
Tel: (020) 8876 3323
Head: Mr J D T Wall
Type: Boys Day 4–13
No of pupils: 186
Fees: (September 01) Day £6690 –
£6870
Special Needs: Level 2: ADD DYP DYS
EBD MLD

SW15

PROSPECT HOUSE SCHOOL
75 Putney Hill, London SW15 3NT
Tel: (020) 8780 0456
Head: Mr B H Evans and Mrs Gerry
Type: Co-educational Day 3–11
No of pupils: B100 G100
Fees: (September 01) Day £1035 –
£2300
Special Needs: Level 1: DYS

SW18

HIGHFIELD SCHOOL
256 Trinity Road, Wandsworth
Common, London SW18 3RQ
Tel: (020) 8874 2778
Head: Mrs V-J Lowe
Type: Co-educational Day 2–11
No of pupils: B41 G33
Fees: (September 01) Day £2595 –
£5535
Special Needs: Level 3: ADD ADHD
DYP DYS

SW19

THE STUDY PREPARATORY
SCHOOL
Camp Road, Wimbledon Common,
London SW19 4UN
Tel: (020) 8947 6969
Head: Mrs L Bond
Type: Girls Day 4–11
No of pupils: G335
Fees: (September 01) Day £5505 –
£6255
Special Needs: Level 2: DEL SPLD
Level 3: ADD ADHD CP DYC DYP
DYS EPI VIS

WIMBLEDON COLLEGE PREP
SCHOOL
Donhead Lodge, 33 Edge Hill,
Wimbledon, London SW19 4NP
Tel: (020) 8946 7000
Head: Mr G C McGrath
Type: Boys Day 7–13
No of pupils: 295
Fees: (September 01) Day £4188
Special Needs: Level 1: ADD DYC
DYP DYS EBD HI MLD SPLD
Level 2: PH SP&LD

W1

QUEEN'S COLLEGE
43–49 Harley Street, London
W1N 2BT
Tel: (020) 7291 7000
Head: Miss M M Connell
Type: Girls Day 11–18
No of pupils: 380
Fees: (September 01) Day £8445
Special Needs: Level 2: DYP DYS
Level 3: PH

W2

CONNAUGHT HOUSE
47 Connaught Square, London
W2 2HL
Tel: (020) 7262 8830
Head: Mr F Hampton and
Mrs J A Hampton
Type: Co-educational Day 4–11
No of pupils: B35 G35
Fees: (September 01) Day £5175 –
£7950
Special Needs: Level 2: DYC DYP DYS

DAVIES LAING AND DICK
INDEPENDENT VI FORM
COLLEGE
10 Pembridge Square, London
W2 4ED
Tel: (020) 7727 2797
Head: Ms E Rickards
Type: Co-educational Day 14–21
No of pupils: B192 G193
Fees: (September 01) Day £4500 –
£12249
Special Needs: Unspecified: DYP DYS

THE HAMPSHIRE SCHOOLS (KENSINGTON GARDENS)
9 Queensborough Terrace, London
W2 3TB
Tel: (020) 7229 7065
Head: Mr A G Bray
Type: Co-educational Day 4–13
No of pupils: B80 G80
Fees: (September 01) Day £5640 –
£8055
Special Needs: Level 2: DYC DYP DYS
Level 3: ADD ADHD Unspecified:
MLD

PEMBRIDGE HALL
18 Pembridge Square, London
W2 4EH
Tel: (020) 7229 0121
Head: Mrs E Marsden
Type: Girls Day 4–11
No of pupils: 250
Fees: (September 01) Day £7605
Special Needs: Unspecified: DYS

TODDLERS AND MUMS MONTESSORI
St Stephens Church, Westbourne
Park Road, London W2 5QT
Tel: 020 7402 1084
Head: Mrs M Molavi
Type: Co-educational Day 2–5
No of pupils: B11 G11
Fees: (September 01) Day £2160 –
£2985
Special Needs: Level 2: DYC DYS HI
SPLD Level 3: ASP CP DYP MLD PH
SP&LD VIS Unspecified: ADD DEL
DOW EBD SLD

WETHERBY SCHOOL
11 Pembridge Square, London
W2 4ED
Tel: (020) 7727 9581
Head: Mrs J Aviss
Type: Boys Day 4–8
No of pupils: 172
Fees: (September 01) Day £7530
Special Needs: Level 2: DYP DYS
SP&LD SPLD

W3

EALING MONTESSORI SCHOOL
St Martins Church Hall, Hale
Gardens, London W3 9SQ
Tel: (020) 8992 4513
Head: Mrs P Jaffer
Type: Co-educational Day 2–6
No of pupils: B12 G24
Fees: (September 01) Day £2280 –
£3480
Special Needs: Level 2: DYC DYS

INTERNATIONAL SCHOOL OF LONDON
139 Gunnersbury Avenue, London
W3 8LG
Tel: (020) 8992 5823
Head: Mrs E Whelen
Type: Co-educational Day 4–18
No of pupils: B165 G123
Fees: (September 01) Day £8450 –
£12450
Special Needs: Level 3: DYS

W4

THE ARTS EDUCATIONAL SCHOOL
Cone Ripman House, 14 Bath Road,
Chiswick, London W4 1LY
Tel: (020) 8987 6600
Head: Mr T Sampson
Type: Co-educational Day 8–18
No of pupils: B23 G92
Fees: (September 01) Day £4836 –
£7245
Special Needs: Level 3: DYP DYS EPI
SPLD

CHISWICK AND BEDFORD PARK PREPARATORY SCHOOL
Priory House, Priory Avenue,
Bedford Park, London W4 1TX
Tel: (020) 8994 1804
Head: Mrs M B Morrow
Type: Co-educational Day Boys 4–8
Girls 4–11
No of pupils: B70 G115
Fees: (September 01) Day £4620 –
£5550
Special Needs: Level 2: DYS SPLD

ELMWOOD MONTESSORI SCHOOL
St Michaels Centre, Elmwood Road,
London W4 3DY
Tel: (020) 8994 8177
Head: Mrs S Herbert
Type: Co-educational Day 2–5
No of pupils: B20 G20
Fees: (September 01) Day £2730
Special Needs: Level 3: ADD ADHD
ASP AUT CP DEL DOW DYC DYP
DYS EBD EPI HI MLD PH PMLD
SLD SP&LD SPLD TOU VIS
Unspecified: W

ORCHARD HOUSE SCHOOL
16 Newton Grove, Bedford Park,
London W4 1LB
Tel: (020) 8742 8544
Head: Mrs S A B Hobbs
Type: Co-educational Day Boys 3–8
Girls 3–11
No of pupils: B80 G140
Fees: (September 01) Day £3450 –
£7350
Special Needs: Level 2: CP DYS
Level 3: ADD ADHD ASP AUT DEL
DOW DYC DYP HI PH SP&LD SPLD

W5

HARVINGTON SCHOOL
20 Castlebar Road, Ealing, London
W5 2DS
Tel: (020) 8997 1583
Head: Dr F Meek
Type: Girls Day 3–16 (Boys 3–5)
No of pupils: B14 G204
Fees: (September 01) Day £4170 –
£5415
Special Needs: Level 2: DYC DYP DYS

W6

THE GODOLPHIN AND LATYMER SCHOOL
Iffley Road, Hammersmith, London
W6 0PG
Tel: (020) 8741 1936
Head: Miss M Rudland
Type: Girls Day 11–18
No of pupils: G707
Fees: (September 01) Day £7380
Special Needs: Level 3: DYP DYS

THE JORDANS NURSERY SCHOOL
Lower Hall, Holy Innocents Church,
Paddenswick Road, London W6 0UB
Tel: (020) 8741 3230
Head: Mrs S Jordan
Type: Co-educational Day 2–5
No of pupils: 50
Fees: (September 01) Day £2250 –
£2715
Special Needs: Level 3: MLD SP&LD
Unspecified: W

LATYMER UPPER SCHOOL
King Street, Hammersmith, London
W6 9LR
Tel: (020) 8741 1851
Head: Mr C Diggory
Type: Boys Day 7–18 (Co-ed VIth
Form)
No of pupils: 1120
Fees: (September 01) Day £8850
Special Needs: Level 3: ASP DYP DYS
HI

ST PAUL'S GIRLS' SCHOOL

Brook Green, London W6 7BS
Tel: (020) 7603 2288
Head: Miss E Diggory
Type: Girls Day 11–18
No of pupils: G670
Fees: (September 01) Day £8823
Special Needs: Unspecified: DYS HI

W8

HAWKESDOWN HOUSE SCHOOL

27 Edge Street, Kensington, London
W8 7PN
Tel: (020) 7727 9090
Head: Mrs C J Leslie
Type: Boys Day 3–8
No of pupils: B150
Fees: (September 01) Day £6375 –
£7185
Special Needs: Level 3: DYS

THOMAS'S PREPARATORY SCHOOL

17–19 Cottesmore Gardens, London
W8 5PR
Tel: (020) 7361 6500
Head: Mrs D Maine
Type: Co-educational Day 4–11
No of pupils: B98 G104
Fees: (September 01) Day £6030 –
£8310
Special Needs: Level 2: DYP DYS

GREATER MANCHESTER

ABBEY COLLEGE

20 Kennedy Street, Manchester
M2 4BY
Tel: (0161) 236 6836
Head: Mrs J Thomas
Type: Co-educational Day and
Boarding 15–21
No of pupils: B90 G90
Fees: (September 01) Day £5700 –
£10500
Special Needs: Level 3: DYS

ABBOTSFORD PREPARATORY SCHOOL

211 Flixton Road, Urmston,
Manchester M41 5PR
Tel: (0161) 748 3261
Head: Mr C J Davies
Type: Co-educational Day 3–11
No of pupils: B77 G59
Fees: (September 01) Day £3060 –
£3885
Special Needs: Unspecified: DYS

CLARENDON COTTAGE SCHOOL

Ivy Bank House, Half Edge Lane,
Eccles, Greater Manchester M30 9BJ
Tel: (0161) 950 7868
Head: Mrs E Bagnall
Type: Co-educational Day 1–11
No of pupils: B120 G100
Fees: (September 01) Day £1000 –
£4150
Special Needs: Level 2: DYS
Level 3: EPI HI

TASHBAR PRIMARY SCHOOL

20 Upper Park Rd, Salford, Greater
Manchester M7 4HL
Tel: (0161) 720 8254
Head: Rabbi C S Roberts
Type: Boys Day 3–11
No of pupils: B270
Fees: (September 01) Day £1020 –
£1620
Special Needs: Level 2: ADD ADHD
ASP AUT DYP DYS EBD PMLD
SP&LD

WITHINGTON GIRLS' SCHOOL

Wellington Road, Fallowfield,
Manchester M14 6BL
Tel: (0161) 224 1077
Head: Mrs J D Pickering
Type: Girls Day 7–18
No of pupils: G650
Fees: (September 01) Day £3789 –
£5418
Special Needs: Level 3: DYS

MERSEYSIDE

CARLETON HOUSE PREPARATORY SCHOOL

Lyndhurst Road, Mossley Hill,
Liverpool, Merseyside L18 8AQ
Tel: (0151) 724 4880
Head: Mrs C Line
Type: Co-educational Day 4–11
No of pupils: B88 G62
Fees: (September 01) Day £3510
Special Needs: Level 2: DYC DYP DYS
SPLD Level 3: ADD ADHD ASP AUT
EPI HI

HESWALL PREPARATORY SCHOOL

Carberry, Quarry Road East,
Heswall, Wirral, Merseyside
CH60 6RB
Tel: (0151) 342 7851
Head: Mrs M Hannaford
Type: Co-educational Day 2–11
No of pupils: B25 G25
Fees: (September 01) Day £1575 –
£3000
Special Needs: Level 2: ADHD DYP
DYS MLD SP&LD

KINGSMEAD SCHOOL
Bertram Drive, Hoylake, Wirral,
Merseyside CH47 0LL
Tel: (0151) 632 3156
Head: Mr E H Bradby
Type: Co-educational Boarding and
Day 2–16
No of pupils: B147 G87
No of Boarders: F24 W4
Fees: (September 01)
FB £8085 – £8790
WB £7785 – £8490
Day £3675 – £5490
Special Needs: Level 2: ADD ASP DYP
DYS EPI SPLD

LIVERPOOL COLLEGE
Liverpool, Merseyside L18 8BG
Tel: (0151) 724 4000
Head: Mrs C Bradley
Type: Co-educational Day 3–18
No of pupils: B600 G400
Fees: (September 01) Day £3990 –
£6255
Special Needs: Level 2: ADD ADHD
DYC DYP DYS SPLD Level 3: ASP
DEL EPI HI SP&LD

MARYMOUNT CONVENT SCHOOL
Love Lane, Wallasey, Merseyside
CH44 5SB
Tel: (0151) 638 8467
Head: Sister C O'Reilly
Type: Co-educational Day 3–11
No of pupils: B41 G120
Fees: (September 01) Day £2100
Special Needs: Level 2: ASP DYP DYS
MLD PH Unspecified: W

TOWER DENE PREPARATORY SCHOOL
59–76 Cambridge Road, Southport,
Merseyside PR9 9RH
Tel: (01704) 228556
Head: Mrs A Lewin
Type: Co-educational Day 0–11
No of pupils: B70 G60
Fees: (September 01) Day £1950 –
£2750
Special Needs: Unspecified: DYS

MIDDLESEX

DENMEAD SCHOOL
41–43 Wensleydale Road, Hampton,
Middlesex TW12 2LP
Tel: (020) 8979 1844
Head: Mr M T McKaughan
Type: Boys Day 2–13 (Girls 2–7)
No of pupils: B189 G12
Fees: (September 01) Day £2565 –
£5985
Special Needs: Level 2: DYS

EILMAR MONTESSORI SCHOOL & NURSERY
Sidmouth Drive, Ruislip Gardens,
Ruislip, Middlesex HA4 0BY
Tel: (01895) 635796
Head: Ms M A Portland
Type: Co-educational Day 2–5
No of pupils: B34 G34
Fees: (September 01) Day £2791 –
£5016
Special Needs: Unspecified: MLD PH
SPLD W

HAMPTON SCHOOL
Hanworth Road, Hampton,
Middlesex TW12 3HD
Tel: (020) 8979 5526
Head: Mr B R Martin
Type: Boys Day 11–18
No of pupils: B1050
Fees: (September 01) Day £7555
Special Needs: Level 2: DYS

HARROW SCHOOL
Harrow on the Hill, Middlesex
HA1 3HW
Tel: (020) 8872 8000
Head: Mr B J Lenon
Type: Boys Boarding 13–18
No of pupils: B790
No of Boarders: F790
Fees: (September 01) FB £17955
Special Needs: Level 2: DYS VIS

LITTLE EDEN SDA SCHOOL & EDEN HIGH SDA SCHOOL
Fortescue House, Park Road,
Hanworth, Middlesex TW13 6PN
Tel: (020) 8751 1844
Head: Mrs L A Osei
Type: Co-educational Day 3–16
No of pupils: B18 G25
Fees: (September 01) Day £2250 –
£2775
Special Needs: Level 2: DOW DYP
SP&LD Level 3: ADD ADHD

NORTHWOOD COLLEGE
Maxwell Road, Northwood,
Middlesex HA6 2YE
Tel: (01923) 825446
Head: Mrs A Mayou
Type: Girls Day 3–18
No of pupils: 782
Fees: (September 01) Day £3897 –
£6996
Special Needs: Level 2: DYS
Level 3: ASP CP DYP EPI HI PH VIS

ST CATHERINE'S SCHOOL
Cross Deep, Twickenham, Middlesex
TW1 4QJ
Tel: (020) 8891 2898
Head: Miss D Wynter
Type: Girls Day 3–16
No of pupils: G348
Fees: (September 01) Day £4710 –
£6165
Special Needs: Level 2: DYP DYS

NORFOLK

ALL SAINTS SCHOOL
School Road, Lessingham, Norwich,
Norfolk NR12 0DJ
Tel: (01692) 582083
Head: Mrs J Gardiner
Type: Co-educational Day 2–16
No of pupils: B35 G35
Fees: (September 01) Day £1680 –
£2760
Special Needs: Level 2: ASP DYP DYS
MLD SPLD Level 3: DOW

BEESTON HALL SCHOOL
West Runton, Cromer, Norfolk
NR27 9NQ
Tel: (01263) 837324
Head: Mr I K MacAskill
Type: Co-educational Boarding and
Day 7–13
No of pupils: B103 G72
No of Boarders: F110
Fees: (September 01) FB £10920 –
£11670 Day £8160 – £8730
Special Needs: Level 3: DYC DYP
Unspecified: DYS PH

HETHERSETT OLD HALL
SCHOOL
Hethersett, Norwich, Norfolk
NR9 3DW
Tel: (01603) 810390
Head: Mrs J M Mark
Type: Girls Boarding and Day 4–18
(Boys 4–7)
No of pupils: B4 G271
No of Boarders: F47
Fees: (September 01)
FB £10590 – £13140
Day £4185 – £6600
Special Needs: Level 2: ADD CP DYC
DYP DYS SPLD

LANGLEY PREPARATORY
SCHOOL & NURSERY
Beech Hill, 11 Yarmouth Road,
Thorpe St Andrew, Norwich, Norfolk
NR7 0EA
Tel: (01603) 433861
Head: Mr P J Weeks
Type: Co-educational Day 2–11
No of pupils: B95 G55
Fees: (September 01) Day £3450 –
£5070
Special Needs: Level 2: ASP DYC DYP
DYS EBD SP&LD SPLD Level 3: MLD
Unspecified: EPI

LANGLEY SCHOOL
Langley Park, Loddon, Norwich,
Norfolk NR14 6BJ
Tel: (01508) 520210
Head: Mr J G Malcolm
Type: Co-educational Boarding and
Day 10–18
No of pupils: B240 G85
No of Boarders: F72 W11
Fees: (September 01)
FB £11400 – £13800
WB £10500 – £12600
Day £5580 – £7200
Special Needs: Level 2: ADD AUT
DEL DYC DYP DYS EPI SPLD
Unspecified: W

THE NORWICH HIGH
SCHOOL FOR GIRLS GDST
95 Newmarket Road, Norwich,
Norfolk NR2 2HU
Tel: (01603) 453265
Head: Mrs V C Bidwell
Type: Girls Day 4–18
No of pupils: 900
Fees: (September 01) Day £3951 –
£5442
Special Needs: Level 2: DYS SPLD

NORWICH SCHOOL
School House, 70 The Close,
Norwich, Norfolk NR1 4DQ
Tel: (01603) 623194
Head: Mr C D Brown
Type: Boys Day 8–18 (Co-ed VIth
Form)
No of pupils: B780 G64
Fees: (September 01) Day £6033 –
£6273
Special Needs: Level 2: DYP DYS

RIDDLESWORTH HALL
Diss, Norfolk IP22 2TA
Tel: (01953) 681246
Head: Mr C Campbell
Type: Co-educational Boarding and
Day Boys 2–11 Girls 2–13 (day boys
only)
No of pupils: B13 G104
No of Boarders: F14 W13
Fees: (September 01) FB £11400
WB £10650 Day £4650 – £6825
Special Needs: Level 1: DYC DYP DYS
SPLD

TAVERHAM HALL
Taverham, Norwich, Norfolk
NR8 6HU
Tel: (01603) 868206
Head: Mr W D Lawton
Type: Co-educational Boarding and
Day 3–13
No of pupils: B121 G88
No of Boarders: W25
Fees: (September 01) WB £9405
Day £1575 – £8175
Special Needs: Level 1: DYS
Level 2: ADD ADHD DYP
Unspecified: MLD

THETFORD GRAMMAR
SCHOOL
Bridge Street, Thetford, Norfolk
IP24 3AF
Tel: (01842) 752840
Head: Mr J R Weeks
Type: Co-educational Day 5–18
No of pupils: B163 G134
Fees: (September 01) Day £4890 –
£5910
Special Needs: Level 2: DYS

THORPE HOUSE SCHOOL
7 Yarmouth Road, Norwich, Norfolk
NR7 0EA
Tel: (01603) 433055
Head: Mrs R McFarlane
Type: Girls Day 3–16
No of pupils: G280
Fees: (September 01) Day £2790 –
£4185
Special Needs: Level 2: DYS SPLD
Level 3: EPI

TOWN CLOSE HOUSE
PREPARATORY SCHOOL
14 Ipswich Road, Norwich, Norfolk
NR2 2LR
Tel: (01603) 620180
Head: Mr R Gordon
Type: Co-educational Day and
Boarding 3–13
No of pupils: B297 G103
No of Boarders: W10
Fees: (September 01) WB £8790
Day £3915 – £6240
Special Needs: Level 2: DYS

NORTHAMPTONSHIRE

BOSWORTH INDEPENDENT COLLEGE
Nazareth House, Barrack Road,
Northampton NN2 6AF
Tel: (01604) 239995
Head: Mr M McQuin
Type: Co-educational Boarding and
Day 14–19
No of pupils: B132 G98
No of Boarders: F166 W1
Fees: (September 01) FB £13350
Day £6990
Special Needs: Level 2: DYS
Level 3: ADD ADHD ASP DYP HI VIS

MAIDWELL HALL
Maidwell, Northampton NN6 9JG
Tel: (01604) 686234
Head: Mr R A Lankester
Type: Co-educational Boarding and
Day 3–13 (Girls day only)
No of pupils: B123 G15
No of Boarders: F80
Fees: (September 01) FB £12870
Day £4200 – £9300
Special Needs: Level 2: DYC DYP DYS
SPLD

NORTHAMPTON CHRISTIAN SCHOOL
The Parish Rooms, Park Avenue
North, Northampton NN3 2HT
Tel: (01604) 715900
Head: Mrs Z Blakeman
Type: Co-educational Day 4–16
No of pupils: B7 G11
Fees: (September 01) Day £1986 –
£2216
Special Needs: Level 1: ADD ADHD
DYC DYP DYS MLD SP&LD
Unspecified: EBD EPI

NORTHAMPTON PREPARATORY SCHOOL
Great Houghton Hall, Northampton
NN4 7AG
Tel: (01604) 761907
Head: Mr M T E Street
Type: Co-educational Day 4–13
No of pupils: B178 G85
Fees: (September 01) Day £3435 –
£6600
Special Needs: Level 2: DYC DYP DYS
MLD SP&LD SPLD Level 3: DEL HI

OUR LADY'S CONVENT PREPARATORY SCHOOL
Hall Lane, Kettering,
Northamptonshire NN15 7LJ
Tel: (01536) 513882
Head: Mrs L Burgess
Type: Co-educational Day 2–11
No of pupils: B83 G66
Fees: (September 01) Day £3540
Special Needs: Level 2: DYS EBD MLD

WELLINGBOROUGH SCHOOL
Wellingborough, Northamptonshire
NN8 2BX
Tel: (01933) 222427
Head: Mr F R Ullmann
Type: Co-educational Day 3–18
No of pupils: B470 G280
Fees: (September 01) Day £4095 –
£7386
Special Needs: Level 2: DYP DYS

NORTHUMBERLAND

ST OSWALD'S SCHOOL
Spring Gardens, South Road,
Alnwick, Northumberland
NE66 2NU
Tel: (01665) 602739
Head: Mr R Croft
Type: Co-educational Day 3–16
No of pupils: B55 G53
Fees: (September 01) Day £3100 –
£4650
Special Needs: Level 3: DYS MLD

NOTTINGHAMSHIRE

ATTENBOROUGH PREPARATORY SCHOOL
The Strand, Attenborough, Beeston, Nottingham NG9 6AU
Tel: (0115) 943 6725
Head: Mrs M Cahill
Type: Co-educational Day 4–11
No of pupils: B59 G28
Fees: (September 01) Day £1815 – £2400
Special Needs: Level 2: DYC DYP DYS MLD Level 3: ADD ADHD EBD HI SP&LD Unspecified: W

DAGFA HOUSE SCHOOL
Broadgate, Beeston, Nottingham NG9 2FU
Tel: (0115) 913 8330
Head: Mr A Oatway
Type: Co-educational Day 3–16
No of pupils: B165 G115
Fees: (September 01) Day £2640 – £4640
Special Needs: Level 2: DYS Level 3: ADD ADHD ASP AUT DYC DYP EPI SPLD

GROSVENOR SCHOOL
Edwalton, Nottingham NG12 4BS
Tel: (0115) 923 1184
Head: Mr C G J Oldershaw
Type: Co-educational Day 4–13
No of pupils: B107 G64
Fees: (September 01) Day £3855 – £4260
Special Needs: Level 1: DYC DYP Level 2: DYS SPLD

HIGHFIELDS SCHOOL
London Road, Newark, Nottinghamshire NG24 3AL
Tel: (01636) 704103
Head: Mr P F Smith
Type: Co-educational Day 2–11
No of pupils: B95 G89
Fees: (September 01) Day £3525 – £3585
Special Needs: Level 2: DYP DYS EPI

THE KING'S SCHOOL
Collygate Road, The Meadows, Nottingham NG2 2EJ
Tel: (0115) 953 9194
Head: Mr R Southey
Type: Co-educational Day 4–16
No of pupils: B90 G68
Fees: (September 01) Day £2484
Special Needs: Level 2: DYS Level 3: ADD ASP AUT DEL DYP EBD MLD

LAMMAS SCHOOL
Lammas Road, Sutton in Ashfield, Nottinghamshire NG17 2AD
Tel: (01623) 516879
Head: Mr C M Peck
Type: Co-educational Day 4–16
No of pupils: B80 G70
Fees: (September 01) Day £2775 – £3075
Special Needs: Unspecified: DYS MLD

PLUMTREE SCHOOL
Church Hill, Plumtree, Nottingham NG12 5ND
Tel: (0115) 937 5859
Head: Mr N White
Type: Co-educational Day 3–11
No of pupils: B76 G51
Fees: (September 01) Day £3075
Special Needs: Level 2: DYS

RANBY HOUSE
Retford, Nottinghamshire DN22 8HX
Tel: (01777) 703138
Head: Mr A C Morris
Type: Co-educational Day 3–13
No of pupils: B201 G134
No of Boarders: F75
Fees: (September 01) FB £9375 Day £4050 – £7200
Special Needs: Unspecified: ADD DYC DYP DYS

ST JOSEPH'S SCHOOL
33 Derby Road, Nottingham NG1 5AW
Tel: (0115) 941 8356
Head: Mr J Crawley
Type: Co-educational Day 1–11
No of pupils: B115 G72
Fees: (September 01) Day £3900
Special Needs: Level 1: W Level 2: DYC DYP DYS MLD

TRENT COLLEGE
Long Eaton, Nottingham NG10 4AD
Tel: (0115) 849 4949
Head: Mr J S Lee
Type: Co-educational Boarding and Day 3–18
No of pupils: B490 G300
No of Boarders: F60 W105
Fees: (September 01)
FB £13384 – £14241
WB £9510 – £13160
Day £3940 – £8773
Special Needs: Level 2: DYC DYP DYS MLD SPLD

WAVERLEY HOUSE PNEU SCHOOL
13 Waverley Street, Nottingham NG7 4DX
Tel: (0115) 978 3230
Head: Mr T J Collins
Type: Co-educational Day 3–11
No of pupils: B65 G63
Fees: (September 01) Day £500 – £1594
Special Needs: Level 2: DYC DYP DYS SPLD Level 3: AUT DEL EBD EPI HI PH VIS

WORKSOP COLLEGE
Worksop, Nottinghamshire S80 3AP
Tel: (01909) 537127
Head: Mr R A Collard
Type: Co-educational Boarding and Day 13–18
No of pupils: B255 G125
No of Boarders: F120 W95
Fees: (September 01) F/WB £14460 Day £9900
Special Needs: Level 1: DYS Level 2: ADD MLD SPLD Level 3: ADHD ASP CP DYP HI VIS

OXFORDSHIRE

THE CARRDUS SCHOOL
Overthorpe Hall, Banbury,
Oxfordshire OX17 2BS
Tel: (01295) 263733
Head: Miss S Carrdus
Type: Girls Day 3–11 (Boys 3–8)
No of pupils: B25 G120
Fees: (September 01) Day £1845 –
£5730
Special Needs: Level 2: ADD ADHD
ASP DYP DYS EPI HI PH SP&LD
SPLD VIS Level 3: AUT CP DEL
DOW DYC EBD MLD Unspecified:
PMLD SLD TOU

CHERWELL COLLEGE
Greyfriars, Paradise Street, Oxford
OX1 1LD
Tel: (01865) 242670
Head: Mr A Thompson
Type: Co-educational Day and
Boarding 16+
No of pupils: B85 G65
No of Boarders: F90 W10
Fees: (September 01) F/WB £15750
Day £10500
Special Needs: Unspecified: ADD
ADHD DYC DYP DYS

COKETHORPE SCHOOL*
Witney, Oxfordshire OX29 7PU
Tel: (01993) 703921
Head: Mr P J S Cantwell
Type: Co-educational Boarding and
Day 7–18 (Day girls only)
No of pupils: B330 G180
No of Boarders: F20 W20
Fees: (September 01)
F/WB £15750 Day £5310 – £9480
Special Needs: Level 2: DEL DYC DYP
DYS PH SP&LD SPLD

CRANFORD HOUSE SCHOOL
Moulsford, Wallingford, Oxfordshire
OX10 9HT
Tel: (01491) 651218
Head: Mrs A B Gray
Type: Girls Day 3–16 (Boys 3–7)
No of pupils: B49 G224
Fees: (September 01) Day £4485 –
£7215
Special Needs: Level 2: DYC DYP DYS
SPLD Unspecified: CP DEL

D'OVERBROECK'S COLLEGE
1 Park Town, Oxford OX2 6SN
Tel: (01865) 310000
Head: Mr S Cohen and
Dr R M Knowles
Type: Co-educational Day and
Boarding 13–19 (Day only 13–16)
No of pupils: 280 *No of Boarders:* F100
Fees: (September 01) FB £15555 –
£17655 Day £7995 – £11655
Special Needs: Level 3: ADD ADHD
EBD HI Unspecified: DYC DYP DYS
SPLD

DRAGON SCHOOL
Bardwell Road, Oxford OX2 6SS
Tel: (01865) 315400
Head: Mr R S Trafford
Type: Co-educational Boarding and
Day 3–13
No of pupils: B568 G268
No of Boarders: F280
Fees: (September 01) FB £13830
Day £6210 – £9660
Special Needs: Level 2: DYC DYP DYS
SPLD Unspecified: EPI

EDWARD GREENE'S
TUTORIAL ESTABLISHMENT
45 Pembroke Street, Oxford OX1 1BP
Tel: (01865) 248308
Head: Mr E P C Greene
Type: Co-educational Day 12–20
No of pupils: B14 G22
No of Boarders: F18
Fees: (September 01) Day £3360 –
£16800
Special Needs: Level 2: DYC DYS MLD
SPLD VIS Level 3: DEL DYP EBD EPI
HI PH TOU

EMMANUAL CHRISTIAN
SCHOOL
Sandford Road, Littlemore, Oxford
OX4 4PU
Tel: (01865) 395236
Head: Mrs R J Stokes
Type: Co-educational Day 4–11
No of pupils: B27 G36
Fees: (September 01) Day £2616
Special Needs: Level 2: MLD
Unspecified: W

KINGHAM HILL SCHOOL†
Kingham, Chipping Norton,
Oxfordshire OX7 6TH
Tel: (01608) 658999
Head: Mr M J Morris
Type: Co-educational Boarding and
Day 11–18
No of pupils: B182 G70
No of Boarders: F205
Fees: (September 01)
F/WB £12711 – £13740
Day £7905 – £8568
Special Needs: Level 2: DYC DYP DYS
SPLD

MANOR PREPARATORY
SCHOOL
Faringdon Road, Abingdon,
Oxfordshire OX13 6LN
Tel: (01235) 523789
Head: Mrs D A Robinson
Type: Co-educational Day Boys 3–7
Girls 3–11
No of pupils: B38 G322
Fees: (September 01) Day £3000 –
£6000
Special Needs: Level 2: ADD ASP DEL
DYC DYP DYS PH SPLD Level 3: HI
VIS

OUR LADY'S CONVENT
JUNIOR SCHOOL
St John's Road, Abingdon,
Oxfordshire OX14 2HB
Tel: (01235) 523147
Head: Sister J Frances
Type: Co-educational Day 4–11
No of pupils: B55 G75
Fees: (September 01) Day £3525 –
£3615
Special Needs: Level 2: DYS MLD

RUPERT HOUSE
90 Bell Street, Henley-on-Thames,
Oxfordshire RG9 2BN
Tel: (01491) 574263
Head: Mrs G M Crane
Type: Co-educational Day Boys 4–7
Girls 4–11
No of pupils: B54 G173
Fees: (September 01) Day £2415 –
£5850
Special Needs: Level 2: DYC DYP DYS
Level 3: HI SP&LD

ST CLARE'S, OXFORD

139 Banbury Road, Oxford OX2 7AL
Tel: (01865) 552031
Head: Mr Boyd Roberts
Type: Co-educational Boarding and
Day 16–20
No of pupils: B231 G119
No of Boarders: F325
Fees: (September 01) FB £18010 –
£18300 Day £11258
Special Needs: Level 3: ADHD DYS
EPI HI PH VIS

ST EDWARD'S SCHOOL

Woodstock Road, Oxford OX2 7NN
Tel: (01865) 319200
Head: Mr D Christie
Type: Co-educational Boarding and
Day 13–18
No of pupils: B410 G215
No of Boarders: F440
Fees: (September 01) FB £17490 Day
£13125
Special Needs: Level 1: DYP DYS
SPLD

ST HUGH'S SCHOOL

Carswell Manor, Faringdon,
Oxfordshire SN7 8PT
Tel: (01367) 870223
Head: Mr D Cannon
Type: Co-educational Boarding and
Day 4–13
No of pupils: B168 G110
No of Boarders: W40
Fees: (September 01) F/WB £9990 –
£10650 Day £4980 – £8760
Special Needs: Level 2: DYC DYP DYS
MLD SPLD Level 3: HI

ST JOHN'S PRIORY SCHOOL

St John's Road, Banbury, Oxfordshire
OX16 5HX
Tel: (01295) 259607
Head: Mrs J M Walker
Type: Co-educational Day 2–11
No of pupils: B75 G85
Fees: (September 01) Day £1200 –
£4050
Special Needs: Unspecified: DYS MLD

SHIPLAKE COLLEGE

Henley-on-Thames, Oxfordshire
RG9 4BW
Tel: (0118) 940 2455
Head: Mr N V Bevan
Type: Boys Day and Boarding 13–18
(Day Girls 16–18)
No of pupils: B278 G12
No of Boarders: F100 W110
Fees: (September 01) FB £15405
Day £10392
Special Needs: Level 1: DYS MLD
Level 3: DYP EPI

SIBFORD SCHOOL†

Sibford Ferris, Banbury, Oxfordshire
OX15 5QL
Tel: (01295) 781200
Head: Ms S Freestone
Type: Co-educational Boarding and
Day 5–18
No of pupils: B223 G152
No of Boarders: F54 W60
Fees: (September 01) FB £13524
WB £9591 – £12597
Day £4205 – £6705
Special Needs: Unspecified: DEL DYC
DYP DYS EPI SP&LD SPLD

SUMMER FIELDS

Mayfield Road, Oxford OX2 7EN
Tel: (01865) 454433
Head: Mr R Badham-Thornhill
Type: Boarding and Day 8–13
No of pupils: B250 *No of Boarders:* F240
Fees: (September 01) FB £13200
Day £9750
Special Needs: Level 2: DYP DYS HI
SPLD Unspecified: W

TUDOR HALL SCHOOL

Banbury, Oxfordshire OX16 9UR
Tel: (01295) 263434
Head: Miss N Godfrey
Type: Girls Boarding 11–18
No of pupils: G262 *No of Boarders:* F233
Fees: (September 01) FB £14700
Day £9180
Special Needs: Level 2: DYS
Level 3: DYP

SHROPSHIRE

BELLAN HOUSE PREPARATORY SCHOOL

Bellan House, Church Street,
Oswestry, Shropshire SY11 2ST
Tel: (01691) 653453
Head: Mrs S L Durham
Type: Co-educational Day 9–18
No of pupils: B91 G92
Fees: (September 01) On application
Special Needs: Level 1: ADD ASP
SP&LD Level 2: DYP DYS EPI MLD
Level 3: CP DEL PH

ELLESMERE COLLEGE*†

Ellesmere, Shropshire SY12 9AB
Tel: (01691) 622321
Head: Mr B J Wignall
Type: Co-educational Boarding and
Day 9–18
No of pupils: 465 *No of Boarders:* F99
Fees: (September 01) FB £14700
WB £12600 Day £9600
Special Needs: Unspecified: ADD
ADHD ASP DYC DYP SPLD

KINGSLAND GRANGE

Old Roman Road, Shrewsbury,
Shropshire SY3 9AH
Tel: (01743) 232132
Head: Mr M C James
Type: Boys Day 4–13
No of pupils: B150
Fees: (September 01) Day £3885 –
£6240
Special Needs: Level 2: DYS MLD
SPLD

THE OLD HALL SCHOOL
Holyhead Road, Wellington, Telford, Shropshire TF1 2DN
Tel: (01952) 223117
Head: Mr R J Ward
Type: Co-educational Day 3–13
No of pupils: B162 G162
Fees: (September 01) Day £3975 – £6225
Special Needs: Level 1: DYC DYS MLD SPLD Level 2: ADD ADHD ASP AUT DYP

OSWESTRY SCHOOL
Upper Brook Street, Oswestry, Shropshire SY11 2TL
Tel: (01691) 655711
Head: Mr P D Stockdale
Type: Co-educational Boarding and Day 2–18
No of pupils: 426
No of Boarders: F97 W2
Fees: (September 01) FB £12500 – £13362 Day £5472 – £7968
Special Needs: Level 1: DYC DYP DYS Level 2: ASP SPLD Level 3: HI

PRESTFELDE PREPARATORY SCHOOL
London Road, Shrewsbury, Shropshire SY2 6NZ
Tel: (01743) 245400
Head: Mr J R Bridgeland
Type: Co-educational Day and Boarding 3–13
No of pupils: B241 G69
No of Boarders: F25
Fees: (September 01) FB £9150 Day £2310 – £7230
Special Needs: Level 1: DYP DYS SPLD Unspecified: HI SP&LD

SOMERSET

ALL HALLOWS
Cranmore Hall, East Cranmore, Shepton Mallet, Somerset BA4 4SF
Tel: (01749) 880227
Head: Mr C J Bird
Type: Co-educational Boarding and Day 4–13
No of pupils: B170 G110
No of Boarders: F70
Fees: (September 01) F/WB £11130 Day £3720 – £7575
Special Needs: Level 2: ADD ADHD ASP DEL DYP DYS EPI HI SP&LD SPLD VIS Level 3: PH

CHARD SCHOOL
Fore Street, Chard, Somerset TA20 1QA
Tel: (01460) 63234
Head: Mr J G Stotesbury
Type: Co-educational Day 2–11
No of pupils: B60 G60
Fees: (September 01) Day £2640 – £2841
Special Needs: Level 2: DYS

HAZLEGROVE (KING'S BRUTON PREPARATORY SCHOOL)
Hazlegrove House, Sparkford, Yeovil, Somerset BA22 7JA
Tel: (01963) 440314
Head: Mr P Jordon
Type: Co-educational Day and Boarding 3–13
No of pupils: B300 G120
No of Boarders: F85
Fees: (September 01) FB £10290 – £11670 Day £4110 – £8370
Special Needs: Level 1: DYC DYP DYS SPLD Level 3: ADD ASP HI PH SP&LD

KING'S COLLEGE
Taunton, Somerset TA1 3DX
Tel: (01823) 328200
Head: Mr R S Funnell
Type: Co-educational Boarding and Day 13–18
No of pupils: B283 G150
No of Boarders: F301
Fees: (September 01) On application
Special Needs: Level 2: DYC DYP DYS SPLD Level 3: ADD EPI

KING'S HALL SCHOOL
Pyrland, Kingston Road, Taunton, Somerset TA2 8AA
Tel: (01823) 285920
Head: Mr J K Macpherson
Type: Co-educational Boarding and Day 3–13
No of pupils: B215 G175
No of Boarders: F50 W25
Fees: (September 01) FB £6555 – £11025 WB £6195 – £10635 Day £2595 – £7815
Special Needs: Level 2: DYC DYS

MILLFIELD PREPARATORY SCHOOL
Glastonbury, Somerset BA6 8LD
Tel: (01458) 832446
Head: Mr K Cheney
Type: Co-educational Boarding and Day 7–13
No of pupils: B270 G190
No of Boarders: F200
Fees: (September 01) FB £13020 Day £8790
Special Needs: Level 1: DYS MLD SPLD Level 2: DYC

THE PARK SCHOOL
Yeovil, Somerset BA20 1DH
Tel: (01935) 423514
Head: Mr P W Bate
Type: Co-educational Day and Boarding 3–18
No of pupils: B108 G135
No of Boarders: F23 W8
Fees: (September 01) FB £9255 – £10320 WB £8625 – £9690 Day £2850 – £5640
Special Needs: Level 3: ADD ADHD ASP AUT CP DYP DYS MLD PH TOU

ST BRANDON'S SCHOOL
Elton Road, Clevedon, Somerset BS21 7SD
Tel: (01275) 875092
Head: Mrs S Vesey
Type: Co-educational Day 3–11
No of pupils: B70 G70
Fees: (September 01) Day £750 – £3780
Special Needs: Level 1: W Level 2: DYS SPLD Level 3: ADD ASP DYP Unspecified: MLD

TAUNTON SCHOOL
Taunton, Somerset TA2 6AD
Tel: (01823) 349200/349223
Head: Mr J P Whiteley
Type: Co-educational Boarding and Day 13–18
No of pupils: B256 G194
No of Boarders: F177
Fees: (September 01) FB £15195 Day £9765
Special Needs: Level 2: DYC DYS Level 3: ADD ADHD ASP CP DEL DYP EBD EPI HI PH

WELLS CATHEDRAL JUNIOR SCHOOL
8 New Street, Wells, Somerset
BA5 2LQ
Tel: (01749) 672291
Head: Mr N M Wilson
Type: Co-educational Boarding and
Day 3–11
No of pupils: B86 G108
No of Boarders: F9 W1
Fees: (September 01) FB £10434
Day £3612 – £7365
Special Needs: Level 2: DYS
Level 3: DYP

NORTH EAST SOMERSET

DOWNSIDE SCHOOL
Stratton-on-the-Fosse, Radstock,
Bath, North East Somerset BA3 4RJ
Tel: (01761) 235100
Head: Dom A Sutch
Type: Boys Boarding and Day 8–18
No of pupils: B315
No of Boarders: F295
Fees: (September 01)
FB £11988 – £15093
Day £6984 – £7767
Special Needs: Level 2: DYS SP&LD
SPLD Level 3: DYC PH

KINGSWOOD PREPARATORY SCHOOL
College Road, Lansdown, Bath,
North East Somerset BA1 5SD
Tel: (01225) 310468
Head: Miss A Gleave
Type: Co-educational Day and
Boarding 3–11
No of pupils: B177 G128
No of Boarders: F5 W4
Fees: (September 01) FB £10998
Day £4029 – £4791
Special Needs: Level 2: DYP DYS
SPLD Unspecified: W

PARAGON SCHOOL
Lyncombe House, Lyncombe Vale,
Bath, North East Somerset BA2 4LT
Tel: (01225) 310837
Head: Mr D J Martin
Type: Co-educational Day 3–11
No of pupils: B142 G115
Fees: (September 01) Day £3735 –
£4149
Special Needs: Level 2: DYC DYP DYS

THE ROYAL HIGH SCHOOL
Lansdown, Bath, North East
Somerset BA1 5SZ
Tel: (01225) 313877
Head: Mr J Graham-Brown
Type: Girls Boarding and Day 3–18
No of pupils: G925
No of Boarders: F100
Fees: (September 01) FB £10692
Day £3906 – £5010
Special Needs: Level 1: DYP DYS
Level 2: DYC Level 3: ADD ADHD
ASP AUT DEL EBD EPI HI PH VIS

STAFFORDSHIRE

ABBOTSHOLME SCHOOL†
Rocester, Uttoxeter, Staffordshire
ST14 5BS
Tel: (01889) 590217
Head: Dr S D Tommis
Type: Co-educational Boarding and
Day 7–18 (Boarders from 11)
No of pupils: B163 G88
No of Boarders: F65 W24
Fees: (September 01)
F/WB £13125 – £15318
Day £6000 – £10242
Special Needs: Level 1: DYC DYP DYS
SPLD Level 2: ADD

CHASE ACADEMY
St John's Road, Cannock,
Staffordshire WS11 3UR
Tel: (01543) 501800
Head: Mr M D Ellse
Type: Co-educational Day and
Boarding 3–18
No of pupils: B74 G49
No of Boarders: F1
Fees: (September 01) FB £11100
Day £1668 – £5652
Special Needs: Level 2: DYP DYS
Level 3: DEL

EDENHURST SCHOOL
Westlands Avenue,
Newcastle-under-Lyme, Staffordshire
ST5 2PU
Tel: (01782) 619348
Head: Mr N H F Copestick
Type: Co-educational Day 3–14
No of pupils: B118 G122
Fees: (September 01) Day £2994 –
£5055
Special Needs: Level 2: DYS
Level 3: DYC DYP

HOWITT HOUSE SCHOOL
New Lodge, Hanbury, Staffordshire
DE13 8TG
Tel: (01283) 820236
Head: Mr M H Davis
Type: Co-educational Day 3–12
No of pupils: B36 G30
Fees: (September 01) Day £3054
Special Needs: Level 2: VIS
Level 3: DYS MLD Unspecified: W

NEWCASTLE-UNDER-LYME SCHOOL
Mount Pleasant,
Newcastle-under-Lyme, Staffordshire
ST5 1DB
Tel: (01782) 631197
Head: Dr R M Reynolds
Type: Co-educational Day 7–18
No of pupils: B500 G561
Fees: (September 01) Day £4524 –
£5115
Special Needs: Level 2: DYS
Level 3: ASP

ST BEDE'S SCHOOL
Bishton Hall, Wolseley Bridge,
Stafford ST17 0XN
Tel: (01889) 881277
Head: Mr H C Stafford Northcote
Type: Co-educational Boarding and
Day 2–13
No of pupils: B68 G50
No of Boarders: F10 W15
Fees: (September 01) FB £8316
Day £3738 – £6342
Special Needs: Level 1: ASP CP DEL
SPLD Level 2: AUT Unspecified: DYS
PH SP&LD W

ST DOMINIC'S PRIORY SCHOOL
21 Station Road, Stone, Staffordshire
ST15 8EN
Tel: (01785) 814181
Head: Mrs J Hildreth
Type: Girls Day 3–18 (Boys 3–11)
No of pupils: B22 G338
Fees: (September 01) Day £3294 –
£5055
Special Needs: Level 2: DYS
Unspecified: EPI PH

ST DOMINIC'S SCHOOL
32 Bargate Street, Brewood, Stafford
ST19 9BA
Tel: (01902) 850248
Head: Mrs M E K Peakman
Type: Girls Day 2–16 (Co-ed 2–7)
No of pupils: B15 G240
Fees: (September 01) Day £1740 –
£7185
Special Needs: Level 2: DEL DYC DYP
DYS

ST JOSEPH'S PREPARATORY SCHOOL
London Road, Trent Vale,
Stoke-on-Trent, Staffordshire
ST4 5RF
Tel: (01782) 417533
Head: Mrs M B Hughes
Type: Co-educational Day 3–11
No of pupils: B93 G72
Fees: (September 01) Day £2955 –
£3795
Special Needs: Level 1: W Level 2: DYS
SPLD Level 3: ADD ADHD ASP AUT
CP DEL DOW DYC DYP PH

VERNON LODGE PREPARATORY SCHOOL
School Lane, Stretton, Stafford
ST19 9LJ
Tel: (01902) 850568
Head: Mrs P Sills
Type: Co-educational Day 2–11
No of pupils: B67 G38
Fees: (September 01) Day £3690 –
£4440
Special Needs: Level 2: CP DYS
Level 3: ASP Unspecified: DYP

STOCKTON-ON-TEES

RED HOUSE SCHOOL
36 The Green, Norton,
Stockton-on-Tees TS20 1DX
Tel: (01642) 553370
Head: Mr C M J Allen
Type: Co-educational Day 3–16
No of pupils: B236 G196
Fees: (September 01) Day £3516 –
£4479
Special Needs: Level 2: DYC DYP DYS

TEESSIDE HIGH SCHOOL
The Avenue, Eaglescliffe,
Stockton-on-Tees TS16 9AT
Tel: (01642) 782095
Head: Mrs H J French
Type: Girls Day 3–18
No of pupils: G470
Fees: (September 01) Day £3510 –
£5592
Special Needs: Level 2: DYS
Level 3: DYP HI VIS

SUFFOLK

THE ABBEY
The Prep School of Woodbridge
School, Woodbridge, Suffolk
IP12 1DS
Tel: (01394) 382673
Head: Mr N J Garrett
Type: Co-educational Day 4–11
No of pupils: B157 G129
Fees: (September 01) Day £4326 –
£6546
Special Needs: Level 2: DYS

BARNARDISTON HALL
PREPARATORY SCHOOL
Barnardiston, Haverhill, Suffolk
CB9 7TG
Tel: (01440) 786316
Head: Lt Col K A Boulter
Type: Co-educational Day and
Boarding 2–13
No of pupils: B143 G128
No of Boarders: F58 W20
Fees: (September 01) FB £10425
WB £9450 Day £5070 – £6375
Special Needs: Level 1: ADD ADHD
AUT DEL DYC DYP DYS EBD MLD
SPLD

CHERRY TREES SCHOOL
Flempton Road, Risby, Bury St
Edmunds, Suffolk IP28 6QJ
Tel: (01284) 760531
Head: Ms W Compson
Type: Co-educational Day 0–11
No of pupils: B120 G117
Fees: (September 01) Day £4560 –
£5610
Special Needs: Level 2: DYC DYP DYS
EBD HI MLD SP&LD SPLD
Level 3: CP DEL EPI PH Unspecified:
AUT

FRAMLINGHAM COLLEGE
JUNIOR SCHOOL
Brandeston Hall, Brandeston, Suffolk
IP13 7AH
Tel: (01728) 685331
Head: Mr S Player
Type: Co-educational Boarding and
Day 4–13
No of pupils: B153 G105
No of Boarders: F50 W10
Fees: (September 01) FB £11025 Day
£3942 – £6858
Special Needs: Level 2: DYS

HILLCROFT PREPARATORY
SCHOOL†
Walnutree Manor, Haughley Green,
Stowmarket, Suffolk IP14 3RQ
Tel: (01449) 673003
Head: Mr F Rapsey and Mrs G Rapsey
Type: Co-educational Day 2–13
No of pupils: B47 G42
Fees: (September 01) Day £1260 –
£6240
Special Needs: Level 1: DYC DYP DYS
MLD SP&LD SPLD Level 3: ASP AUT
DEL EPI PH Unspecified: ADD
ADHD CP DOW EBD HI PMLD SLD
TOU VIS W

IPSWICH HIGH SCHOOL
GDST
Woolverstone, Ipswich, Suffolk
IP9 1AZ
Tel: (01473) 780201
Head: Miss V C MacCuish
Type: Girls Day 3–18
No of pupils: G700
Fees: (September 01) Day £3174 –
£5442
Special Needs: Level 3: DYS EPI HI PH
VIS

IPSWICH PREPARATORY
SCHOOL
Henley Road, Ipswich, Suffolk
IP1 3SQ
Tel: (01473) 408301
Head: Mrs J M Jones
Type: Co-educational Day 3–11
No of pupils: B211 G82
Fees: (September 01) Day £4251 –
£4908
Special Needs: Level 2: DYC DYS
Level 3: CP DYP EPI HI SP&LD SPLD

IPSWICH SCHOOL
Henley Road, Ipswich, Suffolk
IP1 3SG
Tel: (01473) 408300
Head: Mr I G Galbraith
Type: Co-educational Day and
Boarding 11–18
No of pupils: B481 G179
No of Boarders: F25 W22
Fees: (September 01)
FB £10341 – £12030
WB £9867 – £11334
Day £6231 – £6930
Special Needs: Level 3: DEL DYS EBD
EPI HI PH

ROYAL HOSPITAL SCHOOL
Holbrook, Ipswich, Suffolk IP9 2RX
Tel: (01473) 326200
Head: Mr N K D Ward
Type: Co-educational Boarding 11–18
(VIth form day pupils)
No of pupils: B420 G260
No of Boarders: F680
Fees: (September 01)
FB £150 – £13119 Day £7758
Special Needs: Level 3: DYS

ST FELIX SCHOOL
Southwold, Suffolk IP18 6SD
Tel: (01502) 722175
Head: Mr R Williams
Type: Girls Boarding and Day 11–18
No of pupils: G150
No of Boarders: F76 W12
Fees: (September 01)
F/WB £11805 – £13905
Day £7290 – £9180
Special Needs: Level 2: DYP DYS
Level 3: EPI HI

ST GEORGE'S SCHOOL
Southwold, Suffolk IP18 6SD
Tel: (01502) 723314
Head: Mrs W H Holland
Type: Co-educational Day 2–11
No of pupils: B102 G104
Fees: (September 01) Day £3240 –
£5700
Special Needs: Level 1: W Level 2: ASP
AUT DYP DYS MLD PH SLD SP&LD
SPLD TOU

SOUTH LEE PREPARATORY SCHOOL
Nowton Road, Bury St Edmunds,
Suffolk IP33 2BT
Tel: (01284) 754654
Head: Mr D Whipp
Type: Co-educational Day 2–13
No of pupils: B125 G166
Fees: (September 01) Day £4725 –
£5895
Special Needs: Level 2: DYP DYS
SP&LD

STOKE COLLEGE
Stoke by Clare, Sudbury, Suffolk
CO10 8JE
Tel: (01787) 278141
Head: Mr J Gibson
Type: Co-educational Day and
Boarding 3–16
No of pupils: B155 G90
No of Boarders: W25
Fees: (September 01)
WB £10575 – £11775
Day £4785 – £6675
Special Needs: Level 2: DYS MLD

WOODBRIDGE SCHOOL
Woodbridge, Suffolk IP12 4JH
Tel: (01394) 385547
Head: Mr S H Cole
Type: Co-educational Day and
Boarding 11–18
No of pupils: B298 G292
No of Boarders: F35 W3
Fees: (September 01) F/WB £13752
Day £7728 – £7932
Special Needs: Level 2: DYP DYS
Level 3: ADD ADHD ASP PH
Unspecified: DYC SPLD W

SURREY

ABINGER HAMMER VILLAGE SCHOOL
Hackhurst Lane, Abinger Hammer,
Dorking, Surrey RH5 6SE
Tel: (01306) 730343
Head: Mrs P A Hammond
Type: Co-educational Day 3–8
No of pupils: B3 G7
Fees: (September 01) On application
Special Needs: Level 3: MLD
Unspecified: W

BOX HILL SCHOOL†
Mickleham, Dorking, Surrey
RH5 6EA
Tel: (01372) 373382
Head: Dr R A S Atwood
Type: Co-educational Boarding and
Day 11–18
No of pupils: B208 G115
No of Boarders: F104 W55
Fees: (September 01) FB £13926
WB £11115 Day £5685 – £7527
Special Needs: Level 2: DYS

BRAMLEY SCHOOL
Chequers Lane, Walton-on-the-Hill,
Tadworth, Surrey KT20 7ST
Tel: (01737) 812004
Head: Mrs B Johns
Type: Girls Day 3–11
No of pupils: G130
Fees: (September 01) Day £2250 –
£5550
Special Needs: Level 3: DYS

BROOMFIELD HOUSE
10 Broomfield Road, Kew Gardens,
Richmond, Surrey TW9 3HS
Tel: (020) 8940 3884
Head: Mr N O York
Type: Co-educational Day 3–11
No of pupils: B73 G87
Fees: (September 01) Day £2505 –
£5980
Special Needs: Level 3: SLD

CABLE HOUSE SCHOOL
Horsell Rise, Woking, Surrey
GU21 4AY
Tel: (01483) 760759
Head: Mr R Elvidge
Type: Co-educational Day 3–11
No of pupils: B60 G60
Fees: (September 01) Day £2200 –
£4530
Special Needs: Level 3: ADD ADHD
DYP DYS EBD

CAMBRIDGE TUTORS COLLEGE
Water Tower Hill, Croydon, Surrey
CR0 5SX
Tel: (020) 8688 5284
Head: Mr D A Lowe
Type: Co-educational Boarding and
Day 16–21
No of pupils: B140 G130
Fees: (September 01) FB £14000 Day
£9750
Special Needs: Unspecified: DEL DYS
EBD HI

CHARTERHOUSE
Godalming, Surrey GU7 2DJ
Tel: (01483) 291501
Head: Rev J S Witheridge
Type: Boys Boarding and Day 13–18
(Co-ed VIth Form)
No of pupils: B614 G97
No of Boarders: F670
Fees: (September 01) FB £17598
Day £14541
Special Needs: Level 3: DYP DYS

CHINTHURST SCHOOL
Tadworth Street, Tadworth, Surrey
KT20 5QZ
Tel: (01737) 812011
Head: Mr T J Egan
Type: Boys Day 3–13
No of pupils: B390
Fees: (September 01) Day £1950 –
£5580
Special Needs: Level 2: ASP DYC DYS
Level 3: ADD ADHD DYP PH SPLD

COLLINGWOOD SCHOOL
3 Springfield Road, Wallington,
Surrey SM6 0BD
Tel: (020) 8647 4607
Head: Mr G M Barham
Type: Co-educational Day 2–11
No of pupils: B112 G64
Fees: (September 01) Day £1770 –
£3675
Special Needs: Level 2: DYS
Level 3: ADD ADHD ASP AUT CP
DEL DYC DYP EBD EPI HI MLD PH
SP&LD SPLD VIS

COWORTH PARK SCHOOL
Valley End, Chobham, Woking,
Surrey GU24 8TE
Tel: (01276) 855707
Head: Mrs C A Fairbairn
Type: Co-educational Day Boys 3–7
Girls 3–11
No of pupils: B26 G136
Fees: (September 01) Day £2415 –
£5775
Special Needs: Level 2: DYS

CRANLEIGH SCHOOL
Horseshoe Lane, Cranleigh, Surrey
GU6 8QQ
Tel: (01483) 273666
Head: Mr G Waller
Type: Co-educational Boarding and
Day 13–18
No of pupils: B383 G165
No of Boarders: F377
Fees: (September 01) FB £17790
Day £13485
Special Needs: Unspecified: DYS MLD

CRANMORE SCHOOL
West Horsley, Leatherhead, Surrey
KT24 6AT
Tel: (01483) 284137
Head: Mr A J Martin
Type: Boys Day 3–13
No of pupils: 520
Fees: (September 01) Day £2460 –
£6450
Special Needs: Level 2: DYS

CROYDON HIGH SCHOOL GDST
Old Farleigh Road, Selsdon, South
Croydon, Surrey CR2 8YB
Tel: (020) 8651 5020
Head: Miss L M Ogilvie
Type: Girls Day 3–18
No of pupils: G934
Fees: (September 01) Day £5145 –
£6624
Special Needs: Level 3: DYS HI

EPSOM COLLEGE
Epsom, Surrey KT17 4JQ
Tel: (01372) 821004
Head: Mr S R Borthwick
Type: Co-educational Boarding and
Day 13–18
No of pupils: B513 G162
No of Boarders: F156 W164
Fees: (September 01) FB £16611
WB £15216 – £16389
Day £11362 – £12168
Special Needs: Level 2: DYS

EWELL CASTLE SCHOOL
Church Street, Ewell, Epsom, Surrey
KT17 2AW
Tel: (020) 8393 1413
Head: Mr R A Fewtrell
Type: Boys Day 3–18 (Co-ed VIth
Form)
No of pupils: B410 G40
Fees: (September 01) Day £1725 –
£6495
Special Needs: Level 2: DYC DYP DYS
SPLD Level 3: ADD ADHD ASP DEL
EPI HI PH SP&LD VIS

FLEXLANDS SCHOOL
Station Road, Chobham, Woking,
Surrey GU24 8AG
Tel: (01276) 858841
Head: Mrs A Green
Type: Girls Day 3–11
No of pupils: G160
Fees: (September 01) Day £2460 –
£6000
Special Needs: Level 1: ASP EBD EPI
Level 2: ADD ADHD DEL DYC DYP
DYS PH SP&LD SPLD VIS Level 3: HI

FRENSHAM HEIGHTS
Rowledge, Farnham, Surrey
GU10 4EA
Tel: (01252) 792134
Head: Mr P M de Voil
Type: Co-educational Boarding and
Day 3–18
No of pupils: B238 G216
No of Boarders: F72 W50
Fees: (September 01)
FB £14700 – £15900
WB £13950 – £15360
Day £9600 – £10650
Special Needs: Level 2: DYS
Level 3: DYC DYP

GRANTCHESTER HOUSE
5 Hinchley Way, Hinchley Wood,
Esher, Surrey KT10 0BD
Tel: (020) 8398 1157
Head: Mrs A E Fry
Type: Co-educational Day 3–7
No of pupils: B49 G37
Fees: (September 01) Day £2415 –
£4200
Special Needs: Unspecified: DYS

GREENFIELD SCHOOL
Brooklyn Road, Woking, Surrey
GU22 7TP
Tel: (01483) 772525
Head: Mrs J S Becker
Type: Co-educational Day 3–11
No of pupils: B98 G102
Fees: (September 01) Day £2640 –
£4650
Special Needs: Level 2: ADD DYP DYS
Level 3: PH

HALL GROVE SCHOOL
Bagshot, Surrey GU19 5HZ
Tel: (01276) 473059
Head: Mr A R Graham
Type: Boys Day and Boarding 4–13
No of pupils: 252
No of Boarders: W28
Fees: (September 01)
WB £9000 – £9420
Day £5400 – £7170
Special Needs: Unspecified: DYP DYS
EPI MLD PH SPLD

HALSTEAD PREPARATORY SCHOOL
Woodham Rise, Woking, Surrey
GU21 4EE
Tel: (01483) 772682
Head: Mrs S Fellows
Type: Girls Day 3–11
No of pupils: G209
Fees: (September 01) Day £2400 –
£6540
Special Needs: Level 2: ADD ADHD
DYP DYS SPLD

HASLEMERE PREPARATORY SCHOOL
The Heights, Hill Road, Haslemere, Surrey GU27 2JP
Tel: (01428) 642350
Head: Mr K J Merrick
Type: Boys Day 2–14
No of pupils: B150 G2
Fees: (September 01) Day £5775 – £7200
Special Needs: Unspecified: DYS MLD

HAWLEY PLACE SCHOOL
Fernhill Road, Blackwater, Camberley, Surrey GU17 9HU
Tel: (01276) 32028
Head: Mr and Mrs T G Pipe
Type: Girls Day 2–16 (Boys 2–11)
No of pupils: B86 G224
Fees: (September 01) Day £4455 – £5580
Special Needs: Level 2: DYS MLD Level 3: DYP

HAZELWOOD SCHOOL
Wolf's Hill, Limpsfield, Oxted, Surrey RH8 0QU
Tel: (01883) 712194
Head: Mr A M Synge
Type: Co-educational Day 3–13
No of pupils: B248 G134
Fees: (September 01) Day £2550 – £7350
Special Needs: Level 1: ADD ADHD DYP HI Level 2: DYC DYS SPLD

HOLY CROSS PREPARATORY SCHOOL
Coombe Ridge House, George Road, Kingston Hill, Kingston-upon-Thames, Surrey KT2 7NU
Tel: (020) 8942 0729
Head: Mrs K Hayes
Type: Girls Day 4–11
No of pupils: G250
Fees: (September 01) Day £6300
Special Needs: Level 2: DYP DYS Level 3: MLD

KINGSWOOD HOUSE SCHOOL
56 West Hill, Epsom, Surrey KT19 8LG
Tel: (01372) 723590
Head: Mr P Brooks
Type: Boys Day 3–13
No of pupils: B210
Fees: (September 01) Day £4710 – £6360
Special Needs: Level 1: DYC DYP DYS SPLD Unspecified: SP&LD

LANESBOROUGH
Maori Road, Guildford, Surrey GU1 2EL
Tel: (01483) 880650
Head: Mr K S Crombie
Type: Boys Day 3–13
No of pupils: 350
Fees: (September 01) Day £1860 – £6393
Special Needs: Level 2: DYS Level 3: HI

LAVEROCK SCHOOL
19 Bluehouse Lane, Oxted, Surrey RH8 0AA
Tel: (01883) 714171
Head: Mrs A C Paterson
Type: Girls Day 3–11
No of pupils: 150
Fees: (September 01) Day £2250 – £5850
Special Needs: Level 2: DYP DYS SPLD Level 3: ADD ADHD CP DOW PH

LINLEY HOUSE
6 Berrylands Road, Surbiton, Surrey KT5 8RA
Tel: (020) 8399 4979
Head: Mrs S Mallin
Type: Co-educational Day 3–7
No of pupils: B19 G23
Fees: (September 01) Day £2508 – £4440
Special Needs: Level 3: ADD DYC DYP DYS HI PH SP&LD VIS

LYNDHURST SCHOOL
36 The Avenue, Camberley, Surrey GU15 3NE
Tel: (01276) 22895
Head: Mr R L Cunliffe
Type: Co-educational Day 2–12
No of pupils: B132 G72
Fees: (September 01) Day £2040 – £4890
Special Needs: Level 2: DYS Level 3: EPI HI SP&LD SPLD VIS

MARYMOUNT INTERNATIONAL SCHOOL
George Road, Kingston-upon-Thames, Surrey KT2 7PE
Tel: (020) 8949 0571
Head: Sister R Sheridan
Type: Girls Day and Boarding 11–18
No of pupils: 200
No of Boarders: F73 W8
Fees: (September 01)
FB £17300 – £18370
WB £17060 – £18130
Day £9630 – £10700
Special Needs: Level 2: ADD DYS MLD SPLD

NOTRE DAME SCHOOL
Lingfield, Surrey RH7 6PH
Tel: (01342) 833176
Head: Mrs N E Shepley
Type: Co-educational Day 2–18
No of pupils: B312 G374
Fees: (September 01) Day £3540 – £6015
Special Needs: Level 2: DYS

NOWER LODGE SCHOOL
Coldharbour Lane, Dorking, Surrey RH4 3BT
Tel: (01306) 882448
Head: Mrs S Watt
Type: Co-educational Day 3–11
No of pupils: B104 G60
Fees: (September 01) Day £4740 – £5475
Special Needs: Level 2: ADD DYC DYP DYS PH Unspecified: W

OAKHYRST GRANGE SCHOOL
160 Stanstead Road, Caterham, Surrey CR3 6AF
Tel: (01883) 343344
Head: Mr N J E Jones
Type: Co-educational Day 2–11
No of pupils: B117 G35
Fees: (September 01) Day £750 – £4080
Special Needs: Level 2: DYP DYS SP&LD

OLD PALACE SCHOOL OF JOHN WHITGIFT
Old Palace Road, Croydon, Surrey CR0 1AX
Tel: (020) 8688 2027
Head: Mrs J Hancock
Type: Girls Day 4–18
No of pupils: 850
Fees: (September 01) Day £4719 – £6348
Special Needs: Level 3: ADD ADHD ASP DYC DYP DYS EPI HI PH SPLD

OLD VICARAGE SCHOOL
48 Richmond Hill, Richmond, Surrey TW10 6QX
Tel: (020) 8940 0922
Head: Mrs J Harrison
Type: Girls Day 4–11
No of pupils: G168
Fees: (September 01) Day £4794 – £5328
Special Needs: Unspecified: DYS

PARKSIDE SCHOOL
The Manor, Stoke D'Abernon,
Cobham, Surrey KT11 3PX
Tel: (01932) 862749
Head: Mr D Aylward
Type: Boys Day and Boarding 4–14
(Co-ed 2–5)
No of pupils: B390 G30
No of Boarders: W10
Fees: (September 02) WB £10341
Day £5064 – £7611
Special Needs: Level 2: DYS

PARSONS MEAD
Ottways Lane, Ashtead, Surrey
KT21 2PE
Tel: (01372) 276401
Head: Mrs P M Taylor
Type: Girls Day 3–18
No of pupils: G300 No of Boarders: W2
Fees: (September 01)
WB £9954 – £12990
Day £4485 – £7521
Special Needs: Unspecified: DYS HI

PRIOR'S FIELD SCHOOL
Priorsfield Road, Godalming, Surrey
GU7 2RH
Tel: (01483) 810551
Head: Mrs J Dwyer
Type: Girls Boarding and Day 11–18
No of pupils: G300
No of Boarders: F45 W50
Fees: (September 01) F/WB £13980
Day £9348
Special Needs: Level 2: DYP DYS HI

REIGATE ST MARY'S PREPARATORY AND CHOIR SCHOOL
Chart Lane, Reigate, Surrey RH2 7RN
Tel: (01737) 244880
Head: Mr D T Tidmarsh
Type: Co-educational Day 3–13
No of pupils: B155 G28
Fees: (September 01) Day £1155 –
£5823
Special Needs: Unspecified: DYS

ROYAL RUSSELL SCHOOL
Coombe Lane, Croydon, Surrey
CR9 5BX
Tel: (020) 8657 4433
Head: Dr J R Jennings
Type: Co-educational Boarding and
Day 3–18
No of pupils: B497 G274
No of Boarders: F95 W35
Fees: (September 01) F/WB £13444
Day £4170 – £7050
Special Needs: Level 2: DYC DYP DYS

ST ANDREW'S SCHOOL
Church Hill House, Wilson Way,
Horsell, Woking, Surrey GU21 4QW
Tel: (01483) 760943
Head: Mr B Pretorius
Type: Co-educational Day 3–13
No of pupils: 267
Fees: (September 01) Day £4065 –
£7905
Special Needs: Level 2: DYS MLD

ST CATHERINE'S SCHOOL
Park Road, Camberley, Surrey
GU15 2LL
Tel: (01276) 23511
Head: Mr R W Burt and Mrs H M Burt
Type: Girls Day 2–11 (Boys 2–5)
No of pupils: B7 G101
Fees: (September 01) Day £2062 –
£5385
Special Needs: Level 2: ADD DYS EBD
MLD SPLD

ST CATHERINE'S SCHOOL
Station Road, Bramley, Guildford,
Surrey GU5 0DF
Tel: (01483) 893363
Head: Mrs A M Phillips
Type: Girls Day and Boarding 4–18
No of pupils: G692
No of Boarders: F29 W101
Fees: (September 01)
F/WB £12405 – £13875
Day £4230 – £8445
Special Needs: Level 2: ADD DYC
DYP DYS

ST DAVID'S SCHOOL
23 Woodcote Valley Road, Purley,
Surrey CR8 3AL
Tel: (020) 8660 0723
Head: Mrs L Nash
Type: Co-educational Day 3–11
No of pupils: B83 G84
Fees: (September 01) Day £1875 –
£3510
Special Needs: Level 3: ADD DYC
DYP DYS SPLD

ST HILARY'S SCHOOL
Holloway Hill, Godalming, Surrey
GU7 1RZ
Tel: (01483) 416551
Head: Mrs S Bailes
Type: Co-educational Day Boys 2–8
Girls 2–11
No of pupils: B110 G298
Fees: (September 01) Day £4290 –
£6600
Special Needs: Level 2: ADD DYP DYS
SP&LD

ST TERESA'S SCHOOL
Effingham Hill, Dorking, Surrey
RH5 6ST
Tel: (01372) 452037
Head: Mrs M Prescott
Type: Girls Boarding and Day 11–18
No of pupils: G475
No of Boarders: F55 W20
Fees: (September 01) FB £13950
WB £13050 Day £7950
Special Needs: Level 2: DYS
Level 3: DYP EPI HI PH Unspecified:
ADD ADHD ASP AUT CP DEL DOW
DYC EBD MLD PMLD SLD SP&LD
SPLD TOU VIS

ST TERESA'S PREPARATORY SCHOOL
Grove House, Guildford Road,
Effingham, Surrey KT24 5QA
Tel: (01372) 453456
Head: Mrs A Stewart
Type: Girls Day and Boarding 2–11
No of pupils: G160
No of Boarders: F6 W2
Fees: (September 01) FB £12150
WB £11250 Day £1680 – £2050
Special Needs: Level 2: ADD ADHD
DYC DYP DYS SPLD Level 3: ASP
DEL HI PH SP&LD VIS

SHREWSBURY HOUSE SCHOOL
107 Ditton Road, Surbiton, Surrey
KT6 6RL
Tel: (020) 8399 3066
Head: Mr C M Ross
Type: Boys Day 7–13
No of pupils: B280
Fees: (September 01) Day £7725
Special Needs: Level 3: DYS HI VIS

SIR WILLIAM PERKINS'S SCHOOL
Guildford Road, Chertsey, Surrey
KT16 9BN
Tel: (01932) 562161
Head: Miss S Ross
Type: Girls Day 11–18
No of pupils: G580
Fees: (September 01) Day £6645
Special Needs: Level 3: CP DYS HI

STANWAY SCHOOL
Chichester Road, Dorking, Surrey
RH4 1LR
Tel: (01306) 882151
Head: Mr P H Rushforth
Type: Girls Day 3–11 (Boys 3–8)
No of pupils: B32 G118
Fees: (September 01) Day £900 –
£5655
Special Needs: Level 1: DYS

THE STUDY SCHOOL
57 Thetford Road, New Malden,
Surrey KT3 5DP
Tel: (020) 8942 0754
Head: Mrs S Mallin
Type: Co-educational Day 3–11
No of pupils: B73 G67
Fees: (September 01) Day £800 –
£1739
Special Needs: Level 2: DYS SPLD
Level 3: ADD ADHD DYC DYP EBD
HI

SURBITON HIGH SCHOOL
Surbiton Crescent, Kingston-upon-
Thames, Surrey KT1 2JT
Tel: (020) 8546 5245
Head: Dr D J Longhurst
Type: Girls Day 4–18 (Boys 4–11)
No of pupils: B140 G965
Fees: (September 01) Day £4275 –
£7239
Special Needs: Level 2: ADD ADHD
ASP DYP DYS EBD EPI HI SPLD VIS

SURBITON PREPARATORY SCHOOL
3 Avenue Elmers, Surbiton, Surrey
KT6 4SP
Tel: (020) 8546 5245
Head: Mr S J Pryce
Type: Boys Day 4–11
No of pupils: B140
Fees: (September 01) Day £4275 –
£5940
Special Needs: Level 2: ADHD ASP
DYP DYS SPLD Level 3: ADD

SURREY COLLEGE
Administration Centre, Abbot
House, Sydenham Road, Guildford,
Surrey GU1 3RL
Tel: (01483) 565887
Head: Ms L Cody
Type: Co-educational Day 14+
No of pupils: B60 G50
Fees: (September 01) Day £4500 –
£10200
Special Needs: Unspecified: DYS

TORMEAD SCHOOL
27 Cranley Road, Guildford, Surrey
GUI 2JD
Tel: (01483) 575101
Head: Mrs S Marks
Type: Girls Day 4–18
No of pupils: G722
Fees: (September 01) Day £3360 –
£7170
Special Needs: Level 2: DYS

UNICORN SCHOOL*
238 Kew Road, Richmond, Surrey
TW9 3JX
Tel: (020) 8948 3926
Head: Mrs F Timmis
Type: Co-educational Day 3–11
No of pupils: B84 G84
Fees: (September 01) Day £3150 –
£5790
Special Needs: Level 2: DYS

WESTON GREEN SCHOOL
Weston Green Road, Thames Ditton,
Surrey KT7 0JN
Tel: (020) 8398 2778
Head: Mrs J Winser
Type: Co-educational Day 2–8
No of pupils: 180
Fees: (September 01) Day £2550 –
£4500
Special Needs: Unspecified: DYS

WOODCOTE HOUSE SCHOOL
Snows Ride, Windlesham, Surrey
GU20 6PF
Tel: (01276) 472115
Head: Mr N H K Paterson
Type: Boys Boarding and Day 7–14
No of pupils: 100 *No of Boarders:* F75
Fees: (September 01) FB £10425
Day £7350
Special Needs: Level 2: ADD ADHD
ASP DYC DYP DYS MLD SPLD
Level 3: AUT EBD

EAST SUSSEX

ASHDOWN HOUSE SCHOOL
Forest Row, East Sussex RH18 5JY
Tel: (01342) 822574
Head: Mr A J Fowler-Watt
Type: Co-educational Boarding 8–13
No of pupils: B154 G72
No of Boarders: F219
Fees: (September 01) FB £11985
Special Needs: Level 3: DYC DYS

BATTLE ABBEY SCHOOL
High Street, Battle, East Sussex
TN33 0AD
Tel: (01424) 772385
Head: Mr R Clark
Type: Co-educational Boarding and
Day 2–18
No of pupils: B117 G153
No of Boarders: F54
Fees: (September 01)
F/WB £10401 – £12864
Day £4374 – £7971
Special Needs: Level 2: DYC DYP DYS
SPLD

BODIAM MANOR SCHOOL†
Bodiam, Robertsbridge, East Sussex
TN32 5UJ
Tel: (01580) 830225
Head: Mr C Moore
Type: Co-educational Day 2–13
No of pupils: B95 G96
Fees: (September 01) Day £3063 –
£6324
Special Needs: Level 2: DYS

BRICKLEHURST MANOR PREPARATORY
Stonegate, Wadhurst, East Sussex
TN5 7EL
Tel: (01580) 200448
Head: Mrs C Flowers
Type: Co-educational Day Boys 3–8
Girls 3–11
No of pupils: B28 G98
Fees: (September 01) Day £4995 –
£5250
Special Needs: Unspecified: DYP DYS

BRIGHTON COLLEGE PREP SCHOOL
Walpole Lodge, Walpole Road,
Brighton, East Sussex BN2 2EU
Tel: (01273) 704210
Head: Mr B Melia and Mrs H Beeby
Type: Co-educational Boarding and
Day 3–13
No of pupils: 509 *No of Boarders:* W2
Fees: (September 01)
WB £8388 – £10299
Day £1311 – £8685
Special Needs: Level 2: DYS

EASTBOURNE COLLEGE
Old Wish Road, Eastbourne,
East Sussex BN21 4JX
Tel: (01323) 452323
Head: Mr C M P Bush
Type: Co-educational Boarding and
Day 13–18
No of pupils: B348 G179
No of Boarders: F283
Fees: (September 01) FB £16545
Day £10695
Special Needs: Level 2: DYS

MOIRA HOUSE JUNIOR SCHOOL
Upper Carlisle Road, Eastbourne,
East Sussex BN20 7TE
Tel: (01323) 644144
Head: Mrs J Booth-Clibborn
Type: Girls Day and Boarding 2–11
No of pupils: 110 *No of Boarders:* F3
Fees: (September 01) FB £11850
WB £10800 Day £3855 – £7140
Special Needs: Unspecified: DYP DYS

MOIRA HOUSE GIRLS' SCHOOL
Upper Carlisle Road, Eastbourne,
East Sussex BN20 7TE
Tel: (01323) 644144
Head: Mrs A Harris
Type: Girls Boarding and Day 11–18
No of pupils: 220
No of Boarders: F100 W6
Fees: (September 01) FB £13050 –
£15300 WB £11400 – £13650
Day £7710 – £9090
Special Needs: Level 1: EBD
Level 2: DYP DYS

NEWLANDS MANOR SCHOOL†
Sutton Place, Seaford, East Sussex
BN25 3PL
Tel: (01323) 892334 / 490000
Head: Mr O T Price
Type: Boys Boarding and Day 13–18
No of pupils: B125 G66
No of Boarders: F95
Fees: (September 01)
FB £12630 – £14100 WB £12465
Day £7815 – £8145
Special Needs: Level 2: DYC DYP DYS
SPLD

NEWLANDS PREPARATORY SCHOOL†
Eastbourne Road, Seaford,
East Sussex BN25 4NP
Tel: (01323) 892334 / 490000
Head: Mr O T Price
Type: Co-educational Boarding and
Day 2–13
No of pupils: B157 G122
No of Boarders: F58 W2
Fees: (September 01)
FB £10800 – £11550 WB £1140
Day £3510 – £7185
Special Needs: Level 2: DYC DYP DYS
SPLD

ST ANDREW'S SCHOOL
Meads, Eastbourne, East Sussex
BN20 7RP
Tel: (01323) 733203
Head: Mr F Roche
Type: Co-educational Boarding and
Day 3–13
No of pupils: B278 G178
No of Boarders: F28 W16
Fees: (September 01) FB £11910
WB £10890 Day £3390 – £8370
Special Needs: Level 2: DYS SP&LD
SPLD Level 3: ADD ADHD ASP CP
DEL DYC DYP EPI HI

ST AUBYNS
High Street, Rottingdean, Brighton,
East Sussex BNZ 7JN
Tel: (01273) 302170
Head: Mr A G Gobat
Type: Co-educational Boarding and
Day 4–13
No of pupils: B135 G45
No of Boarders: F16 W18
Fees: (September 01) FB £11985
Day £3750 – £9135
Special Needs: Level 2: ADD DYC
DYP DYS SP&LD SPLD

ST BEDE'S
Duke's Drive, Eastbourne,
East Sussex BN20 7XL
Tel: (01323) 734222
Head: Mr C P Pyemont
Type: Co-educational Boarding and
Day 2–13
No of pupils: B280 G150
No of Boarders: F60
Fees: (September 01) F/WB £11520
Day £4905 – £8040
Special Needs: Level 2: ADD ADHD
ASP AUT DEL DYC DYP DYS EBD
MLD PH SP&LD SPLD

ST LEONARDS-MAYFIELD SCHOOL
The Old Palace, Mayfield,
East Sussex TN20 6PH
Tel: (01435) 874614
Head: Mrs J Dalton
Type: Girls Boarding and Day 11–18
No of pupils: G383
No of Boarders: F135 W53
Fees: (September 01) F/WB £15120
Day £9840
Special Needs: Level 1: DYP DYS
SPLD Level 3: HI PH VIS Unspecified:
EPI

SKIPPERS HILL MANOR PREPARATORY SCHOOL
Five Ashes, Mayfield, East Sussex
TN20 6HR
Tel: (01825) 830234
Head: Mr T W Lewis
Type: Co-educational Day 2–13
No of pupils: B98 G60
Fees: (September 01) Day £2256 –
£7755
Special Needs: Level 2: DYS

STONELANDS SCHOOL OF BALLET & THEATRE ARTS
170A Church Road, Hove,
East Sussex BN3 2DJ
Tel: (01273) 770445
Head: Mrs D Carteur
Type: Co-educational Boarding and
Day 5–16
No of pupils: B6 G36
No of Boarders: F10 W10
Fees: (September 01) FB £9825
Day £5520
Special Needs: Level 3: DEL DYS EBD
EPI

TEMPLE GROVE
Heron's Ghyll, Uckfield, East Sussex
TN22 4DA
Tel: (01825) 712112
Head: Mr M H Kneath
Type: Co-educational Boarding and
Day 3–13
No of pupils: B75 G75
No of Boarders: F10
Fees: (September 01) FB £8820 –
£10050 Day £5475 – £7680
Special Needs: Unspecified: DYP DYS
MLD

VINEHALL SCHOOL
Robertsbridge, East Sussex TN32 5JL
Tel: (01580) 880413
Head: Mr D C Chaplin
Type: Co-educational Boarding and
Day 2–13
No of pupils: B248 G150
No of Boarders: F75
Fees: (September 01) FB £11007
Day £4791 – £8463
Special Needs: Level 2: DYS
Unspecified: W

WEST SUSSEX

ARDINGLY COLLEGE
Haywards Heath, West Sussex
RH17 6SQ
Tel: (01444) 892577
Head: Mr J R Franklin
Type: Co-educational Boarding and
Day 13–18
No of pupils: B239 G171
No of Boarders: F253
Fees: (September 01)
FB £11145 – £16125
Day £6000 – £12075
Special Needs: Level 2: DYS
Level 3: ADD ADHD EPI HI PH

ARUNDALE PREPARATORY SCHOOL
Lower Street, Pulborough,
West Sussex RH20 2BX
Tel: (01798) 872520
Head: Miss K Lovejoy
Type: Co-educational Day Boys 2–8
Girls 2–11
No of pupils: B24 G84
Fees: (September 01) Day £1794 –
£5610
Special Needs: Level 2: DYS

BROADWATER MANOR SCHOOL
Broadwater Road, Worthing,
West Sussex BN14 8HU
Tel: (01903) 201123
Head: Mrs E K Woodley
Type: Co-educational Day 2–13
No of pupils: B203 G154
Fees: (September 01) Day £399 –
£4770
Special Needs: Level 2: ADD ADHD
ASP DYP DYS

COPTHORNE SCHOOL
Effingham Lane, Copthorne,
West Sussex RH10 3HR
Tel: (01342) 712311
Head: Mr G C Allen
Type: Co-educational Day and
Boarding 2–13
No of pupils: B150 G104
No of Boarders: W10
Fees: (September 01) WB £9285
Day £4425 – £8025
Special Needs: Level 2: DYC DYP DYS
Level 3: ADD ADHD HI SPLD

FONTHILL LODGE
Coombe Hill Road, East Grinstead,
West Sussex RH9 4LY
Tel: (01342) 321635
Head: Mrs J Griffiths
Type: Co-educational Day 2–11
(Single sex education 8–11)
No of pupils: B127 G115
Fees: (September 01) Day £775 –
£2230
Special Needs: Level 2: DYS
Unspecified: W

GREAT BALLARD SCHOOL
Eartham, Chichester, West Sussex
PO18 0LR
Tel: (01243) 814236
Head: Mr R E Jennings
Type: Co-educational Boarding and
Day 2–13
No of pupils: B103 G97
No of Boarders: F5 W29
Fees: (September 01) F/WB £9789
Day £1623 – £7314
Special Needs: Level 2: DYC DYP DYS
EBD SP&LD SPLD Level 3: ADD DEL
HI PH VIS

LAVANT HOUSE ROSEMEAD
Chichester, West Sussex PO18 9AB
Tel: (01243) 527211
Head: Mrs M Scott
Type: Girls Day and Boarding 4–18
No of pupils: G150
No of Boarders: F10 W10
Fees: (September 02)
F/WB £9525 – £13395
Day £3825 – £7695
Special Needs: Level 2: DYC DYP
DYS SPLD Level 3: ADD ASP CP DEL
EBD EPI HI PH SP&LD VIS
Unspecified: W

OAKWOOD SCHOOL
Oakwood, Chichester, West Sussex
PO18 9AN
Tel: (01243) 575209
Head: Mr A H Cowell
Type: Co-educational Boarding and
Day 2–11
No of pupils: B118 G112
No of Boarders: W12
Fees: (September 01) WB £8580
Day £2100 – £6426
Special Needs: Level 2: DYC DYP DYS

PENNTHORPE SCHOOL
Rudgwick, Horsham, West Sussex
RH12 3HJ
Tel: (01403) 822391
Head: Mr S Moll
Type: Co-educational Day 2–14
No of pupils: B187 G95
Fees: (September 01) Day £780 –
£7680
Special Needs: Level 1: DYS MLD
SPLD

SANDHURST SCHOOL
101 Brighton Road, Worthing,
West Sussex BN11 2EL
Tel: (01903) 201933
Head: Mrs S A Hale
Type: Co-educational Day 2–13
No of pupils: B85 G94
Fees: (September 01) Day £2118 –
£2472
Special Needs: Level 2: DYS

SLINDON COLLEGE†
Slindon House, Slindon, Arundel,
West Sussex BN18 0RH
Tel: (01243) 814320
Head: Mr I P Graham
Type: Boys Boarding and Day 10–16
No of pupils: B100
No of Boarders: F20 W30
Fees: (September 01) F/WB £12840
Day £7935
Special Needs: Level 2: ADD ADHD
DYC DYS SPLD Level 3: DEL DYP
EPI

STOKE BRUNSWICK
Ashurstwood, East Grinstead,
West Sussex RH19 3PF
Tel: (01342) 828200
Head: Mr W M Ellerton
Type: Co-educational Boarding and
Day 3–13
No of pupils: B100 G55
No of Boarders: W10
Fees: (September 01) WB £10215
Day £2235 – £8430
Special Needs: Level 1: DYP DYS

WORTH SCHOOL
Turners Hill, West Sussex RH10 4SD
Tel: (01342) 710200
Head: Fr C Jamison
Type: Boys Boarding and Day 11–18
No of pupils: B428
No of Boarders: F301
Fees: (September 01)
FB £14394 – £15993
Day £10602 – £11778
Special Needs: Level 2: ADD ADHD
DYP DYS Unspecified: MLD

TYNE AND WEAR

ASCHAM HOUSE SCHOOL
30 West Avenue, Gosforth,
Newcastle upon Tyne,
Tyne and Wear NE3 4ES
Tel: (0191) 285 1619
Head: Mr S H Reid
Type: Boys Day 3–13
No of pupils: 270
Fees: (September 01) Day £4800
Special Needs: Level 2: DYC DYP DYS

CENTRAL NEWCASTLE HIGH
SCHOOL GDST
Eskdale Terrace,
Newcastle upon Tyne,
Tyne and Wear NE2 4DS
Tel: (0191) 281 1768
Head: Mrs L J Griffin
Type: Girls Day 3–18
No of pupils: 994
Fees: (September 01) Day £3174 –
£5442
Special Needs: Level 3: DYS

WARWICKSHIRE

ABBOTSFORD SCHOOL
Bridge Street, Kenilworth,
Warwickshire CV8 1BP
Tel: (01926) 852826
Head: Mrs J Adams
Type: Co-educational Day 3–11
No of pupils: B93 G64
Fees: (September 01) On application
Special Needs: Level 2: DEL DYP DYS

BILTON GRANGE
Dunchurch, Rugby, Warwickshire
CV22 6QU
Tel: (01788) 810217
Head: Mr Q G Edwards
Type: Co-educational Boarding and
Day 4–13
No of pupils: B234 G148
No of Boarders: F48 W24
Fees: (September 01) F/WB £11397
Day £7959 – £9096
Special Needs: Level 2: DYP DYS

THE CRESCENT SCHOOL
Bawnmore Road, Bilton, Rugby,
Warwickshire CV22 7QH
Tel: (01788) 521595
Head: Mrs C Vickers
Type: Co-educational Day 2–11
No of pupils: B89 G95
Fees: (September 01) Day £4035 –
£4320
Special Needs: Level 2: ADD ADHD
ASP DYS SPLD Level 3: AUT DYC
DYP EBD HI PH SP&LD

EMSCOTE HOUSE SCHOOL AND NURSERY

46 Warwick Place, Leamington Spa, Warwickshire CV32 5DE
Tel: (01926) 425067
Head: Mrs G J Andrews
Type: Co-educational Day 2–7
No of pupils: B53 G42
Fees: (September 01) Day £700 – £3900
Special Needs: Level 2: DYS MLD

THE KINGSLEY SCHOOL

Beauchamp Avenue, Leamington Spa, Warwickshire CV32 5RD
Tel: (01926) 425127
Head: Mrs C Mannion Watson
Type: Girls Day 2–18 (Boys 2–7)
No of pupils: B12 G582
Fees: (September 01) Day £3825 – £6570
Special Needs: Level 2: DYS SPLD

WEST MIDLANDS

BIRCHFIELD SCHOOL

Albrighton, Wolverhampton, West Midlands WV7 3AF
Tel: (01902) 372534
Head: Mr R P Merriman
Type: Boys Boarding and Day 3–13
No of pupils: 243 *No of Boarders:* W20
Fees: (September 01) WB £8850 Day £4200 – £6600
Special Needs: Level 1: ADD DYC DYP DYS SPLD Level 2: SP&LD Level 3: PH

DAVENPORT LODGE SCHOOL

21 Davenport Road, Earlsdon, Coventry, West Midlands CV5 6QA
Tel: (024) 7667 5051
Head: Mrs M D Martin
Type: Co-educational Day 2–8
No of pupils: B88 G67
Fees: (September 01) On application
Special Needs: Level 2: DYS MLD Unspecified: SP&LD

HALLFIELD SCHOOL

48 Church Road, Edgbaston, Birmingham, West Midlands B15 3SJ
Tel: (0121) 454 1496
Head: Mr J G Cringle
Type: Co-educational Day 2–11
No of pupils: B327 G130
Fees: (September 01) Day £4065 – £6150
Special Needs: Level 2: DYS

KING EDWARD'S SCHOOL

Edgbaston Park Road, Birmingham, West Midlands B15 2UA
Tel: (0121) 472 1672
Head: Mr R M Dancey
Type: Boys Day 11–18
No of pupils: B889
Fees: (September 01) Day £6216
Special Needs: Level 2: ADD ASP DYS Level 3: DYP EPI HI PH

KINGSLEY PREPARATORY SCHOOL

53 Hanbury Road, Dorridge, Solihull, West Midlands B93 8DW
Tel: (01564) 774144
Head: Mrs J A Scott
Type: Co-educational Day 3–11
No of pupils: B20 G20
Fees: (September 01) Day £4500
Special Needs: Level 1: ADD ASP DYP DYS MLD SP&LD SPLD TOU Level 3: DEL HI PH Unspecified: W

MAYFIELD PREPARATORY SCHOOL

Sutton Road, Walsall, West Midlands WS1 2PD
Tel: (01922) 624107
Head: Mrs C M Jones
Type: Co-educational Day 3–11
No of pupils: B108 G88
Fees: (September 01) Day £4185
Special Needs: Level 3: ADD ADHD ASP AUT CP DEL DOW DYC DYP DYS EBD EPI HI MLD PH PMLD SLD SP&LD SPLD TOU VIS

PRIORY SCHOOL

39 Sir Harry's Road, Edgbaston, Birmingham, West Midlands B15 2UR
Tel: (0121) 440 4103
Head: Mrs E C Brook
Type: Girls Day 2–18 (Boys 2–11)
No of pupils: B61 G250
Fees: (September 01) Day £3630 – £5985
Special Needs: Level 2: DYC DYP DYS Level 3: ADD DEL

RUCKLEIGH SCHOOL

17 Lode Lane, Solihull, West Midlands B91 2AB
Tel: (0121) 705 2773
Head: Mrs B M Forster
Type: Co-educational Day 2–11
No of pupils: B119 G101
Fees: (September 01) Day £2430 – £4761
Special Needs: Level 2: DYS

TETTENHALL COLLEGE

Wood Road, Wolverhampton, West Midlands WV6 8QX
Tel: (01902) 751119
Head: Dr P C Bodkin
Type: Co-educational Boarding and Day 7–18
No of pupils: B225 G124
No of Boarders: F73 W12
Fees: (September 01) FB £10104 – £12306 WB £8199 – £10239 Day £5901 – £7374
Special Needs: Level 2: DYC DYP DYS SPLD

WEST HOUSE SCHOOL

24 St James's Road, Edgbaston, Birmingham, West Midlands B15 2NX
Tel: (0121) 440 4097
Head: Mr G K Duce
Type: Boys Day 1–11 (Girls 1–4)
No of pupils: B220 G20
Fees: (September 01) Day £1089 – £6396
Special Needs: Level 2: DYS MLD

WOLVERHAMPTON GRAMMAR SCHOOL
Compton Road, Wolverhampton,
West Midlands WV3 9RB
Tel: (01902) 421326
Head: Dr B Trafford
Type: Co-educational Day 11–18
No of pupils: B457 G282
Fees: (September 01) Day £6795
Special Needs: Level 1: DYS
Level 3: DYP HI

WILTSHIRE

LA RETRAITE SWAN
Campbell Road, Salisbury, Wiltshire
SP1 3BQ
Tel: (01722) 333094
Head: Mrs R A Simmons
Type: Co-educational Day 2–16
No of pupils: B130 G130
Fees: (September 01) Day £3750 –
£6600
Special Needs: Level 2: DYP DYS
Level 3: ADD DEL

MEADOWPARK NURSERY & PRE-PREP
Calcutt Street, Cricklade, Wiltshire
SN6 6BB
Tel: (01793) 752600
Head: Mrs R Kular and Mrs S
Hanbury
Type: Co-educational Day 1–7
No of pupils: B51 G39
Fees: (September 01) Day £4170
Special Needs: Level 2: DYS
Unspecified: W

NORMAN COURT PREPARATORY SCHOOL
West Tytherley, Salisbury, Wiltshire
SP5 1NH
Tel: (01980) 862345
Head: Mr K N Foyle
Type: Co-educational Boarding and
Day 3–13
No of pupils: B118 G172
No of Boarders: F22 W42
Fees: (September 01)
F/WB £10563 – £11409
Day £4290 – £8529
Special Needs: Level 2: DYC DYP DYS
MLD SPLD TOU

SALISBURY CATHEDRAL SCHOOL
1 The Close, Salisbury, Wiltshire
SP1 2EQ
Tel: (01722) 555300
Head: Mr R M Thackray
Type: Co-educational Day and
Boarding 3–13
No of pupils: B129 G113
No of Boarders: F50
Fees: (September 01) FB £11775
Day £2775 – £8025
Special Needs: Level 2: DYS EBD
SPLD Unspecified: ADHD DYC

SANDROYD
Tollard Royal, Salisbury, Wiltshire
SP5 5QD
Tel: (01725) 516264
Head: Mr M J Hatch
Type: Boys Boarding 7–13 (day places
7–11)
No of pupils: B150 *No of Boarders:* F110
Fees: (September 01)
FB £9975 – £12300
Day £7200 – £10200
Special Needs: Level 2: DYP DYS
SPLD

STONAR SCHOOL
Cottles Park, Atworth, Melksham,
Wiltshire SN12 8NT
Tel: (01225) 702795/702309
Head: Mrs S Hopkinson
Type: Girls Boarding and Day 4–18
No of pupils: G400 *No of Boarders:* F200
Fees: (September 01)
F/WB £10881 – £12594
Day £3102 – £6996
Special Needs: Level 1: EBD EPI
Level 2: DYC DYP DYS HI SPLD
Level 3: VIS

STOURBRIDGE HOUSE SCHOOL
Castle Street, Mere, Warminster,
Wiltshire BA12 6JQ
Tel: (01747) 860165
Head: Mrs E Coward
Type: Co-educational Day 2–9
No of pupils: B25 G25
Fees: (September 01) Day £3075 –
£3228
Special Needs: Level 2: ADD ADHD
DEL DYP DYS MLD SPLD

WORCESTERSHIRE

BOWBROOK HOUSE SCHOOL
Peopleton, Pershore, Worcestershire
WR10 2EE
Tel: (01905) 841242
Head: Mr S W Jackson
Type: Co-educational Day 3–16
No of pupils: B85 G54
Fees: (September 01) Day £2763 –
£4875
Special Needs: Level 2: ADD ADHD
ASP DYP DYS

THE DOWNS SCHOOL
Colwall, Malvern, Worcestershire
WR13 6EY
Tel: (01684) 540277
Head: Mr A Ramsay
Type: Co-educational Boarding and
Day 3–13
No of pupils: B70 G70
No of Boarders: F10 W13
Fees: (September 01) FB £10560
WB £10320 Day £2460 – £7620
Special Needs: Level 2: DYP DYS
Level 3: ADD ADHD HI Unspecified:
MLD

THE ELMS
Colwall, Malvern, Worcestershire
WR13 6EF
Tel: (01684) 540344
Head: Mr L A C Ashby
Type: Co-educational Boarding and
Day 3–13
No of pupils: B96 G74
No of Boarders: F83
Fees: (September 01) FB £10560
Day £3900 – £9240
Special Needs: Level 2: ADD ASP AUT
DYP DYS MLD

THE GRANGE
Royal Grammar School Worcester
Pre-Prep, Grange Lane, Claines,
Worcester WR3 7RR
Tel: (01905) 451205
Head: Mrs M Windsor
Type: Co-educational Day 3–8
No of pupils: B130 G70
Fees: (September 01) Day £3276 –
£4152
Special Needs: Level 2: DYP DYS EBD
MLD

THE KING'S SCHOOL
Worcester WR1 2LH
Tel: (01905) 721700
Head: Mr T H Keyes
Type: Co-educational Day 7–18
No of pupils: B581 G376
Fees: (September 01) Day £4305 –
£6681
Special Needs: Level 2: DYS

MALVERN COLLEGE
College Road, Malvern,
Worcestershire WR14 3DF
Tel: (01684) 581500
Head: Mr H C K Carson
Type: Co-educational Boarding and
Day 13–18
No of pupils: 539
Fees: (September 01)
FB £11115 – £17250
Day £6855 – £11085
Special Needs: Level 2: DYC DYP DYS
SPLD Level 3: ADD

MALVERN GIRLS' COLLEGE
Avenue Road, Malvern,
Worcestershire WR14 3BA
Tel: (01684) 892288
Head: Mrs P M C Leggate
Type: Girls Boarding and Day 11–18
No of pupils: G410
No of Boarders: F330
Fees: (September 01) FB £17175
Day £11400
Special Needs: Level 2: DYS MLD
SPLD

MOUNT SCHOOL
Birmingham Road, Bromsgrove,
Worcestershire B61 0EP
Tel: (01527) 877772
Head: Mr S A Robinson
Type: Co-educational Day 3–11
No of pupils: B82 G68
Fees: (September 01) Day £3285 –
£4485
Special Needs: Level 2: DYS SPLD

ST JAMES'S SCHOOL†
West Malvern, Malvern,
Worcestershire WR14 4DF
Tel: (01684) 560851
Head: Mrs S Kershaw
Type: Girls Boarding and Day 10–18
No of pupils: G128
No of Boarders: F45 W40
Fees: (September 01)
F/WB £14985 – £16050
Day £7425 – £9855
Special Needs: Level 1: DYP DYS
SPLD Level 2: ASP DYC Level 3: DEL
EPI HI

WINTERFOLD HOUSE
Chaddesley Corbett, Kidderminster,
Worcestershire DY10 4PL
Tel: (01562) 777234
Head: Mr W C R Ibbetson-Price
Type: Co-educational Day 3–13
No of pupils: B220 G90
Fees: (September 01) Day £3675 –
£6750
Special Needs: Level 2: DYC DYP DYS
SPLD Level 3: EPI HI

EAST RIDING OF YORKSHIRE

HESSLE MOUNT SCHOOL
Jenny Brough Lane, Hessle,
East Riding of Yorkshire HU13 0JX
Tel: (01482) 643371/641948
Head: Mrs Cutting
Type: Co-educational Day 3–8
No of pupils: 160
Fees: (September 01) Day £2640 –
£2880
Special Needs: Level 3: ADD ADHD
ASP AUT CP DEL DOW DYC DYP
DYS EBD EPI HI MLD PH PMLD SLD
SP&LD SPLD TOU VIS

HULL GRAMMAR SCHOOL
Cottingham Road,
Kingston-Upon-Hull,
East Riding of Yorkshire HU5 2DL
Tel: (01482) 440144
Head: Mr R Haworth
Type: Co-educational Boarding and
Day 2–18
No of pupils: B278 G170
No of Boarders: F7
Fees: (September 01) FB £11805
WB £10500 Day £2748 – £5304
Special Needs: Level 2: DYS
Level 3: ADHD

POCKLINGTON SCHOOL
West Green, Pocklington,
East Riding of Yorkshire YO42 2NJ
Tel: (01759) 303125
Head: Mr N Clements
Type: Co-educational Boarding and
Day 7–18
No of pupils: B418 G310
No of Boarders: F127
Fees: (September 01)
FB £10305 – £11970
Day £6090 – £7155
Special Needs: Level 2: DYS SPLD
Level 3: ADD ADHD ASP CP DYC
DYP EBD HI MLD PH SP&LD VIS
Unspecified: AUT DEL DOW EPI
PMLD SLD

NORTH YORKSHIRE

AMPLEFORTH COLLEGE
York, North Yorkshire YO62 4ER
Tel: (01439) 766000
Head: Rev G F L Chamberlain
Type: Co-educational Boarding and
Day Boys 13–18 Girls 16–18
No of pupils: B476 G19
No of Boarders: F467
Fees: (September 01) FB £16908
Day £8859
Special Needs: Level 2: ADD DYP DYS
MLD SPLD Level 3: DYC

ASHVILLE COLLEGE
Harrogate, North Yorkshire HG2 9JP
Tel: (01423) 566358
Head: Mr M H Crosby
Type: Co-educational Day and
Boarding 4–18
No of pupils: B507 G339
No of Boarders: F110 W30
Fees: (September 01)
F/WB £9837 – £11781
Day £3513 – £6330
Special Needs: Level 1: DYP DYS
SPLD Level 3: EPI Unspecified: PH

BOOTHAM SCHOOL
Bootham, York, North Yorkshire
YO30 7BU
Tel: (01904) 623261
Head: Mr I M Small
Type: Co-educational Boarding and
Day 11–18
No of pupils: B245 G175
No of Boarders: F80 W40
Fees: (September 01)
F/WB £9780 – £13596 Day £8889
Special Needs: Level 2: DYS
Level 3: DYP HI PH

BRAMCOTE SCHOOL
Filey Road, Scarborough, North
Yorkshire YO11 2TT
Tel: (01723) 373086
Head: Mr J P Kirk
Type: Co-educational Boarding and
Day 7–13
No of pupils: B60 G26
No of Boarders: F70
Fees: (September 01) FB £11340
Day £8130
Special Needs: Level 1: DYS MLD
SPLD Level 2: SP&LD Level 3: DYC
DYP

CATTERAL HALL
Giggleswick, Settle, North Yorkshire
BD24 0DG
Tel: (01729) 893100
Head: Mr R Hunter
Type: Co-educational Boarding and
Day 3–13
No of pupils: B100 G70
No of Boarders: F50
Fees: (September 01)
FB £10200 – £12000
Day £4113 – £8973
Special Needs: Level 2: ADD ADHD
DYC DYS SPLD Level 3: ASP DYP

CUNDALL MANOR SCHOOL
Helperby, York, North Yorkshire
YO6 2RW
Tel: (01423) 360200
Head: Mr P Phillips
Type: Co-educational Boarding and
Day 2–13
No of pupils: 110 *No of Boarders:* F20
Fees: (September 01) FB £10317
Day £4299 – £7134
Special Needs: Level 1: MLD
Level 2: DYP Unspecified: DYS

GIGGLESWICK SCHOOL
Giggleswick, Settle, North Yorkshire
BD24 0DE
Tel: (01729) 893000
Head: Mr G P Boult
Type: Co-educational Boarding and
Day 11–18
No of pupils: B214 G103
No of Boarders: F255
Fees: (September 01) FB £16443
Day £10911
Special Needs: Level 2: DYC DYP DYS
SPLD Level 3: ADD ADHD ASP DEL
EPI MLD PH

HARROGATE LADIES' COLLEGE
Clarence Drive, Harrogate,
North Yorkshire HG1 2QG
Tel: (01423) 504543
Head: Dr M J Hustler
Type: Girls Boarding and Day 10–18
No of pupils: 378
No of Boarders: F200 W24
Fees: (September 01) F/WB £13365
Day £8190
Special Needs: Level 2: DYS Level 3: HI

HARROGATE TUTORIAL COLLEGE
2 The Oval, Harrogate,
North Yorkshire HG2 9BA
Tel: (01423) 501041
Head: Mr K W Pollard
Type: Co-educational Day and
Boarding 15–20
No of pupils: B46 G44
No of Boarders: F20 W40
Fees: (September 01)
FB £9400 – £11750
WB £8400 – £9900
Day £7000 – £8500
Special Needs: Level 3: ADD DEL DYP
DYS PH

HIGHFIELD PREPARATORY SCHOOL
Clarence Drive, Harrogate,
North Yorkshire HG1 2QG
Tel: (01423) 504543
Head: Mrs P Fenwick and
Dr M J Hustler
Type: Co-educational Day 4–11
No of pupils: B33 G58
Fees: (September 01) Day £4170 –
£4485
Special Needs: Level 2: DYS

THE MOUNT SCHOOL
Dalton Terrace, York, North
Yorkshire YO24 4DD
Tel: (01904) 667500
Head: Mrs D J Gant
Type: Girls Boarding and Day 11–18
No of pupils: G244
No of Boarders: F60 W17
Fees: (September 01)
F/WB £9948 – £13680 Day £8580
Special Needs: Unspecified: DYS

QUEEN MARGARET'S SCHOOL
Escrick Park, York, North Yorkshire
YO19 6EU
Tel: (01904) 728261
Head: Dr G A H Chapman
Type: Girls Boarding and Day 11–18
No of pupils: G363
No of Boarders: F266 W60
Fees: (September 01) F/WB £14148
Day £8964
Special Needs: Level 2: DYS EBD
Level 3: EPI HI PH VIS

QUEEN MARY'S SCHOOL
Baldersby Park, Topcliffe, Thirsk,
North Yorkshire YO7 3BZ
Tel: (01845) 575000
Head: Mr I H Angus and
Mrs M A Angus
Type: Girls Boarding and Day 3–16
(Boys 3–7)
No of pupils: B15 G250
No of Boarders: F10 W55
Fees: (September 01)
F/WB £10650 – £12240
Day £2780 – £8340
Special Needs: Level 2: DYP DYS HI

READ SCHOOL
Drax, Selby, North Yorkshire
YO8 8NL
Tel: (01757) 618248
Head: Mr R Hadfield
Type: Co-educational Boarding and
Day 3–18
No of pupils: B146 G94
No of Boarders: F57 W4
Fees: (September 01)
FB £9795 – £11265
WB £9180 – £10560
Day £4680 – £5205
Special Needs: Unspecified: DYP DYS
PH SPLD

ST MARTIN'S AMPLEFORTH
Gilling Castle, Gilling East, York,
North Yorkshire YO62 4HP
Tel: (01439) 766600
Head: Mr S M Mullen
Type: Co-educational Boarding and
Day 3–13
No of pupils: B120 G60
No of Boarders: F78 W4
Fees: (September 01) F/WB £11895
Day £3270 – £6120
Special Needs: Level 2: DYP DYS
Level 3: EBD Unspecified: SPLD

ST PETER'S SCHOOL
York, North Yorkshire YO30 6AB
Tel: (01904) 623213
Head: Mr A F Trotman
Type: Co-educational Boarding and
Day 13–18
No of pupils: B314 G180
No of Boarders: F149
Fees: (September 01)
FB £13899 – £14271
Day £8094 – £8499
Special Needs: Level 2: DYS
Level 3: ADD DYP EPI

SCARBOROUGH COLLEGE
Filey Road, Scarborough,
North Yorkshire YO11 3BA
Tel: (01723) 360620
Head: Mr T L Kirkup
Type: Co-educational Boarding and
Day 3–18
No of pupils: B268 G241
No of Boarders: F28 W8
Fees: (September 01) F/WB £9150
Day £6495
Special Needs: Unspecified: DYP DYS
SPLD

TERRINGTON HALL
Terrington, York, North Yorkshire
YO60 6PR
Tel: (01653) 648227
Head: Mr J Glen
Type: Co-educational Boarding and
Day 3–13
No of pupils: B110 G70
No of Boarders: F32 W10
Fees: (September 01) F/WB £9750
Day £2985 – £7350
Special Needs: Level 2: DYC DYP DYS
SPLD

SOUTH YORKSHIRE

BIRKDALE SCHOOL*
Oakholme Road, Sheffield,
South Yorkshire S10 3DH
Tel: (0114) 266 8409
Head: Mr R J Court
Type: Boys Day 4–18 (Co-ed VIth
Form)
No of pupils: B752 G41
Fees: (September 01) Day £4380 –
£6225
Special Needs: Level 2: ADD DYP DYS
SPLD

HANDSWORTH CHRISTIAN SCHOOL
231 Handsworth Road, Handsworth,
Sheffield, South Yorkshire S13 9BJ
Tel: (0114) 243 0276
Head: Mrs P Arnott
Type: Co-educational Day 4–16
No of pupils: B55 G63
Fees: (September 01) Day £1860
Special Needs: Level 2: DYC DYS
Level 3: ADD ADHD DYP EBD HI PH
SP&LD SPLD

HILL HOUSE PREPARATORY SCHOOL
Rutland Street, Doncaster,
South Yorkshire DN1 2JD
Tel: (01302) 323563
Head: Mr J Cusworth
Type: Co-educational Day 3–13
No of pupils: B154 G110
Fees: (September 01) Day £4056 –
£5613
Special Needs: Level 2: DYP DYS
Level 3: EPI PH

ST MARY'S SCHOOL
65 Bawtry Road, Doncaster,
South Yorkshire DN4 7AD
Tel: (01302) 535926
Head: Mrs B J Spencer
Type: Co-educational Day 3–16
No of pupils: B74 G106
Fees: (September 01) Day £3897 –
£5967
Special Needs: Level 2: DYS
Level 3: ASP CP HI

WEST YORKSHIRE

ALCUIN SCHOOL
64 Woodland Lane, Leeds,
West Yorkshire LS7 4PD
Tel: (0113) 269 1173
Head: Mr J Hipshon
Type: Co-educational Day 4–11
No of pupils: B25 G38
Fees: (September 01) Day £1500
Special Needs: Level 2: ADD CP DYP
DYS MLD PH

BATLEY GRAMMAR SCHOOL
Carlinghow Hill, Batley,
West Yorkshire WF17 0AD
Tel: (01924) 474980
Head: Mr B Battye
Type: Co-educational Day 4–18
No of pupils: B279 G163
Fees: (September 01) Day £3498 –
£5517
Special Needs: Level 3: ASP CP DYP
DYS PH

BRADFORD GRAMMAR SCHOOL
Keighley Road, Bradford,
West Yorkshire BD9 4JP
Tel: (01274) 542492
Head: Mr S R Davidson
Type: Co-educational Day 7–18
No of pupils: B903 G154
Fees: (September 01) Day £5130 –
£6435
Special Needs: Level 3: ADHD ASP
DYP DYS EPI PH SP&LD TOU

THE FROEBELIAN SCHOOL
Clarence Road, Horsforth, Leeds,
West Yorkshire LS18 4LB
Tel: (0113) 258 3047
Head: Mr J Tranmer
Type: Co-educational Day 3–11
No of pupils: B93 G97
Fees: (September 01) Day £2490 –
£3780
Special Needs: Level 2: DYP DYS MLD
Level 3: ASP SP&LD

FULNECK SCHOOL†
Fulneck, Pudsey, West Yorkshire
LS28 8DS
Tel: (0113) 257 0235
Head: Mrs H S Gordon
Type: Co-educational Day and
Boarding 3–18
No of pupils: B214 G196
No of Boarders: F28 W5
Fees: (September 01)
FB £9690 – £11760
WB £8985 – £10680
Day £2190 – £6390
Special Needs: Level 1: ASP DYP DYS
Unspecified: DEL HI

GHYLL ROYD SCHOOL
Greystone Manor, Ilkley Road,
Burley in Wharfedale, Ilkley, West
Yorkshire LS29 7HW
Tel: (01943) 865575
Head: Mrs J Bonner
Type: Boys Day 2–11
No of pupils: B80
Fees: (September 01) Day £2910 –
£4485
Special Needs: Level 2: DYP DYS
SPLD Level 3: ASP SP&LD

HIPPERHOLME GRAMMAR SCHOOL

Bramley Lane, Hipperholme, Halifax, West Yorkshire HX3 8JE
Tel: (01422) 202256
Head: Mr C C Robinson
Type: Co-educational Day 11–18
No of pupils: B160 G125
Fees: (September 01) Day £5370
Special Needs: Level 2: DYS
Level 3: ADD ASP HI VIS

LADY LANE PARK SCHOOL

Lady Lane, Bingley, West Yorkshire BD16 4AP
Tel: (01274) 551168
Head: Mrs G Wilson
Type: Co-educational Day 2–11
No of pupils: B89 G81
Fees: (September 01) Day £3465 – £3690
Special Needs: Level 2: DYS

LEEDS GIRLS' HIGH SCHOOL

Headingley Lane, Leeds, West Yorkshire LS6 1BN
Tel: (0113) 274 4000
Head: Ms S Fishburn
Type: Girls Day 3–19
No of pupils: 981
Fees: (September 01) Day £4221 – £6312
Special Needs: Level 2: CP
Unspecified: DYS

LEEDS GRAMMAR SCHOOL

Alwoodley Gates, Harrogate Road, Leeds, West Yorkshire LS17 8GS
Tel: (0113) 229 1552
Head: Dr M Bailey
Type: Boys Day 4–18
No of pupils: B1360
Fees: (September 01) Day £3873 – £6873
Special Needs: Level 1: PH
Level 2: DYP DYS Level 3: ASP CP
EPI HI VIS Unspecified: W

MOORFIELD SCHOOL

Wharfedale Lodge, Ben Rhydding Road, Ilkley, West Yorkshire LS29 8RL
Tel: (01943) 607285
Head: Mrs J E Disley
Type: Girls Day 2–11
No of pupils: 150
Fees: (September 01) Day £720 – £4200
Special Needs: Level 2: DYC DYP DYS
MLD SPLD Level 3: HI VIS

MOUNT SCHOOL

3 Binham Road, Edgerton, Huddersfield, West Yorkshire HD2 2AP
Tel: (01484) 426432
Head: Mr N M Smith
Type: Co-educational Day 3–11
No of pupils: B75 G77
Fees: (September 00) Day £2925 – £3450
Special Needs: Level 2: DYS

RASTRICK PREP AND NURSERY SCHOOL

Ogden Lane, Rastrick, Brighouse, West Yorkshire HD6 3HF
Tel: (01484) 400344
Head: Mrs S A Vaughey
Type: Co-educational Day and Boarding 0–13
No of pupils: B93 G99
Fees: (September 01) Day £3585 – £5250
Special Needs: Level 2: ADD ADHD
CP DOW DYC DYP DYS EBD EPI HI
SP&LD VIS

ROSSEFIELD SCHOOL

Parsons Road, Heaton, Bradford, West Yorkshire BD9 4AY
Tel: (01274) 543549
Head: Mrs A M Ball
Type: Co-educational Day 3–11
No of pupils: B90 G45
Fees: (September 01) Day £1680 – £2925
Special Needs: Unspecified: DYS

ST AGNES PNEU SCHOOL

25 Burton Crescent, Leeds, West Yorkshire LS6 4DN
Tel: (0113) 278 6722
Head: Mrs S McMeeking
Type: Co-educational Day 2–7
No of pupils: B35 G19
Fees: (September 01) Day £2235 – £4095
Special Needs: Level 2: DYC DYS
Level 3: HI MLD

ST HILDA'S SCHOOL

Dovecote Lane, Horbury, Wakefield, West Yorkshire WF4 6BB
Tel: (01924) 260706
Head: Mrs A R Mackenzie
Type: Co-educational Day Boys 3–7
Girls 3–11
No of pupils: B48 G90
Fees: (September 01) Day £3600 – £3780
Special Needs: Level 2: DYS

WAKEFIELD GIRLS' HIGH SCHOOL

Wentworth Street, Wakefield, West Yorkshire WF1 2QS
Tel: (01924) 372490
Head: Mrs P A Langham
Type: Girls Day 3–18 (Boys 3–7)
No of pupils: B60 G1035
Fees: (September 01) Day £4086 – £6075
Special Needs: Unspecified: DYS

WAKEFIELD TUTORIAL PREPARATORY SCHOOL

Commercial Street, Morley, Leeds, West Yorkshire LS27 8HY
Tel: (0113) 253 4033
Head: Mrs J A Tanner
Type: Co-educational Day 4–11
No of pupils: B40 G40
Fees: (September 01) Day £2235 – £2400
Special Needs: Level 2: DYC DYS MLD
SPLD Level 3: ADD ADHD ASP DYP
EBD EPI

WESTVILLE HOUSE PREPARATORY SCHOOL

Carters Lane, Middleton, Ilkley, West Yorkshire LS29 0DQ
Tel: (01943) 608053
Head: Mr C A Holloway
Type: Co-educational Day 3–11
No of pupils: B93 G52
Fees: (September 01) Day £2610 – £4860
Special Needs: Level 2: DYC DYP DYS
EBD SPLD Level 3: ADD ADHD ASP
AUT CP DEL DOW EPI HI MLD PH
PMLD SLD SP&LD TOU VIS

WOODHOUSE GROVE SCHOOL

Apperley Bridge, West Yorkshire BD10 0NR
Tel: (0113) 250 2477
Head: Mr D C Humphreys
Type: Co-educational Boarding and Day 11–18
No of pupils: B385 G229
No of Boarders: F80 W15
Fees: (September 01) FB £12405
Day £7050 – £7200
Special Needs: Level 2: DYP DYS

NORTHERN IRELAND

COUNTY ANTRIM

**ROYAL BELFAST
ACADEMICAL INSTITUTION**
College Square East, Belfast,
County Antrim BT1 6DL
Tel: (028) 9024 0461
Head: Mr R M Ridley
Type: Boys Day 4–18
No of pupils: 1050
Fees: (September 01) Day £590 –
£2300
Special Needs: Level 2: DYS

**VICTORIA COLLEGE
BELFAST**
Cranmore Park, Belfast,
County Antrim BT9 6JA
Tel: (028) 9066 1506
Head: Mrs M Andrews
Type: Girls Day and Boarding 4–18
No of pupils: 1020
No of Boarders: F47
Fees: (September 01) FB £4995
Day £280
Special Needs: Level 2: DYC DYS EBD
SP&LD SPLD Level 3: ADD ADHD
ASP AUT CP DEL DOW EPI HI MLD
PH VIS Unspecified: W

SCOTLAND

ABERDEENSHIRE

ALBYN SCHOOL FOR GIRLS
17–23 Queens Road, Aberdeen
AB15 4PB
Tel: (01224) 322408
Head: Miss J Leslie
Type: Girls Day 2–18 (Boys 2–5)
No of pupils: B25 G356
Fees: (September 01) Day £3660 –
£6200
Special Needs: Level 2: DYS

ANGUS

**THE HIGH SCHOOL OF
DUNDEE**
Euclid Crescent, Dundee, Angus
DD1 1HU
Tel: (01382) 202921
Head: Mr A M Duncan
Type: Co-educational Day 5–18
No of pupils: B539 G530
Fees: (September 01) Day £4155 –
£5910
Special Needs: Level 2: DYC DYP DYS
SPLD

LATHALLAN SCHOOL
Brotherton Castle, Johnshaven,
Montrose, Angus DD10 0HN
Tel: (01561) 362220
Head: Mr P Platts-Martin
Type: Co-educational Boarding and
Day 3–13
No of pupils: B80 G50
No of Boarders: F6 W38
Fees: (September 01)
FB £10869 – £11945
WB £10626 – £11688
Day £4794 – £1757
Special Needs: Level 2: DYC DYP DYS
EPI SPLD

ARGYLL AND BUTE

LOMOND SCHOOL
10 Stafford Street, Helensburgh,
Argyll and Bute G84 9JX
Tel: (01436) 672476
Head: Mr A D Macdonald
Type: Co-educational Day and
Boarding 3–19
No of pupils: B268 G234
No of Boarders: F60 W10
Fees: (September 01)
FB £12930 – £13455
WB £12570 – £13095
Day £1980 – £6285
Special Needs: Level 2: DYC DYP DYS
Level 3: HI PH Unspecified: SPLD

BANFFSHIRE

ABERLOUR HOUSE
Aberlour, Banffshire AB38 9LJ
Tel: (01340) 871267
Head: Mr N W Gardner
Type: Co-educational Boarding and
Day 7–13
No of pupils: B54 G35
No of Boarders: F63
Fees: (September 01) FB £12192
Day £8505
Special Needs: Level 2: DYS

CLACKMANNANSHIRE

DOLLAR ACADEMY
Dollar, Clackmannanshire FK14 7DU
Tel: (01259) 742511
Head: Mr J S Robertson
Type: Co-educational Day and
Boarding 5–18
No of pupils: B603 G560
No of Boarders: F76 W14
Fees: (September 01)
FB £11673 – £13131
WB £10980 – £12438
Day £4428 – £5886
Special Needs: Unspecified: ADD
ADHD ASP DYC DYP DYS EBD SPLD
TOU

FIFE

NEW PARK SCHOOL
98 Hepburn Gardens, St Andrews,
Fife KY16 9LN
Tel: (01334) 472017
Head: Mr A Donald
Type: Co-educational Day 3–13
No of pupils: B73 G37
Fees: (September 01) Day £1545 –
£7110
Special Needs: Level 2: DYP DYS MLD
SPLD

**ST KATHARINES
PREPARATORY SCHOOL**
The Pends, St Andrews, Fife
KY16 9RB
Tel: (01334) 460470
Head: Mrs J Gibson
Type: Co-educational Boarding and
Day 3–12
No of pupils: B24 G49
No of Boarders: F8
Fees: (September 01) FB £12294
Day £5055 – £6981
Special Needs: Level 2: DYS SPLD

**ST LEONARDS SCHOOL &
ST LEONARDS VITH FORM
COLLEGE**
St Andrews, Fife KY16 9QJ
Tel: (01334) 472126
Head: Mrs W A Bellars
Type: Co-educational Boarding and
Day 12–19
No of pupils: B18 G213
No of Boarders: F153
Fees: (September 01) FB £16209
Day £9084
Special Needs: Level 2: DYS

GLASGOW

CRAIGHOLME SCHOOL
72 St Andrews Drive, Glasgow
G41 4HS
Tel: (0141) 427 0375
Head: Mrs G Burt
Type: Girls Day 3–18 (Boys 3–5)
No of pupils: B13 G537
Fees: (September 01) Day £2370 –
£5745
Special Needs: Level 2: DYS

THE GLASGOW ACADEMY
Colebrooke Street, Glasgow G12 8HE
Tel: (0141) 334 8558
Head: Mr D Comins
Type: Co-educational Day 2–18
No of pupils: B588 G473
Fees: (September 01) Day £4155 –
£5985
Special Needs: Level 2: DYP DYS
SPLD

**HUTCHESONS' GRAMMAR
SCHOOL**
21 Beaton Road, Glasgow G41 4NW
Tel: (0141) 423 2933
Head: Mr J G Knowles
Type: Co-educational Day 3–18
No of pupils: B1022 G1029
Fees: (September 01) Day £4612 –
£5562
Special Needs: Level 3: ADD ADHD
ASP CP DYP DYS EPI HI PH TOU VIS
Unspecified: W

SOUTH LANARKSHIRE

FERNHILL SCHOOL
Fernbrae Avenue, Rutherglen, South
Lanarkshire G73 4SG
Tel: (0141) 634 2674
Head: Mrs L M McLay
Type: Girls Day 4–18 (Boys 4–11)
No of pupils: B50 G260
Fees: (September 01) Day £3900 –
£4650
Special Needs: Unspecified: DYS MLD

LOTHIAN

**BASIL PATERSON TUTORIAL
COLLEGE**
Dugdale-McAdam House, 23
Abercromby Place, Edinburgh,
Lothian EH3 6QE
Tel: (0131) 556 7698
Head: Mrs I P Shewan
Type: Co-educational Day and
Boarding 14+
No of pupils: B24 G16
No of Boarders: F2 W2
Fees: (September 01)
FB £8200 – £13700
WB £7200 – £12700
Day £5000 – £10500
Special Needs: Level 2: ADD ADHD
ASP DYP DYS Level 3: DEL EPI HI
VIS

BELHAVEN HILL
Dunbar, Lothian EH42 1NN
Tel: (01368) 862785
Head: Mr I M Osborne
Type: Co-educational Boarding and
Day 7–13
No of pupils: B60 G40
No of Boarders: F85
Fees: (September 01) FB £11685
Day £8520
Special Needs: Level 2: DYP DYS MLD
SPLD

THE COMPASS SCHOOL
West Road, Haddington, Lothian
EH41 3RD
Tel: (01620) 822642
Head: Mr M Becher
Type: Co-educational Day 4–11
No of pupils: B56 G62
Fees: (September 01) Day £2844 –
£4626
Special Needs: Level 2: DYS MLD

GEORGE HERIOT'S SCHOOL
Lauriston Place, Edinburgh, Lothian
EH3 9EQ
Tel: (0131) 229 7263
Head: Mr A G Hector
Type: Co-educational Day 4–18
No of pupils: B904 G652
Fees: (September 01) Day £3741 –
£5650
Special Needs: Level 2: DYC DYP DYS
SPLD

LORETTO JUNIOR SCHOOL
North Esk Lodge, Musselburgh,
Lothian EH21 6JA
Tel: (0131) 653 4570
Head: Mr R G Selley
Type: Co-educational Boarding and
Day 5–13
No of pupils: B63 G56
No of Boarders: F32 W5
Fees: (September 01)
FB £11694 – £12474
Day £4164 – £8355
Special Needs: Level 2: DYS SPLD

THE MARY ERSKINE SCHOOL
Ravelston, Edinburgh, Lothian
EH4 3NT
Tel: (0131) 337 2391
Head: Mr J N D Gray
Type: Girls Day and Boarding 12–18
(Co-ed VIth form)
No of pupils: 684 *No of Boarders:* F24
Fees: (September 01) FB £12879
Day £6108
Special Needs: Level 2: DYS
Level 3: DYP

ST MARGARET'S SCHOOL
East Suffolk Road, Edinburgh,
Lothian EH16 5PJ
Tel: (0131) 668 1986
Head: Mrs E M Davis
Type: Girls Day and Boarding 3–18
(Boys 3–8)
No of pupils: B31 G518
No of Boarders: F13 W1
Fees: (September 01)
FB £10815 – £12198
WB £8945 – £11035
Day £3745 – £5835
Special Needs: Level 2: DYP DYS
Level 3: EBD EPI HI MLD PH SPLD
VIS

MORAYSHIRE

ROSEBRAE SCHOOL
Spynie, Elgin, Morayshire IV30 8XT
Tel: (01343) 544841
Head: Mrs B MacPherson
Type: Co-educational Day 2–8
No of pupils: B35 G35
Fees: (September 01) Day £294 –
£2880
Special Needs: Level 2: ASP AUT CP
DYC DYP DYS EBD EPI HI MLD PH
SP&LD SPLD VIS Level 3: ADD
ADHD DEL DOW PMLD SLD TOU

PERTHSHIRE

ARDVRECK SCHOOL
Gwydyr Road, Crieff, Perthshire
PH7 4EX
Tel: (01764) 653112
Head: Mr P Watson
Type: Co-educational Boarding and
Day 3–13
No of pupils: B80 G70
No of Boarders: F110
Fees: (September 01) FB £11610
Day £7420
Special Needs: Level 2: DYS SPLD
Level 3: MLD

BUTTERSTONE SCHOOL
Meigle, Blairgowrie, Perthshire
PH12 8QY
Tel: (01828) 640528
Head: Mr & Mrs B Whitten
Type: Girls Boarding and Day 2–13
(Co-ed 3–7)
No of pupils: B20 G88
No of Boarders: F43
Fees: (September 01) FB £12144
Day £4245 – £8130
Special Needs: Level 2: SPLD
Level 3: ADD CP DYC DYP DYS EPI
HI

CRAIGCLOWAN PREPARATORY SCHOOL
Edinburgh Road, Perth, Perthshire
PH2 8PS
Tel: (01738) 626310
Head: Mr M E Beale
Type: Co-educational Day 4–13
No of pupils: B130 G130
Fees: (September 01) Day £5775
Special Needs: Level 2: ADD ASP DYP
DYS MLD SPLD

GLENALMOND COLLEGE

Perth, Perthshire PH1 3RY
Tel: (01738) 842056
Head: Mr I G Templeton
Type: Co-educational Boarding and Day 12–18
No of pupils: B258 G143
No of Boarders: F349
Fees: (September 01)
FB £12375 – £16485
Day £8250 – £10995
Special Needs: Level 2: DYS

KILGRASTON (A SACRED HEART SCHOOL)

Bridge of Earn, Perth, Perthshire PH2 9BQ
Tel: (01738) 812257
Head: Mrs J L Austin
Type: Girls Boarding and Day 5–18 (Boys day 2–9)
No of pupils: B15 G219
No of Boarders: F109
Fees: (September 01)
F/WB £12441 – £14916
Day £5065 – £8794
Special Needs: Level 2: ADD ADHD ASP DEL DYC DYP DYS PH SPLD
Level 3: EBD EPI

QUEEN VICTORIA SCHOOL

Dunblane, Perthshire FK15 0JY
Tel: (01786) 822288
Head: Mr B Raine
Type: Co-educational Boarding 11–18
No of pupils: B167 G109
No of Boarders: F276
Fees: (January 02) FB £2133 – £2214
Special Needs: Level 2: ADD ADHD DYC DYP DYS EBD HI PH SPLD

RANNOCH SCHOOL

Rannoch, Pitlochry, Perthshire PH17 2QQ
Tel: (01882) 632332
Head: Mr D B McMurray
Type: Co-educational Boarding and Day 10–18
No of pupils: B76 G36
No of Boarders: F110 W2
Fees: (September 01)
FB £12489 – £14775
WB £10113 – £12294 Day £7704
Special Needs: Level 2: ADD ADHD DYC DYP DYS EBD EPI MLD SP&LD SPLD

ROXBURGHSHIRE

ST MARY'S PREPARATORY SCHOOL

Abbey Park, Melrose, Roxburghshire TD6 9LN
Tel: (01896) 822517
Head: Mr J Brett
Type: Co-educational Day 2–13
No of pupils: B60 G64
Fees: (September 01) Day £5250 – £7890
Special Needs: Level 2: DYC DYP DYS SPLD Level 3: ADD ADHD
Unspecified: MLD

WALES

BRIDGEND

ST JOHN'S SCHOOL
Newton, Porthcawl, Bridgend
CF36 5NP
Tel: (01656) 783404
Head: Mrs E D Smith and
Ms D Spearey
Type: Co-educational Day 3–16
No of pupils: B130 G70
Fees: (September 01) Day £3000 –
£6330
Special Needs: Level 2: DYC DYP DYS
SPLD

CARDIFF

THE CATHEDRAL SCHOOL
Llandaff, Cardiff CF5 2YH
Tel: (029) 2056 3179
Head: Mr P L Gray
Type: Co-educational Day 3–16
No of pupils: B336 G121
Fees: (September 01) Day £4140 –
£6240
Special Needs: Level 2: DYS

ELM TREE HOUSE SCHOOL
Clive Road, Llandaff, Cardiff
CF5 1GN
Tel: (029) 2022 3388
Head: Mrs C M Thomas
Type: Co-educational Day 2–11
No of pupils: B24 G136
Fees: (September 01) Day £3135 –
£3915
Special Needs: Level 2: DYS

**HOWELL'S SCHOOL,
LLANDAFF GDST**
Cardiff Road, Llandaff, Cardiff
CF5 2YD
Tel: (029) 2056 2019
Head: Mrs J Fitz
Type: Girls Day 3–18
No of pupils: 729
Fees: (September 01) Day £3174 –
£5442
Special Needs: Level 2: DYS

CONWY

LYNDON SCHOOL
Grosvenor Road, Colwyn Bay,
Conwy LL29 7YF
Tel: (01492) 532347
Head: Mr M B Collins
Type: Co-educational Day 2–11
No of pupils: B41 G50
Fees: (September 01) Day £1830 –
£3810
Special Needs: Level 2: ADD ADHD
DYC DYP DYS MLD SP&LD SPLD
VIS Unspecified: PH

**RYDAL PENRHOS SENIOR
SCHOOL**
Pwllycrochan Avenue, Colwyn Bay,
Conwy LL29 7BT
Tel: (01492) 530155
Head: Mr M S James
Type: Co-educational Boarding and
Day 11–18 (Single sex education)
No of pupils: B196 G196
No of Boarders: F139
Fees: (September 01)
FB £12810 – £14505
Day £8100 – £8655
Special Needs: Level 2: DYS
Unspecified: DYP

ST DAVID'S COLLEGE†
Llandudno, Conwy LL30 1RD
Tel: (01492) 875974
Head: Mr W Seymour
Type: Co-educational Boarding and
Day 11–18
No of pupils: B200 G50
No of Boarders: F160 W5
Fees: (September 01)
FB £12309 – £14592
Day £8004 – £9921
Special Needs: Level 1: DYC DYP DYS
SPLD

MONMOUTHSHIRE

ST JOHN'S-ON-THE-HILL
Tutshill, Chepstow, Monmouthshire
NP16 7LE
Tel: (01291) 622045
Head: Mr I K Etchells
Type: Co-educational Boarding and
Day 2–13
No of pupils: B177 G125
No of Boarders: F27 W2
Fees: (September 01) F/WB £9540
Day £4218 – £7050
Special Needs: Level 2: DYC DYP DYS
SP&LD SPLD

NEWPORT

ROUGEMONT SCHOOL
Llantarnam Hall, Malpas Road,
Newport NP20 6QB
Tel: (01633) 820800
Head: Mr I Brown
Type: Co-educational Day 3–18
No of pupils: B374 G325
Fees: (September 01) Day £3390 –
£5790
Special Needs: Level 2: DYS
Level 3: ADHD Unspecified: W

POWYS

CHRIST COLLEGE
Brecon, Powys LD3 8AG
Tel: (01874) 623359
Head: Mr D P Jones
Type: Co-educational Boarding and
Day 11–18
No of pupils: B205 G100
No of Boarders: F184 W45
Fees: (September 01) F/WB £10710 –
£13695 Day £8025 – £10620
Special Needs: Level 1: DYS
Level 2: DYC DYP SPLD Level 3: EPI
HI

4.3
Profiles of Independent Mainstream Schools with Specialist Provision

The schools in this section offer varying levels of help for students with special needs, from additional tuition on a limited withdrawal basis to specialist units and teaching programmes. For specific details parents should contact individual schools direct.

Akeley Wood School

Akeley Wood, Buckingham MK18 3AE
Tel: 01280 814110   Website: www.gabbitas.net

Head Julian Lovelock
Religious denomination Non-denominational
Special needs provision DYS
Age range 2½–18
Girls 341 *boys* 502
Fees per annum £4,398–£6,450

Akeley Wood School has always helped children with dyslexia and related problems. The pupils are withdrawn from the mainstream timetable for a few hours per week to attend these comprehensive sessions following individual education plans to include study skills, cross curriculum teaching, spelling programmes, reading strategies and writing skills.

Although the school bears much of the cost of employing the experienced staff, an extra charge has to be made for this specialised work. For the more seriously handicapped we have now opened the Charmandean Dyslexia Centre which tackles problems met by children more seriously affected by dyslexia and related learning problems.

Mr Lovelock is the Head Teacher in charge of organising and supervising the work.

Details of our facilities are available from the school secretary.

Bredon School

Pull Court, Bushley, Tewkesbury, Gloucestershire GL20 6AH
Tel: 01684 293156   Fax: 01684 298008
E-mail: enquiries@bredonschool.worcs.sch.uk   enquiries@bredonschool.co.uk
Website: www.bredonschool.ik.org   www.boardingschools.com   www.gabbitas.net

Head Mr M J Newby MA B.Ed(Hons)
Founded 1962
School status DfES approved independent co-educational boarding and day
Religious denomination Church of England
Member of ISA, BSA, DYS
Special needs provision DYC, DYP, DYS, SP&LD, SPLD *Other needs catered for* special dietary needs
Age range 7–18   *boarding from* 8–18
No of pupils (day) 72   *boarding (full)* 83 *(weekly)* 45
Girls 60 *boys* 140
Junior 33; *Senior* 133; *Sixth Form* 41
Fees per annum from September 2002 (boarding) (full) £10,995–£15,690   *(weekly)* £10,710–£14,775   *(day)* £5,595–£10,695

Bredon is a co-educational independent school for 200 pupils with full and weekly boarders and day pupils. The school stands in attractive rural surroundings near the River Severn, on the Worcestershire and Gloucestershire borders in an estate of 85 acres, which includes a school farm. Bredon follows the National Curriculum at all Key Stages and students will sit the national assessment tests at the appropriate stages. In addition Bredon offers GNVQ vocational programmes at Foundation, Intermediate and Advanced level and AVCE courses. Some pupils are able to benefit from the experience of the Learning Support Centre staff and the school is CReSTeD registered.

Excellent facilities exist in craft, design and technology and computer studies, with a farm unit providing the basis for agricultural studies.

Cokethorpe School

Witney, Oxfordshire OX29 7PU
Tel: (01993) 703921   Fax: (01993) 773499
E-mail: admin@cokethorpe.org   Website: www.cokethorpe.org   www.gabbitas.net

Head Mr P J S Cantwell
Founded 1957
School status Co-educational independent boarding and day
Religious denomination Inter-denominational
Member of SHMIS; *accredited by* ISC
Special needs provision DEL, DYC, DYS, DYP, MLD, PH, SP&LD, SPLD
Age range 7–18; *boarders from* 10 (boys only)
No of pupils (day) 470; *(boarding)* 40
Girls 180 *boys* 330
Junior 160; *Senior* 350; *Sixth Form* 70
Fees per annum (full and weekly boarding) £15,750; *(day)* £5,310–£9,480

A broad academic and vocational curriculum is followed to GCSE. A wide range of A Levels are available to the Sixth Form. Small classes provide everyone with the opportunity to fulfil their potential. Extra help is available in the learning support department. Entry requirements are interview and headteacher's report at the age of 7 and 9, interview and assessment at 11, 13 and 16 years.

Examinations: GCSE, A/S Level and A2. New buildings house the library, art and ceramics, information technology and design and technology. There are also modern laboratories, Music School and Sixth Form facilities. The new Sports Hall provides for a large number of indoor sports. There is a wide range of extra-curricular activities within 50 acres of grounds. In 2001, the campus was fully networked and the new Learning Resource Centre with 64 new PCs opened.

Scholarships are awarded on entrance assessment. Bursaries are available on application for details.

Ellesmere College

Ellesmere, Shropshire SY12 9AB   Website: www.gabbitas.net
Tel: 01691 622321   Fax: 01691 623286   E-mail: admin@ellesmere.biblio.net

Head Mr B J Wignall MA MIMgt
Founded 1884
School status Independent co-educational boarding and day
Religious denomination Church of England
Member of HMC Woodard Corporation and corporate member of BDA
Accredited by CreSTeD
Special needs provision ADD, ADHD, DYC, DYP, DYS, SPLD *Other needs catered for* Mild Asperger Syndrome
Age range 9–18   *boarding from* 11
No of pupils 465 *(boarding) (full)* 99
Junior 154; *Senior* 195; *Sixth Form* 116
Boys 321 *girls* 144
Fees per annum (boarding) (full) £14,700; *(weekly boarding)* £12,600; *(day)* £9,600

Ellesmere College is a school of 465 boys and girls set in its own grounds of 70 acres of rural North Shropshire. There are approximately 154 children in the Lower School (9–13). There are 311 in the 13–18 range of whom 174 are boarders. Boarding accommodation has benefited from a recent multi-million pound refurbishment programme and is of the highest quality. There are 116 pupils in the Sixth Form. The college has provided high quality dyslexia support for 30 years; it is a CreSTeD category DU school and is in corporate membership of the British Dyslexia Association.

Grenville College

Bideford, Devon EX39 3JR
Tel: 01237 472212   Fax: 01237 477020
E-mail: info@grenville.devon.sch.uk
Website: www.grenville.devon.sch.uk   www.gabbitas.net

Head Dr Michael Cane BSc, PhD, MRSC
Founded 1954
Needs for which school offers provision DYS
School status Independent
Religious denomination Church of England
Members of GBA, SHMIS, ISA, CReSTeD
Age range 2½–19   *boarders from* 8
No of pupils (day) 300   *(boarding)* 105
Girls 170 *boys* 235
Junior 110   *Senior* 295   *Sixth Form* 70
Fees per annum (boarding) (full) £10,860–
£13,986 *(weekly)* £8,142–£10,485 *(day)*
£2,904–£6,924

Pupils are taught in small groups with their own individual learning programmes, leading to GCSE, GNVQ or A level. The Dyslexia Unit, established in 1969, aims to provide specialist teaching support and to encourage pupils to fulfil their potential.

Entry at all levels is by report and interview. Scholarship and bursary enquiries are welcomed.

The boarding houses stand in 40 acres of gardens and parkland providing excellent opportunities for sporting and extra-curricular activities. The school's coastal location and proximity to Dartmoor and Exmoor make watersports and outdoor pursuits particularly popular. Grenville College provides high quality education in a caring Christian community.

North Bridge House School

1 Gloucester Avenue, London NW1 7AB
Tel: 020 7267 6266   Fax: 020 7284 2508   Website: www.gabbitas.net

Head Hugh Richardson
Founded 1939
School status Co-educational independent day
Religious denomination Non-denominational
Special needs provision DYS
Age range 2 yrs 9 mths–18
Sixth Form opened September 2001
No of pupils 893
Junior 629; *Senior* 264
Girls 395 *boys* 498
Fees per annum Tuition fees £7,425 plus
Dyslexia tuition, lunch and extras

North Bridge House School offers withdrawal tuition for pupils between 7 and 16 years who have special educational needs or who have been classified as dyslexic by educational psychologists.

The pupils are withdrawn from the mainstream timetable for a few hours each week to attend these comprehensive sessions following individual educational plans to include study skills, cross curriculum teaching, spelling programmes, reading strategies and writing skills.

The pupils are taught by a dedicated teacher in a purpose-built department fully equipped with excellent computer facilities.

Mr Richardson is the Head Teacher in charge of organising and supervising the work.

Although the school bears much of the cost of employing the experienced staff, an extra charge has to be made – in addition to the school fees – for this specialised work.

St Joseph's In The Park

St Mary's Lane, Hertingfordbury, near Hertford, Hertfordshire SG14 2LX
Tel: 01992 581378   Fax: 01992 505202   E-mail: admin@stjosephsinthepark.co.uk
Website: www.stjosephsinthepark.co.uk   www.gabbitas.net

Head Mrs J K King
Founded c.1902
School status Independent co-educational day only.
Religious denomination Multi-denominational Christian based
Special needs provision DYS (Woodlands), Gifted and Talented (Parklands)
Other needs catered for Gifted and Talented Special Class
Age range 8–11
No of pupils 177
Girls 87 *boys* 90
Pre-school 28; *Infants* 60; *Junior* 89
Fees per annum (day) £2,700

St Joseph's In The Park offers unique educational opportunities to boys and girls between 8–11 with special needs.
"Woodlands" is a separate class of ten children with Dyslexia, who study in specially equipped accommodation with specialist tutors. ICT and other technological aids are used to teach strategies for learning following the National Curriculum.

"Parklands" is also a class for children with special needs. These children have scores in excess of 120 in nationally standardised tests. They work in greater depth and at a faster pace than their peer group. They study with specialist tutors using modern technological aids and special resources on an enrichment programme following individual education plans.

Both classes are successfully integrated with the mainstream every afternoon sharing sport, music, art, drama, technology and all clubs, societies and recreational periods. Both enjoy extra off-site visits to enhance learning but, most importantly, their self-esteem flourishes in this caring community.

Stanbridge Earls School

Romsey, Hampshire SO51 0ZS
Tel: (01794) 516777   Fax: (01794) 511201
E-mail: stanbridgesec@aol.com

Head N R Hall BSc (London)
Founded 1952
Type Co-educational independent boarding and day
Religious denomination Inter-denominational
Special needs provision DYS, DYC, DYP, SP&LD, ASP, DEL, ADD, ADHD
Member of GBA, SHMIS, BSA; *corporate member* British Dyslexia Association, CReSTeD
Age range 11–18   *boarders from* 11
No of pupils (boarding) 160
Girls 39 *boys* 149
Junior 45; *Senior* 99; *Sixth Form* 44; *Total* 188
Fees per annum (boarding) £14,700–£16,170; *(day)* £10,980–£12,000
Average size of class: 10
Teacher:pupil ratio: 1:6

Curriculum: the National Curriculum, up to the end of Key Stage 4, is enhanced by a daily activities program to develop the strengths and interests of every pupil. Many pupils are dyslexic and all take GCSE. The School has excellent facilities for all academic subjects and has recently opened an ICT/CDT suite and English/Languages block. Sixth Formers are offered a wide choice of courses at Advanced and AVCE level as well as GNVQ and GCSE retakes. The Accelerated Learning Centre, with 16 experienced specialist teachers, for those with literacy difficulties, and the Mathematics Skills Centre, with 7 specialist staff, enhances the learning of pupils with special educational needs.

Leisure: large sports hall, indoor heated swimming pool, squash courts, floodlit tennis courts, vehicle engineering workshop and playing fields. Sailing is at Lymington.

Entry: interview, school report and, where appropriate, educational psychologists report. Registered charity number: 307342.

Wycliffe College

Bath Road, Stonehouse, Gloucestershire GL10 2JQ
Tel: (01453) 822432   Fax: (01453) 827634
E-mail: senior@wycliffe.co.uk   Website: www.wycliffe.co.uk   www.gabbitas.net
Wycliffe Junior School, Ryeford Hall, Stonehouse, Gloucestershire GL10 3LD
Tel: (01453) 820470   Fax: (01453) 825604   E-mail: junior@wycliffe.co.uk

Head Dr R A Collins MA, DPhil
Head of Junior School K Melber BA
Founded 1882
Type Co-educational independent boarding and day
Religious denomination Non-denominational
Member of HMC, IAPS
Special needs provision DYS, DYP
Age range 2½–18+   *boarders from* 8
Fees per annum (full boarding) £8,460–£10,635 (junior school), £16,515–£15,300 (senior school); *(day)* £3,870–£7,545 (junior), £11,160–£10,755

Aims and objectives of special educational needs provision: to provide a continuum of special educational needs in mainstream education for children with Specific Learning Difficulties. To achieve this, we maintain close consultation and partnership with parents and pupils, evaluating and taking into account pupils preferred learning styles and strengths, as well as their learning difficulties.

SEN Specialists and Facilities

We provide a range of facilities, these include:

- Individual Learning Plans, focusing on learning styles, strategies and target setting
- Individual Education Plans to address the specific needs and difficulties of students with SENs
- Differentiated work for students with SpLDs
- Specialist in-class support where needed
- Extra tuition by specialist teachers, in small groups or on a one to one basis, to improve literacy/numeracy skills
- Specialist tuition to improve study skills, organisation and examination technique
- A flexible approach to the curriculum at GCSE
- Small class sizes

Assessment and Screening

All students are screened for dyslexia in Years 2, 4, 7, 9, FY, and D6. Pupils joining the school in other years are screened upon entry. These results are analysed and pupils showing signs of special educational needs are placed on the SEN register. The school then adopts a two-staged approach to intervention. Their progress is closely monitored and reviewed by both teachers and the Special Educational Needs Co-ordinator (SENCO). Students whose difficulties persist are assessed by an educational psychologist.

Admission Arrangements

The school does not operate a selective admissions policy and has a broad ability intake. Admission is by Common Entrance or by Wycliffe Entrance exam. However, in order to ensure that our SEN provision can match the child's need, the SENCO will normally meet parents of prospective entrants to the school, where the child has, or may have, special educational needs. The child's difficulties will be discussed at this meeting, and they may be assessed to determine their ability to cope with the mainstream education offered at Wycliffe. Previous school records are used in the pre-entry assessment. In some cases, the school may require an Educational Psychologist's assessment, before an offer of a place at the school can be confirmed.

Wycliffe College incorporated is a Registered Charity No 311714

4.4
Index of Independent Mainstream Schools with Specialist Provision Classified by Special Need

Note: Schools in London are identified by postal areas.

Attention Deficit Disorder

Level 1

Barnardiston Hall Preparatory School, Suffolk
Bellan House Preparatory School, Shropshire
Birchfield School, West Midlands
Bredon School, Gloucestershire
Hazelwood School, Surrey
Kingsley Preparatory School, West Midlands
Northampton Christian School, Northamptonshire
Rossall School, Lancashire
St Andrew's School, Kent
St Columba's College, Hertfordshire
Stonyhurst College, Lancashire
Wimbledon College Prep School, SW19
Woodside Park International School, N11

Level 2

Abbotsholme School, Staffordshire
Alcuin School, West Yorkshire
All Hallows, Somerset
Ampleforth College, North Yorkshire
Ashbourne PNEU School, Derbyshire
Basil Paterson Tutorial College, Lothian
Beech Hall School, Cheshire
Birkdale School, South Yorkshire
Bowbrook House School, Worcestershire
Brentwood School, Essex
Broadwater Manor School, West Sussex
The Carrdus School, Oxfordshire
Catteral Hall, North Yorkshire
Craigclowan Preparatory School, Perthshire
The Crescent School, Warwickshire
Dean Close Preparatory School, Gloucestershire
Dover College, Kent
Durham School, County Durham
Durlston Court, Hampshire
Elm Grove School, Devon
The Elms, Worcestershire
Filgrave School, Buckinghamshire
Flexlands School, Surrey
Greenfield School, Surrey
Grove Independent School, Buckinghamshire
Halstead Preparatory School, Surrey
Hatherop Castle School, Gloucestershire

Heathcote School, Essex
Hethersett Old Hall School, Norfolk
Holmewood House, Kent
Hordle Walhampton School, Hampshire
Horlers Pre-Preparatory School,
    Cambridgeshire
International Community School, NW1
The Junior School, St Lawrence College,
    Kent
Kilgraston (A Sacred Heart School),
    Perthshire
Kimbolton School, Cambridgeshire
King Edward's School, West Midlands
The King's School, Cheshire
Kingsmead School, Merseyside
Kingswood College at Scarisbrick Hall,
    Lancashire
Kirkstone House School, Cambridgeshire
Langley School, Norfolk
The Leys School, Cambridgeshire
Liverpool College, Merseyside
Lyndon School, Conwy
Mander Portman Woodward,
    Cambridgeshire
Manor Preparatory School, Oxfordshire
Marymount International School, Surrey
Mount St Mary's College, Derbyshire
Nethercliffe School, Hampshire
Northbourne Park School, Kent
Northcote Lodge, SW11
Nower Lodge School, Surrey
Oakhill College, Lancashire
The Old Hall School, Shropshire
The Princess Helena College, Hertfordshire
Queen Victoria School, Perthshire

Rannoch School, Perthshire
Rastrick Prep and Nursery School,
    West Yorkshire
St Aubyns, East Sussex
St Bede's, East Sussex
St Catherine's School, Surrey
St Catherine's School, Surrey
St Christopher's School, Kent
St Crispin's School (Leicester) Ltd.,
    Leicestershire
St Edmund's Junior School, Kent
St Faith's at Ash School, Kent
St Hilary's School, Surrey
St John's College School,
    Cambridgeshire
St Joseph's Convent, Derbyshire
St Margaret's School, Essex
St Mary's Westbrook, Kent
St Michael's, Devon
St Teresa's Preparatory School, Surrey
St Ursula's High School, Bristol
The Schiller International School, SE1
Slindon College, West Sussex
Stanbridge Earls School, Hampshire
Steephill School, Kent
Stourbridge House School, Wiltshire
Surbiton High School, Surrey
Tashbar Primary School, Greater
    Manchester
Taverham Hall, Norfolk
Tower House School, SW14
Woodcote House School, Surrey
Worksop College, Nottinghamshire
Worth School, West Sussex

Level 3

Abbey Gate College, Cheshire
The Abbey School, Gloucestershire
Ardingly College, West Sussex
Ashgrove School, Kent
Attenborough Preparatory School,
    Nottinghamshire
Babington House School, Kent

Baston School, Kent
Bedgebury School, Kent
Benedict House Preparatory School, Kent
Bethany School, Kent
Bishop Challoner RC School, Kent
Bosworth Independent College,
    Northamptonshire

Boundary Oak School, Hampshire
Bow School, County Durham
Bristol Grammar School, Bristol
Butterstone School, Perthshire
Cable House School, Surrey
Carleton House Preparatory School,
    Merseyside
Chinthurst School, Surrey
Chorcliffe School, Lancashire
The Chorister School, County Durham
Churchers College, Hampshire
Claires Court School, Berkshire
Clifton College, Bristol
Collingham, SW5
Collingwood School, Surrey
Copthorne School, West Sussex
d'Overbroeck's College, Oxfordshire
Dagfa House School, Nottinghamshire
Derby Grammar School for boys,
    Derbyshire
The Downs School, Worcestershire
Duke of York's Royal Military School, Kent
Duncombe School, Hertfordshire
Elmwood Montessori School, W4
Ewell Castle School, Surrey
Felsted School, Essex
Giggleswick School, North Yorkshire
Great Ballard School, West Sussex
Haileybury, Hertfordshire
The Hampshire Schools (Kensington
    Gardens), W2
The Hampshire Schools (Knightsbridge
    Under School), SW7
The Hampshire Schools (Knightsbridge
    Upper School), SW7
Handsworth Christian School,
    South Yorkshire
Harrogate Tutorial College,
    North Yorkshire
Hazlegrove (King's Bruton Preparatory
    School), Somerset
Hessle Mount School,
    East Riding of Yorkshire
Highfield School, SW18
Highgate Junior School, N6

Highgate School, N6
Hipperholme Grammar School,
    West Yorkshire
Holme Grange School, Berkshire
Hornsby House School, SW12
Hutchesons' Grammar School, Glasgow
CKHR Immanuel College, Hertfordshire
Keble Preparatory School, N21
Kelly College, Devon
King's College, Somerset
The King's School, Nottinghamshire
King's School, Devon
La Retraite Swan, Wiltshire
Lavant House Rosemead, West Sussex
Laverock School, Surrey
Linley House, Surrey
Little Acorns Montessori School,
    Hertfordshire
Little Eden SDA School & Eden High
    SDA School, Middlesex
Malvern College, Worcestershire
Marist Convent Senior School, Berkshire
Mayfield Preparatory School, West
    Midlands
Mostyn House School, Cheshire
The Mount School, NW7
Norfolk Lodge Nursery & Preparatory
    School, Hertfordshire
Old Palace School of John Whitgift, Surrey
Orchard House School, W4
The Park School, Somerset
Phoenix School, Bedfordshire
Pocklington School,
    East Riding of Yorkshire
Priory School, West Midlands
Ramillies Hall School, Cheshire
Reading Blue Coat School, Berkshire
Rochester Independent College, Kent
Rosebrae School, Morayshire
The Royal High School,
    North East Somerset
The Ryleys, Cheshire
St Andrew's School, East Sussex
St Anne's Nursery & Pre-Preparatory
    School, Hampshire

St Anselm's, Derbyshire
St Bees School, Cumbria
St Brandon's School, Somerset
St David's School, Surrey
St Hilda's School, Essex
St Hugh's School, Lincolnshire
St John's School, Essex
St Joseph's Preparatory School,
  Staffordshire
St Mary's Preparatory School,
  Roxburghshire
St Peter & St Paul School, Derbyshire
St Peter's School, North Yorkshire
St Petroc's School, Cornwall
St Teresa's School, Buckinghamshire
Sancton Wood School, Cambridgeshire
Sedbergh School, Cumbria

The Study Preparatory School, SW19
The Study School, Surrey
Surbiton Preparatory School, Surrey
Talbot Heath, Dorset
Taunton School, Somerset
Thorpe House School, Buckinghamshire
Truro School, Cornwall
Upton House School, Berkshire
Victoria College Belfast, County Antrim
Wakefield Tutorial Preparatory School,
  West Yorkshire
Westminster School, SW1P
Westville House Preparatory School,
  West Yorkshire
Widford Lodge, Essex
Woodbridge School, Suffolk
Yarrells School, Dorset

Unspecified

Annemount School, N2
Bury Lawn School, Buckinghamshire
Cambridge Arts & Sciences (CATS),
  Cambridgeshire
Cherwell College, Oxfordshire
Dollar Academy, Clackmannanshire
Ellesmere College, Shropshire
Glenarm College, Essex
Hillcroft Preparatory School, Suffolk

Homefield School Senior & Preparatory,
  Dorset
Marlin Montessori School, Hertfordshire
Milton Abbey School, Dorset
Oundle School Laxton Junior,
  Cambridgeshire
Ranby House, Nottinghamshire
St Teresa's School, Surrey
Toddlers and Mums Montessori, W2

Attention Deficit/Hyperactivity Disorder

Level 1

Barnardiston Hall Preparatory School,
  Suffolk
Hazelwood School, Surrey
The Leys School, Cambridgeshire

Northampton Christian School,
  Northamptonshire
Rossall School, Lancashire
St Columba's College, Hertfordshire

Level 2

All Hallows, Somerset
Ashbourne PNEU School, Derbyshire
Basil Paterson Tutorial College, Lothian
Bowbrook House School, Worcestershire
Broadwater Manor School, West Sussex

The Carrdus School, Oxfordshire
Catteral Hall, North Yorkshire
The Crescent School, Warwickshire
Dover College, Kent
Durlston Court, Hampshire

Elm Grove School, Devon
Filgrave School, Buckinghamshire
Flexlands School, Surrey
Grove Independent School,
   Buckinghamshire
Halstead Preparatory School, Surrey
Heathcote School, Essex
Heswall Preparatory School, Merseyside
Holmewood House, Kent
Hordle Walhampton School, Hampshire
International Community School, NW1
The Junior School, St Lawrence College,
   Kent
Kilgraston (A Sacred Heart School),
   Perthshire
Kimbolton School, Cambridgeshire
The King's School, Cheshire
Kirkstone House School, Cambridgeshire
Liverpool College, Merseyside
Lyndon School, Conwy
Mander Portman Woodward,
   Cambridgeshire
Nethercliffe School, Hampshire
Northcote Lodge, SW11
The Old Hall School, Shropshire
The Princess Helena College,
   Hertfordshire
Queen Victoria School, Perthshire

Rannoch School, Perthshire
Rastrick Prep and Nursery School,
   West Yorkshire
St Bede's, East Sussex
St Christopher's School, Kent
St Crispin's School (Leicester) Ltd.,
   Leicestershire
St John's College School, Cambridgeshire
St Joseph's Convent, Derbyshire
St Margaret's School, Essex
St Mary's Westbrook, Kent
St Michael's, Devon
St Teresa's Preparatory School, Surrey
St Ursula's High School, Bristol
The Schiller International School, SE1
Slindon College, West Sussex
Stanbridge Earls School, Hampshire
Steephill School, Kent
Stourbridge House School, Wiltshire
Surbiton High School, Surrey
Surbiton Preparatory School, Surrey
Tashbar Primary School,
   Greater Manchester
Taverham Hall, Norfolk
Woodcote House School, Surrey
Worth School, West Sussex
Yarrells School, Dorset

Level 3

Abbey Gate College, Cheshire
Ardingly College, West Sussex
Attenborough Preparatory School,
   Nottinghamshire
Baston School, Kent
Bedgebury School, Kent
Benedict House Preparatory School, Kent
Bishop Challoner RC School, Kent
Bosworth Independent College,
   Northamptonshire
Boundary Oak School, Hampshire
Bow School, County Durham
Bradford Grammar School, West Yorkshire
Bristol Grammar School, Bristol

Cable House School, Surrey
Carleton House Preparatory School,
   Merseyside
Chinthurst School, Surrey
The Chorister School, County Durham
Churchers College, Hampshire
Claires Court School, Berkshire
Collingwood School, Surrey
Copthorne School, West Sussex
d'Overbroeck's College, Oxfordshire
Dagfa House School, Nottinghamshire
Derby Grammar School for boys,
   Derbyshire
The Downs School, Worcestershire

Elmwood Montessori School, W4
Ewell Castle School, Surrey
Giggleswick School, North Yorkshire
The Hampshire Schools (Kensington Gardens), W2
The Hampshire Schools (Knightsbridge Under School), SW7
The Hampshire Schools (Knightsbridge Upper School), SW7
Handsworth Christian School, South Yorkshire
Hessle Mount School, East Riding of Yorkshire
Highfield School, SW18
Highgate Junior School, N6
Highgate School, N6
Holme Grange School, Berkshire
Hornsby House School, SW12
Hull Grammar School, East Riding of Yorkshire
Hutchesons' Grammar School, Glasgow
CKHR Immanuel College, Hertfordshire
Kelly College, Devon
Laverock School, Surrey
Little Acorns Montessori School, Hertfordshire
Little Eden SDA School & Eden High SDA School, Middlesex
Marist Convent Senior School, Berkshire
Mayfield Preparatory School, West Midlands
Mostyn House School, Cheshire
The Mount School, NW7
Norfolk Lodge Nursery & Preparatory School, Hertfordshire
Northbourne Park School, Kent
Old Palace School of John Whitgift, Surrey
Orchard House School, W4
Papplewick, Berkshire

The Park School, Somerset
Phoenix School, Bedfordshire
Pocklington School, East Riding of Yorkshire
Ramillies Hall School, Cheshire
Reading Blue Coat School, Berkshire
Rosebrae School, Morayshire
Rougemont School, Newport
The Royal High School, North East Somerset
St Andrew's School, East Sussex
St Andrew's School, Kent
St Anne's Nursery & Pre-Preparatory School, Hampshire
St Anselm's, Derbyshire
St Clare's, Oxford, Oxfordshire
St Hugh's School, Lincolnshire
St John's School, Essex
St Joseph's Preparatory School, Staffordshire
St Mary's Preparatory School, Roxburghshire
St Peter & St Paul School, Derbyshire
St Petroc's School, Cornwall
St Teresa's School, Buckinghamshire
Sedbergh School, Cumbria
The Study Preparatory School, SW19
The Study School, Surrey
Talbot Heath, Dorset
Taunton School, Somerset
Truro School, Cornwall
Upton House School, Berkshire
Victoria College Belfast, County Antrim
Wakefield Tutorial Preparatory School, West Yorkshire
Westville House Preparatory School, West Yorkshire
Widford Lodge, Essex
Woodbridge School, Suffolk
Worksop College, Nottinghamshire

Unspecified

Annemount School, N2
Cambridge Arts & Sciences (CATS), Cambridgeshire

Cherwell College, Oxfordshire
Dollar Academy, Clackmannanshire
Ellesmere College, Shropshire

Hatherop Castle School, Gloucestershire
Hillcroft Preparatory School, Suffolk
Homefield School Senior & Preparatory,
  Dorset
Milton Abbey School, Dorset

Oundle School Laxton Junior,
  Cambridgeshire
St Teresa's School, Surrey
Salisbury Cathedral School, Wiltshire

Asperger's Syndrome

Level 1

Bellan House Preparatory School,
  Shropshire
Flexlands School, Surrey
Fulneck School, West Yorkshire
Kingsley Preparatory School, West
  Midlands

The Leys School, Cambridgeshire
St Bede's School, Staffordshire
St Mary's Westbrook, Kent
St Petroc's School, Cornwall
Woodside Park International School,
  N11

Level 2

Abbot's Hill, Hertfordshire
All Hallows, Somerset
All Saints School, Norfolk
Ashbourne PNEU School, Derbyshire
Basil Paterson Tutorial College, Lothian
Beech Hall School, Cheshire
Bowbrook House School, Worcestershire
Broadwater Manor School, West Sussex
The Carrdus School, Oxfordshire
Chinthurst School, Surrey
Craigclowan Preparatory School,
  Perthshire
The Crescent School, Warwickshire
Duncombe School, Hertfordshire
Durlston Court, Hampshire
The Elms, Worcestershire
Filgrave School, Buckinghamshire
Friends' School, Essex
Glenhurst School, Hampshire
Grove Independent School,
  Buckinghamshire
Heathcote School, Essex
International Community School, NW1
The Junior School, St Lawrence College,
  Kent
Kilgraston (A Sacred Heart School),
  Perthshire

King Edward's School, West Midlands
Kingsmead School, Merseyside
Langley Preparatory School & Nursery,
  Norfolk
Little Acorns Montessori School,
  Hertfordshire
Manor Preparatory School, Oxfordshire
Marymount Convent School, Merseyside
Northbourne Park School, Kent
The Old Hall School, Shropshire
Oswestry School, Shropshire
Polam Hall, County Durham
The Princess Helena College,
  Hertfordshire
Rosebrae School, Morayshire
St Andrew's Montessori School,
  Hertfordshire
St Bede's, East Sussex
St Christopher's School, Kent
St Christophers School, Devon
St Edmund's Junior School, Kent
St George's School, Suffolk
St James's School, Worcestershire
St John's College School, Cambridgeshire
St John's School, Essex
St Margaret's School, Essex
St Peter & St Paul School, Derbyshire

St Ursula's High School, Bristol
Stanbridge Earls School, Hampshire
Surbiton High School, Surrey
Surbiton Preparatory School, Surrey

Tashbar Primary School, Greater
    Manchester
Woodcote House School, Surrey
Yarrells School, Dorset

Level 3

Abbey Gate College, Cheshire
The Atherley School, Hampshire
Batley Grammar School, West Yorkshire
Benedict House Preparatory School, Kent
Bishop Challoner RC School, Kent
Bosworth Independent College,
    Northamptonshire
Boundary Oak School, Hampshire
Bow School, County Durham
Bradford Grammar School, West Yorkshire
Bristol Grammar School, Bristol
Carleton House Preparatory School,
    Merseyside
Catteral Hall, North Yorkshire
Chorcliffe School, Lancashire
The Chorister School, County Durham
Collingham, SW5
Collingwood School, Surrey
Copthill School, Lincolnshire
Dagfa House School, Nottinghamshire
Derby Grammar School for boys,
    Derbyshire
Elm Grove School, Devon
Elmwood Montessori School, W4
Ewell Castle School, Surrey
The Froebelian School, West Yorkshire
Ghyll Royd School, West Yorkshire
Giggleswick School, North Yorkshire
Gramercy Hall School, Devon
Hazlegrove (King's Bruton Preparatory
    School), Somerset
Hessle Mount School,
    East Riding of Yorkshire
Hillcroft Preparatory School, Suffolk
Hipperholme Grammar School,
    West Yorkshire
Hutchesons' Grammar School, Glasgow
CKHR Immanuel College, Hertfordshire

The King's School, Cheshire
The King's School, Nottinghamshire
Latymer Upper School, W6
Lavant House Rosemead, West Sussex
Leeds Grammar School, West Yorkshire
Liverpool College, Merseyside
Mayfield Preparatory School,
    West Midlands
The Montessori House, N10
The Mount School, NW7
Newcastle-under-Lyme School,
    Staffordshire
Northwood College, Middlesex
Old Palace School of John Whitgift,
    Surrey
Orchard House School, W4
Papplewick, Berkshire
The Park School, Somerset
Phoenix School, Bedfordshire
Pocklington School,
    East Riding of Yorkshire
Rochester Independent College, Kent
The Royal High School, North East
    Somerset
St Andrew's School, East Sussex
St Andrew's School, Kent
St Anselm's, Derbyshire
St Bees School, Cumbria
St Brandon's School, Somerset
St Columba's College, Hertfordshire
St Hilda's School, Essex
St Joseph's Preparatory School,
    Staffordshire
St Mary's School, South Yorkshire
St Mary's School, Cambridgeshire
St Teresa's Preparatory School, Surrey
St Teresa's School, Buckinghamshire
Sedbergh School, Cumbria

Snaresbrook College Preparatory School,
E18
Taunton School, Somerset
Thorpe House School, Buckinghamshire
Toddlers and Mums Montessori, W2
Upton House School, Berkshire
Vernon Lodge Preparatory School,
Staffordshire

Victoria College Belfast, County Antrim
Wakefield Tutorial Preparatory School,
West Yorkshire
Westville House Preparatory School,
West Yorkshire
Widford Lodge, Essex
Woodbridge School, Suffolk
Worksop College, Nottinghamshire

Unspecified

Annemount School, N2
Cransley School, Cheshire
Dollar Academy, Clackmannanshire
Ellesmere College, Shropshire
Highgate School, N6
Marlin Montessori School, Hertfordshire

Milton Abbey School, Dorset
Norfolk Lodge Nursery & Preparatory
School, Hertfordshire
St Philomena's Preparatory School,
Essex
St Teresa's School, Surrey

Autism

Level 1

Barnardiston Hall Preparatory School,
Suffolk
Dolphin School, SW11

St Mary's Westbrook, Kent
Woodside Park International School,
N11

Level 2

Ashbourne PNEU School, Derbyshire
The Elms, Worcestershire
Filgrave School, Buckinghamshire
International Community School, NW1
The Junior School, St Lawrence College,
Kent
Langley School, Norfolk
Little Acorns Montessori School,
Hertfordshire

The Old Hall School, Shropshire
Rosebrae School, Morayshire
St Bede's, East Sussex
St Bede's School, Staffordshire
St Christopher's School, Kent
St Christophers School, Devon
St George's School, Suffolk
Tashbar Primary School,
Greater Manchester

Level 3

Abbey Gate College, Cheshire
Benedict House Preparatory School, Kent
Bishop Challoner RC School, Kent
Boundary Oak School, Hampshire
Carleton House Preparatory School,
Merseyside

The Carrdus School, Oxfordshire
The Chorister School, County Durham
Collingwood School, Surrey
The Crescent School, Warwickshire
Dagfa House School, Nottinghamshire
Duncombe School, Hertfordshire

Elm Grove School, Devon
Elmwood Montessori School, W4
Hessle Mount School,
    East Riding of Yorkshire
Hillcroft Preparatory School, Suffolk
The King's School, Nottinghamshire
Mayfield Preparatory School,
    West Midlands
The Montessori House, N10
Norfolk Lodge Nursery & Preparatory
    School, Hertfordshire
Orchard House School, W4
The Park School, Somerset
Phoenix School, Bedfordshire

The Royal High School,
    North East Somerset
St Andrew's School, Kent
St Joseph's Preparatory School,
    Staffordshire
St Teresa's School, Buckinghamshire
Victoria College Belfast, County Antrim
Waverley House PNEU School,
    Nottinghamshire
Westville House Preparatory School,
    West Yorkshire
Widford Lodge, Essex
Woodcote House School, Surrey

Unspecified

Cherry Trees School, Suffolk
Gatehouse School, E2
Highgate School, N6

Pocklington School,
    East Riding of Yorkshire
St Teresa's School, Surrey

Cerebral Palsy

Level 1

St Bede's School, Staffordshire

St Joseph's Convent, Derbyshire

Level 2

Abbot's Hill, Hertfordshire
Alcuin School, West Yorkshire
Ashbourne PNEU School, Derbyshire
Hethersett Old Hall School, Norfolk
Hordle Walhampton School, Hampshire
Leeds Girls' High School, West Yorkshire
Loreto Preparatory School, Cheshire
Orchard House School, W4

Polam Hall, County Durham
Rastrick Prep and Nursery School, West
    Yorkshire
Rosebrae School, Morayshire
St Christophers School, Devon
St Ursula's High School, Bristol
Vernon Lodge Preparatory School,
    Staffordshire

Level 3

Abbey Gate College, Cheshire
Airthrie School, Gloucestershire
The Atherley School, Hampshire
Batley Grammar School,
    West Yorkshire

Bellan House Preparatory School,
    Shropshire
Benedict House Preparatory School, Kent
Boundary Oak School, Hampshire
Butterstone School, Perthshire

The Carrdus School, Oxfordshire
Cherry Trees School, Suffolk
Collingwood School, Surrey
Elmwood Montessori School, W4
Friends' School, Essex
Hessle Mount School,
    East Riding of Yorkshire
Hornsby House School, SW12
Hutchesons' Grammar School,
    Glasgow
Ipswich Preparatory School, Suffolk
Lavant House Rosemead, West Sussex
Laverock School, Surrey
Leeds Grammar School, West Yorkshire
The Lyceum, EC2A
Mayfield Preparatory School,
    West Midlands
The Montessori House, N10
The Mount School, NW7
Northwood College, Middlesex
The Park School, Somerset

Phoenix School, Bedfordshire
Pocklington School,
    East Riding of Yorkshire
St Andrew's School, East Sussex
St Andrew's School, Kent
St Joseph's Preparatory School,
    Staffordshire
St Mary's School, South Yorkshire
St Mary's School, Cambridgeshire
Sir William Perkins's School, Surrey
Snaresbrook College Preparatory School,
    E18
The Study Preparatory School, SW19
Taunton School, Somerset
Toddlers and Mums Montessori, W2
Upton House School, Berkshire
Victoria College Belfast, County Antrim
Westville House Preparatory School,
    West Yorkshire
Widford Lodge, Essex
Worksop College, Nottinghamshire

Unspecified

Bury Lawn School, Buckinghamshire
Cranford House School, Oxfordshire
Highgate School, N6
Hillcroft Preparatory School, Suffolk

Marlin Montessori School, Hertfordshire
St Teresa's School, Surrey
Yateley Manor Preparatory School,
    Hampshire

Delicate

Level 1

Barnardiston Hall Preparatory School,
    Suffolk

The Mulberry House School, NW2
St Bede's School, Staffordshire

Level 2

Abbotsford School, Warwickshire
All Hallows, Somerset
Ashbourne PNEU School, Derbyshire
Cokethorpe School, Oxfordshire
Flexlands School, Surrey
Friends' School, Essex

Glenhurst School, Hampshire
Heathcote School, Essex
Kilgraston (A Sacred Heart School),
    Perthshire
Langley School, Norfolk
Loreto Preparatory School, Cheshire

Manor Preparatory School, Oxfordshire
Polam Hall, County Durham
St Bede's, East Sussex
St Christopher's School, Kent
St Dominic's School, Staffordshire

St Margaret's School, Essex
Stanbridge Earls School, Hampshire
Stourbridge House School, Wiltshire
The Study Preparatory School, SW19
Upton House School, Berkshire

Level 3

Abbey Gate College, Cheshire
The Abbey School, Gloucestershire
The Atherley School, Hampshire
Basil Paterson Tutorial College,
    Lothian
Bellan House Preparatory School,
    Shropshire
Benedict House Preparatory School,
    Kent
Bishop Challoner RC School, Kent
Boundary Oak School, Hampshire
The Carrdus School, Oxfordshire
Chase Academy, Staffordshire
Cherry Trees School, Suffolk
The Chorister School, County Durham
Collingham, SW5
Collingwood School, Surrey
Edward Greene's Tutorial Establishment,
    Oxfordshire
Elm Grove School, Devon
Elmwood Montessori School, W4
Ewell Castle School, Surrey
Giggleswick School, North Yorkshire
Great Ballard School, West Sussex
Harrogate Tutorial College, North
    Yorkshire
Hessle Mount School, East Riding of
    Yorkshire
Hillcroft Preparatory School, Suffolk
Ipswich School, Suffolk
The King's School, Nottinghamshire
Kingsley Preparatory School, West
    Midlands
La Retraite Swan, Wiltshire
Lavant House Rosemead,
    West Sussex
Liverpool College, Merseyside

Mayfield Preparatory School, West
    Midlands
The Mount School, NW7
Northampton Preparatory School,
    Northamptonshire
Orchard House School, W4
Phoenix School, Bedfordshire
Priory School, West Midlands
Rosebrae School, Morayshire
The Royal High School,
    North East Somerset
Rudolf Steiner School, Devon
The Ryleys, Cheshire
St Andrew's Montessori School,
    Hertfordshire
St Andrew's School, East Sussex
St Andrew's School, Kent
St James's School, Worcestershire
St Joseph's in the Park, Hertfordshire
St Joseph's Preparatory School,
    Staffordshire
St Mary's School, Cambridgeshire
St Teresa's Preparatory School, Surrey
Sancton Wood School, Cambridgeshire
Slindon College, West Sussex
Stonelands School of Ballet & Theatre Arts,
    East Sussex
Talbot Heath, Dorset
Taunton School, Somerset
Victoria College Belfast,
    County Antrim
Waverley House PNEU School,
    Nottinghamshire
Westonbirt School, Gloucestershire
Westville House Preparatory School,
    West Yorkshire
Widford Lodge, Essex

Unspecified

Abbot's Hill, Hertfordshire
Cambridge Tutors College, Surrey
Cranford House School, Oxfordshire
Fulneck School, West Yorkshire
Glenarm College, Essex
Highgate School, N6
Marlin Montessori School, Hertfordshire
Norfolk Lodge Nursery & Preparatory School, Hertfordshire
Pocklington School, East Riding of Yorkshire
St Christophers School, Devon
St Nicholas House, Hertfordshire
St Teresa's School, Surrey
Sibford School, Oxfordshire
Toddlers and Mums Montessori, W2

Down's Syndrome

Level 2

Ashbourne PNEU School, Derbyshire
Little Eden SDA School & Eden High SDA School, Middlesex
Rastrick Prep and Nursery School, West Yorkshire
St Andrew's Montessori School, Hertfordshire
St Christopher's School, Kent
St Christophers School, Devon

Level 3

Abbey Gate College, Cheshire
All Saints School, Norfolk
Benedict House Preparatory School, Kent
Boundary Oak School, Hampshire
The Carrdus School, Oxfordshire
Elmwood Montessori School, W4
Hessle Mount School, East Riding of Yorkshire
Laverock School, Surrey
Little Acorns Montessori School, Hertfordshire
Mayfield Preparatory School, West Midlands
The Montessori House, N10
Mostyn House School, Cheshire
Orchard House School, W4
Phoenix School, Bedfordshire
Princes Avenue School, N10
Rosebrae School, Morayshire
St Andrew's School, Kent
St Joseph's Preparatory School, Staffordshire
Upton House School, Berkshire
Victoria College Belfast, County Antrim
Westville House Preparatory School, West Yorkshire
Widford Lodge, Essex

Unspecified

Gatehouse School, E2
Highgate School, N6
Hillcroft Preparatory School, Suffolk
Marlin Montessori School, Hertfordshire
Norfolk Lodge Nursery & Preparatory School, Hertfordshire
Pocklington School, East Riding of Yorkshire
St Teresa's School, Surrey
Toddlers and Mums Montessori, W2

Dyscalculia

Level 1

Abbotsholme School, Staffordshire
Airthrie School, Gloucestershire
Barnardiston Hall Preparatory School, Suffolk
Birchfield School, West Midlands
Bredon School, Gloucestershire
Clifton College, Bristol
Grosvenor School, Nottinghamshire
Hazlegrove (King's Bruton Preparatory School), Somerset
Hillcroft Preparatory School, Suffolk
Kingswood House School, Surrey
Northampton Christian School, Northamptonshire
The Old Hall School, Shropshire
Oswestry School, Shropshire
Riddlesworth Hall, Norfolk
St Anne's Nursery & Pre-Preparatory School, Hampshire
St Bees School, Cumbria
St Columba's College, Hertfordshire
St David's College, Conwy
St John's School, Devon
Stanbridge Earls School, Hampshire
Stonyhurst College, Lancashire
Thornlow Preparatory School, Dorset
Wimbledon College Prep School, SW19
Woodside Park International School, N11

Level 2

The Abbey School, Gloucestershire
Abbot's Hill, Hertfordshire
Annemount School, N2
Ascham House School, Tyne and Wear
Ashbourne PNEU School, Derbyshire
Attenborough Preparatory School, Nottinghamshire
Babington House School, Kent
Battle Abbey School, East Sussex
Bedgebury School, Kent
Beech Hall School, Cheshire
Berkhampstead School, Gloucestershire
Boundary Oak School, Hampshire
Broadmead School, Bedfordshire
Carleton House Preparatory School, Merseyside
Catteral Hall, North Yorkshire
Cherry Trees School, Suffolk
Chesham Preparatory School, Buckinghamshire
Chinthurst School, Surrey
Christ College, Powys
Claires Court School, Berkshire
Cobham Hall, Kent
Cokethorpe School, Oxfordshire
Colchester High School, Essex
Collingham, SW5
Connaught House, W2
Copthorne School, West Sussex
Cranford House School, Oxfordshire
Dover College, Kent
Dragon School, Oxfordshire
Duncombe School, Hertfordshire
Durlston Court, Hampshire
Ealing Montessori School, W3
Edward Greene's Tutorial Establishment, Oxfordshire
Egerton-Rothesay School, Hertfordshire
Elliott Park School, Kent
Elm Grove School, Devon
Ewell Castle School, Surrey
Filgrave School, Buckinghamshire
The Firs School, Cheshire
Flexlands School, Surrey
George Heriot's School, Lothian
Giggleswick School, North Yorkshire
Great Ballard School, West Sussex
Greenbank, Cheshire
The Hampshire Schools (Kensington Gardens), W2

Handsworth Christian School,
South Yorkshire
Harvington School, W5
Hatherop Castle School, Gloucestershire
Hazelwood School, Surrey
Hethersett Old Hall School, Norfolk
The High School of Dundee, Angus
Highgate School, N6
Holmwood House, Essex
Hordle Walhampton School, Hampshire
Horlers Pre-Preparatory School,
Cambridgeshire
Hornsby House School, SW12
CKHR Immanuel College, Hertfordshire
Ipswich Preparatory School, Suffolk
The Junior School, St Lawrence College,
Kent
Keble Preparatory School, N21
Kelly College, Devon
Kilgraston (A Sacred Heart School),
Perthshire
Kimbolton School, Cambridgeshire
King's College, Somerset
King's Hall School, Somerset
King's Preparatory School, Rochester, Kent
Kingham Hill School, Oxfordshire
Kingswood College at Scarisbrick Hall,
Lancashire
Kirkstone House School, Cambridgeshire
Langley Preparatory School & Nursery,
Norfolk
Langley School, Norfolk
Lathallan School, Angus
Lavant House Rosemead, West Sussex
Lincoln Minster School, Lincolnshire
Liverpool College, Merseyside
Lomond School, Argyll and Bute
The Lyceum, EC2A
Lyndon School, Conwy
Maidwell Hall, Northamptonshire
Malvern College, Worcestershire
Mander Portman Woodward,
Cambridgeshire
Manor Preparatory School, Oxfordshire
Marist Convent Senior School, Berkshire

Millfield Preparatory School, Somerset
Moorfield School, West Yorkshire
Newlands Manor School, East Sussex
Newlands Preparatory School, East Sussex
Norman Court Preparatory School,
Wiltshire
Northampton Preparatory School,
Northamptonshire
Northbourne Park School, Kent
Northcote Lodge, SW11
Nower Lodge School, Surrey
Oakhill College, Lancashire
Oakwood School, West Sussex
Paragon School, North East Somerset
Polam Hall, County Durham
Port Regis, Dorset
Priory School, West Midlands
Queen Victoria School, Perthshire
Ramillies Hall School, Cheshire
Rannoch School, Perthshire
Rastrick Prep and Nursery School,
West Yorkshire
Red House School, Stockton-on-Tees
Rickmansworth PNEU School,
Hertfordshire
Rosebrae School, Morayshire
The Royal High School,
North East Somerset
Royal Russell School, Surrey
Rupert House, Oxfordshire
The Ryleys, Cheshire
Sacred Heart Preparatory School, Bristol
St Agnes PNEU School, West Yorkshire
St Anselm's, Derbyshire
St Aubyn's School, Devon
St Aubyns, East Sussex
St Bede's, East Sussex
St Catherine's School, Surrey
St Christopher's School, Kent
St Crispin's School (Leicester) Ltd.,
Leicestershire
St Dominic's School, Staffordshire
St Edmund's Junior School, Kent
St George's School, Berkshire
St Hugh's School, Oxfordshire

St Hugh's School, Lincolnshire
St James's School, Worcestershire
St John's College School,
  Cambridgeshire
St John's School, Bridgend
St John's-on-the-Hill, Monmouthshire
St Joseph's Convent, Derbyshire
St Joseph's in the Park, Hertfordshire
St Joseph's School, Nottinghamshire
St Martin's Preparatory School,
  North East Lincolnshire
St Mary's Preparatory School,
  Roxburghshire
St Michael's, Devon
St Michael's School, Kent
St Nicholas House, Hertfordshire
St Teresa's Preparatory School, Surrey
St Teresa's School, Buckinghamshire
St Ursula's High School, Bristol
The Schiller International School, SE1
Sevenoaks School, Kent

Slindon College, West Sussex
Steephill School, Kent
Stonar School, Wiltshire
Taunton School, Somerset
Terrington Hall, North Yorkshire
Tettenhall College, West Midlands
Toddlers and Mums Montessori, W2
Treliske School, Cornwall
Trent College, Nottinghamshire
Upton House School, Berkshire
Victoria College Belfast,
  County Antrim
Wakefield Tutorial Preparatory School,
  West Yorkshire
Waverley House PNEU School,
  Nottinghamshire
Westminster School, SW1P
Westville House Preparatory School,
  West Yorkshire
Winterfold House, Worcestershire
Woodcote House School, Surrey

Level 3

Abbey Gate College, Cheshire
Ampleforth College, North Yorkshire
Ashdown House School, East Sussex
Ashford School, Kent
Ashgrove School, Kent
Bancroft's School, Essex
Beeston Hall School, Norfolk
Benedict House Preparatory School, Kent
Bishop Challoner RC School, Kent
Bramcote School, North Yorkshire
Bristol Grammar School, Bristol
Butterstone School, Perthshire
The Carrdus School, Oxfordshire
Chorcliffe School, Lancashire
Churchers College, Hampshire
Collingwood School, Surrey
Copthill School, Lincolnshire
The Crescent School, Warwickshire
Dagfa House School, Nottinghamshire
Derby Grammar School for boys,
  Derbyshire

Downside School, North East Somerset
Edenhurst School, Staffordshire
Elmwood Montessori School, W4
Emanuel School, SW11
Falkner House, SW7
Felsted School, Essex
Frensham Heights, Surrey
Haileybury, Hertfordshire
Hessle Mount School,
  East Riding of Yorkshire
Linley House, Surrey
Longwood School, Hertfordshire
Mayfield Preparatory School,
  West Midlands
Mostyn House School, Cheshire
Old Palace School of John Whitgift, Surrey
Orchard House School, W4
Pocklington School,
  East Riding of Yorkshire
Rochester Independent College, Kent
St Andrew's School, East Sussex

St Andrew's School, Kent
St Aubyn's School, Essex
St David's School, Surrey
St Hilda's School, Essex
St John's School, Essex
St Joseph's Preparatory School,
  Staffordshire

Sedbergh School, Cumbria
The Study Preparatory School, SW19
The Study School, Surrey
Talbot Heath, Dorset
Wentworth College, Dorset
Widford Lodge, Essex

Unspecified

Cambridge Arts & Sciences (CATS),
  Cambridgeshire
Cherwell College, Oxfordshire
Cransley School, Cheshire
d'Overbroeck's College, Oxfordshire
Dollar Academy, Clackmannanshire
Ellesmere College, Shropshire
The Hampshire Schools (Knightsbridge
  Upper School), SW7
Homefield School Senior & Preparatory,
  Dorset

Milton Abbey School, Dorset
Ranby House, Nottinghamshire
St Christophers School, Devon
St George's School, Berkshire
St Teresa's School, Surrey
Salisbury Cathedral School, Wiltshire
Sibford School, Oxfordshire
Sunninghill Preparatory School,
  Dorset
Woodbridge School, Suffolk

Dyslexia

Level 1

Abbotsholme School, Staffordshire
Airthrie School, Gloucestershire
Akeley Wood Junior School,
  Buckinghamshire
Ashville College, North Yorkshire
Austin Friars, Cumbria
Barnardiston Hall Preparatory School,
  Suffolk
Bethany School, Kent
Birchfield School, West Midlands
Bramcote School, North Yorkshire
Bredon School, Gloucestershire
Chiltern Tutorial Unit, Hampshire
Christ College, Powys
Clifton College, Bristol
The Dominie, SW11
Dulwich Preparatory School, Cranbrook,
  Kent
Friends' School, Essex

Fulneck School, West Yorkshire
Hazlegrove (King's Bruton Preparatory
  School), Somerset
Hillcroft Preparatory School, Suffolk
Hopelands School, Gloucestershire
Kingsley Preparatory School,
  West Midlands
Kingswood House School, Surrey
Lambrook Haileybury, Berkshire
The Leys School, Cambridgeshire
Mayville High School, Hampshire
Millfield Preparatory School, Somerset
Mostyn House School, Cheshire
Mount St Mary's College, Derbyshire
The Mulberry House School, NW2
Northampton Christian School,
  Northamptonshire
The Old Hall School, Shropshire
Oswestry School, Shropshire

Pennthorpe School, West Sussex
Prestfelde Preparatory School, Shropshire
Prospect House School, SW15
Riddlesworth Hall, Norfolk
Rossall School, Lancashire
The Royal High School,
    North East Somerset
St Andrew's School, Kent
St Anne's Nursery & Pre-Preparatory
    School, Hampshire
St Bees School, Cumbria
St Columba's College, Hertfordshire
St David's College, Conwy
St Edward's School, Oxfordshire
St James's School, Worcestershire
St Leonards-Mayfield School, East Sussex

St Mary's Westbrook, Kent
Sedbergh School, Cumbria
Shiplake College, Oxfordshire
Stanbridge Earls School, Hampshire
Stanway School, Surrey
Stoke Brunswick, West Sussex
Stonyhurst College, Lancashire
Taverham Hall, Norfolk
Thornlow Preparatory School, Dorset
Tockington Manor School, Bristol
Uplands School, Dorset
Wimbledon College Prep School,
    SW19
Wolverhampton Grammar School,
    West Midlands
Worksop College, Nottinghamshire

Level 2

Abbey Gate School, Cheshire
The Abbey School, Gloucestershire
The Abbey, Suffolk
Abbot's Hill, Hertfordshire
Abbotsford School, Warwickshire
Aberlour House, Banffshire
Akeley Wood School, Buckinghamshire
Albyn School for Girls, Aberdeenshire
Alcuin School, West Yorkshire
All Hallows, Somerset
All Saints School, Norfolk
Ampleforth College, North Yorkshire
Annemount School, N2
Ardingly College, West Sussex
Ardvreck School, Perthshire
Arundale Preparatory School, West Sussex
Ascham House School, Tyne and Wear
Ashbourne PNEU School, Derbyshire
The Atherley School, Hampshire
Attenborough-Preparatory School,
    Nottinghamshire
Babington House School, Kent
Basil Paterson Tutorial College, Lothian
Baston School, Kent
Battle Abbey School, East Sussex
Beaudesert Park, Gloucestershire

Bedales School, Hampshire
Bedford Modern School, Bedfordshire
Bedgebury School, Kent
Beech Hall School, Cheshire
Belhaven Hill, Lothian
Bellan House Preparatory School,
    Shropshire
Berkhampstead School, Gloucestershire
Bilton Grange, Warwickshire
Birkdale School, South Yorkshire
Bishop Challoner RC School, Kent
Blundell's School, Devon
Bodiam Manor School, East Sussex
Bootham School, North Yorkshire
Bosworth Independent College,
    Northamptonshire
Boundary Oak School, Hampshire
Bow School, County Durham
Bowbrook House School, Worcestershire
Box Hill School, Surrey
Brabyns School, Cheshire
Brentwood School, Essex
Brighton College Prep School, East Sussex
Bristol Grammar School, Bristol
Broadmead School, Bedfordshire
Broadwater Manor School, West Sussex

Giggleswick School, North Yorkshire
The Glasgow Academy, Glasgow
Glenalmond College, Perthshire
Glenhurst School, Hampshire
Godstowe Preparatory School,
    Buckinghamshire
The Grange, Worcestershire
Great Ballard School, West Sussex
Greenbank, Cheshire
Greenfield School, Surrey
Grey House Preparatory School,
    Hampshire
Grosvenor School, Nottinghamshire
Grove Independent School,
    Buckinghamshire
Haileybury, Hertfordshire
Hallfield School, West Midlands
Halstead Preparatory School, Surrey
The Hampshire Schools
    (Kensington Gardens), W2
The Hampshire Schools
    (Knightsbridge Under School), SW7
The Hampshire Schools
    (Knightsbridge Upper School), SW7
Hampton School, Middlesex
Handsworth Christian School,
    South Yorkshire
Harecroft Hall School, Cumbria
Haresfoot Preparatory School,
    Hertfordshire
Harrogate Ladies' College,
    North Yorkshire
Harrow School, Middlesex
Harvington School, W5
Hatherop Castle School, Gloucestershire
Hawley Place School, Surrey
Hazelwood School, Surrey
Heath Mount School, Hertfordshire
Heathcote School, Essex
Heathfield School, Berkshire
Hendon Preparatory School, NW4
Heswall Preparatory School, Merseyside
Hethersett Old Hall School, Norfolk
High March School, Buckinghamshire
The High School of Dundee, Angus

Highfield Preparatory School,
    North Yorkshire
Highfield School, Hampshire
Highfields School, Nottinghamshire
Highgate School, N6
Hill House Preparatory School,
    South Yorkshire
Hillcrest Grammar School, Cheshire
Hipperholme Grammar School,
    West Yorkshire
Holme Grange School, Berkshire
Holmewood House, Kent
Holmwood House, Essex
Holy Cross Preparatory School, Surrey
Hordle Walhampton School, Hampshire
Horlers Pre-Preparatory School,
    Cambridgeshire
Hornsby House School, SW12
Howell's School, Llandaff GDST, Cardiff
Hull Grammar School,
    East Riding of Yorkshire
CKHR Immanuel College, Hertfordshire
International Community School, NW1
Ipswich Preparatory School, Suffolk
The Junior School, St Lawrence College,
    Kent
Keble Preparatory School, N21
Kelly College, Devon
Kilgraston (A Sacred Heart School),
    Perthshire
Kimbolton School, Cambridgeshire
King Edward VII and Queen Mary School,
    Lancashire
King Edward's School, West Midlands
King's College, Somerset
King's Hall School, Somerset
King's Preparatory School, Rochester, Kent
The King's School, Cheshire
The King's School, Gloucestershire
The King's School, Nottinghamshire
King's School, Devon
King's School Rochester, Kent
The King's School, Worcestershire
Kingham Hill School, Oxfordshire
Kingshott, Hertfordshire

Parkside School, Surrey
Peterborough High School,
    Cambridgeshire
Plumtree School, Nottinghamshire
Pocklington School,
    East Riding of Yorkshire
Polam Hall, County Durham
Port Regis, Dorset
The Princess Helena College,
    Hertfordshire
Prior's Field School, Surrey
Priory School, West Midlands
Queen Elizabeth's Hospital, Bristol
Queen Margaret's School, North Yorkshire
Queen Mary's School, North Yorkshire
Queen Victoria School, Perthshire
Queen's College, W1N
Ramillies Hall School, Cheshire
Rannoch School, Perthshire
Rastrick Prep and Nursery School, West
    Yorkshire
Red House School, Stockton-on-Tees
The Richard Pate School, Gloucestershire
Rickmansworth PNEU School,
    Hertfordshire
Rose Hill School, Kent
Rosebrae School, Morayshire
Rougemont School, Newport
Royal Belfast Academical Institution,
    County Antrim
Royal Russell School, Surrey
Ruckleigh School, West Midlands
Rupert House, Oxfordshire
Rydal Penrhos Senior School, Conwy
The Ryleys, Cheshire
Sacred Heart Preparatory School, Bristol
St Agnes PNEU School, West Yorkshire
St Andrew's Montessori School,
    Hertfordshire
St Andrew's School, East Sussex
St Andrew's School, Surrey
St Anselm's, Derbyshire
St Aubyn's School, Devon
St Aubyns, East Sussex
St Bede's, East Sussex

St Bernard's Preparatory School, Berkshire
St Brandon's School, Somerset
St Catherine's School, Surrey
St Catherine's School, Middlesex
St Catherine's School, Surrey
St Christopher's School, Kent
St Christophers School, Devon
St Crispin's School (Leicester) Ltd.,
    Leicestershire
St Dominic's Priory School, Staffordshire
St Dominic's School, Staffordshire
St Edmund's Junior School, Kent
St Faith's at Ash School, Kent
St Felix School, Suffolk
St George's School, Suffolk
St George's School, Berkshire
St Hilary's School, Surrey
St Hilda's School, Essex
St Hilda's School, West Yorkshire
St Hugh's School, Lincolnshire
St Hugh's School, Oxfordshire
St John's College School,
    Cambridgeshire
St John's School, Devon
St John's School, Bridgend
St John's School, Essex
St John's-on-the-Hill, Monmouthshire
St Joseph's Convent, Derbyshire
St Joseph's in the Park, Hertfordshire
St Joseph's Preparatory School,
    Staffordshire
St Joseph's School, Nottinghamshire
St Joseph's School, Cornwall
St Katharines Preparatory School, Fife
St Leonards School & St Leonards VIth
    Form College, Fife
St Margaret's School, Essex
St Margaret's School, Lothian
St Martin's Ampleforth, North Yorkshire
St Martin's Preparatory School,
    North East Lincolnshire
St Mary's Preparatory School,
    Roxburghshire
St Mary's Preparatory School, Lincolnshire
St Mary's School, South Yorkshire

St Mary's School, Ascot, Berkshire
St Michael's, Devon
St Michael's School, Kent
St Nicholas House, Hertfordshire
St Olave's Preparatory School, SE9
St Peter & St Paul School, Derbyshire
St Peter's School, North Yorkshire
St Petroc's School, Cornwall
St Philip's School, SW7
St Piran's Preparatory School, Berkshire
St Teresa's School, Surrey
St Teresa's Preparatory School, Surrey
St Teresa's School, Buckinghamshire
St Ursula's High School, Bristol
Salcombe School, N14
Salisbury Cathedral School, Wiltshire
Sancton Wood School, Cambridgeshire
Sandhurst School, West Sussex
Sandroyd, Wiltshire
The Schiller International School, SE1
Sevenoaks School, Kent
Silchester House School, Berkshire
Skippers Hill Manor Preparatory School,
    East Sussex
Slindon College, West Sussex
Snaresbrook College Preparatory School,
    E18
South Lee Preparatory School, Suffolk
Southbank International School,
    Hampstead, NW3
Steephill School, Kent
Stoke College, Suffolk
Stonar School, Wiltshire
Stourbridge House School, Wiltshire
The Study School, Surrey
Summer Fields, Oxfordshire
Sunningdale School, Berkshire
Surbiton High School, Surrey
Surbiton Preparatory School, Surrey
Talbot Heath, Dorset
Tashbar Primary School, Greater
    Manchester
Taunton School, Somerset
Teesside High School, Stockton-on-Tees
Terrington Hall, North Yorkshire

Tettenhall College, West Midlands
Thetford Grammar School, Norfolk
Thomas's Preparatory School, W8
Thorngrove School, Berkshire
Thorpe House School, Norfolk
Thorpe House School,
    Buckinghamshire
Toddlers and Mums Montessori, W2
Tormead School, Surrey
Tower House School, SW14
Town Close House Preparatory School,
    Norfolk
Treliske School, Cornwall
Trent College, Nottinghamshire
Truro School, Cornwall
Tudor Hall School, Oxfordshire
Twyford School, Hampshire
Unicorn School, Surrey
University College School, NW3
Upton House School, Berkshire
Vernon Lodge Preparatory School,
    Staffordshire
Victoria College Belfast,
    County Antrim
Vinehall School, East Sussex
Wakefield Tutorial Preparatory School,
    West Yorkshire
Walthamstow Hall, Kent
Waverley House PNEU School,
    Nottinghamshire
Waverley School, Berkshire
Wellingborough School,
    Northamptonshire
Wells Cathedral Junior School,
    Somerset
Wentworth College, Dorset
West House School, West Midlands
Westminster School, SW1P
Westonbirt School, Gloucestershire
Westville House Preparatory School,
    West Yorkshire
Wetherby School, W2
White House Preparatory School,
    Berkshire
Whitehall School, Cambridgeshire

Winterfold House, Worcestershire
Woodbridge School, Suffolk
Woodcote House School, Surrey
Woodhouse Grove School,
    West Yorkshire

Worth School, West Sussex
Wycliffe College, Gloucestershire
Yarrells School, Dorset
York House School, Hertfordshire

Level 3

Abbey College, Greater Manchester
Abbey Gate College, Cheshire
The Arts Educational School, W4
Ashdown House School, East Sussex
Ashford School, Kent
Ashgrove School, Kent
Bancroft's School, Essex
Batley Grammar School, West Yorkshire
Benedict House Preparatory School, Kent
Bolton School (Girls' Division),
    Lancashire
Bradford Grammar School,
    West Yorkshire
Bramley School, Surrey
Bury Grammar School (Girls'),
    Lancashire
Butterstone School, Perthshire
Cable House School, Surrey
Central Newcastle High School GDST,
    Tyne and Wear
Charterhouse, Surrey
Chorcliffe School, Lancashire
Colston's Girls' School, Bristol
Croydon High School GDST, Surrey
The Dixie Grammar School,
    Leicestershire
Elmwood Montessori School, W4
Eltham College, SE9
Emanuel School, SW11
Falkner House, SW7
Francis Holland School, SW1W
The Godolphin and Latymer School, W6
Gramercy Hall School, Devon
Haberdashers' Aske's Boys' School,
    Hertfordshire
Harrogate Tutorial College,
    North Yorkshire

Hawkesdown House School, W8
Hessle Mount School,
    East Riding of Yorkshire
Highfield School, SW18
Highgate Junior School, N6
Howitt House School, Staffordshire
Hutchesons' Grammar School,
    Glasgow
International School of London, W3
Ipswich High School GDST, Suffolk
Ipswich School, Suffolk
Latymer Upper School, W6
Leicester Grammar School,
    Leicestershire
Linley House, Surrey
Longwood School, Hertfordshire
Loughborough Grammar School,
    Leicestershire
Mander Portman Woodward, SW7
Mayfield Preparatory School, West
    Midlands
The Mead School, Kent
The Montessori House, N10
More House, SW1X
The Mount School, NW7
Old Palace School of John Whitgift, Surrey
The Park School, Somerset
Phoenix School, Bedfordshire
Princes Avenue School, N10
Reading Blue Coat School, Berkshire
Rochester Independent College, Kent
Roselyon Preparatory School, Cornwall
Royal Hospital School, Suffolk
St Aubyn's School, Essex
St Clare's, Oxford, Oxfordshire
St Colette's School, Cambridgeshire
St David's School, Surrey

St Mary's School, Buckinghamshire
St Mary's School, Cambridgeshire
St Oswald's School, Northumberland
Sands School, Devon
Shrewsbury House School, Surrey
Sir William Perkins's School, Surrey
Stonelands School of Ballet & Theatre Arts, East Sussex

The Study Preparatory School, SW19
Victoria College, Channel Islands
Widford Lodge, Essex
Withington Girls' School, Greater Manchester
Woodside Park International School, N11

Unspecified

Abbotsford Preparatory School, Greater Manchester
Beeston Hall School, Norfolk
Bricklehurst Manor Preparatory, East Sussex
Broomwood Hall School, SW12
Bury Lawn School, Buckinghamshire
Cambridge Arts & Sciences (CATS), Cambridgeshire
Cambridge Tutors College, Surrey
Cherwell College, Oxfordshire
Clifton College Preparatory School, Bristol
Colfe's School, SE12
Cranleigh School, Surrey
Cransley School, Cheshire
Cundall Manor School, North Yorkshire
d'Overbroeck's College, Oxfordshire
Davies Laing and Dick Independent VI Form College, W2
Dollar Academy, Clackmannanshire
Dolphin School, SW11
Eaton House The Manor, SW4
Ellesmere College, Shropshire
Exeter Tutorial College, Devon
Farringtons & Stratford House, Kent
Fernhill School, South Lanarkshire
Foxley PNEU School, Berkshire
Gatehouse School, E2
Glenarm College, Essex
Grantchester House, Surrey
Grenville College, Devon
Hall Grove School, Surrey
Haslemere Preparatory School, Surrey

Hellenic College of London, SW1X
Homefield School Senior & Preparatory, Dorset
Kent College, Kent
The Kerem School, N2
Lammas School, Nottinghamshire
Leeds Girls' High School, West Yorkshire
Marlin Montessori School, Hertfordshire
Milton Abbey School, Dorset
Moira House Junior School, East Sussex
North Bridge House School, NW1
Old Vicarage School, Surrey
The Oratory School, Berkshire
Oundle School Laxton Junior, Cambridgeshire
Parsons Mead, Surrey
Pembridge Hall, W2
Ranby House, Nottinghamshire
Read School, North Yorkshire
Reigate St Mary's Preparatory and Choir School, Surrey
Rossefield School, West Yorkshire
St Bede's School, Staffordshire
St George's School, Berkshire
St Hilda's School, Hertfordshire
St John's Priory School, Oxfordshire
St Paul's Girls' School, W6
St Philomena's Preparatory School, Essex
Scarborough College, North Yorkshire
Sibford School, Oxfordshire
Stamford School, Lincolnshire
Stanborough School, Hertfordshire

Stockton House School, Hampshire
The Stroud School, Hampshire
Sunninghill Preparatory School, Dorset
Surrey College, Surrey
Temple Grove, East Sussex
The Mount School, North Yorkshire

Tower Dene Preparatory School, Merseyside
Wakefield Girls' High School, West Yorkshire
Weston Green School, Surrey
Yateley Manor Preparatory School, Hampshire

Dyspraxia

Level 1

Abbotsholme School, Staffordshire
Akeley Wood Junior School, Buckinghamshire
Ashville College, North Yorkshire
Barnardiston Hall Preparatory School, Suffolk
Birchfield School, West Midlands
Bredon School, Gloucestershire
Clifton College, Bristol
The Dominie, SW11
Dulwich Preparatory School, Cranbrook, Kent
Fulneck School, West Yorkshire
Grosvenor School, Nottinghamshire
Hazelwood School, Surrey
Hazlegrove (King's Bruton Preparatory School), Somerset
Hillcroft Preparatory School, Suffolk
Kingsley Preparatory School, West Midlands
Kingswood House School, Surrey
Lambrook Haileybury, Berkshire
The Leys School, Cambridgeshire

Mostyn House School, Cheshire
Northampton Christian School, Northamptonshire
Oswestry School, Shropshire
Prestfelde Preparatory School, Shropshire
Riddlesworth Hall, Norfolk
Rossall School, Lancashire
The Royal High School, North East Somerset
St Anne's Nursery & Pre-Preparatory School, Hampshire
St Aubyn's School, Devon
St Columba's College, Hertfordshire
St David's College, Conwy
St Edward's School, Oxfordshire
St James's School, Worcestershire
St John's School, Devon
St Leonards-Mayfield School, East Sussex
Stoke Brunswick, West Sussex
Stonyhurst College, Lancashire
Wimbledon College Prep School, SW19
Woodside Park International School, N11

Level 2

Abbey Gate School, Cheshire
The Abbey School, Gloucestershire
Abbot's Hill, Hertfordshire
Abbotsford School, Warwickshire
Alcuin School, West Yorkshire
All Hallows, Somerset
All Saints School, Norfolk

Ampleforth College, North Yorkshire
Annemount School, N2
Ascham House School, Tyne and Wear
Ashbourne PNEU School, Derbyshire
Attenborough Preparatory School, Nottinghamshire
Babington House School, Kent

Basil Paterson Tutorial College, Lothian
Battle Abbey School, East Sussex
Beaudesert Park, Gloucestershire
Bedales School, Hampshire
Bedford Modern School, Bedfordshire
Bedgebury School, Kent
Beech Hall School, Cheshire
Belhaven Hill, Lothian
Bellan House Preparatory School,
  Shropshire
Berkhampstead School, Gloucestershire
Bilton Grange, Warwickshire
Birkdale School, South Yorkshire
Bishop Challoner RC School, Kent
Boundary Oak School, Hampshire
Bowbrook House School, Worcestershire
Brentwood School, Essex
Broadwater Manor School, West Sussex
Cameron House, SW3
Carleton House Preparatory School,
  Merseyside
The Carrdus School, Oxfordshire
Chase Academy, Staffordshire
Cheam School, Berkshire
Cherry Trees School, Suffolk
Chesham Preparatory School,
  Buckinghamshire
The Chorister School, County Durham
Christ College, Powys
Claires Court School, Berkshire
Cobham Hall, Kent
Cokethorpe School, Oxfordshire
Colchester High School, Essex
Collingham, SW5
Connaught House, W2
Copthorne School, West Sussex
Craigclowan Preparatory School,
  Perthshire
Cranford House School, Oxfordshire
Cundall Manor School, North Yorkshire
Dallington School, EC1V
Dean Close Preparatory School,
  Gloucestershire
Dean Close School, Gloucestershire
Dover College, Kent

The Downs School, Worcestershire
Dragon School, Oxfordshire
Duncombe School, Hertfordshire
Dunhurst (Bedales Junior School),
  Hampshire
Durlston Court, Hampshire
Egerton-Rothesay School, Hertfordshire
Elm Grove School, Devon
The Elms, Worcestershire
Ewell Castle School, Surrey
Filgrave School, Buckinghamshire
The Firs School, Cheshire
Flexlands School, Surrey
Friends' School, Essex
The Froebelian School, West Yorkshire
George Heriot's School, Lothian
Ghyll Royd School, West Yorkshire
Giggleswick School, North Yorkshire
The Glasgow Academy, Glasgow
Glenhurst School, Hampshire
Godstowe Preparatory School,
  Buckinghamshire
The Grange, Worcestershire
Great Ballard School, West Sussex
Greenbank, Cheshire
Greenfield School, Surrey
Grove Independent School,
  Buckinghamshire
Haileybury, Hertfordshire
Halstead Preparatory School, Surrey
The Hampshire Schools
  (Kensington Gardens), W2
The Hampshire Schools
  (Knightsbridge Under School), SW7
The Hampshire Schools
  (Knightsbridge Upper School), SW7
Harecroft Hall School, Cumbria
Haresfoot Preparatory School,
  Hertfordshire
Harvington School, W5
Hatherop Castle School, Gloucestershire
Heathcote School, Essex
Hendon Preparatory School, NW4
Heswall Preparatory School, Merseyside
Hethersett Old Hall School, Norfolk

Waverley School, Berkshire
Wellingborough School,
   Northamptonshire
Westminster School, SW1P
Westville House Preparatory School,
   West Yorkshire
Wetherby School, W2
Whitehall School, Cambridgeshire

Winterfold House, Worcestershire
Woodbridge School, Suffolk
Woodcote House School, Surrey
Woodhouse Grove School, West Yorkshire
Worth School, West Sussex
Wycliffe College, Gloucestershire
Yarrells School, Dorset
York House School, Hertfordshire

Level 3

Abbey Gate College, Cheshire
The Arts Educational School, W4
Ashgrove School, Kent
Bancroft's School, Essex
Batley Grammar School, West Yorkshire
Beeston Hall School, Norfolk
Benedict House Preparatory School, Kent
Bethany School, Kent
Bolton School (Girls' Division), Lancashire
Bootham School, North Yorkshire
Bosworth Independent College,
   Northamptonshire
Bradford Grammar School, West Yorkshire
Bramcote School, North Yorkshire
Bristol Grammar School, Bristol
Butterstone School, Perthshire
Cable House School, Surrey
Catteral Hall, North Yorkshire
Charterhouse, Surrey
Chinthurst School, Surrey
Chorcliffe School, Lancashire
Churchers College, Hampshire
Collingwood School, Surrey
Colston's Girls' School, Bristol
Copthill School, Lincolnshire
The Crescent School, Warwickshire
Dagfa House School, Nottinghamshire
Derby Grammar School for boys,
   Derbyshire
Edenhurst School, Staffordshire
Edward Greene's Tutorial Establishment,
   Oxfordshire
Elmwood Montessori School, W4
Eltham College, SE9

Emanuel School, SW11
Falkner House, SW7
Felsted School, Essex
Frensham Heights, Surrey
The Godolphin and Latymer School, W6
Gramercy Hall School, Devon
Haberdashers' Aske's Boys' School,
   Hertfordshire
Handsworth Christian School,
   South Yorkshire
Harrogate Tutorial College,
   North Yorkshire
Hawley Place School, Surrey
Heathfield School, Berkshire
Hessle Mount School,
   East Riding of Yorkshire
Highfield School, SW18
Highgate Junior School, N6
Holme Grange School, Berkshire
Hutchesons' Grammar School, Glasgow
Ipswich Preparatory School, Suffolk
King Edward's School, West Midlands
The King's School, Nottinghamshire
Latymer Upper School, W6
Linley House, Surrey
Long Close School, Berkshire
Longwood School, Hertfordshire
Loughborough Grammar School,
   Leicestershire
Mander Portman Woodward, SW7
The Mary Erskine School, Lothian
Mayfield Preparatory School, West
   Midlands
The Mead School, Kent

The Mount School, NW7
New School, Devon
Northwood College, Middlesex
Old Palace School of John Whitgift, Surrey
Orchard House School, W4
The Park School, Somerset
Phoenix School, Bedfordshire
Pocklington School,
    East Riding of Yorkshire
Reading Blue Coat School, Berkshire
Rochester Independent College, Kent
Roselyon Preparatory School, Cornwall
St Andrew's Montessori School,
    Hertfordshire
St Andrew's School, East Sussex
St Aubyn's School, Essex
St Brandon's School, Somerset
St Colette's School, Cambridgeshire
St David's School, Surrey
St Hilda's School, Essex
St Joseph's Preparatory School,
    Staffordshire
St Peter & St Paul School, Derbyshire
St Peter's School, North Yorkshire
St Teresa's School, Surrey

St Teresa's School, Buckinghamshire
Sancton Wood School, Cambridgeshire
The Schiller International School, SE1
Sedbergh School, Cumbria
Shiplake College, Oxfordshire
Slindon College, West Sussex
Snaresbrook College Preparatory School,
    E18
The Study Preparatory School, SW19
The Study School, Surrey
Talbot Heath, Dorset
Taunton School, Somerset
Teesside High School, Stockton-on-Tees
Toddlers and Mums Montessori, W2
Truro School, Cornwall
Tudor Hall School, Oxfordshire
Wakefield Tutorial Preparatory School,
    West Yorkshire
Wells Cathedral Junior School,
    Somerset
Wentworth College, Dorset
Widford Lodge, Essex
Wolverhampton Grammar School,
    West Midlands
Worksop College, Nottinghamshire

Unspecified

Airthrie School, Gloucestershire
Bricklehurst Manor Preparatory,
    East Sussex
Bury Lawn School, Buckinghamshire
Cambridge Arts & Sciences (CATS),
    Cambridgeshire
Cherwell College, Oxfordshire
Clifton College Preparatory School, Bristol
Colfe's School, SE12
d'Overbroeck's College, Oxfordshire
Davies Laing and Dick Independent VI
    Form College, W2
Dollar Academy, Clackmannanshire
Eaton House The Manor, SW4
Ellesmere College, Shropshire
Gatehouse School, E2
Hall Grove School, Surrey

Hellenic College of London, SW1X
Homefield School Senior & Preparatory,
    Dorset
The Kerem School, N2
King's School, Devon
Marlin Montessori School, Hertfordshire
Milton Abbey School, Dorset
Moira House Junior School, East Sussex
The Oratory School, Berkshire
Oundle School Laxton Junior,
    Cambridgeshire
Ranby House, Nottinghamshire
Read School, North Yorkshire
Rydal Penrhos Senior School, Conwy
St Faith's at Ash School, Kent
St George's School, Berkshire
Scarborough College, North Yorkshire

Sibford School, Oxfordshire
Stanborough School, Hertfordshire
Sunninghill Preparatory School,
    Dorset

Temple Grove, East Sussex
Vernon Lodge Preparatory School,
    Staffordshire

Emotional/Behavioural Difficulties

Level 1

Barnardiston Hall Preparatory School,
    Suffolk
Flexlands School, Surrey
The Leys School, Cambridgeshire
Moira House Girls' School, East Sussex

St Columba's College, Hertfordshire
Stonar School, Wiltshire
Stonyhurst College, Lancashire
Wimbledon College Prep School,
    SW19

Level 2

Annemount School, N2
Ashbourne PNEU School, Derbyshire
Beech Hall School, Cheshire
Cherry Trees School, Suffolk
Elm Grove School, Devon
The Grange, Worcestershire
Great Ballard School, West Sussex
Grove Independent School,
    Buckinghamshire
Hatherop Castle School, Gloucestershire
The Junior School, St Lawrence College,
    Kent
Langley Preparatory School & Nursery,
    Norfolk
Norfolk Lodge Nursery & Preparatory
    School, Hertfordshire
Our Lady's Convent Preparatory School,
    Northamptonshire
Queen Margaret's School, North Yorkshire

Queen Victoria School, Perthshire
Rannoch School, Perthshire
Rastrick Prep and Nursery School, West
    Yorkshire
Rosebrae School, Morayshire
St Bede's, East Sussex
St Catherine's School, Surrey
St Christopher's School, Kent
St John's College School, Cambridgeshire
Salisbury Cathedral School, Wiltshire
Steephill School, Kent
Surbiton High School, Surrey
Tashbar Primary School, Greater
    Manchester
Tower House School, SW14
Upton House School, Berkshire
Victoria College Belfast, County Antrim
Westville House Preparatory School, West
    Yorkshire

Level 3

Abbey Gate College, Cheshire
Attenborough Preparatory School,
    Nottinghamshire
Bancroft's School, Essex
Benedict House Preparatory School, Kent
Cable House School, Surrey

The Carrdus School, Oxfordshire
Chorcliffe School, Lancashire
Churchers College, Hampshire
Collingwood School, Surrey
The Crescent School, Warwickshire
d'Overbroeck's College, Oxfordshire

Derby Grammar School for boys, Derbyshire
Durlston Court, Hampshire
Edward Greene's Tutorial Establishment, Oxfordshire
Elmwood Montessori School, W4
Felsted School, Essex
Friends' School, Essex
Handsworth Christian School, South Yorkshire
Hessle Mount School, East Riding of Yorkshire
Highgate Junior School, N6
Highgate School, N6
Hornsby House School, SW12
Ipswich School, Suffolk
Kilgraston (A Sacred Heart School), Perthshire
The King's School, Nottinghamshire
Lavant House Rosemead, West Sussex
Little Acorns Montessori School, Hertfordshire
Longwood School, Hertfordshire
Mayfield Preparatory School, West Midlands
Oriel Bank, Cheshire

Phoenix School, Bedfordshire
Pocklington School, East Riding of Yorkshire
Reading Blue Coat School, Berkshire
The Royal High School, North East Somerset
The Ryleys, Cheshire
St Andrew's School, Kent
St Anne's Nursery & Pre-Preparatory School, Hampshire
St Margaret's School, Lothian
St Martin's Ampleforth, North Yorkshire
St Peter & St Paul School, Derbyshire
St Petroc's School, Cornwall
St Teresa's School, Buckinghamshire
Stonelands School of Ballet & Theatre Arts, East Sussex
The Study School, Surrey
Taunton School, Somerset
Wakefield Tutorial Preparatory School, West Yorkshire
Waverley House PNEU School, Nottinghamshire
Whitehall School, Cambridgeshire
Widford Lodge, Essex
Woodcote House School, Surrey

Unspecified

Bury Lawn School, Buckinghamshire
Cambridge Arts & Sciences (CATS), Cambridgeshire
Cambridge Tutors College, Surrey
Dollar Academy, Clackmannanshire
Foxley PNEU School, Berkshire
Gatehouse School, E2
Hillcroft Preparatory School, Suffolk

Horlers Pre-Preparatory School, Cambridgeshire
International Community School, NW1
Northampton Christian School, Northamptonshire
St Christophers School, Devon
St Teresa's School, Surrey
Toddlers and Mums Montessori, W2

Epilepsy

Level 1

Flexlands School, Surrey
The Leys School, Cambridgeshire
Oakhill College, Lancashire

St Edmund's Junior School, Kent
Stonar School, Wiltshire
Stonyhurst College, Lancashire

Level 2

All Hallows, Somerset
Ashbourne PNEU School, Derbyshire
Bellan House Preparatory School, Shropshire
Boundary Oak School, Hampshire
The Carrdus School, Oxfordshire
Highfields School, Nottinghamshire
Kingsmead School, Merseyside
Langley School, Norfolk
Lathallan School, Angus
Little Acorns Montessori School, Hertfordshire

Loreto Preparatory School, Cheshire
Polam Hall, County Durham
Rannoch School, Perthshire
Rastrick Prep and Nursery School, West Yorkshire
Rosebrae School, Morayshire
St Christopher's School, Kent
St Ursula's High School, Bristol
Surbiton High School, Surrey
Upton House School, Berkshire

Level 3

Abbey Gate College, Cheshire
Airthrie School, Gloucestershire
Ardingly College, West Sussex
The Arts Educational School, W4
Ashford School, Kent
Ashville College, North Yorkshire
The Atherley School, Hampshire
Bancroft's School, Essex
Basil Paterson Tutorial College, Lothian
Benedict House Preparatory School, Kent
Bishop Challoner RC School, Kent
Bolton School (Girls' Division), Lancashire
Bradford Grammar School, West Yorkshire
Bristol Grammar School, Bristol
Butterstone School, Perthshire
Carleton House Preparatory School, Merseyside
Cherry Trees School, Suffolk
Christ College, Powys
Churchers College, Hampshire
Clarendon Cottage School, Greater Manchester
Collingham, SW5
Collingwood School, Surrey
Dagfa House School, Nottinghamshire
Derby Grammar School for boys, Derbyshire
Dulwich Preparatory School, Cranbrook, Kent

Duncombe School, Hertfordshire
Durlston Court, Hampshire
Edward Greene's Tutorial Establishment, Oxfordshire
Elmwood Montessori School, W4
Ewell Castle School, Surrey
Felsted School, Essex
Friends' School, Essex
Giggleswick School, North Yorkshire
Gramercy Hall School, Devon
Hessle Mount School, East Riding of Yorkshire
Highgate School, N6
Hill House Preparatory School, South Yorkshire
Hillcroft Preparatory School, Suffolk
Hornsby House School, SW12
Hutchesons' Grammar School, Glasgow
Ipswich High School GDST, Suffolk
Ipswich Preparatory School, Suffolk
Ipswich School, Suffolk
Keble Preparatory School, N21
Kilgraston (A Sacred Heart School), Perthshire
King Edward's School, West Midlands
King's College, Somerset
The King's School, Cheshire
Lavant House Rosemead, West Sussex
Leeds Grammar School, West Yorkshire

Lincoln Minster School, Lincolnshire
Liverpool College, Merseyside
Longwood School, Hertfordshire
Lyndhurst School, Surrey
Mander Portman Woodward, SW7
Mayfield Preparatory School, West
  Midlands
Norfolk Lodge Nursery & Preparatory
  School, Hertfordshire
Northwood College, Middlesex
Old Palace School of John Whitgift, Surrey
Phoenix School, Bedfordshire
Queen Margaret's School,
  North Yorkshire
Reading Blue Coat School, Berkshire
Rochester Independent College, Kent
The Royal High School,
  North East Somerset
The Ryleys, Cheshire
St Andrew's School, East Sussex
St Andrew's School, Kent
St Anne's Nursery & Pre-Preparatory
  School, Hampshire
St Clare's, Oxford, Oxfordshire
St Columba's College, Hertfordshire
St Felix School, Suffolk
St Hugh's School, Lincolnshire

St James's School, Worcestershire
St Margaret's School, Lothian
St Mary's School, Cambridgeshire
St Peter's School, North Yorkshire
St Teresa's School, Surrey
Sedbergh School, Cumbria
Shiplake College, Oxfordshire
Slindon College, West Sussex
Snaresbrook College Preparatory
  School, E18
Stonelands School of Ballet & Theatre Arts,
  East Sussex
The Study Preparatory School, SW19
Talbot Heath, Dorset
Taunton School, Somerset
Thorpe House School, Norfolk
Truro School, Cornwall
Victoria College Belfast, County Antrim
Wakefield Tutorial Preparatory School,
  West Yorkshire
Waverley House PNEU School,
  Nottinghamshire
Westminster School, SW1P
Westville House Preparatory School,
  West Yorkshire
Winterfold House, Worcestershire
Yarrells School, Dorset

Unspecified

Abbot's Hill, Hertfordshire
Bury Lawn School, Buckinghamshire
Cambridge Arts & Sciences (CATS),
  Cambridgeshire
Dragon School, Oxfordshire
Hall Grove School, Surrey
Langley Preparatory School & Nursery,
  Norfolk

Moorland School, Lancashire
Northampton Christian School,
  Northamptonshire
Pocklington School,
  East Riding of Yorkshire
St Dominic's Priory School, Staffordshire
St Leonards-Mayfield School, East Sussex
Sibford School, Oxfordshire

Hearing Impairment
Level 1

Hazelwood School, Surrey
The Leys School, Cambridgeshire

St Michael's School, Kent
Wimbledon College Prep School, SW19

Level 2

Abbot's Hill, Hertfordshire
All Hallows, Somerset
Annemount School, N2
Ashbourne PNEU School, Derbyshire
Bedgebury School, Kent
Beech Hall School, Cheshire
Boundary Oak School, Hampshire
The Carrdus School, Oxfordshire
Cherry Trees School, Suffolk
Duncombe School, Hertfordshire
Egerton-Rothesay School, Hertfordshire
Elm Grove School, Devon
Horlers Pre-Preparatory School,
    Cambridgeshire
The Junior School, St Lawrence College,
    Kent
Little Acorns Montessori School,
    Hertfordshire

The Lyceum, EC2A
The Princess Helena College, Hertfordshire
Prior's Field School, Surrey
Queen Mary's School, North Yorkshire
Queen Victoria School, Perthshire
Rastrick Prep and Nursery School,
    West Yorkshire
Rosebrae School, Morayshire
St Aubyn's School, Devon
St Christopher's School, Kent
St Christophers School, Devon
St Margaret's School, Essex
Sancton Wood School, Cambridgeshire
Stonar School, Wiltshire
Summer Fields, Oxfordshire
Surbiton High School, Surrey
Toddlers and Mums Montessori, W2
Upton House School, Berkshire

Level 3

Abbey Gate College, Cheshire
Ardingly College, West Sussex
Ashford School, Kent
Attenborough Preparatory School,
    Nottinghamshire
Babington House School, Kent
Basil Paterson Tutorial College, Lothian
Baston School, Kent
Benedict House Preparatory School, Kent
Bethany School, Kent
Bishop Challoner RC School, Kent
Bolton School (Girls' Division), Lancashire
Bootham School, North Yorkshire
Bosworth Independent College,
    Northamptonshire
Bury Grammar School (Girls'), Lancashire
Butterstone School, Perthshire
Carleton House Preparatory School,
    Merseyside
Christ College, Powys
Churchers College, Hampshire
Claires Court School, Berkshire
Clarendon Cottage School,

    Greater Manchester
Collingham, SW5
Collingwood School, Surrey
Colston's Girls' School, Bristol
Copthill School, Lincolnshire
Copthorne School, West Sussex
The Crescent School, Warwickshire
Croydon High School GDST, Surrey
d'Overbroeck's College, Oxfordshire
Derby Grammar School for boys,
    Derbyshire
The Downs School, Worcestershire
Durlston Court, Hampshire
Edward Greene's Tutorial Establishment,
    Oxfordshire
Elmwood Montessori School, W4
Ewell Castle School, Surrey
Falkner House, SW7
Felsted School, Essex
Flexlands School, Surrey
Francis Holland School, SW1W
Friends' School, Essex
Gramercy Hall School, Devon

Great Ballard School, West Sussex
Handsworth Christian School,
    South Yorkshire
Harrogate Ladies' College, North Yorkshire
Hazlegrove (King's Bruton Preparatory
    School), Somerset
Hessle Mount School,
    East Riding of Yorkshire
High March School, Buckinghamshire
Highgate School, N6
Hipperholme Grammar School,
    West Yorkshire
Holmewood House, Kent
Hordle Walhampton School, Hampshire
Hornsby House School, SW12
Hutchesons' Grammar School, Glasgow
Ipswich High School GDST, Suffolk
Ipswich Preparatory School, Suffolk
Ipswich School, Suffolk
King Edward VII and Queen Mary School,
    Lancashire
King Edward's School, West Midlands
Kingsley Preparatory School, West
    Midlands
Lanesborough, Surrey
Latymer Upper School, W6
Lavant House Rosemead, West Sussex
Leeds Grammar School, West Yorkshire
Linley House, Surrey
Liverpool College, Merseyside
Lomond School, Argyll and Bute
Longwood School, Hertfordshire
Lyndhurst School, Surrey
Mander Portman Woodward, SW7
Manor Preparatory School, Oxfordshire
Mayfield Preparatory School, West
    Midlands
The Mead School, Kent
Moorfield School, West Yorkshire
The Mount School, NW7
New School, Devon
Northampton Preparatory School,
    Northamptonshire
Northbourne Park School, Kent
Northwood College, Middlesex

Old Palace School of John Whitgift,
    Surrey
Orchard House School, W4
Oswestry School, Shropshire
Phoenix School, Bedfordshire
Pocklington School,
    East Riding of Yorkshire
Polam Hall, County Durham
Port Regis, Dorset
Queen Margaret's School, North Yorkshire
Reading Blue Coat School, Berkshire
The Royal High School,
    North East Somerset
Rupert House, Oxfordshire
The Ryleys, Cheshire
St Agnes PNEU School, West Yorkshire
St Andrew's Montessori School,
    Hertfordshire
St Andrew's School, East Sussex
St Andrew's School, Kent
St Bees School, Cumbria
St Clare's, Oxford, Oxfordshire
St Columba's College, Hertfordshire
St Felix School, Suffolk
St Hugh's School, Oxfordshire
St James's School, Worcestershire
St Leonards-Mayfield School,
    East Sussex
St Margaret's School, Lothian
St Mary's School, South Yorkshire
St Teresa's School, Surrey
St Teresa's Preparatory School, Surrey
St Ursula's High School, Bristol
Sedbergh School, Cumbria
Shrewsbury House School, Surrey
Sir William Perkins's School, Surrey
The Study School, Surrey
Talbot Heath, Dorset
Taunton School, Somerset
Teesside High School, Stockton-on-Tees
Thorpe House School, Buckinghamshire
Truro School, Cornwall
Victoria College Belfast, County Antrim
Waverley House PNEU School,
    Nottinghamshire

Westminster School, SW1P
Westville House Preparatory School,
    West Yorkshire
Widford Lodge, Essex
Winterfold House, Worcestershire

Wolverhampton Grammar School,
    West Midlands
Worksop College, Nottinghamshire
Yarrells School, Dorset
York House School, Hertfordshire

Unspecified

Cambridge Tutors College, Surrey
Fulneck School, West Yorkshire
Gatehouse School, E2
Hellenic College of London, SW1X
Hillcroft Preparatory School, Suffolk
The Mulberry House School, NW2

Parsons Mead, Surrey
Prestfelde Preparatory School, Shropshire
St Hilda's School, Hertfordshire
St Paul's Girls' School, W6
Yateley Manor Preparatory School,
    Hampshire

Moderate Learning Difficulties

Level 1

Barnardiston Hall Preparatory School,
    Suffolk
Bramcote School, North Yorkshire
Bredon School, Gloucestershire
Cundall Manor School, North Yorkshire
Egerton-Rothesay School, Hertfordshire
Hillcroft Preparatory School, Suffolk
Hopelands School, Gloucestershire
Kingsley Preparatory School,
    West Midlands

Millfield Preparatory School, Somerset
Northampton Christian School,
    Northamptonshire
The Old Hall School, Shropshire
Pennthorpe School, West Sussex
Polam Hall, County Durham
St Joseph's in the Park, Hertfordshire
Shiplake College, Oxfordshire
Wimbledon College Prep School, SW19
Woodside Park International School, N11

Level 2

Alcuin School, West Yorkshire
All Saints School, Norfolk
Ampleforth College, North Yorkshire
Ashbourne PNEU School, Derbyshire
Attenborough Preparatory School,
    Nottinghamshire
Beech Hall School, Cheshire
Belhaven Hill, Lothian
Bellan House Preparatory School,
    Shropshire
Bow School, County Durham
Cherry Trees School, Suffolk
Clifton College, Bristol
The Compass School, Lothian

Craigclowan Preparatory School,
    Perthshire
Davenport Lodge School, West Midlands
Duncombe School, Hertfordshire
Edward Greene's Tutorial Establishment,
    Oxfordshire
Elm Grove School, Devon
The Elms, Worcestershire
Emmanual Christian School,
    Oxfordshire
Emscote House School and Nursery,
    Warwickshire
The Froebelian School, West Yorkshire
The Grange, Worcestershire

Grove Independent School, Buckinghamshire
Harecroft Hall School, Cumbria
Hatherop Castle School, Gloucestershire
Hawley Place School, Surrey
Heathcote School, Essex
Heswall Preparatory School, Merseyside
Hordle Walhampton School, Hampshire
Horlers Pre-Preparatory School, Cambridgeshire
International Community School, NW1
The Junior School, St Lawrence College, Kent
King's School, Devon
Kingsland Grange, Shropshire
Kirkstone House School, Cambridgeshire
Knighton House, Dorset
Loreto Preparatory School, Cheshire
Lyndon School, Conwy
Malvern Girls' College, Worcestershire
Manor House School, Devon
Manor House School, Leicestershire
Marist Convent Senior School, Berkshire
Marymount Convent School, Merseyside
Marymount International School, Surrey
Moorfield School, West Yorkshire
Moorland School, Lancashire
New Park School, Fife
Norman Court Preparatory School, Wiltshire
Northampton Preparatory School, Northamptonshire
The Oratory Preparatory School, Berkshire
Oriel Bank, Cheshire
Our Lady's Convent Junior School, Oxfordshire
Our Lady's Convent Preparatory School, Northamptonshire
Rannoch School, Perthshire

Rosebrae School, Morayshire
Sacred Heart Preparatory School, Bristol
St Andrew's Montessori School, Hertfordshire
St Andrew's School, Surrey
St Bede's, East Sussex
St Catherine's School, Surrey
St Christopher's School, Kent
St Christophers School, Devon
St Crispin's School (Leicester) Ltd., Leicestershire
St George's School, Suffolk
St Hugh's School, Oxfordshire
St Ia School, Cornwall
St John's School, Devon
St Joseph's School, Cornwall
St Joseph's School, Nottinghamshire
St Margaret's School, Essex
St Michael's, Devon
St Peter & St Paul School, Derbyshire
St Ursula's High School, Bristol
Salcombe School, N14
Steephill School, Kent
Stoke College, Suffolk
Stourbridge House School, Wiltshire
Thorpe House School, Buckinghamshire
Tower House School, SW14
Treliske School, Cornwall
Trent College, Nottinghamshire
Upton House School, Berkshire
Victoria College Preparatory School, Channel Islands
Wakefield Tutorial Preparatory School, West Yorkshire
West House School, West Midlands
Whitehall School, Cambridgeshire
Woodcote House School, Surrey
Worksop College, Nottinghamshire

Level 3

Abbey Gate College, Cheshire
The Abbey School, Gloucestershire
Abinger Hammer Village School, Surrey

Ardvreck School, Perthshire
Benedict House Preparatory School, Kent
The Carrdus School, Oxfordshire

Collingwood School, Surrey
Copthill School, Lincolnshire
Derby Grammar School for boys, Derbyshire
Elmwood Montessori School, W4
Giggleswick School, North Yorkshire
Gramercy Hall School, Devon
Hessle Mount School, East Riding of Yorkshire
Holy Cross Preparatory School, Surrey
Howitt House School, Staffordshire
The Jordans Nursery School, W6
The King's School, Nottinghamshire
Langley Preparatory School & Nursery, Norfolk
Little Acorns Montessori School, Hertfordshire
Longwood School, Hertfordshire
Mayfield Preparatory School, West Midlands

The Montessori House, N10
The Park School, Somerset
Pocklington School, East Riding of Yorkshire
Princes Avenue School, N10
Reading Blue Coat School, Berkshire
St Agnes PNEU School, West Yorkshire
St Andrew's School, Kent
St Anne's Nursery & Pre-Preparatory School, Hampshire
St Aubyn's School, Devon
St Margaret's School, Lothian
St Oswald's School, Northumberland
St Petroc's School, Cornwall
Toddlers and Mums Montessori, W2
Victoria College Belfast, County Antrim
Westville House Preparatory School, West Yorkshire
Widford Lodge, Essex

Unspecified

Annemount School, N2
Broomwood Hall School, SW12
Bury Lawn School, Buckinghamshire
Cambridge Arts & Sciences (CATS), Cambridgeshire
Cranleigh School, Surrey
The Downs School, Worcestershire
Eilmar Montessori School & Nursery, Middlesex
Fernhill School, South Lanarkshire
Foxley PNEU School, Berkshire
Gatehouse School, E2
Glenarm College, Essex
Hall Grove School, Surrey
The Hampshire Schools (Kensington Gardens), W2
Haslemere Preparatory School, Surrey

Highgate School, N6
Hillcrest Grammar School, Cheshire
Lammas School, Nottinghamshire
Marlin Montessori School, Hertfordshire
St Brandon's School, Somerset
St George's School, Berkshire
St John's Priory School, Oxfordshire
St Mary's Preparatory School, Roxburghshire
St Philomena's Preparatory School, Essex
St Teresa's School, Surrey
St Teresa's School, Buckinghamshire
Taverham Hall, Norfolk
Temple Grove, East Sussex
Welsh School of London, NW10
Worth School, West Sussex

Physical Impairment
Level 1

Leeds Grammar School, West Yorkshire
Oakhill College, Lancashire

St Joseph's in the Park, Hertfordshire

Level 2

Alcuin School, West Yorkshire
Ashbourne PNEU School, Derbyshire
Beech Hall School, Cheshire
Boundary Oak School, Hampshire
The Carrdus School, Oxfordshire
Cokethorpe School, Oxfordshire
Derby Grammar School for boys,
    Derbyshire
Egerton-Rothesay School, Hertfordshire
Elm Grove School, Devon
The Firs School, Cheshire
Flexlands School, Surrey
Grove Independent School,
    Buckinghamshire
Kilgraston (A Sacred Heart School),
    Perthshire
Little Acorns Montessori School,
    Hertfordshire
Loreto Preparatory School, Cheshire
Manor Preparatory School, Oxfordshire
Marymount Convent School, Merseyside
Nower Lodge School, Surrey
Polam Hall, County Durham
Queen Victoria School, Perthshire
Rosebrae School, Morayshire
St Bede's, East Sussex
St Christophers School, Devon
St George's School, Suffolk
St Margaret's School, Essex
Upton House School, Berkshire
Walthamstow Hall, Kent
Wimbledon College Prep School, SW19

Level 3

Abbey Gate College, Cheshire
All Hallows, Somerset
Ardingly College, West Sussex
Ashford School, Kent
The Atherley School, Hampshire
Babington House School, Kent
Bancroft's School, Essex
Batley Grammar School, West Yorkshire
Bellan House Preparatory School,
    Shropshire
Benedict House Preparatory School,
    Kent
Birchfield School, West Midlands
Bolton School (Girls' Division),
    Lancashire
Bootham School, North Yorkshire
Bradford Grammar School, West Yorkshire
Cherry Trees School, Suffolk
Chinthurst School, Surrey
Churchers College, Hampshire
Colchester High School, Essex
Collingwood School, Surrey
Copthill School, Lincolnshire
The Crescent School, Warwickshire
Downside School, North East Somerset
Durham School, County Durham
Edward Greene's Tutorial Establishment,
    Oxfordshire
Elmwood Montessori School, W4
Ewell Castle School, Surrey
Felsted School, Essex
Friends' School, Essex
Giggleswick School, North Yorkshire
Gramercy Hall School, Devon
Great Ballard School, West Sussex
Greenfield School, Surrey
Handsworth Christian School,
    South Yorkshire
Harrogate Tutorial College,
    North Yorkshire
Hazlegrove (King's Bruton Preparatory
    School), Somerset
Heathcote School, Essex
Hessle Mount School,
    East Riding of Yorkshire
Hill House Preparatory School,
    South Yorkshire
Hillcroft Preparatory School, Suffolk

Hornsby House School, SW12
Hutchesons' Grammar School, Glasgow
Ipswich High School GDST, Suffolk
Ipswich School, Suffolk
Keble Preparatory School, N21
King Edward VII and Queen Mary School,
  Lancashire
King Edward's School, West Midlands
Kingsley Preparatory School,
  West Midlands
Lavant House Rosemead, West Sussex
Laverock School, Surrey
Lincoln Minster School, Lincolnshire
Linley House, Surrey
Lomond School, Argyll and Bute
Longwood School, Hertfordshire
Mayfield Preparatory School,
  West Midlands
The Mount School, NW7
New School, Devon
Northwood College, Middlesex
Old Palace School of John Whitgift, Surrey
Orchard House School, W4
Oriel Bank, Cheshire
The Park School, Somerset
Phoenix School, Bedfordshire
Pocklington School,
  East Riding of Yorkshire
Port Regis, Dorset
Queen Margaret's School,
  North Yorkshire
Queen's College, W1N
Roselyon Preparatory School, Cornwall
The Royal High School,
  North East Somerset

The Ryleys, Cheshire
St Andrew's Montessori School,
  Hertfordshire
St Andrew's School, Kent
St Anne's Nursery & Pre-Preparatory
  School, Hampshire
St Aubyn's School, Essex
St Clare's, Oxford, Oxfordshire
St Columba's College, Hertfordshire
St Joseph's Preparatory School,
  Staffordshire
St Leonards-Mayfield School,
  East Sussex
St Margaret's School, Lothian
St Teresa's School, Surrey
St Teresa's Preparatory School, Surrey
St Teresa's School, Buckinghamshire
Sancton Wood School, Cambridgeshire
Sedbergh School, Cumbria
Snaresbrook College Preparatory School,
  E18
Talbot Heath, Dorset
Taunton School, Somerset
Toddlers and Mums Montessori, W2
Victoria College Belfast,
  County Antrim
Waverley House PNEU School,
  Nottinghamshire
Westminster School, SW1P
Westonbirt School, Gloucestershire
Westville House Preparatory School,
  West Yorkshire
Widford Lodge, Essex
Woodbridge School, Suffolk

Unspecified

Annemount School, N2
Ashville College, North Yorkshire
Beeston Hall School, Norfolk
Eilmar Montessori School & Nursery,
  Middlesex
Hall Grove School, Surrey
High March School, Buckinghamshire

Highgate School, N6
Horlers Pre-Preparatory School,
  Cambridgeshire
Lyndon School, Conwy
Read School, North Yorkshire
St Bede's School, Staffordshire
St Dominic's Priory School, Staffordshire

Profound/Multiple Learning Difficulties

Level 2

Ashbourne PNEU School, Derbyshire

Tashbar Primary School, Greater
Manchester

Level 3

Abbey Gate College, Cheshire
Benedict House Preparatory School,
Kent
Elmwood Montessori School, W4
Hessle Mount School,
East Riding of Yorkshire

Mayfield Preparatory School,
West Midlands
Phoenix School, Bedfordshire
Rosebrae School, Morayshire
St Andrew's School, Kent
Westville House Preparatory School,
West Yorkshire

Unspecified

The Carrdus School, Oxfordshire
Highgate School, N6
Hillcroft Preparatory School, Suffolk

Pocklington School, East Riding of
Yorkshire
St Teresa's School, Surrey

Severe Learning Difficulties

Level 2

Ashbourne PNEU School, Derbyshire
Beech Hall School, Cheshire
Brabyns School, Cheshire

Cranbrook School, Kent
St George's School, Suffolk

Level 3

Abbey Gate College, Cheshire
Benedict House Preparatory School,
Kent
Broomfield House, Surrey
Elmwood Montessori School, W4
Hessle Mount School, East Riding of
Yorkshire

Mayfield Preparatory School,
West Midlands
Phoenix School, Bedfordshire
Rosebrae School, Morayshire
St Andrew's School, Kent
Westville House Preparatory School,
West Yorkshire

Unspecified

The Carrdus School, Oxfordshire
Highgate School, N6
Hillcroft Preparatory School,
Suffolk

Pocklington School,
East Riding of Yorkshire
St Teresa's School, Surrey
Toddlers and Mums Montessori, W2

Speech and Language Difficulties

Level 1

Bellan House Preparatory School, Shropshire
The Dominie, SW11
Hillcroft Preparatory School, Suffolk
Kingsley Preparatory School, West Midlands
Northampton Christian School, Northamptonshire
St Michael's School, Kent
Woodside Park International School, N11

Level 2

All Hallows, Somerset
Annemount School, N2
Ashbourne PNEU School, Derbyshire
Beech Hall School, Cheshire
Birchfield School, West Midlands
Boundary Oak School, Hampshire
Bramcote School, North Yorkshire
Bredon School, Gloucestershire
Broadmead School, Bedfordshire
The Carrdus School, Oxfordshire
Cherry Trees School, Suffolk
Cokethorpe School, Oxfordshire
Downside School, North East Somerset
Duncombe School, Hertfordshire
Egerton-Rothesay School, Hertfordshire
Elm Grove School, Devon
The Firs School, Cheshire
Flexlands School, Surrey
Friends' School, Essex
Great Ballard School, West Sussex
Grove Independent School, Buckinghamshire
Haresfoot Preparatory School, Hertfordshire
Hatherop Castle School, Gloucestershire
Heswall Preparatory School, Merseyside
Holme Grange School, Berkshire
International Community School, NW1
The Junior School, St Lawrence College, Kent
King's School, Devon
Kirkstone House School, Cambridgeshire
Langley Preparatory School & Nursery, Norfolk
Little Acorns Montessori School, Hertfordshire
Little Eden SDA School & Eden High SDA School, Middlesex
Loreto Preparatory School, Cheshire
The Lyceum, EC2A
Lyndon School, Conwy
Manor House School, Devon
The Mulberry House School, NW2
Nethercliffe School, Hampshire
Northampton Preparatory School, Northamptonshire
Oakhill College, Lancashire
Oakhyrst Grange School, Surrey
Oriel Bank, Cheshire
Port Regis, Dorset
Rannoch School, Perthshire
Rastrick Prep and Nursery School, West Yorkshire
Rosebrae School, Morayshire
St Andrew's Montessori School, Hertfordshire
St Andrew's School, East Sussex
St Aubyns, East Sussex
St Bede's, East Sussex
St Christopher's School, Kent
St Crispin's School (Leicester) Ltd., Leicestershire
St George's School, Suffolk
St Hilary's School, Surrey
St John's-on-the-Hill, Monmouthshire

St Joseph's in the Park, Hertfordshire
St Margaret's School, Essex
St Michael's, Devon
St Teresa's School, Buckinghamshire
Salcombe School, N14
Sancton Wood School, Cambridgeshire
South Lee Preparatory School, Suffolk
Stanbridge Earls School, Hampshire

Steephill School, Kent
Tashbar Primary School, Greater
  Manchester
Victoria College Belfast,
  County Antrim
Wetherby School, W2
Wimbledon College Prep School, SW19
Yarrells School, Dorset

Level 3

Abbey Gate College, Cheshire
The Abbey School, Gloucestershire
Attenborough Preparatory School,
  Nottinghamshire
Babington House School, Kent
Bedgebury School, Kent
Benedict House Preparatory School, Kent
Bradford Grammar School,
  West Yorkshire
Collingwood School, Surrey
Copthill School, Lincolnshire
The Crescent School, Warwickshire
Dallington School, EC1V
Elmwood Montessori School, W4
Ewell Castle School, Surrey
The Froebelian School, West Yorkshire
Ghyll Royd School, West Yorkshire
Handsworth Christian School,
  South Yorkshire
Hazlegrove (King's Bruton Preparatory
  School), Somerset
Hessle Mount School,
  East Riding of Yorkshire
High March School, Buckinghamshire
Ipswich Preparatory School, Suffolk
The Jordans Nursery School, W6

Lavant House Rosemead, West Sussex
Linley House, Surrey
Liverpool College, Merseyside
Longwood School, Hertfordshire
Lyndhurst School, Surrey
Mayfield Preparatory School,
  West Midlands
New School, Devon
Orchard House School, W4
Phoenix School, Bedfordshire
Pocklington School,
  East Riding of Yorkshire
Polam Hall, County Durham
Rupert House, Oxfordshire
The Ryleys, Cheshire
St Andrew's School, Kent
St Anne's Nursery & Pre-Preparatory
  School, Hampshire
St Columba's College, Hertfordshire
St Mary's Westbrook, Kent
St Teresa's Preparatory School, Surrey
Snaresbrook College Preparatory School,
  E18
Toddlers and Mums Montessori, W2
Westville House Preparatory School,
  West Yorkshire

Unspecified

Abbot's Hill, Hertfordshire
Beaudesert Park, Gloucestershire
Bury Lawn School, Buckinghamshire
Claires Court School, Berkshire
Cobham Hall, Kent

Davenport Lodge School, West Midlands
Foxley PNEU School, Berkshire
Highgate School, N6
Horlers Pre-Preparatory School,
  Cambridgeshire

Kingswood House School, Surrey
Marlin Montessori School, Hertfordshire
Norfolk Lodge Nursery & Preparatory
  School, Hertfordshire
Prestfelde Preparatory School, Shropshire
St Bede's School, Staffordshire

St Christophers School, Devon
St John's College School,
  Cambridgeshire
St Peter & St Paul School, Derbyshire
St Teresa's School, Surrey
Sibford School, Oxfordshire

Specific Learning Difficulties

Level 1

Abbotsholme School, Staffordshire
Airthrie School, Gloucestershire
Ashville College, North Yorkshire
Barnardiston Hall Preparatory School,
  Suffolk
Bedgebury School, Kent
Birchfield School, West Midlands
Bramcote School, North Yorkshire
Bredon School, Gloucestershire
The Dominie, SW11
Friends' School, Essex
Hazlegrove (King's Bruton Preparatory
  School), Somerset
Hillcroft Preparatory School, Suffolk
Kingsley Preparatory School,
  West Midlands
Kingswood House School, Surrey

Mayville High School, Hampshire
Millfield Preparatory School, Somerset
The Old Hall School, Shropshire
Pennthorpe School, West Sussex
Prestfelde Preparatory School, Shropshire
Riddlesworth Hall, Norfolk
St Bede's School, Staffordshire
St Bees School, Cumbria
St Columba's College, Hertfordshire
St David's College, Conwy
St Edward's School, Oxfordshire
St James's School, Worcestershire
St Leonards-Mayfield School,
  East Sussex
Thornlow Preparatory School, Dorset
Wimbledon College Prep School, SW19
Woodside Park International School, N11

Level 2

The Abbey School, Gloucestershire
Abbot's Hill, Hertfordshire
All Hallows, Somerset
All Saints School, Norfolk
Ampleforth College, North Yorkshire
Ardvreck School, Perthshire
Ashbourne PNEU School, Derbyshire
Babington House School, Kent
Battle Abbey School, East Sussex
Beaudesert Park, Gloucestershire
Beech Hall School, Cheshire
Belhaven Hill, Lothian
Birkdale School, South Yorkshire
Boundary Oak School, Hampshire

Butterstone School, Perthshire
Cameron House, SW3
Carleton House Preparatory School,
  Merseyside
The Carrdus School, Oxfordshire
Catteral Hall, North Yorkshire
Cheam School, Berkshire
Cherry Trees School, Suffolk
Chiswick and Bedford Park Preparatory
  School, W4
Christ College, Powys
Churchers College, Hampshire
Claires Court School, Berkshire
Cokethorpe School, Oxfordshire

Westville House Preparatory School,
  West Yorkshire
Wetherby School, W2
Whitehall School, Cambridgeshire

Winterfold House, Worcestershire
Woodcote House School, Surrey
Worksop College, Nottinghamshire

Level 3

Abbey Gate College, Cheshire
The Arts Educational School, W4
Benedict House Preparatory School, Kent
Chinthurst School, Surrey
Chorcliffe School, Lancashire
Collingwood School, Surrey
Copthill School, Lincolnshire
Copthorne School, West Sussex
Dagfa House School, Nottinghamshire
The Dixie Grammar School, Leicestershire
Elmwood Montessori School, W4
Handsworth Christian School,
  South Yorkshire
Hessle Mount School,
  East Riding of Yorkshire
Highgate Junior School, N6
Ipswich Preparatory School, Suffolk
Longwood School, Hertfordshire
Lyndhurst School, Surrey

Mayfield Preparatory School,
  West Midlands
The Montessori House, N10
Mostyn House School, Cheshire
The Mount School, NW7
Old Palace School of John Whitgift, Surrey
Orchard House School, W4
Phoenix School, Bedfordshire
Princes Avenue School, N10
Reading Blue Coat School, Berkshire
Rochester Independent College, Kent
Roselyon Preparatory School, Cornwall
St Colette's School, Cambridgeshire
St David's School, Surrey
St Hilda's School, Essex
St Margaret's School, Lothian
St Mary's School, Cambridgeshire
Talbot Heath, Dorset
Widford Lodge, Essex

Unspecified

d'Overbroeck's College, Oxfordshire
Dollar Academy, Clackmannanshire
Eaton House The Manor, SW4
Eilmar Montessori School & Nursery,
  Middlesex
Ellesmere College, Shropshire
Exeter Cathedral School, Devon
Hall Grove School, Surrey
Highgate School, N6
Hillcrest Grammar School, Cheshire
Horlers Pre-Preparatory School,

  Cambridgeshire
Lomond School, Argyll and Bute
The Oratory School, Berkshire
Oundle School Laxton Junior,
  Cambridgeshire
Read School, North Yorkshire
St Martin's Ampleforth, North Yorkshire
St Teresa's School, Surrey
Scarborough College, North Yorkshire
Sibford School, Oxfordshire
Woodbridge School, Suffolk

Tourette Syndrome

Level 1

Kingsley Preparatory School,
  West Midlands

Level 2

Heathcote School, Essex
Norman Court Preparatory School,
   Wiltshire

The Princess Helena College, Hertfordshire
St George's School, Suffolk
St Ursula's High School, Bristol

Level 3

Abbey Gate College, Cheshire
Benedict House Preparatory School, Kent
Bradford Grammar School,
   West Yorkshire
Edward Greene's Tutorial Establishment,
   Oxfordshire
Elmwood Montessori School, W4
Gramercy Hall School, Devon
Hessle Mount School,
   East Riding of Yorkshire
Hutchesons' Grammar School, Glasgow

Mayfield Preparatory School, West
   Midlands
The Park School, Somerset
Phoenix School, Bedfordshire
Rosebrae School, Morayshire
The Ryleys, Cheshire
St Andrew's School, Kent
St Columba's College, Hertfordshire
Upton House School, Berkshire
Westville House Preparatory School,
   West Yorkshire

Unspecified

The Carrdus School, Oxfordshire
Dollar Academy, Clackmannanshire
Highgate School, N6

Hillcroft Preparatory School, Suffolk
St Philomena's Preparatory School, Essex
St Teresa's School, Surrey

Visual Impairment

Level 1

St Joseph's in the Park, Hertfordshire

Level 2

All Hallows, Somerset
Ashbourne PNEU School, Derbyshire
Beech Hall School, Cheshire
The Carrdus School, Oxfordshire
Collingham, SW5
Duncombe School, Hertfordshire
Edward Greene's Tutorial Establishment,
   Oxfordshire
Flexlands School, Surrey
Harrow School, Middlesex

Howitt House School, Staffordshire
The Lyceum, EC2A
Lyndon School, Conwy
Polam Hall, County Durham
Rastrick Prep and Nursery School,
   West Yorkshire
Rosebrae School, Morayshire
St Bees School, Cumbria
St Ursula's High School, Bristol
Surbiton High School, Surrey

Level 3

Abbey Gate College, Cheshire
Babington House School, Kent
Basil Paterson Tutorial College, Lothian
Benedict House Preparatory School, Kent
Bolton School (Girls' Division), Lancashire
Bosworth Independent College, Northamptonshire
Bury Grammar School (Girls'), Lancashire
Churchers College, Hampshire
Claires Court School, Berkshire
Collingwood School, Surrey
Colston's Girls' School, Bristol
Copthill School, Lincolnshire
Derby Grammar School for boys, Derbyshire
Elmwood Montessori School, W4
Ewell Castle School, Surrey
Felsted School, Essex
Friends' School, Essex
Great Ballard School, West Sussex
Heathcote School, Essex
Hessle Mount School, East Riding of Yorkshire
Hipperholme Grammar School, West Yorkshire
Hornsby House School, SW12
Hutchesons' Grammar School, Glasgow
Ipswich High School GDST, Suffolk
Lavant House Rosemead, West Sussex
Leeds Grammar School, West Yorkshire
Lincoln Minster School, Lincolnshire
Linley House, Surrey
Longwood School, Hertfordshire
Lyndhurst School, Surrey

Manor Preparatory School, Oxfordshire
Mayfield Preparatory School, West Midlands
Moorfield School, West Yorkshire
The Mount School, NW7
Northwood College, Middlesex
Phoenix School, Bedfordshire
Pocklington School, East Riding of Yorkshire
Queen Margaret's School, North Yorkshire
The Royal High School, North East Somerset
The Ryleys, Cheshire
St Andrew's Montessori School, Hertfordshire
St Andrew's School, Kent
St Clare's, Oxford, Oxfordshire
St Leonards-Mayfield School, East Sussex
St Margaret's School, Lothian
St Teresa's Preparatory School, Surrey
Shrewsbury House School, Surrey
Stonar School, Wiltshire
The Study Preparatory School, SW19
Teesside High School, Stockton-on-Tees
Thorpe House School, Buckinghamshire
Toddlers and Mums Montessori, W2
Upton House School, Berkshire
Victoria College Belfast, County Antrim
Waverley House PNEU School, Nottinghamshire
Westville House Preparatory School, West Yorkshire
Widford Lodge, Essex
Worksop College, Nottinghamshire
York House School, Hertfordshire

Unspecified

Abbot's Hill, Hertfordshire
Highgate School, N6
Hillcroft Preparatory School, Suffolk

Horlers Pre-Preparatory School, Cambridgeshire
St Teresa's School, Surrey
Sevenoaks School, Kent

Wheelchair access

Level 1

St Brandon's School, Somerset
St George's School, Suffolk
St Joseph's Preparatory School,
　Staffordshire

St Joseph's School, Nottinghamshire
St Peter & St Paul School,
　Derbyshire

Level 3

Upton House School, Berkshire

Unspecified

Abinger Hammer Village School, Surrey
The Atherley School, Hampshire
Attenborough Preparatory School,
　Nottinghamshire
Beaudesert Park, Gloucestershire
Broomwood Hall School, SW12
Churchers College, Hampshire
Eilmar Montessori School & Nursery,
　Middlesex
Elmwood Montessori School, W4
Emmanual Christian School, Oxfordshire
Fonthill Lodge, West Sussex
Heathcote School, Essex
Hillcrest Grammar School, Cheshire
Hillcroft Preparatory School, Suffolk
Homefield School Senior & Preparatory,
　Dorset
Hornsby House School, SW12
Howitt House School, Staffordshire
Hutchesons' Grammar School, Glasgow
The Jordans Nursery School, W6
Kingsley Preparatory School, West
　Midlands
Kingswood Preparatory School,
　North East Somerset
Langley School, Norfolk
Lavant House Rosemead, West Sussex
Leeds Grammar School, West Yorkshire

Long Close School, Berkshire
Longwood School, Hertfordshire
Lord Wandsworth College, Hampshire
Marist Convent Senior School, Berkshire
Marymount Convent School, Merseyside
Meadowpark Nursery & Pre-Prep,
　Wiltshire
New School, Devon
Nower Lodge School, Surrey
Phoenix School, Bedfordshire
The Richard Pate School, Gloucestershire
Rougemont School, Newport
St Andrew's Montessori School,
　Hertfordshire
St Anne's Nursery & Pre-Preparatory
　School, Hampshire
St Bede's School, Staffordshire
St Christophers School, Devon
St Margaret's School, Essex
Summer Fields, Oxfordshire
Treliske School, Cornwall
Victoria College Belfast, County Antrim
Vinehall School, East Sussex
Walthamstow Hall, Kent
Woodbridge School, Suffolk
Yateley Manor Preparatory School,
　Hampshire

PART FIVE: REFERENCE SECTION

5.1
Index of Establishments Classified by Special Need

(Independent and Non-maintained Special Schools and Colleges only)

Note: Schools listed in bold specify that the heading under which they appear is a principal special need.

Asperger's Syndrome

Alderwasley Hall School, Derbyshire
Aran Hall School, Gwynedd
Arden College, Merseyside
Banham Marshalls College, Norfolk
Birkdale School for Hearing Impaired Children, Merseyside
Breckenbrough School, North Yorkshire
Brewood Education Centre, Kent
The Camphill Rudolf Steiner Schools, Aberdeenshire
Chelfham Mill School, Devon
Chelfham Senior School, Devon
Church Hill School, Norfolk
Coleg Elidyr, Carmarthenshire
Cotswold Chine School, Gloucestershire
Coxlease School, Hampshire
Cruckton Hall, Shropshire
Delamere Forest School, Cheshire
Derwen College, Shropshire
Dilston College of Further Education, Northumberland
Don Buss Learning Centre Primary, Kent
Don Buss Learning Opportunities, Kent
Doncaster College for the Deaf, South Yorkshire
Doucecroft School, Essex
Eden Grove School, Cumbria

Fairfield Opportunity Farm, Wiltshire
Farleigh College, Somerset
Farleigh Sixth Form College, Somerset
Farney Close School, West Sussex
Fortune Centre of Riding Therapy, Dorset
Grateley House School, Hampshire
Green Laund F.E. Centre, Derbyshire
Harmeny School, Lothian
Helen Allison School, Kent
Henshaw's College, North Yorkshire
Hereward College, West Midlands
Home School of Stoke Newington, N16
Hope Lodge School, Hampshire
I Can's Dawn House School, Nottinghamshire
Ivers, Dorset
Kisharon Day School, NW11
Lindeth College of Further Education, Cumbria
The Link Primary School, Surrey
The Link Secondary School, Surrey
Linkage Further Education College, Lincolnshire
Linn Moor Residential School, Aberdeenshire
The Marchant-Holliday School, Somerset
Minstead Training Project, Hampshire

The Mount Camphill Community, East Sussex

The National Star Centre's College of Further Education, Gloucestershire

NCH Action for Children, Vale of Glamorgan

The New Learning Centre, NW6

The New School, Perthshire

North Hill House, Somerset

Nugent House School, Lancashire

Oakwood Court, Devon

Ochil Tower (Rudolf Steiner) School, Perthshire

Overley Hall School, Shropshire

Peterhouse School for Pupils with Autism, Merseyside

Philip Green Memorial School, Dorset

Philpots Manor School, West Sussex

Pield Heath School, Middlesex

Pontville School, Lancashire

Potterspury Lodge School, Northamptonshire

Queen Alexandra College of Further Education, West Midlands

Radlett Lodge School for Autistic Children, Hertfordshire

Red Brae School, South Ayrshire

Riverside School, Cumbria

RNIB Condover Hall School, Shropshire

RNIB Redhill College, Surrey

The Robert Ogden School, South Yorkshire

Rossendale Special School, Lancashire

The Ryes School, Suffolk

St Andrews School, Norfolk

St Dominic's School, Surrey

The St John Vianney School, Cheshire

St John's College, East Sussex

St Loye's College, Devon

St Mary's School, East Sussex

St Rose's School, Gloucestershire

St Vincent's School, Merseyside

Southern England Psychological Services, Hampshire

Southlands School, Hampshire

Spring Hill School (Barnardo's), North Yorkshire

Starley Hall, Fife

Strathmore College, Staffordshire

Sunfield, West Midlands

Swalcliffe Park School, Oxfordshire

Thornhill Park School, Tyne and Wear

Underley Garden School, Lancashire

The Unicorn School, Oxfordshire

Wargrave House School, Merseyside

Weelsby Hall Further Education College, North East Lincolnshire

West Kirby Residential School, Merseyside

Westgate College for Deaf People, Kent

Woodcroft School, Essex

Yateley Industries for the Disabled Ltd, Hampshire

Attention Deficit Disorder

Appleford School, Wiltshire

Aran Hall School, Gwynedd

Arden College, Merseyside

Belgrave School, Bristol

Breckenbrough School, North Yorkshire

Brewood Education Centre, Kent

Bryn Melyn Group, Gwynedd

The Camphill Rudolf Steiner Schools, Aberdeenshire

Centre Academy, SW11

Chaigeley School, Cheshire

Chartwell House School, Cambridgeshire

Chelfham Mill School, Devon

Coleg Elidyr, Carmarthenshire

Cotswold Chine School, Gloucestershire

Coxlease School, Hampshire

Delamere Forest School, Cheshire

Don Buss Learning Centre Primary, Kent

Don Buss Learning Opportunities, Kent

Eastwood Grange School, Derbyshire

Eden Grove School, Cumbria
Fairley House School, SW1P
Farney Close School, West Sussex
Fortune Centre of Riding Therapy, Dorset
Grateley House School, Hampshire
Harmeny School, Lothian
Hillcrest Pentwyn School, Herefordshire
Hillside School, Fife
Kings Manor Education Centre,
  East Sussex
Lindeth College of Further Education,
  Cumbria
Linkage Further Education College,
  Lincolnshire
Linn Moor Residential School,
  Aberdeenshire
Loddon School, Hampshire
Maple Hayes Hall Dyslexia School,
  Staffordshire
The Marchant-Holliday School, Somerset
Minstead Training Project, Hampshire
NCH Action for Children,
  Vale of Glamorgan
The New School, Perthshire
Nugent House School, Lancashire
Overley Hall School, Shropshire
Owlswick School, East Sussex
Philip Green Memorial School, Dorset

Philpots Manor School, West Sussex
Pield Heath School, Middlesex
Pontville School, Lancashire
Raddery School, Highland
Riverside School, Cumbria
St Dominic's School, Surrey
St Edwards School, Hampshire
The St John Vianney School, Cheshire
St John's College, East Sussex
St Phillip's School, North Lanarkshire
Southern England Psychological Services,
  Hampshire
Spring Hill School (Barnardo's), North
  Yorkshire
Starley Hall, Fife
Sunfield, West Midlands
Swalcliffe Park School, Oxfordshire
Underley Garden School, Lancashire
Underley Hall School, Lancashire
The Unicorn School, Oxfordshire
Westgate College for Deaf People, Kent
West Kirby Residential School, Merseyside
Whitstone Head School, Devon
Woodcroft School, Essex
Woodlands School, Dumfries & Galloway
Yateley Industries for the Disabled Ltd,
  Hampshire

Attention Deficit/Hyperactivity Disorder

Appleford School, Wiltshire
Aran Hall School, Gwynedd
Arden College, Merseyside
Barnardo's Lecropt Project, Stirling
Bessels Leigh School, Oxfordshire
Breckenbrough School, North Yorkshire
Brewood Education Centre, Kent
Caldecott Community, Kent
The Camphill Rudolf Steiner Schools,
  Aberdeenshire
Cedar House School, Lancashire
Centre Academy, SW11
Chaigeley School, Cheshire

Chelfham Mill School, Devon
Coleg Elidyr, Carmarthenshire
Cotswold Chine School, Gloucestershire
Coxlease School, Hampshire
**Crowthorn School (NCH Action for
  Children), Lancashire**
Cruckton Hall, Shropshire
Delamere Forest School, Cheshire
Didsbury School, Greater Manchester
Don Buss Learning Centre Primary, Kent
Don Buss Learning Opportunities, Kent
Eden Grove School, Cumbria
Fairley House School, SW1P

Farney Close School, West Sussex
Grateley House School, Hampshire
Harmeny School, Lothian
Hillcrest Pentwyn School, Herefordshire
Hillside School, Fife
**Kings Manor Education Centre,
  East Sussex**
Kisharon Day School, NW11
Lindeth College of Further Education,
  Cumbria
Linkage Further Education College,
  Lincolnshire
Linn Moor Residential School,
  Aberdeenshire
Loddon School, Hampshire
Maple Hayes Hall Dyslexia School,
  Staffordshire
The Marchant-Holliday School, Somerset
Meadows School (Barnardo's), Kent
Muntham House School, West Sussex
NCH Action for Children, Vale of
  Glamorgan
The New Learning Centre, NW6
The New School, Perthshire
Nugent House School, Lancashire
Oakbank School, Aberdeenshire
Oakwood Court, Devon
**Ochil Tower (Rudolf Steiner) School,
  Perthshire**
Overley Hall School, Shropshire
Ovingdean Hall School, East Sussex
Owlswick School, East Sussex

Philpots Manor School, West Sussex
Potterspury Lodge School,
  Northamptonshire
Raddery School, Highland
Red Brae School, South Ayrshire
Riverside School, Cumbria
Rossendale Special School, Lancashire
The Ryes School, Suffolk
St Dominic's School, Surrey
The St John Vianney School, Cheshire
St John's College, East Sussex
St Phillip's School, North Lanarkshire
The Sheiling School, Bristol
Southern England Psychological Services,
  Hampshire
Starley Hall, Fife
Sunfield, West Midlands
Swalcliffe Park School, Oxfordshire
Talbot House Independent Special School,
  Newcastle Upon Tyne
Underley Garden School, Lancashire
Underley Hall School, Lancashire
The Unicorn School, Oxfordshire
Weelsby Hall Further Education College,
  North East Lincolnshire
Westwood School, Kent
Whitstone Head School, Devon
Witherslack Hall, Cumbria
Woodcroft School, Essex
Woodlands School, Dumfries & Galloway
Yateley Industries for the Disabled Ltd,
  Hampshire

Autism

Aran Hall School, Gwynedd
Arden College, Merseyside
Beech Tree School, Lancashire
Bladon House School, Staffordshire
Broomhayes School, Devon
Broughton House College, Lincolnshire
Camphill Blair Drummond Trust, Stirling
The Camphill Rudolf Steiner Schools,
  Aberdeenshire

Church Hill School, Norfolk
Cintre Community, Bristol
Coleg Elidyr, Carmarthenshire
 Corbenic Camphill Community,
  Perthshire
Cotswold Chine School, Gloucestershire
Cruckton Hall, Shropshire
Daldorch House School, East Ayrshire
Delrow College, Hertfordshire

Sutherland House School (Secondary Department), Nottinghamshire
The Sybil Elgar School, Middlesex
Thornhill Park School, Tyne and Wear
Tree House, WC1
Wargrave House School, Merseyside
Weelsby Hall Further Education College, North East Lincolnshire

The Wessex Autistic Society, Portfield School, Dorset
Westgate College for Deaf People, Kent
Westwood, Staffordshire
Wilsic Hall School, South Yorkshire
Woodcroft School, Essex
Yateley Industries for the Disabled Ltd, Hampshire

Cerebral Palsy

Beaumont College of Further Education, Lancashire
Birtenshaw Hall, Lancashire
Burton Hill School, Wiltshire
The Camphill Rudolf Steiner Schools, Aberdeenshire
Chailey Heritage School, East Sussex
Coney Hill School, Kent
Craig-y-Parc School, Cardiff
Dame Hannah Rogers School, Devon
Delrow College, Hertfordshire
Derwen College, Shropshire
Doncaster College for the Deaf, South Yorkshire
East Park Home School, Glasgow
Exhall Grange School, Warwickshire
Finchale Training College, County Durham
Fortune Centre of Riding Therapy, Dorset
Fourways Assessment Unit, Greater Manchester
Furze Mount, Conwy
The Grange Centre for People with Disabilities, Surrey
Henshaw's College, North Yorkshire
Hereward College, West Midlands
Hinwick Hall College of Further Education, Northamptonshire
Holly Bank School, West Yorkshire
Hornsey Conductive Education Centre, N10
Ingfield Manor School, West Sussex
Ivers, Dorset

Kisharon Day School, NW11
Langside School, Dorset
Linkage Further Education College, Lincolnshire
Loppington House Further Education & Adult Centre, Shropshire
Meldreth Manor School, Hertfordshire
Mordaunt School, Hampshire
Nash College of Further Education, Kent
National Institute of Conductive Education, West Midlands
The National Star Centre's College of Further Education, Gloucestershire
Oakwood Court, Devon
Ovingdean Hall School, East Sussex
The Papworth Trust, Cambridgeshire
Pengwern College, Denbighshire
Penhurst School, Oxfordshire
Penn School, Buckinghamshire
Pennine Camphill Community, West Yorkshire
Percy Hedley School, Tyne and Wear
Philpots Manor School, West Sussex
Pield Heath School, Middlesex
Portfield School, Pembrokeshire
Portland College, Nottinghamshire
Queen Alexandra College of Further Education, West Midlands
Queen Elizabeth's Training College, Surrey
RNIB Alwyn House, Fife
RNIB Condover Hall School, Shropshire
RNIB Redhill College, Surrey

RNIB Rushton Hall School,
Northamptonshire
Royal Blind School, Lothian
Royal School for the Deaf (Manchester),
Cheshire
Rutherford School, Surrey
Rutland House School, Nottinghamshire
The St John Vianney School, Cheshire
St Margaret's School, Surrey
St Mary's School, East Sussex
St Rose's School, Gloucestershire
St Vincent's School, Merseyside
seeABILITY (formerly Royal School for the
Blind), Surrey

Sense East, Cambridgeshire
**Stanmore House Residential School,
South Lanarkshire**
Treloar School, Hampshire
Trengweath School, Devon
Vranch House School, Devon
Weelsby Hall Further Education College,
North East Lincolnshire
Westgate College for Deaf People,
Kent
Woodcroft School, Essex
Yateley Industries for the Disabled Ltd,
Hampshire

Delicate

Birtenshaw Hall, Lancashire
Breckenbrough School, North Yorkshire
Calder House School, Wiltshire
The Camphill Rudolf Steiner Schools,
Aberdeenshire
Dame Hannah Rogers School, Devon
Delamere Forest School, Cheshire
East Park Home School, Glasgow
Exhall Grange School, Warwickshire
Finchale Training College,
County Durham
Hereward College, West Midlands
Hillside School, Fife
Kings Manor Education Centre,
East Sussex
Langside School, Dorset
Linkage Further Education College,
Lincolnshire
The National Star Centre's College of
Further Education, Gloucestershire
The New School, Perthshire
Ochil Tower (Rudolf Steiner) School,
Perthshire

Penn School, Buckinghamshire
Pennine Camphill Community,
West Yorkshire
Philip Green Memorial School, Dorset
Philpots Manor School, West Sussex
Pield Heath School, Middlesex
Royal Blind School, Lothian
St Dominic's School, Surrey
St Mary's School, East Sussex
St Rose's School, Gloucestershire
St Vincent's School, Merseyside
The Sheiling School, Bristol
Southern England Psychological Services,
Hampshire
Spring Hill School (Barnardo's),
North Yorkshire
Treloar School, Hampshire
Weelsby Hall Further Education College,
North East Lincolnshire
Westgate College for Deaf People, Kent
Whitstone Head School, Devon
Woodcroft School, Essex

Down's Syndrome

Arden College, Merseyside
**Camphill Blair Drummond Trust,
Stirling**

The Camphill Rudolf Steiner Schools,
Aberdeenshire
Cintre Community, Bristol

Corbenic Camphill Community, Perthshire
Delamere Forest School, Cheshire
Derwen College, Shropshire
Dilston College of Further Education,
    Northumberland
Easter Auguston Training Farm,
    Aberdeenshire
Fairfield Opportunity Farm, Wiltshire
Fortune Centre of Riding Therapy, Dorset
Henshaw's College, North Yorkshire
Hereward College, West Midlands
Hinwick Hall College of Further
    Education, Northamptonshire
Ivers, Dorset
Kisharon Day School, NW11
Kisimul School, Lincolnshire
Lindeth College of Further Education,
    Cumbria
Linkage Further Education College,
    Lincolnshire
Loppington House Further Education &
    Adult Centre, Shropshire
Minstead Training Project, Hampshire
The Mount Camphill Community,
    East Sussex
Nash College of Further Education,
    Kent
Oakwood Court, Devon
Orchard School, Shropshire

Overley Hall School, Shropshire
The Papworth Trust, Cambridgeshire
Parayhouse School, W12
Pengwern College, Denbighshire
Philip Green Memorial School, Dorset
Philpots Manor School, West Sussex
Pield Heath School, Middlesex
RNIB Redhill College, Surrey
Rowden House School, Herefordshire
The St John Vianney School, Cheshire
St John's College, East Sussex
St Joseph's School, Surrey
St Mary's School, East Sussex
The Sheiling School, Bristol
The Sheiling School, Dorset
Southern England Psychological Services,
    Hampshire
Spring Hill School (Barnardo's),
    North Yorkshire
Strathmore College, Staffordshire
Sunfield, West Midlands
Weelsby Hall Further Education College,
    North East Lincolnshire
Westgate College for Deaf People, Kent
Wilsic Hall School, South Yorkshire
Woodcroft School, Essex
Yateley Industries for the Disabled Ltd,
    Hampshire

Dyscalculia

Appleford School, Wiltshire
Belgrave School, Bristol
Brewood Education Centre, Kent
Calder House School, Wiltshire
Centre Academy, SW11
The Charmandean Dyslexia Centre,
    Buckinghamshire
Coxlease School, Hampshire
Cruckton Hall, Shropshire
East Court School, Kent
Edington and Shapwick School, Somerset
Fortune Centre of Riding Therapy, Dorset
Harmeny School, Lothian

Hereward College, West Midlands
Home School of Stoke Newington, N16
The Knowl Hill School, Surrey
Mark College, Somerset
The Moat School, SW6
Moor House School, Surrey
NCH Action for Children,
    Vale of Glamorgan
The New Learning Centre, NW6
Overley Hall School, Shropshire
Penn School, Buckinghamshire
Philpots Manor School, West Sussex
Portland College, Nottinghamshire

RNIB Vocational College, Leicestershire
St Dominic's School, Surrey
St Joseph's School, Surrey

The Unicorn School, Oxfordshire
Westgate College for Deaf People, Kent

Dyslexia

Alderwasley Hall School, Derbyshire
Appleford School, Wiltshire
Arden College, Merseyside
Belgrave School, Bristol
Bessels Leigh School, Oxfordshire
Birkdale School for Hearing Impaired
   Children, Merseyside
Breckenbrough School, North Yorkshire
Brewood Education Centre, Kent
Bridgend College, Bridgend
Bruern Abbey School, Oxfordshire
Caldecott Community, Kent
Calder House School, Wiltshire
The Camphill Rudolf Steiner Schools,
   Aberdeenshire
Centre Academy, SW11
The Charmandean Dyslexia Centre,
   Buckinghamshire
Chartwell House School, Cambridgeshire
Cintre Community, Bristol
Coxlease School, Hampshire
Cruckton Hall, Shropshire
Delamere Forest School, Cheshire
Derwen College, Shropshire
Doncaster College for the Deaf,
   South Yorkshire
Doncaster School for the Deaf,
   South Yorkshire
East Court School, Kent
Edington and Shapwick School, Somerset
Enham, Hampshire
Exhall Grange School, Warwickshire
Fairley House School, SW1P
Finchale Training College, County Durham
Fortune Centre of Riding Therapy, Dorset
Frewen College, East Sussex
The Grange Centre for People with
   Disabilities, Surrey

Harmeny School, Lothian
Hereward College, West Midlands
Hillcrest Pentwyn School, Herefordshire
Home School of Stoke Newington, N16
I Can's Dawn House School,
   Nottinghamshire
Kings Manor Education Centre,
   East Sussex
The Knowl Hill School, Surrey
Lindeth College of Further Education,
   Cumbria
Linkage Further Education College,
   Lincolnshire
Maple Hayes Hall Dyslexia School,
   Staffordshire
The Marchant-Holliday School, Somerset
Mark College, Somerset
Merton House (Downswood), Cheshire
The Moat School, SW6
Moon Hall School, Surrey
Moor House School, Surrey
More House School, Surrey
NCH Action for Children,
   Vale of Glamorgan
The New Learning Centre, NW6
The New School, Perthshire
Northease Manor, East Sussex
Nugent House School, Lancashire
**Nunnykirk Centre for Dyslexia,
   Northumberland**
Oakwood Court, Devon
The Old Rectory School, Suffolk
Overley Hall School, Shropshire
Ovingdean Hall School, East Sussex
Owlswick School, East Sussex
Penn School, Buckinghamshire
Pennine Camphill Community,
   West Yorkshire

Philpots Manor School, West Sussex
Portland College, Nottinghamshire
The Portsmouth Grammar School, Hampshire
Queen Elizabeth's Training College, Surrey
Raddery School, Highland
Riverside School, Cumbria
RNIB Redhill College, Surrey
Rossendale Special School, Lancashire
Royal National College for the Blind, Herefordshire
St Andrews School, Norfolk
St Dominic's School, Surrey
St Edwards School, Hampshire
St Joseph's School, Surrey
St Loye's College, Devon
St Mary's School, East Sussex
Southern England Psychological Services, Hampshire
Thornby Hall School, Northamptonshire
Treloar School, Hampshire
The Unicorn School, Oxfordshire
Weelsby Hall Further Education College, North East Lincolnshire
Westgate College for Deaf People, Kent
Willoughby Hall Dyslexia Centre, NW3
Woodcroft School, Essex
Wychbury House Residential School, Devon
Yateley Industries for the Disabled Ltd, Hampshire

Dyspraxia

Alderwasley Hall School, Derbyshire
Appleford School, Wiltshire
Belgrave School, Bristol
Birkdale School for Hearing Impaired Children, Merseyside
Blossom House School, SW20
Brewood Education Centre, Kent
Bruern Abbey School, Oxfordshire
Bryn Melyn Group, Gwynedd
Calder House School, Wiltshire
The Camphill Rudolf Steiner Schools, Aberdeenshire
The Charmandean Dyslexia Centre, Buckinghamshire
Cotswold Chine School, Gloucestershire
Coxlease School, Hampshire
Cruckton Hall, Shropshire
Delamere Forest School, Cheshire
Doncaster College for the Deaf, South Yorkshire
East Court School, Kent
Edington and Shapwick School, Somerset
Fairfield Opportunity Farm, Wiltshire
Fairley House School, SW1P
Finchale Training College, County Durham
Fortune Centre of Riding Therapy, Dorset
Frewen College, East Sussex
Grateley House School, Hampshire
Hereward College, West Midlands
Hillcrest Pentwyn School, Herefordshire
Home School of Stoke Newington, N16
I Can's Dawn House School, Nottinghamshire
Kings Manor Education Centre, East Sussex
The Knowl Hill School, Surrey
Linkage Further Education College, Lincolnshire
Mark College, Somerset
The Moat School, SW6
Moor House School, Surrey
National Institute of Conductive Education, West Midlands
The National Star Centre's College of Further Education, Gloucestershire
NCH Action for Children, Vale of Glamorgan
The New Learning Centre, NW6

The New School, Perthshire
Northease Manor, East Sussex
Oakwood Court, Devon
The Old Rectory School, Suffolk
Overley Hall School, Shropshire
Penn School, Buckinghamshire
Philip Green Memorial School, Dorset
Philpots Manor School, West Sussex
Pield Heath School, Middlesex
Portland College, Nottinghamshire
Potterspury Lodge School, Northamptonshire
Rossendale Special School, Lancashire
Royal Blind School, Lothian
St Andrews School, Norfolk
St Dominic's School, Surrey
The St John Vianney School, Cheshire
St John's Catholic School for the Deaf, West Yorkshire
St Joseph's School, Surrey
St Mary's School, East Sussex
St Rose's School, Gloucestershire
The Speech, Language & Hearing Centre, NW1
Talbot House Independent Special School, Newcastle Upon Tyne
Treloar School, Hampshire
The Unicorn School, Oxfordshire
Weelsby Hall Further Education College, North East Lincolnshire
Westgate College for Deaf People, Kent
Willoughby Hall Dyslexia Centre, NW3
Woodcroft School, Essex
Yateley Industries for the Disabled Ltd, Hampshire

Emotional/Behavioural Difficulties

Arden College, Merseyside
Ballikinrain Residential School, Stirling
Balnacraig School, Perth and Kinross
Banham Marshalls College, Norfolk
Banstead Place Brain Injury Rehabilitation, Surrey
Barnardo's Lecropt Project, Stirling
Beech Tree School, Lancashire
Belmont School, Wiltshire
Bessels Leigh School, Oxfordshire
Bramfield House, Suffolk
Breckenbrough School, North Yorkshire
Brewood Education Centre, Kent
Bryn Melyn Group, Gwynedd
Caldecott Community, Kent
Camphill Blair Drummond Trust, Stirling
The Camphill Rudolf Steiner Schools, Aberdeenshire
Cedar House School, Lancashire
Cerrig Camu, Gwynedd
Chaigeley School, Cheshire
Chartwell House School, Cambridgeshire
Chelfham Mill School, Devon
Chelfham Senior School, Devon
Cintre Community, Bristol
Clarence House School, Merseyside
Coleg Elidyr, Carmarthenshire
Cornerstones Independent School, East Sussex
Cotsbrook Community, Shropshire
Cotswold Chine School, Gloucestershire
Coxlease School, Hampshire
Crookhey Hall School, Lancashire
Crowthorn School (NCH Action for Children), Lancashire
Cruckton Hall, Shropshire
Delamere Forest School, Cheshire
Didsbury School, Greater Manchester
Don Buss Learning Centre Primary, Kent
Don Buss Learning Opportunities, Kent
Doncaster College for the Deaf, South Yorkshire
Doncaster School for the Deaf, South Yorkshire

West Kirby Residential School, Merseyside
Westwood School, Kent
Whitstone Head School, Devon
William Henry Smith School, West Yorkshire

Witherslack Hall, Cumbria
Woodcroft School, Essex
Woodlands School, Dumfries & Galloway
Wychbury House Residential School, Devon

Epilepsy

Aran Hall School, Gwynedd
Arden College, Merseyside
Banstead Place Brain Injury Rehabilitation, Surrey
Beaumont College of Further Education, Lancashire
Beech Tree School, Lancashire
Birtenshaw Hall School, Lancashire
Bryn Melyn Group, Gwynedd
Camphill Blair Drummond Trust, Stirling
The Camphill Rudolf Steiner Schools, Aberdeenshire
Chelfham Mill School, Devon
Cintre Community, Bristol
Coleg Elidyr, Carmarthenshire
Coney Hill School, Kent
Cotswold Chine School, Gloucestershire
Coxlease School, Hampshire
Cruckton Hall, Shropshire
Dame Hannah Rogers School, Devon
The David Lewis School, Cheshire
Delamere Forest School, Cheshire
Derwen College, Shropshire
Dilston College of Further Education, Northumberland
East Park Home School, Glasgow
Eden Grove School, Cumbria
Exhall Grange School, Warwickshire
Fairfield Opportunity Farm, Wiltshire
Finchale Training College, County Durham
Fortune Centre of Riding Therapy, Dorset
Fullerton House School, South Yorkshire
Furze Mount, Conwy
The Grange Centre for People with Disabilities, Surrey
Henshaw's College, North Yorkshire

Hereward College, West Midlands
Hinwick Hall College of Further Education, Northamptonshire
Holly Bank School, West Yorkshire
Ivers, Dorset
Kings Manor Education Centre, East Sussex
Kisimul School, Lincolnshire
Langside School, Dorset
Lindeth College of Further Education, Cumbria
Linkage Further Education College, Lincolnshire
Linn Moor Residential School, Aberdeenshire
Loddon School, Hampshire
Loppington House Further Education & Adult Centre, Shropshire
MacIntyre School Wingrave, Buckinghamshire
Meldreth Manor School, Hertfordshire
Mordaunt School, Hampshire
Nash College of Further Education, Kent
The National Centre for Young People with Epilepsy (NCYPE), Surrey
The National Star Centre's College of Further Education, Gloucestershire
NCH Action for Children, Vale of Glamorgan
Oakwood Court, Devon
Ochil Tower (Rudolf Steiner) School, Perthshire
Orchard School, Shropshire
Overley Hall School, Shropshire
The Papworth Trust, Cambridgeshire
Parayhouse School, W12

Pengwern College, Denbighshire
Penhurst School, Oxfordshire
Penn School, Buckinghamshire
Pennine Camphill Community,
    West Yorkshire
Philpots Manor School, West Sussex
Pield Heath School, Middlesex
Portfield School, Pembrokeshire
Portland College, Nottinghamshire
Queen Alexandra College of Further
    Education, West Midlands
Queen Elizabeth's Training College,
    Surrey
RNIB Condover Hall School,
    Shropshire
RNIB Redhill College, Surrey
RNIB Rushton Hall School,
    Northamptonshire
Rossendale Special School, Lancashire
Rowden House School, Herefordshire
Royal Blind School, Lothian
Royal School for the Deaf (Manchester),
    Cheshire
Rutherford School, Surrey
Rutland House School, Nottinghamshire
St Christopher's School, Bristol
St Dominic's School, Surrey
St Elizabeth's School, Hertfordshire

St John's College, East Sussex
St Loye's College, Devon
St Margaret's School, Surrey
St Mary's School, East Sussex
St Rose's School, Gloucestershire
St Vincent's School, Merseyside
seeABILITY (formerly Royal School for the
    Blind), Surrey
Sense East, Cambridgeshire
The Sheiling School, Dorset
Southern England Psychological Services,
    Hampshire
Spring Hill School (Barnardo's),
    North Yorkshire
Stanmore House Residential School,
    South Lanarkshire
Strathmore College, Staffordshire
Stroud Court, Gloucestershire
Thornby Hall School, Northamptonshire
Treloar School, Hampshire
Trengweath School, Devon
Weelsby Hall Further Education College,
    North East Lincolnshire
Westgate College for Deaf People, Kent
Woodcroft School, Essex
Yateley Industries for the Disabled Ltd,
    Hampshire

Hearing Impairment

Arden College, Merseyside
Beech Tree School, Lancashire
Birkdale School for Hearing Impaired
    Children, Merseyside
Brewood Education Centre, Kent
Bridgend College, Bridgend
Camphill Blair Drummond Trust, Stirling
The Camphill Rudolf Steiner Schools,
    Aberdeenshire
Delrow College, Hertfordshire
Derby College For Deaf People,
    Derbyshire
Derwen College, Shropshire

Dilston College of Further Education,
    Northumberland
Doncaster College for the Deaf,
    South Yorkshire
Doncaster School for the Deaf,
    South Yorkshire
Eden Grove School, Cumbria
Exhall Grange School, Warwickshire
Fairfield Opportunity Farm, Wiltshire
Finchale Training College, County Durham
Fortune Centre of Riding Therapy, Dorset
The Grange Centre for People with
    Disabilities, Surrey

Hamilton Lodge School for Deaf Children, East Sussex
Henshaw's College, North Yorkshire
Hereward College, West Midlands
Hinwick Hall College of Further Education, Northamptonshire
Homefield Residential College, Leicestershire
Jordanstown Schools, County Antrim
Lindeth College of Further Education, Cumbria
Linkage Further Education College, Lincolnshire
Loppington House Further Education & Adult Centre, Shropshire
The Mary Hare Grammar School for the Deaf, Berkshire
Meldreth Manor School, Hertfordshire
Northern Counties School for the Deaf, Tyne and Wear
Ovingdean Hall School, East Sussex
The Papworth Trust, Cambridgeshire
Penhurst School, Oxfordshire
Penn School, Buckinghamshire
Pennine Camphill Community, West Yorkshire
Philpots Manor School, West Sussex
Portland College, Nottinghamshire
Queen Alexandra College of Further Education, West Midlands
Queen Elizabeth's Training College, Surrey
RNIB Condover Hall School, Shropshire
RNIB Redhill College, Surrey
RNID Poolemead, North East Somerset
Royal National College for the Blind, Herefordshire
The Royal School for Deaf Children Margate, Kent
Royal School for the Blind, Merseyside
Royal School for the Deaf, Devon
Royal School for the Deaf (Manchester), Cheshire
Royal School for the Deaf, Derby, Derbyshire
Royal West of England School for the Deaf, Devon
Rutherford School, Surrey
Rutland House School, Nottinghamshire
St John's Catholic School for the Deaf, West Yorkshire
St Loye's College, Devon
St Margaret's School, Surrey
St Mary's School, East Sussex
St Vincent's School, Merseyside
seeABILITY (formerly Royal School for the Blind), Surrey
Sense East, Cambridgeshire
The Speech, Language & Hearing Centre, NW1
Stanmore House Residential School, South Lanarkshire
Treloar School, Hampshire
Trengweath School, Devon
Weelsby Hall Further Education College, North East Lincolnshire
Westgate College for Deaf People, Kent
Whitstone Head School, Devon
Woodcroft School, Essex
Yateley Industries for the Disabled Ltd, Hampshire

Moderate Learning Difficulties

Arden College, Merseyside
Banstead Place Brain Injury Rehabilitation, Surrey
Beaumont College of Further Education, Lancashire
Belgrave School, Bristol
Birkdale School for Hearing Impaired Children, Merseyside
Birtenshaw Hall, Lancashire
Bladon House School, Staffordshire

Bramfield House, Suffolk
Brewood Education Centre, Kent
Broomhayes School, Devon
Bryn Melyn Group, Gwynedd
Burton Hill School, Wiltshire
Caldecott Community, Kent
Camphill Blair Drummond Trust, Stirling
The Camphill Rudolf Steiner Schools, Aberdeenshire
Cerrig Camu, Gwynedd
Chailey Heritage School, East Sussex
Chelfham Mill School, Devon
Chelfham Senior School, Devon
Cintre Community, Bristol
Coleg Elidyr, Carmarthenshire
Cotswold Chine School, Gloucestershire
Coxlease School, Hampshire
Crowthorn School (NCH Action for Children), Lancashire
Cruckton Hall, Shropshire
Dame Hannah Rogers School, Devon
The David Lewis School, Cheshire
Delamere Forest School, Cheshire
Delrow College, Hertfordshire
Derby College For Deaf People, Derbyshire
Derwen College, Shropshire
Didsbury School, Greater Manchester
Dilston College of Further Education, Northumberland
Doncaster College for the Deaf, South Yorkshire
Doncaster School for the Deaf, South Yorkshire
Dorton College of Further Education, Kent
Easter Auguston Training Farm, Aberdeenshire
Eastwood Grange School, Derbyshire
Eden Grove School, Cumbria
Enham, Hampshire
Fairfield Opportunity Farm, Wiltshire
Farney Close School, West Sussex
Finchale Training College, County Durham
Fortune Centre of Riding Therapy, Dorset
Geilsland School, North Ayrshire

Good Shepherd Centre, Renfrewshire
The Grange Centre for People with Disabilities, Surrey
Green Laund F.E. Centre, Derbyshire
Harmeny School, Lothian
The Hatch, South Gloucestershire
Henshaw's College, North Yorkshire
Hereward College, West Midlands
High Close School (Barnardo's), Berkshire
Hillcrest Pentwyn School, Herefordshire
Hillside School, Fife
Hinwick Hall College of Further Education, Northamptonshire
Holly Bank School, West Yorkshire
Homefield Residential College, Leicestershire
Ivers, Dorset
Kibble School, Renfrewshire
Kings Manor Education Centre, East Sussex
Kisharon Day School, NW11
Lambs House School, Cheshire
Lindeth College of Further Education, Cumbria
Linkage Further Education College, Lincolnshire
Linn Moor Residential School, Aberdeenshire
Loppington House Further Education & Adult Centre, Shropshire
Lufton Manor College, Somerset
Meadows School (Barnardo's), Kent
Minstead Training Project, Hampshire
The Mount Camphill Community, East Sussex
The National Centre for Young People with Epilepsy, Surrey
National Institute of Conductive Education, West Midlands
NCH Action for Children, Vale of Glamorgan
The New School, Perthshire
Oakwood Court, Devon
Ochil Tower (Rudolf Steiner) School, Perthshire

Overley Hall School, Shropshire
Ovingdean Hall School, East Sussex
Owlswick School, East Sussex
The Papworth Trust, Cambridgeshire
Parayhouse School, W12
Pengwern College, Denbighshire
Penn School, Buckinghamshire
Pennine Camphill Community,
    West Yorkshire
Philip Green Memorial School, Dorset
Philpots Manor School, West Sussex
Pield Heath School, Middlesex
Pontville School, Lancashire
Portland College, Nottinghamshire
Queen Alexandra College of Further
    Education, West Midlands
Queen Elizabeth's Training College,
    Surrey
Riverside School, Cumbria
RNIB Redhill College, Surrey
RNIB Rushton Hall School,
    Northamptonshire
RNIB Vocational College, Leicestershire
The Robert Ogden School, South Yorkshire
Royal Blind School, Lothian
Royal School for the Blind, Merseyside
Royal School for the Deaf (Manchester),
    Cheshire
The Ryes School, Suffolk
St Andrews School, Norfolk
St Edwards School, Hampshire
St Elizabeth's School, Hertfordshire
St Francis Day Boy Unit, Glasgow
The St John Vianney School, Cheshire
The St John Vianney School,
    Greater Manchester
St John's College, East Sussex
St John's RC School, Essex

St Joseph's School, Surrey
St Mary's School, East Sussex
St Phillip's School, North Lanarkshire
St Rose's School, Gloucestershire
St Vincent's School, Merseyside
seeABILITY (formerly Royal School for
    the Blind), Surrey
Sense East, Cambridgeshire
The Sheiling School, Bristol
The Sheiling School, Dorset
Solden Hill House, Northamptonshire
Southern England Psychological Services,
    Hampshire
Spring Hill School (Barnardo's),
    North Yorkshire
Strathmore College, Staffordshire
Stroud Court, Gloucestershire
Swalcliffe Park School, Oxfordshire
Thornby Hall School, Northamptonshire
Underley Garden School, Lancashire
Underley Hall School, Lancashire
Vranch House School, Devon
Weelsby Hall Further Education College,
    North East Lincolnshire
West Kirby Residential School,
    Merseyside
Westgate College for Deaf People,
    Kent
Westmorland School, Lancashire
Westwood School, Kent
Whitstone Head School, Devon
Woodcroft School, Essex
Woodlands School, Dumfries & Galloway
Wychbury House Residential School,
    Devon
Yateley Industries for the Disabled Ltd,
    Hampshire

Physical Impairment

Banstead Place Brain Injury Rehabilitation,
    Surrey
Beaumont College of Further Education,
    Lancashire

Beech Tree School, Lancashire
Birtenshaw Hall School, Lancashire
Bridge College, Cheshire
Burton Hill School, Wiltshire

The Camphill Rudolf Steiner Schools,
Aberdeenshire
Cerrig Camu, Gwynedd
Chailey Heritage School, East Sussex
Coney Hill School, Kent
Corseford School, Strathclyde
Craig-y-Parc School, Cardiff
Dame Hannah Rogers School, Devon
The David Lewis School, Cheshire
Derby College For Deaf People,
Derbyshire
Derwen College, Shropshire
Doncaster College for the Deaf,
South Yorkshire
Doncaster School for the Deaf,
South Yorkshire
Enham, Hampshire
Exhall Grange School, Warwickshire
Finchale Training College,
County Durham
Fourways Assessment Unit,
Greater Manchester
Furze Mount, Conwy
The Grange Centre for People with
Disabilities, Surrey
Henshaw's College, North Yorkshire
Hereward College, West Midlands
Hinwick Hall College of Further
Education, Northamptonshire
Holly Bank School, West Yorkshire
Hornsey Conductive Education Centre,
N10
Kings Manor Education Centre,
East Sussex
Langside School, Dorset
Linkage Further Education College,
Lincolnshire
Love Walk, SE5
**Meldreth Manor School,
Hertfordshire**
Mordaunt School, Hampshire
Nash College of Further Education,
Kent
**The National Star Centre's College of
Further Education, Gloucestershire**

Northern Counties School for the Deaf,
Tyne and Wear
The Papworth Trust, Cambridgeshire
Penhurst School, Oxfordshire
Penn School, Buckinghamshire
Portland College, Nottinghamshire
The Portsmouth Grammar School,
Hampshire
**Queen Alexandra College of Further
Education, West Midlands**
Queen Elizabeth's Training College,
Surrey
RNIB Condover Hall School,
Shropshire
RNIB Manor House, Devon
RNIB Redhill College, Surrey
RNID Poolemead, North East Somerset
Royal Blind School, Lothian
Royal School for the Blind, Merseyside
Royal School for the Deaf (Manchester),
Cheshire
Rutherford School, Surrey
Rutland House School,
Nottinghamshire
St Loye's College, Devon
St Mary's School, East Sussex
St Rose's School, Gloucestershire
St Vincent's School, Merseyside
seeABILITY (formerly Royal School for the
Blind), Surrey
Sense East, Cambridgeshire
Southern England Psychological Services,
Hampshire
Stanmore House Residential School, South
Lanarkshire
Treloar School, Hampshire
Trengweath School, Devon
Vranch House School, Devon
The West of England School and College
for Pupils with Little or No Sight,
Devon
Westgate College for Deaf People, Kent
Woodcroft School, Essex
Yateley Industries for the Disabled Ltd,
Hampshire

Profound/Multiple Learning Difficulties

Annie Lawson School, Berkshire
Birtenshaw Hall School, Lancashire
Bridge College, Cheshire
Broomhayes School, Devon
Camphill Blair Drummond Trust, Stirling
The Camphill Rudolf Steiner Schools, Aberdeenshire
Coney Hill School, Kent
Craig-y-Parc School, Cardiff
Dame Hannah Rogers School, Devon
East Park Home School, Glasgow
Holly Bank School, West Yorkshire
Kibble School, Renfrewshire
Langside School, Dorset
Linn Moor Residential School, Aberdeenshire
Lufton Manor College, Somerset
MacIntyre School Wingrave, Buckinghamshire
MacIntyre School Womaston, Powys
Meldreth Manor School, Hertfordshire
Mordaunt School, Hampshire
Nash College of Further Education, Kent
The National Star Centre's College of Further Education, Gloucestershire
Northern Counties School for the Deaf, Tyne and Wear

Ochil Tower (Rudolf Steiner) School, Perthshire
Pengwern College, Denbighshire
Penhurst School, Oxfordshire
Pield Heath School, Middlesex
Portfield School, Pembrokeshire
RNIB Condover Hall School, Shropshire
RNIB Rushton Hall School, Northamptonshire
Rowden House School, Herefordshire
Royal Blind School, Lothian
Royal School for the Blind, Merseyside
Royal School for the Deaf (Manchester), Cheshire
Rutherford School, Surrey
Rutland House School, Nottinghamshire
St Christopher's School, Bristol
St Margaret's School, Surrey
seeABILITY (formerly Royal School for the Blind), Surrey
The Sheiling Curative Schools, Hampshire
Stanmore House Residential School, South Lanarkshire
Sunfield, West Midlands
Trengweath School, Devon
Vranch House School, Devon
Westgate College for Deaf People, Kent
Woodcroft School, Essex

Severe Learning Difficulties

Annie Lawson School, Berkshire
Aran Hall School, Gwynedd
Arden College, Merseyside
Beaumont College of Further Education, Lancashire
Beech Tree School, Lancashire
Birtenshaw Hall, Lancashire
Bridge College, Cheshire
Broomhayes School, Devon
Broughton House College, Lincolnshire
Burton Hill School, Wiltshire

Camphill Blair Drummond Trust, Stirling
The Camphill Rudolf Steiner Schools, Aberdeenshire
Cerrig Camu, Gwynedd
Chailey Heritage School, East Sussex
Coleg Elidyr, Carmarthenshire
Cotswold Chine School, Gloucestershire
Dame Hannah Rogers School, Devon
The David Lewis School, Cheshire
Derby College For Deaf People, Derbyshire
Derwen College, Shropshire

Specific Learning Difficulties

Appleford School, Wiltshire
Arden College, Merseyside
Banstead Place Brain Injury Rehabilitation, Surrey
Barnardo's Lecropt Project, Stirling
Belgrave School, Bristol
Bessels Leigh School, Oxfordshire
Bladon House School, Staffordshire
Blossom House School, SW20
Bridgend College, Bridgend
Broomhayes School, Devon
Bruern Abbey School, Oxfordshire
Calder House School, Wiltshire
Camphill Blair Drummond Trust, Stirling
The Camphill Rudolf Steiner Schools, Aberdeenshire
Cedar House School, Lancashire
Centre Academy, SW11
Corbenic Camphill Community, Perthshire
Cotswold Chine School, Gloucestershire
Coxlease School, Hampshire
Crookhey Hall School, Lancashire
Cruckton Hall, Shropshire
Delamere Forest School, Cheshire
Derby College For Deaf People, Derbyshire
Dilston College of Further Education, Northumberland
Doncaster College for the Deaf, South Yorkshire
Doncaster School for the Deaf, South Yorkshire
East Court School, Kent
Edington and Shapwick School, Somerset
Fairfield Opportunity Farm, Wiltshire
Fairley House School, SW1P
Farney Close School, West Sussex
Fortune Centre of Riding Therapy, Dorset
Green Laund F.E. Centre, Derbyshire
Harmeny School, Lothian
Hereward College, West Midlands
Hillcrest Pentwyn School, Herefordshire
Hillside School, Fife

Hinwick Hall College of Further Education, Northamptonshire
Home School of Stoke Newington, N16
Kibble School, Renfrewshire
Kisimul School, Lincolnshire
The Knowl Hill School, Surrey
Lakeside School, Merseyside
Lindeth College of Further Education, Cumbria
The Link Primary School, Surrey
Linkage Further Education College, Lincolnshire
Loppington House Further Education & Adult Centre, Shropshire
Lowgate House School, Cumbria
MacIntyre School Wingrave, Buckinghamshire
Maple Hayes Hall Dyslexia School, Staffordshire
The Marchant-Holliday School, Somerset
Moon Hall School, Surrey
Mordaunt School, Hampshire
More House School, Surrey
Nash College of Further Education, Kent
NCH Action for Children, Vale of Glamorgan
The New Learning Centre, NW6
The New School, Perthshire
Northease Manor, East Sussex
Nunnykirk Centre for Dyslexia, Northumberland
Oakwood Court, Devon
The Old Rectory School, Suffolk
Ovingdean Hall School, East Sussex
Penn School, Buckinghamshire
Pennine Camphill Community, West Yorkshire
Philpots Manor School, West Sussex
Pield Heath School, Middlesex
Queen Elizabeth's Training College, Surrey
RNIB Redhill College, Surrey
Royal Blind School, Lothian

Royal National College for the Blind,
Herefordshire
Royal School for the Deaf (Manchester),
Cheshire
St Andrews School, Norfolk
St Dominic's School, Surrey
St Mary's School, East Sussex
St Vincent's School, Merseyside
Southern England Psychological Services,
Hampshire
Strathmore College, Staffordshire
Treloar School, Hampshire
Underley Garden School, Lancashire
Underley Hall School, Lancashire

The Unicorn School, Oxfordshire
Weelsby Hall Further Education College,
North East Lincolnshire
Westgate College for Deaf People, Kent
Westmorland School, Lancashire
Whitstone Head School, Devon
Wilsic Hall School, South Yorkshire
Witherslack Hall, Cumbria
Woodcroft School, Essex
Woodlands School, Dumfries & Galloway
Wychbury House Residential School,
Devon
Yateley Industries for the Disabled Ltd,
Hampshire

Speech and Language Difficulties

Alderwasley Hall School, Derbyshire
Appleford School, Wiltshire
Arden College, Merseyside
Banham Marshalls College, Norfolk
Banstead Place Brain Injury Rehabilitation,
Surrey
Barnardo's Lecropt Project, Stirling
Beaumont College of Further Education,
Lancashire
Beech Tree School, Lancashire
**Birkdale School for Hearing Impaired
Children, Merseyside**
Birtenshaw Hall, Lancashire
Blossom House School, SW20
Brewood Education Centre, Kent
Broomhayes School, Devon
Bruern Abbey School, Oxfordshire
Camphill Blair Drummond Trust, Stirling
The Camphill Rudolf Steiner Schools,
Aberdeenshire
Centre Academy, SW11
Chailey Heritage School, East Sussex
Cotswold Chine School, Gloucestershire
Coxlease School, Hampshire
Craig-y-Parc School, Cardiff
Dame Hannah Rogers School, Devon
The David Lewis School, Cheshire
Delamere Forest School, Cheshire

Derwen College, Shropshire
Dilston College of Further Education,
Northumberland
**Doncaster College for the Deaf,
South Yorkshire**
Doncaster School for the Deaf,
South Yorkshire
Easter Auguston Training Farm,
Aberdeenshire
Eastwood Grange School, Derbyshire
Eden Grove School, Cumbria
Fairfield Opportunity Farm, Wiltshire
Fortune Centre of Riding Therapy, Dorset
Fullerton House School, South Yorkshire
Green Laund F.E. Centre, Derbyshire
Harmeny School, Lothian
Hereward College, West Midlands
**Hinwick Hall College of Further
Education, Northamptonshire**
Holly Bank School, West Yorkshire
Hope Lodge School, Hampshire
**I Can's Dawn House School,
Nottinghamshire**
I CAN's John Horniman School,
West Sussex
I CAN's Meath School, Surrey
Ivers, Dorset
Kibble School, Renfrewshire

Kisharon Day School, NW11
Kisimul School, Lincolnshire
Lakeside School, Merseyside
Lindeth College of Further Education,
   Cumbria
The Link Primary School, Surrey
The Link Secondary School, Surrey
**Linkage Further Education College,
   Lincolnshire**
Loddon School, Hampshire
Loppington House Further Education &
   Adult Centre, Shropshire
MacIntyre School Wingrave,
   Buckinghamshire
Meldreth Manor School, Hertfordshire
Moor House School, Surrey
Mordaunt School, Hampshire
The National Centre for Young People with
   Epilepsy (NCYPE), Surrey
The National Star Centre's College of
   Further Education, Gloucestershire
The New Learning Centre, NW6
Oakwood Court, Devon
Overley Hall School, Shropshire
Ovingdean Hall School, East Sussex
Parayhouse School, W12
Pengwern College, Denbighshire
Penhurst School, Oxfordshire
Penn School, Buckinghamshire
Pennine Camphill Community,
   West Yorkshire
Percy Hedley School, Tyne and Wear
**Philip Green Memorial School,
   Dorset**
Philpots Manor School, West Sussex
Pield Heath School, Middlesex
Portfield School, Pembrokeshire
Portland College, Nottinghamshire
Riverside School, Cumbria

RNIB Condover Hall School, Shropshire
RNID Poolemead, North East Somerset
Royal Blind School, Lothian
Royal School for the Deaf (Manchester),
   Cheshire
Rutland House School, Nottinghamshire
St Catherine's School, Isle of Wight
St Dominic's School, Surrey
St Elizabeth's School, Hertfordshire
The St John Vianney School,
   Cheshire
**St John's Catholic School for the Deaf,
   West Yorkshire**
St John's College, East Sussex
St John's RC School, Essex
St Joseph's School, Surrey
St Mary's School, East Sussex
St Rose's School, Gloucestershire
St Vincent's School, Merseyside
The Sheiling School, Dorset
The Speech, Language & Hearing Centre,
   NW1
Stanmore House Residential School,
   South Lanarkshire
Stroud Court, Gloucestershire
The Sybil Elgar School, Middlesex
Treloar School, Hampshire
Trengweath School, Devon
Vranch House School, Devon
Weelsby Hall Further Education College,
   North East Lincolnshire
**West Kirby Residential School,
   Merseyside**
Westgate College for Deaf People, Kent
Wilsic Hall School, South Yorkshire
Woodcroft School, Essex
Woodlands School, Dumfries & Galloway
Yateley Industries for the Disabled Ltd,
   Hampshire

Tourette Syndrome

Brewood Education Centre, Kent
The Camphill Rudolf Steiner Schools,
   Aberdeenshire

Chelfham Mill School, Devon
Chelfham Senior School, Devon
Cotswold Chine School, Gloucestershire

Coxlease School, Hampshire
Delamere Forest School, Cheshire
Eden Grove School, Cumbria
Grateley House School, Hampshire
Hereward College, West Midlands
Linkage Further Education College,
    Lincolnshire
NCH Action for Children, Vale of
    Glamorgan
The New Learning Centre, NW6
The New School, Perthshire
Nugent House School, Lancashire
Oakwood Court, Devon
Overley Hall School, Shropshire
Penn School, Buckinghamshire

Philpots Manor School, West Sussex
Pontville School, Lancashire
Potterspury Lodge School,
    Northamptonshire
Riverside School, Cumbria
Rossendale Special School, Lancashire
Rowden House School, Herefordshire
Royal Blind School, Lothian
Royal School for the Deaf (Manchester),
    Cheshire
The Ryes School, Suffolk
St Mary's School, East Sussex
Starley Hall, Fife
West Kirby Residential School, Merseyside

Visual Impairment

Banstead Place Brain Injury Rehabilitation,
    Surrey
Beech Tree School, Lancashire
Brewood Education Centre, Kent
Bridgend College, Bridgend
The Camphill Rudolf Steiner Schools,
    Aberdeenshire
Chailey Heritage School, East Sussex
Coney Hill School, Kent
Derby College For Deaf People, Derbyshire
Derwen College, Shropshire
Doncaster College for the Deaf,
    South Yorkshire
Doncaster School for the Deaf,
    South Yorkshire
Dorton College of Further Education,
    Kent
Exhall Grange School, Warwickshire
Finchale Training College, County Durham
Fortune Centre of Riding Therapy, Dorset
Henshaw's College, North Yorkshire
Hereward College, West Midlands
Jordanstown Schools, County Antrim
Langside School, Dorset
Linkage Further Education College,
    Lincolnshire

Loppington House Further Education &
    Adult Centre, Shropshire
Meldreth Manor School, Hertfordshire
Mordaunt School, Hampshire
The National Star Centre's College of
    Further Education, Gloucestershire
**Northern Counties School for the Deaf,
    Tyne and Wear**
Ovingdean Hall School, East Sussex
Penhurst School, Oxfordshire
Penn School, Buckinghamshire
Pennine Camphill Community, West
    Yorkshire
Pield Heath School, Middlesex
Portfield School, Pembrokeshire
**Queen Alexandra College of Further
    Education, West Midlands**
Queen Elizabeth's Training College, Surrey
RNIB Alwyn House, Fife
RNIB Condover Hall School, Shropshire
RNIB Manor House, Devon
RNIB New College, Worcestershire
RNIB Redhill College, Surrey
RNIB Rushton Hall School,
    Northamptonshire
RNIB Sunshine House School, Middlesex

RNIB Vocational College, Leicestershire
RNID Poolemead, North East Somerset
Royal Blind School, Lothian
Royal London Society for the Blind, Kent
Royal National College for the Blind,
   Herefordshire
The Royal School for Deaf Children
   Margate, Kent
Royal School for the Blind, Merseyside
Royal School for the Deaf (Manchester),
   Cheshire
Rutherford School, Surrey
Rutland House School, Nottinghamshire
St Loye's College, Devon
St Margaret's School, Surrey
St Mary's School, East Sussex

St Rose's School, Gloucestershire
St Vincent's School, Merseyside
seeABILITY (formerly Royal School for the
   Blind), Surrey
Sense East, Cambridgeshire
Stanmore House Residential School,
   South Lanarkshire
Treloar School, Hampshire
Trengweath School, Devon
The West of England College for Students
   with Little or No Sight, Devon
The West of England School and College
   for Pupils with Little or no Sight,
   Devon
Westgate College for Deaf People, Kent
Woodcroft School, Essex

Wheelchair access

Annie Lawson School, Berkshire
Banham Marshalls College, Norfolk
Banstead Place Brain Injury Rehabilitation,
   Surrey
Barnardo's Lecropt Project, Stirling
Beech Tree School, Lancashire
Birtenshaw Hall School, Lancashire
Burton Hill School, Wiltshire
The Camphill Rudolf Steiner Schools,
   Aberdeenshire
Chailey Heritage School, East Sussex
Coney Hill School, Kent
Cotswold Chine School, Gloucestershire
Craig-y-Parc School, Cardiff
Dame Hannah Rogers School, Devon
The David Lewis School, Cheshire
Derby College For Deaf People, Derbyshire
Derwen College, Shropshire
Doncaster College for the Deaf,
   South Yorkshire
Doncaster School for the Deaf,
   South Yorkshire
East Park Home School, Glasgow
Eden Grove School, Cumbria
Enham, Hampshire

Finchale Training College, County Durham
Furze Mount, Conwy
The Grange Centre for People with
   Disabilities, Surrey
Harmeny School, Lothian
High Close School (Barnardo's), Berkshire
Hinwick Hall College of Further
   Education, Northamptonshire
Holly Bank School, West Yorkshire
Jordanstown Schools, County Antrim
Langside School, Dorset
Linkage Further Education College,
   Lincolnshire
Meadows School (Barnardo's), Kent
Meldreth Manor School, Hertfordshire
Mordaunt School, Hampshire
Nash College of Further Education, Kent
**The National Star Centre's College of
   Further Education, Gloucestershire**
Northern Counties School for the Deaf,
   Tyne and Wear
Oakwood Court, Devon
The Papworth Trust, Cambridgeshire
Parayhouse School, W12
Pengwern College, Denbighshire

5.2

Council for the Registration of Schools Teaching Dyslexic Pupils (CReSTeD)

Registered charity number 1052103
Information supplied by CReSTeD, February 2002

CReSTeD (the Council for the Registration of Schools Teaching Dyslexic Pupils) produces a twice yearly (Spring and Autumn) register of schools that provide for dyslexic children. The aim is to help parents and those who advise them to choose a school that has been approved to published criteria. CReSTeD was established over eleven years ago - its main supporters are the British Dyslexia Association and The Dyslexia Institute. Schools wishing to be included in the Register are visited by a CReSTeD consultant whose report is considered by the CReSTeD Council before registration can be finalised.

Consulting the Register should enable parents to decide which schools they wish to approach for further information. Dyslexic students have a variety of difficulties and so have a wide range of special needs. An equally wide range of teaching approaches is necessary. CReSTeD has therefore grouped schools together under four broad categories, which are designed to help parents match their child's needs to an appropriate philosophy and provision.

The four categories of the schools are described below:

Specialist Provision (SP) schools are specifically established to teach pupils with dyslexia and related specific learning difficulties.

The other three categories offer special help to dyslexic children within or alongside mainstream provision:

Dyslexia Unit (DU) schools offer a designated unit that provides specialist tuition for a small group on an individual basis, according to need;

Specialist Classes (SC) schools teach dyslexic pupils in separate classes within the school for some lessons (often English and Mathematics);

Withdrawal System (WS) schools help dyslexic children by withdrawing them from appropriately selected lessons for specialist tuition.

A school in one category may also offer the sort of care found in a different, less intensive category. For example, a Dyslexia Unit category school may offer a Withdrawal System. If a school seems appropriate in other ways, parents should check directly with the school.

CReSTeD only examines the adequacy of a school's provision for dyslexic pupils. Registration with or approval by other educational associations, or status with the

Department for Education and Skills (DfES), Office for Standards in Education (Ofsted) or the Local Education Authority, takes account of a school's general competence and administration.

A free copy of the Register can be obtained by contacting CReSTeD on 01242 604852 or by email at **admin@crested.org.uk**, or by writing to The Administrator, Greygarth, Litttleworth, Winchcombe, Cheltenham, GL54 5BT. Alternatively, visit the website at www.crested.org.uk

SPECIALIST PROVISION SCHOOLS – SP

These cater for dyslexic students whose difficulties are most severe. These students are a small section of the dyslexic population and do not relish close liaison with non-dyslexic colleagues because they are seen to fail very publicly in the curriculum. They prefer to be in a school where everyone has a similar difficulty. These schools are small in size, with small classes, offering a whole school approach and a broad, balanced but suitable restricted curriculum which ensures a high level of individual skills directed teaching, using multi-sensory principles.

Appleford School
Shrewton, Salisbury, Wiltshire SP3 4HL
Tel: (01980) 621020
Independent; rural; boarding, weekly
boarding and day
90 boys and girls 7–13

Brown's School
Cannock House, Hawstead Lane,
Chelsfield, Orpington, Kent BR6 7PH
Tel/Fax: (01689) 876816
Independent; rural; day
33 boys and girls 6–12

Calder House School
Colerne, Bath, Wiltshire SN14 8BN
Tel: (01225) 742329
Independent; day
32 boys and girls 5–13

The Dominie
142 Battersea Park Road, London
SW11 4NB
Tel: (020) 7720 8783
Independent; city; day
32 boys and girls 6–13

East Court School
Victoria Parade, Ramsgate, Kent CT11 8ED
Tel: (01843) 592077
Independent; town; boarding, weekly
boarding and day
67 boys and girls 8–13

Edington and Shapwick School
Shapwick Manor, Shapwick, Bridgwater,
Somerset TA7 9NJ
Tel: (01458) 210384
Independent, rural; boarding, weekly
boarding and day
169 boys and girls 8–17

Fairley House School
30 Causton Street, London SW1P 4AU
Tel: (020) 7976 5456
Independent; city; day
95 boys and girls 6–12

Frewen College
Brickwall, Northiam, Rye, East Sussex
TN31 6NL
Tel: (01797) 252494
Independent; village; boarding; day
69 boys 11–17

Knowl Hill School
School Lane, Pirbright, Surrey GU24 0JN
Tel: (01483) 797032
Independent; village; day
40 boys and girls 7–16

Laleham School
Northdown Park Road, Cliftonville,
Margate, Kent CT9 2TP
Tel: (01843) 221946
Local education authority; edge of town;
boarding, weekly boarding and day
104 boys and girls 9–16

Mark College
Mark, Highbridge, Somerset TA9 4NP
Tel: (01278) 641632
DfEE Beacon School; independent, rural;
boarding, weekly boarding and day
80 boys 11–16

Moon Hall School
'Feldemore', Holmbury St Mary, Dorking,
Surrey RH5 6LQ
Tel: (01306) 731464
Independent; rural; weekly boarding and
day
80 boys and girls 7–13

More House School
Moons Hill, Frensham, Farnham, Surrey
GU10 3AP
Tel: (01252) 792303
Independent; rural; boarding, weekly
boarding and day
150 boys 9–16

Northease Manor School
Rodmell, Lewes, East Sussex BN7 3EY
Tel: (01273) 472915
Independent; rural; weekly boarding and
day
85 boys and girls 10–17

Nunnykirk Centre for Dyslexia
Netherwitton, Morpeth, Northumberland
NE61 4PB
Tel: (01670) 772685
Independent; rural; boarding and day
40 boys and girls 9–16

The Old Rectory School
Brettenham, Ipswich, Suffolk IP7 7QR
Tel: (01449) 736404
Independent; rural; boarding, weekly
boarding and day
48 boys and girls 7–13

Sunnydown School
Portley House, 152 Whyteleafe Road,
Caterham, Surrey CR3 5ED
Tel: (01883) 342281
Local education authority; edge of town;
weekly boarding and day
74 boys 11–16

The Unicorn School
Whitefield, Park Crescent
Abingdon, Oxfordshire, OX14 1DD
Tel: (01235) 530222
Independent, village, day
36 boys and girls 6–12

DYSLEXIA UNIT – DU

DU schools are larger and offer education to a limited number of dyslexic students in an *ordinary education setting*. These schools usually operate an initial screening system to ensure that the dyslexic student intake can cope with the breadth and pace of curriculum development, and that the facilities offered by the unit are appropriate to meet the less serious special needs of these students.

Abbotsholme School
Rocester, Uttoxeter, Staffordshire ST14 5BS
Tel: (01889) 590217
Independent; rural; boarding, weekly
boarding and day
235 boys and girls 9–18

Avon House School
490 High Road, Woodford Green, Essex
IG8 0PN
Tel: (020) 8504 1749
Independent; edge of town; day
280 boys and girls 2–11

Bethany School
Curtisden Green, Goudhurst, Cranbrook,
Kent TN17 1LB
Tel: (01580) 211273
Independent; rural; boarding and day
280 boys and girls 11–18

Bloxham School
Bloxham, Near Banbury, Oxfordshire
OX15 4PE
Tel: (01295) 720222
Independent; rural; boarding and day
385 boys and 44 girls 11–18

Bredon School
Pull Court, Bushley, Tewkesbury,
Gloucestershire GL20 6AH
Tel: (01684) 293156
Independent; rural; boarding; weekly
boarding and day
200 boys and girls 7–18

Clayesmore Preparatory School
Iwerne Minster, Blandford Forum, Dorset
DT11 8PH
Tel: (01747) 811707
Independent; village; boarding and day
260 boys and girls 5–13

Clayesmore School
Iwerne Minster, Blandford Forum, Dorset
DT11 8LL
Tel: (01747) 812122
Independent; rural; boarding and day
305 boys and girls 13–18

Clifton College Preparatory School
The Avenue, Clifton, Bristol BS8 3HE
Tel: (0117) 973 7264
Independent; edge of town; boarding,
weekly boarding and day
400 boys and girls 8–13

Cobham Hall
Cobham, Gravesend, Kent DA12 3BL
Tel: (01474) 823371
Independent; rural; boarding and day
190 girls 11–18

Ellesmere College
Ellesmere, Shropshire SY12 9AB
Tel: (01691) 622321
Independent; rural; boarding and day
410 boys and girls 9–18

Ercall Wood Technology School
Golf Links Lane, Wellington, Telford,
Shropshire TF1 2DU
Tel: (01952) 417800
Local authority; town; day
825 boys and girls 11–16

Fulneck School
Fulneck, Pudsey, Leeds, West Yorkshire
LS28 8DS
Tel: (0113) 257 0235
Independent; semi-rural; boarding, weekly
boarding and day
424 boys and girls 3–18

Grenville College
Bideford, Devon EX39 3JR
Tel: (01237) 472212
Independent; rural town; boarding and day
380 boys and girls 8–18

Hillcroft Preparatory School
Walnut Tree Manor, Haughley Green,
Stowmarket, Suffolk IP14 3RQ
Tel: (01449) 673003
Independent; rural; day
86 boys and girls 2–13

Holmwood House School
Lexden, Colchester, Essex CO3 5ST
Tel: (01206) 574305
Independent; edge of town; boarding and
day
338 boys and girls 4–13

Hurst Lodge
Bagshot Road, Ascot, Berkshire SL5 9JU
Tel: (01344) 622154
Independent; town; boarding, weekly
boarding and day
160 girls 2–18, 40 day boys 2–11

Kingham Hill School
Kingham, Chipping Norton, Oxfordshire
OX7 6TH
Tel: (01608) 658999
Independent; rural; boarding, weekly
boarding and day
210 boys and girls 11–18

King's School Rochester
Satis House, Boley Hill,
Rochester, Kent ME1 1TE
Tel: (01634) 843913
Independent; city; boarding; weekly
boarding and day
550 boys and girls 8–18

Kingswood College at Scarisbrick Hall
Southport Road, Ormskirk,
Lancashire L40 9RQ
Tel: (01704) 880200
Independent; rural; day
500 boys and girls 2½–19

Kingswood House School
56 West Hill, Epsom, Surrey KT19 8LG
Tel: (01372) 723590
Independent; urban; day
200 boys 3–13

Merchiston Castle School
Colinton, Edinburgh E13 0PU
Tel: (0131) 312 2200
Independent; edge of town; boarding; day
390 boys 8–18

Newlands Preparatory School
Eastbourne Road, Seaford, East Sussex
BN25 4NP
Tel: (01323) 892334
Independent; edge of town; boarding,
weekly boarding and day
200 boys and girls 2–13

New Hall School
Chelmsford, Essex CM3 3HT
Tel: (01245) 467588
Independent, town, day
250 boys and girls 4–11
boarding, weekly boarding and day
370 girls 11–18

Roundhay School
Gledhow Lane, Leeds LS8 1ND
Tel: (0113) 293 7711
Local education authority; city; day
1192 boys and girls 11–18

St David's College
Llandudno, Conwy LL30 1RD
Tel: (01492) 875974
Independent; rural; boarding, weekly
boarding and day
210 boys and girls 11–18

Sibford School
Sibford Ferris, Banbury, Oxfordshire
OX15 5QL
Tel: (01295) 781200
Independent; rural; boarding, weekly
boarding and day
320 boys and girls 5–18

Sidcot School
Winscombe, North Somerset BS25 1PD
Tel: (01934) 843102
Independent; rural; boarding, weekly
boarding and day
74 boys and girls 3–8, 405 boys and
girls 9–18

Stanbridge Earls School
Romsey, Hampshire SO51 0SZ
Tel: (01794) 516777
Independent; boarding and day
184 boys and girls 11–18

Stowford College
95 Brighton Road, Sutton, Surrey
SM2 5SJ
Tel: (020) 8661 9444
Independent; urban; day
70 boys and girls 7–16+

St James's School
West Malvern, Worcestershire,
WR14 4DF
Tel: (01684) 560851
Independent, semi-rural, boarding,
weekly boarding and day
120 girls 10–18

Thornlow Preparatory School
Woodsford House, Connaught Road,
Weymouth, Dorset DT4 0SA
Tel: (01305) 785703
Independent; rural; boarding, weekly
boarding and day
70 boys and girls 3–13

SPECIALIST CLASSES – SC

These schools meet the needs of dyslexics in the ordinary classroom through support, differentiation of the curriculum, and special tuition within the classroom setting; or, where necessary, through limited withdrawal. Many of these schools are maintained and can call on the expertise of the psychology and special needs support services of the education authority.

Bodiam Manor School
Bodiam, Robertsbridge, East Sussex
TN32 5UJ
Tel: (01580) 830225
Independent; rural; day
170 boys and girls 2–13

Box Hill School
Mickleham, Dorking, Surrey RH5 6EA
Tel: (01372) 373382
Independent; edge of town; boarding,
weekly boarding and day
268 boys and girls 11–18

Brontë House School
Apperley Bridge, Bradford, Yorkshire
BD10 0PQ
Tel: (0113) 250 2811
Independent; edge of city; boarding,
weekly boarding and day

Danes Hill School
Leatherhead Road, Oxshott, Surrey
KT22 0JG
Tel: (01372) 842509
Independent, rural, day
800 boys and girls 3–13

The Hugh Christie Technology College
Norwich Avenue, Tonbridge, Kent
TN10 4QL
Tel: (01732) 353544
Local education authority; town; day
1100 boys and girls 11–18

King's School Junior School
Ely, Cambridgeshire CB7 4DB
Tel: (01353) 660730
Independent; small city; boarding, weekly
boarding and day
320 boys and girls 8–13

Llandovery College
Llandovery, Carmarthenshire SA20 0EE
Tel: (01550) 723000
Independent; town; boarding; weekly
boarding; day
220 boys and girls 11–18

Mayville High School
35 St Simon's Road, Southsea, Hampshire
PO5 2PE
Tel: (023) 9273 4487
Independent; city; day
55 boys 4–11, 193 girls 4–16

Mount St Mary's College
Spinkhill, Derbyshire
S21 3YL
Tel: (01246) 433388
Independent, rural, boarding, weekly
boarding and day
285 boys and girls 11–18

Newlands Manor Senior School
Eastbourne Road, Seaford,
Sussex BN25 4NP
Tel: (01323) 892334
Independent; edge of town; boarding; day
160 boys and girls 13–18

**Newlands Pre-Preparatory and Nursery
School**
Eastbourne Road, Seaford, East Sussex
BN25 4NP
Tel: (01323) 892334
Independent; edge of town; day
150 boys and girls 2–8

Ramillies Hall School
Cheadle Hulme, Cheadle, Cheshire
SK8 7AJ
Tel: (0161) 485 3804
Independent, edge of town, boarding
weekly boarding and day
89 boys and girls 4–13

Slindon College
Slindon House, Arundel, West Sussex
BN18 0RH
Tel: (01243) 814320
Independent; village; boarding, weekly
boarding and day
110 boys 11–18

WITHDRAWAL SYSTEM – WS

These are usually larger schools with only a very small minority of much less seriously affected dyslexic students enrolled. These schools offer a broad academic curriculum where individual needs are met by limited withdrawal, either within the working day, or outside the timetabled curriculum to an unsupported specialist teacher.

Hordle Walhampton School
Lymington, Hampshire SO41 5ZG
Tel: (01590) 672013
Independent; rural; boarding, weekly
boarding and day
177 boys and girls 7–13

Monkton Combe School
Bath BA22 7HG
Tel: (01225) 721102
Independent; village; boarding, weekly
boarding and day
346 boys and girls 11–18

Mowden Hall School
Newton, Stocksfield, Northumberland
NE43 7TD
Tel: (01661) 842147
Independent; rural; boarding, weekly
boarding and day
170 boys and girls 4–13

Newlands School
34 The Grove, Gosforth, Newcastle upon
Tyne NE3 1NH
Tel: (0191) 285 2208
Independent; city; day
252 boys 3–13

Prior Park Preparatory School
Cricklade, Calcutt Street, Wiltshire
SN6 6BB
Tel: (01793) 750275
Independent; edge of town; boarding,
weekly boarding and day
187 boys and girls 2–13

St Bees School
St Bees, Cumbria CA27 0DS
Tel: (01946) 822263
Independent; village; boarding, weekly
boarding and day
300 boys and girls 11–18

Windlesham House School
Washington, Pulborough, West Sussex
RH20 4AY
Tel: (01903) 873207
Independent; rural; boarding
290 boys and girls 4–13

Woodhouse Grove School
Apperley Bridge, West Yorkshire
BD10 0NR
Tel: (0113) 250 2477
Independent; edge of town; boarding,
weekly boarding and day
555 boys and girls 11–16

Woodleigh School
Langton Hall, Langton, Malton, North
Yorkshire YO17 9QN
Tel: (01653) 658215
Independent; rural; boarding, weekly
boarding and day
55 boys and girls 7–13

Woodside Park International School
Friern Barnet Road, London N11 3DR
Tel. (020) 8368 3777
Independent; city; day
250 boys and girls 7–16

Ysgol Rhydygors
Llanstephan Road, Johnsown, Carmarthen
SA31 3NQ
Tel. (01267) 231171
LEA Special School
Semi-rural; boarding
45 boys and girls 8–16

5.3
Useful Addresses and Associations

Action for Blind People
14–16 Verney Road
London SE16 3DZ
Tel: (020) 7635 4800
Fax: (020) 7635 4900

Services include an information and advice service, including welfare rights advice and a national mobile service. Publications include "Disability Living Allowance for visually impaired children" and "Young people in full-time education: a guide for visually impaired people" (benefit information).

Action for Sick Children
c/o National Children's Bureau
8 Wakely Street
London EC1V 7QE
Tel: (020) 7843 6444
Helpline: (0800) 074 4519
Contact: Pamela Barnes, Chairman

Aims to join parents and professionals in promoting high quality health care for children in hospital and at home. Services include: library and information service, publications, research and a branch network which offers advice and support.

Advice Service Capability Scotland (ASCS)
11 Ellersly Road
Edinburgh EH12 6HY
Tel: (0131) 313 5510
Fax: (0131) 346 1681
Textphone: (0131) 346 2529
Email: ascs@capability-scotland.org.uk
Website: www.capability-scotland.org.uk

Advisory Centre for Education (ACE) Ltd
1C Aberdeen Studios
22–24 Highbury Grove
London N5 2DQ
Exclusion Advice: (020) 7704 9822
Tel: Advice Lines (0808) 800 5793
Monday–Friday 2–5pm

The Advisory Centre for Education is an independent national education advice centre which offers free and confidential telephone advice to parents every weekday from 2–5pm on (0808) 800 5793. ACE helps explain the school system, formal procedures, and aspects of education law, particularly in the areas of admission and exclusion appeals, and special educational needs issues. ACE has a full range of publications described in a free publication leaflet and offers training to parents groups, governors, LEA officers and teachers.

Contact the business line (020) 8354 8318 for these services or write to ACE at the above address. Information on all these issues is also available on the ACE website www.ace-ed.org.uk

Afasic
69–85 Old Street
London EC1V 9HX
Helpline: (0845) 355 5577
Administration (020) 841 8900
e-mail: info@afasic.org.uk
Website: www.afasic.org.uk

Afasic represents children and young adults with speech, language and communication difficulties and supports and provides information to parents/carers and professionals.

Association of Educational Psychologists
26 The Avenue
Durham, DH1 4ED
Tel: (0191) 384 9512
Fax: (0191) 386 5287
Secretary: Mary Jenkin

Trade union and professional body representing educational psychologists.

Association of National Specialist Colleges (NATSPEC)
PO Box 358
Grimsby DN34 4YA
Tel/Fax: (01472) 594014
email: chriswberry@ntlworld.com
Secretariat: Chris Berry

NATSPEC member colleges seek to offer the widest choice of innovative, high quality, cost-effective and appropriate further education and training, in

residential or day settings, for young people and adults with learning difficulties and/or disabilities.

Association for Spina Bifida and Hydrocephalus (ASBAH)
ASBAH House
42 Park Road
Peterborough PE1 2UQ
Tel: (01733) 555988
Fax: (01733) 555 985
e-mail: gillw@asbah.org

Executive Director: Andrew Russell, MA
Specialist Education Advisers: Three advisers cover England, Wales and Northern Ireland.

ASBAH provides information, advice and advocacy for people with Spina Bifida and or Hydrocephalus, promotes strategies which reduce their dependence on others, and funds educational and social research.

The Association of Workers for Children with Emotional and Behavioural Difficulties
Charlton Court
East Sutton
Maidstone
Kent ME17 3DQ
Tel: (01622) 843104
e-mail: awcebd@mistral.co.uk
Website: www.awcebd.co.uk
Administrative Officer: Allan Rimmer

The Bobath Centre For Children with Cerebral Palsy –
Registered Charity No. 229663
250 East End Road
London N2 8AU

Tel: (020) 8444 3355
Fax: (020) 8444 3399
Consultant Paediatrician:
Dr Andrew Lloyd Evans MA, MD, FRCP

The Bobath treatment concept was developed by Dr and Mrs Bobath in the 1940s and is a holistic interdisciplinary approach involving occupational physio- and speech and language therapists. Treatment provided on an individual basis (outpatient only), and therapists teach parents and carers how to continue therapy at home/or in school. A letter of referral is required from the child's consultant paediatrician or general practitioner giving full medical history and birth details. Letters should be addressed to the Director. On the basis of this information an application for funding may be made to the NHS. When the Centre has been notified in writing that its fees will be met, a consultation or course of treatment will be offered. If you would like further information this may be obtained from the Appointments & Funding Organiser.
The Centre organises post-graduate training courses in the Bobath treatment approach for physio-, occupational and speech and language therapists who are working with children who have cerebral palsy.
Details may be obtained from the Course Organiser.
For a list of the Centre's publications and teaching films please send a s.a.e. to the address above.

**Break, Special Needs, Special Care
(Registered Charity No. 286650)**
1 Montague Road, Sheringham
Norfolk NR26 8LN
Tel: (01263) 823170
Fax: (01263) 825560
email: office@break-charity.org
Contact: Judith Davison

Break provides holidays and respite care for children and adults with learning disabilities and other special needs. Full 24-hour care and a varied holiday programme, including outings, are provided. Special dietary requirements can be met. Centres are fully accessible, have numerous aids and adaptations, heated indoor swimming pool and adapted bus with wheelchair lift.

Breakthrough Deaf-Hearing Integration
National Office, Alan Geale House
The Close, Westhill Campus
Bristol Road
Birmingham B29 6LN
Tel: (0121) 415 2289
Text: (0121) 415 2289
Fax: (0121) 415 2323
Contact: Gill Winstanley,
National Services Manager

Developing innovative work between deaf and hearing people of all ages through partnership. Operates through four regional centres, London, Southern Counties, West Midlands and the North East (Gateshead) offering a programme of Contact, Information and Training. Meetings and activities vary in each region. For further information contact

	Text	Telephone
London	020 8269 0287	020 8269 0242
Southern Counties	01252 313 882	01252 313 882
West Midlands	0121 415 5900	0121 472 5488
North	0191 478 6963	0191 478 4369

British Association of Teachers of the Deaf (BATOD)
21 The Haystacks, High Wycombe
Buckinghamshire HP13 6PY
Tel: (01494) 464 190
email: secretary@batod.org.uk
Website: www.batod.org.uk
Secretary: Mr Paul Simpson

The British Association for Teachers of the Deaf (BATOD) is the only Association representing the interests of Teachers of the Deaf in this country. BATOD promotes the educational interests of all hearing-impaired children, young people and adults and safeguards the interests of Teachers of the Deaf. Nationally, conferences are organised to develop the professional expertise of Association members and to promote issues connected with the education of hearing-impaired children. There are seven Regions which organise workshops and activities locally. Courses and conferences are open to non-members. Associate membership is open to those who are not qualified Teachers of the Deaf.

British Colostomy Association
15 Station Road, Reading
Berkshire RG1 1LG
Tel: (0800) 328 4257
Fax: (0118) 956 9095
email: sue@bcass.org.uk
Website: www.bcass.org.uk

British Deaf Association
1–3 Worship Street
London EC2A 2AB
Textphone: (0800) 6522 965
Voice: (0870) 770 3300
Fax: 020 7588 3527
Videophone: 020 7496 9539
Email: helpline@bda.org.uk
Website: www.bda.org.uk

The BDA is a democratic, membership-led national charity campaigning on behalf of nearly 70,000 deaf sign language users in the UK. It exists to advance and protect the interests of the deaf community, to increase deaf people's access to facilities and lifestyles that most hearing people take for granted and to ensure greater awareness of their rights and responsibilities as members of society. The Association has several main service areas, with teams covering education and youth, information, health promotions, video production and community services, offering advice and help. We have a national Helpline that provides information and advice on a range of subjects such as Welfare Rights, Disability Discrimination Act (DDA) and Education. The BDA also publish the 'British Deaf News'.

British Dyslexia Association
98 London Road
Reading RG1 5AU
Tel: (0118) 966 8271
Fax: (0118) 925 1927
email: info@dyslexiahelp-bda.demon.co.uk
Website: www.bda-dyslexia.org.uk
Helpline/Information Service 10am–12.45pm & 2pm–4.45pm weekdays

British Epilepsy Association
New Anstey House, Gate Way Drive
Leeds LS19 7XY
Tel: (0113) 210 800
Helpline Tel: (0808) 800 5050
Website: www.epilepsy.org.uk

British Institute for Brain Injured Children
Knowle Hall, Knowle, Bridgwater
Somerset TA7 8PJ
Tel: (01278) 648 060
email: info@bibic.org.uk
Website: www.bibic.org.uk
Family Service Manager: Jeanette Saunders

Teaches the parents of brain injured children programmes of stimulation therapy which they carry out at home in order to improve their children's abilities.

Initially three days are spent at the Institute for assessment, evaluation and teaching. The family then returns at four-monthly intervals for reassessment and programming adjustment. Periods of specialised treatment therapy are offered when appropriate.

British Institute of Learning Disabilities (BILD)
Campion House, Green Street, Kidderminster
Worcestershire DY10 1JL
Tel: (01562) 723 010
Fax: (01562) 723 029
Email: enquiries@bild.org.uk
Website: www.bild.org.uk

BILD works towards improving the quality of life of people with learning disabilities.

The British Kidney Patient Association
Bordon
Hampshire GU35 9JZ
Tel: (01420) 472 021
Contact: Mrs Elizabeth Ward, OBE

The BKPA was founded in 1975 by Elizabeth Ward, whose son was diagnosed with kidney failure at the age of 13 years. At that time there was no national association concerned with the plight of Britain's kidney patients. Now kidney patients can turn to the BKPA for support, advice and, perhaps more importantly, financial help and a much needed break with their families at the BKPA holiday dialysis centres. The work of the BKPA falls roughly into two halves engendered by two quite separate needs: on the one hand the material and physical needs of the patients and their relatives, and on the other the

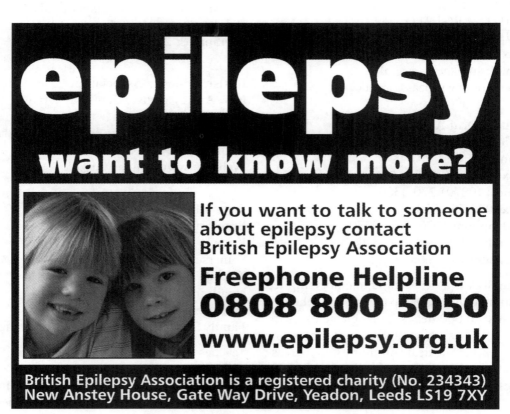

necessity to lobby for more and improved facilities and increased governmental funding, so that all parents may benefit from improvements in technology and pharmaceutical achievements.

British Psychological Society

48 Princes Road East
Leicester LE1 7DR
Tel: (0116) 254 9568

The British Psychological Society is the professional body incorporated by Royal Charter to maintain standards for the profession of psychology in the United Kingdom. The Directory of Chartered Psychologists, published by the Society, contains the names and addresses of Chartered Educational Psychologists who can provide services for parents and children with Special Educational Needs.

The British Stammering Association

15 Old Ford Road
London E2 9PJ
Tel: (020) 8983 1003 (3 Lines)
Helpline: (0845) 603 2001
Fax: (020) 8983 3591
Schools' Liaison Officer Tel/Fax:
(01606) 77374 (Visits and training arranged without charge)

The BSA is the largest charity in Europe helping children who stammer. It provides free information for parents, teenagers and teachers, and a counsellor is available to discuss specific problems. It also offers a mail-order service on specialist publications and a video pack for teachers. The Schools' Liaison Officer is able to offer training to education staff, and advice and guidance on oral assessment for public examinations to schools and parents.

Brittle Bone Society

30 Guthrie Street
Dundee DD1 5BS
Tel: (01382) 204446
Fax: (01382) 206771
Helpline: 08000 282459
email: bbs@brittlebone.org
Website: www.brittlebone.org

The Society seeks to promote research into the causes, inheritance and treatment of osteogenesis imperfecta and similar disorders characterised by excessive fragility of the bones. It also provides advice, encouragement and practical help for patients and their relatives living with difficulties caused by brittle bones.

Cancerlink
MacMillan Cancer Relief

89 Albert Embankment
London SE1 7UQ
Tel: (020) 7840 7840
Fax: (020) 7840 7841
Freephone Support Line: (0808) 808 0000
Email: cancerlink@cancerlink.org.uk
Website: www.cancerlink.org.uk

Cancerlink provides free confidential support services for people affected by cancer, and is part of national cancer charity Macmillan Cancer Relief. Cancerlink works with UK cancer self-help and support groups, to help people with cancer, their families and carers offering emotional and practical support close to home.

Centre for Studies on Inclusive Education (CSIE)

Room 25203, S Block
Frenchay Campus
Coldharbour Lane
Bristol BS16 1QU
Tel: (0117) 344 4007
Fax: (0117) 344 4005
Website: www.inclusion.org.uk

Advice and publications for parents wishing their children with special needs to be included in mainstream schools.

The Child Psychotherapy Trust
Star House, 104–108 Grafton Road
London NW5 4BD
Tel: (020) 7284 1355
Fax: (020) 7284 2755
email: cpt@globalnet.co.uk
Website:
www.childpsychotherapytrust.org.uk

Launched in 1987, the Child Psychotherapy Trust is a national charity dedicated to increasing the number of child psychotherapists available throughout the UK to treat emotionally damaged children, adolescents and their families. It is convinced of the benefits of treating emotional difficulties early, before they become entrenched.
The Trust publishes a range of material including a series of *Understanding Childhood* leaflets, written by child psychotherapists, for parents, carers and people working with children and families, which aim to promote understanding of children's emotional health, development and behaviour. They also publish a newsletter available for £10 per year. The Trust supports and manages various outreach projects, but does not itself offer psychotherapy or referral services.

Children's Legal Centre
The University of Essex, Wivenhoe Park
Colchester
Essex CO4 3SQ
Tel: (01206) 873820 Advice Line
Tel: (01206) 872466 General Enquiries
(Mon–Fri 10am–12.30pm & 2–4.30pm)

CLAPA (Cleft Lip and Palate Association)
235–237 Finchley Road
London NW3 6LS
Tel: (020) 7431 0033
Fax: (020) 7431 8881
email: info@clapa.com
Website: www.clapa.com
Chief Executive: Gareth Davies

CLAPA was set up in 1979 as a partnership between parents and professionals involved with the treatment of Cleft lip and/or Palate to provide specialist support for parents, the growing child, the adolescent and the adult. As well as practical parent-to-parent support services, CLAPA runs a helpline, dispatches feeding equipment, publishes a range of information leaflets, organises workshops for health professionals and, through its 50 branches, raises money towards facilities for local hospital treatment.

Contact a Family
209–211 City Road
London EC1V 1JN
Tel: (020) 7608 8700
Fax: (020) 7608 8701
email: info@cafamily.org.uk
Website: www.cafamily.org.uk

Support for families who care for children with disabilities and special needs. The organisation also publishes "The Contact a Family Directory of Specific Conditions and Rare Syndromes in Children".

Council for the Advancement of Communication with Deaf People
Durham University Science Park
Block 4, Stockton Road
Durham DH1 3UZ
Tel: (0191) 383 1155
Fax: (0191) 383 7914
Text: (0191) 383 7915
email: durham@cacdp.demon.co.uk
Chief Executive: Miranda Pickersgill

CACDP aims to improve communication between deaf and hearing people by the development of curricula and examinations in communication skills. CACDP offers certification in British Sign Language, Lipspeaking, Communication with Deafblind People and Deaf Awareness, and carries out the selection, training, monitoring and registration of examiners.

Council for Disabled Children
8 Wakeley Street
London EC1V 7QE
Tel: (020) 843 6061

The Council for Disabled Children is an independently elected council established under the aegis of the National Children's Bureau. The Council promotes collaborative work between different organisations providing services and support for children and young people with disabilities and special educational needs.

CReSTeD (Council for the Registration of Schools Teaching Dyslexic Pupils)
Registered Charity No: 1052103
Greyarth, Littleworth
Winchcombe
Cheltenham GL54 5BT
Tel/Fax: (01242) 604852
Administrator: Ms Christine Manser

The CReSTeD Register aims to help parents and those who advise them choose schools for Dyslexic children. Its main supporters are the British Dyslexia Association and the Dyslexia Institute who, with others, established CReSTeD to produce an authoritative list of schools, both maintained and independent, which have been through an established registration procedure, including a visit by a CReSTeD-selected consultant. For a list of schools see pages 495–503.

CReSTeD

Council for the Registration of Schools Teaching Dyslexic Pupils

Are you looking for a school with excellent provision for your dyslexic child?

- CReSTeD produces a Register of schools that are approved for their dyslexia provision
- CReSTeD schools are visited regularly to ensure standards are maintained
- Only schools visited and approved by CReSTeD are on the CReSTeD Register
- Look for the school with the CReSTeD logo - a symbol of quality of dyslexia provision

Registers are available free of charge from CReSTeD, Greygarth, Littleworth, Winchcombe, Cheltenham, GL54 5BT. Tel/Fax: 01242 604852
E: admin@crested.org.uk; www.crested.org.uk
Registered Charity No. 1052103

Cystic Fibrosis Trust
11 London Road
Bromley
Kent BR1 1BY
Tel: (020) 8464 7211
Fax: (020) 8313 0472
email: enquiries@cftrust.org.uk
Website: www.cftrust.org.uk

The Cystic Fibrosis Trust Support Service provides emotional, practical, and financial advice to families who have a child with CF and adults with CF. The full-time staff are supported by a network of trained volunteer workers who operate on a local basis. The Trust offers advice on welfare benefits, insurance, employment, holidays, housing, equipment and other matters.

Disability Alliance
Universal House
88–94 Wentworth Street
London E1 7SA
Office (minicom available):
(020) 7247 8765
Fax: (020) 7247 8776
Rights advice helpline (minicom available): (020) 7247 8763
The helpline is open on Monday 2–4pm and on Wednesday 2–4pm

The Disability Alliance is committed to breaking the link between poverty and disability. It provides information to disabled people about their entitlements, and campaigns for improvements to the social security system and for increases in disability benefits.

It publishes the *Disability Rights Handbook* and three issues of the *Disability Rights Bulletin* every year, as well as other publications and information briefings. The Disability Alliance also runs training courses on benefits and provides a free telephone helpline.

The Disability Law Service
39–45 Cavell Street
London E1 2BP
Tel: (020) 7791 9800
Minicom: (020) 7791 9801
Fax: (020) 7790 9802
email: advice@dls.org.uk

Provides a broad range of free legal advice and assistance on education, children and many other matters specifically for disabled people, their families and carers.

Disability Sport England
Unit 4G
784–788 High Road
Tottenham
London N17 0DA
Tel: (020) 8801 4466
Fax: (020) 8801 6644
email: sharon@dse.org.uk

DSE aims to provide, develop and co-ordinate opportunities in sport and recreation for people with disabilities. We co-ordinate 12 National championships and over 200 regional events for people with all disabilities.

Disabled Living Foundation
380–384 Harrow Road
London W9 2HU
Helpline: (0845) 130 9177
Minicom: (020) 7432 8009
Fax: (020) 7266 2922
email: advice@dlf.org.uk
Website: www.dlf.org.uk
Head of Services: Mary Queally

The Disabled Living Foundation is a national charity, which aims to provide advice and information on equipment to enable disabled and elderly people manage daily living activities. Its services are open to all: disabled people, carers, relatives, students and professionals working in the disability field.
The organisation runs a telephone, letter, email enquiry service and an equipment demonstration centre. It also publishes a range of fact sheets.

Dogs for the Disabled
(Registered Charity No 700454)
The Frances Hay Centre
Blacklands Hill, Banbury
Oxon OX17 2BS
Tel: (01295) 252 600
Fax: (01295) 252 688
email: dfd@dial.pipex.com

Specially-selected dogs are trained to perform tasks which disabled people find difficult or impossible. Tasks include retrieving articles, opening and closing doors, activating light switches and helping people with a balance problem to rise from a chair or walk independently of other aids. Dogs are trained to suit individual needs providing independence, security and companionship.

Down's Syndrome Association
155 Mitcham Road
London SW17 9PG
Tel: (020) 8682 4001
email: info@downs-syndrome.org.uk
Website: www.downs-syndrome.org.uk

The Down's Syndrome Association is the only national charity, covering England Wales & Northern Ireland, which works exclusively with people with Down's Syndrome. It exists to provide support, information, advice and counselling to people with Down's Syndrome, their parents/carers, families and those with a professional interest. The Association has a network of parent-led branches and groups, a national office and resource centre in London and resource centres in Belfast & Cardiff.

Down's Syndrome Scotland
158–160 Balgreen Road
Edinburgh
EH11 3AU
Tel: (0131) 313 4225
Fax: (0131) 313 4285
Website: www.dsscotland.org.uk
Children's worker: Karen Bain

Dyslexia Institute (Head Office)
133 Gresham Road, Staines
Middlesex TW18 2AJ
Tel: (01784) 463851
Fax: (01784) 460747
Executive Director: Mrs E J Brooks

Through its national network of 25 centres and over 120 outposts the Dyslexia Institute offers assessments and specialist teaching programmes, as well as a wide range of courses and resource materials for all teachers. Staff also provide advice and counselling to dyslexic individuals and their families. The Dyslexia Institute's professional body, the Dyslexia Institute Guild, publishes a membership journal, "Dyslexia Review" and organises an annual symposium.

The Dyslexia Institute (Scotland)
74 Victoria Crescent Road, Dowanhill
Glasgow G12 9JN
Tel: (0141) 334 4549
Contact: Mrs Elizabeth Mackenzie

The Institute in Scotland provides psychological assessment, specialist teaching, short courses and teacher training to postgraduate diploma level.

Dyspraxia Foundation (Registered Charity No. 1058352)
8 West Alley, Hitchin
Herts SG5 1EG
Tel: (01462) 455016
Helpline: (01462) 454986
Fax: (01462) 455052

Dyspraxia is an impairment or immaturity of the organisation of movement, perception and thought, sometimes known as "Clumsy Child Syndrome". The Foundation offers advice, information, support, professional and parental conferences and much more.

Eating Disorders Association
First floor, Wensum House
103 Prince of Wales Road, Norwich
Norfolk NR1 1DW
Helpline: (01603) 621414
Mon–Fri 9am–6.30pm

Youth Helpline: (01603) 765050
Mon–Fri 4pm–6.30pm (18 years & under)
Admin: (0870) 770 3256
Media: (0870) 770 3221
Fax: (01603) 624915
Email: info@edauk.com
Website: ww.edauk.com

The Eating Disorders Association offers information and understanding through telephone help-lines, guidelines, newsletters and a national network of self-help groups for people with anorexia or bulimia, their families and friends. Telephone helplines operate on 01603 621414 (Mon–Fri 9am–6.30pm). The Youth Helpline operates Mon–Fri, 4pm–6pm, on 01603 765050 and is specifically for callers aged 18 years or under. Membership includes a newsletter every quarter.

Electronic Aids for the Blind
Suite 4B, 71–75 High Street
Chislehurst
Kent BR7 5AG
Tel: (020) 8295 3636
Fax: (020) 8295 3737

A national charity helping blind and
partially sighted people of all ages to
achieve their fullest potential by awarding
partial grants and arranging fund-raising
appeals to third parties to purchase
specialist or suitably-adapted equipment
for personal use where no statutory
obligations exist and where there is
financial hardship.

emPOWER
c/o Limbless Association
Rehabilitation Centre
Queen Mary's Hospital
Roehampton Lane

London SW15 5PR
Tel: (020) 8788 1777
Fax: (020) 8788 3444
email: enquiries@empowernet.org
Website: www.empowernet.org

A consortium of users of prosthetics,
orthotics, wheelchairs and electronic
assistive technology which campaigns for a
"natural look" based on individual needs.

ENABLE
6th Floor, 7 Buchanan Street
Glasgow G1 3HL
Tel: (0141) 226 4541

ENABLE can provide information and legal
advice about educational issues affecting
children with learning disabilities in
Scotland. It has a network of local branches
across Scotland offering mutual support to
parents and runs a range of services
including housing for adults with complex

The Disability Rights Handbook
A must for all special needs staff

A fully comprehensive guide to all social security benefits
for disabled children and young people, including:

Disability living allowance
Child benefit
Financing studies- grants and loans
Income support
Severe disablement allowance/incapacity benefit
Help for carers
Community care/Residential care
How to challenge decisions
Housing Benefit and much, much more

This book is essential for anyone working with
16-19 year olds

Published May 2002. Price £13.00 (postfree) or £9.00 for
people on benefit. Also available on CD price £15.28 (incl
VAT). Order now by sending payment by cheque or postal
order to:- Disability Alliance, (ref.GAB),
              88-94 Wentworth Street,
              London E1 7SA

Please allow 28 days for delivery
Registered Charity number 1063115

---

difficulties, employment training and support, day services and family-based respite care.

Family Fund Trust
PO Box 50
York YO1 9ZX
Tel: (01904) 621115
Text Tel: (01904) 658085
Fax: (01904) 652625
Information Manager: Allison Cowen

The purpose of the Family Fund Trust is to ease the stress on families who care for very severely disabled children under 16, by providing grants and information related to the care of the child. Further details are available from the Information Office at the above address.

The Foundation for Conductive Education
The National Institute of Conductive Education,
Cannon Hill House
Russell Road, Moseley
Birmingham B13 8RD
Tel: (0121) 449 1569
Fax: (0121) 449 1611
email: foundation@conductive-education.org.uk
Website: www.conductive-education.org.uk
Monday–Friday, 9.00am–5.00pm

A national charity formed in 1986 "to establish and develop the science and skill of Conductive Education in the UK". The National Institute of Conductive Education provides direct services to children and adults with motor disorders; cerebral palsy, multiple sclerosis, Parkinson's disease, children with dyspraxia and those who have suffered strokes and head injuries. Through a system of positive teaching and learning support, Conductive Education maximises its control over bodily movement in ways that are relevant to daily living.
The National Institute also undertakes research and offers a comprehensive range of professionally oriented, skills-based training courses at all levels. Covers UK and overseas.

FYD (Friends for Young Deaf People)
Community Development Office, South East Court Mansion
College Lane
East Grinstead
West Sussex RH19 3LT
Tel: (01342) 300080
Minicom: (01342) 324164
Fax: (01342) 410232
Development Officer: Martin Broomfield
Family Officer: Geoff Harbor

The aim of the FYD is to promote an active partnership between deaf and hearing people which will enable young deaf people to develop themselves and become active members of society.

The Guide Dogs for the Blind Association
Hillfields
Burghfield Common
Reading RG7 3YG
Tel: (0870) 600 2323
Contact: Stephen Kirk
email: guidedogs@gdba.org.uk
Website: www.guidedogs.org.uk

Helen Arkell Dyslexia Centre
Frensham
Farnham
Surrey GU10 3BW
Tel: (01252) 792400
email: general_enquiries@arknellcentre.org.uk
Director: Mrs Rosie Wood

A registered charity providing comprehensive help and care for children with specific learning difficulties, including assessment, tuition, speech and language therapy and short courses as well as teacher training and schools support. Financial help is available. Specialist books on dyslexia for parents and teachers are available by mail order.

Hornsey Conductive Education Centre
54 Muswell Hill
London N10 3ST
Tel: (020) 8444 7242

Provides Conductive Education for children with Cerebral Palsy, and courses for professionals working with children who have Cerebral Palsy in mainstream education.

Hyperactive Children's Support Group (HACSG)
71 Whyke Lane
Chichester
West Sussex PO19 2LD
Tel: (01243) 551313
Fax: (01243) 55219
Contact: Mrs Sally Bunday

I CAN (Invalid Children's Aid Nationwide)
4 Dyer's Buildings, Holborn
London EC1N 2QP
Tel: (0870) 010 4066
Fax: (0870) 010 4067
Email: ican@ican.org.uk
Fax: www.ican.org.uk

I CAN is the national educational charity for children with speech and language difficulties. ICAN's services include an Early Years Programme, Special Schools, a Mainstream Programme, a national Training Programme, innovative partnership projects and an information service for parents, professionals and the general public.

In Touch
10 Norman Road
Sale
Cheshire M33 3DF
Tel: (0161) 905 2440

Information and contacts for all types of special needs in children, especially those with rare disorders. Newsletters and publications available.

Independent Panel for Special Education Advice
6 Carlow Mews
Woodbridge
Suffolk
IP12 1EA
Advice Line: (0800) 0184016
Admin: (01394) 380518
Co-ordinator: John Wright

IPSEA provides:
- Free independent advice on LEAs' legal duties towards children with special educational needs.
- Free professional second opinions for parents who disagree with an LEA's assessment of their child's special educational needs.
- Free representation at the Special Educational Needs Tribunal for parents who want to appeal against an LEA decision.

The Institute for Neurophysiological Psychology
4 Stanley Place
Chester
Cheshire CH1 2LU
Tel: (01244) 311414
Director: Peter Blythe
Co-Director: Sally Goddard-Blythe

Established in 1975 to research into the effects of central nervous system dysfunctions on children with learning difficulties, and to develop appropriate CNS remedial and rehabilitation programmes. INPP can diagnose what underlies dyslexia, dyspraxia and other specific learning difficulties, and then devise an appropriate physical correction programme to be done each day at home or school. The children are regularly monitored, and as the basic causes are corrected the children begin to benefit from teaching and the educational process.

LDA (Learning Development Aids)
Duke Street, Wisbech
Cambridgeshire PE13 2AE
Tel: (01945) 463441
Fax: (01945) 587361

Learning and Teaching Scotland
74 Victoria Crescent Road
Glasgow
G12 9JN
Tel: (0141) 337 5000
Fax: (0141) 337 5050
Development Officer: Mrs M Watson

Advice on the use of technology for those with special needs. Development of software for special needs.

The Leukaemia Care Society
14 Kingfisher Court
Venny Bridge
Pinhoe
Exeter
Devon EX4 8JN
Tel: (0345) 673203 (Local call rate)
Chief Administrative Officer:
Mrs S J Brown
email: leukaemia.care@ukonline.co.uk
Website: www.leukaemiacare.org

Supports children, and their families, suffering from leukaemia and allied blood disorders. Information is available from the Exeter office.

Limbless Association
Roehampton Rehabilitation Centre
Roehampton Lane
London SW15 5PR
Tel: (020) 8788 1777
Fax: (020) 8788 3444
email: enquiries@limbless-association.org
Website: www.limbless-association.org

Information on a disabled football team run in co-operation with Wimbledon Football Club also available.

Makaton Vocabulary Development Project (MVDP)
31 Firwood Drive
Camberley
Surrey GU15 3QD
Tel/Fax: (01276) 61390/681368
Email: mvdp@makaton.org
website: www.makaton.org

Makaton Vocabulary is a language programme which provides basic means of communication and encourages the development of language and literacy skills in children and adults with learning and communication difficulties. The MVDP provides training and advice for parents, carers and professionals who wish to use Makaton through a national network of local and regional tutors. A wide range of resource materials is also available from the MVDP: these include books of signs and symbols, videos, pictures, guidelines and computer databases. A translation service into symbols and signs is also available to enable access to information.

Marfan Association UK
Rochester House
5 Aldershot Road
Fleet
Hampshire GU51 3NG
Tel: 01252) 810472
Fax: (01252) 810473

Chairman/Support Co-ordinator:
Mrs Diane L Rust

Marfan Syndrome is an inherited disorder of connective tissue, which may affect the eyes, skeleton, lungs, heart and blood vessels and may be life-threatening. The Marfan Association UK exists to support those with the condition, providing educational material about Marfan Syndrome for both medical and lay sectors and encouraging research projects.

MIND (The Mental Health Charity)
15–19 Broadway
London E15 4BQ
Tel: (020) 8519 2122
Information Line: (0845) 766 0163
email: contact@mind.org.uk
Website: www.mind.org.uk
Chief Executive: Richard Brook

MIND, the leading mental health charity, works for a better life for people in mental distress, campaigning for their right to lead an active and valued life. Founded in 1946, MIND has become the largest charitable provider of quality community care and an influential voice on mental health issues.

Muscular Dystrophy Campaign
7–11 Prescott Place
London SW4 6BS
Tel: (020) 7720 8055
Fax: (020) 7498 0670

The Muscular Dystrophy Group is the national charity funding research into treatments and cures for the muscular dystrophies and allied muscle wasting conditions. The Group also supports adults and children affected by these conditions with expert clinical care and grants towards

equipment. The charity relies on voluntary donations to fund its work.

National Association for Gifted Children
Suite 14, Challenge House
Sherwood Drive, Bletchley
Milton Keynes MK3 6DP
Tel: (0870) 770 3217
Fax: (0870) 770 3219
email: amazingchildren@nagcbritain.co.uk
Website: www.nagcbritain.org.uk

NAGC provides services and support to gifted children, their families and those involved in their education through its information service, branch activities, counselling services and in-service training. It works to increase awareness and understanding of the social, emotional and education needs of gifted children and to improve provision.

National Association of Independent and Non-Maintained Special Schools (NAIMS)
c/o Holly Bank School
Far Common Road
Mirfield
West Yorkshire WF14 0DQ
Tel: (01924) 490833
Fax: (01924) 491464
Secretary: Mr S Hughes

The National Association for Special Educational Needs (NASEN)
NASEN House
4/5 Amber Business Village
Amber Close
Amington
Tamworth B77 4RP
Tel: (01827) 311500
Fax: (01827) 313005
email: welcome@nasen.org.uk
Hon General Secretary: Sue Pearson

The National Association for Special Educational Needs promotes the development of children and young people with special educational needs, and influences the quality of provision through strong and cohesive policies and strategies for parents and professionals.

The National Autistic Society
393 City Road
London EC1V 1NG
Tel: (020) 7833 2299
Fax: (020) 7833 9666
email: nas@nas.org.uk

The National Autistic Society aims to offer families and carers information, advice and support, to improve awareness amongst key decision-makers, professionals and the general public, to provide training and to promote research into autism. The Society currently owns and manages six schools for children with autism offering daily, weekly, termly and 52 week a year placements. Local affiliated autistic societies run a further nine schools. The society also runs the Centre for Social and Communication Disorders which provides a diagnosis and assessment service.

National Children's Bureau
8 Wakeley Street
London EC1V 7QE
Tel: (020) 7843 1900
Fax: (020) 7278 6313
Website: www.ncb.org.uk

National Deaf Children's Society
15 Dufferin Street
London EC1Y 8PD
Information & Helpline: (020) 7250 0123 (voice and text)
Tel: (020) 7251 5020 (fax)

The National Deaf Children's Society is the leading national charity especially concerned with the needs of deaf children and their families. The society provides advice on education and welfare, health, technology and audiology and publishes information on all aspects of childhood deafness.

National Reye's Syndrome Foundation of the UK
15 Nicholas Gardens
Pyford, Woking
Surrey GU22 8SD
Tel: (01932) 346843
Fax: (01932) 343920
Contact: Mr Gordon Denney

Reye's Syndrome is a children's disease that affects the liver and brain. It is an acute disorder which affects children when they seem to be recovering from a viral illness. The National Reye's Syndrome Foundation of the United Kingdom was formed to provide funds for research into the cause, treatment, cure and prevention of Reye's Syndrome and Reye-like illnesses, to inform both the public and medical communities, and to provide support for parents whose children have suffered from the diseases.

Network 81
1–7 Woodfield Terrace
Chapel Hill, Stansted
Essex CM24 8AJ
Tel: (01279) 647415
Fax: (01279) 814908
National Co-ordinator: John Pashley
Administrator: Val Rosier

The National Autistic Society

The National Autistic Society seeks to meet the needs of children across the autistic continuum from those diagnosed as having Asperger syndrome or autism to children with severe challenging behaviour. Provision varies from day through to weekly, termly and full 52 week boarding.

Broomhayes School and Children's Centre
Kingsley House, Alverdiscott Road,
Bideford, North Devon, EX39 4PL
Tel: 01237 473 830 Fax: 01237 421 097
E-mail: Broomhayes@nas.org.uk
Principal: Barbara Dewar
Type of school: Mixed, full boarding

Daldorch House School
Sorn Road, Catrine, East Ayrshire, KA5 6NA
Tel: 01290 551 666 Fax: 01290 553 399
E-mail: Daldorch@nas.org.uk
Principal: Shona Pinkerton
Type of school: Mixed, full boarding and day

The Helen Allison School
Longfield Road, Meopham, Kent, DA13 0EW
Tel: 01474 814 878 Fax: 01474 812 033
E-mail: Helen.Allison@nas.org.uk
Principal: Jacqui Ashton-Smith
Type of school: Mixed, weekly boarding and day

Radlett Lodge School
Harper Lane, Radlett, Hertfordshire, WD7 9HW
Tel: 01923 854 922 Fax: 01923 859 922
E-mail: Radlett.Lodge@nas.org.uk
Principal: Lynda Tucker
Type of school: Mixed, weekly boarding and day

Robert Ogden School
Clayton Lane, Thurnscoe, Rotherham, South Yorkshire,
S63 0BE
Tel: 01709 874 443 Fax: 01709 870 701
E-mail: Robert.Ogden@nas.org.uk
Principal: Andrea Dishman
Type of school: Mixed, weekly boarding, full boarding

The Sybil Elgar School
Havelock Road, Southall, Middlesex, UB2 4NR
Tel: 020 8813 9168 Fax: 020 8571 7332
E-mail: Sybil.Elgar@nas.org.uk
Principal: Chloe Phillips
Type of school: Mixed, termly, weekly boarding and day

Further details can be obtained from:
Director of Services, The National Autistic Society,
Church House, Church Road, Filton, Bristol, BS34 7BD;
Tel: 0117 974 8400; Fax: 0117 987 2576; E-mail:
services@nas.org.uk

Network 81 is a national organisation supporting parents through the assessment and statementing process contained in the Education Act 1996. Services offered include a national helpline, literature for parents, and links with local Network 81 groups and other organisations. Individual, family and group membership is available.

OAASIS
Office for Advice, Assistance, Support and Information on Special Needs
Brock House
Grigg Lane
Brockenhurst
Hampshire SO42 7RE
Helpline: (09068) 633201*
Fax: (01590) 622687
email: oaasis@hesleygroup.co.uk
Website: www.oaasis.co.uk
Co-ordinator: Lesley Durston

OAASIS is an information and advice centre set up by the Hesley Group, an independent company running ten residential special schools and colleges. It offers advice, information and training on many learning disabilities, including ADHD, Asperger Syndrome and autism. OAASIS also produces a range of literature on these disorders, from free Information Sheets, to its 'First Guide to ...' series, for which a small charge is made.
Write to OAASIS or telephone the helpline* if you would like information about the Hesley Group schools and colleges, information about any aspect of special education, an information pack, publications list, forthcoming training day dates, or if you would like to go on the OAASIS mailing list.

(*calls to the Helpline cost 60p a minute)

THE NATIONAL
DEAF CHILDREN'S
SOCIETY

THE NATIONAL DEAF CHILDREN'S SOCIETY

is the leading UK charity providing on-going support, information, advice and advocacy on all aspects of childhood deafness. It is an organisation of families, parents and carers which exists to enable deaf children and young people to maximise their skills and abilities, and works to facilitate this process by every possible means.

Services include freephone helpline, specialist advisors in audiology, education and technology, a network of regional staff, loan of equipment, *The Listening Bus*® – a mobile travelling technology exhibition, family information days and more.

Contact the NDCS:
* Freephone helpline: 0808 800 8880 (voice/text) open mon-fri, 10am-5pm
* Fax: 020 7251 5020
* Email: helpline@ndcs.org.uk
* Visit our website: www.ndcs.org.uk

Paget Gorman Society (Registered Charity No 1008041)
2 Downlands Bungalows, Downlands Lane
Smallfield
Surrey RH6 9SD
Tel: (01342) 842308
email: PruP@compuserve.com
Website: www.pgss.org

Advice and information for parents and professionals concerned with speech and language-impaired children. The Society runs courses in Paget Gorman Signed Speech (PGSS). Publications and a video are available.

Perthes Association
15 Recreation Road
Guildford
Surrey GU1 1HE
Tel: (Admin): (01483) 534431
Tel: (Helpline): (01483) 306637
Fax: (01483) 503213
email: admin@perthes.org.uk
Website: www.perthes.co.uk

The Association advises families of children suffering from Perthes' Disease and associated conditions in all parts of the British Isles and abroad. Perthes' Disease (a potentially crippling disease of the hip) is a form of osteochondritis, which affects 5.5 per 100,000 children (mainly boys) between the ages of 2 and 15 years. Perthes Association volunteers are at the end of the telephone line for any worried or distressed parents, will visit them if possible or put them in touch with a family living locally.

The Physical & Sensory Service
The Education Centre
Church Street, Pensnett, Dudley
West Midlands DY5 4EY
Tel: (01384) 818007
Fax: (01384) 814241

Rathbone
Head Office
Churchgate House, 56 Oxford Street
Manchester M1 6EU
Tel: (0161) 236 5358
Fax: (0161) 238 6356
Special Education Advice Line:
(0800) 917 6790

A national charity working for and on behalf of people with learning difficulties. Provides a wide range of services including youth and adult training, residential services, and advice and information services. Our helpline provides advice on special needs education, statementing and exclusions.

REACH – Association for Children with Hand or Arm Deficiency
25 High Street, Wellingborough
Northamptonshire NN8 4JZ
Tel: (01933) 274126
email: reach@reach.org
Website: www.reach.org.uk

REACH: National Advice Centre for Children with Reading Difficulties (Registered Charity No 297694)
California Country Park
Nine Mile Ride, Finchampstead
Berkshire RG40 4HT
Tel: (0118) 973 7575 (Voice and text)
Helpline: (0845) 604 0414
Fax: (0118) 973 7105
email: reach@reach-reading.demon.co.uk
Website: www.reach-reading.demon.co.uk
Director: Beverly Mathias
Information Officer: Desmond L Spiers

REACH provides a resource and information centre for those who work with children whose disability, illness or learning problem affects their reading, language or communication. The centre contains both printed books and books on tape and video, plus microelectronic equipment and software. The collections are for reference only.

Royal Association for Disability and Rehabilitation (RADAR)
12 City Forum
250 City Road
London EC1V 8AF
Tel: (020) 7250 3222
email: radar@radar.org.uk
Minicom: (020) 7250 4119
Website: www.radar.org.uk

Information on all aspects of disability.

Royal College of Speech and Language Therapists
2 White Hart Yard
London SE1 1NX
Tel: (020) 7378 3013
Fax: (020) 7403 7254

The Royal National Institute for the Blind (RNIB)
224 Great Portland Street
London W1N 6AA
Tel: (020) 7388 1266
Fax: (020) 7388 2034
Website: www.rnib.org.uk
Director General: Ian Bruce
Director of Education and Employment: Eamonn Fetton

RNIB supports blind and partially-sighted children and their families by providing information and advice, books and magazines, schools, education centres, training and support for families.

The Royal National Institute for Deaf People
19–23 Featherstone Street
London EC1Y 8SL
Tel: (0808) 808 0123 – Helpline
Textphone: (0808) 808 9000 – Helpline
Fax: (020) 7296 8199
Chief Executive: James Strachan

The Royal National Institute for Deaf People (RNID) is the largest charity representing the 8.7 million deaf and hard of hearing people in the UK. As a membership charity, we aim to achieve a radically better quality of life for deaf and hard of hearing people. We do this by campaigning and lobbying vigorously, by raising awareness of deafness and hearing loss, by providing services and through social, medical and technical research.

Royal Mencap Society
123 Golden Lane
London EC1Y 0RT
Tel: (020) 7454 0454
Website: www.mencap.org.uk
Chairman: Brian Baldock CBE
Chief Executive: Fred Heddell CBE

- Mencap provides services for, and campaigns with, people who have a learning disability, their families and carers in England, Wales and Northern Ireland. Mencap is the UK's largest disability charity. It is a membership organisation.
- Mencap's leisure arm, Gateway, runs clubs for over 60,000 people around the country.
- *Viewpoint*, the monthly newspaper of the learning disability world, is available on subscription.

SCOPE
Cerebral Palsy Helpline
PO Box 833
Milton Keynes MK12 5NY
Tel: (0808) 800 3333

Scope exists to help all people with cerebral palsy and related disabilities.

**The Scottish Society for Autism
(Formerly Scottish Society for
Autistic Children)**
Hilton House
Alloa Business Park
Whins Road
Alloa
Clackmannanshire FK10 3SA
Tel: (01259) 720044
Fax: (01259) 720051
Website: www.autism-in-scotland.org.uk

SSAC is the leading provider of services for autism in Scotland. They run Struan House School, the only accredited school for autism in Scotland (both residential and day pupils); residential and specialist day services for adults; the only respite care centre for autism in the UK; nationwide family support services; training for carers and professionals; support self-help groups and local societies; and produce information and a members' magazine. They undertake community care assessments and give guidance on diagnosis, assessment and care management. Advice on all aspects of autism is available from their professional staff.

Scottish Spina Bifida Association
190 Queensferry Road
Edinburgh EH4 2BW
Tel: (0131) 332 0743
Fax: (0131) 343 3651
Chief Executive: Andrew H D Wynd

Royal National Institute for the Blind

Services for visually impaired children

RNIB offers a range of services to blind and partially sighted children and young people, their families and the professionals who work with them, including:

- Special schools for blind and partially sighted children, including those with additional disabilities
- Advice on equipment and technology to help children at home and at school
- Support, advice and information for parents and families

For more details call RNIB Education & Employment Information Service on tel: 020-7388 1286
or check www.rnib.org.uk
Registered charity no 226227

RNIB

The Scottish Spina Bifida Association seeks to increase public awareness and understanding of individuals with Spina Bifida/Hydrocephalus and allied disorders. It aims to secure provision for their special needs and those of their families.

Scottish Support for Learning Association
Registered Charity Number: SE026546
2403 Paisley Road West
Glasgow G52 2QH
Tel: (0141) 883 6134
Email: info@ssla.org.uk
Website: www.ssla.org.uk
Secretary: Christina Brownlie

SENNAC: Special Educational Needs – National Advisory Council
Pett Archive & Study Centre
Toddington
Cheltenham
Gloucestershire GL54 5DP
Hon General Secretary: Mr John Cross

Sense, The National Deafblind & Rubella Association
11–13 Clifton Terrace
Finsbury Park
London N4 3SR
Tel: (020) 7272 7774
Fax: (020) 7272 6012
Minicom: (020) 7272 9684
email: enquiries@sense.org.uk
Website: www.sense.org.uk

Sense is the national voluntary organisation supporting and campaigning for people who are deafblind, their families, their carers, and professionals who work with them. People of all ages and with widely varying conditions use Sense's specialist services. Founded as a parents' self-help group in 1955, Sense is now the leading national organisation working with deafblind people.

Sense:

- offers advice, help and information to deafblind people and their families;
- supports families through a national network and local branches;
- runs holiday programme for deafblind children and adults;
- education, residential, respite and day services;
- communicator-guides and one-to-one intervenor support;
- training and consultancy.

Sense West
Midlands Area
Princess Royal Centre
4 Church Road
Edgbaston
Birmingham B15 3TD
Tel: (0121) 687 1564 (voice and text)
Fax: (0121) 687 1656

Sense West provides a regional advisory service to families, deaf-blind people and professionals working with them, an adult service department offering a range of residential provision and learning opportunities based on individual need for deaf-blind and multiply disabled sensory impaired adults, and a Training and Consultancy Service offering advice, assessment and training to people involved with the education and care of deaf-blind children and adults. In addition they also provide a day service for deaf-blind people in the Birmingham area and an information service.

The Sequal Trust
(Special Equipment and Aids for Living)
3 Ploughmans Corner
Wharf Road
Ellesmere
Shropshire SY12 0EJ
Tel/Fax: (01691) 624222

A national charity which aims to assist severely physically disabled people by providing special electronic/electrical communication equipment. SEQUAL is run by severely disabled people who themselves use a variety of electronic equipment and is dedicated to the improvement of conditions for its members and other disabled people.

The SIGNALONG Group
Communication & Language Centre
North Pondside
Historic Dockyard
Chatham
Kent ME4 4TY
Tel: (01634) 819915 (Enquiries & sales)
Tel: (01634) 832469
(Training & development)

SIGNALONG is a sign-supporting system based on British Sign Language intended to promote communication in learning disabilities and autism. The charity has devised a uniform method of presenting signs with drawings and descriptions, and has published the widest range of illustrated signs in Britain, catering for all ages and abilities. Manuals contain full signing instructions, but training and advice are also provided, both by SIGNALONG staff and by independent accredited tutors. SIGNALONG works with other organisations to developed symbol resources and to promote total communication to enable understanding and expression of choice.

Skill – National Bureau for Students with Disabilities
Chapter House
18–20 Crucifix Lane
London SE1 3JW
Tel: (020) 7450 0620
Fax: (020) 7450 0650
Information Service:
(0800) 328 5050, (0800) 068 2422
(Info Service Minicom)
Monday to Friday 1.30–4.30pm
email: info@skill.org.uk
Website: www.skill.org.uk
Director: Ms B Waters
Information Service Manager:
Mr M Sissons

Skill is a voluntary organisation which aims to develop opportunities for young people and adults with any kind of disability or learning difficulty – in further, higher and adult education, in training and employment.

Special Needs Advisory Project Cymru (SNAP)
45 Penarth Road, Cardiff CF1 5DJ
Tel: (029) 2038 8776
Fax: (029) 2038 8776
email: snapcym@aol.com.uk

SNAP Cymru offers information and support to families of children and young people who have, or may have, special educational needs.

Tourette Syndrome (UK) Association
PO Box 26149
Dunfermline
KY12 9WT
Tel/Fax: (01892) 669151
email: enquiries@tsa.org.uk

5.4
Bibliography

The following list has been compiled with the kind assistance of editorial contributors and offers suggested further reading on many aspects on special educational needs.

General

"The Code of Practice for the Identification and Assessment of SEN"

"Special Educational Needs: A Guide for Parents"

"Meeting Special Educational Needs – a programme of action"

"Meeting Special Educational Needs – a programme of action" – a summary, also available in braille, on audio-cassette and in British Sign Language

All the above publications are available from the Department for Education and Employment (DfEE), tel. 0845 602 2260

"Children with Special Educational Needs – Assessment Law and Practice"
J Friel
Jessica Kingsley Publishers
ISBN 185 302460 0

"Telephone Helplines Directory"
Telephone Helplines Association
61 Grays Inn Road, London WC1X 8LT
Tel: 020 7248 3388
£15.00

"Statements: A Handbook for Parents"
Network 81, 1–7 Woodfield Terrace
Chapel Hill, Stansted, Essex CM24 8AJ
Tel: 01279 647415

"How and Why Children Fail"
Edited by: Ved Varma
Jessica Kingsley Publishers
£13.99
ISBN 185 302186 5

"ACE SEN Handbook"
Advisory Centre for Education (ACE)
Tel: 020 7354 8318
£8.00 Plus postage

"Tribunal Toolkit"
Advisory Centre for Education
Tel: 020 7354 8318

"Taking Action: Your Child's Right to Special Education – the definitive guide for parents, teachers, advocates and advice workers"
J White and I Rubain, 2000
Questions Publishing Co Ltd
ISBN 184 190010 9

"Disability Rights Handbook"
A guide to rights, benefits and services for all people with disabilities and their families
Disability Alliance
Universal House
88–94 Wentworth Street, London E1 7SA
Tel: 020 7247 8776
Fax: 020 7247 8765
£13.00 or £9.00 for people on benefit
ISBN: 1 9033 3506X

"Children First"
Royal Association for Disability and
Rehabilitation (RADAR)
Publications Department
12 City Forum, 250 City Road
London EC1V 8AF

"Challenging Decision"
A practical guide to decision making and
the appeal process for social security
benefits
Disability Alliance, 2000
ISBN 0946336873
£4.00

"Children in Difficulty: a Guide to
Understanding and Helping"
J Elliot and M Place
Routledge, 1998
ISBN 0415144590

"Disability Living Allowance – A Guide and
Checklist"
A user-friendly guide to disability living
allowance
Disability Alliance
Tel: 020 7247 8776
Fax 020 7247 8765
ISBN 1903335027

"Hope for the Journey – Helping children
through good times and bad. Story building
for parents, teacher and therapist"
C R Snyder, D McDermott, W Cook and M
A Rapoff
Westview Press, 1997
ISBN 0813331560

"Spelling: Remedial strategies"
Diane Montgomery
Cassell, 1997
ISBN 0304329746

"Understanding and Supporting Children
with Emotional or Behavioural Difficulties"
P Cooper (Ed.)
Jessica Kingsley, 1999
ISBN 1853026662

For students aged 16+ with disabilities

"After Age 16 – What Next?"
The Family Fund, PO Box 50
York YO1 2ZX
Tel: 01904 621115

"COPE Directory: Compendium of
post-16 education and training in
residential establishments for young
people with special needs"
Lifetime Careers (Wiltshire)
7 Ascot Court, Whitehorse Business Park
Trowbridge, Wiltshire BA14 0XA
Tel: 01225 716024

"The Association of National Specialist
Colleges Directory 1997 and 1998 and
1999"
A directory of colleges with specialist
provision for disabled students
£5.00 from NATSPEC
Contact: Olive Ralphes, Trevor Villa
School Lane, St Martins
Oswestry SY11 3BX

"Guide to Training and Benefits for
Young People"
Published by Youthaid, 322 St John Street
London EC1V 4NT
Tel: 020 7833 8499
Email: youthaid@gn.apc.org
ISBN 1907658202
£6.00

"Your Future Needs Assessment"
(Scotland Only)
Published by the Special Needs Forum of
Children in Scotland

Contact: Children in Scotland
5 Shandwick Place, Edinburgh EH2 4RG
Tel: 0131 228 8484
Fax: 0131 228 8585
£2.95

A range of publications covering all aspects of education for disabled students is available from SKILL, The National Bureau for Students with Disabilities
Chapter House, 18–20 Crucifix Lane
London SE1 3JW
Tel: 0800 328 5050 (voice) or
0800 068 2422 (text)

Higher education

"UCAS Handbook"
Available from UCAS or careers offices.

"UCAS Helpline"
Tel: 01242 227788
Minicom: 01242 225857
Website: www.ucas.ac.uk

"The Big Offical UCAS Guide to University and College Entrance"
UCAS Sheedon and Ward

"Into HE: a guide to Higher Education for people with disabilities"
Skill, Chapter House, 19–20 Crucifix Lane
London SE1 3JW
Tel: 0800 328 5050 (voice) or
0800 068 2422 (text)

ADD/ADHD

"The AD/HD Handbook. A guide for parents and professionals on attention deficit/hyperactivity disorder"
A Munden and J Arcelus
Jessica Kingsley Publishers
ISBN 1853027561

"12 Effective ways to Help your ADD/ADHD Child"
Laura J. Stevens
Avery Publishing Group, 2001
ISBN 1583330399

Autism/Asperger's Syndrome

"The Autistic Spectrum: A Guide for Parents and Professionals"
Lorna Wing
Constable, 1996
ISBN 0094751609

"Children with autism and Asperger syndrome: a guide for practitioners and carers"
Patricia Howlin
Wiley, 1998
ISBN: 0471983284

"Autism: The Facts"
Simon Baron-Cohen and Patrick Bolton
Oxford University Press, 1993
ISBN: 0192623273

"Asperger's Syndrome: A Guide for parents and Professionals"
Tony Attwood
Jessica Kingsley Publishers 1998
ISBN 1853025771

"Meeting the Needs of Children with Autistic Spectrum Disorders"
R Jordan and G Jones
David Fulton, 1999
ISBN 1853465828

A range of books, booklets and videos on autism and Asperger's Syndrome is available from the National Autistic Society, 393 City Road, London EC1V 1NG
Tel: 020 7833 Fax: 020 7837 9666

And also from OAASIS
Brock House, Grigg Lane
Brockenhurst, Hampshire SO42 7RE
Tel: 0891 633201 (helpline)
Fax: 01590 622687

Cerebral Palsy

A range of publications on cerebral palsy is available from SCOPE.
Cerebral Palsy Helpline
PO Box 833
Milton Keynes MK12 5NY
Tel: 0808 800 3333
Fax: 01908 321051
Email: Cphepline@scope.org.uk

"The Cerebral Palsy Handbook"
Marion Stanton
Vermilion, 2002
ISBN 0091876761

Cystic Fibrosis

A range of publications on cystic fibrosis is available from the Cystic Fibrosis Trust
11 London Road
Bromley, Kent BR1 1BY
Tel: 020 8464 7211
Fax: 020 8313 0472

"Cystic Fibrosis – A Family Affair"
Jayne Chumbley
Sheldon Press, 1999
ISBN 0859697711

Down's Syndrome

"Down's Syndrome – The Facts"
Mark Selikowitz
Oxford University Press, 1997

"New Approaches to Down's Syndrome"
Edited by Brian Stratford and Pat Gunn
Cassell, 1996

"The Development of Language and Reading Skills in Children with Down's Syndrome"
Sue Buckley, Maggie Emslie
Gilly Haslegrove, Pat leProvost
University of Portsmouth, 1993

"Meeting the Educational Needs of Children with Down's Syndrome"
Gillian Bird and Sue Buckley
The Sarah Duffen Centre
University of Portsmouth, 1994

"Supporting Support Assistants –
A Practical Handbook for SENCOs in Mainstream Primary and Secondary Schools"
Stephanie Lorenz, 1996

"Supporting Special Educational Needs in Secondary School Classrooms"
Jane Lovely
David Fulton Publishers, 1995

Dyscalculia

"Mathematics for Dyslexics:
A Teaching Handbook"
2nd edition
Chinn and Ashcroft
Whurr
ISBN 1861560435
£22.50

"Sum Hope – Breaking the Numbers Barrier"
Steve Chinn
Souvenir Press
ISBN 0285634550

CD-ROM
"What to do when you can't learn the times tables"
Dr S Chinn
Available from
Mark College
Mark, Somerset TA9 4NP
£29.99 + £1.95 p&p

Dyslexia

For parents:

"Dyslexia: A Parent's Survival Guide"
C Ostler, 1999
Ammonite Books
ISBN 1869866134

"Overcoming Dyslexia (A straightforward guide for families and teachers)"
B Hornsby
Macdonald & Co
ISBN 0091813204

"The Scars of Dyslexia (Eight case studies in emotional reactions)"
J Edwards, 1995
Cassell
ISBN 0304329444

"Susan's Story (An autobiographical account of my struggle with words)"
S Hampshire, 1990
Corgi
ISBN 0552135860

"This Book Does not Make Sens, Cens, Sns, Scens, Sense"
J Auger
Better Books

"Reversals"
E Simpson
Gollancz

Dyslexia – General

"Dyslexia: 100 Years On"
Miles T & E, 1999
Open University Press
ISBN 0335200346

"Dyslexia in Children"
Fawcett & Nicholson
Harvester Wheatsheaf

"The Pattern of Difficulties"
Miles T R
Whurr

"Developmental Dyslexia"
Thompson M E
Whurr

"Dyslexia: A Cognitive Developmental Perspective"
Snowling M
Blackwell

"Dyslexia: Speech and Language: A Practitioner's Handbook"
Snowling & Stockhouse
Whurr

"Psychological Assessment of Dyslexia"
Turner M
Whurr

"Specific Learning Difficulites (Dyslexia): Challenges & Responses"
Pumfrey & Reason
Routledge

"Dyslexia: A Practitioner's Handbook"
Gavin Reid
Wiley
ISBN 0471973912

Teaching

"Dyslexia: A Teaching Handbook"
Thompson & Watkins
Whurr
ISBN 1861560397

"Learning Difficulties in
Reading & Writing"
NFER
Nelson

"Specific Learning Difficulties (Dyslexia):
A Teacher's Guide"
Crombie M
Jordanhill College of Education

"Dealing with Dyslexia"
Heaton & Winterson
Better Books, 1996
ISBN 1897635575

"Children with Special Learning
Difficulties"
Tansley & Pankhurst
NFER Nelson

"Reading Writing & Dyslexia:
A Cognitive Analysis"
Ellis A, 1984
Lawrence Erlbaum
ISBN 0863770037

"Children with Special Needs"
Chasty & Friel
Jessica Kingsley

"Instrumental Music for Dyslexics:
A Teaching Handbook"
Ogelthorpe S
Whurr

"Mathematics for Dyslexics:
A Teaching Handbook"
Chinn & Ashcroft
Whurr

Resources

"Learning to Learn"
Malone S
Nasen
ISBN 1874784434

"Alpha to Omega"
Hornsby & Shear, 1999
Heinemann
ISBN 0435103881

"Spotlight on Words"
Aitken G, 1970
Robinswood Press
ISBN 1869981510

"Easy Type"
Kinloch R, 1994
Egon Publishers
ISBN 0905858905

"New Phonic Blending Kit"
Learning Materials Ltd

For the older student:

"Help for the Dyslexic Adolescent"
E G Stirling
St David's College, Llandudno

"Use Your Head"
T Buzan, 1999
BBC
ISBN 056337103X

"Study Skills: A Pupil's Survival Guide"
C Ostler
Ammonite Books

"Adult Dyslexia: Assessment,
Counselling and Training"
McLoughlin, Fitzgibbon & Young
Whurr, 1993
ISBN 1897635354

"Dyslexia at College"
D Gilroy & Prof T Miles, 1995
Routledge
ISBN 0415127785

A range of publications and videos is
available from The Dyslexia Institute
133 Gresham Road, Staines
Middlesex TW18 2AJ
Tel: 01784 463851
Fax: 01784 460747

"How to Detect and Manage Dyslexia"
P Ott
Heinemann, 1997
ISBN 0435104195

"Living with Dyslexia"
B Riddick
Routledge. 1997
ISBN 0415125014

"The Dyslexia Handbook 2001"
A Series of articles on different aspects of
dyslexia.
British Dyslexia Association
ISBN 1872653316
£9.50 (including postage)

Dyspraxia

"Developmental Dyspraxia"
2nd Edition
Madeleine Portwood
£17.50 (inc p&p)

"Take Time"
Mary Nash-Wortham and Jean Hunt

£11.00 (inc p&p)

"Dyspraxia – A Handbook for Therapists"
Michele Lee and Jenny Taylor
£7.00 (inc p&p)

All the above are available from
The Dyspraxia Foundation
8 West Alley, Hitchin
Hertfordshire SG5 1EG
Tel: 01462 455016,
Fax: 01462 455052.

"Praxis Makes Perfect"
A Dyspraxia Foundation Publication
£7.50 (inc p&p)

Epilepsy

Articles:

"Epilepsy, Learning and Behaviour
in Children"
F M Besal
In "Epilepsia" 36 1:1995 58–63
Raven Press, New York

"Established antiepileptic drugs"
M Brodie et al
In "Seizure" 1997 6: 159–174

"Behaviour problems in children with
new-onset epilepsy"
D W Dunn et al
In "Seizure" 1997 4:283–287

"Educational Attainment in Children
and Young People with Epilepsy"
P Thomson
In "Epilepsy and Education –
A Medical Symposium on Changing
Attitudes to Epilepsy in Education"
Edited by Jolyon Oxley and Gregory Stores
Published by Labaz Sanofi UK Ltd
London 1986

Gifted Children

"Gifted or Able"
Peter Young and Colin Tyre
Oxford University Press
ISBN 0335099963
£10.99

"Challenge of the Able Child"
David George
David Fulton Publishers
ISBN 1853463469
£12.99

"Supporting the Child of Exceptional
Ability at Home and at School"
S Leyden
David Fulton, 1998
ISBN 18534516X

The National Association for Gifted
Children (NAGC) publishes a range of
publications and newsletters for its
members.
Contact the NAGC
Elder House, 540 Elder Gate
Milton Keynes, MK9 1LR
Tel: 01908 673677
Fax: 01908 673679

Muscular Dystrophy

"Muscular Dystrophy: The Facts"
Alan E H Emery
Oxford University Press, 2000
ISBN 0192632175

"Childhealth Care Nursing: Concepts,
Theories and Practice"
Edited by B Carter and A K Dearmun
Blackwell Scientific, 1995
ISBN 0632036893
£19.99

"Children with Muscular Dystrophy in
Mainstream Schools"
Factsheet available from the
Muscular Dystrophy Group
7–11 Prescott Place, London SW4 6BS
Tel: 020 7720 8055

Speech and Language difficulties

AFASIC Publications

"Supporting Your Child's Speech and
Language": 12 booklets – price from £1–£2,
full set £12.50

"Glossary Sheets on Speech and Language
Impairments": 26 individual sheets which
explain terms used to describe children
with speech and language impairments
(35p each, £8.00 for the full set)

"Accessing Speech and Language Therapy
for your child – a Guide to the Law"

"Choosing a School – an AFASIC Guide to
Educational Options for Children with
Speech and Language Impairments"
£1.75

Other publications

"Activities for Speaking and Listening and
Confidence in Communicating"
Two publications – Part I (ages 3–7)
Part II (ages 7–11)
Heather Anderson, Frances Graham and
Alison Constable
£4.50

"Help me speak – a parent's guide to
speech and language therapy"
J Barrett
Souvenir Press, 1994
ISBN 0285631802

"Rachel – the 'write' to speak"
S Capelin
Minerva Press, 1998
ISBN 1861066341

"Children with Language Impairment:
an Introduction"
M Donaldson
Jessica Kingsley Publishers, 1995
ISBN 1853023132

"Trouble Talking: a guide for parents of
children with speech and language
difficulties"
J Law and J Elias
Jessica Kingsley Publishers, 1996
ISBN 1853022535

"Let Me Play; Let Me Speak"
D Jefree and R McConkey
Souvenir Press, 1996

"It Takes Two to Talk: a parent's guide to
helping children communicate"
A Manolson
Window Press

"Dyspraxia – A Guide for Teachers
and Parents"
K Ripley, B Daines and J Barrett
David Fulton, 1997
ISBN 1853464449

All the above publications are available
from AFASIC –
Unlocking Speech and Language
347 Central Markets
Smithfield
London EC1A 9NH
Tel: (020) 7236 3632 (helpline)
Fax: (020) 7236 8115

"Communication Difficulties in
Childhood"
Law, Parkinson and Tamnhe
Radcliffe Medical Press, 1999

"Elementary Mathematics and Language
Difficulties – a book for teachers, therapist
and parents"
Eva Grauberg
Whurr, 1997

Spina Bifida and Hydrocephalus

"Teaching the Student with Spina Bifida"
Fern L Rowley – Keith & Donald H Reigel
Paul Brookes Publishing Co,
ISBN 10557660646

"Living with Spina Bifida"
Adrian Sandler MP
University of North Carolina Press, 1997
(obtainable from Trevor Brown Associates,
Tel: (020) 7388 8500
ISBN 1080782352X

"Spinabilities: A Young Person's
Guide to Spina Bifida"
Edited by Marlene Lutkenhoff
Woodbine House (USA) &
Sonya Oppenheimer
ISBN 0933139867

"Children with Spina Bifida and/or
Hydrocephalus"
(Association for Spina Bifida and
Hydrocephalus)
ASBAH House, Peterborough
ISBN 090668711X

"Hydrocephalus and You"
Rosemary Bachelor and Leonie Holgate
ASBAH, Peterborough, 1999
ISBN 090 6687128

"Hydrocephalus Information Pack"
ASBAH, Peterborough, 1999
ISBN 0906687128

"Current Concepts in Spina Bifida
and Hydrocephalus"
Carys Bannister & Brian Tew
MacKeith Press
Distributed by
Blackwell Scientific Publishers Ltd
ISBN 0901260916

"The Statementing Process for
Children with Special Educational
Needs"
Peter Walker
ASBAH, Peterborough

"LINK"
Bi-monthly magazine of ASBAH
obtainable from ASBAH House
Titles available from ASBAH
42 Park Road
Peterborough PE1 2UQ,
Tel: 01733 555988
Fax: 01733 555985

Gilles de la Tourette Syndrome

"Tourette Syndrome: the facts"
Mary Robertson and Simon Baron-Cohen
Oxford University Press, 1998
ISBN 019852398X
£9.99

"Teaching the Tiger: A Handbook for
Individuals Involved in the Education of
Students with Attention Deficit Disorders,
Tourette Syndrome or Obsessive-
Compulsive Disorder"
Marilyn P Dornbush & Sheryl K Pruitt
Hope Press

"Tourette Syndrome"
Amber Carroll, Mary Robertson
David Fulton Publishers, 2000
ISBN 1853466565

Visual Impairment

"Visibility", "Eye Contact"

Both journals published three times a year
by the Royal National Institute for the
Blind.
Subscription: £9.00 for three issues.
Contact: Karen Porter
RNIB Education Information Service
224 Great Portland Street
London W1N 6AA
Tel: 020 7288 1266.

A range of books and videos covering the
needs of visually impaired children and
visually impaired children with additional
needs is available through the RNIB Book
Sales Service. For a catalogue contact:
Des Johnson
RNIB National Education Services
Garrow House, 190 Kensal Road
London W10 5BT
Tel: 020 8968 8600
Fax: 020 8960 3593

"Children with Visual Impairment in
Mainstream Settings"
Christine Arter, et al
David Fulton Publishers, 1999
ISBN 1853465836

Glossary of Abbreviations

Special Needs

ADD	Attention Deficit Disorder
ADHD	Attention Deficit/Hyperactivity Disorder
ASP	Asperger Syndrome
AUT	Autism
CP	Cerebral Palsy
DEL	Delicate
DOW	Down's Syndrome
DYC	Dyscalculia
DYP	Dyspraxia
DYS	Dyslexia
EBD	Emotional and Behavioural Difficulties
EPI	Epilepsy
HI	Hearing Impairment
MLD	Moderate Learning Difficulties
PH	Physical Impairment
PMLD	Profound and Multiple Learning Difficulties
SLD	Severe Learning Difficulties
SP&LD	Speech and Language Difficulties
SPLD	Specific Learning Difficulties
TOU	Tourette's Syndrome
VIS	Visual Impairment
W	Premises should be suitable for wheelchair access

Associations and Accrediting Bodies

AOC	Association of Colleges
ARC	Association for Residential Care
AWCEBD	The Association of Workers for Children with Emotional and Behavioural Difficulties
BDA	The British Dyslexia Association
BILD	British Institute of Learning Disabilities
BSA	Boarding Schools Association
CES	Catholic Education Service
CReSTeD	Council for the Registration of Schools Teaching Dyslexic Pupils
ECIS	European Council of International Schools

EQUALS	Entitlement and Quality Education for Pupils with Severe Learning Difficulties
FEFC	Further Education Funding Council
GBA	Governing Bodies Association
HMC	The Headmasters' and Headmistresses' Conference
IAPS	The Incorporated Association of Preparatory Schools
ISA	The Independent Schools Association
ISC	The Independent Schools Council
ISI	The Independent Schools Inspectorate
ISIS	The Independent Schools Information Service
LSC	Learning & Skills Council
NAES	National Association of EBD Schools
NAIMS	The National Association for Independent and Non-maintained Schools
NAS	National Autistic Society
NASEN	The National Association for Special Educational Needs
NASS	The National Association for Voluntary and Non-maintained Special Schools
NATSPEC	The National Association of Specialist Colleges
NCSE	National Council for Special Education
NCVO	National Council of Voluntary Organisations
NFAC	National Federation of Access Centres
OCR	Oxford, Cambridge and RSA Examinations
OPSIS	National Association for the Education, Training and Support of Blind and Partially Sighted People
SHMIS	The Society of Headmasters and Headmistresses of Independent Schools
SRCON	Surrey Regional Colleges Network
TSC	Training Standards Council
WJEC	Welsh Joint Education Committee

MAIN INDEX

A